LINGUISTIC STRUCTURES OF
NATIVE AMERICA

VIKING FUND
PUBLICATIONS IN ANTHROPOLOGY

Number Six

LINGUISTIC STRUCTURES
OF NATIVE AMERICA

HARRY HOIJER

L. BLOOMFIELD	S. S. NEWMAN
M. R. HAAS	M. SWADESH
A. M. HALPERN	G. L. TRAGER
F. K. LI	C. F. VOEGELIN

B. L. WHORF

New York · 1946

CORNELIUS OSGOOD

Editor

PREFACE

THIS volume, dedicated to the memory of Franz Boas, was planned by Edward Sapir. The contributors have been deprived of the help and encouragement that Sapir would have given; the reader has been deprived of the contribution that Sapir would have written with insight, grace, and power. The dedication is as Sapir intended it, though now we must speak of memory. In our work we have thought of Franz Boas, the pioneer and master in the study of American languages and the teacher, in one or another sense, of us all.

LEONARD BLOOMFIELD

1944.

CONTENTS

INTRODUCTION

HARRY HOIJER

THE term "American Indian languages" refers only to the aboriginal tongues spoken within the continental limits of North and South America and in the West Indies. There is no evidence whatever that these languages are historically interrelated. Indeed, quite the contrary appears to be true: we find in the Americas a region of greater linguistic diversity than any other in the world.

Furthermore, this diversity is found in grammatical structure and phonology as well as in historical origin. There are no structural or phonetic features peculiar to all or a majority of American languages which set them off in comparison to other groups. In brief, then, the term American Indian languages is only a geographical designation, it has neither historical nor a-historical classificatory significance.

As nearly as we can tell at the present time, no linguistic stock of the Americas is related to idioms outside this territory. Numerous suggestions of such relationships have been made from time to time. Thus, Eskimo and the so-called Ural-Altaic stock have been compared, several have attempted to link various American Indian tongues with those of the Malayo-Polynesian group, and Sapir has mentioned once or twice the possibility that his tentative Na-Dene group may have remote connections with Sinitic. None of these proposed wider relationships have at present any validity whatsoever. Much needs to be done in America itself before any remoter connections can reasonably be stated, much less demonstrated.

It is customary to group the American languages into three great geographical classifications: the languages of America north of Mexico, the languages of Mexico and Central America, and the languages of South America and the West Indies. This classification is, however, not a rigid one; there is a good bit of overlapping. Thus, for example, the Piman dialects of northern Mexico, as well as the languages of the Nahuatlan (Aztecan) stock, are clearly related to certain languages north of Mexico; this stock, the Uto-Aztecan, is found in two of our geographical divisions for that reason. It is quite possible that when the remoter relationships between American Indian languages have been established, this geographical classification, a convenient one now, will be abandoned.

Within each geographical area, the languages are classed into genetically related groups or linguistic stocks. There is, however, a considerable difference in the accuracy and completeness with which this can be done in each of the areas.

The languages north of Mexico have been studied more thoroughly than those of the other two groups. As a consequence, the genetic classification of the languages north of Mexico, while not by any means a solved problem, has a completeness and definiteness lacking in the other two areas, particularly in South America. Work now under way in Mexico and Central America will soon bring the classification of those languages to a level comparable with that of the languages to the north. In South America, however, the complexity of the problem of classification and the relatively few scholars working in the field make it unlikely that we shall soon have a solution.

1. THE LANGUAGES NORTH OF MEXICO

The first comprehensive classification of the languages north of Mexico was made by J. W. Powell and his associates, A. S. Gatschet and J. Owen Dorsey, in 1891.[1] Though a number of far-reaching modifications of this classification have been suggested since, the groups set up by Powell still retain their validity. In no case has a stock established by Powell been discredited by later work; the modifications that have been suggested are all concerned with the establishment of larger stocks to include two or more of the Powell groupings. Since most of these modifications have not as yet been indisputably established, we shall list in the following the stocks set up by Powell and indicate where later work has led to larger groupings.

§1. Eskimo-Aleut (Eskimauan).[2]

A large number of dialects extending along the shores of the Arctic from Greenland to the end of the Aleutian chain.[3] There is little knowledge of the interrelationships of the languages included in this stock. On the basis of data presented by Rasmussen, Dall, and Thalbitzer, however, the following major divisions may be set up.[4]

[1] J. W. Powell, *Indian Linguistic Families of America North of Mexico* (7th Annual Report of the Bureau of American Ethnology, Washington, 1891, pp. 7–142).

[2] Powell's terms for each stock are given in parenthesis following the more modern names given here.

[3] The locations of the stocks are taken from the map issued in 1915 by the Bureau of American Ethnology. The locations are those occupied by these groups in pre-Columbian times. At the present time, most of the Indians are segregated on Government Reservations in various parts of the United States and Canada. The Map of North American Indian Languages compiled and drawn by C. F. and E. W. Voegelin (Publication 20, American Ethnological Society, n.d.) was not available when this article was written.

[4] W. H. Dall, *Tribes of the Extreme Northwest* (Contributions to North American Ethnology, vol. 1, Washington, 1877, pp. 7–156); Knud Rasmussen, *Across Arctic America* (New York, 1927); W. Thalbitzer, *The Aleutian Language Compared with Greenlandic, A Manuscript by Rasmus Rask Dating from 1820, now in the Royal Library at Copenhagen* (International Journal of American Linguistics, vol. 2, New York, 1922, pp. 40–57), and *Eskimo* (In *Handbook of American Indian Languages*, Bureau of American Ethnology, Bulletin 40, pt. 1, Washington, 1911, pp. 967–1069).

A. Eskimo.
  1. Central and Greenland Eskimo. Spoken in many mutually intelligible dialects from Greenland to the Yukon River delta in Alaska.
  2. Alaskan Eskimo. The dialects south and west of the Yukon.
B. Aleut.
  1. Eastern Aleut or Unalaskan.
  2. Western Aleut or Atkan.

§2. Athapaskan.

The Athapaskan languages are generally divided into three geographical groupings: the Northern Athapaskan, the Pacific Coast Athapaskan, and the Southern Athapaskan.

The northern languages, which are spoken in western Canada and Alaska, are divided by Sapir and Osgood into the following substocks:

1. Kutchin.	5. Tahltan-Kaska.
2. Tsetsaut.	6. Sekani-Beaver-Sarsi.
3. Tanaina-Ingalik.	7. Chipewyan-Slave-Yellowknife.
4. Carrier-Chilcotin.	8. Dogrib-Bear Lake-Hare.

The precise interrelations of the above eight groups are far from certain. Each appears, however, to be a group of more or less mutually intelligible dialects. Of uncertain classification are the following: Koyukon, Tanana, Nabesna, Ahtena, Han, Tutchona, Mountain, and Nicola.[5]

The Pacific Coast group apparently forms a single substock, though this conclusion has not as yet been fully established. It includes a number of isolated languages spoken along the Pacific Coast from Washington to northern California. Of these, Hupa, Kato, Wailaki, Chasta Costa, Mattole, and Tolowa are still spoken.

The Southern Athapaskan languages (now called Apachean) are definitely a linguistic as well as a geographical grouping. They may be divided into two main groups: Western Apachean (which includes Navaho, San Carlos Apache and a number of other mutually intelligible dialects, Chiricahua Apache, and Mescalero Apache); and Eastern Apachean (which includes Jicarilla, Lipan, and Kiowa-Apache).[6] All except Lipan and Kiowa-Apache were spoken in New Mexico, Arizona, and the northern portions of Mexico which adjoin these states. Kiowa-Apache was spoken in western Kansas, and Lipan in Texas.

§3. Eyak.

A recently discovered language spoken by about 200 people on the Copper River delta in Alaska. Its classification is as yet uncertain, but it may turn out to be a link between Athapaskan and Tlingit.

[5] Cornelius Osgood, The Distribution of the Northern Athapaskan Indians (Yale University Publications in Anthropology, no. 7, New Haven, 1936), p. 22.

[6] H. Hoijer, The Southern Athapaskan Languages (American Anthropologist, n.s., vol. 40, Menasha, Wis., 1938, pp. 75–87).

§4. Tlingit (Koluschan).

A number of loosely related languages spoken on the north Pacific Coast from Alaska to 55 degrees north latitude.

§5. Haida (Skittagetan).

Spoken on the Queen Charlotte Islands off the coast of British Columbia.

Athapaskan, Tlingit, and Haida were grouped together by Sapir in 1915 under the name Na-Dene.[7] Na-Dene is divided into two subgroups: Haida and Continental Na-Dene. Continental Na-Dene, in turn, has two subgroups: Tlingit and Athapaskan.

The complete evidence for this classification is not as yet available. It has however, been attacked by Boas and Goddard, who point out that the similarities listed by Sapir as evidence of genetic relationship may have resulted from borrowing.[8]

§6. Beothukan.

An extinct linguistic stock formerly spoken in Newfoundland. Little data is extant on Beothuk. It was suggested by Latham in 1846 that Beothuk was related to Algonquian.[9] Gatschet, however, on the basis of further data, decided that Beothuk was an independent stock. Lately, Boethuk has generally been considered as remotely related to Algonquian though, since the language is extinct, this hypothesis cannot be proven.

§7. Algonquian.

A widely distributed stock, extending from Labrador and the north Atlantic Coast to Montana. Bloomfield, on page 85 of this volume, states as follows:

"The grouping of the Algonquian languages is uncertain, since most of them are scantily or poorly recorded. Following, in the main, Michelson, we may list them as follows:

"I. Central-Eastern:
   A. Central Type: Cree-Montagnais-Naskapi, Menomini, Fox-Sauk-Kickapoo, Shawnee, Peoria-Miami, Potawatomi, Ojibwa-Ottawa-Algonquin-Salteaux, Delaware, Powhatan.
   B. New England Type: Natick-Narragansett, Mohegan-Pequot, Penobscot-Abnaki, Passamaquoddy-Malecite, Micmac.
"II. Blackfoot.
"III. Cheyenne.
"IV. Arapaho-Atsina-Nawathinehena."

§8. Kutenai (Kitunahan).

This group of languages is spoken on the Kootenay River in Oregon.

[7] Edward Sapir, The Na-Dene Languages, a Preliminary Report (American Anthropologist, n.s., vol. 17, Lancaster, Pa., 1915, pp. 534–558).

[8] Franz Boas, The Classification of American Languages (American Anthropologist, n.s., vol. 22, Lancaster, Pa., 1920), p. 375; P. E. Goddard, Has Tlingit a Genetic Relationship to Athapaskan? (International Journal of American Linguistics, vol. 1, New York, 1917, pp. 266–279).

[9] J. W. Powell, Indian Linguistic Families of America North of Mexico (1891), p. 57.

§9. Salishan.

A large group of languages spoken in the region about Puget Sound and inland. A small enclave, the Bella Coola, is found north of this region on the Dean River.

The classification of the Salishan languages is still unclear. Boas and Haeberlin divided them into a coast group and an inland group, and pointed out that this geographical division was in the main accompanied by significant differences phonetically.[10]

§10. Wakashan.

This stock is composed of two main subgroups: Nootka, Nitinat, and Makah, spoken on Vancouver Island; and Kwakiutl, Bella Bella, and Kitamat, spoken on the coast of British Columbia north of Vancouver Island.

§11. Chimakuan.

A small stock consisting of two languages: Chimakum, spoken about Port Townsend Bay in Puget Sound, and Quileute, which is spoken on the Pacific Coast, south of Cape Flattery.

§12. Yurok (Weitspekan).

Spoken by a small group of tribes occupying the lower Klamath River in northern California.

§13. Wiyot (Wishokan).

Spoken by a small group of tribes in the area just south of the Yurok.

A similarity between Wiyot and Yurok has long been noted. Dixon and Kroeber, in 1913, classed the two together under the name Ritwan.[11] Later, Sapir pointed out a number of similarities between Ritwan and the Algonquian languages and set forth the hypothesis that these two were remotely related.[12] This view was attacked by Michelson.[13]

In a later article in the 14th edition of the *Encyclopedia Britannica*,[14] Sapir listed Beothukan, Algonquian, Kutenai, Salishan, Wakashan, Chimakuan, and Ritwan as substocks in a larger linguistic grouping to which he gave the name Algonkin-Wakashan. No evidence was published for this grouping which was admittedly speculative.

[10] Franz Boas and Herman Haeberlin, *Sound Shifts in Salishan Dialects* (International Journal of American Linguistics, vol. 4, New York, 1927, pp. 117–136).

[11] R. B. Dixon and A. L. Kroeber, *New Linguistic Families in California* (American Anthropologist, n.s., vol. 15, Lancaster, Pa., 1913, pp. 647–655).

[12] Edward Sapir, *Wiyot and Yurok, Algonkin Languages of California* (American Anthropologist, n.s., vol. 15, Lancaster, Pa., 1913, pp. 617–646).

[13] Truman Michelson, *Two Alleged Algonquian Languages of California* (American Anthropologist, n.s., vol. 16, Lancaster, Pa., 1914, pp. 361–367). Sapir's answer to this criticism and Michelson's further discussion will be found in the American Anthropologist (vol. 17, 1915, pp. 188–198).

[14] Under the title "Central and North American Indian Languages," *Encyclopedia Britannica* (14th Edition).

§14. Miwok (Moquelumnan).

Spoken in central California, east of the San Francisco Bay area.

§15. Costanoan.

Spoken in California on the south coast of San Francisco Bay and along the Pacific Coast to the south of the bay. Gatschet, in 1877, classed Costanoan with Miwok, calling the combined stock Mutsun. Powell, however, rejected this synthesis.[15]

§16. Yokuts (Mariposan).

Spoken in the area east of the Costanoan and south of the Miwok.

Kroeber, in 1904,[16] established the following classification of the Yokuts languages.

1. Valley division.
   a. Northern valley group: Chukchansi, Kechayi, Dumna, and a number of extinct languages.
   b. Main valley group: Yauelmani, Wechikhit, Nutunutu, Tachi, Chunut, Wowolasi, Choinok, and a number of now extinct languages.
   c. Chulamni.
2. Foothill division.
   a. Kings River group: Chukaimina, Michahai, Aiticha, and Choinimni.
   b. Tule-Kaweah Rivers group: Yaudanchi, Wükchamni, and possibly two or three others.
   c. Poso Creek group: Paleuyami, and one or two neighboring dialects.
   d. Buena Vista and Kern Lakes group: Tulamni and one other tribe.

Newman, in a recent publication,[17] states that his data completely substantiates the classification made by Kroeber.

§17. Maidu (Pujunan).

Spoken in California in the area directly north of the Miwok.

§18. Wintun (Copehan).

Spoken in north central California directly west of the Maidu.

In 1913, Dixon and Kroeber combined Miwok, Costanoan, Yokuts, Maidu, and Wintun into a single genetically related group which they called Penutian.[18] The evidence for this classification was published in a larger monograph in 1919.[19] Though this evidence is far from conclusive, it presents an hypothesis which deserves further investigation.

[15] J. W. Powell, *Indian Linguistic Families of America North of Mexico* (1891), p. 70.

[16] A. L. Kroeber, *The Yokuts Language of South Central California* (University of California Publications in American Archaeology and Ethnology, vol. 2, no. 5, Berkeley, 1905, pp. 310–313).

[17] Stanley Newman, *Yokuts Language of California* (Viking Fund Publications in Anthropology, no. 2, New York, 1944), pp. 5–6.

[18] R. B. Dixon and A. L. Kroeber, *New Linguistic Families in California* (1913).

[19] R. B. Dixon and A. L. Kroeber, *Linguistic Families of California* (University of California Publications in American Archaeology and Ethnology, vol. 16, no. 3, Berkeley, 1919, pp. 47–118).

§19. Takelma (Takilman).

Spoken on the Rogue River in Oregon.

§20. Coos (Kusan).

Spoken on the coast of middle Oregon, on the Coos River and Bay.

§21. Siuslaw and Yakonan (Yakonan).

Powell included in this group the Yakona, Alsea, Siuslaw, and Lower Umpqua tribes, all of which lived on the northern portion of the Oregon coast.[20] Wissler, in 1938, lists Siuslaw and Lower Umpqua together and puts Yakona and Alsea in a separate group.[21] He gives no authority for this division of the Powell stock.

§22. Kalapuya (Kalapooian).

Spoken in the valley of the Willamette River in Oregon, well up to the head-waters of the river.

§23. Chinook.

Spoken in Washington, at the mouth and along the banks of the Columbia River. There are two major dialect groups: Lower Chinook (now nearly extinct) and Upper Chinook.

In 1918, Frachtenberg published a paper comparing Takelma, Kalapuya, and Chinook and suggested that these languages were sufficiently similar to be classed together.[22] Sapir, in 1921, suggested that these languages, together with certain others, constituted an Oregon Penutian family which was remotely related to Dixon and Kroeber's California Penutian.[23]

§24. Tsimshian (Chimmesyan).

Spoken on the North Pacific Coast directly across from the Queen Charlotte Islands.

§25. Shahaptian.

Spoken over a comparatively large area in southern Washington and northern Oregon.

§26. Waiilatpuan.

A small group in northeastern Oregon, about in the center of the Shahaptian territory.

§27. Lutuamian.

Spoken in south central Oregon, just south of the Shahaptian area.

In 1931, Jacobs suggested that Powell's Shahaptian, Waiilatpuan, and Lu-tuamian stocks be tentatively combined into a single linguistic stock for which

[20] J. W. Powell, *Indian Linguistic Families of America North of Mexico* (1891), p. 70.

[21] Clark Wissler, *The American Indian* (New York, 1938), pp. 398–400.

[22] Leo J. Frachtenberg, *Comparative Studies in Takelman, Kalapuyan, and Chinookan Lexicography* (International Journal of American Linguistics, vol. 1, New York, 1918, pp. 175–182).

[23] Edward Sapir, *A Characteristic Penutian Form of Stem* (International Journal of American Linguistics, vol. 2, New York, 1921, pp. 58–67).

he proposed the name Sahaptin.[24] The complete evidence for this grouping has not as yet been published.

In his *Encyclopedia Britannica* classification, Sapir put into a single linguistic family—also called Penutian—the California Penutian languages, the Oregon Penutian, Chinookan, Tsimshian, the Plateau Penutian (Jacobs' Sahaptin), and a Mexican Penutian group (including Mixe-Zoque and Huave). As in the case of the Algonkin-Wakashan hypothesis, this grouping was tentative and Sapir published no evidence for it.

§28. Karok (Quoratean).

Spoken in northwestern California.

§29. Chimariko.

A small stock in northwestern California.

§30. Shasta-Achomawi (Sastean and Palaihnihan).

A large group of languages spoken in the territory east of the Karok in northern California. This connection was first suggested by Gatschet, who did not, however, have the data to prove it. The relationship was demonstrated by Dixon in 1905.[25]

§31. Yanan.

A small group of dialects spoken in northern California in the area just south of that occupied by the Shasta-Achomawi languages.

§32. Pomo (Kulanapan).

A group of languages spoken on the coast of California north of San Francisco Bay. Dr. A. M. Halpern, who has recently studied the languages of this group, sends me a tentative statement (as yet unpublished) of their interrelationships, which I have summarized as follows:

1. Southeastern Pomo.
2. Eastern and Russian River Pomo.
   a. Eastern Pomo.
   b. Russian River Pomo. Here are included five languages; Northeastern Pomo, Northern Pomo, Central Pomo, Southwestern Pomo, and Southern Pomo. The relationships within this group cannot now be stated with any assurance.

§33. Washoan.

Spoken in the Carson valley, Nevada, just at the Nevada-California state line.

§34. Esselenian.

A now extinct group who formerly lived on the coast of California just south of the Costanoan-speaking peoples.

[24] Melville Jacobs, *A Sketch of Northern Sahaptin Grammar* (University of Washington Publications in Anthropology, vol. 4, Seattle, 1930–1931, pp. 94–95).

[25] R. B. Dixon, *The Shasta-Achomawi; a New Linguistic Stock, with Four New Dialects* (American Anthropologist, n.s., vol. 7, Lancaster, Pa., 1905, pp. 213–217).

§35. Yuman.

A large group of languages spoken in Lower California and in the territory in California and Arizona which centers about the lower Colorado and Gila valleys. The most recent classification has been published by Kroeber, who divides them as follows:

1. Northwest or Upland Arizona: Walapai, Havasupai, the three Yavapai dialects.
2. Colorado River, where this forms the boundary between California and Arizona, and the lower Gila: Mohave, Halchidhoma, Kavelchadom, Maricopa, and Yuma.
3. Colorado Delta, in Mexico: Cocopa, Halyikwamai, Kahwan.
4. Mexican and American California north of 31 degrees: Diegueño, Kamia, Akwa' ala, Kiliwa.[26]

§36. Salinan.

Spoken on the coast of southern California south of the Esselenian group.

§37. Chumashan.

Spoken on the coast of southern California just south of the Salinan group.

In 1913, Dixon and Kroeber set up a new stock which they called Hokan, subsuming under this head, Karok, Chimariko, Shastan, Pomo, Yana, Esselen, and Yuman.[27] Later, Kroeber linked Seri (in northern Mexico) and Tequistlatecan (in southern Mexico) with the original California Hokan.[28]

Chumash and Salinan were also grouped together by Dixon and Kroeber in 1913, under the name Iskoman.[29] Harrington later suggested a relationship between Chumash and Yuman, thereby linking the Iskoman group with the California Hokan.[30]

In 1917, Sapir published a paper on the Hokan affiliations of Yana, in which he presented evidence relating Shasta-Achomawi, Chimariko, Karok, Yana, Pomo, Esselen, Yuman, Salinan, Chumash, Seri, and Chontal.[31] This hypothesis was accepted by Dixon and Kroeber, who later also added Washo to the Hokan group.[32] It must be remembered, however, that all of these later extensions of the Hokan stock were made on the basis of scanty and, in some cases, poorly recorded materials. Before it can definitely be stated that there is a Hokan stock—even in the limited sense in which it was originally set up by Dixon and Kroeber—a good deal

[26] A. L. Kroeber, *Classification of the Yuman Languages* (University of California Publications in Linguistics, vol. 1, no. 3, Berkeley, 1943), p. 21.

[27] R. B. Dixon and A. L. Kroeber, *New Linguistic Families in California* (1913).

[28] A. L. Kroeber, *Serian, Tequistlatecan, and Hokan* (University of California Publications in American Archaeology and Ethnology, vol. 11, no. 4, Berkeley, 1915, pp. 279–290).

[29] R. B. Dixon and A. L. Kroeber, *New Linguistic Families in California* (1913).

[30] J. P. Harrington simply announced in the American Anthropologist (vol. 15, 1913), p. 716, that recent work on these languages had caused him to believe them related.

[31] Edward Sapir, *The Position of Yana in the Hokan Stock* (University of California Publications in American Archaeology and Ethnology, vol. 13, Berkeley, 1917, pp. 1–34).

[32] R. B. Dixon and A. L. Kroeber, *Linguistic Families of California* (1919).

of work remains to be done. The evidences presented so far are far from conclusive and can serve only as a basis for future work.

§38. Tonkawa.

Originally spoken in perhaps three or four dialects in the neighborhood of Austin, Texas. Today there are only about ten speakers of Tonkawa alive, who live in the town of Tonkawa, Oklahoma.

§39. Coahuilteco (Coahuiltecan).

A number of tribes, all of which are now extinct, who lived along the Gulf Coast and inland on both sides of the Rio Grande. The little data on these languages was gathered by Gatschet in 1886 or is known from the records of the Reverend Father Bartolome Garcia.[33]

§40. Karankawa.

A now extinct tribe formerly found in the neighborhood of Matagorda Bay in Texas. A scanty vocabulary was collected by Gatschet in 1884.[34]

In 1917, Sapir presented data relating Tonkawa, the Coahuiltecan languages, and Karankawa to the newly established Hokan group.[35] Later, in 1925, he added the Subtiaba-Tlappanec languages of Nicaragua to this group to which he gave the name Hokan-Coahuiltecan.[36]

§41. Yuki.

Spoken in Round valley, California, north of the San Francisco Bay area.

§42. Keresan.

A group of languages spoken by some of the pueblo-dwellers of New Mexico. The Keresan stock may be divided into two groups: Eastern Keresan (spoken at San Felipe, Santa Ana, Sia, Cochiti, and Santo Domingo) and Western Keresan (spoken at Acoma and Laguna).

§43. Tunican (Tonikan).

A group of languages formerly spoken in northern Louisiana on both sides of the Mississippi River. These languages are now practically extinct, only one speaker surviving.

§44. Atakapa (Attacapan).

A group of languages, now extinct, formerly spoken on the Gulf Coast of Texas and Louisiana. The material extant on Atakapa was collected by Sibley and Gatschet.[37] Though this evidence showed a possible relationship of Atakapa to Chitimacha, Powell listed it as a separate stock.

[33] J. W. Powell, *Indian Linguistic Families of America North of Mexico* (1891), p. 68.

[34] J. W. Powell, *Indian Linguistic Families of America North of Mexico* (1891), p. 82.

[35] Edward Sapir, *The Hokan and Coahuiltecan Languages* (International Journal of American Linguistics, vol. 1, New York, 1917, pp. 280–290). The relationship of the Coahuiltecan languages to Tonkawa and Karankawa was first suggested by John R. Swanton, *Linguistic Position of the Tribes of Southern Texas and Northeastern Mexico* (American Anthropologist, n.s., vol. 17, Lancaster, Pa., 1915, pp. 17–40).

[36] Edward Sapir, *The Hokan Affinity of the Subtiaba in Nicaragua* (American Anthropologist, n.s., vol. 27, Menasha, Wis., 1925, pp. 402–435 and 491–527).

[37] J. W. Powell, *Indian Linguistic Families of America North of Mexico* (1891), p. 56.

§45. Chitimachan.

Formerly spoken in Louisiana, on the Gulf Coast just west of the Mississippi River. Only one speaker now survives.

In 1917, Swanton published a paper in which he compared all the then available material on Tunica, Chitimacha, and Atakapa.[38] On the basis of the similarities so revealed, he concluded that these languages were genetically related and gave the new stock the name Tunican. This hypothesis was accepted by Sapir, who divided Tunican into two subgroups: Tunica-Atakapa and Chitimacha.[39]

§46. Iroquoian.

A large group of languages distributed in two discontinuous areas in eastern North America. The largest group (Seneca, Cayuga, Onondaga, Mohawk, Oneida, and Wyandot) is found from the Lake Erie region northeast along the St. Lawrence River to the Gulf of St. Lawrence. Tuscarora was spoken in western Virginia, and Cherokee in North and South Carolina.

§47. Caddoan.

A widely distributed group of languages spoken on the southern plains. The Caddoan-speaking peoples ranged from southern Texas and Louisiana north and a bit west to central Nebraska. In addition, a small island of Caddoan speech is found on the boundary between North and South Dakota.

Powell divided these languages into three main groups: Northern Caddoan (the Arikara), Middle Caddoan (the Pawnee), and Southern Caddoan (the Caddo, Wichita, Kichai, and others).[40] Lesser and Weltfish, in a paper published in 1932, give us the latest classification of the Caddoan languages.[41] This may be summarized as follows.

I. Pawnee, Kitsai, and Wichita.
  A. Pawnee.
    1. Pawnee proper.
    2. Skiri Pawnee.
    3. Arikara.
  B. Kitsai.
  C. Wichita.
    1. Wichita proper (spoken by six groups).
    2. A dialectically divergent Wichita spoken by two groups.
II. Caddo
  A. Caddo proper.

[38] John R. Swanton, A *Structural and Lexical Comparison of the Tunica, Chitimacha, and Atakapa Languages* (Bureau of American Ethnology, Bulletin 68, Washington, 1918).

[39] *Encyclopedia Britannica* (14th Edition) under the title "Central and North American Indian Languages."

[40] J. W. Powell, *Indian Linguistic Families of America North of Mexico* (1891), p. 50.

[41] A. Lesser and Gene Weltfish, *Composition of the Caddoan Linguistic Stock* (Smithsonian Miscellaneous Collections, vol. 87, no. 6, Washington, 1932, pp. 1–15).

B. Haina.

C. Adai (?)

In his classification of Central and North American Indian languages in the 14th edition of the *Encyclopedia Britannica*, Sapir groups Iroquoian and Caddoan together as one of the substocks of his larger Hokan-Siouan family. As far as we know, no evidence has been published on this relationship.

§48. Siouan.

The Siouan languages are found in three distinct areas in mid-western and eastern United States. The largest group is west of the Mississippi River and extends from the southeastern corner of Saskatchewan south and a bit east to eastern Arkansas. A group of Siouan-speaking people also lived in eastern South Carolina, North Carolina, and Virginia, just east of the southern Iroquois. Finally, a small island of Siouan-speaking people (the Biloxi and Ofo) is found on the Mississippi coast of the Gulf of Mexico.

Voegelin divides the Siouan languages as follows:[42]

1. Eastern (Catawba).
2. Ohio Valley (Ofo, Biloxi, Tutelo).
3. Missouri River (Hidatsa, Crow).
4. Mississippi Valley (Iowa-Oto-Missouri, Winnebago, and possibly Dhegiha, Mandan, and Dakota).

A Siouan-Iroquois connection has been suggested by Louis Allen in a paper published in 1931.[43] The author lists a number of lexical and grammatical similarities between the two groups. His conclusions are as follows:

"The writer does not flatter himself that he has in these few pages definitely established the genetic connection between Siouan and Iroquoian though he is convinced of such a connection, and believes that it can be satisfactorily established. This comparison makes no pretense of being complete."[44]

§49. Yuchi (Uchean).

A small group of languages distributed in two noncontiguous areas in southeastern United States. One island is in northern Alabama, the other on the border between Georgia and South Carolina.

§50. Natchez-Muskogean (Natchesan and Muskogean).

Powell considered these two stocks to be independent of one another. Their connection was first established by Swanton in 1924[45] and has been confirmed by other investigators since.

[42] C. F. Voegelin, *Internal Relationships of Siouan Languages* (American Anthropologist, n.s., vol. 43, Menasha, Wis., 1941, pp. 246–249).

[43] Louis Allen, *Siouan and Iroquoian* (International Journal of American Linguistics, vol. 6, New York, 1931, pp. 185–193).

[44] Allen, *Siouan and Iroquoian* (1931), p. 193.

[45] John R. Swanton, *The Muskhogean Connection of the Natchez Language* (International Journal of American Linguistics, vol. 3, New York, 1924, pp. 46–75).

Mary Haas provides us with the latest classification of the Muskogean group:[46]

A. Western Division.
　　Old Choctaw.
　　　New Choctaw subdialects, including Chickasaw.
B. Eastern division.
　　1. Old Alabama,
　　　a. New Alabama.
　　　b. Koasati.
　　2. Old Hitchiti.
　　　New Hitchiti, including its subdialect Mikasuki.
　　3. Old Creek.
　　　New Creek subdialects, including Seminole.

§51. Timuquan.

An extinct language formerly spoken in northern Florida. Sapir has suggested, in his paper in the *Encyclopedia Britannica*, that Timuquan may be related to the Natchez-Muskogean subgroup of his Hokan-Siouan stock. No evidence for this relationship has been published.

In Sapir's classification of American Indian languages in the *Encyclopedia Britannica*, he sets up the Hokan-Siouan stock in which he brings under one linguistic family all of the groups listed in sections 28 to 51. His classification, summarized, is as follows:

1. Hokan-Coahuiltecan.
2. Yuki.
3. Keres.
4. Tunican.
5. Iroquois-Caddoan.
6. Eastern Group.
　a. Siouan-Yuchi.
　b. Natchez-Muskogean.

This hypothesis is, to the best of our knowledge, not supported by any published data. Since many of the substocks of the proposed Hokan-Siouan are still in question, it is clear that much more data must be made available before this hypothesis can be either confirmed or denied.

§52. Uto-Aztecan.

This stock, which includes the Powell stocks Piman and Shoshonean, as well as a number of Mexican families, was first clearly defined in Sapir's papers on Southern Paiute and Nahuatl.[47] The exact position of its constituent groups with

---

[46] Mary R. Haas, *The Classification of the Muskogean Languages* (In *Language, Culture, and Personality*, Menasha, Wis., 1941), p. 55.

[47] Edward Sapir, *Southern Paiute and Nahuatl, A Study in Uto-Aztecan* (Journal de la Société des Américanistes de Paris, n.s., vol. 10, Paris, 1913, pp. 379–425). Part II of this article begins in Volume 11, 1914, pp. 443–488 of the same journal and is concluded in the American Anthropologist (n.s., vol. 17, Lancaster, Pa., 1915, pp. 98–120 and 306–328).

regard to one another is not yet satisfactorily settled but the validity of the group as a whole has not been seriously challenged.

The most recent classification of the Uto-Aztecan languages is that published by Kroeber in 1934, a summary of which follows:[48]

I. Shoshonean.
    A. Hopi (spoken in northeastern Arizona).
    B. Plateau Shoshonean (spoken in eastern Oregon, Idaho, Nevada, Utah, and in western Wyoming and California).
        1. Ute-Chemehuevi.
        2. Shoshone-Commanche.
        3. Mono-Bannock.
    C. Tubatalabal (spoken in Kern County, California).
    D. Southern California Shoshonean.
        1. Serrano.
        2. Gabrielino.
        3. Luiseño-Cahuilla.
II. Pima-Tepehuan. Spoken in a narrow belt from the Gila River (in Arizona) to the Santiago River in northern Mexico.
III. Cáhita-Opata-Tarahumar. A number of languages spoken in various portions of northwestern Mexico.
IV. Nahuatl or Mexicano, including Pipil. Spoken mainly in the territory south of Mexico City approximately to the state line of Oaxaca and also along the east coast of Mexico south of Vera Cruz. There is also an isolated group on the west coast of Mexico south of the Gulf of Tehuantepec to the Guatemalan border. Pipil is spoken in Salvador.
V. Grouping uncertain: Cora; with Totorame or Pinome of the coast.
VI. Grouping uncertain: Huichol; with Tecual, Guachichil. This may be more similar to Nahuatl than any of the preceding groups.
VII. Unplaced, for lack of evidence: Jumano and Suma; Lagunero or Irritila; Zacatec; Teul and Cazcan; Coca and Tecuexe; languages of Aguas Calientes, Jalisco, Colima, and western Guerrero west of the Otomi and Tarasco, usually known on maps as Mexicano.

§53. Tanoan.

Spoken by many of the pueblo-dwellers of New Mexico. This stock is generally divided into three groups: Tiwa (spoken at the pueblos of Taos, Picuris, Sandia, Isleta, and the extinct Piro); Towa (spoken at Jemez and the extinct pueblo

---

[48] A. L. Kroeber, *Uto-Aztecan Languages of Mexico* (Ibero-Americana, vol. 8, Berkeley, 1934, pp. 16–17). See also J. Alden Mason, *The Classification of the Sonoran Languages* (*with an Appendix by B. L. Whorf*), (In *Essays in Anthropology in Honor of Alfred Louis Kroeber*, Berkeley, 1936, pp. 183–198)

of Pecos); and Tewa (spoken at San Juan, Santa Clara, San Ildefonso, Nambe, Poyoaque, Tesuque, and the Hopi village of Hano).

§54. Kiowan.

Spoken in the territory centering about the junction of the Oklahoma, Kansas, and Colorado state lines.

The relationship of Kiowan and Tanoan was first suggested by Harrington[49] but no considerable amount of evidence has been published on this point. The relationship was accepted by Sapir, who, in his *Encyclopedia Britannica* classification, groups them together under the name Tanoan-Kiowa as a subgroup of his Aztec-Tanoan stock.

Sapir's Aztec-Tanoan group linked Uto-Aztecan with Tanoan-Kiowa and Zuni, though the latter inclusion was queried. Recently, Whorf and Trager have published a paper presenting evidences for the relationship between Tanoan and Uto-Aztecan.[50]

2. THE LANGUAGES OF MEXICO AND CENTRAL AMERICA

The Indian languages of this region are on the whole less well known than those of America north of Mexico. Particularly is this true of their classification, on which we have a vast amount of speculation but very little basic data. Perhaps the most comprehensive and conservative classification was made by Thomas and Swanton in 1910.[51] Sapir, using this as a base, proposes a number of far-reaching changes, none of which have as yet been fully attested, in his *Encyclopedia Britannica* classification.[52] The most recent attempt at listing Middle America stocks has been made by J. Alden Mason.[53] In this, the pertinent literature is carefully reviewed and a classification "proposed merely as representing the weight of present opinion; future researches will doubtless modify it greatly."[54] Mason adds: "There could hardly be a more inauspicious time than the present for an attempt at a classification of Middle American languages with any claim to finality. Following

[49] J. P. Harrington, *On Phonetic and Lexical Resemblances between Kiowan and Tanoan* (Archaeological Institute of America, Papers of the School of American Archaeology, no. 12, Washington, 1910). See also his *Vocabulary of the Kiowa Language* (Bureau of American Ethnology, Bulletin 84, Washington, 1928).

[50] B. L. Whorf and G. L. Trager, *The Relationship of Uto-Aztecan and Tanoan* (American Anthropologist, n.s., vol. 39, Menasha, Wis., 1937, pp. 609–624).

[51] Cyrus Thomas and John R. Swanton, *Indian Languages of Mexico and Central America* (Bureau of American Ethnology, Bulletin 44, Washington, 1911).

[52] Sapir's information, in part from Thomas and Swanton, was in the main from W. Lehmann, *Zentral-Amerika I. Theil, Die Sprachen Zentral-Amerikas* (Berlin, 1920) and P. Rivet, *Langues de l'Amérique Centrale* (pp. 629–639 of A. Meillet and M. Cohen, *Les Langues du Monde*, Paris, 1924).

[53] J. Alden Mason, *The Native Languages of Middle America*, and Frederick Johnson, *The Linguistic Map of Mexico and Central America* (In *The Maya and Their Neighbors*, New York, 1940, pp. 52–114).

[54] J. Alden Mason, *The Native Languages of Middle America* (1940), p. 54.

decades of inactivity, with occasional reworkings of old vocabularies and grammars, a group of trained linguistic students is now investigating a number of
Mexican languages at first hand. Especially is this true of Southern Mexico where
studies are being made, or have recently been made, on Tarascan, Totonac, Mixtec,
Otomi, Matlazinca, Chinantec, Mayan, Cuitlatec, Huaxtec, Mazatec, Zapotec,
Mixe, Nahuatl. Work has also been done on Yaqui and some other northern languages. When these researches are published they will doubtless modify some of
the conclusions herein reached, though I hope they will corroborate most."[55]

Here we can do little more than summarize Mason's work. For more detailed
information and bibliography, the reader is referred to the original article.

§55. The Yuman languages of Mexico.

Most of the languages spoken in the peninsula of Lower California belong
clearly to the Yuman stock. See §35.

§56. Seri.

Spoken on the west coast of Mexico across from Lower California; may be
remotely related to Yuman. See §37.

§57. Tequistlatec (Chontal).

In southern Oaxaca; has also been linked to Yuman and is classed by Sapir
in his larger Hokan-Coahuiltecan group. See §§37, 40.

§58. Subtiaba-Tlappanec (called Supanec by Mason).

Is similarly classed as Hokan-Coahuiltecan by Sapir. (See §40.) The languages
of this group are spoken in Nicaragua (Subtiaba) and Guerrero (Tlappanec.)

§59. Pakawa.

An extinct language of northeastern Mexico, generally regarded as Coahuiltecan.

§60. Tamaulipecan.

An extinct family of Tamaulipas. Swanton has suggested a possible relationship to Coahuiltecan.

§61. Janambrian.

Extinct, and possibly related to Coahuiltecan.

§62. Waicuri.

A group of now extinct languages spoken at the tip of Lower California. It
is probably independent though Yuman affinities have been suggested.

§63. Uto-Aztecan languages of Mexico.

See §52.

§64. Tarascan.

Spoken in Michoacan. No subdivisions or dialects are known and the language
apparently has no wider affiliations.

§65. Otomanguean.

A grouping of three families: Otomi in central Mexico; Popolucan (formerly

[55] J. Alden Mason, *The Native Languages of Middle America* (1940), pp. 54–55.

Mazatec) of Guerrero, Puebla, and Oaxaca; and Chorotegan, spoken in Chiapas, Nicaragua, and Costa Rica. The Trique language is probably to be included as well.

§66. Mixtec.

Including Mixtec proper, Cuicetec, and Amusgo, all spoken in Guerrero and Oaxaca. A relationship to Zapotec (see §68) is suggested by many authorities but is still disputed.

§67. Chinantec.

One language with apparently no dialect divisions. Spoken in Oaxaca and western Vera Cruz.

§68. Zapotec.

A number of related languages spoken in Oaxaca.

§69. Mayan.

A large and important group of languages spoken in Yucatan and the neigh-boring Mexican states, British Honduras, western Honduras, and Guatemala. An isolated northern branch is Huastec, spoken on the coast of Vera Cruz and in the neighboring state of Potosi. Halpern, in working over Andrade's material, has proposed the following tentative grouping of the Maya languages:[56]

  I. Huastec.
 II. Yucatan-Guatemala group.
    A. Yucatec.
    B. Quichoid (Cakchiquel, Tzutuhil, Quiche, Uspantec, Quekchi, and Pokomam).
    C. Mamoid (Mam, Aguacatec, and Jacaltec).
III. Chiapas group (perhaps subdivided into Tzental-Tzotzil, Chontal-Chol-Chorti, Chanabal, and Chuj).

§70. Mizocuavean or the older Mixe-Zoque-Huave.

Mixe-Zoque are spoken in Oaxaca, Vera Cruz, Chiapas, and Tabasco; Huave on the coast of Oaxaca. Two extinct languages, Tapachultec and Aguacatec, are often included in this family. As we have seen, Sapir listed this group as a Mexican Penutian branch of his greater Penutian stock. See §27.

§71. Totonacan.

A small group of languages spoken in Hidalgo, Puebla, and on the coast of Vera Cruz.

§72. Jincan or Xincan.

Spoken in Guatemala.

§73. Lencan.

Spoken in Honduras and Salvador.

§74. Jicaquean.

Spoken in northern Honduras.

[56] A. M. Halpern, A *Theory of Maya tš Sounds* (Notes on Middle American Archaeology and Ethnology, vol. 1, no. 13, Washington, 1942, pp. 51–62).

§75. Payan.

Spoken in Honduras, just east of the Jicaquean group.

§76. Misumalpan or Miskito-Sumo-Matagalpa.

Miskito is spoken on the eastern coasts of Nicaragua and Honduras, Sumo in eastern Nicaragua and southern Honduras, and Matagalpa just west of the Sumo in Nicaragua as well as in Salvador.

§77. Languages in Middle America having South American affinities.

Two South American groups are represented in Middle America: Chibchan and Carib. (See §§78, 90.) There is considerable difference of opinion as to how far north of Panama the Chibchan affiliates extend; some would class Misumalpan as Chibchan. Carib languages are posthispanic intrusions found along the north coast of Honduras and in places on the coast of British Honduras.

3. THE LANGUAGES OF SOUTH AMERICA

The languages of South America, with very few exceptions, are so little known that any classification can be no more than tentative. Investigators vary even in estimating the probable number of independent families, some holding it to be as low as 75, others counting 100 or more. It is probable that Rivet's classification in *Les Langues du Monde*[57] comes as close to accuracy as the material permits. He lists 77 distinct families.

There can be no question but that this number will be greatly reduced when better data becomes available. A number of the stocks now listed as independent are known only from brief vocabularies or from one or two texts. Indeed, excepting only such widely spoken idioms as Quechua, Carib, Arawak, and Tupi-Guarani, it is likely that most of our South American linguistic data is hardly adequate for comparative treatment.

The summary listing below is made on the basis of Rivet's classification. No attempt is made to present all of the stocks contained in his list; the reader requiring more detailed information is referred to the original article.

§78. Chibchan.

A large and important group spoken all over Colombia up to the frontiers of Nicaragua and Costa Rica. Before the Inca invasion of Ecuador and southern Colombia, it is probable that Chibchan was also spoken in Ecuador as far south as the latitude of Guayaquil.

§79. Kechuan.

Spoken on the high plateaus of Ecuador and Peru. It is also spoken in parts of Bolivia (Cochabomba, Chuquisaca, and Potosi) and in northwestern Argentina (Jujuy and Santiago del Estero). Kechua, or a dialect of it, was the language of the

---

[57] A. Meillet and M. Cohen, *Les Langues du Monde* (Paris, 1924), pp. 639–707. See also A. F. Chamberlain, *Linguistic Stocks of South American Indians, with Distribution Map* (American Anthropologist, n.s., vol. 15, Lancaster, Pa., 1913, pp. 236–247) and *Encyclopedia Britannica* (14th Edition) under "South American Languages."

Incas of Peru and owes its wide distribution to their conquests. It is quite certian that numerous other languages, perhaps of entirely different stocks, were made extinct by the Incaic conquests.

Kechuan languages are still spoken by large numbers of people in Peru today; in fact, it would probably not be wholly wrong to regard Kechua as important as Spanish to the native population of modern Peru.

§80. Aymaran.

Found in two provinces of the department of Puno in Peru as well as in the departments of Arequipa and Moquequa. It is also spoken in Bolivia, in the territory centering about the Titicaca Basin. Aymaran is said by some who have worked on it to be related to Kechua. No evidence of this has been published, however.

§81. Araucanian.

Spoken in Chile, in the region between the coast and the Andes and between 27 and 43 degrees south latitude. It is also spoken in Argentina.

§82. Chonean.

Spoken on the islands off the southern coasts of Chile. Possibly related to Alikaluf (§83).

§83. Alikaluf.

South of Chonean.

§84. Yahgan.

Spoken on both sides of Beagal Channel in extreme southern Tierra del Fuego.

§85. Ona.

In the northern and eastern portions of Tierra del Fuego.

§86. Tehuelche.

Spoken by about 2000 people living in the region from the Rio Negro in Patagonia to the Straits of Magellan.

§87. Pehuelche.

From the 34th parallel to the Rio Negro in Patagonia.

From here on the picture becomes increasingly more complex. The region of South America east of the Andes and north of the 34th parallel is probably as complex linguistically as any in the world. The following list makes no pretense at completeness but names only the larger and more important groups.

§88. Chocoan.

Spoken on the Pacific Coast of South America just south of Panama, between the 8th and 4th degrees of latitude.

§89. Tupi-Guarani.

One of the most widespread of the South American stocks. It is spoken in the north in Guiana, in the west up to the slopes of the Andes, in the plains west of the Bolivian Gran Chaco, throughout Paraguay in the south, and, in the east, over a large portion of the Brazilian coast south of the mouth of the Amazon.

§90. Cariban.

Another widely distributed stock and one, moreover, which appears to have

spread fairly recently. The Carib languages, we have seen, are found in portions of Central America. In South America, the center of dispersal of the stock
seems to be in the region between the Upper Xingu and Tapajoz Rivers. From
here it seems to have spread northward to the Lesser Antilles and Florida. Carib-
speaking peoples reached the Andes on the west and small groups entered Colombia and Peru.

§91. Arawakan.

Also widely distributed, has in general a distribution almost identical with
that of the Caribs. In some cases, indeed, the two languages appear to have spread
together. Its center of dispersal is somewhere in the Venezuelan-Brazilian area about
the basins of the Orinoco and Rio Negro. Its northern extension is Florida, its
southernmost boundary Paraguay, it reached Peru on the west, and Arawak-
speaking peoples may be found at the mouth of the Amazon.

§92. Panoan.

Found in three geographical areas. The first and most important is along the
south bank of the Amazon River from the Jutahy on the east to the Huallaga on
the west, on both banks of the Ucayali from its mouth to the 10th parallel, on the
right bank of the Urubamba, a tributary of the Ucayali, and in the entire basin of
the Upper Jurua. The second group is found in the basin of the Inamburi, and the
third on the banks of the Mamore, Beni, and Madre de Dios Rivers.

§93. Gê.

Probably one of the oldest linguistic stocks in South America. Its speakers are
distributed through the whole of the southern half of Brazil, reaching the Xingu
on the west and the Atlantic on the east. Nimuendajú and Lowie give the following classification of the Gê languages, which they describe as a "simplified scheme":[58]

A. Northern and Western Gê.
    1. Timbira branch.
        a. Eastern Timbira.
        b. Western Timbira.
    2. Northern Kayapó.
    3. Southern Kayapó.
    4. Suyá.
B. Central Gê.
    1. Akwe.
    2. Akroá.
C. Southern Gê.
    1. Kaingang.
    2. Ingain.

[58] Curt Nimuendajú and Robert H. Lowie, *The Dual Organizations of the Ramokamekra
(Canella) of Northern Brazil* (American Anthropologist, n.s., vol. 39, Menasha, Wis., 1937), pp.
565–566.

D. Jaicó.

E. Kamakan and others.

§94. Tukano.

May be divided into three groups: the Eastern (found in the basins of the Uaupes, Curicuriary, and the Apaparis), the Western (in the basin of the Napo from its junction with the Amazon to the mouth of the Aguerica, along the Putumayo, and along the upper Caqueta to 74 degrees longitude), and the Northern (found near the sources of the Manacacia).

§95. Katukina.

Covers an immense area south of the Amazon from 72°30′ to 62°30′ longitude and 4° to 7° latitude.

§96. Puinavean.

Another linguistic stock, which, like the Gê, is said to be spoken by a very primitive people. These live in the basin of the Inirida and between the Rio Negro and Yapura between 69°30′ and 61°45′ longitude.

§97. Guaycuruan.

Spoken by a series of tribes along the banks of the Paraguay, the Parana, and their tributaries. It is also spoken in the Chaco.

§98. Matako-Mateguayo.

A smaller group spoken in the lesser Chaco.

The remaining languages are little known and poorly classified. Thus, in Venezuela and on the border between Venezuela and Brazil are found the following groups of uncertain classification: Jirijira, Timote, Yaruro, Otomah, Guahibo, Saliba, Maku, Shiriana, Auake, Kaliana, and the Guarauno. Similarly, along the eastern slopes of the Andes and on the upper tributaries of the Amazon from Colombia to Brazil are the Koche, Kofane, Zaparo, Chirino, Kahuepana, Cholona, Asmuesha, Tuyuneiri, Leko, Moseten, and Yurakare, with the Witoto, Yuri, and Mura living south of this region on the upper and middle Amazon. Finally, in central and southern Brazil, eastern Bolivia, and in Paraguay are found another large group of tribes whose languages are still unclassified: Chiquito, Samuku, Moskoi, Enimaga, Shavante, Guato, Bororo, Trumai, Mobima, Kayuvava, and several others.

SOUTH GREENLANDIC (ESKIMO)

MORRIS SWADESH

THE language of the aboriginal population of Greenland is of the Eskimo stock, which is spoken by about forty thousand individuals in Greenland, Labrador, along the northern coast and islands of Canada, in Alaska, and at the easternmost point of Asia.[1] Numerous dialectic differences, which are phono-logical and lexical rather than structural, are to be found especially between the easternmost and westernmost dialects; in Greenland, Thalbitzer distinguishes five slightly differing dialects. The stock as a whole seems to be related to Aleutian of the region of Bering Strait.[2]

The present sketch is of South Greenlandic (of the second half of the 19th century) as reported by Kleinschmidt.[3] This material is remarkably complete and accurate—a surprising fact considering that it was compiled about eighty-five years ago. There are a few points that Kleinschmidt did not work out or which he states ambiguously, but for the most part he does give the pertinent facts. Only because of this has it been possible to give the present sketch of the language.

In structure, Eskimo is unique among languages of North America in that it employs suffixation as its only morphologic process.[4] There is a certain amount of fusional phonetic change (elision, contraction, apocope), but it is always in connec-tion with suffixation and has no independent significance. Suffixes are used in three ways: in internal syntax, in inflection, in enclisis. The language is profusely poly-synthetic in its use of derivational suffixes, and is at the same time highly inflected; enclisis (addition of derivational and connective suffixes to inflected forms) is rela-tively unimportant.

PHONETICS

Vowel Phonemes:

	Front	Back
High	i	u
Low	a	

Semiconsonant phoneme: y

[1] William Thalbitzer, *Eskimo* (Bureau of American Ethnology, bull. 40, pt. 1, 1911, pp. 967–1069).

[2] William Thalbitzer, *The Aleutian Language Compared with Greenlandic* (International Journal of American Linguistics, vol. 2, 1921, pp. 40 ff.).

[3] S. Kleinschmidt, *Grammatik der Groenlaendischen Sprache* (G. Reimer, Berlin, 1851); *Den Groenlandsk Ordbog* (Louis Kleins Bogtrykkeri, Copenhagen, 1871). Material on other Greenlandic dialects is given by Thalbitzer, *A Phonetical Study of North Greenlandic* (Meddelelser om Grønland, vol. 34, 1904, pp. 1–406).

[4] Nootka and Yana are also profusely suffixing, and Nootka even has considerably more suffixes in number, but these languages employ other processes (reduplication and vowel mutation) in addition to suffixation.

Consonant Phonemes:

	Bilabial	Midpalatal	Velar	Interdental Point	Interdental Lateral	Alveolar Blade	Alveolar Point
Stops (voiceless-fortis)	p	k	q	t			
Normal spirants (voiced and voiceless)	β	γ	γ				
Nasals (voiced)	m	ɲ	ŋ	n			
Lateral spirant (voiced)					l		
Sibilants (voiceless)						s	ş

Vowels occur initially, medially, and finally in the word, and they occur both singly and in clusters. Clusters of two and three vowels are common, of four and five (e.g., auiaiβuq "he removes blood") relatively rarer. Clusters never have more than two like vowels (aa, ii, uu) together, but two like vowels do not occur together between other vowels.

The palatal semiconsonant y occurs only between vowels and never before or after i. y is distinct from intervocalic i, as may be seen from the comparison of such near homonyms as puyak "oxydized blubber" and puiaq "bird's crop"; ·i· has the quality described below, y is always close.[5]

Consonants occur initially, medially, and finally in the word, but not more than one consonant may stand initially and finally and not more than two conso- nants may stand together medially. Only stops, s, m, and n occur initially. Only stops occur in final position, but in the speech of some, especially women, the stop is replaced by the corresponding nasal. Medial clusters may be 1) any geminate cluster (pp, ββ, mm, etc.); 2) tl and ts; 3) the normal-spirant clusters γβ and γβ; 4) the following nongeminate clusters with continuant as first member:

	βq	βk	βt		βn	βs	βş	βl
γp		γk	γt	ɲm	ɲn	γs	γş	γl
γp	γq		γt	γm	γn	γs	γş	γl

ŋ does not occur freely but is limited to word final position in the speech of those who make the substitution of nasals for final stops; it also occurs in general usage in a few phrases, e.g., qanuŋ ippa (also qanuγ ippa) "how is it?"

Each vowel has a range of qualities according to phonetic surroundings. The most important differences are conditioned by the following consonant. The high- est timbres occur before following dental or mid-palatal consonants; middle quali- ties occur before labial consonants, before vowels, and in final position; low tim- bres, including velarized a, occur before velar consonants and before βq. Be- tween a and a following ss, ts, βs, there tends to be a front glide. u is fronted between s and y and is partly fronted whenever unrounded vowels (a or i) occur in both the preceding and following syllables. In clusters of two vowels the first tends to be pronounced with more stress and with greater time value than the second; in longer clusters the same tendency holds.

[5] William Thalbitzer, A Phonetical Study of North Greenlandic (1904).

The phonetic values of the consonants are for the most part sufficiently indicated in the table, but a few additional remarks are necessary. The normal spirants
are voiced lenis except as the second consonant of a cluster (ββ, γγ, γγ, γβ, or γβ),
in which case they are voiceless fortis. l is always voiced; it is lenis except as the
second consonant of a cluster (ll, βl, γl, γl, tl) where it is strongly spirantal. The
stops tend to be aspirated before the high vowels, especially i, but unaspirated
before a. Clusters of like stops (pp, tt, kk, qq) are pronounced with a single closure.
s is produced with the blade and point of the tongue, ş more with the point, so
that it sounds someting like an untrilled tongue-tip r.[6]

Syllabic division is such that a single consonant or the second consonant of a
cluster is always taken with the following syllable; the first consonant of a cluster
or the final consonant of the word goes with the preceding syllable. The treatment
of vowel clusters in syllabication is not clear (perhaps each vowel makes its own
syllable, perhaps certain clusters tend to be unified into one syllable while others
are separated). Closed syllables are more heavily stressed than open ones.

PHONOLOGY

Suffixation is accompanied by certain phonological changes, some of them
fairly complex, but all essentially regular in principle. It is not attempted to treat
the phonology exhaustively here. The following symbols indicating morphological
classification and inflection are used: . . i . intransitive verb; . . t . transitive verb;
. . verb which may be either transitive or intransitive; . . p . noun used only with
pronominal suffixes.

The stem or theme to which suffixes are normally added is either capable of
being used without suffix or at least has a phonetic form like such words; that is,
it ends in a vowel or in a stop consonant. The initial of suffixes is not comparably
limited, but may begin in a vowel, a consonant, or two consonants. According to
their way of uniting with the underlying theme, suffixes fall into three phonological classes. Class one, symbolized by a simple hyphen, spirantizes p, k, q to β, γ, γ
except that k >ɲ before nasals, k+γ >kk, q+γ >γ; t spirantizes to ş before
vowels, undergoes complete assimilation before consonants (i.e., t+p >pp,
t+n >nn, etc.) other than t, s, l, before which it remains. Example, -nïq[7] in:
aunïq "rotten stuff" <au . . i . "to rot," katinnïq "a joint," <katit . . t . "joins
it," uβiγlaγnïq "widow" <uβiγlaq . . i . "to lose one's husband." Class two,
symbolized by wavy hyphen, elides any preceding consonant except that q+γ >γ;
q or k+ş >γ; a, u+γu >ayu, uyu; a, u+γi >ai, ui. Example: saβiqaq . . i . "to
have a knife" <saβik "knife" + ~qaq . . i . Class three, symbolized by ᴘ-, is added
to a modified form of the theme, which may for convenience be called the plural
base. A variant of class three, symbolized ϙ- requires the plural base only in some

---

[6] S. Kleinschmidt, *Grammatik der Groenlaendischen Sprache* (1851), p. 1.
[7] ï is explained below.

cases: suffixes beginning in vowels are added to the plural base of themes ending in ᐟik, ᐟiq; Q᠈ suffixes beginning in consonants are added to the plural base of themes other than those in ᐟik and ᐟiq.

The plural base is formed in various ways, which have to be determined for the particular themes. Common formations are:

1) No change; thus, always when the theme ends in a vowel, also when it ends in ᐟik or ᐟiq preceded by two consonants, and in a few themes in which only one consonant precedes ᐟik or ᐟiq. Examples: iɣlu "house," pl. iɣlut; uɣpĭk "tree," pl. uɣpiɣᐟit; tikĭq "index finger," pl. tikiɣᐟit.

2) With loss of final q or k, e.g., amiq "skin," pl. amiᐟt.

3) By syncope of ĭ of final ᐟik or ᐟiq, with phonologic modification of the conso᠈ nant cluster resulting; limited to themes in which a single (noninitial) con᠈ sonant precedes ᐟik or ᐟiq. Example: alĭq "harpoon᠈line," pl. aɣlᐟit, relative aɣlᐟup.

4) By transposition of final k or q and the vowel preceding it, and alteration of the resulting consonant cluster; the vowel must be other than ĭ and it must be preceded by only one (noninitial) consonant. Example: ukaliq "rabbit," pl. ukatliᐟt, relative ukatliᐟp.

Modifications of consonant clusters are not necessarily the same for the last two formations, as shown in the examples given, but within each formation there is regularity. There are in addition several irregular formations of the plural base, e.g., qayaq "kayak," pl. qainat.[8]

It is necessary to recognize, a unique morphophoneme ĭ, having certain pecu᠈ liarities of phonological behavior. ĭ is replaced by a before vowels, e.g., nipiᐟɣa "my voice," nipaᐟa "his voice" (contrast akiᐟɣa "my coat," akiᐟa "his, its coat"). Prevocalic t >s after i but not after ĭ, e.g., akiᐟsik "the coat of you two" but nipiᐟtik "the voice of you two"; this applies even when a stem final consonant precedes the t, as aɣɣiɣsuq "he who comes" <aɣɣiq . . i . but qanittuq "he who is close" <qanĭt . . i . No vowel but ĭ is subject to syncope in the formation of the plural base.

In certain cases vowels are inserted before suffixes. All nouns ending in t take ĭ before the initial suffix of a consonant. All Q᠈ suffixes beginning in a conso᠈ nant take an insert vowel when they are added to a consonant final; the insert is i in all cases except with relative P᠈p, which takes u, as in aɣlup given above. A certain few plural bases take the vowel insert before pl. Q᠈t, even though they end in vowels, thus inuᐟit plural of inuk "man" (plural᠈base formation 2).

Spirantizing suffixes beginning in two consonants drop the first of them

---

[8] S. Kleinschmidt, *Grammatik der Groenlaendischen Sprache* (1851), pp. 25–29, has fuller data on the plural base. The present treatment differs in plan from Kleinschmidt's, notably in using the concept of the ĭ morphophoneme to help systematize the formations.

when added to a consonant-final theme, uyaɣak "stone" +ɣşuaq "large, evil" >uyaɣaɣşuaq (cf., after vowel, nuna "land," nunaɣşuaq "evil land").

Certain suffixes have alternate forms, ş and t, ɣ and s, according to whether they occur after vowels or consonants, thus -t/şuq "one who . . . -s," -s/ɣaq "what has been . . . -ed." The paradigmatic formatives for the indicative and interrogative modes begin in -p/β- that is, have -β- after vowels, -p- after consonants.

WORD CLASSES

Words may be classified into two inflectional classes, verbs and substantives, and different kinds of uninflected words, or particles. Verbs are inflected for mood and for person and number of subject and object. Substantives are inflected for case, but the class includes a number of subclasses: nouns, including normal type, pronon-modifying type, and numerals; demonstrative-directionals; and interrogatives. Particles may be classed as modifying, relational, predicational, expressive, imitative.

The verb has independent moods and subordinate moods, the former expressing predications, the latter relations. The notion expressed may be of state (e.g., miki . . i . "to be small," aputait . . i . "to be without snow") as well as of action (e.g., pisuk . . i . "to go," tuqut . . t . "to kill," sana . . "to work, to work at"). The inflectional endings indicate the mood and include one or two pronominal references. If there are two pronominal references, one is to the subject, the other to the object; if there is one pronominal reference, it may be either to the subject or the object, depending on the inherent voice of the verb. In this connection, there are the following voice types:

1) Inherently intransitive verbs, e.g., pisuk . . i . "to go," iβiɣsi . . i . "to have bread." Note in the second example that the action may involve an object, if the object is only part of the definition of the verb, and therefore not subject to pronominal expression. Verbs of this type normally occur with one pronominal reference, namely, to the subject, e.g., pisuɣpuq "he went," but are sometimes also used with double pronominal reference, e.g. pisuɣpaa "he went to it." The second pronominal reference, when present, is to an object somehow connected with the action.

2) Inherently transitive verbs, e.g., tuqut . . t . "to kill," mattaq . . t . "to remove the clothes of." A double pronominal reference refers to the subject and the object, e.g., tuquppaa "he kills him." A single proniminal reference is to the object with the subject indefinite or identical with the object: tuquppuq "he gets killed, he kills himself."

3) Doubly transitive verbs, e.g., nuɲuɣqu . . t . "to want one to make an end of." Such verbs, all of which are derived by means of suffixes from transitive verbs, are like transitives except that they involve an intermediary entity which is subject of the underlying transitive; if expressed, the intermediary term is in the allative case, e.g., nuɲuɣquβaa "he wants someone to end it, he wants it to be ended": uβaβnut nuɲuɣquβaa "he wants me to end it."

There are some verbs which are equally transitive and intransitive, e.g., sana . .

"to work, to work at" in: sanaβuq "he works," sanaβaa "he works at it."

Normal nouns refer to entities, concrete and abstract, including names as well as generic terms; examples: nanu "bear," inuk "person," iɣlu "house," sisi "fox's den," iβïk "grass," kayumiɲnïq "desire," annuɣaaɣşaq "material for a garment," unnuk "evening," uummannaq place name, piili man's name. Nouns commonly have a singular, dual, and plural, but there are some nouns that are limited as to their number inflection. Thus nouns referring to substances and qualities (e.g., uɣsuq "blubber," mikinïq "smallness") and names ordinarily are limited to the singular. Some nouns occur only in the plural, and in some cases there is a plural which differs in meaning from the singular; examples: nuɣlut (stem nuɣluq-) "ligature." umiat "boat with people in it" (sg. umiaq "boat"), aɣşat (stem aɣşaq-) "ashes," nuɣβit "bird dart having three auxiliary points" (sg. nuβik "single-pointed dart").

Certain nouns, called dependent nouns, do not occur except with pronominal suffixes; these include 1) location words, 2) words expressing the parts of a whole, 3) relationship terms, 4) transitive agentives. Examples: 1) at . . p . "under part, space beneath" (e.g. ataa "its under part, the space beneath it"; ataani "in its under part, under it"); qulï . . p . "upper part, space above"; suyu . . p . "front end, space before the front end"; sanni . . p . "neighboring thing, proximity"; aki . . p . "space opposite"; 2) isï . . p . "eye" (e.g., işaa "his eye"); uqaq . . p . "tongue"; natïq . . p ."bottom"; 3) aɲut . . p ."father"(e.g., aɲutiɣa "my father"); panik . . p . "daughter"; nukaq . . p . "younger sibling of same sex"; nuliaq . . p . "wife, female mate"; 4) asaşï . . p . "he who loves . . " (e.g., asaşiɣa "he who loves me"); ayuqiɣsuɣtï . . p . "he who teaches . . "; tuqutsişï . . p ."he who killed . . " All dependent nouns of the first group have one usage without pronominal suffix, namely, in the allative case, in the sense of "in . . . direction," e.g., ammut "off, down," qummut "upwards," kiɲumut "back, returning," suyumut "forward," akimut "over, across," etc. Some nouns of the second and third groups have a homonymous independent noun in a slightly different meaning; thus; inuk "person" (. . p . "possessor"), naaq "belly skin" (. . p . "belly").

Pronoun-modifying nouns do not ordinarily occur without pronominal suffixes, and have the peculiarity that they modify or are semantically appositional to the pronominal element. Two stems of this class are those referring to first and second person: uβa-ɲa "I," uβa-ɣut "we"; iβli-t "thou," iliβ-si "you" (stem iliβ- or ilip-), with metathesis in the singular form. Other stems of this class are kisi . . p . "alone" (e.g., kisi-ma "I alone"), tamaq . . p . "all together, all of," iluiɲɲaq . . p . "complete, whole," naliɲinaq . . p . "each" naɲminïq . . p . "self; . . .'s own," ik . . p . "self," katiɲɲaq . . p . "together, in collected piles." The words of this class show various peculiarities and limitations of inflection and usage. uβa- and iliβ- do not formally distinguish the absolute and relative cases; the remaining stems distinguish nominative and accusative cases instead of the normal absolute and relative. naliɲinaq is used without suffix with the meaning "all sorts of things, anything at all." naɲminïq is used without pronouns in apposition to other nouns, e.g., uβaɲa naɲminiq "I myself." ik . . p . is used in the third person only and ordinarily only in adverbial cases, e.g., iɲmini "with himself."

The numerals form a special class of nouns; their meanings are then "one thing," "two things," etc. The first numeral is always singular, the second numeral always dual, and the remaining always plural: atausiq "one," maɣluk "two" (stem maɣluq·), piɲasut "three" (piɲasuq·), sisamat "four" (sisamaq·), tatlimat "five" (tatlimaq·), qulit "ten" (quliq·). These six forms comprise the whole system of simple numerals; the remaining numbers are expressed by derivatives (aɣβiniɣlit "six" <"having on the other hand," aɣqaniɣlit "eleven" <"having on the first foot," aɣβaɣsaniɣlit "sixteen" <"having on the other foot") and by constructions with the particles aɣβinïq "on the other hand," aɣqanïq "on the first foot," aɣβaɣsanïq "on the other foot" and case forms of nouns meaning "on a person's intended second," "on a person's intended third"; "twenty" may be expressed by inuk naaβluɣu "ending a person" or aɣβaɣsaniq tatlimat "on the other foot five." The entire system is based on the notion of counting on the fingers and toes of persons, taking first the fingers and then the toes.

The dual and plural of "one" and a special form of the dual and plural of the other numbers, express the notion of "so and so many groups," e.g., aataat sisamait "four troops of seals," inuiait atautsit "one people"; the duals express the notion of "so and so many groups of two," e.g., ayaɣṣautik atautsik "one (two-pronged) fork."

Ordinals are suyuɣliq "the first," aipaa "the second" (literally "his companion"), and above two, the cardinals with third person plural possessive (i.e., piɲayuat "their three" = "the third," sisamaat "their four" = "the fourth").

The demonstrative-directionals consist of a limited number of stems with peculiarities of inflection and inflectional formation. Their most striking peculiarity is that they may occur affixed to an element tak·, which has an emphasizing force. or indicates greater distance; this is the only case of stems used in suffix position The stems are: (∼)ma· "here" (speaker's position); taṣṣ· "there" (anaphoric reference, also hearer's position)—not used with tak·; (∼)uβ· "here, there" (demonstrative); (∼)ik·, also (∼)iβ· "there, yonder"; (∼)aβ· "north, up-coast"; (·)aqβ· "south, down-coast"; (·)kiɣ "south"; (·)paβ· "east, landward, above"; (∼)sam· "west, seaward, below"; (·)pik· "there above, east, landward"; (∼)kan· "here below, west, seaward"; (·)kam· "inside, outside"; na·, only in naa "where is it?" and naɲa "let's see it! where do you have it?" Each of these stems and their tak-forms has two inflectional bases: a simple base expressing locational notions and limited to the absolutive, locative, ablative, allative, and perlative cases; an extended base (in ·nna·, ·ṣum· for the singular; in ·ku·, ·kun· for the plural) expressing a pronominal reference ("the one who is there, here, in the south, etc."), which is inflected in all the cases of the noun, except that there is no dual and that the plural differentiates nominative and accusative instead of absolutive and subordinate. The absolute of the simple base is used as an exclamatory predicative to give the location of something unexpressed, e.g., uββa "here! here it is!" Not all the simple bases make such an absolutive, the form being limited to uββa and most of the tak- derivatives. taṣṣa (<taṣṣ-) and a related form tamaṣṣa are absolutives used in nonexclamatory sentences expressing an equivalence of one term to another, e.g.,

> naᵧtuᵧalik, taṣṣa tiɲmiṣṣat nunaβtiniⁱttut aɲniᵧṣaat "the eagle, that (is) of the birds in our land the largest."
> nautsiiββik, taṣṣa silaᵧsuaq "the soil, that (is) the world."

The interrogatives are suk- "what?" and kik- "who?" They are inflected like nouns, except that they have no dual and that they do not take pronominal affixes. suk has, in addition to its interrogative use, the function of an ordinary noun with the meaning of "a something."

Particles include all words that are not inflected, comprising several different types of words from the viewpoint of their syntactic function; we may recognize modifying, relational, predicational, expressive, and imitative particles. Many modifying particles are related to substantives, or have formal resemblance to substantives; for example, there are instances of case-forms of substantives used in a specialized sense as modifying particles, e.g. taimaittumik ("in this way") "accordingly, therefore."

Modifying particles express degree and amount, as aᵧsut "very much," iɲma, iɲmaɲɲuaq, iɲmamik "somewhat," imannat, taimannat "thus many"; emphasis, as ila, ilami, ilaβik "certainly, I should think, is it not so?" (e.g., ila nikuβiᵧlutit "now stay away from it!"); reason, cause, circumstance, as suuq "why?" suuᵧmi "but why?" taimaittumik "accordingly, therefore"; manner, as qanuq "how?" ima, imaa, imaaq, imanna, imannak "thus," taima, taimannak "thus"; temporal location as qaɲa "when (in the past)?" qaɲaᵧu, qaquᵧu "when (future)?" maana "now," taimani "then," uβatsiaq "earlier today," tauβa "then," uβatsiaᵧu, uβatsiaᵧami "later today," taṣṣa, tauβa "just before," iᵧpaᵧṣaq "yesterday," taṣṣaɲɲa (inaq) "suddenly, in a moment," itsaq "years ago," aama "again," imanniliᵧami, itsaliᵧami "bye and bye, several days hence," qaqutiᵧut "from time to time," aitsait "just now, just before," aipaaᵧut ("through its companion") "coming year," kiɲuᵧna ("what it has ahead") "hereafter," etc. Certain temporal particles referring to past time have in addition to their customary form an ablative (irregular in formation, in that it has the plural form) used in the sense "as compared with . . . time," e.g., itsaᵧnit tuᵧtuqaqauq "as compared with years ago, there are plenty of reindeer."

Relational particles include: nauk, uβnit "although," used with relative or, occasionally, conjunctive mood, e.g., nauk qaiᵧquɲɲikkiᵧa, uᵧniᵧpaaɲa "although I had not called him, he came to me"; suuᵧlu "like, as" used with substantive or with relative or conjunctive mood of verb, e.g., suuᵧlu una "like this one (it is)," suuγlu uqaγtutit "as you said." suuγlu is also used with the indicative in the sense of "apparently (but not really)," e.g., suγlu nakkassaβuq "to appearances, it will fall (but it won't really)."

Under predicational particles may be included sentence-words as aak, aap, suu, suuγ(n)una "yes," naaγγa "no," quyanaq "thanks"; and predication-forming particles as imaqa "imagine! how would it be?", ussiuββa "I thought (mistakenly) it was . . . " sunauββa "see here, it was . . . ; so it was . . . " imaqa is used ordinarily with the relative mood of the verb or with a substantive, occasionally also with the indicative or optative of the verb; examples: imaqa, tipatsuşşaqaut "imagine (their situation)—they will be very unhappy," imaqa ilua "imagine its interior," imaqa samuɲa "how about (going) westward," ussiuββa is used with substantives or with the relative mood of verbs, e.g., usiuββa inuit "I thought it was people," usiuββa aipaγissaγaatit "I thought he being your companion" = "I thought he would have gone with you." sunauββa is used with substantive or with the relative mood, e.g., sunauββa ayuγtuq "see here, its being bad" = "now, it was bad."

Expressives are, for example, a (amazement), aya "oh!" (sighing), iiq, tiiq (scorn or irony). Imitatives are, for example, qutsiiq (gulls), qau qau (ravens). Such imitatives are used as hunters' calls.[9]

ENCLITICS

Enclitics are a class of suffixes which are semantically like independent words, in that they express notions similar to those of particles, but phonetically dependent in that they are attached to the end of other words and require phonetic modifications similar to those which apply within the word. They do not form a part of the inflectional system, nor are they a part of the normal internal syntax, being appended after all formative suffixes, including verb endings. They include: 1) conjunctive enclitics, as -lu "and, also," tauq (also -tsauq) "also, likewise," -luuniit "or, or also, even," -luuniit . . . -luuniit "either . . . or," -li "but"; 2) emphatic -mi "certainly, indeed"; 3) predication-forming enclitics, as -lusuuq (pl. used with plural noun, -lusuut) "it is as though it were," -γuuq (after vowels), -ɲuuq (after consonants) "he says, they say, they tell me," -tuq (equivalent to the particle qanuγtuq, formed with this enclitic, which is more common) "if only." Examples: iβlittauq "you also," takuɲɲilaγatauq "I also did not see it," iβlitluuniit uβaɲaluuniit "either you or I"; 2) ayuγpuγmi "it is certainly worthless," tikippumi "they came indeed"; 3) qişuγlusuuq "it is as though it were wood," paβaɲɲalusuuq "it seems to be (coming) from above," ayuγmaɲɲuuq "he said (it was) because it was bad," unaluγuuq "this one also, he said" (<una "this one"

---

[9] Examples of imitatives and expressives are taken from Thalbitzer, *Eskimo* (1911), pp. 1051–1052, and are northwest Greenlandic, but at least some are common to south Greenlandic, for they are included in Kleinschmidt's dictionary.

+-lu "and, also" +-ɣuuq), nilaɲɲuamiɣtuq "if only (one were provided) with a piece of ice."

INFLECTIONAL CATEGORIES

The inflectional categories are of pronominal reference, of person, of number, of case, and of mood.[10] These of course apply only to the inflective word types (the verb and the substantive), and are indicated by means of paradigmatic suffixes. There is a considerable amount of formal fusion in the paradigmatic suffixes, so that it is not always possible to isolate particular portions of the paradigmatic increment as expressing given inflectional categories, but the meaning of the para-digmatic form does lend itself to analysis.

There is never more than a double pronominal reference. Substantives have either no pronominal reference or a single pronominal reference, which expresses either the "possessor" or a direct pronominal reference to which the noun stem is appositional, e.g., iɣlu-ɣa "my house"; kisima "I alone." The "possessor" reference can be of various kinds depending on the meaning of the substantive; it may indicate 1) actual possession (e.g., iɣlu-ɣa "my house"), 2) whole-part relation (e.g., iṣi-ɣa "my eye"), 3) kinship (aɲuti-ɣa "my father"), 4) point of reference of loca-tion (suyu-ɣa "my space in front" = "the space in front of me"), 5) basis of com-parison (aɲiqi-ɣa "my larger = "what, he who is larger than I"), 6) the object of one's action (kalitta-ɣa "my towed thing" = "what I towed"), 7) actor whose ac-tion affects one (ayuqiɣsuɣti-ɣa "my teacher" = "he who teaches, taught me").

The verb may have a single or double pronominal reference. In case of double pronominal reference, one reference is to the subject, one to the object. In case of single pronominal reference, the reference is to the subject if the verb is inherently intransitive, to the object if the verb is inherently transitive; in the latter case, the subject remains indefinite or it is implied that the subject is the same as the object. Examples: pisuɣpaɣa "I go to it," pisuɣpuɲa "I go," tuquppaɣa "I kill him," tuquppuɲa "(someone) kills me, I am killed; (I) kill myself."

The number categories of singular, plural, and dual are distinguished in sub-stantives, except that demonstratives and interrogatives have no dual, and in pro-nominal references. Thus

iɣlu "house": iɣlut "houses": iɣluk "two houses"
iɣlua "his house": iɣlui "his houses": iɣluk "his two houses"
iɣlua "his house": iɣluat "their house": iɣluak "the house of them (two)"
tuquppaa "he kills him": tuquppaat "they kill him": tuquppaak "they two kill him"

---

[10] Paradigmatic formations are not indicated in this paper for want of space. See S. Klein-schmidt, *Grammatik der Groenlaendischen Sprache* (1851), particularly pp. 19–20. Terminological equivalences: recurrent person = Kleinschmidt's "third person e-suffixes," absolutive = Klein-schmidt's "objective," relative = Kleinschmidt's "subjective."

tuquppaa "he kills him": tuquppai "he kills them": tuquppak "he kills them (two)"

The singular expresses a single entity (e.g., iɣlu "a house") or a continuous entity (e.g., uɣşuq "blubber") not subject to being counted. The plural expresses more than one (e.g., iɣlut "houses"), except that it may refer to two only when duality is immaterial or when it is self-evident; thus reference to a natural pair of things (e.g., işai "his eyes," talii "his arms") is in the plural, and likewise any set of entities when the numeral for two is actually in the context (e.g., inuit maɣluk "two men" <"men-pl."+"two-du."). The dual refers to two and is used whenever the duality is essential and when it is not otherwise clear in the context. As shown above, certain entities are always treated as plural regardless of any specific rela-tion to a corresponding singular. Pronominal references always agree in number with the substantives expressed or implied, to which they refer.

Four persons, first, second, third, and recurrent, are distinguished in pro-nominal references. The first two refer to speaker and addressed person respec-tively. The third person is used for others than the speaker and the person ad-dressed except in certain cases where the recurrent is used instead.

Within a clause, if a third person subject is also referred to as the possessor of another entity in the context, it is in the recurrent person in the latter refer-ence, e.g.,

aɣqi taiβaa "he mentioned his own[11] name"—contrast aɣqa taiβaa "he men-tioned his (i.e., another's) name"

iɣlumi qaɣmaa uppitippaa "he destroyed his own house's wall"

qituɣnaminut tuniuppaa "he gave it to his own child"

In a clause subordinate to another, the subject is in the recurrent person if it is the same as that of the superordinate clause; and possessive pronominal references are in the recurrent person if they are the same as the subject of the superordinate. Examples:

takuɣamiuk ilisaɣaa "when he himself saw him, he recognized him"

niɣişaɣşaiɣukkunik aɲiɣlaɣumaaɣput "when they themselves are without means of livelihood, they will go home"

uqautiɣiɲɲilaa piɣiɲni "he did not speak of it, that he himself possessed it"

uqautiɣaa aɲuni qimakkaa "he said of him, that he left his own father"

uqautiɣaa nunaminut autlaɣtuq "he said of him, that he had gone to his own (home) land"

Cases like the last two are ambiguous since the recurrent reference applies either to the subject of the same clause or to the subject of the superordinate clause. In

---

[11] "His own," "he himself" are used to translate the recurrent. The Eskimo does not have the emphatic force that the English translation seems to imply.

a series of successive subordinations, the recurrent may have reference to the subject of any of the superordinate clauses; thus,

> isumaqaɣpuq, qataɲɲutaisa maluɣissaɣaani annautiɣiumaaɣitik, kuutip an-
> naukkumaɲmatik "he had the thought, that his brothers would notice
> him, whom they themselves would have as means of rescue, since God
> wanted to save them themselves"

The object can be in the recurrent person only in the case of a subordinate verb,
and then only when the subject of the same verb is identical with the object of the
immediately superordinate one; thus,

> kiββaata uɣniɲmani isiɣkuɲɲilaa "when his servant came to him himself, he
> ordered him not to come in"
> tuniɣuɲni iluaɣissaβaatit "if you give it to him himself, he will approve of
> you"
> tusassaβsi uqautiɣiɣiβtik "they will hear of you that you spoke of them them-
> selves"

The recurrent is used even when its reference is to part of a plural involved
in the subject of the main verb, e.g.,

> tikikkamik tuquβuq "when they arrived, he himself (one of their number)
> died"

The recurrent is sometimes used in cases other than those covered by the rules
given but this is not regular. Examples:

> tuquβuq aɲunila "he died, and also his own father"
> pinni tuɣquɣpai tiɣliɣtup uɣniliɣmani "he locked his things, because a thief
> was approaching him himself"

The third person is often substituted for the recurrent person object of a subordinate verb, when the subject of the subordinate verb is first or second person,
e.g., ilisimaβaaɲa uɣnissaɣiɣa "he knows of me that I will come to him" (instead
of uɣnissaɣiβni "that I will come to him himself").

   If the subject of the main verb is not indicated in its pronominal references,
as happens in a transitive verb with single pronominal reference, it cannot serve
as the basis of a recurrent; thus: saβianik tuniṣauβuq "someone presented him with
his knife" (possessor of the knife, ambiguous).

   The verb has three independent moods, indicative, interrogative, and optative; and four subordinate moods, conjunctive, subjective, subject participial, and
object participial. Of the independent moods, the indicative expresses statement;
the interrogative, question; the optative, wish or command. A subordinate mood
occurs in a clause subordinated to another clause, which may in turn be subordinate
to still another. A subordinate verb may be dependent on a noun, if the latter

involves a verbal meaning, e.g., iṣinnaɣu nappaɣtaliaq "without looking at it, a made barrel " =" a barrel made without looking."

The conjunctive mood expresses in terms of an actual event of the present or past 1) temporal location ("when . . . "), 2) cause, 3) noncondition (i.e., circumstance in spite of which an occurrence takes place). Examples:

> tuniɣaβku nipaɲiɣpuq "when I gave to him, he became silent"
> qaiɣquɣaɲma uɣniɣpaβkit "because you called me, I come to you"

The expression of noncondition requires the use of a verb in ꞏaluaq "although . . . " or of the particle kiɲumut "contrariwise," e.g.,

> iɣluɣput ayuɲɲikkaluaɣami ayuliɣpuq "although our house was not bad (before), it is (now) bad"
> kamiɣlaaɣama kiɲumut kamiɣpuɲa "if I took my boots off (before), I am (now) contrariwise putting them on"

The subjunctive mood expresses in terms of a future or a hypothetical event 1) temporal location, or 2) condition; examples:

> tiniɲɲaɣpat kiβluiaɣtuɣumaaɣpuɣut "when the water is low, we will go out to cut (seaweed)"
> takuɣuβku nalusaɲɲilaɣa "when I see him, I will know him"
> qaiɣqaɣpatiɣut uɣnikumaaɣpaɣput "if, when he calls us, we will go to him"

The participial moods express, roughly speaking, concomitant or connected occurrences, the subject participial when the subject of the concomitant occurrence is the same as that of the superordinate verb, the object participial when the subordinate verb involves either as subject or object, the object of the superordinate verb. The subject participial never has another verb subordinate to it, and the object participial does not ordinarily have a verb subordinate to it.

The semantic relation of a subject participial verb to its superordinate verb may be various, indicating cause, means, concomitant or prior event or circumstance. Examples:

> nakkaiβluɣu asiɣuɣpaa "he letting it fall, he broke it"
> qiβiaɣluɲa takuβaɣa "I turning about, saw him"
> tikitluɣu qimiɣluuɣsiuk "going up to it, examine it"

Verbs made with given suffixes are used to express certain relations more specifically; examples:

> mianiɣṣuɣitsi nakkaɣqunnasi "he is careful, not wishing (=in order not) to fall"
> nunaɣput takuyumaβluɣu tamauɲnaɣpuq "wishing (=in order) to see our land, he has come"
> aputiqaɣtinnaɣu paβuɲnaɣta "letting it not have snowed (=before it has snowed), let's go up"

iɲiulik piβluɣu uniɣpaɣut "bearing in mind (=because of) the tide, we re‑
mained there"

uβaɲa piβluɲa "I bearing me in mind: for my part"

suβluni qiaβa "lacking what (=why) is he crying?"

If the superordinate verb has an object but no subject, the subject participial may
still be used and must then be parallel to the main verb in having an object but no
expressed subject, e.g.,

tuniniqaɣpuq piqaɲaaɣquβluɣu "(someone) gave to him, wishing him to have
much" = "it was given him that he have much"

tukkiɣluɣu natuiiɣpuq "kicking it, (someone) opened it" = "it was opened by
kicking"

The chief use of the object participial is in connection with superordinate
verbs expressing communication, mental process, or perception and its logical func‑
tion is to give the event or circumstance that is communicated, thought of, or per‑
ceived. Thus:

aɣnaa tuquṣuq uqautiɣaat "his mother dying, they tell of her" = "they tell
that his mother died"

nalaɲɲilaaɲa qiɲmia tuqukkiɣa "he is not unaware of me, I killing his dog" =
"he is not unaware that I killed his dog"

qayaq iṣiɣaaɣa uɣnikkaatit "I saw a kayak, it coming to you" = "I saw that
a kayak came to you"

But the object participial is also used to indicate a concomitant action or circum‑
stance of the object of the superordinate verb, e.g.,

aɲumiɣaaɣa tuɣquɣaa "I caught him, he stealing it" = "I caught him as he
stole it"

umiat autlaliɣsut tikippai "the boat (pl.) going away, he reached it" = "he
reached the boat (just) as it was going away"

aataaɣtaɣa tikippaɣa iqaluɣṣuup niɣiliɣaa "I reached my killed seal, a shark
beginning to eat it" = "I reached the seal I had killed, which a shark had
begun to eat"

When the superordinate verb has no subject and the subordinate is intransi‑
tive, the subordinate may be expressed as a subject participial, or an intransitive‑
agentive, formally related to the object participial, may be used. In the latter case,
the agentive noun has the peculiarity of being in the relative case if it is singular,
in the instrumental case if it is dual or plural. "He (they) said (he) they would
come" may thus be expressed with the subject participial:

aɣɣissaβluɣu uqaɣpuq "he wishing to come, (he) said of himself"

aγγissaβlutik uqaγput "they wishing to come, (they) said of themselves"
or with the intransitive agentive noun:

aγγissaṣup uqaγpuq "comer-rel., (he) said of himself"

aγγissaṣumik uqaγput "by a comer, (they) said of themselves"

Certain substitutions of one mood for another are made to modify the tone
of the utterance, to add emphasis or liveliness. Thus:

1) interrogative for indicative, e.g., amiγlapat "are there many?" = "I certainly should say there were many"

2) second person optative (in imperative sense) for the indicative, e.g.,
   amuaγpit "pull up!" = "now, I pulled all my strength" or "there was
   no end to the pulling"; aṣṣakaaɲuaγit "roll a bit!" = "it rolled and
   rolled"

3) subject participial for optative, e.g., nikuβiγlutit "you standing up" =
   "stand up!"; kipiβluγu "cutting it off" = "let's cut it off!"

4) the object participial of a form with ~ssa . . "he will or should . . . " for
   optative, e.g., takuiaγtussaγit "you who should come to see it" = "come
   see it!"; saβtissaγiγa "I who am to feel it" = "let me feel it"

5) the object participial for indicative or interrogative; this substitution gives
   an emotional overtone of pity, wonder, sympathy, friendliness, disap-
   proval, etc., e.g., uγluṣuɲa "I falling" = "I fell!"; quɲasiaγut iγquγiγa
   "I striking him on his throat" = "(imagine it!) I struck him on his
   throat"; sumut pissaṣuq "one who wants to go where?" = "where does
   he want to go?"; ainiassaɲɲikkiγa "I who will not get him" = "should
   I not get him?"

6) indicative of a form with ᴗumaaq "he will . . . " for imperative, e.g.,
   tuγquγmaaγpaγsi "you will lift it" = "lift it!"; mianiγṣuγumaaγputit
   "you will be careful" = "be careful (word of farewell to one departing
   on a trip)"

7) indicative used paratactically instead of object participial, e.g., tusaγpuɲa
   qiɲmip kiiβaatit "I hear a dog bit you"; isumaqaγpuɲa uβlumi sisamaɲ-
   ɲuγpuq "I think it is Thursday today"

In the substantive are distinguished two purely syntactic cases, absolutive
and relative; and six adverbial cases, locative, ablative, allative, perlative, instrumental, and simulative. Pronoun-appositive substantives and the plural of the pronominal demonstratives distinguish nominative and accusative instead of absolutive
and relative. In these words, the nominative expresses the subject of the verb; the
accusative, the object of a transitive verb.

The syntactic cases apply to substantives in apposition with the pronominal
reference attached to nouns and verbs. The relative is used when the substantive
is in apposition to a "possessor" pronominal reference attached to another noun,
or to the subject in a double pronominal reference of a verb. Examples:

tiɣianiap iɣlua "the fox-rel., his house" = "the fox's house"

tiɣianiap takuβaa "the fox-rel., he saw him" = "the fox saw him"

tiɣianiap iɣlu takuβaa "the fox-rel., the house, he saw it" = "the fox saw the house"

aɣβiɣup saɣpata umiap suyua aɣtuɣpaa "the whale-rel. its tail-rel. (subj. of verb), the boat-rel., its front, it struck it" = "the whale's tail struck the boat's forward part"

The absolutive is used in all other cases, namely, in verbless sentences, in apposition to a single pronominal reference in a verb, and in apposition to the object reference in a double pronominal reference of a verb. Examples:

tiɣianiaq "a fox!"

tiɣianiaq iɣlumut pisuɣpuq "the fox, to the house, he went" = "the fox went to the house"

tiɣianiaq tukuβaa "the fox, he saw him" = "he saw the fox"

tiɣianiaq takuβuq "the fox, (someone) saw him" = "(someone) saw the fox, the fox was seen"

inuk tuquppuq "the man, (someone) killed him" = "the man was killed," or "the man killed himself"

In addition the absolutive of nouns referring to a temporal period is used in an adverbial sense to express location in time (but the locative and medial are also used with this force), e.g.,

auṣaq aβalaɣpuq "the summer, he left the country" = "he left the country last summer"

unnuaq siniɲɲilaɲa "the night, I did not sleep" = "I didn't sleep at night"

uβluq tammannaɣpiaq tuqussaβutit "the day, the same one, you will die" = "you will die the same day"

The superordinate has an irrational use in the singular only of intransitive agent nouns referring to the object and the logical subject of a subjectless verb, e.g.,

nappaɣsimasup misiɣiliɣpuq "the sick one-rel., (he) observes himself" = "(he) observes of himself that he is sick"

This usage does not extend to the plural and dual, where (also irrationally) the instrumental singular is used, e.g.,

aɣɣissaṣumik uqaɣput "by the one to come, (they) say of themselves" = "they said of themselves that they would come"

But this construction is not common, the participle being normal in such cases, e.g.,

aɣɣissaβlutik uqaɣput "they wishing to come, (they) say of themselves: they said they would come"

The adverbial cases are normally used as modifiers of verbs, but also occur with nouns having a verbal meaning, including:

1) nouns derived from verbs, e.g., qaβuɲa iɲiɣlaniɣani "to the south, on his trip" = "on his trip to the south"; aɲmaɣṣanik qaluut "with herrings, a raking instru- ment" = "a herring rake"
2) possessor nouns in ∼lik "one having . . . ," e.g., puɣtuṣunik qaqqalik "with high ones, one having mountains" = "a place with high mountains"
3) nouns in ∼liaq "a produced, home-made . . . "
4) nouns in -siaq "an obtained, bought . . . ," e.g., niuβiɣumit saβiɣsiaa "from the merchant, his obtained knife" = "his knife obtained from the merchant"

The locative case expresses:

1) the spatial location of an occurrence, e.g., qaβani tuquβuq "in the south he died"
2) the temporal location of an action when the location is with reference to another occurrence expressed by a -nǐq derivative of a verb stem, and sometimes when the temporal location is given in terms of a noun referring to a temporal period (but in this case, the medial or absolutive is more usual), e.g., qatsuɣniɣani autlaɣit "in its calmness, start out" = "start out while it is calm"; auṣami ayuɣṣaɣnaɲɲilaq "in the summer one does not suffer want"

The ablative case expresses:

1) the starting point of a movement, explicit or implicit, including the starting point of a measurement and the original source of an article, e.g., qaqqamit atiɣput "from the mountain they came down"; nunaβtinit qanippuq "from our land it is near"; tauṣumaɲɲa piβaɣa "from that one I received it"
2) temporal starting point (time of beginning) ,but only when there is also an allative in the context, e.g., uβlaamit unnuɲmut "from morning till evening"
3) basis of comparison, e.g., nanu tuɣtumit aɲiβuq "the bear, from the reindeer, he is large" = "the bear is large beside the reindeer, is larger than the reindeer"
4) cause, e.g., mikiniɣmit tammaɣpuq "from smallness, it got lost" = "it got lost be- cause of its small size"

The allative case expresses:

1) the ending point of a movement, e.g., qaβuɲa iɲiɣlaβuq "to, toward the west he traveled"; iɣluminut isiɣpuq "to his house, he went in" = "he went into his house"
2) temporal ending point, in rare cases, e.g., isuanut inuuβuq "to its end, he lived" = "he lived to the end of (the normal life span)"
3) that toward which an action is directed, e.g., inuɲnut piɣṣauβuq "for the people, it is intended"; naliɲinaɣnut atuɣpuq "for all sorts of things, it is used"
4) the logical subject of an impersonal verb in -naq . . i-, e.g., tamannut takunaɣpuq "to all, one saw it" = "it was seen by all"
5) the intermediary subject of a doubly transitive verb, e.g., pini inuɲnut takuɣquβai "his possessions, to people, he wants one to see them" = "he wants people to see his things"

6) the less directly affected object of an action, e.g., aniɲauṣat inuɲnut tuniuppai "the money (pl.) to the people, he gave them" = "he gave the money to the people"

7) various other uses dependent on the verb employed, e.g., siqiniɣmut ikitsiβuq "to the sun, he made a light" = "he lit it by the sun (i.e., with a sun glass)"

8) the quantity desired, in terms of price, of something to be bought (the article itself is in the instrumental), e.g., aataaɣṣuaɣmut tuamik "twelve shillings worth of to-bacco"

The perlative case expresses:

1) the course of a movement, e.g., nunakkut uɣɲiɣpas "he went by land"; maauna pissaβuɣut "we must go this way"

2) intermediary basis, indicating the way in which a fact applies, e.g., aɣnaβkut iɣqaɣliɣaaɣa "I am related to him through my mother"; taɣniβkut nayuɣpaɣa "I am with him in spirit"

3) the part of a whole affected by an action, e.g., aɣṣaisiɣut tiɣuβaa "through the hand, I took him" = "I took his hand"

4) temporal location indicating a temporal period within which an action takes place, e.g., uβlaakut autlaɣput "we departed in the morning"; qaqutiɣut tikiɣaaɣtaɣput "in the meantime, they visited"

5) agent (the logical subject) of a transitive verb used with single pronominal refer-ence, e.g., iliɣkut siɣniɣiṣauβuɲa "through you, (someone) protected me" = "I was protected through (or by) you"

The instrumental case expresses:

1) the thing used in effecting an action, e.g., aɣṣaminik tiɣuβaa "with his hand he took it"; uyaɣqamik miluuɣpaa "he threw at it with a stone"; piuainniɣnik piβai "he treated them with pleasantness"

2) apposition to the contained or implied object of an internally transitive intransi-tive verb, e.g., maɣluɲnik iɣalaaqaɣpuq "with two, it has windows" = "it has two windows"; qituɣtumik puuɣluɣu "with soft thing, putting it in a wrapper" = "wrapping it in something soft"; uyaɣqamik tiɣusiβuq "with a stone, he took something" = "he took a stone"—this usage has the force of indicating the object as indefinite ("a stone") in contrast with the normal transitive construction uyaɣaq tiɣuβaa "he took the stone" which implies a definite object ("the stone")

3) that which is referred to in communication or thought, e.g., aataanik uqalaɣput "they talk of seals"

4) the name or expression by which a thing is referred to, e.g., naalaɣkaβnik taiβaɣa "by my master, I call him" = "I call him my master"; tauku taiṣaɣaaβut uβkannik "these, we call them, by codfish" = "we call these (fish) codfish"

5) with agentive nouns or words of similar meaning, manner or concomitant action, e.g., kiɣaitsumik aɣɣiɣpuq "with slow one, he comes" = "he comes slowly"; tuniβaaɲa uuɣtuɣniqaɲɲitsumik "he gave it to me, with a not measured thing" = "he gave it to me without measuring it." In the case of the passive agentive, the meaning may be "in accordance with," e.g., piɣquṣaanik "at his command"; naamaɣiṣaanik "to his satisfaction"

6) with numerals, the number of times an action takes place, e.g., atautsimik takuβakka "I saw them once"

7) with ordinals, the ordinally defined place of an occurrence, e.g., aipaγşaanik tusassaβat "you are to hear it for the second time"

The simulative case expresses similarity, e.g., kiββatut "like servant"; iγluγtut "like your house"

The simulative has the peculiarity that it may be combined with the locative, e.g., paβanisut "as though above"; nunamisut "as in the country."

EXTERNAL SYNTAX

Syntactic relations of words are indicated by the inflectional forms of the words, word order serving only to indicate what words belong together. The relation of words in a sentence is either a modifier relation, in which a verb or semantically verb-like substantive is modified by an adverbial particle or a substantive in an adverbial case or a verb in a subordinate mood, or an appositional relation. An appositional relation may apply between two substantives, in which case they agree in number and case, e.g.,

uqautsit makkua tusaγkatit "words, these, your heard ones" = "these words which you heard"

uqautsit makkua tusaγkaβit "words-rel., these-rel., your heard ones-rel." = "these words which you heard (relative)."

uqautsinnik makkuniŋŋa tusaγkaŋnik "by words, by these, by your heard ones" = "by these words which you heard"

Apposition also applies between a substantive and the pronominal reference attached to another substantive or to a verb; in this case, there is agreement as to number between the noun and the pronominal reference but the case of the noun depends on the rules already given as to the use of the absolutive and superordinate cases. Finally, the apposition may apply between a noun and a part of the verb theme; in this case, the noun is either in the instrumental or in the allative, according to rules given in the discussion of these cases, or, in one type of derived verb, in the absolutive. The last mentioned type of case is that of apposition to the noun stem of a verb derived by means of a predicative suffix, e.g.,

manna qişuγşauβuq ayuŋŋitsuq "that, it is firewood, a good one" = "that is good firewood"

Aside from elliptical sentences and sentences consisting of a single sentence-word ("yes," "no," "thanks") or an interjection, one may distinguish three types of sentences:

1) copulative sentences, consisting of two members, a primary member which is a substantive in the absolutive or an equivalent expression and a predicate member which may be either a substantive in the absolutive (or an equivalent expression)

or an adverbial element (an adverbial particle or a substantive in an adverbial case). Examples:

> nunaγput qaqqaliγşuaq "our land (is) one of many mountains"
> siγγua suuγlu tiɲmişap siγγua "his snout (is) like a bird's beak"
> maγγaɲ una "clay, this" = "is this clay?"
> qaɲa una amuşaq "when this, a pulled up thing" = "when was this pulled up?"

Anaphoric taşşa or tamaşşa "that, it" may be used in copulative sentences (see examples, p. 11)

2) particle sentences, made by means of a sentence-forming particle, e.g., imaqa ilua "imagine its interior!"

3) normal, verbal sentences, consisting of a verb in an independent mood with or without appositional elements for its subject and object pronominal references (and for the stem in the cases mentioned), with or without adverbial modifiers, and with or without adverbial and participal clauses (examples are to be found through the discussion).

In copulative sentences, the order of the elements is generally speaking that the primary member precedes in a statement, but follows in a question, but this order is not necessarily adhered to. In particle sentences, the particle generally comes first in the sentence. In the verbal sentence, the normal order for the clause is: 1) subject substantive, 2) object substantive, 3) adverbial elements, 4) verb. The possessing nouns always stands before the possessed, an appositional substantive always after its primary. In a sentence containing a subordinate clause the latter may stand either before or after the main clause, ordinarily before; if the subordinate clause in turn has a subordinate, the subordinate precedes its superordinate if the latter precedes it superordinate, follows its superordinate if the latter follows its superordinate; thus, either of the following may be used: autlassaşuq tusaγaγamiuk tuniɲɲiɲmaγu iluaγiɲɲilaat "he being about to go away, when he himself heard of him, he not giving anything to him, they did not approve of him" = "they did not approve that he did not give anything to him when he himself heard he was going away"; iluaγiɲɲilaat tuniɲɲiɲmaγu tusaγaγamiuk autlassaşuq (clauses in reverse order). When the sentence is particularly complex, the tendency is to use the order of main clause first with subordinate clauses following in their order of subordination.

Elliptical senteices consist of one member only of an implied copulative sentence, of the elements of an implied particle or verbal sentence without the sentence forming particle or verb (subordinate verbs may be present). Common types of elliptical sentences are:

1) attention-calling and identification sentences, consisting of one member of an implied copulative sentence, e.g., naiat "gulls!" = "there are gulls"; naβşaaγa "my found things" = "(that is) the thing I found"

2) allative, perlative, instrumental, or adverbial particle implying optative of move-

ment, transference from one place to another, or other action, e.g., ikuɲa "thither!"; uɣuuna "this way!"; puumik "with a sack" = "take a sack to him, bring me a sack, let's take a sack! etc."; iβşuatsiaamik "moss!"; aɣsut "bravely, energetically!"; iɲmatsiaq "gently!"

3) any independent word given in answer to a question, e.g., sumut pissaβit "where do you want to go?": kitliɣnut "to the western people"; kia takuβauk "who saw it?": uma "this one (rel.))"; qanuŋ iliɲmat tuquβa "when it was how, did he die?": unnuɲmat "when it was evening"

In addition, certain of the uses of the object participial mentioned above may be regarded as elliptical uses involving an implied verb or sentence-forming particle.

INTERNAL SYNTAX

The inflectional base of a word may be made up of a stem solely, or of a stem with one or more suffix glossemes.[12] There are almost two hundred suffix glossemes, which are added both to stems and to themes made by suffixation. The process applies primarily to noun and verb stems and themes, but there is also a limited amount of suffixation on case forms of substantives, and on modifying particles. Suffixes are for the most part limited as to the type of them to which they can be added so that we may distinguish subnominal suffixes, added to noun themes, subverbal suffixes, added to verb themes, and postformative suffixes, added to case forms and particles; some suffixes are used with more than one type of theme. Postformative suffixes, are quite different from enclitics, with which they partly coincide as to position of occurrence, in that the formations they make are normal nouns and verbs; they are also different in never being added to paradigmatic forms of verbs.

On the basis of their semantic relationship with the underlying theme, suffixes are to be classed into restrictive and governing suffixes. Restrictive suffixes modify or limit the meaning of the underlying theme (e.g., uyaɣaɣşuaq "large stone" < uyaɣak "stone" + ɣşuaq "large"); governing suffixes bring about an essential change of meaning so that they refer to something different from the underlying theme, though defined in terms of the latter (e.g., akiliniɣmiut "inhabitants of Labrador" < akiliniɣq "what is on the other side; Labrador" + miut "inhabitants of . . . "). The class (whether noun, verb, etc.) of a word made with a restrictive suffix is the same as that of the underlying theme. The class of a word made with a governing suffix is determined by the suffix; thus, there are, of governing suffixes, governing verb suffixes and governing noun suffixes.

Governing verb suffixes must further be classed according to their peculiarities as to voice. Some governing subverbal verb-suffixes make a verb of the same in-

---

[12] The term glosseme is used here to mean a morpheme having an independent unitary meaning. A glossemic morpheme contrasts with an inflectional morpheme, one which indicates the place of an element in its paradigm.

herent voice as the underlying theme; these may be called neutral as to voice. Certain governing verb suffixes, transitive suffixes, make a transitive verb regardless of the underlying theme (if the theme is itself transitive, a doubly transitive verb results); there are also intransitive governing verb suffixes which make intransitive derivatives, either from nouns (e.g., iɣlu-qaq . . i, "to have a house" <iɣlu "house" + ~qaq . . "to have a . . . ") or from transitive verbs (but suffixes that make intransitives from transitive verbs do so by indefinitizing the object, e.g., tuqut . . t . "kills": tuqutsi . . i . "to kill things"). It is to be noted that intransitive verbs may involve the notion of an object, but such an object is combined in the theme itself and cannot give rise to the use of transitive paradigmatic usage; thus, a verb of the type of tuqutsiβuq "he kills-things" contrasts with one of the type of tuquppaa "he kills him." A peculiar subverbal restrictive suffix from the standpoint of voice is ⌐naq . . " (there is . . . ⌐ing) by someone," which, when added to a transitive theme makes a transitive verb in which the subject may not be expressed, e.g., maluɣaatit "he notices you": maluɳnaɣputit "there is noticing of you by someone" (=one notices you").

The only limitations as to the number of glossemic suffixes that may be added to one stem are the limitations imposed by the semantic and combinatory nature of the suffixes. Rather complex formations may thus result, for example:

qasuiiɣsaɣβiɣşaɣsiɳɳitluinaɣnaɣ-puq "one failed entirely to find a resting place" <[13] ⌐naq . . " (there is . . . ⌐ing) by someone" + ⌐luinaq . . "entirely" + qasuiiɣsaɣβiɣşaɣsiɳɳit . . i . "not to find a resting place" < ~ɳɳit . . + "not to . . . " + qasuiiɣβiɣsi⌐ . . i . "to find a resting place" < ⌐si . . i . "to find . . . " + qasuiiɣsaɣβik "resting place" < ⌐ββik "place of, for . . . ⌐ing" + qasuiiɣsaq . . t . "to cause to rest" < ⌐saq . . t . "cause one to . . . " + qasuiiq . . i . "to be not tired, to rest" < ~iiq . . " "not to be . . . " (also ~iiq . . i . "to be without . . . ") + qasu . . i . "to be tired"

The order in which the suffixes occur is, on the whole, fixed with reference to a sequence of restrictive suffixes, but with governing suffixes different orders are possible with different meanings. However, in the formation of a verb, governing suffixes expressing notions of time, aspect, and modality tend to be used last. A verb temporally, aspectively, or modally defined may take a noun-forming suffix, in which case the suffixes of time, and so on, no longer stand last; and the noun thus formed may then again be verbalized by a further addition of a suffix.

In the following outline summary, are given the kinds of derivational suffixes (expanding the classification already sketched out) with examples:

I. Restrictive suffixes
    1. Subverbal, expressing manner, degree, temporal notions, Examples: ~qï . .

[13] The analysis procedes from the last suffix.

"very much, very badly"; ⸱niɣluk .. "badly"; ⸝βluaq .. "properly"; ⸝luinaq ..
"thoroughly"; ⸝tuinnaq .. "steadily, without interruption"; ∼ɲaaq .. "very
much"; ∼tlaq .. "with energy, more than ordinarily"; ⸝t/ṣaq .. "repeatedly";
⸝ɣumaaq .. "in the future"; ⸝sima .. "in the past"; ⸝t/ṣaɣï .. "customarily"

2. Subnominal, expressing certain notions of size, age, state, provenience, etc.;
many of these are used with the absolute of pronominal demonstratives as well
well as with noun stems; examples: ⸝ɣṣuaq "large" (e.g., uyaɣaɣṣuaq "a large
stone"); ⸝ɲɲuaq "small"; ⸝taaq "new"; ∼tuqaq "old"; ∼ɣpait (pl.) "several";
∼liaq "made, home-made"; ⸝siaq "purchased, obtained"; ∼kuq "ruined, rem-
nant of . . . "

3. Subverbal and subnominal, including mainly the following: ∼inaq(..) "only"
(e.g., iɣluinaq "only a house"; uqainaɣpuq "he just talked"); ∼kasik(..)
"empty, hated; unfortunately, badly"; ∼ɲayak(..) "nearly"; ∼kuluk(..)
"lonely, pitiful; pitifully, unfortunately"

II. Governing suffixes
1. Noun-forming
a. Subnominal; examples: ∼lïk "something having a . . . " (e.g., pilik "one
having goods"); ⸝miu "inhabitant of . . . "; ∼kanniq "place near to . . . "
(used with location nouns, e.g., isukannianut "toward the end" and postformative with adverbial cases); ∼qat .. p. "one's fellow . . . "; ∼ɣṣaq
"that which is destined to be a . . . "

b. Subverbal, including various agentives, instrumentals, abstracts, etc.; the
most important: ⸝t/suq (intrans. agentative) "one who has . . . ed" (e.g.,
autlaɣtuq "one who has gone away"); ∼ɣsaq, ⸝taq (passive agent) "what is,
has been . . . ed"; ⸝t/si .. p. (active agent) "one's . . . er" (usually formed
from the indefinite object intransitive, e.g., tuqutsiṣaa "his killer, the one
who killed him"); ⸝nïq "result of . . . ing, act of . . . ing"; ∼ut "instrument
of . . . ing"; ⸝ββik "location of . . . ing"; ∼ɣlaaq "one who . . . s for the first
time"

2. Verb-forming
a) Subverbal
1) neutral (the voice of the derivative is the same as that of the underlying
theme) including suffixes expressing notions of aspect, of negation and
probability, and of attitude toward or relation to an action; examples:
∼ɣiaq .. "to be . . . ing"; ∼liq .. "to begin to . . ."; ∼ɲɲit .. "not
to . . ."; ∼kanniq .. "to almost . . ."; ⸝uɲnaq .. "to presumably . . .";
∼ɣquuq .. "to probably . . ."; ⸝t/ṣuuṣaaq .. "to seem to . . ."; ∼ssa ..
"should . . .; in the future"; ∼liɣṣaaq .. "to intend to . . ."; ⸝niaq ..
"to seek to . . ."; ⸝umau .. "to like to . . ."; ⸝iaɣtuq .. "to go in order
to . . ."

2) intransitivizing, including five semantically equivalent suffixes which,
added to a transitive verb theme, make the object reference indefinite,
the choice of one or the other of these suffixes is in part optional, in part
dependent on the particular transitive involved. The suffixes: ∼i, ∼ɣi ..,
∼ṣi, ⸝ɲnik, ⸝si, ⸝ɣliq .. i . (For examples, see above)

3) transitive; added to intransitives, the logical subject of the underlying transitive is the object (e.g., pisuɣsaɣpaa "he causes him to go"); added to transitives the object of the underlying transitive is the object of the derivative (e.g., tuqutsaɣpaa "he causes someone to kill him"). Examples: ˏsaq . . t . "to cause (him) to . . ."; ˏt/ṣaili . . t . "to prevent (him) from . . ˏing"; ˏniɣaq . . t . "to say (he) . . ˏs"; it/ṣuɣi . . t . "to think mistakenly (he) . . ˏs"; ∼ɣqu . . t . "to tell, want (him) to . . ."; ˏtit . . t . "to let (him) . . ."; ˏtsiq . . t . "to expect (him) to . . ."

b. Subnominal

1) forming copulative verbs: ∼u . . i . "to be a . . ." (e.g., uɣpiuβuq "it is a tree"), also used with pronouns and pron. demonstratives (e.g., kinauβit "who are you?"); ∼ɳɳuq . . i . "to become a . . ."; ˏɣpaluk . . i . "to appear, sound like a . . ."

2) forming transitive verbs: ∼ɣĭ . . t . "to have as . . ." (e.g., nunaɣaa "he has it as country: that is, his native land"); ᴘ∼iq, ∼liq . . t . "to provide with . . ." (e.g., quuɣqiɣpaa "he puts furrows in it"); ᴘ∼iaq . . t . "to deprive of . . ."

3) forming internally transitive intransitives; examples: ∼qaq . . i . "to have . . ." (e.g., nunaqaɣpuq "he has land"); added to pronouns and pronominal demonstratives in the sense of ". . . exists, is there" (e.g., taunaqaɣmat "because that one was there"); ˏk, ˏq (after vowels), zero . . . i . "to handle, use, act (in customary fashion) with . . ."; ˏsi . . i "to receive . . ."; ˏsiuq . . i . "to seek, be after . . ."; ǫˏiaq, ˏliaq . . i . "to go to . . ."; ˏtuq . . i . "to use . . ."; ∼luk . . i . "to have bad . . ."; ∼it . . i . "to be without . . ."; ∼kit . . i . "to have small . . ."; ∼tuu . . i . "to have large . . ."; ∼ɣnit . . i . "to smell of . . ." ˏk, ˏq, zero . . i . ("to handle, use, act, in customary fashion with . . .") has different meanings according to the noun with which it is used, thus, with animal names "to capture . . ."; with garments, "to dress in . . ."; with interjections "to say . . ."; with instrumentals of body parts, (either trans. or intrans.) "to use . . ., to use . . . on" (e.g., nanuɣpuq "he captures a bear," nasaɣpuq "he puts on a hat," kakakaaɣpuq "he says 'kakakaa' like a fox," ikusiɳmiɣpaa "he strikes it with his elbow")

As has been seen, a number of subnominal and subverbal suffixes also have postformative uses. The rather few purely postformative suffixes are substantially as follows:

ˏɣpasik . . i . "to lie in the direction of," used with location nouns and with the ablative of pure demonstratives (aβaɳnaɣpasiɣpuq "it is somewhat to the north"; kiɣaɳnaɣpasiɣpuq "it comes from a southerly direction") ˏɣqut . . t . "to go past, around . . . " used with location words and with the allative of pure demonstratives (e.g., aβaɣquppaa "he goes past on the outer side," paβuunaɣquppaa "he passes it on the landward side")

ʼuɲnaq . . i . (cf. ʼuɲa abl. of demonstratives) "to go toward . . . " (e.g.,
samuɲnaɣpuq "he goes down, seawards")

~uq . . used with perlative of numerals, "to do . . . (number) of times (to)"
(e.g., atautsikkuuɣpai "he handles them [all] at once")

~kaaq . . i . used with allative of location nouns "goes toward . . . " (e.g.,
kuyammukaaɣpuq "he goes southward").

CHIRICAHUA APACHE

HARRY HOIJER

THE Chiricahua Apache, in aboriginal times, ranged through southwestern New Mexico, southeastern Arizona, and the northern parts of Sonora and Chihuahua. The present day Chiricahua live on the Mescalero Reservation in New Mexico.

The material upon which this sketch is based was gathered in 1930 and 1931 under grants from the Committee on Research in Native American Languages and the University of Chicago. A volume of textual material has already been published[1] and a detailed grammatical treatment is now in preparation.

1. INTRODUCTION

§1:1. The morphemes making up Chiricahua Apache words are of three basic types: prefixes (including proclitics), stems, and enclitics. There are three main form classes in Chiricahua; these may be distinguished on the basis of their essential structure and by the degree of inflection to which they are subject. In the list which follows, the morphemes not set in parentheses are necessary to all forms in the class, whereas those in parentheses are found with only some members of the class.

I. Nouns:
    A. Simple nouns
        1. (Prefixes)-Stem-(Enclitics)
        2. Prefix-Stem-(Enclitics)
    B. Nouns derived from verbs
        (Prefixes)-Verb form-(Enclitics)
    C. Compound nouns
        A combination of two or more nouns of any of the above types to which may be added prefixes and enclitics.
II. Verbs:
    Prefixes-Stem-(Enclitics)
III. Particles:
    A. (Prefixes)-Stem-(Enclitics)
    B. Unanalyzable polysyllabic forms

Nouns only vary in structure when possessive prefixes are added but, in the

---

[1] Harry Hoijer, *Chiricahua and Mescalero Apache Texts* (*with Ethnological Notes by Morris Edward Opler*), (Chicago 1938).

majority of cases, this process is unaccompanied by variation in the essential structure. Particles are never inflected and only occasionally may prefixes or enclitics be added. Verbs, however, are complexly inflected, both by variation in their essential form and by the addition and subtraction of prefixes.

§1:2. The prefixes employed with the noun and particle, and a majority of those found with the verb may be distinguished, phonologically and morphologically, from certain prefixes peculiar to the verb alone. Prefixes of the former type we shall call derivational prefixes, and those of the latter group, paradigmatic prefixes.

Derivational prefixes found with the noun are of two kinds: proclitics (which may also be added to verbs and particles), and possessive pronouns (which are identical in form with the object pronouns prefixed to verbs). Particles may take only proclitics.

The prefix complex of the verb, however, is decidedly more complex. Following is a list of the verb prefixes in the order in which they occur in the verb form:

1. Proclitics
2. Adverbial prefixes (rare in this position)
3. Object pronouns (when they denote the indirect object of the verb)
4. Adverbial prefixes (most adverbial prefixes appear in this position)
5. The prefix for the iterative mode
6. The prefix for the distributive
7. Object pronouns (when they denote the direct object of the verb)
8. Deictic prefixes
9. Adverbial prefixes (rare in this position)
10. Tense-modal prefixes
11. Subject pronouns
12. Classifiers

Prefixes of positions one to nine, inclusive, are classed as derivational prefixes, and those of positions ten to twelve, inclusive, as paradigmatic prefixes. The minimum verb form must include a classifier (though this may be zero), a subject pronoun (or a deictic prefix), a tense-modal prefix which may, however, be zero, and a stem.

2. PHONOLOGY

§2:1. The Chiricahua Apache utterance, phonetically considered, is a succession of evenly stressed syllables separated from one another by "valleys" or minima of prominence. Between some syllables the point of minimal prominence is not far below the adjacent maxima of prominence; thus, for example, in the normal pronunciation of such words as tó-è· "at the water hole" the voice merely falls slightly in intensity as it passes from the final vowel of the first syllable to the initial vowel of the last. A similarly slight variation of vocal intensity differentiates, syllables terminating in a vowel or syllabic n from following syllables beginning with a syllabic n: bà-ń-ʔà· "you give a round object to him," ǹ-ǹš-ʔà· "I put a round object down."

Much more distinct minima of prominence may be noted between syllables terminating in a vowel, syllabic n, or consonant and one beginning with a consonant: dì-bé "sheep," nà·-dá·ʔ "corn," ǹ-dà· "he sits down," and sàh-dè "handle." Where the vowel of an open first syllable is short (as the dì- of dì-bé "sheep") the point of syllabic division appears to lie in, not before, the following consonant (thus [dìb-bé]). In all other cases the point of minimal prominence is just before the following consonant. It is evident from this rule that all intervocalic consonants following a short-voweled open syllable are mechanically lengthened.

Finally, it should be emphasized that the minima of prominence separating the syllables of a single word do not differ appreciably in magnitude from those which separate syllables belonging to different words in the same utterance. Pauses of greater or less duration may, to be sure, separate the words or phrases of an utterance but similar pauses may quite often fall within the word. Consequently, in the absence of any other special characteristics of a phonetic nature setting off the word or the phrase, it is a reasonable conclusion that the syllable is the smallest phonetic group in Chiricahua Apache.

The syllable in Chiricahua Apache has the following phonetic characteristics:

1) It most often begins with a consonant or syllabic n. Exceptions to this rule are certain rarely occurring syllables beginning with a consonantal cluster (e.g., šdì-bá "he starts off to war") and other, even less frequently occurring, syllables which begin with a vowel (e.g., kǫ̀-bà̧·è· "at the fireside").

2) The syllabic may be a vowel (short or long), a two-vowel cluster, or a syllabic n.

3) The syllable may terminate in a vowel or syllabic n, in a consonant, or, rarely, in a consonantal cluster.

4. Each syllable possesses a toneme.

Chiricahua Apache words are minimum free forms composed of one or more syllables. It is evident, then, that words exhibit the following phonetic characteristics:

1) All words begin with a consonant, a syllabic n, or, rarely, a bi-consonantal cluster.

2) Medial consonantal clusters never exceed three consonants and are most often composed of only two. Such clusters always occur at a syllable division.

3) Vowel clusters are usually within syllables and may occur medially and finally in the word. Some vowel clusters occur at a syllable division.

4) The word may terminate in a vowel, a syllabic n, or a consonant. Consonantal clusters never terminate the word.

5) The pitch accent of a word is built up of the tonemes of its constituent syllables.

§2:2. The consonants.

	Labial	Alveolar	Blade Alveolar	Lateral	Palatal	Faucal
STOPS						
Unaspirated	b	d	—	—	g	—
Aspirated	—	t	—	—	k	—
Glottalized	—	ṭ	—	—	ḳ	ʔ
NASALS						
Continuant	m	n	—	—	—	—
Exploded	ⁿb	ⁿd	—	—	—	—
SPIRANTS						
Unvoiced	—	s	š	ł	x	h
Voiced	—	z	ž	l	γ	—
SEMI-VOWEL	—	—	—	—	y	
AFFRICATES						
Unaspirated	—	ӡ	ž̌	λ	—	—
Aspirated	—	c	č	ƛ	—	—
Glottalized	—	ċ	č̣	ƛ̇	—	—

§2:3. The distribution of the consonants is summarized in the following. Examples will be given later.

1) All consonants may occur as syllable initials.

2) Only ʔ, s, z, š, ž, ł, l, and h may terminate a syllable. These also occur as word finals.

3) All consonants except ƛ (this exception is probably fortuitous) occur as word initials. Except for s and š, which as word initials may be followed by d or a vowel, a consonantal word initial is always followed by a vowel.

4) Medially in the word, all consonants may occur between vowels and between another consonant and a vowel. However, only the syllable finals listed in (2) above are found between a vowel and a consonant, and only s, š, and ł between two consonants.

§2:4. b, d, and g are voiceless unaspirated lenes. g before a and o is back palatal and before e and i is front palatal. Sometimes g is followed by a voiced palatal glide: [gγ] before a and o, [gᶦ] before e and i. Examples: báˑʔ "thirst," béˑš "knife," dìˑbòˑl "it is round," hàˑdèˑsˑbìʔ "it is full"; dàˑ "cup," ʔìłdǫ́ "also"; gàh "rabbit," dìˑgèˑ "he swoops down," dìˑšˑgìs "I am lazy," gó "snake."

t and k are unvoiced fortes and are always followed by a heavy spirantal aspiration similar to the consonant x. Before a and o the aspiration is back palatal and before e and i it is front palatal. Examples: táˑí [txáˑí] "three," sìˑtéˑž [šìˑtx̣éˑž] "two beings lie," hàˑsˑtìˑ [hàˑsˑtx̣ìˑ] "old man," tó [txóh] "water"; kàˑ [kxàˑ] "disease," šìˑkèˑ [šìˑkx̣èˑ] "my shoes," hídìšˑkì [hídìšˑkx̣ìh] "I ask him," dìˑkòs [dìˑkxòs] "cough."

ṭ and ḳ are unvoiced and glottalized. The glottal closure is simultaneous with (in rapid speech) or follows (in slow speech) the oral closure. Examples: t̬ǫ́·yá "backward," ná·té·žè "eyebrow," ʔáš·t̬í "I am so," ná·t̬òh "tobacco"; k̬à· "arrow," cé·k̬èh "firepit," bì·cà·s·k̬ì·dè "his lap," k̬òs "cloud."

The glottal stop (ʔ) is strongly articulated and may be heard without difficulty in any position. Examples: ʔá "fog," bì·ʔé·dè "his coat," nà·ṅ̬ł·ʔį̀ "he has it hidden," bé·ʔ·dìš·ʔà "I sing about him," žǫ́·ʔòł "Douglas spruce," bá·ʔ "thirst."

§2:5. m and n are essentially the same as English m and n. The exploded nasals are best described [mb] and [nd], respectively, though, in a majority of oc-currences, the stopped element is only lightly pronounced. ⁿb is rare, found only in the word ⁿbàiʔ (or ⁿbà·ʔyè) "coyote" and its derivatives. m is somewhat more frequent but occurs only before the vowel a and, except in borrowed words, never as a word initial: mà·dé··yà "bottle" (<Span. botella), šì·má "my mother," yì·ł·màs "he rolls it up."

ⁿd is found before the vowels a, e, and i but only in stem syllables: ⁿdá·sá "further on," ʔì·ⁿdè· "it is new," ʔá·dìš·ⁿdí "I speak thus." n is very common but, except before o, is limited to affixed syllables: nà·k̬ì "two," bì·čì·né "his father's mother," nà·nì·h·dá "we fall off," nà··nó·k̬à· "I have fainted," šìł·nà··ʔà·š "my spouse," nòn "grave, cache."

Intervocalically after a short vowel and between syllabic n and a vowel, ⁿb and ⁿd are ambisyllabic: šì·ⁿbàʔ·yè [šìm·bàʔ·yè] "my coyote," ṅ̀·ⁿbàʔ·yè [m̀·bàʔ·yè] "your coyote," ʔì·ⁿdè· [ʔìn·dè·] "it is new," ṅ̀·ⁿdè·z [ṅ̀·dè·z] "he is tall."

§2:6. s and z are pronounced as in English sip and zipper, respectively. Examples: sà· "language," sdìł·té·ł "(sand, water) begins to stream," nô··sé·ł "they were moving in a circle," yì·bàʔ·sì·dá "he waits for him," sǫ̀·s "star," yì·yè·s·xį́ "he has killed him," k̬à·ʔs·dà·dà··yá "he got away from them," dì··gìs "he is lazy"; zàs "snow," bì·zégé "his sweetheart," ʔí·ṅš·zìs "I am the main one," ṅ̀·X̬ìs·ná·ʔà "it is hard, they say," ʔì·zòh "he draws a line," ná·nè·s·dìz "he lies curled up."

š and ž are similar to the initials of English ship and French gendarme, re-spectively. Examples: šá "sun," šdì·bá "he starts off to war," yì·šé "he cuts it," xà·ʔ·šé·šį̀ "in some way," šòʔ "dew, frost," dìš·bá "I start off to war," bé·ʔ·šdìł·ʔà "he sings about him," bé·š "knife, metal"; žî·gò "rich" (<Span. rico), ʔì·žá "he goes off hunting," ʔì·žé "saliva" ʔìš·žìš "I dance," ʔì·žǫ́··ʔá·ž·dą́ "when they two had gone away," sì·bé·ž "it has boiled," hò·žòł "it is being dragged."

ł is a voiceless alveolar lateral spirant: łàʔ "one," ʔì·łé·hì·ká "we come to-gether," łį́ "horse," łó "sore, scab," dìš·łé "I start to carry a rope-like object," žìł·bá "he is gray," X̬é·ʔł·ⁿdí "midnight," bìł "sleep."

l is a voiced alveolar lateral similar to English "clear" l. In final position, it becomes syllabic. Examples: là··cíń "wrist," bì·lè·žè "its dirt, dust," dì·lìʔ "it burns," ló·ʔs·cò "wood rat," gò·s·lį́ "it has become" sì·ⁿdìl·ná·ʔa [sì·ⁿdìl·ná·ʔàl] "several objects lie, it is said," dè·s·bàl [dè·s·bàl] "he has begun to swing."

x and γ are back palatal before a and o, front palatal before e and i. x before o is sometimes labialized. γ before o is always strongly labialized and very often resembles closely a [w] with slight velar attack. Examples: xàˀ "winter," hà‑xàˀ "you two shake it," xé·ł [x̣é·ł] "pack," dìł‑xìł [dìł‑x̣ìł] "black," xòš (sometimes [xʷòš]) "cactus"; bì‑γà· "its wool," γé·ˀ‑yè [γé·ˀ‑yè] "Giant," bì‑γò· [bì‑γwò·] "his teeth."

As in English, the Chiricahua faucal spirant h varies in pronunciation depending upon the quality of the following vowel (when h is a syllable initial) or the preceding vowel (whe h is a syllable final). In general, however, h is more clearly articulated in Chiricahua than in English. Before or after the vowels a and o, it is always more spirantal than the English h; sometimes, indeed, it approaches the pronunciation of [x] in this position. Before or after e and i, however, h is less spirantal and not greatly different from the h's of English hem and him. Examples: hà‑dè·s‑bìˀ "it is full," dì‑bé‑hé "sheep," hí‑tò· "it is striped red," dàˀ‑hŏ·ké·z "a long rigid object has moved up," łì‑nàh‑k̃à· "you two are fat," gàh "rabbit."

cv syllables, when final in an utterance, are always pronounced [cvh]. This inorganic h disappears when the syllable is in included position whereas a true h remains. Thus, łì‑bá [łì‑báh] "it is gray" and łì‑bá‑gò "it being gray" but gàh "rabbit" and gàh‑gò "there being a rabbit."

§2:7. y is pronounced somewhat as in English young, except that it always has a slightly "rubbed" or spirantal quality. Examples: yà· "louse," ˀì‑yé‑zìł‑ⁿdì "he knocks it off," yà·‑yí‑ˀà· "he gives a round object to him," ˀìˀ‑nó·‑yò· "he has driven them away," ˀì‑γèˀ‑yá "into it."

§2:8. ʒ, ẓ̌, and λ are combinations of Chiricahua d and s, š, and ł, respectively. They are, therefore, unvoiced, unaspirated, lenis affricates. Examples: ʒà· "here,' ʒé "choke‑cherries," ʒìł "mountain," tâi‑dì‑ʒó "he threshes, winnows it," ˀìs‑ʒán "woman"; ẓ̌à· "pitch, gum," ẓ̌è·‑ẓ̌í‑ķẹ "little girl," yì‑ẓ̌ò·‑ⁿdè "he helps him," n̂ł‑ẓ̌į́ "he sits down"; λè·š "white clay," λì·‑dè "hawk (Sp.)," λọ́·ˀ‑yè "prairie dog," hà‑gò‑dì‑λà· "a noise is heard," nà·ł‑λò·š "he trots about."

c, č, and ƛ are phonetically Chiricahua t released into the spirants s, š, and ł, respectively. In contrast to ʒ, ẓ̌, and λ, they are aspirated and fortis. Examples: càˀ "awl," bì‑cè· "his tail," cí‑dí "glowing coals," dá‑ˀàł‑cò "every (one)"; čà· "beaver," čé·ł‑čá‑yé "beetle (Sp.)," čí "red clay," bì‑čó "his mother's brother"; ˀì‑ˀì‑ƛà· "he shovels a mud‑like mass away," dì‑ƛè· "he gets wet," cá‑dì‑ƛí·š "he falls down dead," nà·ł‑ƛò "he waves his arms about."

ċ, č̣, and ƛ̓ are [c], [č], and [ƛ] pronounced with a simultaneous (in rapid speech) or a following (in slow speech) glottal stop. Examples: ċà· "shallow basket," ˀì‑ċì‑dè "sinew," nàił‑ċọ̀· "he pulls it"; č̣àh "hat," č̣é‑ń‑ˀá "a rigid object extends out," ˀì‑gò‑č̣ì· "he digs a hole," gò‑dìł‑č̣òš "he makes a noise"; ƛ̓éˀ "night," hà‑n̂‑ƛ̓àh "he is left‑handed," bé‑ʒìł‑ƛ̓é "he runs into him," ƛ̓ì·š "snake," yè·‑ˀì‑ƛ̓ó "he ties it up."

§2:9. An s‑consonant (i.e., s, z, ʒ, c, or ċ) preceding an š‑consonant (i.e., š, ž, ẓ̌, č, or č̣) in a prefinal or stem syllable of the same word assimilates to the corresponding š‑consonant. Similarly, an š‑consonant preceding an s‑consonant in a prefinal or stem syllable of the same word assimilates to the corresponding s-con-sonant.

In both cases the assimilation is optional. The frequency with which assimi-lated forms occur, however, is determined by two factors: the distance of the two consonants from one another and the rapidity of speech. Taking the first factor as primary, we may set up the following conditions under which assimilation may take place.

1) If the two consonants are members of the same syllable, the first will always as-similate to the second except in very slow and precise speech. Thus, ʔìɫ-čéš-dọ̀· "I straighten it" and nà·-ʐ̧ìʾs-bị́ "he has swum" are always pronounced [ʔìɫ-čéš-dọ̀·] and [nà·-ʐ̧ìʾs-bị́h], respectively.

A reverse assimilation sometimes occurs in the case of the š-phoneme. A final š in certain prefinal syllables beginning with s, z, or ʐ̧ appears to assimilate to s. There are only a few examples of this alternation: hà-sìš-tìʔ [hà-sìs-tìʔ] "I am old," sìš-xé [sìs-xéh] "I kill him," ná-ʐ̧ìš-xé [ná-ʐ̧ìs-xéh] "I kill him again," gò-tà·-ʐ̧ìš-ⁿdì [gò-tà·-ʐ̧ìs-ⁿdì·] "I knock them down."

2) If the two consonants are members of different but contiguous syllables, the as-similation will take place in rapid and normal speech but not in slow speech. Thus, ʔìɫ-čé-ʐ̧ìɫ-dọ̀· "he straightens it" and čé-má·s "he rolls out" are usually pronounced [ʔìɫ-čé-ʐ̧ìɫ-dọ̀·] and [čé-má·s], respectively, but, in deliberate speech, may be heard [ʔìɫ-čé-ʐ̧ìɫ-dọ̀·] and [čé-má·s].

3) If the two consonants are separated by one or more syllables, the assimilation will more often take place when the separation is slight and speech is rapid, and will be less likely to take place as the distance between the two consonants increases and speech be-comes more deliberate. Thus, in a form like sí-ǹ-čá "you have buried it," the pronunciation [ší-ǹ-čáh] will be most frequent in normal speech since only a syllabic n separates the con-sonants s and č. But in any of the following examples, we may hear two pronunciations in normal speech (the most frequently occurring variant is given first): šà·-dà-ʔìʾs-ʔą́ [sà·-dà-ʔìʾs-ʔą́h] or [šà·dà-ʔìʾs-ʔą́h] "there is a bump on me," šà·ʔ-dà·-sí-ǹ-yá [sà·ʔ-dà·-sí-ǹ-yáh] or [šà·ʔ-dà·-sí-ǹ-yáh] "you went away from me," šà·ʔ-ɫé-ń-ʐ̧ị̀ [sà·ʔ-ɫé-ń-ʐ̧ị̀h] or [sà·ʔ-ɫé-ń-ʐ̧ị̀h] "you are happy over me."

4) s- and š-consonants never appear as members of the same stem syllable.

5) An s- or š-consonant in a stem syllable never assimilates to a following š- or s-con-sonant, respectively, in a postfinal syllable. Thus, ʐ̧ìɫ-šị́ "from the mountain" is never pro-nounced *[ʐ̧ìɫ-šị́].

6) In compound words, an s- or š-consonant in a stem syllable will assimilate to š- or s-consonant, respectively, in a following stem syllable. The conditions under which such assimilation takes place are essentially the same as those stated in (2) and (3) above. Ex-amples: cị̀-ʐ̧ì-né [čị̀-ʐ̧ì-nèh] "a variety of bush," cè·-ʐ̧ìn [čè·-ʐ̧ìn] "eagle" (Sp.), cé-ʔí-čị̀ [čé-ʔí-čị̀h] or [cé-ʔí-čị̀h] "Guadalupe Mountain," cè-ɫ-kì-ʐ̧è [čè-ɫ-kì-ʐ̧èh] or [čè-ɫ-kì-ʐ̧èh] "golden eagle," ʐ̧ì-ɫá-tà·-ʐ̧è [ʐ̧ì-ɫá-txà·-ʐ̧èh], rarely [ʐ̧ì-ɫá-txà·-ʐ̧èh] "turkey."

§2:10. Three types of consonant combination occur in Chiricahua: 1) bi-consonantal clusters found initially and finally in the syllable, 2) bi-consonantal

combinations (separated by a hiatus) at a point of syllable division, and 3) triconsonantal combinations (type (1) cluster plus hiatus plus consonant).

Only sd and šd are found as syllable initials. Syllables containing such clusters
always begin a word. Examples: sdè·s·tè·l "it has begun to stream," šdì·ʔì· "he
begins to carry them."

Consonant clusters ending the syllable are ʔs, ʔš, and ʔł. Syllables containing
such clusters never occur in final position and are always followed by a syllable
beginning with a consonant. Examples: ló·ʔs·cò "wood rat," bì·čè·ʔš·ké "his children," dáʔł·k̀èh "both of them." These, too, are the only circumstances under
which triconsonantal combinations occur in Chiricahua.

The most frequently occurring consonant combinations are those of type (2).
These are found whenever a syllable ending in a consonant immediately precedes
one beginning with a consonant. Only ʔ, s, z, š, ž, ł, l, and h may begin such combinations though any consonant may complete one.

§2:11. Syllabic n occurs initially, medially, and finally in the word. In the
initial position it is always followed by a consonant or another syllabic n, never
by a vowel: ǹ·cà· "it is big," ǹ·ń·ʔà· "you put a round object down."

In medial position syllabic n may occur:

1) Between another syllabic n and a vowel: ʔìs·z̧ą́·ń·ń·è· "to that particular woman."
2) Between another syllabic n and a consonant: ǹ·ń·ʔà· "you put the round object
down."
3) Between a vowel and another syllabic n: ʔìs·z̧ą́·ń·ń "that particular woman."
4) Between two vowels: sì·ʔą́·ǹ·è· "to the place where a round object had lain."
5) Between a vowel and a consonant: bà·ń·ʔà· "you give a round object to him."
6) Between a consonant and another syllabic n: gò·γ̧à̧ʔ·ń·ń "her actual husband."
7) Between a consonant and a vowel: bè·ʹz̧à·ʔà· š·ǹ·í "that by means of which they
had been traveling."
8) Between two consonants: náʔ·ǹ·ⁿdìł "he makes a brush corral."

The pronunciation of syllabic n varies with its position in the word and with
the speed of utterance. In normal and rapid speech, all syllabic n's are pronounced
[hn̥] in the initial position and [n] in the medial and final positions.

In slow and precise speech, however, several variant pronunciations appear:
[ni] and [hn] initially, [ni], [dn̥], and [n̥] medially, and [n̥], [dn̥], and [hn̥] in final position. These variations result from the disparate origins of syllabic n. Those which
are optional contractions of an original ni are pronounced [ni] in slow speech, regardless of position; those which are from di+ni are pronounced [hn̥] initially
and [dn̥] in medial and final positions; and those which go back to an original syllabic n are pronounced [n̥] medially and [hn̥] finally (they do not occur initially).

In final position syllabic n may be preceded by a vowel, a consonant, or by
another syllabic n: čí·ń "ghost," nàh·č̀ì·hò·gá·ł·ń "he who keeps coming toward
us," ʔìs·z̧ą́·ń·ń "that particular woman."

n̥ plus n̥, as we have seen does not contract to a long syllabic n but is pro-

nounced as two separate syllables. However, as a result of certain archaic contractions, a long syllabic n does occur as a separate phoneme. It is found in the following positions in the word:

1) Initially, where it is always followed by a consonant: ǹ·gìs "you are lazy."
2) Between another syllabic n and a consonant: ǹ·ǹ·t̬ì· "we two put them down."
3) Between a vowel and a consonant: ná·ǹ·ʔà· "you pick up a round object."
4) Between two consonants: náš·ǹ·ʔà· "he picks up a round object."

In normal and rapid speech, ṇ· is always pronounced [hṇ·] in the initial position and [ṇ·] in the medial position. In slow speech, ṇ· resulting from a reduced
and lengthened ni is pronounced [ṇ·] but one derived from a contracted and
lengthened di·ni· is heard [dṇ·].

When ṇ immediately precedes m, ⁿb, or b, it assimilates to syllabic m:
ǹ·má [hm·máh] "your mother," ǹⁿbàʔyè [hm̀·bàʔ·yèh] "your coyote," nà·ǹ·má·s
[nà·m̀·má·s] "you roll off."

§2:12. The vowel phonemes may be listed as follows.

Position of Articulation	Un·nasalized		Nasalized	
	Short	Long	Short	Long
Low·central unrounded	a	a·	ą	ą·
Mid·front unrounded	e	e·	ę	ę·
High·front unrounded	i	i·	į	į·
Mid·back rounded	o	o·	ǫ	ǫ·

a and a· vary from the low central position to the low front position. The
variation is apparently haphazard. Examples: gàh "rabbit," kà· "disease, illness."

e and e· are usually half open vowels, very similar to the vowels of English
met and bed, respectively (Midwestern American dialect). Before i in vowel clusters, however, their quality approaches that of the half close vowel of standard
German Weh. Examples: ké "shoes, moccasins," tè·ł "tule," bì·ẓéiʔ "his heart."

i is usually half close, similar to the vowel of English bit. Before voiced consonants and in the final position of the word, however, it approaches the close
pronunciation of i·. Examples: bì·tà· "his father," bì·má "his mother," bí "he,
him," bì·šeʔ "a variety of bird," dí· "this one."

o varies from the half open position, as of the vowel of standard German voll,
to the half close position of the vowel of English book. Similarly, o· varies from a
half close o, similar to that of German Sohn, to the high u of English soothe. These
variations are entirely random; the same informant will accept either [txɔ́h[or
[txúh] for tó "water" and either [txò·] or [txù·] for tò· "hundred."

§2:13. Short vowels occur as syllable initials only in a few medial and final syllables. Consequently, they are only medial and final in the word, never initial. In the medial position, short vowels may be found:

1) Between consonants: šàš "bear," bì·té·lè "the front of his body," gìš "cane, staff," bì·tò? "his water."

2) Between a consonant and syllabic n: ʔìs·ẓá·ń "woman," yé·ǹ·t̨í "he bewitches him," yì·ǹ·λá·s "he helps him," gò·ǹ·są́ "I am wise."

3) Between a consonant and vowel: tà·ˑnâi·gìs "he washes it," k̇èi·dì·cé "he slips it on," ń·dói "puma." i is not found in this position.

4) Between a vowel and consonant: i and o are most frequent in this position; e does not occur here at all: ʔêał·ⁿdí "you two are jealous," ʔì·gòi·ʔá·ń "holes, dens," nào·λìž "we two have fallen off."

In the final position, a short vowel may be preceded by:

1) A consonant: nà·ˑdà "mescal," dì·bé "sheep," bí "he," gó "snake.'

2) A syllabic n: only i may occupy this position: ẓò·ˑγé·ǹ·í "he who used to be called by name."

3) Another short vowel: only i and o are found in this position: ʔái "he, that one," ʔào "yes."

§2:14. Like the short vowels, long vowels never begin the word but are found only medially and finally. Medially, they occupy the following positions:

1) Between consonants: bá·ʔ "thirst," bé·š "knife," t̂ì·s "cottonwood tree," gó·ʔ·yè "all living creatures except man."

2) Between consonant and syllabic n: bà·ˑǹ·ˑʔà· "you take a round object off it," k̇è·ń·ⁿdì· "you dislike him," gò·ⁿdì·ń "shaman," dá·lè·ǹ·tò·ˑǹ "one hundred times."

3) Between consonant and vowel: t̂ì·k̇à·ˑí "these who are fat," bì·k̇è·ˑí "those which are his shoes," ⁿdì·ˑí "all the earth," hí·tò·ˑí "that which is striped red."

In the final position, long vowels are preceded by:

1) A consonant: bì·tà· "his father," bì·dè· "his horn," dí· "this one," ʔì·tò· "juice, soup."

2) A syllabic n. Only e· is found in this position: sì·ʔą́·ǹ·è· "that round object which had been there."

3) Another vowel. Again only e· occurs in this position: tó·è· "at the water."

Long vowels in high-toned syllables appear to be appreciably shorter (i.e., half long) in contrast with long vowels in low-toned syllables. Thus, for example, the vowels of dí· "this one" and bé·š "knife," though distinctly longer than those of bí "he" and dì·bé "sheep," are about half the duration of the long vowels of gò·ⁿdì· "shaman" and t̂è·š "charcoal."

§2:15. Nasalized vowels are found:

1) Between consonants: bì·k̨à? "male," nà·ˑdą́·ʔ "corn," bì·ẓè·k̨èʔ "his daughter," kì·sì·ẓà· "town," ʔí·šì·š "salt," bé·ʔ·k̨òs "arrow·shaft straightener," dì·k̨ò·ˑhé "novice on the war·path."

2) Between consonant and syllabic n: ʔìł-čą́-ń-gìž "you cut it in two," yò·kạ̀·ń "he who begs of him," žè·kę́ń "the girl," dì-γì·ń "he who is holy," bì-čì·ń-λá·s "you help him," ǹ-tọ̀-ń "he who is worthless," zé·ʔ-nà·-gò-čọ̀·ń "he whose mouth stretches."

3) Between a consonant and vowel: ʔìł-čą́o-gé·š "would that you cut it in two," bì-bą̀·í "that which is its edge," žè·-ží-kę́-í "the girl," bì-ǹ-cà·í "elk," bì·í "the deer," λóiʔ "prairie dog," kọ̀·í "the fire."

In the final position, nasalized vowels occur only after a consonant: ʔá-dą́ "at that time," bì-bą̀· "its edge, border," žè·-ží-kę̀· "girl," hę̀· "yes," ʔé-dì "it is gone," bì· "deer," ʔìł-dǫ́ "also," kọ̀· "fire."

§2:16. Vowel clusters are of two types: 1) clusters which function as syllabics and 2) those in which the vowels are separated by a point of syllable division.

The most frequently occurring clusters of the first kind are: ea, ai, ei, oi, ọi, ao, ạo, and eo. These are pronounced much like the English diphthongs except that the second vowels of Chiricahua clusters have a marked syllabic quality. Examples: ʔêał-ⁿdí "you two are jealous," sái "sand," bì-žéiʔ "his heart," ń-dói "puma," λóiʔ "prairie dog," ʔào "yes," ʔìł-čą́o-gé·š "would that you cut it in two," yéoł-žòł "he has rubbed it on him."

Vowel combinations of the second type occur when a syllable beginning with vowel immediately follows one ending in a vowel. Only two syllables begin with vowels, so all combinations of this type end in either -í or -è·. Any vowel but ę· may begin the cluster. Examples: łì-bá-í "those who are gray," nà·-dà·-bà·í "those who raid," sì·ʔą́-í "that round object which lies," bì-bą̀·í "that which is its edge," dì-bé-í "the sheep," bì-dè·-í "that which is his horn," žè·-ží-kę́-í "the girl," yáł-tì-í "those who are talking," bì-cì·í "that which is his head," dì-γì-í "that which is holy," ʔì-ǹ-ʔì·í "that which is stolen," tó-í "the water," ʔì-tò·í "that which is soup," gó-žǫ́-í "the place which is beautiful," kọ̀·í "the fire," dì-bá-è· "where he started off to war," ʔà·-è· "at that place," sì·ʔą́-è· "where the round object lay," bì-bą̀·è· "at its edge," dì-bé-è· "to the sheep," bì-dè·è· "on his horns," tá·-ʔá-ⁿdí-è· "just as he spoke thus," bì-cì·è· "on his head," sì·tį́-è· "where he lay," ná-dì·tì̧·è· "where he picked up a long slender object," tó-è· "at the water," sàs-bì-tò·è· "at Bear Springs," gó-žǫ́-è· "at the beautiful place," kọ̀·è· "at the fire."

In deliberate speech, an inorganic h is often inserted between the vowels of clusters of this type. In rapid speech, however, and particularly when both vowels are short, the cluster is often pronounced like one of type 1, or, if the vowels are identical, as a single long vowel.

§2:17. Each syllable of a Chiricahua utterance possesses, in addition to its segmental phonemes, certain distinctive features of pitch accent which constitute its prosodic or suprasegmental phonemes. There are four such prosodic phonemes (or tonemes): the low tone, indicated by a grave accent (e.g., gàh "rabbit"); the high tone, indicated by an acute accent (e.g., tó "water"); the high-low or falling tone, indicated by an inverted circumflex (e.g., ⸯⁿdâ· "eye"); and the low-high or rising tone, indicated by a circumflex (e.g., hǒ·ʔá "a rigid object juts out").

It should be emphasized that it is not possible to define the tonemes in terms of specific musical or physical descriptions. As for all other phonemes, the pronunciation of tonemes varies from speaker to speaker and in accordance with emotional and other factors affecting each speaker. Not only are the level (i.e., high and low) tones not always pronounced alike but there is never precisely the same interval between the two registers. Two factors, however, are constant: 1) whenever an utterance contains syllables differing in tone, an interval may always be heard between them, and 2) this interval is always such that syllables characterized as high-toned are pronounced on a higher pitch than those characterized as low-toned.

High and low tones occur in syllables of all kinds: ń-lį̇ "it flows," bí "he, him," bá·ʔ "thirst," bì-ǯéiʔ "his heart," ǹ-bèʔ "your breast," ǹ-bá "we two start off to war," nà·-bà· "he goes about on the war-path," nài-ʔà· "he goes about carrying a round object."

Syllables with inflected tones, however, always have a long vowel, a vowel cluster, or a long syllabic n: bì-ⁿdâ· "his eyes," ʔâiɫ-ċà "a noise is heard," ǹ-n̂·-ʔì̇· "you have put them down," hǒ·-tì "it extends upward," běo-ⁿdá·ɫ "you travel by means of it."

3. MORPHOPHONEMICS

§3:1. The Chiricahua word has three major syllable positions: prefinal, final, and postfinal. The final position is occupied in all words by one and only one syllable. Prefinal and postfinal positions, however, may be filled by zero, one, or more syllables. Proclitics, prefixes, and stems may occupy the prefinal position. The final position can only be taken by a stem syllable. Postfinals may include enclitic syllables and, rarely, certain stems.

The phonetic elements which make up a Chiricahua utterance are of two types: primary syllables and augments. Primary syllables may occur unmodified (in any of the three positions) or they may be reduced, augmented, contracted, or modified internally. Augmentation may apply to syllables in all three positions, contraction and reduction to prefinals and finals, and internal modification only to stem syllables in the final position. Augments are never syllabic but always appear as part of another syllable.

The material of the preceding two paragraphs may be summarized and illustrated as follows:

1. Primary syllables
   a) Prefinal. The syllable bì- (<bi- "his") in bì-cì-gò "[that] being his head."
   b) Final. The stem -cì- "head" in bì-cì-gò "[that] being his head."
   c) Postfinal. The enclitic -gò, subordinating, in bì-cì-gò "[that] being his head."
2. Reduced syllables
   a) Prefinal. The prefix ǹ- (<nì- "you") in ǹ-cì- "your head."

b) Final. The syllable -ʔé- (<the stem -ʔéd- "clothing") in bì-ʔé-dè "his clothing."
3. Augmented syllables
  a) Prefinal. The syllable dìš- (<the prefix dì- "to begin to" plus the augment š-, first person), in dìš-bá "I start off to war."
  b) Final. The syllable -ła·ł (<the augment d-, classifier, plus the stem -ʔà·ł "to chew") in hì-ła·ł "it is being chewed."
  c) Postfinal. The syllable -dè (<d, final consonant of the preceding stem -ʔéd-, plus the vocalic possessive enclitic -è) in bì-ʔé-dè "his clothing."
4. Contracted syllables
  a) Prefinal. The syllable dé- (<di- "to begin to" plus si-, perfective, and í-, first person) in dé-bà· "I have begun to go to war."
  b) Final. The syllable dí· "this one" (<the stem dí- "this" and the enclitic -í, referring to nonhuman objects).
5. Internally modified syllables
    Stem syllables which have several phonetic alternatives. Examples: ʔé·ʔ "clothing" (absolute form), -ʔéd- "clothing" (possessed form); -ʔà·š "two move" (imperfective mode), -ʔá·ž "two move" (perfective mode).

§3:2. Primary syllables always have the form cv or cvc plus a toneme. They are usually made up of a single morpheme having a similar phonetic form except that it may in some cases lack a toneme. In other words, morphemes in general are of two sorts with respect to tone: neutral-toned (i.e., lacking a toneme) and inherent-toned (possessing a toneme) (see §3:9). When a neutral-toned morpheme functions as a primary syllable, it takes on a low tone. Examples: bi- "his" becomes the syllable bì- in bì-cì· "his head" while nàh- "our" is unchanged in nàh-cì· "our heads."

Some primary syllables may be composed of part of a disyllabic morpheme. Thus, the morpheme -ná-ʔà "it is said" has two syllables: -ná-ʔà.

§3:3. Reduced syllables are primary syllables minus one segmental phoneme. The principal example of this process in prefinals is found in syllables having the form nì- or ní-. Such syllables in normal and rapid speech always reduce to ǹ- and ń-, respectively. Examples: ǹ-kè· (<nì-kè·) "your foot," ǹ-ń-ʔà· (<nì-ní-ʔà·) "you put a round object down."

Augmented and contracted prefinals containing nì- or ní- are also subject to similar reduction. See §§3:4, 3:5.

Primary prefinals ending in h are reduced when they immediately precede prefinals beginning with a spirant. Examples: dàh- in dà-sì-ẓà· "they lie in a bunch" (cf. dàh-gò·s-ẓà· "they [fourth person] lie in a bunch"), and in dà-sí-yá "I have become of a certain age" (cf. dàh-ẓì·-yá "he [fourth person] has become of a certain age").

Stem (i.e., final) syllables are reduced when followed by certain vocalic enclitics. Thus, the stem -ʔéd- in bì-ʔé-dè "his clothing" loses its final consonant which then augments the enclitic syllable.

When stem syllables having the form cvc are followed by the enclitics -í and ·ń, they may be pronounced either cv·cí, cv·cń, or cvc·í, cvc·ń. In the former pronunciation, which is perhaps more frequent in rapid speech, the stem syllable is of course reduced. Examples: ·gá·ł· in hò·gá··łń or hò·gá·ł·ń "he who is coming," ·bì?· in hài·dìł·bì·?í or hài·dìł·bì?·í "those who fill it."

§3:4. Augmented syllables are primary syllables which have combined with one or more nonsyllabic augments. They may be formed in all three syllable positions.

The augments most commonly occurring in prefinal position are the prefixes: à·· "to, from"; á· "for benefit of"; è· "by means of"; é· "on, against, at"; š·, first person subject pronoun (in all modes but the perfective); '· (i.e., high tone), conjunct second person subject pronoun (in all modes but the perfective); '·h· (i.e., low tone and length plus h) first person dual subject pronoun; ah·, second person dual subject pronoun (in all modes but the perfective); àh· or à·h·, second person dual pronoun (perfective mode); í·, first person pronoun (perfective mode); ł, classifier.

The postpositions à··, á·, è··, and é· unite only with the object pronoun prefixes ši·, first person; ni·, second person; bi· or yi·, third person; go·, fourth person; ?i·, indefinite; nà·hi·, first or second person dual; ?ád·, reflexive; and ?ìł·, reciprocal. The following rules of combination may be observed:

1) When the pronoun ends in i, the vowel of the postposition replaces i. The tone of the augmented syllable is that of the postposition. Examples: šà··yì·?à· (šà··>ši·+à··) "he gives a round object to me," ná·?á·gó·là· (ná·>ni·+á·) "he made it for you," bè··ža·gá·ł (bè··>bi·+è··) "he travels along by means of it," yè··?í·ɣą́ (yè··>yi·+è··) "he kills by means of it," ?à··yí·?à· (?à··>?i·+à··) "he gives a round object to someone," nà·hé·dìł·ɣòš (nà·hé·>nà·hi·+é·) "he shouts at us."

2) When the pronoun is go·, the g becomes k and the vowel o is replaced by the vowel of the postposition. The syllable takes the tone of the postposition. Examples: kà··yí·?à· (kà··>go·+à·) "he gives a round object to him," kè··žì·λí (kè··>go·+è··) "he acts like him," ká·?á·gó·là· (ká·>go·+á·) "he made it for him," ké·dìł·ɣòš (ké·>go·+é·) "he shouts at him."

3) When the pronoun ends in a consonant, the postposition forms a new syllable with the final consonant of the prefix. The pronoun syllable is thereby reduced. Examples: ?á·dè··ná·gó·λá (?á·dè··>?ád·+è··) "restore it by means of your own (power)," ?ì··łà··hài·λé (?ì·łà··>?ìł·+à··) "they pull a rope·like object from one another."

The subject pronouns and classifiers only augment primary syllables of the type cv. The rules of combination are as follows:

4) š· and ł· are simply added as final consonants: dìš· (<dì·+š·) in dìš·čá "I begin to hop," dìł· (<dì·+ł·) in dìł·λé "he begins to trot." Sometimes both š· and ł· may augment a syllable; in such cases, they combine to š·: dìš· (<dì·š·ł·) in dìš·λé "I begin to trot."

5) ah· plus a primary syllable yields càh· or cáh·, depending on the tone of the primary syllable: dàh· (<di·+ah·) in dàh·žá·š "you two begin to carry a mass," náh· (<ná·+ah·) in náh·žì· "you two are being cured." When both ·ah and ł· augment a syllable, the result

is càɬ or cáɬ: dàɬ (<dì·+ah̥+ɬ) in dàɬ·ᴋ̌é "you two begin to trot," náɬ (<ná·+ah̥+ɬ) in náɬ·ᴋ̌à· "you two wet it."

6) àh·, à·h· only augment the morphemes si·, ho·, and ni·, all of which designate the perfective mode (see §4:7). The resultant forms are sàh·, hà·h·, and nàh·, respectively. If ɬ also aguments these syllables we have sàɬ·, hà·ɬ·, and nàɬ·. Examples: ná·sàh·ᴋ̌é "you two have become wet," ná·sàɬ·ᴋ̌é "you two have wet it," hà·h·bé·ž "you two boil," hà·ɬ·bé·ž "you two boil it," ǹ·nàh·ẓà· "you two have put a mass down," šà·nàɬ·tį́ "you two have given him to me."

7) í· augments the morphemes si·, ho·, and ni·. The resultant forms are sí·, hó·, and ní·, respectively. It should be noted that the augmented syllable ní· never reduces to ń· (cf. §3:3). When ɬ also augments these syllables, the forms síɬ·, hó·ɬ·, and níɬ· result. Examples: sí·tį́ "I lie," síɬ·tį́ "I have him lying," hó·bé·ž "I boil," hó·ɬ·bé·ž "I boil it," ǹ·ní·ẓà· "I have put a mass down," nà··níɬ·tį́ "I have given him to you."

8) ·h· may augment any neutral or high·toned primary syllable of the type cv. The result is cv̀·h· when the primary syllable is neutral·toned and cv́·hì·h· when the syllable is high·toned. Reduced syllables of the type ǹ· and ń· become ǹ·h· and n̂·h·, respectively, when augmented by ·h·. When ɬ is also an augment, the resultant forms are cv̀·ɬ·, cv́·hì·ɬ·, ǹ·ɬ·, and n̂·ɬ·. Examples: ʔì·h· (<ʔì·+·h·) in ʔì·ʔì·h·ᴋ̌à· "we two shovel a mud·like mass away," ʔì·ɬ· (<ʔì·+·h·+ɬ) in ʔì·ɬ·gòš "we two sleep," náhì·h· (<ná·+·h·) in ná·hì·h·ẓì· "we two are being cured," ná·hì·ɬ· (<ná·+·h·+ɬ) in ná·hì·ɬ·ẓì· "we two cure him," ǹ·h· (<nì·+·h·) in ǹ·n̂·h·kè·s "we two faint," ǹ·ɬ· (<nì·+·h·+ɬ) in ǹ·ɬ·ⁿdá "we two be· come wrinkled," n̂·ɬ· (<ní·+·h·+ɬ) in n̂·ɬ·t̀àh "we two butcher it."

Certain primary syllables derived from a morpheme di·, when combined with ·h· and ·h·+ɬ, become ǹ·h· and ǹ·ɬ·, respectively: ǹ·h·kè· "we begin to run" (cf. dì·kè· "they begin to run"), ǹ·ɬ·ᴋ̌é "we two begin to trot" (cf. dì·ᴋ̌é "he begins to trot").

§3:5. Stem syllables are augmented by nonsyllabic consonants or final con· sonants of prefinals which appear directly before them. There are five such conso· nants: d (classifier or final consonant of the augment ·h·, first person dual subject, which appears before certain stems as ·d·), h (final consonant of the second person subject pronouns ah·, àh·, and à·h·), s (final consonant of the contracted prefinal cv·s·, see §3:8), š (the first person pronoun subject), and ɬ (a classifier). Not all stem syllables are augmented by these but where they are it is evident that the preceding prefinal is correspondingly reduced.

1) The classifier d· drops out (or survives as h) before all stem syllable initials but ʔ, h, ɣ, y, z, ž, and l. d· unites with these to produce t̀, d, g, d or ẓ, ẓ, ž, and λ, respectively. Examples: hì·t̀à·ɬ (<hì·d·ʔà·ɬ) "it is being chewed," ná·dá (<ná·d·há) "he returns," ʔì·gą́ (<ʔì··d·ɣą́) "we two kill them," hì·dą́ (<hi·d·yą́) "it is being eaten," gò·ǹ·ẓą́ (<go·ni··d·yą́) "we two are wise," nà··ʔì·ẓì· (<nà··ʔi··d·zì·) "we two work," ǹ·ží·š (<di··d·žì·š) "we two begin to pull it," ʔá·hì··λá (<ʔá··d·lá) "we two make it so."

2) h before the stem syllable initials ɣ, y, z, ž and l unites with them to produce x, s, s, š, and ɬ, respectively. Before any other stem syllable initial, h remains as final conso· nant of the preceding prefinal (see §3:4, 5, 6). Examples: hà·xàʔ (<hi·ah·ɣàʔ) "you two shake it," gà·sà· (<go·ah·yà·) "you two are becoming wise," bà··yá·nà·sì (<bi·à··yá·ni·

ah·zį̀) "you two are ashamed of it," hà·šìž (<hi·ah·žìž) "you two break it off," ʔá·là·
(<ʔá·ah·là·) "you two have made it so."

3) There are morphophonemically two final s consonants occurring before the stem syllable. One is a simple s, the other an s+ł. In a few instances, the single s (historically from an old z) assimilates completely to a following stem syllable initial y, z, and ž; in most cases, it remains. s+ł, however, always combines with the stem syllable initials y, z, and ž to form s, s, and š, respectively. Examples: ná·dè··zą́ (<ná·dè·s·zą́) "a movement of peoples has begun," nà··yá (<nà·s·yá) "he has moved about," dè··žó (<dè·s·žó) "a dragging has begun" (but note dè·s·yòl "he has blown," nà·s·zì "it has flown through the air," and dè·s·žì·ž "he has begun to crouch"), yì·sòl (<yì·s·ł·zòl) "he has blown it," n̓·ná·hè··są́ (<nì·ná·hè·s·ł·zą́) "they have camped," yì·dè··šó (<yì·dè·s·ł·žó) "he has begun to drag it."

4) Similarly, there are morphophonemically two š augments; simple š and š derived from š+ł (see §3:4, 4). Simple š combines with the stem sylalble initial h to form š. Both š augments unite with the stem syllable initials y, z, and ž to form s, s, and š, respectively. Examples: dì·šá (<dì·š·há) "I start off," gò·sà· (<gò·š·yà·) "I am becoming wise," bì·łn̓·sì (<bì·ł·nì·š·zì) "I am sleepy," hì·šìž (<hì·š·žìž) "I break it," hì·sòl (<hì·š·ł·zòl) "I blow it," ʔì·ʔì·sí (<ʔì·ʔì·š·ł·zí) "I shoot it through the air," hì·šé (<hì·š·ł·žé) "I cut it."

In a few cases, however, an š appears which does not combine with the stem syllable initials y, z, and ž: hìš·yà·ł "I yawn," ʔí·nš·zìs "I am the main one," ʔì·dìš·ží·š "I begin to dance." It seems likely that this š represents a combination of š plus a ł derived from an older l.

5) ł, as we have already seen, may be from an original ł or from h+ł (see §3:4, 5, and 6). Both, however, combine with the stem syllable initials y, z, ž, and l to form s, s, š, and ł, respectively. Examples: yì·sòl (<yì·ł·yòl) "he blows it," hà·sòl (<hì·ah·ł·yòl) "you two blow him," ʔì·ʔì·sí (<ʔì·ʔì·ł·zí) "he shoots it through the air," ʔì·ʔà·sí (<ʔì·ʔì·ah·ł·zí) "you two shoot it through the air," yì·šé (<yì·ł·žé) "he cuts it," hà·šé (<hì·ah·ł·žé) "you two cut it," yì·dì·łìʔ (<yì·dì·ł·lìʔ) "he burns it," dà·łìʔ (<dì·ah·lìʔ) "you two burn it."

§3:6. Augmented postfinals occur only when a vocalic enclitic follows a stem syllable ending in a consonant: bì·ʔé·dè (<bì·ʔéd·è) "his clothing." As indicated previously, the enclitics ·í and ·n̓ may, in rapid speech, be similarly augmented. See §3:3.

§3:7. The great majority of contracted syllables (combinations of two or more primary syllables) are found among the prefinals. Stem syllables occasionally contract with a following postfinal, but such contractions are nearly always optional whereas the prefinal contractions are, in most cases, mandatory.

Insofar as stem syllables are concerned, contraction is largely between stems of the type cv followed by a postfinal syllable composed of a vowel or syllabic n. Such contraction, however, takes place only in comparatively rapid speech. Thus, for example, the forms łì·bá·í "the gray ones" (·bá, stem syllable; ·í, postfinal) and łì·bá·n̓ "he who is gray" (·n̓, postfinal) may be heard, when spoken rapidly, łì·bái and łì·bán, respectively. Less often in rapid speech the postfinal ·gò may contract with an immediately preceding stem syllable. Thus, łì·bá·gò "it being gray" may be heard łì·bâo.

§3:8. Contractions of prefinals are so numerous and complex that we can do little here but describe some of the more frequently occurring examples:

1) Syllables of the type ʔì- frequently become ʔ and combine with an immediately preceding syllable type cv. Such contractions are optional but usually occur in normal and rapid speech. Examples: nà·ʔ-sí-zì· (or nà·-ʔì-sí-zì·) "I have worked," nà·ʔ-ñš-ʔì̀ (or nà·-ʔì-ñš-ʔì̀) "I lend them to you," hàʔ-ẑìł-γè· (or hà-ʔì-ẑìł-γè·) "he walks off."

2) Syllables of the type zì- or ẑì- frequently reduce to s and š, respectively. The reduced forms may then combine with a following syllable of the type di- or, more often, with a preceding syllable of the type cv. The contraction is optional through it usually takes place in normal and rapid speech. Examples: sdì-té·ł (or zì-dìł-té·ł)"it is about to stream," nà·s-dàł-tìł (or nà·-zì-dàł-tìł) "it will slide off," šdì-bá·ł (or ẑì-dìł-bá·ł) "he swings," náš-dì·-ẓá (or ná-ẑì-dì·-ẓá) "he stands up."

3) The syllable ẑì-, between a syllable type cv and zì-, reduces to i and contracts with the preceding syllable. Examples: ʔì-bêi-zìł-ⁿdí (<ʔì-bé-ẑì-zìł-ⁿdì) "he knocks it off," gò-tài-zìł-ⁿdì (<gò-tà·-ẑì-ẑì-ⁿdì) "he knocks them down one after another."

4) Syllables of the type yì- or yí-, in normal or rapid speech and when preceded by a syllable type cv, reduce to i and become part of the preceding syllable. Examples: tà·-nâi-gìs (or tà·-ná-yì-gìs) "he washes him," nài-dì-λó (or nà·-yì-dì-λó) "he tries it on," nái-ń-ʔą́ (or ná-yí-ń-ʔą́) "he has brought a round object back."

5) Certain prefinals having the form nì- (<morphemes ni- or nì-), occurring after a syllable type cv, disappear entirely leaving a high tone on the vowel of the preceding syllable. Examples: ʔí-lį́ (<ʔì-nì-lį́) "it is valuable," yà·-ʔí-ʔì̀ (<yà·-ʔì-nì-ʔì̀) "he gives them to him," ʔí-ń-łą́ (<ʔí-nì-nì-łą́) "you raise crops."

When the syllable preceding such a ni- has the form di-, the resultant contracted syllable is ń-, not dí-: ń-bá (<dì-nì-bá) "you start off to war," ʔá-ń-ⁿdí (<ʔá-dì-nì-ⁿdí) "you speak so." See §3:4, (8).

di- syllables may also unite with ni- syllables that remain to form a long syllabic n. Thus: ná-ǹ·-ʔà· (<ná-dì-nì-ʔà·) "you pick up a round object." It will be remembered that syllabic n syllables having this origin display certain peculiarities of pronunciation. See §2:11.

6) The element characteristic of the disjunct imperfective (hi-) combines with prefinals type cv to form a syllable cv with a long vowel. Examples: hà·-čà (<hà-hì-čà) "he burst out crying," dì·-γòš (<dì-hì-γòš) "there is shouting."

7) A number of prefixes having the form hò-, hó-, or hó·- combine with a preceding cv syllable. When the vowel of the preceding syllable is a, the vowel of the contracted syllable is either ao or o·; where the vowel is other than a, the contracted syllable has o (if combined with hò- or hó-) or o· (if combined with hó·-). Examples: nào-yàʔ or nò·-yàʔ (<nà·-hò-yàʔ) "would that he go about," nà·-ẑó-yàʔ (<nà·-ẑì-hó-yàʔ) "would that he (fourth person) go about," nǎo-λìž or nǒ·-λìž (<nà·-hó-λìž) "he has fallen off," dó-lìʔ (<dì-hó-lìʔ) "would that it burn," dó·-lìʔ (<dì-hó·-lìʔ) "it has burned."

8) The syllable sì- (derived from the morpheme si-, perfective mode) unites in different ways with a preceding cv syllable. In a majority of cases, sì- reduces to s- and becomes the final consonant of the syllable preceding. The vowel of the syllable preceding, if originally short, is lengthened. Examples: hà·s-ʔá (<hà-sì-ʔá) "a rigid object extends upward,

k̓à·s·k̓èh (<k̓à·ˑsì·k̓èh) "he has been wounded," gò·s·lį́ (<gò·sì·lį́) "he has been born," yì·s·k̓àš (<yì·sì·k̓àš) "he has sharpened it."

Certain prefixes like those formed from the prefixes di·, hi·, and ni· contract with si· to form de·, he·, and ne·, respectively. Examples: dé·ṅ·ẓ̌à· (<dì·sí·ṅ·ẓ̌à·) "you have started to carry a mass," né·ṅ·yá (<nì·sí·ṅ·yá) "you have grown," nì·hé·ṅ·čà̰· (<nì·hì·sí·ṅ·čà̰·) "you have defecated."

9) The prefinals dì·, hì·, and nì· also combine with a prefinal derived from a morpheme ni· (meaning uncertain) to de·, he·, and ne·: dà·dè·ɫé (<dà·dì·ni·ɫé) "it (a string) is stretched across," nì·nè·ɫà· (<nì·nì·ni·ɫà·) "he turns his head about," nì·hè··dá (<nì·hì· ni·dá) "he makes a wager."

10) Contracted prefinals may be augmented as well. In general, the rules for the augmentation of contracted prefinals are the same as those for primary syllables; see §3:4. The following examples will serve to illustrate the process: dé·ẓ̌à· (<dì·sì·í·ẓ̌à·) "I have started to carry a mass," dè·h·ẓ̌à· (<dì·sì·ˑh·ẓ̌à·) "we two have started to carry a mass," dáh·ẓ̌à· (<dì·sì·ah·ẓ̌à·) "you two have started to carry a mass," déɫ·xìz (<dì·sì·í·ɫ·xìz) "I have twirled it."

§3:9. By internal modification we refer to changes in vowels, consonants, or tonemes by which syllables morphologically related in function may alternate. In Chiricahua Apache such modifications are highly irregular and we can do little here but indicate some of the more frequently occurring processes.

Noun stems sometimes alternate phonetically depending upon their use in the absolute or possessed form. Thus, initial voiceless spirants may become voiced in the possessed form: xé·ɬ "pack, burden," bì·γé·lè "his pack," ɬì "smoke," bì·lì·dè "his smoke."

Note, too, that the final consonants of noun stems vary. Thus, noun stems having a zero final in the absolute may take a ʔ or d final in the possessed form. The toneme and vowel duration may change as well. Examples: tó "water," bì·tòʔ "his water"; k̓à· "arrow," bì·k̓àʔ "his arrow"; ɬì "smoke," bì·lì·dè "his smoke."

By far the most important changes of this sort occur in verb stems. These may vary according to the tense and mode of the verb and the variations, briefly summarized, are of the following types: changes in the final consonant of the stem (e.g., ·có·s, imperfective; ·cò·z, perfective "to handle a fabric-like object"), changes in the pitch accent of the stem (e.g., ·ʔà·, momentaneous imperfective, ·ʔá, continuative imperfective "to handle a round object"), changes in the quality of the stem vowel (e.g., ·ʔà·, imperfective, ·ʔą̄, perfective "to handle a round object"), and changes in the length of the stem vowel (e.g., ·ʔà·š, imperfective, ·ʔàš, progressive "two people move"). In some verbs, as may be seen from the examples given above, more than one of these variations may take place. The stem variations are highly irregular and it will be impossible to list here all of the possible patterns of variation. The following list, however, will suffice to illustrate the commoner types. Stems are given in this order: imperfective, perfective, progressive, iterative, and optative. Where variant forms for aspect are listed, these are marked (mom. = momentaneous, cont. = continuative).

-ʔàh; -ʔàh; -ʔàh; -ʔàh; "to butcher" (act. tr.)

-ťè·; -ťè·; -ťè·ł; -ťè·; -ťè· "to handle a board-like object" (act. tr.)

-ʔà·; -ʔá; -ʔá·ł; -ʔá; -ʔà· "a noise is heard" (act. intr.)

-ká (mom.), -kà (cont.); -kà; -kàł; -kà; -ká "several move" (act. intr.)

-ɣè· (mom.), -ɣò (cont.); -ɣò; -ɣòł; -ɣò; -ɣè· "to move quickly, to run" (act. intr.)

-lé; -lá; -lé·ł; -lé; -lé (mom.), -là ʔ (cont.) "to handle a rope-like object" (act. tr.)

-čì·; -čà·; -čì·ł; -čì·; -čì· "to defecate" (act. intr.)

-ƛó; -ƛǫ́; -ƛó·ł; -ƛó; -ƛó "to tie" (act. tr.)

-ʔà· (mom.), -ʔá (cont.); -ʔǫ́; -ʔá·ł; -ʔá; -ʔà· "to handle a round object" (act. tr.)

-ɣé; -ɣí; -ɣé·ł; -ɣé; -ɣé "to kill one" (act. tr.)

-zé; -zǫ́; -zé·ł; -zé; -zà ʔ "a movement of peoples takes place" (act. tr.)

-ɣè· (mom.), -ɣé (cont.); -ɣí; -ɣé·ł; -ɣé; -ɣè· "to carry a burden" (act. tr.)

-bì· (mom.), -bì ʔ (cont.); -bǫ́; -bí·ł; -bí; -bì· "to win a game" (act. tr.)

-tàł; -tàł; -tàł; -tàł; -tàł "to burst" (act. intr.)

-ʔòł; -ʔè·l; -ʔòł; -ʔòł; -ʔòł "to spread out" (act. tr.)

-dè·s; -dè·z; -dìs; -dìs; -dè·s "to singe" (act. tr.)

-ʔè·š; -ʔè·ž; -ʔìš; -ʔìš; -ʔè·š "to string beads" (act. tr.)

-bà·ł; -bà·l; -bàł; -bàł; -bà·ł "to hang suspended" (act. intr.)

-bà·s; -bǫ́·z; -bàs; -bàs; -bà·s "to become round" (act. intr.)

-ʔà·š; -ʔá·ž; -ʔàš; -ʔàš; -ʔà·š "two persons move" (act. intr.)

-ʔè·ł; -é·l; -ʔòł; -ʔòł; -ʔè·ł "to float" (act. intr.)

-ʔé·s; -ʔè·z; -ʔìs; -ʔìs; -ʔé·s "to step about" (act. intr.)

-ká·š (mom.), -kàš (cont.); -kà·ž (mom.), -kàš (cont.); -kàš; -kàš; -ká·š (mom.), -kàš (cont.) "to sharpen" (act. tr.)

-ʔí·ł; -ʔì·l; -ʔí·ł; -ʔí·ł; -ʔí·ł "to copulate" (act. tr.)

The stem initials ɣ and l become x and ł, respectively, when preceded by s (<s+ł, see §3:5, [3]) or š (<š or <š+ł, see §3:5, [4]). ɣ also becomes x when preceded by ł (<ł or <h+ł, see §3:5, [5]). Examples: yì·s-xàš (<yì·s-ł-ɣàš) "he has bitten it," nàis-łì ʔ (<nàis-ł-lì ʔ) "he has burned it here and there," hìš-xǫ́ (<hìš-ɣǫ́) "I kill them," ʔáš-là· (< ʔáš-là·) "I have made it so," hì·š-xàš (<hì·š-ł-ɣàš) "I bite it," nà·š-łì ʔ (<nà·š-ł-lì ʔ) "I burn it here and there," yì·ł-xàš (<yì·ł-ɣàš) "he bites it," hà·ł-xàš (<hà·h-ł-ɣàš) "you two bite it."

Parenthetically, it may be noted that this assimilation does not always take place. Note, for example, dì·š-ɣá·š "I shout," nà·š-lǫ̀· "I waddle," yìł-ɣàl "he eats it," gò·s = lí "he has been born." Comparative evidence makes it clear that š may be from an earlier *š+l, l from an earlier *l, and s from an earlier *z. The lack of assimilation noted in the examples just quoted is a trace of these archaisms in Chiricahua.

§3:10. Pitch accent is, as we have said, a syllable phenomenon. The pitch of a given syllable, however, is determined by the tones of the morpheme or morphemes which compose that syllable. Morphemes may be without pitch (e.g., š‑, first person; ł‑, classifier), neutral‑toned, or possess inherent tone. The morphophonemic processes by which the toneme of a syllable is determined may be summarized as follows:

1) A syllable consisting of one or more neutral‑toned morphemes ordinarily takes the low tone: sì‑ (<si‑) in sì‑ʔą́ "a round object lies," bì‑ (<bi‑) in bì‑tò? "his water," nàh‑ (<ni‑ah‑) in nàh‑ⁿdè·z "you two are tall," hài‑ (<ha‑yi‑) in hài‑ʔà· "he takes a round object out."

When a syllable consisting of one neutral‑toned morpheme immediately precedes a high‑toned syllabic n, it assimilates in tone: yí‑ (<yi‑) in yà·‑yí‑ń‑ʔą́ "he has given a round object to him."

2) Syllables consisting of one or more inherently low‑ or inherently high‑toned morphemes have a low or high tone, respectively. Examples: nàh‑ (<nàh‑) in nàh‑tò? "our water," ná‑ (<ná‑) in ná‑mà·s "it rolls around," ná‑ <ná·‑) in ná‑mà·s "you roll around."

3) Syllables combining low‑ and neutral‑toned morphemes have the low tone: nà·h‑ (<nà·‑hi‑ah‑) in nà·h‑ʔà· "you carry a round object about," hì·h‑ (<hi·‑·h‑) in hì·h‑bé·ž "we two boil."

4) Syllables in which a neutral‑toned morpheme precedes one with an inherent high tone have the high tone: sí‑ (<si‑í‑) in sí‑tį́ "I lie (there)," ń‑ (<di‑·) in ń‑bá "you start off to war."

5) Syllables in which a high‑toned morpheme precedes a low‑ or neutral‑toned morpheme have the falling tone: n̂‑ł‑ (<ní‑·‑h‑ł‑) in n̂‑ł‑t̯àh "we two butcher it," ‑bâo (<‑bá‑gò) in łì‑bâo "it being gray," nâi‑ (<ná‑yi‑) in tà·‑nâi‑gìs "he washes him," bêi‑ (<bi‑é‑ži‑) in ʔì‑bêi‑ži‑ł‑ⁿdí "he knocks it off."

In some cases, a neutral‑toned morpheme following one with a high tone assimilates to it in pitch: náh‑ (<ná‑ah‑) in náh‑ži‑ "you two are cured," ʔá‑ (<ʔá‑ah‑) in ʔá‑łà· "you two have made it so."

6) Syllables in which a low‑toned morpheme precedes a high‑toned morpheme have the rising tone: nǎo‑ (<nà·‑ho‑·‑) in nǎo‑yà? "would that you would wander about."

4. MORPHOLOGY

THE NOUN

§4:1. Chiricahua Apache nouns may be divided into the following groups: monosyllabic nouns, nouns requiring a constant possessive prefix, thematic nouns, nouns formed from verbs, and compound nouns.

Monosyllabic nouns are those composed of a single free theme: ʔá "fog", ʔé·? "coat," tó "water," k̓òs "cloud," k̓à· "arrow."

Included in this class are certain nouns composed of a stem plus a suffix which cannot be isolated: tà·žè "chicken," tàłé "cedar," gą́hé "supernaturals of the mountain," kéhè· "moccasin game."

When monosyllabic nouns are preceded by a possessive pronoun prefix, they sometimes alter in phonetic form. These alternations involve the following types of changes: an initial voiceless spirant may be voiced, a final voiceless spirant may become voiced, a zero final may be replaced by a consonantal final, and a vocalic suffix may be added. Examples: ʔé·ʔ "coat," bì·ʔéd·è "his coat" (bì· "his"); ťá "feather," bì·ťàʔ "his feather," k̯à· "arrow," bì·k̯àʔ "his arrow"; bé·š "knife," bì·béž·è "his knife"; xè·ł "pack," bì·ɣél·è "his pack"; łì "smoke," bì·lìd·è "his smoke."

Nouns requiring a constant possessor are composed of a single bound stem or of a bound stem plus vocalic suffix and a possessive prefix. Nouns of this classification generally denote body parts, kinship terms, or localities. Examples: bì·cì· "his head," bì·kè· "his foot" (cf. ké "moccasin, shoe"), bì·ⁿdâ· "his eye," bì·tà· "his father," bì·k̯ìs "his sibling of the same sex," bì·bé·žè "his stepfather," bì·ɣèʔ "its inside; inside it," bì·ká "its surface; on top of it," bì·čą́ "away from it."

With some nouns of this sort, particularly those denoting body parts, it is possible to distinguish between alienable and inalienable possession. Thus, for example, bì·cì· "his head" denotes the head which is a part of the individual's body but bì·ʔì·cì·, which means literally "his someone's head" (ʔì·, indefinite possessive), denotes a head once the inalienable part of another's body but now in the possession of the individual referred to by the pronoun bì·.

In compounds, nouns requiring constant possessors may sometimes occur without the possessive prefix: cì·ťá "top of the head" (cì· "head," ·ťá "top," both of which require the possessive prefix when used independently), dá·ɣèʔ "throat" (dá· "chin," ·ɣèʔ "inside"), dá·ɣà· "beard" (·ɣà· "hair, wool").

Thematic nouns are composed of a prefix plus a stem. The prefix cannot be isolated from the stem in meaning. Examples: dì·béhé "sheep," yá·tì "talk, conversation," ná·ťòh "tobacco," gò·tál "ceremony," kò·ɣà̀ "home, camp" (cf. ɣà̀ "home"), kò·tà "encampment."

These nouns do not alter their form in the possessive: šì·dìbéhé "my sheep," šì·kò·ɣà̀ "my home," šì·náťòh "my tobacco."

Nouns formed from verbs are of two kinds: those which are composed of a verb form alone, and those which are composed of a verb form plus relative enclitic. Examples: nà·ťá "chief; he commands," ʔéńťį "witch; he bewitches him," gòłgà "a plain, clearing; it (a place) is white," dìɣì "ceremony, shaman; it is holy," šìłnà·ʔà·š "my spouse; he lives with me," łìbá·ń "a class of supernaturals; he who is gray," hà·ʔdì·ʔá·ń "singer; he who sings."

More complex nouns of this class are formed from clauses. These consist of a clause plus relative enclitic: bé·š·ńX̯ìz·í "steel; that metal (bé·š) which is hard" (ńX̯ìz "it is hard"), bì·ńcà·í "elk; that deer (bì·) which is big" (ńcà· "it is big"), ńłčìʔ·dìłxìł·í "cyclone; that wind (ńłčìʔ) which is black" (dìłxìł "it is black").

Noun compounds are very common in Chiricahua Apache. They may be divided into four groups: noun plus noun compounds, noun plus particle, noun plus verb stem, and noun (or particle) plus verb. Examples: tó·ⁿdé "all water creatures" (tó "water," ⁿdé "beings"), gòlgà ʔìžáš̀è· "horned lark" (gòlgà "plains," ʔìžáš̀è· "bird"), k̄à· ɣé·ł "quiver" (k̄à· "arrows," ɣé·ł "burden"), k̄à· bé·š "arrow point" (bé·š "metal"), nì·šž̧à· dábádé "pygmy owl" (nì·šž̧à· "owl," dábádé "small, insignificant"), ńłcą̀ bìʔá "a light rain" (ńłcą̀ "rain," bìʔá "female"), čís tè·ł "terrapin" (čís "body," tè·ł "to be wide"), cè· ž̧ìn "a species of eagle" (cè· "tail," ž̧ìn "to be black"), cį̀ skà· "a place name" (cį̀ "trees," skà· from sìkà· "a clump [of trees] lies"), góč̨į dàgìž̧ "the cutting of the nose, a punishment for adultery" (góč̨į "his nose," dàgìž̧ "it has been cut").

§4:2. Only one set of prefixes may be combined with the noun. These are the possessive pronoun prefixes.

Person	Singular	Dual	Distributive
1	ši·	{ nàhi· or	{ dà·nàhi· or
2	ni·	{ nàh·	{ dà·nàh
3	bi·	bi·	dà·bi·
4	go·	go·	dà·go·
indef.	ʔi·	ʔi·	dà·ʔi·

Five persons are distinguished: first, second, third, fourth, and the indefinite. The fourth person is used when reference is made to certain relatives by marriage with whom a respect relationship is maintained. It may also be used in a context in which it is necessary to distinguish two third persons. The indefinite possessor is employed when it is necessary to indicate that a thing is possessed but it is not necessary to specify the possessor.

In the dual, there is no difference between the pronouns for the first and second persons. The distinction between nàhi· and nàh· seems to be purely phonetic but no rule can be given regarding their use.

Ordinarily, the third person singular forms are used in the dual as well. Where, however, it is necessary to specify the third person dual, the form góbi· may be used.

THE VERB

§4:3. All verbs may be divided into a prefix complex (composed of one or more prefixes) and a theme. The theme may consist of a single stem (e.g., ʔà· "a round object moves," gà "to be white") or of a prefix (called a "thematic prefix") plus a stem (e.g., ná·...t̓òh "to smoke," go·...tà·ł "to conduct a ceremony"). The thematic prefix generally occupies position four in the prefix complex (see §1:2). It remains the same in all forms of the verb.

The verb stem, however, may vary according to the tense and mode of the verb. These variations have already been described; see §3:8.

Five tense-modes are recognized, each of which may theoretically be varied for aspect as well. In no case, however, does a verb have a distinct form for each tense-mode and aspect. For most verbs, there are perhaps only three distinct stems; in a few cases, there may be as many as five or six.

§4:4. In §1:2 was given a list of the prefixes to the verb in the order in which they occurred in the complex. These prefixes, for the purposes of the morphological description, may be divided into the following groups: adverbial prefixes (occupying positions 2, 4, and 9), object pronoun prefixes (occupying positions 3 and 7), subject pronouns and deictic prefixes (occupying positions 8 and 11), tense-modal prefixes (occupying positions 5 and 10), and the classifiers (occupying position 12).

The adverbial prefixes, as the name implies, add a measure of concrete significance to the theme. They differ from the thematic prefixes in that they are not indissolubly a part of the theme but may be found with a number of themes. There are probably as many adverbial prefixes and prefix combinations as there are stems. To illustrate their use, let us take the theme -ʔà·, -ʔá̧, -ʔá·ł, -ʔá, -ʔà· "to handle a round object" and see the variety of meanings obtainable by varying the adverbial prefixes:

O-à·-ni·. . . "to give a round object to someone" (O, any object pronoun, à- "to"; ni-, completive).

ʔáh-. . . "to put a round object inside" (ʔáh- "in, inside").

dàh-yí-. . . "to put a round object on top" (dàh-yi- "up, on top").

di-. . . "to begin to carry a round object" (di- "to begin to").

nà·-. . . "to carry a round object here and there" (nà- "about, here and there").

ná-di-. . . "to pick up a round object" (ná-di- "movement upward").

ná-ni-. . . "to bring a round object back" (ná- "back," ni-, completive; see the first example above).

nì-ni-. . . "to put a round object down" (nì- "down, to a stop"; ni-, completive).

hà-. . . "to take a round object out" (hà- "out of an enclosed space").

céh-. . . "to put a round object in the fire" (céh- "into the fire").

Most of the prefixes and prefix combinations above may be used with more than one theme. Thus, for example, the prefix combination ná-di- "movement upward" forms the following verbs:

ná-di-. . .-ł-tè· "to pick up an animate object" (stem: "to handle an animate object").

ná-di-. . .-ʔà·š "two persons get up, arise" (stem: "two persons move").

ná-di-. . .-tì· "to pick up a slender object" (stem: "to handle a slender object").

ná-di-. . .-ká "several stand up, arise" (stem: "several persons move").

ná-di-. . .-γè· "to carry a burden up" (stem: "to carry a burden").

Though the adverbial prefixes are not conjugated, they do have some relational significance. Thus, certain adverbial prefixes require the conjunct form of the imperfective paradigm whereas others require the disjunct form (see §4:7, [1]). Similarly, the adverbial prefixes determine the type of perfective paradigm required by the verb form. Thus, for example, the prefixes di- "to begin to" and nà- "about, here and there" always require the verb to take the si- perfective paradigm, whereas the prefixes di-, referring to noise or sound, and nà- "down, off, into" require the hi- perfective paradigm.

Finally, the determination of aspect seems definitely a function of the adverbial prefix. The prefix di- "to begin to" always requires the momentaneous aspect and the prefix nà- "about, here and there" the continuative aspect. Contrast this with the prefix di-, referring to repetetive action, which always requires the repetetive verb stem, and the prefix nà- "down, off, into" which takes the momentaneous stem. In many cases, however, the prefix does not specifically require a particular aspectival form.

§4:5. The object pronoun prefixes are as follows:

Person	Singular	Dual	Distributive
1	ši-		
		nàhi-	dà·nàhi-
2	ni-		
3	bi-	bi-, góbi-	dà·bi-, dà·góbi-
	yi-	yi-, góyi-	dà·yi, dà·góyi-
4	go-	go-	dà·go-
indef.	ʔi-	ʔi-	dà·ʔi-

The reflexive prefix is ʔá- or ʔád-, the former preceding a consonant, the latter a vowel. The reciprocal prefix is ʔìł-.

The third person object is ordinarily indicated by zero in all forms but the third person. When the subject is also the third person, the third person object is indicated by the prefix yi-. bi- is used only to denote the indirect object of a verb form in persons other than the third person.

The same distinction between the third and fourth persons applies here as in the case of the possessive pronouns (see §4:2).

§4:6. There are two sets of subjective pronouns in Chiricahua Apache:

Person	Set (a)	Set (b)
Sing. 1	š-	í-
2	ǹ- or -ʼ-	n̂-
3	zero	zero
Dual 1	ì·(d)-	ì·(d)-
2	ah-	àh- or à·h-

Set (a) is used in the imperfective, progressive, iterative, and optative modes. It is also used in the perfective paradigms when the verb has the d or l class (see §4:8). Set (b) is used only in the perfective paradigms of zero and ł class verbs.

In the second person singular, n̓- is used in the disjunct imperfective paradigm and the high tone (which is attached to the adverbial prefix preceding) in the conjunct imperfective paradigm.

In set (b), àh- is used in the si- and ni- perfective paradigms, while à·h- is used only in the ho- perfective paradigm.

The fourth person subject, a place or time subject, and an indefinite subject are indicated by the deictic prefixes ǯi-, go-, and ʔi-, respectively.

§4:7. The Chiricahua verb is conjugated in five principal modes: imperfective, perfective, progressive (from which the future is formed), iterative (also the base for the customary), and the optative. We have already dealt with stem variations for mode; here we shall deal with the prefix complex.

1) The imperfective mode, in a large majority of cases, is indicated by the absence of a modal prefix. In a verb which has adverbial prefixes, then, these prefixes are combined directly with the subject pronouns of set (a), the second person singular pronoun being a high tone. Thus, for example, the verb ná-ni-. . .-ʔà· "to bring back a round object" is conjugated as follows in the imperfective mode: náǹšʔà· (<*ná-ni-š-ʔà·) "I bring back a round object," náńʔà· (<*ná-ni-´-ʔà·) "you . . . ," náiʔà· (<*ná-yi-ni- -ʔà·) "he . . . ," náǯíʔà· (<*ná-ǯi-ni-ʔà·) "he (fourth person) . . . ," náǹ·tʼà· (<*ná-ni-i-d-ʔà·) "we two . . . ," nánàhʔà· (<*ná-ni-àh-ʔà·) "you two . . . ."

When the verb has no thematic or adverbial prefixes, the second person singular is indicated by a pronoun n̓-, and a prefix hi- appears before the pronoun in each of the other persons: hìšbé·ž (<*hi-š-bé-ž) "I boil," ǹ-bé·ž "you boil," hì-bé·š "he boils," ǯì-bé·š "he (fourth person) boils" (here the fourth person deictic element makes hi- unnecessary), hì·bé·ž (<*hi-ì-d-bé·ž) "we two boil," hàhbé·ž (<*hi-àh-bé·ž) "you two boil." If such a verb is transitive, the object pronoun will replace the hi- element: nìšbé·ž (<*ni-š-ł-bé·ž) "I boil you," yìlbé·ž "he boils him."

Certain adverbial prefixes require the disjunct form of the imperfective. This means that a prefix hi- is inserted between the adverbial prefix and the subject pronoun in all but the second person singular and where deictic or object pronouns are used. The second person singular of such conjugations is marked by the prefix n̓-. Thus, for example, the verb ha-. . .-ʔà· "to take out a round object" is conjugated as follows in the imperfective mode: hà·šʔà· (<*ha-hi-š-ʔà·) "I take out a round object," hàǹʔà· (<*ha-ǹ-ʔà·) "you . . . ," hàiʔà· (<*ha-yi-ʔà·) "he . . . " (here the required third person object yi- replaces the hi- prefix), hà-ǯ̀ìʔà· "he (fourth person) . . . " (ǯi- makes hi- unnecessary), hàhì·tʼà· (<*ha-hi-ì-d-ʔà·) "we two . . . ," hà·hʔà· (<*ha-hi-àh-ʔà·) "you two . . . ."

The imperfective mode denotes activities in the process or activities about to fulfill themselves. Examples: k̇ìdàsàh ?à· "you two tie a fabric on him," ǹń?à· "put the round object down," náǹšá "I am going home," nádì· ?à· "he picks up the round object." Neuter verbs denoting states and qualities undefined as to time are also conjugated in the imperfective paradigm: łìgà "it is white," ǹšⁿdè·z "I am tall," ?áťé "it is so."

2) There are three perfective paradigms: the si- perfective, the ho- perfective, and the ni- perfective. When the verb has a zero or ł classifier, the pronouns of set (b) are used; and when the verb has a d or l classifier, the pronouns are of set (a). The forms are as follows:

Person	si- perfective		ho- perfective		ni- perfective	
	zero and ł	d and l	zero and ł	d and l	zero and ł	d and l
Sing. 1	sí-	sìš-	hó··	hòš-	ní-	nìš-
2	síǹ-	síǹ-	hóǹ-	hóǹ-	n̂·-	n̂·-
3	sì-	sì-	hó··	hà-	ń-	ń-
4	ǯì̀·s-	ǯì̀·s-	ǯó··	ǯà-	ǯíń-	ǯíń-
Place	gò·s-	gò·s-	gò··	gà-	góń-	góń-
Indef.	?ì·s-	?ì·s-	?ó··	?à-	?íń-	?íń-
Dual 1	sì·(d)-	sì·(d)-	hò·(d)-	hò·(d)-	ǹ·(d)-	ǹ·(d)-
2	sàh-	sàh-	hà·h-	hà·h-	nàh-	nàh-

The above are the characteristic forms of each of the paradigms. When the verb employs adverbial prefixes, these often unite with the tense-modal prefixes in such a way as to obscure the forms quoted. For a summary of some of the more important contractions of this sort, see the phonology, §§3:4–3:7.

The perfective paradigms, like those for the imperfective, serve two functions: to form neuter verbs and to form the perfective mode of active verbs. Perfective neuters define states or qualities which have resulted from previous action. The si- perfective is employed when a durative static notion is implied: sì?ą́ "a round object has position," sìdá "he is sitting," sìzį́ "he is standing." The ho- perfective is used when an inceptive static notion is implied: dìcì·?ó·?á-í "a standing tree" (dìcì "tree," ?ó·?á "a rigid object has extension"), zà·hǒ·?á-í "a bridle bit" (zà·- "mouth"; hǒ·?á "a rigid object extends out from an enclosed space"). Finally, the ni- perfective is used when a completive static notion is implied: nà·?ń?á "bridge; a rigid object extends across (to the other side)," góń?á "arroyo; a rigid object (the reference is to a place) extends off (but with definite end)."

The perfective mode of the active verb distinguishes an action that has become complete. The form of the perfective paradigm is determined by the meaning of the adverbial prefixes and the theme. Thus, nà·síyá "I have moved about" (nà·- "here and there"; -yá "one person moves") may be contrasted with hǎoyá

"I have come out of an enclosed space" (ha- "out of an enclosed space"), and ṅníyá "I have arrived, I have stopped moving" (nì- "to an end").

3) The progressive, future, iterative, and optative paradigms are all formed by adding certain prefixes (ho- for the progressive, do- or da- for the future, ná- for the iterative, and ho- for the optative) to the conjunct imperfective pronouns. The forms are as follows:

Person	Progressive	Future	Iterative	Optative
Sign. 1	hòš-	dò·š-	náš-	hóš-
2	hó-	dó·-	ná-	hó·-
3	hò-	dà-	ná-	hó-
4	ǯà-	ǯìdà-	náǯì-	ǯó-
Place	gà-	gòdà-	nágò-	gó-
Indef.	ʔà-	ʔìdà-	náʔì-	ʔó-
Dual 1	hò·(d)-	dò·(d)-	nâ·(d)-	hò·(d)-
2	hàh-	dà·h-	náh-	hà·h-

Adverbial prefixes often unite with those denoting the progressive and optative modes in such a way as to obscure their form.

The progressive paradigm functions in the progressive mode of active verbs. It signifies action carried on while moving along: hòšʔá·ł "I am carrying a round object" (literally: "I handle a round object while moving along"), hòžàh "he is hunting" (lit: "he hunts while moving along").

The future seems to be formed from the progressive by the addition of an element di- or de- to the progressive prefixes. The same stem form is used in both paradigms.

The future is the only obligatory tense form in Chiricahua Apache. All other tenses are expressed periphrastically by means of enclitics.

The iterative mode expresses repeated or habitual activity: nádìšdá "I begin to go home again and again," náššá "I hunt repeatedly, I am a hunter." Another mode, the usitative, may be formed by combining the prefix complex of the imperfective with the stem of the iterative. This mode expresses usual or customary activity.

The optative mode expresses a wish or desire that some activity be performed. nò·ká "would that we go; let's go," gòdóyàʔ "would that [the ceremony] begin."

§4:8. Chiricahua Apache verbs may be divided into four classes. These classes are in part distinguished by the classifier contained in the prefix complex, and in part by certain modifications in the pronoun subjects employed.

Zero class verbs are distinguished by the lack of a classifier and the fact that subject pronouns of set (a) are employed in all modes but the perfective, which uses the pronouns of set (b). Zero class verbs may be neuter or active, transitive or intransitive: sìʔą́ "a round object lies" (neuter intr.), yàʔį̀ "he sees it" (neuter trans.), ʔìdìʔà· "a round object begins to move" (act. intr.), yìdìʔà· "he begins to carry a round object" (act. tr.).

Some zero class intransitives may be made transitive by the addition of the -ł- classifier: sí-ł-ʔą́ "I have a round object lying" (cf. sìʔą́ "a round object lies"), sí-ł-tį̀ "I have an animate object lying" (cf. sítį̀ "I lie"), nài-ł-tè· "I carry an animate object about" (cf. nà·tè· "an animate object moves about"), yì-ł-bé·ž "he boils it" (cf. hìbé·ž "it boils").

This, however, is not true in all cases. Some transitives formed from intransitives do not add the -ł- classifier but retain the zero class: cf. ʔìdìʔà· "a round object begins to move" with yìdìʔà· "he begins to carry a round object"; sìtą́ "a long slender object has position" with ǹyį́ńtą́ "he has put a long slender object down." Furthermore, there are a number of intransitive verbs which have the -ł- classifier: hìłkà· "day is dawning," ʔìłxòš "he is sleeping," ʔì·łxá·š "he is about to fall asleep." Verbs with -ł- classifiers (these also have the pronouns characteristic of the zero verbs), then, may also be either transitive or intransitive, neuter or active.

All passive and mediopassive verbs have either a -d- or an -l- classifier. These classifiers, however, do not always appear in the verb form. -d- is indicated only when certain consonants are initial in the stem (see §3:5), or by an h before the stem, or by the fact that the perfective paradigm employs subject pronouns of set (a). Similarly, the -l- classifier becomes -ł- in all Chiricahua verbs and -l- verbs can only be distinguished from -ł- verbs by the effect of the -l- classifier on certain stem initials (see §3:10), and the fact that subject pronouns of set (a) are employed in the perfective paradigm.

Passives and mediopassives derived from zero class verbs employ the -d- classifier: hìʔà·l "it is being chewed" (cf. yìʔà·l "he chews it"), nè·sʔį̀ "it has been stolen" (cf. yìnè·sʔį̀ "he stole it"), dà·hìhⁿdí·ł "several objects are being scattered about" (cf. dà·yìndí·ł "he scatters several objects about"), ńdèšʔį̀ "I have hidden" (cf. ńdéłʔį̀ "I have hidden it"). Passives and mediopassives derived from -ł- verbs employ the -l- classifier: nìłʔàh "it is being butchered" (cf. ǹyìłʔàh "he butchers it"), hòšⁿdá "I have been licked" (cf. hó·lⁿdá "I have licked it").

Not all -d- and -l- class verbs are passives. There are a number of prefixes which require the -d- or -l- class regardless of the voice of the verb: nádìsdá "I begin to go again and again" (cf. dìšá < *di-š-há "I begin to go"), ʔìłgóžǫ́ "they love one another" (cf. bìłⁿžǫ́ "he loves you"), nádìšgá·ł "I look again" (cf. dìšxá·ł "I look"), nánšgè· "I carry it back" (cf. dìšxè· "I start to carry it").

The classifiers and their functions may, then, be summarized as follows:

    I. Zero class verbs
        A. Intransitives
        B. Transitives
    II. -ł- class verbs
        A. Transitives derived from verbs of class I A

    B. Intransitives
III. ˗d˗ class verbs
    A. Passives derived from verbs of class I B
    B. Other ˗d˗ class verbs
IV. ˗l˗ class verbs
    A. Passives derived from verbs of class II A
    B. Other ˗l˗ class verbs

THE PARTICLE

§4:9. Particles are of two kinds: pronouns (independent personal pronouns, demonstratives, and interrogatives), and those particles which function as numerals, connectives, adverbs, and adjectives.

1) The independent personal pronouns are as follows: ší, first person singular; ⁿdí, second person singular; bí, third person; kí, fourth person; nàhí, first or second person dual; and góbí, third person dual. Distributive forms of these pronouns are formed by prefixing the distributive dà·: dà·nàhí, first or second person distributive; dà·bí or dà·góbí, third person distributive; and dà·kí, fourth person distributive. None of these forms may be inflected; their syntactic function may be indicated by their position in the sentence or may be inferred from the context.

2) Demonstrative pronouns are composed of a bound stem plus an enclitic. There are eight principal demonstrative stems: ʔì·˗ "here" (position nearest the speaker), z̧à·˗ "here," ʔá˗ (or ʔá·˗) "there," γà˗ (or γàh˗) "there; over yonder," kò˗ "hereabout, thereabout," dí˗ "this," ʔá˗ "that," and ʔáγá˗ (or ʔáγà˗) "that yonder." The first five, referring to places, are usually found in combination with the following postpositions: ˗è· "at, in, on," ˗ší "from," ˗z̧ì "to," and ˗yá, a generalized postposition functioning to link the verb with the indirect object. The last three demonstrative stems, which refer to persons or things, are always combined with one of the following relative enclitics: ˗í, referring to things, actions, or collectivities, and ˗ń, referring to persons. The following table summarizes the more frequently occurring demonstratives:

Stems	˗è·	˗ší	˗z̧ì	˗yá
ʔì·˗	ʔì·è·	ʔì·ší		
z̧à·˗	z̧à·è·	z̧à·ší	z̧à·z̧ì	
ʔá˗	ʔáè·	ʔáší	ʔáz̧ì	
ʔà·˗	ʔà·è·	ʔà·ší		
γà˗	γàè·	γàší	γàz̧ì	γàhyá
kò˗		kòší		kòyá or kòʔyá

Stems	˗í	˗ń
dí˗	dí·	díń
ʔá˗	ʔáí	ʔáń
ʔáγá˗	ʔáγáí	ʔáγáń
ʔáγà˗	ʔáγàí	ʔáγàń

3) The interrogative and indefinite pronouns are expressed by identical forms, a context being necessary to distinguish them. Four of the stems, xà?·, xà·, and xà·d·, occur only with enclitics; the fifth, yâ· or ?ìyâ·, may occur alone. xà?šį "where from, from somewhere," xà?yá "where; somewhere," xá·ń "who; someone," xá·dą́ "at what place; someplace," yâ·, ?ìyâ· "what; something," xà·d·í "what thing; something."

4) The remainder of the particles exhibit a variety of forms, from the monosyllabic structure characteristic of some numerals to the polysyllabic constructions of the adverbs. Particles may not be inflected or otherwise altered in structure. They function as numerals, connectives, adverbs, and adjectives: dáłè·?é "one," nà·kì "two," tá·? "three," dį·? "four," ?ákò· "and, then," ?áńdè·dà "and so, just then," nágò "then," ?ìłkìdą́ "long ago," xąh "in a hurry," ǹdàh "but," dá·ⁿdí "truly, certainly."

§4:10.   Proclitics and enclitics are bound forms which may be added to words of any form class. The commoner proclitics are as follows: dá· "just, only," dò·, always used with the enclitic ·dà to express the negative, dásí· "very much, exceedingly."

Enclitics are more numerous and may be divided into three groups: postpositions, relatives, and tensemodal enclitics. Examples: ·è· "at, in," ·šį "from," ·í, relative referring to things, actions, and collectivities, ·ń, relative referring to persons, ·ⁿdè "people of . . . group," ·ǹ, past tense, ·gò, subordinating enclitic, ·ná?à, narrative enclitic.

ALGONQUIAN

LEONARD BLOOMFIELD

§1. The grouping of the Algonquian languages is uncertain, since most of them are scantily or poorly recorded. Following, in the main, Michelson, we may list them as follows:[1]

I. Central-Eastern:
- A. Central Type: Cree-Montagnais-Naskapi, Menomini, Fox-Sauk-Kicka-poo, Shawnee, Peoria-Miami, Potawatomi, Ojibwa-Ottawa-Algonquin-Salteaux, Delaware, Powhatan.
- B. New England Type: Natick-Narragansett, Mohegan-Pequot, Penob-scot-Abnaki, Passamaquoddy-Malecite, Micmac.

II. Blackfoot.

III. Cheyenne.

IV. Arapaho-Atsina-Nawathinehena.

Two languages of California, Wiyot and Yurok, have been suspected of kin-ship with Algonquian.[2]

§2. Our reconstructions are based, to begin with, on the four best-known languages: Fox, Cree, Menomini, and Ojibwa. Michelson's brilliant study of the divergent western languages (Blackfoot, Cheyenne, and the Arapaho group), showed that these reconstructions will, in the main, fit all the languages and can accordingly be viewed as Proto-Algonquian.[3] Since then, however, Siebert has shown that F, C, M, O have all merged two consonant clusters, θk and xk, which

---

[1] Truman Michelson, *Preliminary Report on the Linguistic Classification of Algonquian Tribes* (28th Annual Report of the Bureau of American Ethnology, Washington, 1912, pp. 221-290).

[2] A. L. Kroeber, *The Languages of the Coast of California North of San Francisco* (University of California Publications in American Archaeology and Ethnology, vol. 9, Berkeley, 1910-1911, pp. 384-412, and 414-426); Truman Michelson, *Two Alleged Algonquian Languages of California* (American Anthropologist, n.s., vol. 16, Lancaster, Pa., 1914, pp. 361-367) and *Rejoinder* [to Sapir] (American Anthropologist, n.s., vol. 17, Lancaster, Pa., 1915, pp. 194-198); Gladys Reichard, *Wiyot Grammar and Texts* (University of California Publications in American Archaeology and Ethnology, vol. 22, Berkeley, 1925, pp. 1-215); Edward Sapir, *The Algonkin Affinity of Yurok and Wiyot Kinship Terms* (Journal de la Société des Américanistes, n.s., vol. 15, Paris, 1923, pp. 37-74); C. C. Uhlenbeck, *Infigeering op het gebied der Algonkin-Talen* (Mededeelingen der Koninklijke Akademie van Wetenschappen, Afdeeling Letterkunde, Ser. A., vol. 69, Amsterdam, 1930, pp. 111-116).

[3] Truman Michelson, *Phonetic Shifts in Algonquian Languages* (International Journal of American Linguistics, vol. 8, New York, 1935, pp. 131-171).

are distinct in Delaware and the New England languages;[4] for this feature, at any rate, an eastern language is necessary in the reconstruction of PA.[5]

3–15. SOUNDS

§3. PA had four vowels, each in short and long quantities: high front i, ii; low front e, ee; high back o, oo; low back a, aa.

We use the term *nonsyllabic* of any phoneme other than a vowel and of any sequence of phonemes not containing a vowel.

The PA vowel system is preserved in F; only initial PA e- >F i-, form 13, and F has a few assimilative (?) changes of short vowels, as in form 100.

PA i and e are merged to i in C and O.

PA i, ii are broken up in M into a high vowel, M i, ii and a mid vowel, M e, ee. Similarly, PA o, oo yield M u, uu and M o, oo. PA e appears in M partly as e (coinciding with e from PA i) and partly as a very open vowel, M ɛ. PA ee >M ɛɛ. Moreover, M has made complex but regular changes of vowel quantity.

Examples of PA vowels: *1* *aθemwa "dog": Kickapoo anemwa, C atim, M anɛɛm, O anim. *2* *pemaatesiwa "he lives": F pemaatesiwa, C pimaatisiw, M pemaatesew, O pimaatisi. *3* *seekesiwa "he is afraid": F seekesiwa, C seekisiw, M sɛɛkesew, O seekisi. *4* *wentenamwa "he takes it from there": F otenamwa, C ohtinam, M ohtɛɛnam, O ontinank.[6] *5* *poosiwa "he embarks": F poosiwa, C poosiw, M poosew, O poosi. *6* *kiiškahamwa "he chops it through": F kiiškahamwa, C kiishakam, M keeskaham, O kiiškaqank.

§4. Before syllabic vowels, PA i, o are nonsyllabic; we write y, w:[7]   *7* *wii-yawi "his body": F wiiyawi, C wiyaw, M weeyaw, O wiiyaw.

§5. PA ya between consonants >F yee, O ii: *8* *aqsenyali "stones": F asenyeeni, C asiniya, M aqsɛnyak (an. form), O assiniin.

PA yaa >F aa after č, š and C, O aa after all nonsyllabics. PA yaa, waa >M

---

[4] Frank T. Siebert, Jr., *Certain Proto-Algonquian Consonant Clusters* (Language, vol. 17, Baltimore, 1941, pp. 298–303).

[5] Forms are cited in uniform inflection; especially, verbs are cited in the third person singular independent indicative (transitive verbs with obviative object), except for Ojibwa transitive verbs, where we give the conjunct form, because there the independent indicative has been replaced by another inflection (§42). Often, therefore, the cited inflectional form has been made by me from stems recorded in some other form of the paradigm.

Starred forms or forms with hyphens at the beginning or end are Proto-Algonquian. (Etymologies are preceded by numbers in *italics* for reference.) Abbreviations: > ="became"; < ="coming from"; ∼ ="is replaced in alternation by"; an. ="animate"; C ="Cree"; exc. = "exclusive"; F ="Fox"; inan. ="inanimate"; inc. ="inclusive"; intr. ="intransitive"; M ="Menomini"; O ="Ojibwa"; obv. ="obviative"; PA ="Proto-Algonquian"; pl. ="plural"; sg. = "singular"; tr. ="transitive"; V ="vowel."

[6] The O form is in conjunct mode: "if he takes it from there"; cf. footnote 5.

[7] We use y, w because it is likely that in some of the languages the syllabic and nonsyllabic values are no longer mechanically determined. Also, we set up such theoretical elements as nyeeww- "four."

ia, ua (falling diphthongs) after nonsyllabics when not shortened: *9* *neniičya-anehsa "my child": F neniičaanesa, M neniičianeh, O niniičaaniss.   *10* *kyaataawa "he hides it": C kaataaw, M kiataaw, O kaatoot; reshaped in F kyaatamwa.

PA yee >F ee after č, š; C ee after all nonsyllabics; M ii after all nonsyllabics; O ee after š, 86, ii after other nonsyllabics: *11* *pyeetaawa "he brings it": F pyeetoowa (inflectional ending reshaped), M piitaaw, O piitoot.

PA wee >M ii after nonsyllabic: *12* *pyeetweeweekesiwa "he comes with noise": F pyeetweeweekesiwa, M piitiiweekesew, O piitweeweekisi.

PA yi >i after nonsyllabic in all the languages for which we have data, but in M this i is distinct from e <PA i: *13* *elenyiwa "man": F ineniwa, C iyiniw, M eneeniw, O inini.

PA wi >F, O i after t, l (the exact conditions are obscured by new forma-tions); C o, M i (o before w) after all nonsyllabics: *14* *piintwikeewa "he enters a dwelling": F piitikeewa, C piihtokeew, M piihtikew, O piintikee.[8]

PA yii >ii in all the languages for which we have data, but in M this ii is distinct from ee <PA ii: *15* *kešyiipisowa "he speeds": M kesiipesow, O kišiipiso.

PA wii >M ii after nonsyllabic: *16* *kwiiθomeewa "he longs for him": F kwiinomeewa, M kiinomew, O kwiinomaat.

In word initial, PA we >o in most of the languages, 4.

§6. The PA simple consonants were p, t, k, č, s, š, θ, l, m, n. The last three were voiced. The rest were voiceless, probably lenis; in some dialects of O they are largely voiced. Medial k is often voiced in F and C. In O, PA h appears as a glottal stop, for which we write q.

PA θ (unvoiced interdental or lateral?) and l coincide in most languages. Shawnee, Delaware, the Peoria group, and the New England languages have l. Blackfoot, Cheyenne, and Nawathinehena have t, coinciding with PA t; M, F, O, and Potawatomi have n, coinciding with PA n, but differing from the latter in morphologic treatment, §20. The remaining languages distinguish as follows:

	PA θ	PA l
Atsina	t	n
Arapaho (except Atsina and Nawathinehena)	θ	l
Cree-Montagnais	t	y

Northern C dialects represent PA l variously by n, l, r, or by an interdental voiced spirant.

C has PA t, θ >č originally in diminutives, secondarily also in some other forms.[9]

C and M merge PA s and š in s, an intermediate sound. PA s >Shawnee θ.

The consonants appear in 1 to 16.

[8] In setting up postconsonantal wi, yi for PA, we depart from earlier conclusions, which were prompted, at bottom. by the mistaken assumption that in PA l alternated with š.

[9] Recognition of this fact dispenses with the cluster θš formerly set up for PA.

§7. Clusters of two consonants occur medially. They consist of ordinary consonants preceded by obscure elements which we render by arbitrary symbols.

Where northern O dialects represent the prior element of a cluster as h, there most O dialects have a fortis or ambisyllabic unvoiced consonant, e.g., PA hs > northern O hs, general O ss.

§8. Clusters with second member p:

PA	F	C	M	O
mp	p	hp	hp	mp
hp	?	hp	hp	pp
xp	hp	sp	hp	pp
čp	?	sp	čp	pp
šp	hp	sp	sp	šp

17 *wempenamwa "he lifts it up": C ohpinam, O ompinank: compare F opaaškeewi "it flies up" and M ohpεεqnen "it is blown upward." *18* *koohpačiheewa "he ruins him": C koohpačiheew, M koohpačehεεw, O kooppačihaat. *19* *axpeelemowa "he places reliance": F ahpeenemowa, C aspeeyimow, M ahpεεnemow, O appeenimo. *20* *noočpinatamwa "he pursues it": C noospinatam, O nooppinatank; compare M noočpenεεhtaw. *21* *ešpemenki "up above": F ahpemeki, C ispimihk, O išpimink; reshaped M espεεmiah (<ʿiiwenki).

§9. Clusters with second member t:

PA	F	C	M	O
nt	t	ht	ht	nt
ht	ht	ht	ht	tt
qt	ht	st	qt	tt
št	?	st	?	št

For nt, see 4. *22* *ešihtaawa "he makes it so": F išihtoowa (ending reshaped), C, isiihtaaw, M eseehtaw, O išittoot. *23* *peqtenamwa "he takes it by error": C pistinam, M pεqtεnam, O pittinank; compare F pehtenaweewa "he shoots him by error." *24* *weštikwaani "his head": C ostikwaan, O oštikwaan.

§10. Clusters with second member k:

PA	F	C	M	O	
nk	k	hk	hk	nk	
hk	hk	hk	hk	kk	
xk	hk	sk	hk	kk	Delaware hVk, New England hk
θk	hk	sk	hk	kk	Delaware xk, New England sk
çk	šk	hk	hk	sk	Northern Cree htk[10]
čk	hk	sk	čk	šk	
šk	šk	sk	sk	šk	

[10] The fuss and trouble behind my note in Language (Vol. 4, pp. 99–100, 1928) would have been avoided if I had listened to O, which plainly distinguishes sk (<PA çk) from šk (<PA šk); instead, I depended on printed records which failed to show the distinction.

25 *tankeškaweewa "he kicks him": F takeškaweewa, C tahkiskaweew, M tahkɛɛskawɛw, O tankiškawaat. *26* *noohkomehsa "my grandmother": F noohᵜkomesa, C noohkom (without diminutive suffix), M noohkomɛh, O nookkomiss. *27* *axkyi "earth, land": F ahki, C askiy, M ahkeew (ending reshaped), O akki, Penobscot kki (nətahki "my land"). *28* *nemeθkawaawa "I find him": F nemehᵜkawaawa, C nimiskawaaw, M nemɛɛhkawaw, O nimikkawaa, Penobscot nəməsᵜkawɑ. *29* *meçkosiwa "he is red": F meškosiwa, C mihkosiw (Swampy Cree mihtkosiw), O miskosi; compare M mɛhkoon. *30* *nooçkwaatamwa "he licks it": F nooškwaatamwa, C noohkwaatam, M nuuhkwatam, O nooskwaatank. *31* *nalakačkwi "my palate": C nayakašk; the first syllable is reshaped in M neᵜnaakačkon (plural only), O ninakašk; compare M kakiipanakačkow "he is dumb." *32* *kečkyeewa "he is old": F kehkyeewa, M kečkiiw. šk in 25.

There were perhaps other clusters with k. M has qk, as in poohkeqkow "he is one-eyed." There are quite a few discrepant sets, but some of them are doubtless due to reshaping of words in one or another language: F eemehkwaahi "spoon," C eemihkwaan, O eemikkwaan, but M ɛɛmeskwan; F nehtooškwani "my elbow," M nɛhtuuhkwan, O nintooskwan, but C nitooskwan; M kayaah "gull" (plural kayaahkok), but O kayaašk.[11]

§11. Clusters with second member č:

PA	F	C	M	O
nč	č	hč	hč	nč
hč	hč	hč	hč	čč
qč	hč	sč	qč	čč

33 *wenčiiwa "he comes from there": F očiiwa, C ohčiiw, M ohčeew, O ončii. *34* *ešihčikeewa "he makes things so": F išihčikeewa, C isiihčikeew, M eseehčekɛw, O išiččikee. *35* *keqči "big, much": F kehči, C kisči, M kɛɛqč, O kičči.

§12. Clusters with second member s:

PA	F	C	M	O
ns	s	s	hs	ns
hs	s	s	hs	ss
qs	s	s	qs	ss

36 *wensaapameewa "he sees him from there": F osaapameewa, C osaapameew, M ohsaapamɛw, O onsaapamaat. *37* *nemihsa "my elder sister": F nemiseeha (diminutive), C nimis, M nemeeh (pl. nemeehsak), O nimisseenq (diminutive). *38* *nekwiqsa "my son": F nekwisa, C nikosis (diminutive), M nekiiqs, O ninkwiss.

---

[11] James A. Geary, *Proto-Algonquian *çk: Further Examples* (Language, vol. 17, p. 307, 1941) shows what may lie behind some of the apparent discrepancies.

§13. Clusters with second member š.

PA	F	C	M	O
nš	š	s	hs	nš
hš	š	s	hs	šš
qš	š	s	qs	šš

39 *neškiinšekwi "my eye": F neškiišekwi, C niskiisik, M neskeehsek, O niškiinšik.   *40* *wemehšoomehsali "his grandfather": F omešoomesani, C omo-sooma (without diminutive suffix), M omɛɛhsomɛɛhsan, O omiššoomissan.   *41* *kawenkwaqšiwa "he is sleepy": F kawekwašiwa, C kawihkwasiw, M kakuuh-kwaqsew (reduplicated and contracted, §19), O kawinkwašši.

§14. Clusters with second member θ.

PA	F	C	M	O
nθ	?	ht	hn	n
hθ	s	ht	hn	ss
qθ	s	st	qn	ss

42 *wanahanθeewa "he loses the trail of him": C wanahahteew, M wawaanahaahnew (reduplicated); compare O pimaqanaat "he tracks him" (with root pem-).   *43* *ešihθenwi "it falls or lies thus": F išisenwi, C isihtin, M eseehnen, O išissin.   *44* *koqθeewa "he fears him": F koseewa, C kosteew, M koqnɛw, O kossaat.

§15. Clusters with second member 1.

PA	F	C	M	O
nl	n	hy	hn	n
hl	s	hy	hn	ss
ql	s	hy	qn	ss

In C hy, the h or the y mostly drops; the conditions have been obscured by leveling.

45 *wiinleewa "he names him": F wiineewa, C wiiheew, M weehnɛw, O wiinaat.   *46* *leehleewa "he breathes": F neeseewa "he is saved," C yeehyeew "he breathes," M nɛɛhnɛw, O neessee.   *47* *aqleewa "he places him": F aseewa, C aheew, M aqnɛw, O assaat.

16–24. INTERNAL COMBINATION

§16. In the combination of word-forming elements, when an element ending in a nonsyllabic is followed by an element beginning with a consonant or cluster, a *connective* -i- appears between them. Thus, the root poon- "cease" combines directly with a suffix like -eele "think":   *48* *pooneelemeewa "he stops thinking of him": F pooneenemeewa, C pooneeyimeew, M poonɛɛnemɛw, O pooneenimaat. Similarly, a root like kiihkaa- "berate" combines directly with a suffix such as -m

"act by speech on an animate object": *49* *kiihkaameewa "he berates him":
C kiihkaameew, M keehkamɛw, O kiikkaamaat. But when poon- combines with -m,
the connective -i- appears between them: *50* *poonimeewa "he stops talking to
him": F poonimeewa, C poonimeew, M poonemɛw, O poonimaat.

§17. Irregularly, in certain combinations, the connective -i- is not used before p, t, k. In these combinations, t-p, θ-p ∼xp; t-k ∼θk; nasal is assimilated as to
position. Our examples show first the root eθ- "thither, thus" before a suffix with
initial vowel, then the suffix -pahtoo "run" preceded by connective -i-, and then
the irregular combination of eθ- with -pahtoo: *51* *eθahkamikesiwa "he carries
on so": F inahkamikesiwa, C itahkamikisiw, M enaahkamekɛsew, O inakkamikisi;
52 *pemipahtaawa "he runs by": C pimipahtaaw, M pemeepahtaw, O pimipattoo
(inflection reshaped); compare F pemipahowa; *53* *expahtaawa "he runs thither":
C ispahtaaw, M ehpaahtaw, O ippattoo; compare F ihpahowa. The root atoot-
"on something," as in M atootapew "he sits on something," combines thus with
-po "eat": *54* *atooxpowa "he eats from upon something": F atoohpowa, C
atoospow, M atoohpow, O atooppo. The root, wiit- "along, with," §103, combines with a unique suffix -pee "sleep": *55* *wiixpeewa "he sleeps with someone":
F wiihpeewa, M weehpɛw; *weexpeemeewa "he sleeps with him": F wiih-
peemeewa, M weehpemɛw; but C has here hp (loanword?): wiihpeemeew. Our
next examples show first a verb stem in t, then the ending -ki after a verb stem in
vowel, and then the combination, always made without connective -i-, of a verb
stem in t with the ending -ki: *56* *kiišekatwi "it is day": F kiišekatwi, M
keesekat, O kiišikat; *57* *aqteeki "when it is there": F ahteeki, C asteek, M
aqtɛk, O atteek; *58* *kiišekaθki "when it is day": F kiišekahki, M keesekah,
O kiišikakk.

Similarly after n: *59* *kemiwanwi "it rains": C, O kimiwan, M kemeewan;
60 *kemiwanki "when it rains": C kimiwahk, M kemeewah, O kimiwank.

§18. Between consonants, ye ∼i and we ∼o. Thus, the local suffix of nouns
is -enki-: *61* *wiikenki "at his house": F owiikeki, C wiikihk, M weekeh. With the
noun stem aqseny-, 8: *62* *aqseninki "on the stone": F aseniki, M aqsɛneh. On
a noun in consonant plus w it appears as follows: *63* *meqtekwi "stick": F
mehtekwi, C mistik (pl. -wa), M mɛqtek (pl. -wan), O mittik (pl. -oon); *64*
*meqtekonki "on a stick or tree": F mehtekoki, C mistikohk, M mɛqtekoh, O
mittikonk.

After consonants, wiiw ∼oow, as illustrated in §67.

In all positions, apparently, woo ∼oo. Thus, the prefixes ne- of the first person and we- of the third appear as n-, w- before ii: *65* *niiyawi "my body":
F niiyawi, C niyaw, M neeyaw, O niiyaw; *wiiyawi "his body," 7; but as n-
and zero in *noohkomehsa "my grandmother," 26, and *66* *oohkomehsali "his
grandmother": F oohkomesani, C oohkoma, M oohkomɛɛhsan, O ookkomissa.

After consonant plus w, y is dropped; thus, with suffix -yaa: *67* *takhyaaki
"when it is cool": F tahkyaaki, C tahkaak, O takkaak; reshaped M tahkiik (repre-

senting ⁓yee, transferred from a different inflectional form); *68* *meçkwaaki "when it is red": F meškwaaki, C mihkwaak, O miskwaak; reshaped in M mɛhkiik.

§19. Irregularly, in certain forms, awe ∼aa before t, k, s, and ∼oo before other consonants. This *contraction* always takes place when the e begins an inflec⁓ tional ending. We illustrate first the endings ⁓ekwa "he—me" and ⁓eθene "I— thee," then a verb stem ending in aw, and then its combination with these endings: *69* *newaapamekwa "he looks at me": F newaapamekwa, C, O niwaapamiik, M newaapamek; *70* *kewaapameθene "I look at thee": C kewaapamitin; the other languages have haplologic forms: F kewaapamene, M kewaapamen, O kiwaapamin; *71* *newiintamawaawa "I tell it to him": F newiitamawaawa, C niwiihtamawaaw, M neweehtamowaaw, O niwiintamawaa; *72* *newiintamaakwa "he tells it to me": F newiitamaakwa, C niwiihtamaak, M neweehtamak, O niwiintamaak; *73* *kewiintamooθene "I tell it to thee": F kewiitamoone, M kɛwɛehtamon, O kewiintamoon (all haplologic); C kiwiihtamaatin has analogic aa for oo.

In general, however, the sequence awe is undisturbed: *74* *kaweneewa "he prostrates him by hand": F kaweneewa, C kawineew, M kawɛɛnɛɛw, O kawinaat. M has various other contractions of Vwe; some may date from PA.

§20. Before i, ii, y, PA t∼č and θ∼š: *75* *pemaačiheewa "he makes him live, restores him to life": C pimaačiheew, M pemaačehɛw, O pimaačiqaat; com⁓ pare pemaat⁓, 2. *76* *pyeečimeewa "he calls him hither": C peečimeew, M piičemɛw; compare pyeet⁓, 12. *77* *piinčihšinwa "he falls into an enclosed place": C piihčisin, M peehcehsen; compare piint⁓, 14. Similarly, compare went⁓, 4, and wenč⁓ii⁓, 33; ⁓htoo⁓, ⁓htaa⁓, 22, with ⁓hč⁓i⁓kee, 34. *78* *miikaaθeewa "he fights him": F miikaaneewa, M meekaanɛɛw, O miikaanaat; *79* *miikaaši "fight thou him": F miikaaši, M meekaasin (extended by particle *na or otherwise reshaped), O miikaaš. With eθ⁓, 51, compare eš⁓i⁓, 22, 43.

This alternation distinguishes n <PA θ, in F, M, O, and Potawatomi, from n <PA n. Thus, the imperative "thou—him" form of a stem like kawen⁓, 74, keeps n before i: *80* *kaweni "lay thou him prostrate": F kaweni, C, O kawin, M kawɛɛnen. These languages, however, have extended the alternation analogi⁓ cally to forms with n <PA l: *81* *milileewa "he gives it to him": F miineewa, C miyeew (Woodland C miineew), M meenɛɛw, O miinaat; compare Shawnee nimiila "I give it to him"; *82* *miili "give thou it to him": C miyi (Woodland C miini), Shawnee miili; but reshaped in F miiši, M meesen, O miiš.

§21. Irregularly, in certain forms, PA t∼s before aa and e; so always before the suffixes ⁓ehk by "foot" and ⁓aap "look." Thus, compare went⁓, 4, with wens⁓ aap⁓, 36.

The same alternation appears in the sequence iitii ∼iisii: *83* *miiten⁓ kwaamwa "he defecates in his sleep": C miitihkwaamiw (ending reshaped), M miitehkwamow (ending reshaped), O miitinkwaam; *84* *miisiiwa "he defecates": F miisiiwa, C miisiiw, M meeseew, O miisii.

§22. A short vowel drops before or after a long vowel. Thus, the prefix ne-, 9, 28, 37, appears as n- where it is added to ii-, 65, and to oo-, 26; similarly, we-, 24, 40, appears as w- before ii-, 7, 61, and as zero before oo-, 66. The suffix -en "by hand," 74, loses its vowel after such roots as nakaa- "stop," ašyee- "back": *85* *nakaaneewa "he stops him by hand": C nakaaneew, M nakaanεεw, O nakaanaat; *86* *ašyeenamwa "he pushes it back, rejects it": C aseenam, M asiinam, O ašeenank.

§23. Between long vowels the sound y is inserted, at least if one is a front vowel. Thus, F has pemaamowa "he flees by," but ašeeyaamowa "he flees back"; and M has pemεεqnen "it is blown by," but asiiyεεqnen "it is blown back."

§24. In word final position, PA apparently shortened long vowels: F nepaate "if he sleeps," stem nepaa-, but, with zero ending, nenepa "I sleep."

25. THE WORD

§25. In PA the word began with a vowel or with a simple nonsyllabic or with consonant plus y, w. Between the vowels of a word there was a semivowel, or a consonant, or a cluster, or one of these followed by y or w. The word ended in a short vowel. The vowel of the first syllable was never i.

Members of compound words were treated phonetically like words.

Before an initial vowel of the next word or compound-member, the final vowel dropped or else h was inserted: F pešekesiw-owiiwina, pešekesiwih-owiiwina "deer-horn."

Many of the languages (not F, Shawnee, Peoria) lost the final vowel as well as a preceding postconsonantal w, 1. M and O lost also a preceding postconso- nantal y, but C has iy: *87* *aqsenya "stone": F asenya, C asiniy, M aqsen, O assin. C lost also a preceding h or l, 8.[12] M further lost all but the first sound of a preceding cluster, 9, except qč, qs, 35.

However, in two-syllable words with short vowels (C also in others) these languages keep the final intact, M adding h: *88* *ehkwa "louse": F, C ihkwa, M ehkuah, O ikkwa. *89* *nepyi "water": F nepi, C nipiy, O nimpi; reshaped M nepeew.

Most types of O insert a nasal after initial m, n, plus short vowel before a simple stop, 38, 89, but not, apparently, in nak-, 85.

Particles which precede nouns and verbs in composition keep their final vowel (mostly it is the particle final suffix -i) not only in F and Shawnee, but also in C and O; in M they are treated like other words. *90* *weepi "begin": F weepi-pyeetoseewa "he starts to walk hither," M weεp-piitohnεw, O weepi-kimiwan "it starts to rain." *91* *meeqči "to exhaustion": C meešci-nipaheew "he kills them all," M nemεεqč-aqsekεnan "I pick it all up." *92* *weški "new": C oski-wiikihtowak "they are newly married," M oskeeh-weekehtowak.

---

[12] Actually, all final vowels of C have an h-like off-glide.

26–29. INFLECTION

§26. The inflectional types are *noun, verb* (in four subtypes), and (unin-flected) *particle*, including *pronouns*.

Nouns are in two *gender* classes, *inanimate* and *animate;* the latter includes all persons, animals, spirits, and large trees, and some other objects, such as to-bacco, maize, apple, raspberry (but not strawberry), calf of leg (but not thigh), stomach, spittle, feather, bird's tail, horn, kettle, pipe for smoking, snowshoe.

Number is *singular* and *plural*.

Person is *first, second,* and *third,* with distinction of exclusive and inclusive first person plural: M netaanenaw "our daughter" (parent speaking to another person), ketaanen "our daughter" (one parent speaking to the other). If an animate third person occurs in a phrase, any other animate third person and any inanimate verb in this phrase has a distinguishing form, the *obviative.* Thus, C, talking about a chief (okimaaw): okimaaw iskweewa kitoteew "the chief talks to a woman," okimaaw iskweewa kitotik "a woman talks to the chief," where iskweewa is the obviative of iskweew "woman"; okimaaw nikitotaaw "I speak to the chief," okimaaw okosisa nikitotimaawa "I speak to the chief's son," tipiskaaw "it was dark," eeh-takohteet tipiskaayiw "when he arrived it was dark." A few inflec-tional forms distinguish a nearer and a farther obviative: C okimaaw oteema "the chief's horse (obv.)," okimaaw okosisa oteemiyiwah "the chief's son's (obv.) horse (farther obv.)." C, M, and most O dialects have lost the distinction of number in the obviative; in C this is due to phonetic development. In general, the finer distinctions of obviation (such as transitive verb forms for "I—obv.," "thou—obv.," "obv—me," and so on) have been lost in most of the languages; C and O best preserve them.

§27. The noun is inflected for number, with different endings for the two genders; the animate noun also for obviation and for address. All inflected forms, except unpossessed nouns, contain personal-anaphoric reference (by gender, per-son, and number) to some object: possessed nouns to a *possessor,* verbs (except in the *passive*) to an *actor,* transitive verbs also to a *goal-object.* These can be named specifically by words in cross-reference: M okeemaaw otaanan "(the chief his-daughter), the chief's daughter"; nenah neneewaaw enoh okeemaaw "I I-see-him that chief (as for me, I see the chief)."

Verbs are *intransitive* and *transitive.* The former are divided into those which refer to an animate actor, *animate intransitive* verbs, M paapɛhcen "he falls," and those which refer to an inanimate actor, *inanimate intransitive* verbs, M paapɛhnɛn "it falls." Transitive verbs are divided into those which refer to an animate goal, *transitive animate* verbs, M nemuawak "I eat them" (as, anoohkanak "raspberries," animate) and those which refer to an inanimate goal, *transitive inanimate* verbs, M nemeečenan "I eat them" (as, atɛehemenan "strawberries," inanimate).

However, some intransitive verbs are used habitually with *implied goals* thus M menuah "he drinks (it)" is intr. in form, but in general makes sense only with a pseudo-object: nepeew menuah "he drinks some water," and M netooweematem "I have a friend" is freely used also with a pseudo-object: čaan netooweematem "I have John as a friend." About half the tr. an. verbs are matched not by tr. inan. verbs, but by *pseudo-transitive* verbs, namely intr. verbs formed mostly with the suffixes ⁻too, ⁻htoo and taking implied objects: F wiikiyaapyeeni ašihtoowa "he builds houses," where the verb is intr. in form. Some of the languages, however, as M and O, have reshaped these verbs into a special tr. inan. type. Some tr. an. verbs (*double-goal* verbs) imply a second goal in addition to the one for which they are inflected: M soopomah eneesenamaaq "hand me the sugar," where the verb is inflected for "thou—me," but its structure implies a second goal, here soopomah "sugar."

Conversely, some tr. inan. verbs refer to no identifiable object, but have a merely *formal* goal: M noqnonam "he swims"; also M nemaamiiqtehkooskanan "I go bare-legged," with the formal goal in plural inflection. These forms, too, have been reshaped in O.

§28. There are four inflectional prefixes. Three of them, ke⁻ "thou," ne⁻ "I," we⁻ "he, it," appear on both noun and verb. The fourth, me⁻, appears only on certain nouns, §32. Where more than one person is involved as possessor, actor, or goal, the preference is in the order given; thus "we inc." has ke⁻, but "we exc." has ne⁻; tr. forms for "I—thee" and "thou—me" both have ke⁻: M kenian "I see thee," keneewem "thou seest me."

The prefixes add t before a vowel: *93* *netaqlaawa "I place him": F netasaawa, C nitahyaa, M netaaqnaw, O nintassaa; compare *aqleewa "he places him," 47; contrast *nemeθkawaawa "I find him," 28. However, before the vowels of certain stems no t was added, 7, 26, 31 (where C probably preserves the old form), 61, 65, 66.

§29. Among endings common to noun and verb are those of the third person: an. sg. ⁻a, pl. ⁻aki, obv. sg. ⁻ali, pl. ⁻ahi; inan. sg. ⁻i, pl. ⁻ali: F ineniwa "man," ineniwaki "men"; ineniwani "(other) man," ineniwahi "(other) men"; miišaami "sacred bundle," miišaamani "sacred bundles."

30–32. INFLECTION OF THE NOUN

§30. In addition to the forms just cited, the an. noun has forms for address: F ineniwe "man!" ineniwetike "men!"

The noun makes *possessed themes*, which are then inflected like unpossessed nouns, except that an an. noun with third person an. possessor is necessarily obviative. Possessed themes take a suffix ⁻em. Thus *ehkwa "louse," 88, gives rise to forms like the following: *94* *netehkoma "my louse": F netehkoma, C nitihkom, M neteehkom, O nintikkom; *95* *ketehkomaki "thy lice": F ketehkomaki, C

kitihkomak, M keteehkomak, O kitikkomak;   *96* *wetehkomali "his louse": F
ohtehkomani, C otihkoma, M oteekhoman, O otikkoman;   *97* *wetehkomahi "his
lice": F otehkomahi, C otihkoma, O (Lake Superior) otihkomaq; M and most O
dialects use the singular form for both numbers.

The forms for plural possessor add ᐧenaan for the first person, ᐧwaaw ᐧ for
the second and third: F ketehkomenaanaki "our (inc.) lice," ketehkomwaawaki
"your lice," otehkomwaawahi "their lice." An obv. possessor is indicated by ᐧeliw:
C otihkomiyiwa "the other's (sg. or pl.) louse or lice."

§31. There are many irregularities in the formation of possessed themes. Some
do not take ᐧem; so especially the abstract nouns derived from verbs with the suffix
ᐧn and various extensions of it: *98* *pemaatesiweni "life": F pemaatesiweni, C,
O pimaatisiwin, M pemaatesewen;   *99* *wepemaatesiweni "his life": F opemaate
siweni, C, O opimaatisiwin, M opeemaatesewen. Also, certain objects of intimate possession do not take ᐧem: *100* *axkehkwa "kettle": F ahkohkwa, C askihk,
M ahkeeh (pl. ᐧkok), O akkikk;   *101* *netaxkehkwa "my kettle": F netahkohkwa,
C nitaskihk, M netaahkeh, O nintakkikk.

§32. Certain stems, *dependent* nouns, occur only in possessed form, nearly all
without ᐧem.

One type, denoting parts of the body and a few intimate possessions, uses
the prefix meᐧ for an indefinite personal possessor; so 24, 31, 39, 61;   *102* *keteehi
"thy heart": F keteehi, C kitee, M keteeh, O kiteeq; compare M meteeh "a (human) heart," meteehyan "(human) hearts." The form with third person singular
possessor is used as an indefinite possessor form for parts of animals' bodies:
M oteeh "his heart, its heart; an animal's heart (as, at the butcher's)," oteehyan
"animals' hearts," contrasting with oteehowawan "their hearts." Some languages,
such as O, have lost the form with meᐧ.

The other class of dependent nouns, terms of relationship, have no form with
meᐧ, but use verbal derivatives, §82. Thus, beside *nekwiqsa "my son," 38, there
are such derived forms as M okiiqsemaw "a son, the son," weekiqset "one who has
a son." Examples in 26, 37, 40, 66. Some of these have irregular forms for address:
103 *noohko "O my grandmother": F anoohko, C noohko, M nohkoq, O nookko;
compare 26.

Some dependent nouns have irregularities of prefixation. Some of the stems
begin with a cluster, impossible in word initial, 24, 39. Some that begin with ii do
not add t to the prefixes, 7, 61, 65;   *104* *niiθemwa "my sister-in-law (man
speaking), my brother-in-law (woman speaking)": F niinemwa, C niitim, M
neenem, O niinim. Three terms of relationship have initial oo with the same peculiarity: *noohkomehsa 26, 66;   *105* *oohθali "his father": F oosani, C oohtaawiya
(reshaped), M oohnan, O oossan;   *106* *noohšihsema "my grandchild": F
noošisema, C noosisim, M noohsehseh (diminutive ᐧehs replacing ᐧem), O kooošiss
(ᐧem lacking). In PA, t was absent also in some that began with other vowels;
C has many traces of this, as in 31.

Dependent nouns are formable from the pseudo-root -iit- and by composition with the dependent prenoun -iiči, §100.

33. INFLECTION OF THE VERB

§33. Intransitive verb stems end in a vowel, transitive verb stems in a non-syllabic.

The forms of the verb fall into five *orders*. Each order consists of one or more *modes*, each with a full set of forms. The *independent* order takes prefixes; its principal mode, however, the *indicative*, has zero instead of we- for the third person. The other orders take no prefixes. The *imperative* has forms for second person actor only, and only one mode. The *prohibitive* has two modes with the same restriction, but also a third mode, the *potential*, with a full set of forms. The *conjunct* and *interrogative* orders are used only in subordinate clauses and as participles. The languages differ widely in their stock of modal forms; all seem to have lost a few, and some languages have created new ones.

34–42. INDEPENDENT ORDER

§34. The chief mode of the independent order is the *indicative*, used in ordinary statements.

The an. intr. verb here has the ending -w in the third person, with -li before it in the obviative; then come the usual third person endings. Thus, *pemaatesiwa "he lives," 2;   *107* *pemaatesiwaki "they live": F pemaatesiwaki, C pimaatisiwak, M pemaatesewak, O pimaatisiwak;   *108* *pemaatesiliwali "the other lives": F pemaatesiniwani, C pimaatisiyiwa; simplified in M pemaatesewan, O pimaatisiwan; *109* *pemaatesiliwahi "the others live": F pemaatesiniwahi, C pimaatisiyiwa. The first and second persons singular have no ending; M adds an m, C an n: *110* *kepemaatesi "thou livest": F kepemaatesi, C kipimaatisin, M kepεεmaatesem, O kipimaatis.

The languages disagree as to the plural forms of first and second persons. For the first pl. F has -pena (some eastern languages agree with this); C has exc. -naan, inc. -naw or -naanaw; M exc. -menaw, inc. -q; O -min. The second person is pluralized by F -pwa (so also in some eastern languages), C -naawaaw, M -muaw, O -m.

Before the -w of the third person endings the final vowel of the stem is subject to alternations; these have been largely leveled out in the different languages, least so perhaps in M. Thus, the numerous (pseudo-tr.) stems in oo: *111* *nepyeeto "I bring it": F nepiito, M nepiitoon, O nimpiitoon (here M and O have added a tr. inan. ending), but *pyeetaawa "he brings it," 11. Some stems in aa have ee before w: *112* *nenepa "I sleep": F nenepa, C ninipaan, M nenεεpaam, O ninipaa;   *113* *nepeewa "he sleeps": F nepeewa, M nepεεw, O (Algonquin) nipee; leveled out in C nipaaw, O nimpaa. Stems in e drop it before w: *114* *ninepe "I die": F nenepe, C ninipin, M nenεεpem, O ninip;   *115* *nepwa "he

dies": F nepwa, M nepuah, O nimpo (reshaped with o for wa); leveled out in C
nipiw.   *116* *nemene "I drink (it, implied goal)": F nemene, M nemεεnem;
117 *menwa "he drinks (it)": F menwa, M menuah.   *118* *nenaate "I fetch it"
(pseudo-tr.): F nenaate, C ninaatin, M nenaaten, O ninaatin; the last three with
tr. inan. ending added;   *119* *naatwa "he fetches it": F naatwa, M naatwah
(second syllable restored on the model of stems with short vowel in the first syllable), O naati (leveled out), C naatam (reshaped into tr. inan. inflection).

The stem si- "say so" is entirely irregular: *120* *nesi "I say so": F nesi,
M neseem;   *121* *ewa "he says so": F iwa, M ewaah.

§35. The inan. intr. verb is like the third person of the an. intr., with inan.
endings: sg. -wi, F pyeemikatwi "it comes": pl. -wali, F pyeemikatooni "the things
come"; obv. sg. -liwi, F pyeemikateniwi; obv. pl. -liwali, F pyeemikateniwani.

The preceding F example shows a stem in e dropping this vowel before w.
The alternation of aa~ee appears, for instance in a stem like meçkwaa-, 68:
122 *meçkweewi "it is red": M mεhkiiw; leveled out in F meçkwaawi, C mih-
kwaaw, O miskwaa.

§36. The independent indicative forms of the tr. an. verb fall into four sets.
The first two sets involve not more than one of the first two persons; the other two
sets involve both first and second person as actor and goal.

§37. In the first set of forms the prefix, determined by §28, accords with the
actor: first or second person acts on third; third acts on obviative. The ending
-aa~ee is added to the stem, and the *theme* so formed is inflected much like an an.
intr. verb: *123* *newaapamaawa "I look at him": F newaapamaawa, C newaa-
pamaaw, M newaapamaw, O niwaapamaa;   *124* *kewaapamaawaki "thou lookest at them": F kewaapamaawaki, C kiwaapamaawak, M kewaapamawak, O
kiwaapamaak;   *125* *waapameewa "he looks at the other one": F waapameewa,
C waapameew, M waapamεw; O has lost this form, replacing it by one of a different mode, §42.

The forms with first and second person plural actors diverge: F kewaapamaa-
pena "we (inc.) look at him or them," C kiwaapamaanawak "we (inc.) look at
them," M kewaapamonawak, O kiwaapaminaanik. Here belong also the passive
forms of the third person: *126* *waapamaawa "he is looked at": C waapamaaw,
M waapamaw, O waapamaa. Forms with obv. goal take -em before the -aa: C
niwaapamimaawa "I see the other one."

§38. In the second set of forms the prefix, determined by §28, accords with
the goal: third person acts upon first or second, obv. upon third. Here belong also
the forms for inan. actor and the passives of first and second person. The theme
is formed by the ending -eke, with inflection like an an. intr. verb, with loss of e
before -w. Thus, *newaapamekwa "he looks at me," 69;   *127* *waapamekwa "the
other looks at him": F waapamekwa, C waapamik, M waapamek; O uses a form
originally of different mode, §42.

The stem eθ- "say so to" is reduced to zero before -eke: *128* *eθeewa "he says so to him": F eneewa, C iteew, M enɛɛw, O inaat; *129* *ketekwa "he says so to thee": F ketekwa, C, O kitik, M ketɛɛkwah; *130* *ekwa "the other says so to him": F ekwa, M ekuah; C (regularized) itik.

§39. In the third set of forms the actor is the second person (agreeing with the prefix) and the goal the first person. The theme is formed with suffix -i: *131* *kewaapami "thou lookest at me": F kewaapami, C kiwaapamin, M kewaapamem, O kiwaapam; *132* *keteši "thou sayest so to me": F keteši, C kitisin, M ketɛɛsem, O kitiš. As before, the plural forms diverge: F kewaapamipwa "ye look at me," C kewaapaminaawaaw, M kewaapamemuaw, O kiwaapamim.

§40. In the fourth set of forms the actor is the first person and the goal (agreeing with the prefix) is the second person. The theme is made with a suffix -eθene, which, especially when final, is largely reduced by haplology in the n-languages: *kewaapameθene, 70. The plural forms are discrepant: F kewaapamenepwa "I look at you," C kiwaapamitinaawaaw, M kewaapamenenɛmuaw (without haplology), O kiwaapamininim, kiwaaapaminim. The stem eθ- is here, as in §38, reduced to zero: *133* *keteθene "I say so to thee": F ketene (haplologic), C kititin, M ketɛɛnen, O kitinin.

§41. The tr. inan. verb has an ending -am for the third person; this is followed by -w and the usual third person endings: *134* *waapantamwa "he looks at it": F waapatamwa, C, M waapahtam. O here uses a form of a different mode, §42, but has -am in verbs with formal goal: ineentam "he thinks so." The first and second persons singular have an ending -aa: *135* *newaapanta "I look at it": F newaapata, M newaapahtan, O niwaapantaan; leveled out, C niwaapahteen. The first and second persons plural have -ee, followed by plural endings: C kiwaapahteenaawaaw "ye look at it," M kewaapahtɛmuaw.

§42. The languages differ greatly as to modes of the independent order other than the indicative.

A mode which took all three prefixes and had apparently an l in its endings appears in C as a preterit, in M as a negative, and in O tr. verbs replaces the old third person forms of the indicative: C opimaatisi "he once lived," kipee-waapamiti "I came to see thee (but thou wast not there)"; M kan opɛɛmaatesenan "he is not living," kan owaapamanan "he does not look at him"; kan owaapahtanan "he does not look at it"; O owaapamaan "he sees him, owaapantaan "he sees it."

C, M, O have an emphatic preterit with -pa: *136* *pemaatesipanyeeki "they once lived": C, O, pimaatisipaniik, M pemaatesyapanik (reshaped; -sya- represents -siwe-).

F, C, O have a dubitative mode with -tok: *137* *pemaatesitoke "he probably lives": F. pemaatesitoke, C pimaatisitokee (extended ending, perhaps < -tokeeli), O pimaatisitok; *138* *pemaatesitokeeniki "they probably live": C, O pimaatisito-keenik.

M has an interrogative mode: kewaapahtɛmet "dost thou look at it?" and an emphatic present: pemaatesyasah "so he is alive!" pemaatesyasapanik" so they are alive!"

O has a negative mode with -ssii (perhaps in origin a diminutive suffix): kaa wiin pimaatisissii "he is not alive."

43. IMPERATIVE ORDER

§43. In the imperative order, an. intr. verbs have the ending -lo for the singu-lar: *139* *poosilo "embark thou": F. poosino, C poosi, M poosenon (extended, perhaps with particle *na), O poosin. The plural ending is -ko: *140* *poosiko "embark ye": F poosiko, C, O poosik, M (extended) poosekon.

The tr. an. verb has the following endings: "thou—me" -ilo; "ye—me" -iko; "thou—us, ye—us" -inaanke; "thou—him, thou—them" -i, 79, 80, 82; "ye—him, ye—them" -ehko: *141* *waapamehko "look ye at him, them": F waapamehko, C waapamihk, M (extended) waapamɛɛkhon, O waapamikk.

The tr. inan. verb has sg. -anlo: *142* *waapantanlo "look thou at it": F waapatano, C waapahta, M waapahtah, O waapantan. The plural ending is -amoko.

44. PROHIBITIVE ORDER

§44. The forms of the prohibitive order have hk in most of the endings. F has a *prohibitive* mode, used in negative commands and in statements of undesired occurrence; corresponding forms, for second person actor only, appear in C and O for future commands: *143* *maačyiihkani: F kaata maačiihkani "do thou not move"; maačiihkani "thou mightst move"; C maačiihkan "do thou later go on a hunt"; O maačiikkan "do thou later go away." F has forms for all persons:pyaahkiči "he might (undesiredly) have come"; the endings, after the -hk, resemble those of the conjunct order.

F has also a *potential* mode for statements of hypothetical occurrence: maačiihkapa "thou wouldst go," ukimaawisa "he would be chief."

O has second person forms with longer endings in negative commands: keekwa maačiikkeen "do thou not go away."

45–49. CONJUNCT ORDER

§45. The verb forms of the conjunct order have personal endings quite differ-ent from those of the independent order. These endings are followed by various mode signs.

The *indicative* mode used in ordinary subordinate clauses, ends in -i (though F, which best preserves these endings, has -e in some of the inflections): F pemaatesiči "that he lives; when he lives."

The *changed* mode has the same ending, together with *initial change*, a modi-fication of the first vowel of the verb stem: a, e∼ee; o∼oo; to a long vowel ay is prefixed (but F leaves long vowels unchanged; O and, in traces C, has ii~aa). The changed conjunct is used in *when*-clauses of a single past occurrence, and as a *relative* conjunct, §102: *144* *neqθaawa "he was killed": M nɛqnaw, O nissaa; *145* *neeqθenči "when he was killed": F neeseči, M nɛɛqneh, O neessint (final consonant restored, t for č). Stems beginning with the roots tahθ- "so many" and taθ- "there," and the an. intr. stem taa- "exist, dwell," 248, prefix een- for initial change: *146* *tahšiwaki "they (an.) are so many": F tašiwaki, C tasiwak, M tahseewak, O taššiwak; *147* *eentahšiwaači "as many as they are": F eetašiwaači, C eehtasiwaat (final consonant restored), M ɛɛhtahsetuaq (ending reshaped), O eentaššiwaat (in some dialects eentaššiwaač).

The changed conjunct of stems containing a particle eeh (this is the changed form; the simple form does not occur) is common in C: eeh-takohteet "when he arrived." It occurs occasionally in O; in F this form serves also for nonsubordinate statements in hearsay narrative: eeh-pyaači "when he came; he came (it is said)."

The *subjunctive* mode ends in -e; it is used in subordinate clauses of events which have not yet occurred: F kiiši-nepaate "when he has gone to sleep" (then do you . . .); M piat "if, when he comes."

The *iterative* mode ends in -ini and has initial change; it is used in clauses of repeated occurrence: F peemaatesičini "whenever one lives," M pɛɛmaatesečen. In F these forms, without initial change, are used in negative non-subordinate sentences: aakwi pemaatesičini "he does not live."

The *participle* of the conjunct order has the ending -a for the animate singular and -i for the inanimate singular, with initial change. The participle denotes an actor, a goal, or an implied goal: F peemaatesita "one who lives," neesaata "he who killed the other," miinaki "that which I gave to him" (ending -ak "I—him"). The plural forms are not made with the usual conjunct endings, but are derived from the singulars with endings like those of §29: an. pl. -iki: F peemaatesičiki "they who live," inan. pl. -ili: F miinakini "those which I gave him." The obviatives are based on the usual conjunct endings, the singular adding -ili, the plural -ihi: F peemaatesiničini "the other who lives," peemaatesiničihi "those others who live."

C and O have a preterit conjunct with -pa; O has also a negative conjunct with -ssi.

§46. In the an. intr. verb, the personal endings (which precede the mode signs of §45) are: "I" -aan; "thou" -an; "we exc." -aank; "we inc." -ankw; "ye" -eekw; "he" -t; passive -nk. The third person is pluralized by -waa before or after the -t, and made obviative (without distinction of number) by -li before the -t. After a vowel, the first five prefix y: *148* *pemaatesiyaane "if I live": F pemaatesiyaan, C, O pimaatisiyaan, M pemaateseyan; *149* *pemaatesite "if he lives": F pemaatesite, C, O pimaatisit, M pemaateset.

Many stems in ne drop e; for instance, those ending in -hšine "fall, lie": *150* *šenkihšinaane "if I lie down": F šekišinaane, M sɛhkeehsenan, O šinkiššinaan.

These and most other stems in e have ‑k for "he": *151* *šeenkihšinka "one who lies down": F šeekišika, M sɛɛhkehseh, O šeenkiššink; *152* *nepeke "if he dies": F nepeke, M nepɛɛk.

§47. The inan. intr. conjunct has, for both sg. and pl., ‑k, obv. ‑lik: 57, 58, 60, 67, 68.

§48. The personal endings of the tr. an. verb fall into four sets. In each set the third person is pluralized by ‑waa and made obviative by ‑em.

The first set, with no theme sign, has the following endings: "I—him" ‑ak; "thou—him" ‑at; "we exc.—him" ‑akent; "we inc.—him" ‑ankw; "ye—him" ‑eekw; "he—obv." ‑aat; "he, passive" ‑ent ("I—obv." ‑emak, "they—obv." ‑aawaat or ‑aatwaa, and so on): *153* *waapamate "if thou lookest at him": F waapamate, C, M, O waapamat.

The second set has the theme sign ‑eke, as in §38, followed by ‑w wherever a third person is involved. Here belongs the form for "obv.—him," ‑ekot: *154* *waapamekote "if the other looks at him": F waapamekote, C, O waapamikot, M waapamekot. Here belong also the forms for inanimate actor; these have the endings of §46, but the languages differ as to the vowel after the ‑ek: F nesekwiči "if it kills him," M nɛqnekot. C, M, O have similar formations for the passives of the first and second persons, but F has special forms for these in the third and fourth sets.

The third set of forms has the theme sign ‑i, as in §39: "he—me" ‑it; "he—us exc." ‑iyament; "thou—me" ‑iyan; "thou—us, ye—us" ‑iyaank; "ye—me" ‑iyeekw: *155* *waapamiyamente "if he looks at us exc.": F waapamiyamete, C waapamiyamiht, M waapameyameh, O waapamiyamint.

The fourth set of forms has the theme sign ‑eθ, as in §40: "he—thee" ‑eθk; "he—us inc." ‑eθankw; "he—you" ‑eθaakw; "I—thee" ‑eθaan; "we—thee, we—you" ‑eθaank; "I—you" ‑eθakokw: *156* *waapameθankwe "if he looks at us inc.": F waapamenakwe, C waapamitahk, M waapamʹenah, O waapaminank.

§49. The tr. inan. verb has ‑am, followed by the endings of §46: "I—it" ‑amaan; "thou—it" ‑aman; "we exc.—it" ‑amaank; "we inc.—it" ‑amankw; "ye—it" ‑ameekw; "he—it" ‑ank; "they—it" ‑amowaat; "obv.—it" ‑amilit; "it, passive" ‑amenk; except for participles, sg. and pl. objects are not distinguished. *157* *waapantameekwe "if ye look at it": F waapatameekwe, C waapahtameek, M waapahtamɛɛk, O waapantameek; *158* *waapantanke "if he looks at it": F waapatake, C waapahtahk, M waapahtah, O waapantank; *159* *waapantamenke "if it is looked at": F waapatameke, C waapahtamih, M waapahtamɛh, O waapantamink.

50. INTERROGATIVE ORDER

§50. The forms of the *interrogative* order, used in subordinate clauses of question or probability, have an ending ‑eeli, added to personal endings which resemble those of the conjunct, the chief differences being extensive use of a theme sign

ᐧaaw for the third person, and of ᐧkw instead of ᐧt (or ᐧk) as a third person ending. In C and O there is only one mode, with initial change; F has also a mode without initial change and a participle. C and O have a preterit with ᐧpa; O has also a negaᐧ tive with ᐧssi. *160* *peemaatesikweeli "whether he live": F peemaatesikweeni, C peemaatisikwee, O peemaatisikween; *161* *wayaapamaawateeli "whether thou lookest at him": F waapamaawateeni, C wayaapamaawatee, O wayaapamaawateen.

51. WORD FORMATION

§51. In *composition*, one or more *prior members* are prefixed to a noun stem, a verb stem, or a particle; the members are treated phonetically like words in a phrase, suffering little or no modification. In *derivation*, suffixes are added to stems (*secondary* derivation) or to roots (*primary* derivation), and these components are subject to internal sandhi. Both compound stems and derived stems are subject to inflection; prefixes and initial change appear at the beginning (in compounds, on the first member) and inflectional endings at the end.

The distinction between compounds and derived words is not removed by the fact that some suffixes are homonymous with independent stems. Thus, beside the an. intr. stem apiᐧ (C apiw "he sits") there is a suffix ᐧapi "sit," forming an. intr. verbs; yet there is a sharp formal distinction between, say, C isihᐧapiw "and thus he sits" (nitisihᐧapin "and so I sit," eesihᐧapit "when he accordingly sat") and C itapiw "he sits so" (nititapin "I sit so," eetapit "the way he sits"). The former is a compound, with the particle isi (<PA *eši) "thus" as prior member; this particle is formed from the root eθᐧ "thither, thus" with the particle-forming suffix ᐧi. The latter is a primary derivative in which the root eθ is followed by the suffix ᐧapi, which is deverbal from the stem apiᐧ, §56.

52–54. COMPOSITION

§52. Certain particles, *preverbs*, freely precede verb stems: M keesᐧpesᐧ neeweew "he has seen him on the way," nekeesᐧpesᐧneewaaw "I saw him on the way," kayeesᐧpesᐧneewak "when I had seen him on the way": kees "completion," pes (used only as a preverb) "hither"; F weepiᐧpyeečiᐧteteposeewa "he begins to approach walking in a circle." Particles and even longer words are often *included* between the members of such compounds: M nekeesᐧpesᐧtɛhᐧwenahᐧneewaaw "but I did see him on the way," with tɛh wenah "however" included; F nepyeečiᐧ ketaanesaᐧnaanaawa "I have come to fetch thy daughter," with ketaanesa "thy daughter" included.

Some particles occur only as prior members: wiih "future" in F, C, O; kiih "past" in C and O; eeh in F, C, O, §45. On the other hand, particles formed with suffix ᐧi added to roots are freely formed (§91) and freely used as preverbs.

§53. Noun stems with an ending ᐧi and an. intr. verb stems with an ending ᐧwi (properly, agent nouns formed with ᐧw) are used as prior members with nouns:

F manetoowi-wiikiyaapi "a manitou lodge" (manetoowa "manitou"); niimihetiwi-nakamooni "dancing song" (niimihetiwaki "they dance together").

Particles (*prenouns*) appear before nouns in less variety than before verbs: *162* *waapi "white": F waapi-nenoswa "white buffalo," C waapi-maakwa "white loon," M waap-mianiiw "white owl," O waapi-kaak "white porcupine"; *163* *mači "bad": F mači-metemooha "bad old woman," C mači-mahkisin "worthless shoe," M mačeeq-mahkɛɛsen, O mači-očiččaak "evil spirit." The prenoun -iiči "fellow" yields dependent compound nouns, §100.

§54. Certain particles, denoting position or number, form *exocentric* particle compounds with a following noun stem; the suffix -e is added: F ahkwič-asenye "on top of a stone," nesw-eesepane "three raccoons' worth."

55–58. DERIVATION

§55. In general, the same suffixes are used for both primary and secondary derivation, though some are predominantly secondary.

Final suffixes appear at the end of the stem; without a sharp boundary, we can distinguish between *abstract* finals, which merely determine the form-class (noun, four types of verbs, or particle) and *concrete* finals, which add some more palpable meaning. Thus, -esi an. intr., 2, 3, is abstract, but -piso an. intr. "move without obstruction, glide," 15, is concrete. Unanalyzable stems, such as aθemw- "dog" in 1, are sometimes conveniently described as having a final of the form *zero*.

In primary derivation, the final suffix is often preceded by a *medial* suffix, such as -weeweek- "noise," 12. Medial suffixes have concrete meaning. Dependent noun stems contain a medial suffix but no root; thus -teeh- "heart," 102.

§56. Some concrete finals and some medials are *deverbal*, resembling a word-stem either in the way of homonymy or with some formal deviation, most usually loss of an initial nonsyllabic: *164* *apiwa "he is in place, he sits": F apiwa, C apiw, M apeew, O api, stem api-; *165* *eθapiwa "he sits so": F inapiwa, C itapiw, M enaapew, O inapi; final suffix -api. Beside the tr. an. stem *waapam-, 125, there is the tr. an. final suffix -aapam, 36.

§57. Suffixes appear in divergent forms, so that we set off *accretive elements*: *premedials, postmedials, prefinals.* Some prefinal elements appear in more than one final and in part carry a meaning; we call them *significant* prefinals. Thus, the an. intr. finals -enkwaqši, 41, and -enkwaame, 83, both mean "sleep" and have a common prefinal -enkw-. More often, a significant prefinal appears in a set of four verb finals; thus, -hθ "fall, lie" appears in an. intr. -hšine, 77, 150; inan. intr. -hθen, 43; tr. an. -hšim and pseudo-tr. inan. -hθetoo: *166* *ešihšimeewa "he lays him so": C isisimeew, M eseehsemɛw, O išiššimaat; *167* *ešihθetaawa "he lays it so": F išisetoowa, C isihtitaaw, M eseehnetaw, O išissitoot.

§58. Noun stems often lose final w when a secondary derivative suffix is added, as in 198. An. intr. verb stems, on the other hand, often add w to their final vowel before a suffix of secondary derivation, as in 197.

Dependent nouns take the prefix we´ when secondary derivation is made from them, 184; those which take the prefixes without t (before ii and oo, §32) here prefix wew´; see, for instance, §68.

59–65. NOUN FINALS

§59. Many primary nouns show no analysis; we may say that they consist of a noun root and a final suffix of the form zero, 27, 63, 87–89; *168* *miinali "berries, blueberries" (sg. rarely used): C miinisa (diminutive), M meenan, O miinan; *169* *šiiqšiipa "duck": F šiišiipa, C siisiip, M seeqsep, O šiiššiip; *170* *aakima "snowshoe": M aakem, O aakim. Many such nouns end in w: 1, 88, 100; *171* *wekimaawa "chief": F okimaawa, C okimaaw, M okeemaaw, O okimaa; *172* *eškoteewi "fire": F aškoteewi, C iskoteew, M eskootεεw, O iškotee; *173* *eθkweewa "woman": F ihkweewa, C iskweew, O ikkwee, Dela-ware xkweew; *174* *atehkwa "caribou": C atihk, M atεεh (pl. ´kok), O atikk.

A very few nouns appear in sets, with a common noun root and different finals: *175* *nameewa "sturgeon": C nameew, M namεεw, O namee; *176* *nameeqsa "fish": F nameesa, M namεεqs; this is perhaps to be described as an irregularly formed diminutive of the preceding; *177* *nameekohsa "trout": C nameekos, M namεεkoh (pl. ´sak), O nameekoss, diminutive of a stem nameekw´, compare §65; *178* *nameepila "carp, sucker": C nameepiy, M namεεpen, O nameepin.

§60. Scarcely any primary nouns are formed from general roots (that is, from roots which appear in primary verbs and particles) with an abstract final suffix. A noun of this exceptional kind is *elenyiwa "man," 13, with root elen´ "ordinary, plain": *179* *eleni (prenoun) "ordinary, plain": C iyini, M enεεn (as enεεn´apuan "ordinary roast: corn bread"); *180* *eleneqšipa "ordinary duck, mallard": C iyinisip, O ininiššip.

In contrast with this, many nouns consist of a general root with a concrete suffix. The concrete suffix may be a noun final deverbal from a noun stem; thus ´eqšip "duck," 180, deverbal from *šiiqšiipa, 169. Similarly, ´aqθemw "dog," de-verbal from *aθemwa, 1: *181* *waapaqθemwa "white dog": C waapastim, M waapeskaaqnem (longer form of the root), O waapassim. Or the concrete suffix may be a medial suffix followed by an abstract noun final, as ´aapeθk´ "stone, metal," with noun final ´w: *182* *piiwaapeθkwi "iron": F piiwaapehkwi, C piiwaapisk, O piiwaapikk; compare M enεεnaapεh (pl. ´kon) 'axe," Penobscot wɑpahpeskʷ "white rock." Or, finally, the concrete suffix may be a medial with noun final zero, as ´aaxkw´ "wood, tree, solid": *183* *šenkwaaxkwa" pine tree": F šekwaahkwa, O šinkwaakk; compare M askaah (pl. ´kok) "white pine."

Among the noun stems that are formed with a medial are the dependent nouns, §32; the medial suffixes which appear in dependent nouns of relationship, however, do not occur elsewhere. A few noun stems consist of a medial suffix with the third person prefix we´ or, less often, me´, §103.

§61. Noun final ⁻w is freely added to intr. verb stems, forming agent nouns, as M čeepaahkow "he cooks"; as noun, "cook," nečeepaahkom "my cook, my wife." As a primary suffix it appears after some medials, as in 182.

Final ⁻aa⁻w is added to tr. an. verb stems, forming nouns of undergoer: *184* *wekwiqsemeewa "he has him as a son": F okwisemeewa, M okiiqsemεw, O okwissimaat; *185* *wekwiqsemaawa "one who is a son": F okwisemaawa, M okiiqsemaw.

§62. Noun final ⁻n forms actions, products, and instruments from an. intr. stems: *186* *meteewiwa "he takes part in the Mystic Rite": C miteewiw, M metεεwew, O miteewi; *187* *meteewini "the Mystic Rite": M metεεwen, O miteewin; here C miteewiwin has a longer suffix; see below. Before this ⁻n, the an. intr. final ⁻kee has replacement of ee by a: *188* *paaškesikeewa "he shoots with a gun": F paaškesikeewa, C paaskisikeew, O paaškisikee; compare, with medial ⁻ečyee⁻, M paaskečisekεw; *189* *paaškesikani "gun": F paaškesikani, C paaskisikan, O paaškisikan; compare M paaskečisekan.[13] Otherwise, ee∼aa, as in M ahpεεsaawaan "bark mixed with tobacco," from ahpεεsaawεεw "he mixes something into his tobacco"; O kittikaan "field, farm" from kittikee "he farms" (<keqt⁻wik⁻ee⁻).

An extension of this ⁻n is ⁻wen, as in *peemaatesiweni "life," 98, from the an. intr. stem pemaatesi⁻, 2.

Another extended form is ⁻kan, as in F išiteehaakani "thought," from išitee⁻heewa "he thinks so."

An extended form ⁻aakan is added to some tr. an. stems, forming undergoers: *190* *wiičyeeweewa "he accompanies him": F wiičeeweewa, C wiičeeweew, M wiičiiwεεw, O wiičiiwaat; *191* *wiičyeewaakana "companion": C wiičeewaakan, O wiičiiwaakan.

Some unanalyzable nouns end in ⁻n: *192* *maxkesini "moccasin": F mahⁿkeseehi (diminutive), C maskisin, M mahkεεsen, O makkisin, Penobscot maksən.

§63. Diminutive formations differ in the different languages; s⁻clusters and, less often, h, appear in the suffixes, e.g., from *aθemwa, 1, we find F anemooha, C ačimosis, M anεεmoohsεh, O animoonss and pejorative animošš. Finals of this type are ⁻ehs, 9, 26, 40; ⁻hs, 37, 106; ⁻qs, 38, 176.

§64. Few concrete noun finals are unanalyzable; the commonest is perhaps ⁻aahtekw "stick, wood, tree": *193* *elenaahtekwa "ordinary wood or tree": M enεεnaahtek "hardwood," O ininaattik "maple." This is common as a secondary suffix, as M kohkaanaahtek "fish pole" from kohkaan "fish hook."

More commonly, concrete noun finals contain medials, as in 182, 183. Common in secondary derivation is ⁻wikamikw "house," with medial ⁻wik⁻ "dwell": *194* *ataaweewa "he trades, sells": F ataaweewa, C ataaweew, M ataawεεw, O ataawee; *195* *ataaweewikamikwi "trading post, store": C, O ataaweewikamik,

---

[13] Here, as in some other examples, the meaning is modern, but the habit of formation is old.

M ataaweewikamek (with i generalized from cases where -wik- comes after a consonant, §5).

Common in secondary formations is -aapoow "liquid," with medial -aapw-;
thus, from *eškoteewi "fire," 172:   *196* *eškoteewaapoowi "fire water, whisky":
C iskoteewaapoy, M eskooteewaapoh (ending reshaped), O iškoteewaapoo.

§65. Most concrete noun finals are deverbal, as -eqšip, 180, from šiiqšiip-
"duck," 169; -aqθemw, 181, from aθemw- "dog," 1. These occur also in secondary
derivation, as M aweetokaaqnem "bloodhound," from aweetok "spirit." From
elenyiw- "man," 13, there is the final -lenyiw, common in secondary use; thus,
from ataawee- "trade," 194:   *197* *ataaweewilenyiwa "trader": M ataawee-
weneniw, O ataaweewinini; compare F ataaweeneniwa, without addition of -w,
§58. From eθkweew- "woman," 173, there is deverbal -eθkweew; thus, added to
wekimaaw-, 171:   *198* *wekimaaθkweewa "chief's woman": C okimaaskweew,
O okimaakkwee; compare M okiimuuhkiw, without dropping of the final w of the
underlying stem, §58, and with contraction. From miin- "berry," 168, there is
-min: *199* *waapimina (an.), *waapimini (inan.): F waapimini "maize," C
waapimin "white bead," M waapemen (an.) "maize," O (Cuoq) waapimin "apple."
From nameekw- "fish," in 177, there is formed -aameekw: *200* *myaalameekwa
"catfish": F myaanameekwa, C maayameek, O maanameek;   *201* *aθameekwa
"dead fish": C atameek, M anaameek. Secondary, from atehkw- "caribou," 174,
with unusual loss of postconsonantal w: *202* *atehkameekwa C atihkameek,
O atikkameek. Another deverbal noun final is -aapeew "male, man":   *203*
*meqθaapeewa "giant": C mistaapeew, M meqnapeew, O missaapee. This is de-
verbal from   *204* *naapeewa "male, man": F naapeewa, C naapeew, M naapeew,
O naapee.

66–73. INTRANSITIVE VERB FINALS, SECONDARY

§66. Intransitive verb finals go largely in pairs, for an. and inan. actors.
Where there is no special inan. formation, an inan. intr. stem is derived from the
an. intr. with -makate: *205* *pyeewa "he comes": F pyeewa, M piiw;   *206*
*pyeemakatwi "it comes": F pyeemikatwi, M piimakat. Similarly, M pemaatese-
makat "it lives," from 2.

§67. In both genders -i added to noun stems in vowel plus w makes verbs of
being. Thus, an. intr. meteewi-, 186, is derived from the noun   *207**meteewa
"shaman": C miteew, M meteew, O mitee. From wekimaaw-, 171:   *208*
*wekimaawiwa "he is a chief": F okimaawiwa, C okimaawiw, M okeemaawew,
O okimaawi. To noun stems not ending in vowel plus w, suffix -eewi is added for
verbs of being, as M meniikaaneewew "it is a town," from meniikaan "town."
Similarly, from aθemw- 1, M aneemoowew "he is a dog," §18.

§68. An. intr. -i is added to possessed noun themes with third person singular possessor, making verbs of possession. Thus from wetehkom- "his louse," 94–97:
209 *wetehkomiwa "he has lice": C otihkomiw, M oteehkomew, O otikkomi. De-

pendent nouns which have this theme in wii- prefix we- to it: M oweeyawew "he has a body," from weeyaw, 7; those which have oo- prefix wew-: M owoohkomεεh- sew "he has a grandmother," from oohkomεεhsan, 66; see §58.

§69. An. intr. verbs of gathering and producing are derived from nouns with final -ehkee: *210* *wiikopihkeewa "he gathers basswood bark": F wiikopih- keewa, M weekopeehkεw; the underlying noun is *211* *wiikopyi "basswood bark": F wiikopi, M weekop, O wiikop.

§70. An. intr. verbs of action on indefinite inanimate objects are derived from tr. inan. stems by means of -kee. Thus, paaškesikee-, 188, is derived from *212* *paaškesamwa "he shoots it": C paaskisam, O paaškisank; compare M paaskečisam. Pseudo-tr. inan. stems in -too, -htoo drop oo; thus ešihčikee-, 34, is derived from ešihtoo-, 22.

However, the tr. inan. stems whose tr. an. pendant has -aw, §85, take -aakee: *213* *noontaakeewa "he hears something": F nootaakeewa, O noontaakee, from *214* *noontamwa "he hears it": M noohtam, O noontank; the tr. an. pendant of this is *215* *noontaweewa "he hears him": F nootaweewa, M noohtawεw, O noontawaat.

§71. An. intr. verbs of action on indefinite animate objects are derived from tr. an. verbs by means of -iwee: *216* *niimyiheewa "he makes him dance": F niimiheewa, C niimiheew, M niimihεw, O niimihaat; *217* *niimyihiweewa "he makes people dance": F niimihiweewa, M niimihewεεw. From some stems, how- ever, these an. intr. derivatives are made in other ways; thus to miikaaθ-, 78, suffix -kyee is added without connective: *218* *miikaaθkyeewa "he fights people": M meekaahkow (inflection reshaped, compare the conjunct miikaahkit "if he fights"), O miikaakkii.

§72. An. intr. verbs of *reciprocal action* are derived with -etwi from tr. an. verbs; thus, from 216: *219* *niimyihetwiwaki "they make each other dance, they dance together": F niimihetiwaki, C niimihitowak, M niimihεtowak, O niimihitiwak. In some cases, however, this derivative is made with -wi from the tr. inan. verb; so in the case of 78: *220* *miikaatamwa "he fights it": M meekaatam, O miikaatank; *221* *miikaatwiwaki "they fight each other": F miikaatiwaki, M meekaatowak, O miikaatiwak. Similarly, beside tr. an. waapam-, 125; tr. inan. waapant-, 134: *222* *waapantwiwaki "they look at each other": F waapatiwaki, M waapahtowak, O waapantiwak.

§73. Reflexive an. intr. verbs are derived with -eso from tr. an. stems. Thus, from pemaačih-, 75: *223* *pemaačihesowa "he restores himself to life, he saves his (own) life": C pimaačihisow, M pemaačehεsow. However, there are quite a few special formations, such as -wiso added to the tr. inan. stem; from 134: *224* *waapantwisowa "he looks at himself": F waapatisowa, O waapantiso.

Some of these special formations occur in both genders and show primary rather than secondary structure. These have a less explicitly reflexive meaning; we call them *middle reflexives*. Thus, beside tr. an. -esw, tr. inan. -es "by heat," there are middle reflexives in an. intr. ⸗eso, inan. intr. ⸗etee: *225* *kiišesweewa "he cooks him done": C kiisisweew, M kiisesiw, O kiišiswaat; *226* *kiišesamwa "he cooks it done": F kiišesamwa, C kiisisam, M keesesam, O kiišisank; *227* *kiišesowa "he is cooked done": F kiišesowa, C kiisisowa, M keesesow, O kiišiso; *228* *kiišeteewi "it is cooked done": F kiišeteewi, C kiisiteew, M keesetεw, O kiišitee. Similarly, beside divergent forms (§84) of these tr. finals: *229* *wens⸗weewa "he brings him to boiling": M ohsiiw, O onswaat; *230* *wensamwa "he brings it to boiling": M ohsaam, O onsank; *231* *wensowa "he comes to a boil": M ohsoow, O onso; *232* *wenteewi "it comes to a boil": M ohtεεw, O ontee.

Beside tr. an. ⸗θ, tr. inan. ⸗t or pseudo⸗tr. ⸗too, there is very often a middle reflexive pair with an. intr. ⸗so, inan. intr. ⸗tee: *233* *kyaaθeewa "he hides him": C kaateew, M kianεεw, O kaanaat; pseudo⸗tr. inan. kyaatoo⸗, 10; *234* *kyaasowa "he hides himself, he is hidden": F kyaasowa, C kaasow, M kiasow, O kaaso; *235* *kyaateewi "it is hidden": C kaateew, M kiatεεw.

In some instances, tr. an. ⸗m, tr. inan, ⸗nt are matched by middle reflexive an. intr. ⸗nso, inan. intr. ⸗ntee: *236* *eθakimeewa "he counts, values him so": C itakimeew, M enaakemεw, O inakimaat; *237* *eθakintamwa "he counts, values it so": C itakihtam, M enaakehtam, O iinakintank; *238* *eθakinsowa "he is counted, valued so": C itakisow, M enaakehsow, O inakiso (reshaped from ⸗inso); *239* *eθakinteewi "it is counted, valued so": F inakihteewi, M enaakehtεw, O inakintee.

Beside tr. an aql⸗, 47, pseudo⸗tr. inan. aqtoo⸗: *240* *aqtaawa "he places it, has it": F ahtoowa, C astaaw, M aqtaw, O attoot, the middle reflexive inan. intr. is aqtee⸗, 57, but the middle reflexive an. intr. is suppletive api⸗, 164.

A freely formed type of middle reflexive, *verbs of undergoing*, adds an. intr. ⸗kaaso, inan. intr. ⸗kaatee to tr. inan. stems. In structure, these verbs are mid⸗dle reflexives of stems in tr. an. ⸗θ, tr. inan. ⸗t, ⸗too, §81, based on an. intr. stems in ⸗kee, §70. Thus, from pseudo⸗tr. inan. ešihtoo⸗, 22, and beside the an. intr. derivative ešihčikee⸗, 34, the verbs of undergoing are: *241* *ešihčikaasowa "he is (generally) made so": M eseehčekasow, O išiččikaaso; *242* *ešihčikaateewi "it is (generally) made so": C isiihčikaateew, M eseehčekatεεw, O išiččikaatee.

Some an. middle reflexives merely add ⸗o to the tr. an. stem. The commonest verb of this sort is *243* *aačimeewa "he tells of him": F aačimeewa, C aačimeew, M aačemεw, O aačimaat; *244* *aačimowa "he tells of himself, he narrates (his own experience)": F aačimowa, C aačimow, M aačemow, O aačimo. Similarly ⸗po, 54, beside ⸗pw, 311, 312; ⸗eelemo, 19, beside ⸗eelem, 48.

74–78. INTRANSITIVE VERB FINALS, PRIMARY

§74. The final vowels of an. intr. stems can always be described as suffixal. Often enough, however, the part of the stem which precedes the final vowel seems to occur in no other primary word. Thus, ⸗i appears in esi⸗ (si⸗, e⸗) "say so," 120, 121, and in poosi⸗ "embark," 5. Similarly: *245* *niimyiwa "he dances": F niimiwa,

C niimiw, M neemow (inflection reshaped), O niimi. The pseudo-tr. inan. in -i that serves as pendant to tr. an. amw- "eat," 317, is of this character: *246* *miičiwa "he eats it": F miičiwa, C miičiw, M miičwah (inflection reshaped), O miiči.

In other instances, -i is added to a recurring root: *247* *waapiwa "he looks on": F waapiwa, C waapiw, M waapew, O waapi.

The final vowel is -e in a few, such as nepe- "die," 114, 115; mene- "drink (it)," 116, 117; naate- "fetch (it)," 118, 119.

Final -aa (replaced by -ee before -w in inflection) appears in pyaa- "come," 205. Similarly, taa-:   *248* *teewa "he exists": M teew, O tee; compare M netaam "I exist," O eentaat "where he dwells" (with irregular initial change, §45); M has a corresponding inan. intr. takuah "it exists," takiik "if it exists"; compare O eentakween "I wonder whether it is the case."

An. intr. -ee appears in leehlee- "breathe," 46. Similarly: *249* *ahkeewa (prior element of cluster uncertain) "he extracts marrow": M ahkeew, O akkee. In analyzable stems, -ee is very common after medials, as in *piintwikeewa "he enters a dwelling," 14, with medial -wik-.

An intr. -ii appears after recognizable roots, for instance in 33, 84.

§75. More recognizable abstract finals, mostly occurring in pairs, an. and inan., are fairly numerous.

A very common pair in primary derivation is an. intr. -esi, inan. intr. -ate: *250* *sanakesiwa "he is difficult, he is hard to get": F sanakesiwa, M sanaakesew, O sanakisi;   *251* *sanakatwi "it is difficult": F sanakatwi, M sanaakat, O sanakat.

Another such pair is an. intr. -esi, inan. intr. -yaa. Thus, beside inan. meçkwaa-, 68, 122, there is an. meçkosi-, 29;   *252* *kenosiwa "he is long": F kenosiwa, C kinosiw, M kenoosew, O kinosi;   *253* *kenweewi "it is long": M keniiw; reshaped in C kinwaaw, O kinwaa.

A less common pair is -esi, -ete, as in M mateesew, mateet "he, it is bad, ugly."

Another an. final appears in -aθe, inan. -ane: *254* *kosekwaθwa" he is heavy": M koseekwan, O kosikwan; inflection reshaped in C kosikwatiw;   *255* *kosekwanwi "it is heavy": C, O kosikwan, M koseekwan. In C, this inan. -ane everywhere replaces -ate.

Somewhat different is -eθe, inan. -ane, as in M weehken, weehkan "he, it tastes good"; M has this -eθe in mehkoon "he is red," 29.

A few pairs have -ekeθe, inan. -yaa: *256* *meqθekeθwa "he is big": M -meqneken, C (reshaped) misikitiw;   *257* *meqšyeewi "it is big": M meqsiw; inflection reshaped in F mešaawi, C misaaw.

Suffixes of this kind appear after medials; thus, -esi appears after -weeweek- "noise" in 12, and after -ahkamik- "place, space" in 51.

Suffixes like these are not always paired; thus, an. intr. -esi occurs without an inan. pendant in pemaatesi-, 2, seekesi-, 3, and inan. intr. -ane without an an. pendant in kemiwane-, 59. This last has a unique root; a root found also in other words appears in the following, without an. pendant: *258* *waapanwi "it dawns": F waapanwi, M, C, O waapan.

§76. More concrete finals are largely analyzable into prefinal and final parts; often also the same prefinal appears in transitive suffixes. Thus, prefinal -k appears in intr. verbs for growth and shape, an. intr. -ki, inan. intr. -kene: *259* *ešikiwa "he grows so, is so, fares so": F išikiwa, M eseekew; *260* *ešikenwi "it grows so, is so": F išikenwi, M eseeken. Prefinal -at "cold" appears with the same finals in an. -ači, inan. -atene: *261* *kawačiwa "he freezes to prostration": C kawačiw, M kawaačew, O kawači; *262* *kepatenwi "it freezes over": F kepatenwi, M kepaaten, O kipatin.

Very common is -hšine, -hθene with prefinal -hθ "fall, lie," 77, 150. The pendant of inan. ešihθene-, 43, is *263* *ešihšinwa "he falls so, he lies so": C isisin, M eseehsen, O išiššin.

Prefinal -nt "in water" is followed by an. -ne, inan. -ee: *264* *akwinčinwa "he is in water": C akohčin, M akiihčen, O akwinčin; *265* *akwinteewi "it is in water": F akwiteewi, C akohteew, M akiihtɛw, O akwintee.

Prefinal -ešk "movement of foot or body" appears in -eškaa, for both genders: *266* *papaameškaawa "he goes about": C papaamiskaaw, M papaameskaw, O papaamiškaa. There is also a form -ehk of this prefinal, with apparently dissimilative distribution, though the languages differ: *267* *peesehkaawa "he, it moves slowly": M pɛɛsɛhkaw, O peesikkaa, but C peesiskaaw, probably reshaped; the root is peet-. Compare §85.

§77. Other finals have fairly definite meanings but are not analyzable. Thus, an. intr. -eente "stay away": *268* *eθeentwa "he stays away so long": F ineetwa, M enɛɛhtwah, O (inflection reshaped) eneenti. Very common is an. intr. -ohθee "walk": *269* *pemohθeewa "he walks along": F pemoseewa, C pimohteew, M pemoohnɛw, O pimossee.

§78. Deverbal finals are numerous. Thus, from an. intr. waapi-, 247, there is an. intr. -aapi "look": *270* *eθaapiwa "he looks thither or thus": F. inaapiwa, C itaapiw, O inaapi; *271* *natawaapiwa "he looks to see": F natawaapiwa, C nitawaapiw, M nataawaapew, O nantawaapi; root nataw- "try, seek." From this last stem M in turn derives an an. intr. -atawaapi: menuatawapew "he has good eyesight," root melw- "good." Similarly, from inan. intr. waapane-, 258, there is a deverbal -aapane "dawn": *272* *pyeetaapanwi "dawn approaches": F pyeetaa-panwi, C peetaapan, O piitaapan.

79–87. TRANSITIVE FINALS

§79. Transitive verb finals or *instrumentals* go in pairs, tr. an. and tr. inan.; hence some analysis always presents itself. Instead of a tr. inan. there is often a pseudo-tr. in -too or -htoo, with inflection reshaped in M and O in the direction of tr. inan. endings.

§80. The most abstract pair is tr. an. -h, tr. inan. -htoo. In secondary use it is added to an. intr. stems. Thus, niimyih- "cause to dance," 216, is derived from niimyi- "dance," 245; the pseudo-tr. inan. is *273* *niimyihtaawa "he makes it dance": F niimihtoowa, M niimihtaw, O niimittoot.

This pair freely makes primary verbs: *274* *ešiheewa "he makes him so": C isiiheew, M eseeheew, O išiqaat; pseudo-tr. inan. ešihtoo-, 22. *275* *pooniheewa "he ceases from him, leaves him alone": C pooniheew, M poonehew, O pooniqaat; *276* *poonihtaawa "he ceases from it": F poonihtoowa, C poonihtaaw, M poonehtaw, O poonittoot. Other examples are 18, 52 (pseudo-tr. with formal object, so also 53), 75.

§81. Quite abstract also is tr. an. -θ, tr. inan. -t (often pseudo-tr. inan. -too). In secondary use it is added to an. intr. stems in -ee; this vowel is replaced in some words by aa, in others by a. Thus, from piintwikee-, 14: *277* *piintwikaθeewa "he brings him inside": F piitikaneewa, M piihtikanεεw, O piintikanaat; here C has the reshaped piihtokaheew, with -h, §80; *278* *piintwikataawa "he brings it inside": F piitikatoowa, C piihtokataaw, M piihtkataaw, O piintikatoot. This pair is added to pyaa- "come," 205, with the unique irregularity of aa~ee: *279* *pyeeθeewa "he brings him": F pyeeneewa, M piinεεw, O piinaat; tr. inan. pyeetoo-, 11, 111.

There are may primary formations, such as miikaaθ-, 78, miikaat-, 220, "fight." Similarly, kyaaθ-, 233, kyaatoo-, 10, "hide." *280* *nooçkwaaθeewa "he licks him": C noohkwaateew, M nuuhkwanεw, O nooskwaanaat; tr. inan. nooçkwaat-, 30.

An odd pseudo-tr. inan. is naate-, 118, 119, which goes with tr. an naaθ: *281* *naaθeewa "he fetches him": F naaneewa, C naateew, M naanεεw, O naanaat. Another odd pair is tr. an. eθ- (with irregularity of inflection, §§38, 40) and tr. inan. et-: *282* *etamwa "he says so to it, calls it so, says it so": F itamwa, C itam, M etaam, O itank. Somewhat different are tr. an. koqθ- "fear," 44, and neqθ- "kill," 144. The tr. inan. mates are not alike: *283* *koqtamwa "he fears it": F kohtamwa, C kostam, M koqtam, O kottank; *284* *neqtaawa "he kills it": F nehtoowa (with the usual leveling of the vowel), M neqtaw, O nittoot.

Longer forms, analyzable into prefinal plus final, have definite meanings, as -ahanθ "track, trail," 42; the tr. inan is -ahantoo: M wawaanahaahtaw "he loses track of it," O pimaqatoot "he follows the track of it."

§82. Tr. an. -m, with various tr. inan. pendants, has the specialized meaning "by speech, by thought." Commonest is tr. inan. -nt; thus, to kiihkaam-, 49, there corresponds *285* *kiihkaantamwa "he berates it": C kiihkaahtam, M keehkaahtam, O kiikkaantank; *286* *akimeewa "he counts him, them": C akimeew, M akeemεεw, O akimaat; *287* *akintamwa "he counts it, them": C akihtam, M akeehtam, O akintank. From this there is a deverbal pair -akim, -akint, 236, 237.

Other instances, of tr. an. -m are 16, 50, 76.

Peculiar is -m, -ot in aačim-, 243, and *288* *aatotamwa "he tells of it": C, M aatotam, O aatotank.

The longer form ⸱am, ⸱ant means "by mouth, eat, bite": *289* *eθameewa "he bites or eats him so": M enaameɛw, O inamaat; *290* *eθantamwa "he bites or eats it so": F inatamwa, M enaahtam, O inantank.

With a longer prefinal, ⸱eelem, ⸱eelent means "by thought," as in 48; *291* *pooneelentamwa "he ceases thinking of it": F pooneenetamwa, C pooneeyihtam, M pooneenehtam, O pooneentank.

In many formations, however, tr. an. ⸱m, with its various inan. pendants, has not this specialized meaning; thus, waapam⸱, 125, waapant⸱, 134, mean "look at." From this pair there is derived a pair of deverbal suffixes ⸱aapam, ⸱aapant: *292* *eθaapameewa "he looks at him so": F inaapameewa, C itaapameew, M enaapamɛw, O inaapamaat; *293* *eθaapantamwa "he looks at it so": F inaapatamwa, C itaapah⸱tam, M enaapahtam, O inaapantank.

Another common pair with unspecialized meaning, is *294* *pakameewa "he strikes him": F pakameewa, M pakaameɛw; *295* *pakantamwa "he strikes it": F pakatamwa, M pakaahtam.

A common extended form is ⸱oom, ⸱oont "carry on one's back": *296* *pyeetoomeewa "he carries him hither on his back": F pyeetoomeewa, M piitoomɛw, O piitoomaat; *297* *pyeetoontamwa "he carries it hither on his back": F pyeetootamwa M piitoohtam, O piitoontank.

The common pair ⸱hšim, ⸱hθetoo has the prefinal part ⸱hθ which occurs also in other formations, §57, examples 166, 167. Similarly, with prefinal ⸱nt, 264, 265, the tr. suffixes are ⸱nčim, ⸱nčitoo: *298* *akwinčimeewa "he puts him in water": M akiihčemɛw, O akwinčimaat; *299* *akwinčitaawa "he puts it in water": M akiihčetaw, O akwinčitoot.

Tr. an. ⸱em is added to possessed noun themes: from wekwiqs⸱ "his son," 38, there is tr. an. wekwiqsem⸱ "have or treat as a son," 184.

Tr. an. ⸱m is added to an. intr. stems that contain the root wiit⸱ "along with," §103, making verbs of accompaniment; thus, from wiixpee⸱ "sleep with others," there is wiixpeem⸱ "sleep with," 55. The underlying stem need not occur in in⸱flected forms. Thus, an an. intr. stem wiitapi⸱ "sit with others" is not quotable, but the derived tr. an. is usual: *300* *wiitapimeewa "he sits with him" (espe⸱cially, "with her," as a symbol of marriage): C wiitapimeew, M weetapemɛw, O wiitapimaat. Often the underlying stem is a compound with the preverb *wiiči "along": O anokkii "he works," wiiči⸱anokkiimaat "he works along with him"; C meetaweew "he contends, he plays," wiiči⸱meetaweemeew "he contends or plays with him."

§83. A very common pair is tr. an. and inan. ⸱en "by hand." Thus, our ex⸱amples, 4, 17, 23, 74, 85, 86, are matched as follows: *301* *wenteneewa "he takes him from there by hand": F oteneewa, C ohtineew, M ohteeneɛw, O ontinaat; *302* *wempeneewa "he lifts him up": C ohpineew, O ompinaat; *303* *peqteneewa "he takes him by mistake": C pistineew, M peqteneɛw; *304* *kawenamwa "he

knocks it down by hand": C kawinam, M kawɛɛnam, O kawinank;   *305*
*nakaanamwa "he stops it by hand": C, M nakaanam;   *306* *ašyeeneewa "he
pushes him back, rejects him": C aseeneew, M asiinɛɛw, O ašeenaat.

§84. In some pairs the tr. an. differs from the tr. inan. by a plus of w.

Very common is ᴗahw, ᴗah "by tool, instrument, or medium." Thus, beside 6,
there is   *307* *kiiškahweewa "he chops him through": C kiiskahweew, M
keeskahɛw, O kiiškawaat.[14]

Also common is ᴗesw, ᴗes "by heat," 225, 226. With 212 compare the tr. an.
308 *paaškesweewa "he shoots him with a gun": F paaškesweewa, C paaskisweew,
O paaškiswaat; M, with medial ᴗečyeeᴗ "whole body, belly," paaskecisiiw. In some
stems the suffixes are ᴗsw, ᴗs, preceded by various consonants; thus wenswᴗ, wensᴗ,
229, 230.

Another common pair of this type is ᴗcšw, ᴗeš "by cutting edge":   *309*
*kiiškešweewa "he slices him through": F kiiškešweewa, C kiiskisweew, M
kiiskesiw, O kiiškišwaat;   *310* *kiiškešamwa "he slices it through"; F kiiškešamwa,
C kiiskisam, M keeskesam, O kiiškišank.

Somewhat different and far less common is the pair ᴗpw, ᴗpot "by mouth":
311 *sakipweewa "he bites him": M sakiipiiw, Shawnee neθakipwa "I bite him";
312 *sakipotamwa "he bites it": M sakeepotam, Shawnee neθakipota "I bite it."
These last two pairs also have variants with clusters instead of simple š and p.

There are a few short verbs of this general type: *313* *mešweewa "he hits
him with a missile": F mešweewa, C misweew, M mesiiw, O mišwaat;   *314*
*mešotamwa "he hits it with a missile": M mesootam, O mišotank; for C Lacombe
gives misam.   *315* *pemweewa "he shoots him": F pemweewa, C pimweew,
M pemiiw, O pimwaat;   *316* *pemotamwa "he shoots it": F pemotamwa, C
pimotam, M pemootam, O pimotank. Tr. an. only is the common verb   *317*
*amweewa "he eats him": F amweewa, O amwaat; C moweew, M miiw lack the
initial vowel, but it is present in the deverbal suffix ᴗamw: C kitamweew "he eats
all of him," M ketaamiiw; M mɛɛqtamiw "he eats them till all are gone." The place
of a tr. inan. is taken by the pseudo-transitive an. intr. miičiᴗ, 246.

§85. In various pairs the tr. an. has a plus of ᴗaw. Some of these admit of no
plain analysis. Thus, beside tr. an. meθkawᴗ, 28, there is tr. inan. meθkᴗ: *318*
*meθkamwa "he finds it": F mehkamwa, C miskam, M mɛkhaam, O mikkank.
Another unique pair is noontawᴗ, noontᴗ, 214, 215.

Other pairs have more clear-cut suffixes. Thus, ᴗqtaw, ᴗqt is added to an. intr.
stems, for action relative to an object, as in the following set: *319* *aθoxkyeewa
"he works": F anohkyeewa, C atoskeew, M anohkiiw (with irregular vowel quantities, perhaps borrowed from O) O anokkii, Penobscot alohke;   *320* *aθoxkyeeqᴗ
taweewa "he works for or at him": C atoskeestaweew, M anohkiiqtawɛw, O

[14] Wherever the w of the suffix tr. an. ᴗahw is not merged with a following e to yield PA o
§18), there O drops the preceding q (<h) and M drops the w.

anokkiittawaat; *321* *aθoxkyeeqtam "he works at it": M anohkiiqtam, O anokkiittank.

Very common in primary derivation is -eškaw, -ešk "by foot or body-movement," with a probably dissimilative variant -ehkaw, -ehk; -ešk, -ehk reappear in the intransitive finals -eškaa, -ehkaa, 266, 267. Thus, beside tankeškaw-, 25, the tr. inan. is *322* *tankeškamwa "he kicks it": F takeškamwa, C tahkiskam, M tahkeeskam, O tankiškank; *323* *neqtaasehkaweewa "he comes to him relieving his loneliness": C nistaasihkaweew, M neqtasehkaweew, O nittaasikkawaat.

Another common pair is -ehtaw, -eht "hear": *324* *natohtaweewa "he tries to hear him, listens for him": C nitohtaweew, M natoohtawew, O nantottawaat; *325* *natohtamwa "he listens for it": C natohtam, M natoohtam, O nantottank.

The pair -naw, -n has to do with perception, especially "by sight": *326* *ešinaweewa "he sees him so": C isinaweew, O išinawaat; *327* *ešinamwa "he sees it so": C isinam, O išinank.

The pair -elaw, -el means "shoot (with arrow or gun)": *328* *wentelaweewa "he shoots him from there": F otenaweewa, M ohteenawew, O ontinawaat; compare C niisoyaweew "he shoots two of them" (root niišw- "two"): *329* wentelamwa "he shoots it from there": M ohteenam, O ontinank.

§86. Tr. an. -amaw is added to tr. inan. stems, forming double-goal verbs, §27. This, from waapant- "look at," 134: *330* *waapantamaweewa "he looks at something for or on him": F waapatamaweewa, C waapahtamaweew, O waapantamawaat. Similarly, wiintamaw-, 71, is made from wiint-, 334.

One common verb has no underlying tr. inan. and diverges in having no second object: *331* *naatamaweewa "he helps him": C naatamaweew, M naatamoweew, O naatamawaat.

The few recorded tr. inan. forms corresponding to tr. an. -amaw (e.g., M naatamatam "he helps it") diverge too greatly to permit of a reconstruction.

When the tr. inan. member of a pair is pseudo-transitive, the double-object derivative is made with -aw (M has the phonetically queer -uw), before which the final vowel of the pseudo-tr. is dropped. Thus, from ešihtoo-, 22: *332* *ešihtaweewa "he makes it so for him": F išihtaweewa, M esiihtuwew, O išittawaat. Similarly, from naate-, 118, 119: *333* *naataweewa "he fetches it for him": F naataweewa, M naatuwew.

§87. We come now to a number of common but isolated verbs. Tr. an. miil- "give something to," 81, has no tr. inan. by its side and functions as a double-object verb. A few tr. an. verbs end in clusters with l, as aql- "place," 47; its pendant is the pseudo-tr. aqtoo-, 240. Beside wiinl- "name," 45, there is *334* *wiintamwa "he names it, tells it": C wiihtam, M weehtam, O wiintank. No tr. inan. is recorded for *335* *noonleewa "she suckles him": C nooheew, M noohnew, O noonaat.

Other divergent verbs end in w, as wiičyeew-, 190: *336* *neeweewa "he

sees him": F neeweewa, M neeweew. F has here the tr. inan. neetamwa "he sees
it"; M has a pseudo-tr. neemwah (representing a stem neeme-).

88, 89. PRONOUNS

§88. A set of *personal* pronouns is based on a suffix -iil- with prefixes. Singulars have an ending -a; plurals have endings like those of §30, in part differing in
the different languages: *337* *niila "I": F niina, C niya, M nenah, O niin;
338 *wiila "he, it": C wiya, M wenah, O wiin; *339* *niilaana "we excl.": F
niinaana, C niyaan; *340* *kiilwaawa "ye": F kiinwaawa, C kiyawaaw, M
kenuaq, O kiinawaa.

§89. The languages agree in having other sets of pronouns: *demonstrative,*
indefinite, and *interrogative,* each in several varieties, but there is little agreement
among them. The following are some of the few agreements. *341* *awiyaka
"someone, anyone" (sg. or pl.): C awiyak, M weyak; but O awiya. C and M have
a special obviative form for this: *342* *awiyali "some (other) one, any (other)
one": C awiyah, M weyan. *343* *keekoohi "something, anything" (sg. or pl.):
F keekoohi, M keekooh, O keekoo; but C keekwa, kiikwa diverges. *344* *aween-
"who is it?": F weeneeha; M aweeq, aweeniq, O aweeneešš; but C awiina. *345*
*weekw- "what is it?": F weekoneehi, M weekiq, O weekoneešš. The interroga-
tive pronouns are predicative, hence an accompanying verb is in conjunct or interrogative order: M piiw "he comes"; aweeq payiat? "who (is it that) comes?"

In general, pronouns are capable of predicative use: F iin ee-nepeyaani "this
(is) when I die." In M, pronouns have special predicative inflections: eneh "that,"
but eneq as nepeeyan "this (is) when I die." O has a special predicative particle
mii: mii šikwa wii-ni-maačaayaan "now (is when) soon I must go."

90–93. PARTICLE FINALS

§90. Many particles, differing from language to language, cannot be referred
to recurrent roots. There are a very few correspondences: *346* *keehi "additive
limiting" (placed after the first word of the modified expression): F keehi, M keeh;
for instance M eneq keeh nenah "that is enough for me" (eneq "it is that," nenah
"I").

Especially as to particles of negation there is great discrepancy: F aakwi,
awita (with potential), kaata (with prohibitive); C nama (nama wiya), eekaa (in
clause and prohibition); M kan, kat (in clause), poon (in prohibition); O kaa (kaa
wiin), keekwa (in prohibition); Shawnee mata; Potawatomi čoo.

§91. Many particles were made from roots with suffix -i. Thus, from eθ-
"thus, thither": *347* *eši "thus, thither": F iši (preverb), C isi (also preverb and
prenoun), M es (preverb), eseeh (prenoun), O iši (preverb and prenoun). Other
examples 35, 90, 91, 92, 162, 163, 179.

The lower numeral particles are of this form: *348* *nekotwi "one": F nekoti,
M nekot. C and O have this root in other words, but for the independent particle

O has peešik (which appears also in some of the New England languages) and C the unique peeyak. *349* *niišwi "two": F niišwi, C niiso, M niis, O niiš. *350* *neqθwi "three": F neswi, C nisto, M neqniw, O nisswi. *351* *nyeewwi "four": F nyeewi, C neewo, M niiw, O niiwin. *352* *nyaalanwi "five": nyaananwi, M nianan, O naanan; C niyaanan is probably a borrowed form.

The higher numbers are made with longer suffixes, partly from the same roots, but there is much divergence among the languages: *353* *nekotwaašika "six": F nekotwaašika, C nikotwaasik; but M nekuutuasetah and O ninkotwaasso diverge. *354* *neqšwaašika "eight": F nešwaašika, M suasek (reshaped initial); but O niššwaasswi. *355* *metaatahθe "ten": C mitaataht, M metaatah; but F metaaswi, O mintaasswi.

§92. Particles of place are derived from noun stems by suffix ⸝enki, 61, 62, 64; ⸝enki is less common as a primary final, 21.

§93. The suffix ⸝e is added to combinations of root and medial, forming particles of exocentric meaning, parallel with the compound noun forms of §54. *356* *nekotwikamike "in one houseful": F nekotikamike, M nekuutikamek, O ninkotokamik. *357* *piintwike "in the house, inside": F piitike, M piihtik, O piintik. Some formations of this kind had ⸝i, if we may judge by F: *358* *niišwaapyeeki "in two strings": F niišwaapyeeki, C niiswaapeek, M niisuapiik. *359* *aθaamepyeeki "under the water": F naamepyeeki, C ataamipeek, M anaamepik; O anaamipiink has the ending reshaped, as though with ⸝enki, §92.

94–100. MEDIAL SUFFIXES

§94. Medial suffixes appear in nouns, either with a noun final (182, ⸝aapeθk⸝ "stone, metal" with noun final ⸝w) or alone (183, ⸝aaxkw⸝ "wood solid"). No line can be drawn between medials in this use and concrete noun finals; we call a suffix medial when it appears also in other uses. When no root is present, the noun is dependent (⸝yaw⸝ "body," 7; ⸝štikwaan⸝ "head," 24; ⸝alakačkw⸝ "palate," 31; ⸝škiinšekw⸝ "eye, face," 39; ⸝teeh⸝ "heart," 102). In intransitive verbs, medials appear before final suffixes, mostly an. intr. ⸝ee (⸝wik⸝ "dwelling," 14) and ⸝esi, ⸝at (⸝ahkamik⸝ "space," 51) or else suffixes of more concrete meaning. In transitive verbs, medials appear before the finals (as in the M forms of 188, 189, 212, 308, with ⸝ečyee⸝ "whole body, belly"). In particles they appear in the types of §93 (⸝wik⸝, ⸝wikamik⸝ "dwelling," ⸝aapyeek⸝ "elongated thing, string, row," ⸝epyeek⸝ "water, liquid").

Some medials do not form dependent nouns; others, especially those in dependent nouns of relationship, appear only here (26, 37, 38, 40, 104, 105, 106). In a dependent noun a medial often has a divergent form, especially a premedial extension.

§95. An extremely common medial is ⸝aaxkw⸝ "wood, solid"; its shape is entirely stable and it makes no dependent noun. In nouns it appears with zero final, as in 183. Occasionally it (that is, strictly speaking, the combination of medial ⸝aaxkw⸝ plus noun final *zero*) serves as a secondary suffix. Thus, from aakim⸝, 170:

360 *aakimaaxkwa "white ash tree": C aakimaask,[15] O aakimaakk, Penobscot ɑkəmahkw. Similarly, from the theme with prefix we- of a dependent noun, M oseetaah (pl. -kon) "axe handle" (possessed netoosetah "my ax handle") from oseet "his foot," 377. With an. intr. -ee it appears in such forms as M keeskahaahkow "he fells trees," O kiiškaqaakkwee. With other intr. finals: *361* *pemaaxkwihšinwa "he lies lengthwise as or on a solid": M pemaahkihsen, O pimaakkwiššin; *362* *pemaaxkwihθenwi "it lies lengthwise as or on a solid": F pemaahkwisenwi, M pemaahkihnɛn, O pimaakkwissin. *363* *kenwaaxkosiwa "he is a tall tree": C kinwaaskosiw, M kenuahkosew, O kinwaakkosi; *364* *kenwaaxkwatwi "it is a long stick": M kenuahkwat, O kinwaakkwat. With transitive finals: *365* *eθaaxkoneewa "he places him thus by hand as or on a solid; he thus arranges for him": M enaahkonɛw, O inaakkonaat. *366* *sakaaxkwahamwa "he fastens it by tool to or as a solid": F sakaahkwahamwa, C sakaaskwaham, M sakaahkwaham, O sakaakkwaqank. With particle final -e, it appears in forms like F otaahkwe "from the wood, on that side of the wood," čiikaahkwe "close to the solid."

Similar to this is -aapeθk- "stone, metal." It, however, takes final -w in nouns, 182. With intr. final: *367* *kiiškaapeθkyaa- "be a cut-off rock": C kiiskaapiskaaw, O kiiškaapikkaa. With tr. finals: *368* *kešyaapeθkesweewa "he heats him as stone or metal": C kisaapiskisweew, M kesiapɛhkesiiw, O kišaapikkiswaat; *369* *kešyaapeθkesamwa "he heats it as stone or metal": C kisaapiskisam, M kesiapɛhkɛsam, O kišaapikkisank. In particles: *370* *niišwaapeθke "two pieces of metal; two coins, two dollars": C niiswaapisk, M niisuapɛh, O niišwaapikk.

§96. As an example of a medial with variable form we may cite -kamy- "liquid," which appears also with premedial -aa; in M, for instance, only this extended form is used in new formations. *371* *keqčikamyi "sea": M kɛqčekam, Shawnee kčikami; compare C kihčikamihk "in the sea" and F kehčikamiiwi "sea." *372* *tahkikamyiwi "it is cold water": C tahkikamiw, M tahkiikamiw, O takkikami. With premedial -aa: *373* *meçkwaakamyiwi "it is red liquid": C mihkwaakamiw, M mɛhkuakamiw, O miskwaakamiw.

§97. Among postmedial accretions, -ee and -ak are frequent, the latter especially before an. intr. -esi and inan. intr. -at. Both are present, for instance, in -epyeek- "water, liquid," 359; the simple form -epy- appears in forms like M omaanep (pl. -yan) "spring of water," mooskenɛpiiw "he, it is full of liquid" (with intr. final -ee); -epyee- appears in forms like M siinepinam "he wrings it out" (with tr. inan. final -en "by hand"). Postmedial -ak is present in -aapyeek- "string," 358; compare -aapy- in forms like M mɛqtekuap "bowstring" and -aapyee- in forms like M sakaapiinɛɛw "he holds him by a string, by reins" (with tr. an. -en "by hand"). Similarly, -weeweek- "noise," 12, has -ee and -ak added to -weew-, as in M piitiiwɛɛw "it sounds hither" (<pyeet-weew-ee-); this, in turn, is an extension of -wee-, as in M eniitam "he makes it sound so" (<eθ-wee-t-). Similarly, -ekon-

---

[15] Cited Language (vol. 17, p. 307, 1941); not known to me.

"day" appears in particles: *374* *nyeewokoni" four days": F nyeewokoni, M niiwokon, O niiyokon; and ˒ekonak˒ in verbs: *375* *nyeewokonakatwi "it is four days": F nyeewokonakat, M niiwokonakat, O niiyokonakat.

§98. Deverbal medials are largely the same as deverbal noun finals. Thus, the noun final ˒eθkweew "woman," 198, appears as a medial before an. intr. ˒ee: *376* *pyeeteθkweeweewa "he brings a woman or women": F pyeetehkweeweewa, M piitɛhkiwɛɛw, O piitikkweewee; compare C nootiskweeweew "he seeks a woman." Similarly, ˒aqθemw "dog," 181, in C sinikonastimweew "he pets his dog(s)"; ˒eqšip "duck," 180, in C nootisipeew "he hunts ducks."

§99. Some medials occur unchanged as dependent noun stems, thus, ˒sit˒ "foot": *377* *nesitali "my feet": F nesitani, C nisita, M neseetan, O nisitan. This medial appears as a noun final, for instance, in M nekɛɛqčeset "my big toe" (normaly in possessed form, but not a dependent noun, since it has the root keqt˒ "big"); before an. intr. ˒ee, M keeskesetɛɛw "he is cut off at the foot"; with postmedial ˒ee before tr. an. ˒ahw in M keeskesetɛɛhɛɛw "he chops off his foot," O kiiškisiteepinaat "he tears off his foot"; with premedial ˒tala in F teewitanasiteekaapaawa "he stands with aching feet."

Other medials have a discrepant form in dependent noun stems. Thus, ˒iipit˒ occurs as a dependent noun: *378* *niipitali "my teeth": F niipitani, C niipita, M neepetan, O niipitan, but everywhere else the suffix is ˒aapit˒: *379* *saakaapiteewa "he teethes": M saakaapetɛw, O saakaapitee. Extended ˒aapitak˒ appears in M nɛqnwapetakat "it is three˒pronged."

Some medials which begin with p, t, k have xp, ht, θk or xk in dependent nouns: *380* *nexkaatali "my legs": F nehkaatani, C niskaata, M nɛkhaatan, O nikkaatan; compare Penobscot nkɑt "my leg." In all other uses the form is ˒kaat˒: C kiiskikaat "person or animal with a leg cut off"; *381* *kiiškikaateewa "he is cut off at the leg": C kiiškikaateew, M keeskekatɛɛw. Extended ˒kaatee˒, for instance in M čeeqčepekaatɛɛqtaw "he jerks his legs."

§100. The *pseudo˒root* ˒iit˒ "along, with, fellow" behaves like a root in every way except that, like medials, it never begins a word. It forms dependent nouns, such as M keetaqnɛm "thy fellow cur," weetaqnɛmon "his fellow cur"; and it forms the dependent prenoun particle ˒iiči: *382* *niiči˒elenyiwa "my fellow man": C niiči˒iyiniw, M neeč˒enɛɛniw, O niiči˒inini.

A pseudo˒root ˒iil˒ appears in the personal pronouns, §88.

101–107. ROOTS

§101. Roots are the most numerous type of morphologic element. Noun roots appear in a single primary noun, mostly with no plain suffix (miin˒, 168), though many such stems end in w (aθemw˒, 1). Rarely there is more than one noun (namee˒, 175, 177, 178). General roots appear in primary verbs and particles and in nouns with concrete suffixes (elen˒, 180, 193). Some general roots, especially some short ones, occur in only one primary form or one pair or set of verbs: a˒, 317; a˒ or aqʻ, 47, 57, 240; eʻ, 128, 282; keehʻ, 346; koʻ or koqʻ, 44, 283; miiʻ, 81; neʻ or neqʻ, 144, 284; neeʻ, 336; peʻ, 315; pyʻ, 205; tʻ, 248. A root meʻ is demanded by 28, 318, but also, with divergent meaning, by 313. Other roots range through all degrees of freedom, with much difference among the languages. The following are examples of freely used roots: akwʻ "adhere, be on," 264, 265, 298, 299; ašyeeʻ "reverse direction, back," 86, 306; atootʻ "on something," 54; aθaamʻ "underneath," 201, 359; elenʻ "ordinary," 13, 179, 180, 193; ešpʻ "high," 21; kawʻ "prostrate," 41, 74, 261, 304; kenwʻ "long," 252, 253, 363, 364; kepʻ "cover up," 262; keqtʻ "big," 35, 371; kešyʻ "hot," 368, 369; kešyiiʻ "speedy," 15; kiišʻ "finish, done," 225–228; kiiškʻ "cut through, sever," 6, 307, 309, 310, 367, 381; koohpatʻ "useless," 18; maatʻ "move," 142; matʻ "bad," 163; meçkwʻ "red," 29, 68, 373; meeqtʻ "exhaust," 91; melwʻ "good," 397; meqθʻ "big," 203, 256, 257; miitʻ "defecate," 83, 84; myaalʻ "spotted," 200; nakaaʻ "stop," 85, 305; nekotwʻ "one," 348, 353, 356; niišwʻ "two," 349, 358, 370; paaškʻ "burst," 188, 189, 212, 308; peetʻ "slow," 267; pemʻ "along in space or time," 52, 269, 361, 362; peqtʻ "by accident," 23, 303; poonʻ "cease," 48, 50, 275, 276, 291; saakʻ "protrude, emerge," 379; sakʻ "seize hold," 311, 312, 366; sanakʻ "difficult," 250, 251; seekʻ "fright," 3; tahkʻ "cool," 67, 372; waapʻ "look; white; dawn," 125, 134, 162, 181, 199, 247, 258; wanʻ "disappear," 42; weepʻ "begin," 90; wempʻ "upward," 17, 302; weškʻ "new, young," 92.

No root is present in dependent stems and in certain verb inflections, 129, 130, 133.

§102. *Relative* roots refer to an *antecedent* in the phrase. For instance, a word containing the relative root eθʻ "thither, thus," 22 (34, 241, 242, 332), 43, 51, 53, 165–167, 236–239, 259, 260, 263, 268, 270, 274, 289, 290, 292, 293, 326, 327, 347, 365, 392, such as M eseekew "he is thus, fares thus" or eseemen "such fruit," makes sense only in phrases like kamaač eseekew "he is contrary," kakiihkih eseemen "all kinds of fruit." The antecedent is sometimes a particle in composition: M meehnow-eseekew "he is of good disposition." However, the changed conjunct of a verb containing a relative root serves without an antecedent as a *relative conjunct*: M ɛɛseket "the way he is, the way he fares," ɛɛs-pemaateset "the way he lives." These forms appear especially as complements of nonverbal predicative forms (§89): F iin eeši-kanoonaači "that was the way he spoke to him"; M eneq ɛɛseket "that is the way he is," taaq ɛɛs-pemaateseyan "how is it that thou farest?" The relative roots are ahkwʻ (cluster uncertain) "so far," ahpiihtʻ (clusters uncertain) "to such intensity," eθʻ "thither, thus," taθʻ "there," tahθʻ "so many," 146, 147, wentʻ "from there, therefore," 4, 33, 36, 301, 328, 329: *383* *eehkopyeekaθki "as far as the water extends": F eehkopyeekahki, M eehkopikah, O eekkopiikakk. *384* *eehpiihtesiyaani "as powerful or as old as I am": F eehpiihtesiyaani, M eehpeehteseyan, O eeppiittisiyaan. *375* *eentaθesiyani "where thou art active, where thou dwellest": F eetanesiyani, M eehtaneseyan, O eentanisiyan.

§103. Some roots in the several languages are derived from stems and themes, largely from nouns with the third person prefix we-; some such forms are inherited.

The most important instance is the root wiit- "along, with others," 55, 190, 300, derived from the pseudo-root -iit-, §100; it appears also in the common preverb, *386* *wiiči "along, with": C, O wiiči, §82, M weeč, as in weeč-asaaqsow "he is enrolled along with the others."

Similarly, beside the dependent noun stem -iik- "dwelling," 61, there is a root wiik- "dwell": *387* *wiikiwa "he dwells": C wiikiw, M weekew (neweekem "I dwell"). This verb is distinct from the verb of possession, §68: *388* *wewiikiwa "he owns a dwelling": C owiikiw, M oweekew (netooweekem "I own a dwell-ing"). M has also wiikiahtam "he dwells on the bank of it (a body of water"). Nouns containing this root seem once to have been dependent: *389* *wiikiwaami "house": M weekewam, O wiikiwaam, but O (Algonquin) miikiwaam. Similarly F wiikiyaapi "house," but C miikiwaahp. There is some confusion between second-ary derivatives of the dependent noun -iik- and derivatives of the root wiik-; thus F has owiikiwa "he dwells" and M makes rare possessed themes of the shape netooweekewam "the house I own" (in contrast with neek "my dwelling").

Similarly, a few noun stems consist of a medial suffix with third person prefix, as though a theme of a dependent noun had been isolated: *390* *wexpenya "tuber, potato": F ahpenya, M ohpɛɛn, O oppin, Penobscot ppən "ground nut." Compare with this the medial suffix -xpeny-: M moonehpɛniiw "he digs potatoes."

Occasionally a theme with prefix me- is elevated into a root. Thus, M meewahkapetaw "he ties it up in a pack" (<miiwaθkaa- ?) and F nemiiwašiweni "my pack" appear beside the dependent stem -iiwaθ-: *391* *niiwaši "my pack": C niiwas (pl. niiwata), M neewas "my pack" (pl. neewanan), meewas "someone's pack, a pack"; O wiiwaš "his pack"; the F noun is not quotable, but the verb of possession (§68) is recorded as owiiwašiwa "he has a pack."

§104. Some roots appear with *postradical* extensions, In a few cases these are meaningful, thus, pemaat- "live," 2, 75, beside pem-, §101. Similarly, beside eθ-, §102, there is eθaat-: *392* *eθaatesiwa "he is of that character": C itaatisiw, M enaatesew, O inaatisi.

Most postradicals, however, have no clear meaning. Thus, beside waap- "white," 162, 181, 199, there is waapešk-: *393* *waapeškesiwa "he is white": F waapeškesiwa, C waapiskisiw, O waapiškisi; compare M waapeskɛn; *394* *waapeškyeewi "it is white": F waapeškyaawi, C waapiskaaw, M waapeskiw, O waapiškaa.

A plus of postconsonantal w is especially common. Thus, some forms have kep-, 262, but others kepw-: *395* *kepahamwa "he closes the opening of it with something:" C kipaham, M kepaaham, O kipaqank; compare F kepahikani "stop-per"; *396* *keponamwa "he covers the opening of it with his hand": C kiponam, M kepoonam. There are various such pairs; most roots in consonant plus w, on the

other hand, never lack the w, as, for instance, the very common root melw-
"good": *397* *melweelemeewa "he likes him": F menweenemeewa, C miywee-
yimeew, M meniinemɛw, O minweenimaat.

Quite a few roots appear sometimes with postconsonantal w and sometimes
with aw. Thus, beside kwiiθw-, 16, certain stems have kwiiθaw-: *398* *kwiiθawee-
lemeewa "he yearns for him": C kwiitaweeyimeew, O kwiinaweenimaat. A common
pair of this kind is natw- "seek," 324, 325, nataw-, 271.

§105. Often the extended root has the shape of a stem, especially of a tr.
inan. stem, as M keeskahaahkow "he fells trees," §95, formed from a root M
keeskah-, homonymous with (and historically no doubt abstracted from) the stem
of tr. inan. keeskaham, 6. In a number of instances the simple root occurs only in
one or two stems and it is only the extended root, with the shape of a tr. inan.
stem, that is freely used. Thus, naa- "fetch" occurs only in tr. an. naaθ-, 281, and
pseudo-tr. inan. naate-, 119, but the extended naat- is freely used: *399*
*naatoontamwa "he fetches it carrying it on his back": F naatootamwa, M
naatoohtam. Similarly, py- "come" occurs only in an. intr. pyaa-, 205; this has the
secondary derivatives tr. an. pyeeθ-, 279, pseudo-tr. inan. pyeetoo-, 11, but, resembling this last stem, the extended root pyeet- is freely used, 12, 76, 272, 296,
297, 376. An odd but important root of this sort is pii- "enclose, inside." The simple root occurs only in a pair of middle reflexive verbs: *400* *piinsowa "he is enclosed": M peehsow, O piinso; *401* *piinteewi "it is enclosed": M peehtɛw,
O piintee. The corresponding tr. verbs would be tr. an. piinl-, tr. inan. piint-;
these forms occur nowhere, apparently, as verb stems, but everywhere as extended
roots. The form piinl- appears in one pair of tr. verbs: *402* *piinlahweewa "he
encloses him in something": F piinahweewa, M peehnahɛw, O piinawaat; *403*
*piinlahamwa "he encloses it in something": F piinahamwa, M peehnaham, O
piinaqank. Except for these forms, all stems are made from the extended root piint-,
14, 77, 357.

§106. *Reduplicated* roots occur especially in verb forms, with meanings such
as repetition, plurality, or intensity. The regular type of reduplication prefixes the
initial nonsyllabic plus aa: F waawaapameewa "he keeps looking at him" (beside
125), M naaniis "two each" (beside 349); before a vowel, aay- is prefixed M
aayaačemow "he keeps narrating" (beside 244). There are various irregular types
of reduplication: F kehkahweewa "he decides about him," kekyeehkahweewa "he
repeatedly decides about him"; M keeskeeskaham "he repeatedly chops it through"
(beside 6); M poohkonam "he breaks it across by hand," pooqpoohkonam "he repeatedly breaks it across." More remote is papaam-, 266, beside pem-, §101. The
noun šiiqšiip-, 169, seems to show reduplication in a noun root.

§107. In some cases the reduplicated root tends to suppletive use for plurals.
Beside kenw- "long," 252, 253, 363, 364, the irregularly reduplicated kakaanw- is
used where more than one long thing is involved, as M kakaanuahkosewak "they
are tall trees" (beside 363 for the singular), kakaanuahkwaton "they are long sticks"

(sg. 364);   *404* *kakaanwaanexkweewa "he has long hair": M kakaanuanεhkow, O kakaanwaanikkwee; compare F kakaanohkweewa, Natick quanonuhquoant "having long hair" (Trumbull). Similarly M enεεken "he is so big," ayiinekεnok "they are so big" (would be ayyeeθ beside eθ); mεqnekεn "he is big," 256, mamaahkekεnok "they are big"; mεqsiw "it is big," 257, mamaahkiwan "they (inan.) are big"; nahεεnesew "he is small," nahεεnet "it is small," papiasewak "they are small," papeewaton "they (inan.) are small"; likewise the prenouns: mεεqčenεεniw "big man," mamaah-enεεniwak "big men."

BIBLIOGRAPHY OF ALGONQUIAN ACCORDING TO LANGUAGE GROUPS

GENERAL SOURCES

MURDOCK, G. P., *Ethnographic Bibliography of North America* (Yale Anthropological Studies, vol. 1, New Haven, 1941).

PILLING, J. C., *Bibliography of the Algonquian Languages* (Bureau of American Ethnology, Bulletin 13, Washington, 1891).

VOEGELIN, C. F., *Bibliography of American Indian Linguistics 1938–41* (Language, vol. 18, pp. 133–139, Baltimore, 1942).

Items from these sources are in general not repeated below.

COMPARATIVE STUDIES

BLOOMFIELD, LEONARD, *A Note on Sound-Change* (Language, vol. 4, pp. 99–100, Baltimore, 1928).

Proto-Algonquian -iit- 'Fellow' (Language, vol. 17, pp. 292–297, Baltimore, 1941).

On the Sound System of Central Algonquian (Language, vol. 1, pp. 130–156, Baltimore, 1925).

The Word-Stems of Central Algonquian (In Festschrift Meinhof, pp. 393–402, Hamburg, 1927).

GEARY, JAMES A., *Proto-Algonquian *çk: Further Examples* (Language, vol. 17, pp. 304–310, Baltimore, 1941).

MICHELSON, TRUMAN, *Algonquian Linguistic Miscellany* (Journal of the Washington Academy of Sciences, vol. 4, pp. 402–409, Washington, 1914).

Algonquiana Parerga (International Journal of American Linguistics, vol. 8, pp. 39–44, New York, 933).

An Archetype Vindicated (Language, vol. 11, p. 148, Baltimore, 1935).

The Fundamental Principles of Algonquian Languages (Journal of the Washington Academy of Sciences, vol. 16, pp. 369–371, Washington, 1926.

Miscellanea Algonquiana (International Journal of American Linguistics, vol. 7, p. 93, New York, 1932).

Notes on Algonquian Languages (International Journal of American Linguistics, vol. 1, pp. 50–57, New York, 1917).

The Proto-Algonquian Archetype of "Five" (Language, vol. 9, pp. 270–272, Baltimore, 1933).

Remarks on Terms of Relationship (Journal of the Washington Academy of Sciences, vol. 7, pp. 181–184, Washington, 1917).

Some Algonquian Kinship Terms (American Anthropologist, n.s., vol. 34, pp. 357–359 Menasha, Wis., 1932).

Terms of Relationship and Social Organization (Proceedings of the National Academy of Sciences, vol. 2, pp. 297–300, Washington, 1916).

Two Phonetic Shifts Occurring in Many Algonquian Languages (International Journal of American Linguistics, vol. 1, pp. 300–304, New York, 1920).

Two Proto-Algonquian Phonetic Shifts (Journal of the Washington Academy of Sciences, vol. 9, pp. 333–334, Washington, 1919).

Varia Algonquiana (International Journal of American Linguistics, vol. 5, pp. 116–117, New York, 1929).

SIEBERT, FRANK T. JR., *Certain Proto-Algonquian Consonant Clusters* (Language, vol. 17, pp. 298–303, Baltimore, 1941).

UHLENBECK, C. C., *Ontwerp van Eene Vergelijkende Vormleer van Eenige Algonkin-Talen* (Verhandelingen der Koninklijke Akademie van Wetenschappen, Afdeeling Letterkunde, n.s., vol. 11, no. 3, pp. 1–67, Amsterdam, 1910).

Het Passieve Karakter van het Verbum Transitivum of van het Verbum Actionis in Talen van Noord-Amerika (Verslagen en Mededeelingen der Koninklijke Akademie van Wetenschappen, Afdeeling Letterkunde, ser. 5, vol. 2, pp. 187–216, Amsterdam, 1917).

CREE

BLOOMFIELD, LEONARD, *The Plains Cree Language* (Proceedings of the Twenty-second International Congress of Americanists, vol. 2, pp. 427–431, Rome, 1928).

Plains Cree Texts (Publications of the American Ethnological Society, vol. 16, pp. 1–309, New York, 1934).

Sacred Stories of the Sweet Grass Cree (National Museum of Canada, Bulletin 60, Ottawa, 1930).

COOPER, J. M., *Some Notes on the Waswanipi* (Proceedings of the Twenty-second International Congress of Americanists, vol. 2, pp. 459–461, Rome, 1928).

MICHELSON, TRUMAN, *Indian Language Studies on James and Hudson's Bays, Canada* (Explorations and Field Work of the Smithsonian Institution in 1935, pp. 75–80, Washington, 1936).

The Linguistic Classification of Rupert's House and East Main Cree (American Anthropologist, n.s., vol. 26, p. 295, Menasha, Wis., 1924).

The Linguistic Classification of Tete de Boule (American Anthropologist, n.s., vol. 35, p. 396, Menasha, Wis., 1933).

A Report on a Linguistic Expedition to James and Hudson's Bays (Language, vol. 12, pp. 135–136, Baltimore, 1936).

Some Linguistic Features of Speck's "Naskapi" (American Anthropologist, n.s., vol. 39, pp. 370–372, Menasha, Wis., 1937).

Studies among the Montagnais-Naskapi Indians of the Northern Shore of the St. Lawrence River (Explorations and Field Work of the Smithsonian Institution in 1937, pp. 119–122, Washington, 1938).

SPECK, F. G., *Naskapi* (Norman, Oklahoma, 1935).

MENOMINI

BLOOMFIELD, LEONARD, *The Menomini Language* (Proceedings of the Twenty-first International Congress of Americanists, vol. 2, pp. 336–343, Hague, 1924).

Menomini Texts (Publications of the American Ethnological Society, vol. 12, pp. 1–607, New York, 1928).

MICHELSON, TRUMAN, Review of *Menomini Texts* by Leonard Bloomfield (Language, vol. 5, pp. 189–190, Baltimore, 1929).

SWADESH, MORRIS, Unpublished data.

FOX GROUP

BLOOMFIELD, LEONARD, *Notes on the Fox Language* (International Journal of American Linguistics, vol. 3, pp. 219–232, 1925, and vol. 4, pp. 181–219, New York, 1927).

Review of *The Owl Sacred Pack of the Fox Indians* by Truman Michelson (American Journal of Philology, vol. 43, pp. 276–281, Baltimore, 1922).

JONES, WILLIAM, *Algonquian (Fox)*, (Bureau of American Ethnology, Bulletin 40, pt. 1, pp. 735–873, Washington, 1911).

Fox Texts (Publications of the American Ethnological Society, vol. 1, pp. 1–9, New York, 1907); compare H. M. Rideout, *William Jones* (New York, 1912).

Kickapoo Ethnological Notes (American Anthropologist, n.s., vol. 15, pp. 332–335, Lancaster, Pa., 1913).

Some Principles of Algonquian Word-Formation (American Anthropologist, n.s., vol. 6, pp. 369–411, Lancaster, Pa., 1904).

MICHELSON, TRUMAN, *The Autobiography of a Fox Indian Woman* (40th Annual Report of the Bureau of American Ethnology, pp. 291–349, Washington, 1925).

Contributions to Algonquian Grammar (American Anthropologist, n.s., vol. 15, pp. 470–476, Lancaster, Pa., 1913).

Contributions to Fox Ethnology (Bureau of American Ethnology, Bulletin 85, Washington, 1927, and Bulletin 95, Washington, 1930).

Fox Kemiyāwi "It Rains" (Language, vol. 13, pp. 73–75, Baltimore, 1937).

Fox Linguistic Notes (In Festschrift Meinhof, pp. 403–408, Hamburg, 1927).

Fox Miscellany (Bureau of American Ethnology, Bulletin 114, Washington, 1937).

On the Future of the Independent Mode in Fox (American Anthropologist, n.s., vol. 13, pp. 171–172, Lancaster, Pa., 1911).

Linguistic Miscellany (In *Studies in Honor of H. Collitz*, pp. 37–40, Baltimore, 1930).

Mesawi'ka, and Fox Sociology (American Anthropologist, n.s., vol. 35, p. 397, Menasha, Wis., 1933).

Notes on the Buffalo-Head Dance of the Thunder Gens of the Fox Indians (Bureau of American Ethnology, Bulletin 87, Washington, 1928).

Notes on the Fox Negative Particle of the Conjunctive Mode (American Anthropologist, vol. 15, p. 364, Lancaster, Pa., 1913).

Notes on the Fox Wapanowiweni (Bureau of American Ethnology, Bulletin 105, Washington, 1932).

Notes on the Social Organization of the Fox Indians (American Anthropologist, n.s., vol. 15, pp. 691–693, Lancaster, Pa., 1913).

Observations on the Thunder Dance of the Bear Gens of the Fox Indians (Bureau of American Ethnology, Bulletin 89, Washington, 1929).

The Owl Sacred Pack of the Fox Indians (Bureau of American Ethnology, Bulletin 72, Washington, 1921).

Rejoinder (to the Bloomfield review of *Owl Sacred Pack*) (American Journal of Philology, vol. 44, pp. 285–286, Baltimore, 1923).

Review of *Observations on the Ethnology of the Sauk Indians* by Alanson Skinner (American Anthropologist, n.s., vol. 26, pp. 93–100, Menasha, Wis., 1924).

The So-Called Stems of Algonquian Verbal Complexes (Proceedings of the Nineteenth International Congress of Americanists, pp. 541–544, Washington, 1917).

Some General Notes on the Fox Indians (Journal of the Washington Academy of Sciences, vol. 9, pp. 483–494; 521–528; 593–596, Washington, 1919).

Vocalic Harmony in Fox (American Journal of Philology, vol. 41, pp. 181–183, Baltimore, 1920)

Who Were the Padouca? (American Anthropologist, n.s., vol. 23, p. 101, Menasha, Wis., 1921).

SHAWNEE

VOEGELIN, C. F., *Productive Paradigms in Shawnee* (In *Essays in Anthropology in Honor of Alfred Louis Kroeber*, pp. 391–403, Berkeley, 1936).
Shawnee Phonemes (Language, vol. 11, pp. 23–37, Baltimore, 1935).

PEORIA GROUP

VOEGELIN, C. F., *Shawnee Stems and the Jacob P. Dunn Miami Dictionary* (Indiana Historical Society, Prehistory Research Series, vol. 1, pp. 63–108; 135–167; 289–341; 345–406; 409–478, Indianapolis, 1937–1940).

POTAWATOMI

HOCKETT, C., *Potawatomi Syntax* (Language, vol. 15, pp. 235–248, Baltimore, 1939).
Unpublished data.
MICHELSON, TRUMAN, *The Linguistic Classification of Potawatomi* (Proceedings of the National Academy of Sciences, vol. 1, pp. 450–452, Washington, 1915).

OJIBWA GROUP

CUOQ, J. A., *Grammaire de la Langue Algonquine* (Proceedings and Transactions of the Royal Society of Canada, 1st ser., vol. 9, pp. 85 ff., 1891, and vol. 10, pp. 41 ff., Ottawa, 1892).
HALLOWELL, IRVING, *Was Cross-Cousin Marriage Practised by the North-Central Algonquian?* (Proceedings of the Twenty-third International Congress of Americanists, pp. 519–544, New York, 1930).
JONES, WILLIAM, *Ojibwa Texts* (Publications of the American Ethnological Society, vol. 7, pt. 1, pp. 1–501, 1917; pt. 2, pp. 1–771, New York, 1919).
JOSSELIN DE JONG, J. P. B. de, *A Few Otchipwe Songs* (Internationales Archiv für Ethnographie, vol. 20, pp. 189–190, Leiden, 1912).
Original Odzibwe Texts (Baessler Archiv, Beiheft 5, pp. 1–54, Leipzig and Berlin, 1913).
MICHELSON, TRUMAN, Review of *The Ojibwa Indians of Parry Island, Their Social and Religious Life* by Diamond Jenness (American Anthropologist, n.s.., vol. 38, pp. 657–659, Menasha, Wis., 1936).
VOEGELIN, C. F., Unpublished data.

DELAWARE

SPECK, F. G., *Oklahoma Delaware Ceremonies, Dances and Feasts* (Memoirs of the American Philosophical Society, vol. 7, pp. 1–161, Philadelphia, 1937).
A Study of the Delaware Big House Ceremony (Publications of the Pennsylvania Historical Commission, vol. 2, pp. 5–192, Harrisburg, 1931).
VOEGELIN, C. F., *Proto-Algonquian Consonant Clusters in Delaware* (Language, vol. 17, pp. 143–147, Baltimore, 1941).

POWHATAN

GERARD, W. R., *The Tapehanek Dialect of Virginia* (American Anthropologist, n.s., vol. 6, pp. 313–330, Lancaster, Pal, 1904).
MICHELSON, TRUMAN, *The Linguistic Classification of Powhatan* (American Anthropologist, n.s., vol. 35, p. 549, Menasha, Wis., 1933).

NATICK GROUP

GERARD, W. R., *The Root Kompau: Its Forms and Meaning* (American Anthropologist, n.s., vol. 14, pp. 574–576, Lancaster, Pa.

MICHELSON, TRUMAN, *On the Etymology of the Natick Word Kompau*, '*He Stands Erect*' (American Anthropologist, n.s., vol. 13, p. 339, Lancaster, Pa., 1911).

Mr. Gerard and the Root "Kompau" (American Anthropologist, n.s., vol. 14, p. 577, Lancaster, Pa., 1912).

TRUMBELL, J. H., *Natick Dictionary* (Bureau of American Ethnology, Bulletin 25, Washington, 1903).

PENOBSCOT GROUP

MICHELSON, TRUMAN, *The Linguistic Classification of the Shinnecock Indians* (American Anthropologist, n.s., vol. 26, p. 427, Menasha, Wis., 1924).

The Passamaquoddy Indians of Maine (Explorations and Field Work of the Smithsonian Institution in 1934, pp. 85–88, Washington, 1935).

Review of *Penobscot Transformer Tales* by F. G. Speck (American Journal of Philology, vol. 41, pp. 305–306, Baltimore, 1920).

PRINCE, J. D., *The Differentiation between the Penobscot and the Canadian Abenaki Dialects* (American Anthropologist, n.s., vol. 4, pp. 17–32, New York, 1902).

The Modern Dialect of the Canadian Abenakis (In *Miscellanea Linguistica in onore di Graziadio Ascoli*, pp. 343–362, Turin, 1901).

A Passamaquoddy Tobacco Famine (International Journal of American Linguistics, vol. 1, pp. 58–63, New York, 1917).

The Penobscot Language of Maine (American Anthropologist, n.s., vol. 12, pp. 183–208, Lancaster, Pa., 1910).

A Tale in the Hudson River Indian Language (American Anthropologist, n.s., vol. 7, pp. 74–84, Lancaster, Pa., 1905).

PRINCE, J. D. AND F. G. SPECK, *Dying American Speech-Echoes from Connecticut* (Proceedings of the American Philolosphical Society, vol. 42, pp. 346–352, Philadelphia, 1903).

Glossary of the Mohegan-Pequot Language (American Anthropologist, n.s., vol. 6, pp. 18–45, Lancaster, Pa., 19044).

The Modern Pequots and Their Language (American Anthropologist, n.s., vol. 5, pp. 193–212, Lancaster, Pa., 1903).

SPECK, F. G., *A Modern Mohegan-Pequot Text* (American Anthropologist, n.s., vol. 6, pp. 469–476, Lancaster, Pa., 1904).

Native Tribes and Dialects of Connecticut: A Mohegan-Pequot Diary (43rd Annual Report of the Bureau of Americau Ethnology, pp. 199–287, Washington, 1928).

Penobscot Transformer Tales (International Journal of American Linguistics, vol. 1, pp. 187–244, New York, 1920).

Wawenock Myth Texts from Maine (43rd Annual Report of the Bureau of American Ethnology, pp. 165–197, Washington, 1928).

MICMAC

SPECK, F. G., *Beothuk and Micmac* (Indian Notes and Monographs, ser. 2, no. 22, New York, 1922).

BLACKFOOT

JOSSELIN DE JONG, J. P. B. de, *Social Organization of the Southern Piegans* (Internationales Archiv für Ethnographie, vol. 20, pp. 191–197, Leiden, 1912).

KROEBER, A. L., Review of *The Adverbial and Prepositional Prefixes in Blackfoot* by G. J. Geers (International Journal of American Linguistics, vol. 1, pp. 184–185, New York, 1918).

MICHELSON, TRUMAN, *Notes on the Piegan System of Consanguinity* (In *Holmes Anniversary Volume*, pp. 320–333, Washington, 1916).

Notes on Some Word-Comparisons between Blackfoot and Other Algonquian Languages (International Journal of American Linguistics, vol. 3, pp. 233–235, New York, 1925).

Review of *Original Blackfoot Texts* by C. C. Uhlenbeck (American Anthropologist, n.s., vol. 13, pp. 326–330, Lancaster, Pa., 1911).

UHLENBECK, C. C., *De Afwezigheid der Datief-Conceptie in het Blackfoot* (In *Symbolae Rozwadowski*, pp. 72–82, Cracow, 1927).

Blackfoot Notes (International Journal of American Linguistics, vol. 2, p. 181, 1923; vol. 5, pp. 119–120, 1929; and vol. 9, p. 76, New York, 1936).

A Concise Blackfoot Grammar (Verhandlingen der Koninklijke Akademie van Wetenschappen, Afdeeling Letterkunds, n.s., vol. 41, pp. 1–240, Amsterdam, 1938).

Het Emphatisch Gebruik van Relatief Pronominale Uitgangen in het Blackfoot (In *Festschrift P. W. Schmidt*, pp. 148–156, Vienna, 1928).

Infigeering op het Gebied der Algonkin-Talen (Mededeelingen der Koninklijke Akademie van Wetenschappen, Afdeeling Letterkunde, ser. A, vol. 69, no. 3, pp. 11–116, Amsterdam, 1930).

Some Word-Comparisons between Blackfoot and Other Algonquian Languages (International Journal of American Linguistics, vol. 3, pp. 103–108, New York, 1924).

UHLENBECK, C. C. AND R. H. VAN GULICK, *A Blackfoot-English Dictionary* (Verhandlingen der Koninklijke Akademie van Wetenschappen, Afdeeling Letterkunde, n.s., vol. 33, no. 2, pp. 1–380, Amsterdam, 1934).

An English-Blackfoot Dictionary (Verhandlingen der Koninklijke Akademie van Wetenschappen, Afdeelnig Letterkunde, n.s., vol. 29, no. 4, pp. 1–261, Amsterdam, 1930).

CHEYENNE

GRINNELL, G. B., *Notes on Some Cheyenne Songs* (American Anthroploogist, n.s., vol. 5, pp. 312–322, Lancaster, Pa., 1903).

MICHELSON, TRUMAN, *American Linguistics* (Science, vol. 76, pp. 55–56, New York, 1932).

Anthropological Studies in Oklahoma and Iowa (Explorations and Field Work of the Smithsonian Institution in 1932, pp. 89–92, Washington, 1933).

Anthropological Studies in Oklahoma, Iowa, and Montana (Explorations and Field Work of the Smithsonian Institution in 1931, pp. 179–182, Washington, 1932).

Phonetic Shifts in Cheyenne (International Journal of American Linguistics, vol. 8, p. 78, New York, 1933).

Studies of the Algonquian Tribes of Iowa and Oklahoma (Explorations and Field Work of the Smithsonian Institution in 1929, pp. 207–212, Washington, 1930).

Studies of the Cheyenne, Kickapoo, and Fox (Explorations and Field Work of the Smithsonian Institution in 1930, pp. 207–210, Washington, 1931).

PETTER, R., *Sketch of the Cheyenne Grammar* (Memoirs of the American Anthropological Association, vol. 1, pp. 443–478, Lancaster, Pa., 1907).

SAPIR, E., *Algonkin p and s in Cheyenne* (American Anthropologist, n.s., vol. 15, pp. 538–439, Lancaster, Pa., 1913).

ARAPAHO GROUP

KROEBER, A. L., *The Arapaho* (Bulletin of the American Museum of Natural History, vol. 18, pp. 1–229, New York, 1902).

Arapaho Dialects (University of California Publications in American Aracheology and Ethnology, vol. 12, no. 3, pp. 71–138, Berkeley, 1916).

MICHELSON, TRUMAN, *Algonquian Tribes of Oklahoma and Iowa* (Explorations and Field Work of the Smithsonian Institution in 1928, pp. 183–188, Washington, 1929).

Language Studies among the Fox and Northern Arapaho Indians (Explorations and Field Work of the Smithsonian Institution in 1927, pp. 179–182, Washington, 1928).

Some Arapaho Kinship Terms and Social Usages (American Anthropologist, n.s., vol. 36, pp. 137–139, Menasha, Wis., 1934).

UHLENBECK, C. C., *Additional Blackfoot-Arapaho Comparisons* (International Journal of American Linguistics, vol. 4, pp. 227–228, New York, 1927).

DELAWARE, AN EASTERN ALGONQUIAN LANGUAGE[1]

C. F. VOEGELIN

1. SOUNDS AND PHONEMES

§1:1. Phonemes.

Consonants:

Stops:	p	t(T)	č	k	
Ambisyllabic stops:	P	T	c	K	
Spirants:		s(S)	š		
Fricatives:				x	h
Ambisyllabic fricative:					H
Nasals and Lateral:	m	n	l		
Ambisyllabic nasals and Lateral:	M	N	L		

Vocalics:

Semivowels:	w		y	
Ambisyllabic semivowel:	w			
Short vowels		i	ə	u
		e	a	o
Long vowels:		i·	(ə·)	u·
		e·	a·	o·
Stress (marked over vowel):				'

STOPS

§1:2. Points of articulation are identical for p, t, č, k and the corresponding but distributionally restricted ambisyllabic stops (§1:6) and T (§1:10). All stops are voiceless in all positions except one (§1:9). The affricate č (as in English "hatch" rather than "hats") patterns as a stop in Delaware. Velar k appears fairly stable but fronts noticeably after a long high front vowel. The k in ší·ki "good" is somewhat more fronted than the k in kí·spu "he is full of food."

---

[1] The dialect represented in this sketch is largely from the speech of one individual, Willie Longbone (74 years old) of Dewey, Oklahoma. The Delaware Indians around Dewey are said to speak Lenape Delaware as opposed to Munsee Delaware. Besides working with a few Lenape informants in Oklahoma, I was fortunate in having Mr. Longbone go with me to Ann Arbor for the Linguistic Institute at the University of Michigan, where he served as informant for a group of students. Reading galley now, several years after our Linguistic Institute discussions, I would offer another solution to the phonemic problem treated then in terms of large cap T and S. I would now write small cap ᴛ and s, and make a new statement of distribution: these ambisyllabic consonants also appear in clusters, and when they do they have the phonetic features formerly attributed to large cap T and S (voiceless in clusters; prior n actualized as consonant).

130

§1:3. Stops in prevocalic word-initial are unaspirated and quite lenis even when preceding a stressed vowel, as pénkwsu "he is dry," típa·s "chicken."

§1:4. A rather delayed release is audible after stops in word-final, but this release cannot be counted as aspiration. However, w is whispered after k in word-final, and this gives an aspirated effect: máxkw "bear," kúmpakw "leaf," entapá·e·kw "when you fellows came." Likewise, w between voiceless consonants is whispered, giving an aspirated effect: təkwčé·su "he is round," kwsí·yok "they are mowing in a group."

§1:5. As a prior member of a cluster, a stop is weakly aspirated, as k before p and before š, and t before s in kpaxkši·kanə́na "our knives," mi·tsúwak "they are eating." In contrast to ambisyllabic stops which do not occur in clusters, two identical normal stops may be juxtaposed, with the prior stop released and aspirated: amankká·ᴛe· "he has big legs," wsí·ttət "his little foot," nəmattu·nhá·la "I talk mean to him."

§1:6. Stops in intervocalic position may be ambisyllabic (ᴛ), normal (t), or normal juxtaposed (tt). Only normal consonants occur in clusters and at the beginning and end of words. Ambisyllabic stops (§1:7) and ʜ (§1:16) and ᴍ, ɴ, ʟ, w (§1:19) are restricted to intervocalic position. While stops offer a contrast, as between ᴛ and tt (§1:5; 7), continuants lack this contrast. Voiced consonants in general do not serve as the final members of medial clusters (§1:32). But as an initial cluster, nn and ll are possible: nni·sktəlínko "I have a dirty face," lle·la·ó·kwsi·t "one who is in the middle." Initial nn and ll are produced with two impulses of voicing, sometimes suggesting nən and ləl, while medial ɴ and ʟ are relatively fortis and produced with a single impulse of voicing.

§1:7. Ambisyllabic stops tend to be long and rather fortis after stressed vowels. The second ᴛ is longer than the first ᴛ in nkaᴛá·ᴛamən "I want it," and both are more fortis than the ᴛ in nkaᴛapá "I want to come." However, exceptional instances occur, as in háᴛe· "it is there," when an ambisyllabic stop is neither long nor fortis despite what would usually constitute optimum stressing for ambisyllabic emphasis. The minimum distinction between ambisyllabic stops and normal stops is to be heard in the vocalic on-glide. The vowel before an ambisyllabic stop continues in full force until the stop is reached which appears to close the syllable, and belongs also to the following syllable. The vowel before a normal stop falls slightly in intensity before the stop is reached (§1:29).

In a random word list, well over half the stops in intervocalic position appear to be ambisyllabic. Doublets of the same element may apear with a normal stop in one form, an ambisyllabic stop in another: ntá·ki "my land," háᴋi "land"; ləpwé· "he is smart," kələ́ᴩo "you are smart."

But ambisyllabic ᴩ is possible before w: nkaᴛú·ᴩwi "I am hungry." So also is the sequence ᴋw possible: toᴋwí·ma·n "he blamed him for it." If w is granted the status of a vowel in this sequence, ᴩ and ᴋ may still be said to be in intervocalic position (§1:25).

§1:8. Normal stops in intervocalic position are unaspirated without giving the pseudo-voiced effect associated with unaspirated stops in some languages: ne·petané· "I also," íkali "out yonder," me·čitá "through already."

§1:9. Stops are fully voiced only in the sequence homorganic nasal-stop-vocalic (§1:20; 21; 22). Compare maxálankw "evening star," mpənškinkwé·na "I put my finger in his eye," háкink ntəlipánči "I went in the ground." The k of the sequences nkw are fully voiced but the k of the sequence nk in word-final is only partly voiced; p and t are just as fully voiced as č even though mp and nt are in word initial while nč is intervocalic.

When a nonhomorganic nasal precedes a stop, the stop is not voiced: šuwánpi "sea water," naxámtət "my little daughter-in-law," ntaкwí·mkwəm "he blamed me for it." Neither is the stop fully voiced when followed by a voiceless consonant in an extended cluster: hémpsa "dresses," ahkontká·тe· "he is long legged," xinkwká·тe· "he has one big leg" (w, being voiceless in the sequence kwk, unvoices the preceding k).

§1:10. Defective T is written for a t which is not voiced in the sequence homorganic nasal-stop-vowel. Besides mahtánTu "devil," other instances found involve a by-form of the diminutive suffix (§6:39): ntá·nTət "my little daughter," nəwi·skónTət "my little elbow."

SPIRANTS AND FRICATIVES

§1:11. The spirants s and š and the velar fricative x have much the same distribution as normal stops, but lack a distinctive ambisyllabic-normal contrast in intervocalic position. They are fairly short in word-initial and word-final, but long between vowels, especially long after a stressed vowel: xáxa·kw "sycamore." As prior member of a medial cluster they are long, but short after a prior member in a cluster: ké·šte·k "the heat" but kwənščənáman "he pushed it." The long and short positional variants are always in complementary distribution.

§1:12. Prevocalic spirants are fully voiced after word initial n (§1:21): nša·kwsíhina "we are stingy," nsakhoté·nami "'I am worried."

§1:13. When the sequence ns or nš occurs medially before a vowel or finally, the spirant has a voiced timbre, but is by no means fully voiced; the preceding n is not actualized as a consonant but functions as an anusvara, nasalizing the preceding vowel which is always long: alú·ns "arrow," lo·кamhú·nši "elm tree," ši·má·nši "hickory tree" (but sí·mi·n "hickory nut"), naxá·ns "my elder brother," xá·nsa· "oh elder brother," nko·nši·phúwe "I'm hiding," ló·ke·ns "dish."

§1:14. Defective S is written for an s which is not at all voiced in the intervocalic sequence nS; it is known for only one word, e·mhó·nSak "spoons." The n before S is actualized as a consonant.

§1:15. Many words begin in a vowel without any suggestion of an h on-glide (§1:34). These are never confused with words beginning in h-vowel; the vowel is short and usually stressed: húpwe·w "he smokes," húкo·n "pot hook," háкi "land," hóĸe·s "bark," hópan "lung," hópəni·s "potato," hápi·s "tump-line," hírukw "tree" and hítku·k "trees"; but hupó·ĸan "pipe," hakí·he·w "he is farm-ing" (§1:33).

In the following, initial x appears where one would expect h in Delaware: xáni·kw "squirrel." Both x and h appear before w in word-initial: xwi·səmə́sa "his younger brother," hwíkxkona "his shin." Clusters of x plus stop are found in word-initial (xkú·k "snake"), but not of h plus stop (§1:18). Velar x occurs freely in word-final (kí·šu·x "sun"), h in artificially slow speech (wté· beside wté·h "heart"), and in some exclamations (yúh "all right").

§1:16. Both normal h, which sounds very much like h in an English phrase ("now help me"), and the longer ambisyllabic н occur intervocalically: nkarahúpo "I want to smoke," weнuponkwšá·tay "smoking tobacco," eнakí·he·t "farmer."

§1:17. Normal h between vowels is in syllabic-initial except when the vowels before and after h are short and identical; then h appears to be associated more closely with the preceding vowel, which may be stressed, than with the following vowel, which is never stressed. The entire sequence is best regarded as a single interrupted syllable, having the value of two morae (§1:33). Interrupted syllables are most often medial, never final, sometimes initial: kənihini·šantpáhamo "you fellows have two heads each," kopšéhemən "he closed it," kəna·ni·sktəlinkóhomo "you fellows have dirty faces," úhuma "his grandmother." Except for pohohší·ĸan "his dried meat," interrupted syllables have been found only before single conso-nants, not before consonant clusters.

§1:18. Clusters of h plus stop or spirant are distributionally restricted to intervocalic position, not unlike an ambisyllabic consonant (§1:6), but are nonethe-less analyzed as two juxtaposed phonemes (§1:33). These clusters characteristi-cally follow short vowels, usually unstressed: tahkócu "he is cold," ntákohči "I'm cold," pehpomorú·nhe·s "preacher," hwíkahša "his fingernail" (nhíĸaš "my finger-nail"), pásahpo·n "light, puffed up bread," tahkóx "turtle," but tíhtəs "red ham-mer wood pecker." The semivowel w occurs after hk, and thereby patterns as a vowel (§1:25): we·entahkwí·i "both sides, both ends." In rare instances an under-lying sequence of two short vowels may be actualized as a long vowel before h-consonant: entá·hpi·t beside entaáhpi·t "one who is born."

NASALS AND LATERAL

§1:19. In intervocalic position ambisyllabic м, н, ʟ, w are distinguished from m, n, l, w in being distinctly long, with one impulse of voicing (§1:6): aʟəní·xsu "he talks Delaware," kəмankka·ráhana "we have big legs," ikaktaнáwo "you fel-lows sieze him." In contrast to stops (§1:7), ambisyllabic continuants are rare in-deed; only w appears after a long vowel: po·tama·wó·o "they pray to him."

§1:20. Of the nasals, m is always bilabial. The n phoneme has two posi-tional variants, alveolar and velar.

Velar n occurs only before k (§1:9). It is this allophone of the n phoneme which is homorganic to k.

Alveolar n occurs in all positions except before k. With some slight assimilation, alveolar n is homorganic to t, č, s, š in the clusters nt, nč (§1:9) and ns, nš (§1:12; 13), and to n in nn (§1:6).

§1:21. In word-initial clusters of nasal plus homorganic consonant, the nasal is extremely short and even somewhat unvoiced if the consonant is voiceless (§1:9; 12), but merely short before n (§1:6).

§1:22. Nasal syllables, that is, syllables closed by prevocalic or word-final mp, nt, nč, nk have the value of two morae (§1:33). The preceding vowel is short but the nasal is very long, longer than an ambisyllabic nasal (§1:19). The two morae length of a nasal syllable is distributed between the fixed short vowel and the following nasal which is long only if the homorganic stop is voiced (§1:9; 10). Compare nasal syllable in hémpəs "dress," and syllables with length determined by vowel in hémpsa "dresses," maxke·mpsé·yok "they have red dresses."

§1:23. Clusters of ns and nš after a vowel (§1:13) yield two morae nasalized syllables (§1:33) in which the n serves to nasalize the preceding long vowel: čú·lə·ns "bird." If the spirant is replaced by an homorganic stop, the n is actualized as a consonant in a nasal syllable (§1:22) rather than a nasalized syllable: ču·léntət "little bird" (§6:39). Nor does a nasalized syllable result when n precedes defective S (§1:14) or when the sequence ns is followed by other consonants in an extended cluster: mpənstu·né·na "I put my finger in his mouth."

§1:24. Fully voiced l (like the first rather than the second l in English "little") occurs in word-initial and intervocalically. In word-final and in clusters before voiceless consonants, l is slightly fronted and, like w in the same positions, begins with a voiced on-glide but ends in a voiceless off-glide; in contrast, n and m in these positions are not at all unvoiced: nu·ltu·nhéhena "we talk well," pá·lsu "he is sick," ntahitkáwsi "I am very gentle," ksaka·ʀéhu·l "I am leading you," i·lá·wke·w "he is dancing the war dance," ntəma·kwe·wxé·semak "my beaver hides."

SEMIVOWELS

§1:25. When the cluster w plus consonant is in word-initial, w is completely unvoiced. Compare eheliwsí·ka·k "to the west" and wsí·ka "sun-down." When the sequence kw is in word-final or precedes a voiceless consonant, w is completely voiceless (§1:4; 9). Postvocalic w is partly voiceless in word-final and as a prior member of a cluster (§1:24). In clusters, w patterns as a consonant when voiceless, as a vowel when voiced (§1:7; 18; 28). When not in word-final, and not preceding a voiceless consonant, w as well as y is voiced (§1:26; 27; 28). There seems to be no voiceless allophone for y. In one example noted of y before consonant, y is voiced: ntu·lháytət "my little breast." Likewise, y is voiced in word-final: kwšá·tay "tobacco." No examples of y following a consonant have been found.

§1:26. In word-initial, y occurs before u and u· while w occurs before i, i·, e·, o·, ə: yúkwe "now," yú·k "those," wí·xa "his hair," we·yó·psi·t "one who is white," wələtú·nhe· "he talks well," wo·kahté·səma "his paunch." One example gives y before a· and only a few instances show w before a: ya·ká·un "shade house," waní·ṛi·s "that one, my friend."

§1:27. Likewise in intervocalic position there is a tendency toward comple-mentary distribution in vowel sequences which permit the intrusion of one semi-vowel to the exclusion of the other. Only y appears between two vowels if the first vowel is e· or if the second is u· or u: me·xke·yohkǿsi·t "one who has red flesh, an Indian," wiyú·s "meat." Only w appears if the first vowel is ə: kahé·səwa "the mother of all of you." However, both y and w may appear between two vowels if the first vowel is not e·, and not ə, and the second vowel is not u· or u. Thus, both oyə and owə are possible: toyəmǿna "he bought them," powənəməné·yo "they sieved it."

§1.28. The semivowel w has been found to occur after prior member p, ᴘ, ᴋ (§1:7; 18) and k (but not after t or č); after h and x (but not after s or š); after m (but not after n or l): šinka·lkwǿsu "he is hateful," wí·shwi "his gall," mú·xwe·s "worm," tataentaša·wəla·mwíhti·t "until they starve to death." Syllabic bounda-ries remain undetermined here; the prior consonant was heard indifferently as in syllabic initial (with w) and in syllabic final. While t, č, s, š never precede w, w pre-cedes these and other consonants but has not been noted before p, m, n, l (§1:24).

CLUSTERS

§1:29. All consonants except members of restricted series (§1:6; 10; 14) ap-pear in word-initial, in word-final, and in clusters. One gains a general impression (but see §1:6; 7; 17; 28) that prevocalic consonants syllabify with the following vowel, while one or more prior members of a cluster syllabify with a preceding vowel; clusters at the beginning or end of a word are, respectively, in syllabic-initial and syllabic-final.

§1:30. Only x, s, and n have been noted as prior members before k, kw and s in word-final (§1:9; 11; 13): ó·ᴘaskw "cornshuck."

§1:31. Word-initial clusters show n, k, w as prior members before t, č, s, š; m instead of n, and k but not w before p; n but not k or w before k; n and k but not w before h; k but not n or w before x (§2:21 ff.). There are besides kwč, kwš, xkw, khw, nhw, kw, hw, xw, mw, mh, nh, th, ph, ll, tk, čk, sk, xk, and doubt-less other clusters in word-initial.

§1:32. Medial clusters are less restricted than clusters in word-final or word-initial. All consonants except p and l appear prior to p; all consonants, including t, appear prior to t; t, č, s, x, m and l have not been noted before č; all consonants.

including k but not p, appear prior to k; all consonants except s, š, č appear prior to s; t, č, s, š, m and l have not been noted before š; all consonants except č, x, h appear prior to h; č, s, x, h, m, n have not been noted before x. A voiced consonant may serve as prior member but not as the final member of a medial cluster; however, the semivowel w (not y) appears freely both as prior and final member (§1:28). Medial clusters of more than two consonants include at least xkp, ntp; skt, xpt, xkt, nst, nkwt, mskt, mxkwt; kwč, nšč; ntk, nkk, nkwk, psk, ksk, msk, nšk, pxk, kxk, nxk; sks, skws, xkws, nkws, nks, mps; xkš, kwš; nkh, pskh; stx, xtx, ntx, nkx, nktx, xktx.

VOWELS

§1:33. Interrupted syllables (§1:17), nasal syllables (§1:22), and nasalized syllables (§1:23) have a fixed length of two morae. Sequences of h plus stop or spirant appear to follow short vowels (§1:18); compare éhsak "mussels" and é·həs "mussel." So also, word-initial h appears before short vowels (§1:15); compare hatá·ᴘi "bow" and nta·ta·ᴘí·wəna "our bow."

§1:34. Other syllables show a contrast between short and long, depending on whether the vowel of the syllable is short or long. Thus, when a word begins in a vowel, the vowel may be short a (as in English "father") or long a·, amánki "it is big," á·me· "he is fishing" (compare namé·s "fish"); short e (as in English "met") or long e· (as in English "mad"), eʟí·i "both," e·ᴋó·ᴋoles "raspberry"; short i (more like English "feet" than "fit") or long i·, íka "there," í·la "brave man"; short o (as in English "thought") or long o·, ókahte·s "paunch," o·pe·ksí·ᴘu "White River"; short u (as in English "fool") or long u·, ú·ce "fly," úpxkon "his back." Short u occurs with less frequency than other vowels; its favorite positions are before w, and in word-final: wewtənúwe·s "mermaid," kéku "something," təkwčé·su "he is round." In general, short vowels occur more freely in word-final than long vowels; in other positions both lengths occur freely.

§1:35. Short ə (as in English "butter") does not occur in word-initial nor in word-final, and is also avoided in interrupted syllables (§1:17) and in syllables having a fixed length of one mora (§1:33). In other syllables, ə is a favorite vowel.

§1:36. Only long vowels are nasalized; the phonetic long ə· is found only in a nasalized syllable (§1:23).

§1:37. Front vowels (long and short i, e, a) are freely juxtaposed without the intrusion of a semivowel, and thereby form two syllables, the second syllable beginning in a vowel. Of back vowels, only o or o· appears as the first member of a juxtaposed pair. Back vowels occasionally appear after front vowels, but more often a semivowel intrudes in such a sequence (§1:27 and 2:2). If the pair of juxtaposed vowels is of the same quality, one is usually long; if of different qualities, both vowels may be short or both may be long. Compare entatəntewhé·enk "when he and I made a fire," entapá·ᴛia "when I came," entapali·a·ᴛíhti·t "when they went away" but ikapa·á·ne "when you get there."

§1:38. In rare instances three vowels are juxtaposed, and thereby form three syllables: nəmaipənaó·ok "I go to see them."

§1:39. A few words are distinguished only by a difference in stress. Compare the independent mode káwi "you are sleeping" (§2:23), and the imperative kawí "sleep!" (§2:8 and 6:3).

Each word receives one stress. A particle may be stressed in a certain collocation, and thereby count as a separate word, but in another collocation may precede or follow a stressed word as an unstressed procliic or enclitic (§4:1 and 5:3; 8).

The favorite position for stress is on the third mora from the end of the word (§1:22). Accordingly, a two morae penult is stressed (§6:2); but the antepenult would be stressed when the penult and the ultima each have the value of one mora (§6:4).

A less favored position for stress is on the second mora from the end of the word. Accordingly, a two morae ultima is stressed; but the penult would be stressed before a one mora ultima (§6:3).

A small class of words shows stress arbitrarily on the theme-final vowel, even when this vowel is the word-end mora (§6:5).

2. PHONOLOGY

MORPHEME ALTERNANTS: IN SUFFIXATION

§2:1. Person pluralizing suffix -na[·n]- appears as -na·n- before another suffix, as -na in word-final. Thus, nkahé·səna "our mother"; but before suffixes -ak, -a, and -inka, nkahe·səná·nak "our mothers," nkahe·səná·na "our mother, now deceased," nkahe·səna·nínka "our mothers, now deceased."

Intrusive ə appears between a theme ending in certain consonants and -na[·n]- (see above). But if the theme ends in a vowel, the vowel is expanded to a two morae interrupted syllable (§1:17) before -na[·n]-: nəməsiliáhana "we are moving about"; and before person pluralizer -mo (§3:8).

Some elements ending in -m or underlying -w are followed by intrusive -hu- and -hum- before -mo and -na[·n]- respectively. The negative suffix -i[·w]- provides an example of underlying -w (§5:4): ku·takaʀakwtəki·húmo "no, you fellows don't want to go back," ku·taki·lú·na kaʀakwtəki·húməna "not us, we don't want to go back." Compare theme-final in -m (§6:10): nkaʀunko·mhúməna "we are sleepy."

§2:2. Third person suffix -w is usually not heard in word final, but appears as such between theme-final -u and a following suffix: péhewe·w beside péhewe· "he is waiting," kənthu "he is flying" but kənthúwak "they are flying."

Between theme-final -e· or -i· and suffix in -a, third person -w- contracts with the following -a to -o, and an intrusive y appears between the theme-final -e· or -i· and -o (§1:37): pehewé·yok "they are waiting." Likewise, inanimate suffix -w contracts with thing pluralizer -a after -e·-, but remains as -w after -n- (§4:3).

§2:3. After a theme in -m, third person -w is dropped in word-final, but with suffix ·ak contracts to uˑ: kahtúnkoˑm "he is sleepy," kahtunkóˑmuˑk "they are sleepy."

Inverse marker ·əkw (§3:14) plus ·ak, ·ə·na[·n]·, ·a, and ·wa[·w]· contracts, respectively, to ·kuˑk, ·kuˑna[·n]·, ·ku, and ·kuwa (when ·wa[·w]· is in word-final, otherwise ·kəwoˑoˑ). But subordinate mode suffixes in ·e follow ·əkw without contraction, while those in ·a contract with ·əkw to ·əko (§2:9 and 4:4): entawəlál·kwenk "when we are kept by him or them" (with suffix ·enk), entawəlálkon "when you are kept by him or them" (with suffix ·an).

Animate noun final ·kw plus pluralizer ·ak contracts to ·kuˑk, but plus obviative ·a contracts to ·ko (§3:12).

§2:4. Person pluralizing suffix ·wa[·w]· appears as ·wa in word-final, but contracts with following suffix vowel ·a· to ·woˑoˑ: kahéˑsəwa "the mother of all of you," but kaheˑsəwóˑok "the mothers of all of you" (with following suffix ·ak) and koheˑsəwóˑo "their mother" (with following suffix ·a). It contracts with following suffix vowel ·i· to ·woˑuˑ: kaheˑsəwoˑúnka "the mothers, now deceased, of all of you."

Preceding suffix ·a[·w]· (§2:5) plus pluralizing suffix ·wa[·w] contracts to ·awo: kwiˑcəmáwo "you fellows are helping him." But ·a[·w]· plus ·wa[·w]· followed by a suffix in ·a contracts to ·awoˑoˑ: kuˑlhalawóˑok "you fellows keep them" (§2:3 and 3:14). Theme-final in ·aw· plus ·a[·w]· plus ·wa[·w]· plus suffix in ·a contracts to ·a·woˑoˑ: wšiˑxwiˑtaˑwóˑo "they robbed him."

§2:5. The direct marker, ·a[·w]· (§3:14), appears as ·a in word-final, as ·a·w· before intrusive ·ə·, as ·a·· before suffix beginning in a consonant, as ·a· before a preaspirated consonant (§4:7), as ·a·o in contraction with following ·a (§2:4).

Theme-finals in ·e·w and ·aw contract with ·a[·w]· as ·e·yo and ·ao respectively. Compare kwihilúˑraw "run after him!", néˑw "see him!" (with zero suffix); and nnéˑyo "I see him," nkwihilúˑrao "I ran after him" (with direct marker ·a[·w]).

§2:6. Speaker-addressee suffix ·i appears as ·i in word-final (§3:15) and before another suffix beginning in a vowel (§4:4), but is extended to two morae before a consonant (§2:10).

§2:7. Speaker-addressee suffix ·əl[u]· appears without vowel in word-final (§3:15) and before a suffix beginning in a vowel (§4:4), but with vowel extended to two morae before consonant (3:15). In contraction with the negative suffix ·i[·w], ·əluˑwi results (§2:12 and 5:4): kuˑkəneˑwəlúˑwi "no, I do not see you."

§2:8. Imperative singular ·l appears after transitive animate themes in ·i· (§4:2). It is dropped after animate intransitive themes in i, sometimes leaving a shift in stress as a reflex (§6:3). It appears after other theme-final vowels (§6:1). Compare laˑləmátahpi "sit down!" and lapipáˑl "come back again!"

The m of imperative suffix ·ram is replaced by n before element in k (§5:8).

§2:9. When third person subordinate ·k follows a theme in ·m, m is replaced by n, and a preceding long vowel is replaced by a short vowel, but a short vowel remains (§4:8). Compare independent kahtúnkoˑm "he is sleepy," and subordinate

entakahtúnkonk "when he is sleepy"; independent wi·cə́ntamu·k "they are helping," wəlú·səmən "he burned it"; and subordinate entawi·cə́ntank "when he
helps," entalú·sənk "when he burned it."

But third person -k and preceding -əkw combine as kuk: entawelálkuk "when
he is kept by him or them" (§2:3 and 4:8).

An intrusive -ə- follows theme in -l before third person -k: entame·čimaxakí·lək
"when she got big."

§2:10. When a theme in -m or -l precedes intrusive -i- and -hti·t (§4:8), the h
before t is transposed to precede the intrusive -i-: entakahtunko·mhíti·t "when they
are sleepy," entawi·cəntamhíti·t "when they helped it," entame·čimaxaki·lhíti·t
"when they got big."

Theme-final vowels which are long before other subordinate suffixes are short
before -hti·t (§6:2 ff.): entako·nši·phuwéhti·t "when they are hiding."

Suffixes ending in -t replace t by c before i or i· (§4:9 ff.): e·lanku·máci·k "the
ones to whom you are related."

§2:11. First person singular -a[·n]- appears as -a in word-final (§4:4), as -a·n-
before -e (§5:2). Compare entalú·sia "when I burned" and xulu·siá·ne "if I should
burn."

§2:12. The negative suffix -i[·w] appears as -i in word-final: ku·taní·
nkaʀakwtəkí·i "not me, I don't want to go back." It contracts with preceding
theme final in -i and following suffix in -a as -i·yo (with intrusive y). Compare
entakwtə́ʀia "when I went back" and entamatakwtəkí·yo "when I did not go
back." But after underlying third person suffix -w (§3:5), -i·í·yo- results:
ku·takahtakwtəki·í·yok "they didn't go back." Before preconsonantic intrusive -ə-,
-i·w- results: ni·ntəlimatakwtəkí·wən "I, indeed I did not go back," ku·kəne·hku·-
wí·wəna "we are not seen by him." In the last example, the theme -ne·w- plus inverse marker -əkw- before the negative suffix yields -ne·hku·wi·w- (§2:1 and 5:4).

§2:13. Preterite -əp[an] appears as -əp in word-final, as -pan- before a vowel
(§5:5; 6). Syncope of syllable-final -ə- in medial position is regular.

§2:14. Intrusive -y occurs between theme-final -e·- and suffixes in a (§6:2):
entatəmi·ʀé·yankw "when we went in the house" (§2:2). Intrusive y is also found
within the theme (§6:7): ohtawé·yu "he is talking Ottawa."

§2:15. The independent person particle -i·[lu·]- appears as -i· in word-final,
as -i·lu·- before person pluralizers (§5:10): ní· "I," ni·lú·na "we," ki·lú·wa "you
fellows."

§2:16. After theme-final -o·-, the vowel -a is replaced by -o, but -e remains
(§6:9): entaahke·pinkó·o "when I was blind" (§4:4).

§2:17. Syllables with long vowels may be replaced by two morae interrupted
syllables (§1:17). Thus, the stem pe·w- appears as pehew- before intransitive
formative, as pe·- before transitive formatives (§6:15), with -w lost before the consonants of the latter.

§2:18. The transitivizer -aw- plus -əkw contracts to -a·kw (§6:18):

nəmáxka·kw "he found me." In another formation with theme in ·am, ·am appears
as ·un before ·t: entamáxkunt "when he has found his way." Themes in ·aw plus ·i
appear as ·ai, but contract with ·əl as ·u·l (§3:15): kša·khwíkai "you kicked me,"
kša·khwíku·l "I kicked you."

§2:19. Themes in ·uw, as those formed with the transitivizer ·šuw (§6:16;
and occasionally other themes in spirants which add ·uw as a by-form), contract
with ·əkw or ·əl to ·u·kw or ·u·l (§3:14; 15). Compare kpé·šuwi "you brought me"
with mpé·šu·kw "he brought me," kpé·šu·l "I brought you"; nəmóhu·kw "he ate
me," kəmóhu·l "I ate you," mhú·we "Cannibal" (proper name).

MORPHEME ALTERNANTS: IN PREFIXATION

§2:20. The person prefixes, nə·, kə·, wə· (§3:1 ff.), remain as such before
stems beginning in certain consonants but undergo change of form or position before stems beginning in other consonants and before stems beginning in vowels
(§2:21 ff.). While wə· is frequently subject to metathesis, nə· and kə· are never
transposed.

§2:21. Stem-initials in m· prefix nə· and kə· with prefix vowel preserved:
kəmathaká·la héč "did you fight him?," kəma·kháko "your bottles," nəməkəná··
kwələnč "my little finger," kəmihilú·səm "your husband," kəmí·ci·n "you ate it,"
nəmé·kən "I gave it away," kəmú·kum "your blood," nəmo·kəláma "my mauls."

§2:22. Stem-initials in p· prefix nə· and kə· with prefix vowel lost (and n-
is replaced by m· before p·): kpé·tu·n héč "are you waiting for it?" mpi·kənámən
"I crumbled it," kpaxkši·kanána "our knife," mpa·lsuwa·kanána "our sickness,"
mpó·ma "my thighs," kpu·kí·xtu·n "you broke it," mpəmú·tamən "I shot him."

§2:23. Stem-initials in k· prefix nə· and kə· with prefix vowel lost (and k·
contracts with k· to a single k·): nkí·tələnč "my thumb," kišipənae·lántamən héč
"have you finished thinking about it?" nke·nahkíha "I take care of him," kátukw
"your knee," nkanthála "I hid him," ka·xksámən "you dried it," kəpšéhemən "you
closed it," nkwántamən "I swallowed it," ki·kwántamən beside kwántamən "you
swallowed it," kohó·kanəm beside ki·kohó·kanəm "your mortar" (§2:26).

§2:24. When stem-initials in m·, p·, k· are followed by the vowels i, i·, e·,
the prefix wə·, with loss of prefix vowel, is transposed after the stem-initial consonant. Compare §2:21 and mwihilú·səma "her husband," mwí·ci·n "he ate it,"
mwé·kəna "he gave it away." Compare §2:22 and pwé·tu·n "he waited for it,"
pwi·kanámən "he crumbled it." Compare §2:23 and kwi·tələnča "his thumb,"
kwišipənae·lántamən "he has finished thinking about it," kwe·nahkihá·o "he takes
care of him," kwátko "his knee."

§2:25. But when m·, p·, k· are followed by a, a·, the prefix wə· is not only
transposed after the stem-initial consonant but also contracts with the following
vowel as o, without influencing the length of this vowel. Compare 2:22 and
poxkší·kan "his knife," po·lsuwá·kan "his sickness." Compare §2:21 and mothaka··
lá·o "he was fighting him," mo·kháko "his bottles," mokəna·kwəlánča "his fingers."

Compare §2:23 and konthalá·o "he hid him," ko·xksə́mən "he dried it," kopšéhemən "he closed it."

§2:26. When the vowel following the stem-initial consonant is u·, o, o·, or when the initial sequence is kw- or pə- (followed by a nasal), an underlying meta- thesis of wə- may be assumed, with the resulting contraction leaving the stem- initial sequence in its original form. Compare §2:21 and mú·kum "his blood," mo·kələ́ma "his mauls." Compare §2:22 and pó·ma "her thighs," pu·kí·xtu·n "he broke it," pəmú·Tamən "he shot it." Compare §2:23 and kwə́ntamən "he swal- lowed it," kohó·ᴋanəm "his mortar."

§2:27. Stem-initials in t-, č-, š-, s- and h- (followed by i or wi) prefix nə- and kə- with loss of prefix vowel: ktá·n "your daughter," ntú·n "my mouth," ktehená·- nak "our hearts," ktə́ᴋi "your shoulder," ntə́la "I told him," kčí·ᴋəni·n "you took it away from me," nšinká·la "I hate him," nša·khwíka·kw "he kicked me," ksí·səna héč "did you pinch him?" ksu·kháməne·n "we poured it," nsí·Ta "my feet," nsəpú·Ti "my anus," nsaᴋa·ᴩého "I am leading him," nsa·ᴋi·má·yum "my chief," nhikí·yon "my nose," khika·Tə́ná·na "our legs," nhwícu "my calf."

§2:28. So also, wə- appears as w- before stem-initials in tu·, te·, tə-, či·-, ši·-, si·-, su·-, sə·: wtú·n "his mouth," wté·ha "his heart," wtə́ᴋi "his shoulder" (but təlá·o "he told him," with stem-initial unchanged after prefixation of wə-), wčí·ᴋəna·n "he took it away from him," wšinka·lá·o "he hates him," wsí·Ta "his feet," wsi·səná·o "he pinched him," wsu·khámən "he poured it," wsəpú·Ti "his anus."

§2:29. Stem-initials t-, š-, s- followed by a, a· permit the usual metathesis of wə- with contraction to o, o· (§2:25): tó·na "his daughter," šo·khwika·wó·o "they kicked them," soᴋa·ᴩehó·o "he is leading him," so·ᴋi·má·yuma "his chief."

§2:30. The prefix wə- never occurs in metathesis without contraction after stem-initials in t-, č-, š-, s- (§2:24); but note such metathesis after stem-initial hi·: hwikí·yon "his nose," hwíka·t "his leg." Stem-initial hw- remains unchanged after wə- (§2:26): hwícuwa "his calf of leg." The prefix vowel is preserved before stem- initial cluster šk·: nə́škinkw "my eye," kə́škinkw "your eye," wə́škinkw "his eye."

§2:31. Both kə- and wə- precede stem-initials in l- and n-, with prefix vowel preserved. Metathesis of wə- occurs only with contraction of following a, a· to o, o· (§2:25): wəle·la·o·kwələ́nča "his middle finger," kəla·ptu·né·na "you put your finger in his mouth," lo·ptu·ne·ná·o "he put his finger in her mouth," kənaxkú·məl "I answered you," noxku·má·o "he answered him," no·wəlá·o "he followed her," kənúhula héč "are you nursing him?" wənu·ná·ᴋan "her nipple."

§2:32. But nə- suffers loss of prefix vowel before l- and n- (and n- is replaced by l- before l-): lle·la·ó·kwələnč "my middle finger," lla·ptu·né·na "I put my finger in his mouth," nnaxkú·ma "I answered him," nná·wəla "I followed her," nnúhula "I nursed him."

§2:33. Before stem-initials in we·- and wi·-, nə- preserves prefix vowel, kə- suffers loss of prefix vowel, and wə- disappears in contraction: nəwe·Tanə́mən "I took it," kwe·ᴛanə́mən "you took it," we·ᴛanə́mən "he took it"; nəwí·si "I am fat."

§2:34. Stem-initials in wə- contract with the prefixes to nu·-, ku·-, and u·-: wəli·ᴛé·he·w "he is good hearted" (§3:5 and 6:5), nu·li·ᴛe·háhana "we are good hearted." A pleonastic wə- is prefixed to the absolute form of some words with the usual contraction when person prefixes precede: wiyú·s "meat," u·yú·səm "his meat," ku·yú·səm "your meat."

§2:35. Stems in x- appear as such in absolute forms, and also, in one class of stems, after kə- with loss of prefix vowel: kxí·səməs "your younger brother" (in this class, nə- contracts with a stem-extending vowel, and wə- is transposed: naxí·səməs "my younger brother," xwi·səmə́sa "his younger brother"). Usually a- or wə- precede stems in x- before the person prefixes: xáskwi·m "corn," ntaxaskwi·məmə́na "our corn"; xkwə́n "liver," ú·xkwənəm "his liver" (§2:34; 39).

§2:36. Many possessed nouns without absolute forms (§3:6), show prefix vowel and stem-initial vowel contracting as i·-: wí·l "his head," ni·ᴘí·ᴛa "my teeth," kí·ᴛi·s "your friend." But compare í·la· "brave man" and kti·la·íhina "we are brave" (§6:36).

§2:37. Stem-initials in hu- contract with the prefixes to nu·-, ku·-, and u·- (§2:34): húᴋo·n "pot hook," u·ᴋó·nəma "his pot hook"; hupwé·yok "they are smoking," ku·póhona "we smoke" (§6:9).

§2:38. The prefix vowel contracts to o· with stem-initials in ho-, o-, o·-: hópəni·s "potato," no·pəní·səmak "my potatoes"; hópan "lung," wo·panə́ma "his lung"; ókahte·s "paunch," wo·kahté·səma "his paunch"; o·ᴘínkw "opossum," ko·ᴘínkum "your opossum."

§2:39. Other vowels are preceded by intrusive -t- before person prefixes: éhsak "mussels, clams," ntéhsəmak "my clams"; ntəla·ší·mwi "I am dreaming" but la·ši·muwá·kan "dream" (with ə- not appearing in word-initial); a·lu·kwé·ᴘi "hat," kta·lu·kwe·ᴘí·si "you are wearing a hat"; ayəmú·k "they are buying," toyəmə́na "he is buying things."

§2:40. A few instances show h- before -a- replaced by intrusive -t- with vowel lengthened before person prefixes: hatá·ᴘi "bow," nta·tá·ᴘi "my bow," to·tá·ᴘia "his bow"; haki·hé·yok "they are farming," nta·ki·héhena "we are farm-ing."

3. PREFIX PARADIGMS

§3:1. Prefix paradigms are sets of elements (used in the inflection of certain word classes, in part or exclusively) which mark at least the first person (speaker) and second person (addressee) by prefixes while number and other categories are marked by suffixes. Word classes (parts of speech) include nouns, verbs, and particles. Nouns are inflected only by prefix paradigms. The independent mode of verbs is inflected chiefly by prefix paradigms, while the independent with inanimate actor as well as all other modes is inflected by suffix paradigms (a correlative paradigm type which marks all categories, including person, by suffixes to the ex-

clusion of prefixes). Particles are generally uninflected,—at most, partially inflected (§5:10).

§3:2. Prefix paradigms are used in the inflection of inanimate, animate, and
preterite animate nouns; and independent mode verbs which are intransitive with
animate actor, or transitive with animate goal, or transitive with inanimate goal.
These six paradigms all employ the person prefixes nə- and kə-.

§3:3. As a result, a given form used in the expression of person serves to
marks the possessor in the case of nouns, the actor in the case of verbs. Thus, the
prefix nə-, without person pluralizing suffix, expresses "my" or "I": nšé·ᴛu·n "my
lip" (inanimate noun), nkáhe·s "my mother" (animate noun), nkahé·sa "my mother,
now deceased" (preterite noun), nčí·ᴘuwe "I am whistling" (animate intransitive),
nu·lhála "I keep him" (transitive animate), nu·lhátu·n "I keep it" (transitive inanimate). If kə- instead of nə- were prefixed to the preceding examples, the translations would be "your" in place of "my," and "you" in place of "I" (§2:20 ff.)

§3:4. However, when both prefix nə- and person pluralizer -na[·n]- are employed, first person plural exclusive is expressed: "our" (mine and his) or "we"
(he and I); likewise, prefix kə- and pluralizer -na[·n]- yield first person plural inclusive: "our" (your and mine) or "we" (you and I). See §2:1 and §3:15 for examples.
All of the prefix paradigms employ -na[·n] except the transitive inanimate, which
employs a by-form for this element, namely -e·n: nkwihilu·ᴛamə́ne·n "we (he and I)
ran after it." Compare imperative -ne·n (§4:2). Supplementary paradigms in -n also
employ the by-form -e·n (§5:9 ff.).

§3:5. Of prefix paradigms (§3:2), only animate intransitive verbs employ the
third person suffix -w (§2:2; 3), and the obviative suffix, -luwa (in an anecdote
about a man and his wife, the "man" as the more prominent actor is third person
while "his wife" as the less prominent actor is obviative). In Delaware the obviative is indifferent as to number (§3:13 and 4:6). Compare kə́ntke·w "he is dancing"
and kəntké·luwa "she (his wife) is dancing."

§3:6. Other prefix paradigms employ the third person prefix wə-: wšé·ᴛu·n
"his lip," wənihilá·o "he killed him" (§2:5).

For things not ordinarily spoken of as belonging to anyone there are animate
and inanimate nouns which may be said to employ an absolute zero prefix in contrast to forms marked by person prefix. Some names for things which are ordinarily
possessed, as body parts, occur only with person prefix, and if the context calls for
an absolute meaning, a form with third person prefix is used: wí·xa "his hair" or
"a hair."

Other nouns make a formal distinction between possessed and absolute forms;
a special suffix, -m- is not necessarily included in the possessed forms but is never
used in the absolute forms: u·xkanə́ma "his bones" and xkána "bones," wəlakšía
"guts" and u·lahkə́šia "his guts." Different words are used in a few instances:
alú·ns "arrow," wí·p "his arrow"; mwe·ᴋané·yok "dogs," ntaləmú·sak "my dogs,
pets."

The locative suffix ∙nk generally follows absolute nouns. Any person prefix may precede, but pluralizing suffixes do not follow locative nouns. Compare kwátko "his knee" and kátkunk "on the knee" but ksí·sənəl kánanunk "I pinched you on your cheek."

§3:7. Person pluralizer ∙wa[·w]∙ is used with kə∙ prefixed and wə∙ prefixed nouns and verbs in all paradigms (§3:2) except two (§3:8; 9) in the expression of second and third person plural: kpaxkší·kanəwa "your (plural) knife," poxkší·kanəwa "their knife" (§2:4).

§3:8. Person pluralizer ∙mo is used with kə∙ prefixed animate intransitive and transitive animate verbs in the expression of second person plural: ktəspeheláhamo héč "do you fellows have smallpox?" ku·lhalíhimo héč "are you fellows keeping me?" (§2:1 and 3:15).

§3:9. Person pluralizer ∙e·yo is used with kə∙ and wə∙ prefixed transitive in∙animate verbs in the expression of second and third person plural: ktayəməné·yo "you fellows bought it," toyəməné·yo "they bought it." It is also used after the directive predicator (§5:9 ff.).

§3:10. Thing pluralizer ∙a is used in inanimate noun and transitive inanimate verb paradigms: nše·Tú·na "my lips," wəlu·səmə́na "he burned the things." Person pluralizers ∙na[·n]∙ (§3:4) and ∙wa[·w]∙ (§3:7) precede thing pluralizer ∙a: kše·Tu·nəná·na "our lips." But the person pluralizers of transitive inanimate verbs, ∙e·yo (§3:9) and ∙e·n (§3:4), are the same whether the goal is singular or plural: wəlu·səmə́né·yo "they burned the thing or the things." Compare also §4:3.

Some animate intransitive verbs always appear in association with a noun as implied goal. This is somewhat parallel to the loss of the transitive inanimate formative in collocation with a noun which serves as goal. Thus, when the noun is not given, the goal is explicitly marked by the verb: nna·Təmə́na "I went after it (plural)." But when the noun is given in the sentence, the same verb appears in animate intransitive form: nná·Təm tə́ntay "I'm going after the fire."

§3:11. Preterite noun pluralizer ∙inka follows animate noun stems or person pluralizers (§3:4; 7), and has been occasionally noted with verbs where the actors are no longer existing, as ankəlúnka "they are dead" (§5:6). The preterite noun paradigm is unique in having an explicit singular suffix ∙a, as well as the plural suffix ∙inka, for nə∙ and kə∙ prefixed nouns (§2:1); however, in third person ∙inka serves indifferently for singular or plural (compare §3:13 and 5:6).

§3:12. The pluralizer for animate nouns and for third person of verbs is ∙ak in all prefix paradigms except those employing thing pluralizer ∙a (§3:10) or pret∙erite pluralizer ∙inka (§3:11).

With animate nouns, ∙ak follows the noun stem or the person pluralizer (§3:4; 7) and marks the plurality of the noun rather than the person or the pos∙sessor in the case of nə∙ and kə∙ prefixed forms: ni·mahtə́sak "my brothers," ku·xwi·səná·nak "our grandchildren." Zero and wə∙ prefixed nouns use ∙ak only when the noun is not followed by an obviative suffix (§3:6; 13): alú·nsak "arrows," kwə́tku·k "the knees" but kwə́tko "his knee or knees."

In contrast, -ak after verbs serves to mark third person plural. With animate intransitives, -ak follows -w (§2:2; 3 and 3:5). With transitive animates, -ak appears after the direct or inverse goal markers (§2:3 and 3:14) and after person pluralizers (§3:4; 7), but only when nə- or kə- prefixed forms are involved, not when wə- prefixed forms are used (§3:13).

§3:13. Besides the obviative suffixes -luwa (§3:5) and -li·- (§4:6) there is another obviative suffix, namely -a (not to be confused with the homonymous thing pluralizer, §3:10, or the homonymous preterite singular, §3:11).

Obviative -a may follow absolute animate nouns (§3:6), but necessarily follows wə- prefixed possessed nouns. While the possessor is third person, marked by wə-, the noun itself (as the less prominent of the two) is obviative person and marked by -a: wtəxkwé·yəma "his (third person) sister or sisters (obviative)."

Likewise in transitive animate verbs, obviative -a is necessarily used for wə- prefixed verbs, for the actor is then third person, marked by wə-, while the goal (as the less prominent of the two persons) is obviative and marked by -a: wənihilá·o "he (third person) killed him or them (obviative)." See also §2:5 and §3:14.

§3:14. Transitive animate direct (active) and inverse (passive) third persons are marked, respectively, by suffixes -a[·w]- and -əkw (§2:3; 5). The two voice types are parallel, enjoying much the same possibilities of person and number affixation.

Thus, in the direct (active), the prefixed person is actor while a third person is goal: nu·hála "I keep him," nu·lhalá·ok "I keep them," ku·lhalá·wəna "we keep him," ku·lhala·wəná·nak "we keep them."

But in the inverse (passive), the prefixed person may be regarded as a psychological subject with a third person agentive actor, or more briefly, the prefixed person may be translated as a goal with third person as actor: nu·lhálǝkw "I am kept by him," or what amounts to the same thing in Delaware, "he keeps me," nu·lhálku·k "they keep me," ku·lhalkú·na "she keeps us," ku·halku·ná·nak "they keep us."

For wə- prefixed verbs (§3:13), compare the direct (active), u·lhalawó·o "they (third person) keep him or them (obviative)"; and the inverse (passive), u·lhalkəwó·o "they (third person) are kept by him or them (obviative)."

§3:15. When transitive animate personal relations do not include third person, all forms are kə- prefixed. Second person actor with first person goal is marked by the addition of suffix -i: ku·lháli "you keep me." First person actor with second person goal is marked by the addition of suffix -əl[u]-: ku·lhálǝl "I keep you." Whether serving as actor or goal, plurality of second person is marked by -mo, plurality of first person by -na[·n]-: ku·lhalíhimo "you fellows keep me," ku·lhalǝlúhumo "I keep you fellows"; ku·lhalíhina "you keep us," ku·lhalǝlúhuna "we keep you." See also §2:6; 7 and 4:2; 4; 6.

4. SUFFIX PARADIGMS

§4:1. Suffix paradigms mark all categories by suffixes to the exclusion of pre-fixes (compare §3:1 ff.). The imperative and the inanimate independent modes are formed without a preceding modal particle or initial syllable change characteristic of the remaining suffix paradigms.

Imperatives occasionally show initial syllable reduplication of a type which is also used to mark aspect (§4:2 and 5:7).

A wide variety of introductory modal particles precede subordinate forms of verbs; these particles vaguely suggest relative time or mode (§4:4 and 5:2 ff.).

In initial syllable change characteristic of the participle mode, the first vowel of a syllable is replaced by -e·- (§4:9 ff.).

§4:2. With animate intransitives, the imperative is marked by -l (§2:8) when one person is addressed, by -kw when plural persons are addressed. Compare im-perative la·ləmátahpi·kw "sit down, you fellows!" and independent kələmatahpí-himo héč "did you fellows sit down?"

Singular -l and plural -kw follow transitive animate themes in -i·- (§2:6): mí·li·l či·ranəsəwá·ҡan "you give me strength!" (a form used in prayer), né·wi·kw "see me, you fellows!" A goal pluralizer -ne·n may replace the imperative suffix, when the goal is first person: ne·wí·ne·n "see us!" mi·lí·ne·n "give us!" (with num-ber of person addressed not specified). The imperative is also marked by a zero suffix when the goal is an indefinite third person: né·w "see him!" mí·l "give him!" But if plural persons are addressed, the imperative is marked by -u·, as né·yu· "see him, you fellows," mí·lu· "give him something, you fellows!" Exhortive suffix -ram (§2:8) follows the transitive animate direct marker -a[·w] (§2:5) as a kind of first person imperative: nhilá·ram "let's kill him," ne·yó·ram "let's see him."

The negative imperative in part shares regular subordinate mode suffixes (§4:4), with a special introductory particle (§5:4).

Transitive inanimate verbs formed by -am- mark singular addressee by -a, plural by -amu·kw, exhortative by -amu·ramu·kw: kwihilú·ra "run after it!" kwihilú·ramu·kw "run after it, you fellows!" kwihilu·ramú·ramu·kw "let's take after it!"

§4:3. When the singular of inanimate intransitive verbs is in -t, the plural is marked by -u·l: wəlát "it is good," əwəltú·l "they are good." More commonly, the singular ends in -w, and the plural is formed by the addition of the regular thing pluralizer -a (§2:2 and 3:10): máxke·w "it is red," ame·xké·yo "they are red"; ní·ske·w "it is dirty," ni·ské·yo "they are dirty," wi·sú·uwa "they are large, fat." There are still other types, including forms ending in -n: wáskən "it is new." Only one participle form, marked by -k, has been noted, serving for both singular and plural: máxke·k "that which is red," wáskink "that which is new."

§4:4. In subordinate mode verbs involving speaker or addressee, one suffix is employed for both person and number as follows: -an and -e·kw for second person

singular and plural; ·a[·n]·, ·enk, ·ankw for first person singular, exclusive, and inclusive, respectively.

Thus, with animate intransitives: e·lipi·lsían "while you are clean,"
entapá·pie·kw "when you fellows play," ne·likawíenk "while we were sleeping (stems preceded by modal particles e·li-, enta-, ne·li-). See also §2:11 and 5:2.

The suffixes listed above may follow the inverse marker of transitive animate
verbs (§2:3 and 3:4); ·an, ·enk, ·e·kw may follow transitive animate suffixes -i and
·əl[u]· (§3:15): entawəlahalíe·kw "when you fellows kept me," entawəlahalóle·kw
"when I kept you fellows."

Transitive inanimate verbs employ all the suffixes used by animate intransitives (those above, and §4:7; 8), and in the subordinate do not distinguish between
a singular and plural goal. Compare independent mode kəlú·si "you are burning,"
kəlú·səmən "you burned it," kəlu·səmə́na "you burned many things" (§3:2; 10);
and subordinate mode entalú·sian "when you are burning," entalú·səman "when
you burned one or many things."

§4:5. Certain suffixes do not follow the direct marker (§3:14) but are appended directly to the transitive animate theme. These include all but two of the
suffixes given (§4:4): entawəláhalankw "when we (you and I) kept him." The
singular of first and second person is marked by ·ak and ·at in place of ·a[·n]· and
·an, respectively: entawəláhalat "when you kept him or them," entawəláhalak
"when I kept him or them."

§4:6. In contrast to the last example, compare entawəlálko "when I am kept
by him or them (obviative?)," and entawəláhali·t "when he kept me" beside
entawəlahalíhti·t "when they kept me." Suffixation in the first example includes
the inverse marker ·əkw (§3:14), plus first person singular ·a[·n]· (§4:4), possibly
appearing as though in word-final but actually before obviative ·a (§3:13), with
the usual contraction (§2:3). If correct, this instance of obviative with first person
is unique; other instances combine only third person with obviative (§3:5; 13).

With animate intransitive verbs, the form of the obviative suffix both after
vowel and after consonant plus intrusive ·ə· is ·li·: entame·čimaxakí·ləli·t "when
obviate person ('his wife') got big."

§4:7. Third person subordinates, singular ·t, and plural ·hti·· plus ·t, may
follow animate intransitive themes ending in a vowel (§4:8), and transitive animate verbs with preceding goal suffix ·i· (§4:6) or direct marker ·a[·w]· (§2:5 and
3:14). Compare entapə́nči·t "when he went in," entako·nši·puwéhti·t "when they
are hiding," entapali·á·t "when he went away," entahupóhti·t "when they were
smoking"; and entawəláhala·t "when she keeps him or them," entawəlahaláhti·t
"when they keep him or them."

§4:8. The by-form ·k is used in place of ·t (§4:7) after themes ending in a
consonant and after the inverse marker ·əkw (§2:9). However, the regular subordinate plural, ·hti··t, follows these consonant ending forms after an intrusive ·i·
(§2:10): entawəlalkwíhti·t "when they are kept by him or them."

§4:9. For third person singular, participles employ the subordinate suffix (-t after vowel and -k after consonant) but are also marked by a distinctive initial syllable change. Compare the subordinate entawəle·lə́ntank "when he is glad" and the participle we·le·lə́ntank "one who is glad." Initial change is omitted in some participle forms: mi·kəmó·si·t alúmske· "the worker went away." In addition to subordinate suffixes serving in participle formation, an agentive suffix -s is used where the actor is characteristically occupied in a certain way. Compare participle pe·pomoтú·nhe·t "one who is preaching (at the moment)" and pehpomoтú·-nhe·s "preacher."

Some participle forms add -i to the subordinate suffix (§2:10 and 4:11): e·lanku·má·ci "the one or ones to whom he is related."

§4:10. A participle pluralizer -i·k follows suffixes -k and -t (§2:10): we·le·lə̀ntánki·k alumské·yok "the ones who were glad went away," mi·kəmo·sí·ci·k "workers." The plural of agentive forms in -s is marked by the regular animate pluralizer -ak (§3:12): pehpomoтu·nhé·sak "preachers."

When third person participle is in -i (§4:9), plural is formed by the subordinate pluralizer -hti·- (§4:7): e·lanku·mahtí·ci "the one or ones to whom they are related" (§4:11).

§4:11. Productive participle formation is limited to third person forms (§4:9; 10). However, certain transitive verbs undergo initial syllable change (§4:1) and form plurals in -i·k (§4:10) with speaker and addresssee suffixes (§4:4; 5). These are formally participles but are usually translated as possessed nouns. Compare the independent verb ntəlankú·ma "I am related to him," and the following participles: e·lankú·mak "my relative" (the one to whom I am related), e·lankú·mat "'your relative," e·lanku·mé·кwi·k "the ones to whom you fellows are related," e·lankú·mankw "our relative" (the one to whom you and I are related).

5. SUPPLEMENTARY PARADIGMS

§5:1. Both prefix paradigms (§3:1 ff.) and suffix paradigms (§4:1 ff.) may be elaborated by the addition of certain elements. In expression of categories as in formation, supplementary paradigms are characterized by some addition to paradigms already described.

§5:2. Thus, the subordinate mode suffixes (§4:4 ff.) followed by -e express subordinate mode of improbable event (generally translated as an "if" clause). Compare entalú·sian "when you burn" and xulu·siáne "if you should burn"; entalú·si·t "when he burns" and xulu·sí·тe "if he should burn" (both enta- and xu- are modal particles; the latter is used for future event. See §4:1; 4).

§5:3. The modal element -á· is always stressed. Base forms of verbs without suffixes (§6:1) are not stressed before -á· while other forms retain their normal stress (§5:8). Compare nkwə́tki "I went back" and nkwətkiá· "I ought to go back," but kwətaкí·w "he went back" and kwətaкí·w á· "he ought to go back." Examples show ⸢á· after the improbable subordinate in ⸢e (§5:2) without an introductory modal particle (§4:1): kwətəκiá·ne á· "I should go back." Apparently ⸢á· is the only stressed member in a group of particles before the following negative verb: nahali·á·mata nkwətkí·i "I shouldn't go back."

§5:4. The negative particle ⸢mata is used only after another introductory particle. Beside this noninitial negative, ku·, ku·ta, and the imperative negative kači occur initially, often as unstressed proclitics, before a negative verb which is formed by suffixing ⸢i[·w]⸢ in word-final or before a person pluralizer (§2:1; 7; 12). Compare kəne·yó·wəna "we saw him" and ku·kəne·yo·wí·wəna "we did not see him."

The negative of independent and subordinate verbs is formed by the addition of ⸢i[·w]⸢; the negatives of imperative verbs are formed partly by supplementary suffixes, partly by suffixes which supplant the affirmative imperative (§4:2): kačine·wié·κač "don't see him!" kačine·wé·κe·k "don't see him, you fellows!" The imperative negative particle, kači, before a subordinate negative verb, appears to count as an imperative: kačine·í·enk "don't see us!"

§5:5. The preterite in ⸢əp[an]⸢ (§2:13), as a final suffix in subordinate verb usually suggests a past momentaneous (§5:6). Compare entané·yok "when I see him" and entane·yóκəp "since I had seen him"; entane·yóhti·t "when they saw him" and entane·hohtí·Təp "since they had seen him."

§5:6. Noun preterite singular ⸢a and plural ⸢inka (§3:11) follow participle verb suffixes in supplementary paradigm: e·lanku·máκa "the one, now deceased, to whom I was related" (compare §4:11). More commonly, ⸢a and ⸢inka follow participles already marked for momentaneous preterite (§2:13 and 5:5): e·lanku·makpána "the one, suddenly deceased, to whom I had been related," e·lanku·makpanínka "the deceased ones to whom I had been related," e·lanku·ma·tpanínka "the deceased one or ones to whom he had been related," e·lanku·mahti·tpanínka "the deceased one or ones to whom they had been related."

§5:7. The past habituative element ma follows independent verbs without causing a forward shift in stress (compare §5:5). The preceding verb may show initial syllable reduplication (§4:1). Compare nne·yó·ok "I see them" and nnihine·yó·okma "I used to see them."

§5:8. The reflexive is formed by a transitive animate verb preceding a possessed noun, ⸢haκay "self," as goal. Compare nníhila "I killed him" and nníhila nháκay "I killed myself," kənihilá·wəna khaκayə́na "we killed ourselves." In subordinate and imperative forms, the collocation of verb and noun receives only one stress (§4:3): entanhilaκenháκay "if I would kill myself," nhila·Tankhaκayə́na "let's kill ourselves!" (§2:8 and 4:2).

§5:9. The directive predicator ⸢n, suffixed to independent mode verbs, directs attention to a collocated noun or particle as the focus of attention; the predication assumes significance, as it were, by virtue of the noun or particle to which the verb in ⸢n points.

Attention may be directed to a place rather than a person: nanətə́nta aləmí·ки·n "right there, there indeed she began to grow."

Usually attention is directed to a person: naniskí·xkwe moipahkí·la·n "that young woman, she indeed went and threw her away." Here the verb, with directive predicator ⁀n, points to the actor (that young woman) for special attention as the instigator of the event (throwing her away) while the goal (her) is relatively unimportant and is known only from context to be a certain child mentioned in a preceding sentence. By way of contrast note kwəriskínu təlá·o wi·rí·sa "one young man told his friend," where the verb without ⁀n (təlá·o "he told him") simply states the relationship of telling between the young man as actor and his friend as goal, with attention equally divided between actor, event, and goal.

§5:10. The independent person particle ⁀i·[lu·]⁀ (§2:15), with first and second person and number affixes, often appears unstressed before verbs with directive predicator ⁀n. These verbs usually include ⁀əli⁀ "thus, indeed" after the person prefix of the verb proper with the result that person is pleonastically expressed. Compare kəlú·si "you are burning" and ki·ktəlilú·si·n "you, you indeed are burning"; kəlu·síhimo "you fellows are burning" and ki·lu·waktəlilu·si·né·yo "you fellows, you fellows indeed are burning."

§5:11. Transitive inanimate verbs with themefinal in ⁀ən do not apparently add another ⁀n for directive predicator. Compare kəlú·səmən héč "did you burn it?" and ni·ntəlilú·səmən "I, indeed I burned it." When an inanimate person is to be indicated in the inverse (§3:14), ⁀ən follows ⁀əkw: nu·lhálkwən "I am kept by it" (compare §5:12: directive predicator after ⁀əkw).

§5:12. Animate intransitive verbs add the directive predicator ⁀n to the verb stem (§5:10), but in the case of transitive animate verbs ⁀n follows ⁀a[·w]⁀ or ⁀əkw (§3:14), or ⁀i or ⁀əl[u]⁀ (§3:15). In all cases person pluralizers ⁀e·n or ⁀e·yo (§3:4; 9) follow after ⁀n: šé·nan ntəliwəlálkwən "that one, he indeed kept me," ni·lu·nantəliwəlahalá·ne·n "we, we indeed kept him or them," ki·lu·waktəliwəlahali·né·yo "you fellows, you fellows indeed kept me," ni·ktəliwəlahalələné·yo "I, I indeed kept you fellows."

6. THEMES

§6:1. Animate intransitive themes appear in two characteristic forms, base form and wordinitial form. The wordinitial form is used before the suffix ⁀w or ⁀luwa (§3:5). The base form is used with all other affixes, as after the prefixes nə⁀ or kə⁀ (§3:3 ff.), before one of the subordinate or participle mode suffixes (§4:4 ff.), before the directive predicator (§5:9 ff.).

Themes of all classes except one end in a vowel (§6:2 ff.). The themefinal vowel is short in wordfinal and before ⁀hti·t (§2:10); it has the value of two morae when followed by a suffix beginning in a single consonant. Themefinal vowel before a suffix beginning in a vowel (§4:4) is long when the base form ends in a, e, or o, but short when the base ends in i.

In general, any theme is taken to be a form ready for inflection; analysis of this form may reveal a stem, or stems in composition, with or without derivative or formative suffixes.

§6:2. For many verbs, theme-final vowel remains a or e in both word-initial and base forms (§2:14): entapopsi·ká·an "when you had feathers on your head," entapa·tamá·e·kw "when you fellows were praying," entatəntewhé·enk "when we made a fire," nkəsínkwe "I am washing," pahóke·w "he is friendly."

§6:3. In a less extensive group of verbs, theme-final vowel remains i in both word-initial and base forms. The vowel is stressed before suffixes: né·li kawía "while I was sleeping," né·li kawíenk "while we were sleeping," entakawí·t "when he was sleeping," kawí·w "he was sleeping," but nkáwi "I am sleeping." In all cases stress falls on the second mora, counting from the end of the word (§1:39). An apparent exception is kawí "sleep," where the imperative suffix, -l, of the under-lying form, *kawí·l, is dropped (§2:8).

§6:4. A few verbs differ from the preceding class only in conforming to the favorite third mora stress pattern (§1:39): háᴋink lipə́nči·w "he went in the ground," entapə́nčia "when I went in," entapə́nči·t "when he went in."

§6:5. In this class, theme-final vowels are of different qualities for the two forms: a for base form, e for word-initial form. The theme-final vowel is stressed without respect to mora count (§1:39): kahtapé·w "he wants to come," nəwinkia·pá "I like to come," me·čimpá "I have come," entapá·enk "when we came." While vowels preceding the theme-final are never stressed, vowels follow-ing the theme-final in extended suffixation may be stressed: entapa·ᴛíhti·t "when the little ones came."

§6:6. Some verbs differ from the preceding only in conforming to the usual stress patterns (§1:39): kə́ntke·w "he is dancing," nkə́ntka "I am dancing."

§6:7. Many verbs appear with theme-final i in base form, u in word-initial form: nohtawé·i "I am talking Ottawa," pi·lsúwak "they are clean."

Some of these show stress on the second, others on the third mora from the end of the word (§1:39). Compare né·li pi·lsía "while I am clean" and entatahkócia "when I am cold."

§6:8. Other verbs appear with word-initial form in -u, and differ from the preceding only in that the base form is in postconsonantic -wi: nkə́nthwi "I am flying," kənthúwak "they are flying." Compare second mora stress in entaki·spwía "when I am full of food" and third mora stress in entakahtú·ᴘwia "when I am hungry" (§1:39).

§6:9. A somewhat similar class appears with -o in base form but with post-consonantic -we in word-initial form: ahke·pínkwe·w "he is blind," entaahke·-pinkó·enk "when we were blind" (§2:16).

§6:10. Theme-final in consonant remains the same for word-initial and for base forms (§2:1; 9 and 4:8 ff.). Relatively few animate intransitive themes end in a consonant.

§6:11. Inanimate intransitives (§4:3) are not as extensively used as animate intransitives. Certain parallel themes can be analyzed as stem, or stems in composition, plus animate formative in one case, plus inanimate formative in the other. A highly productive example is a noninitial (-s-, -t-) which appears in animate forms as -si or -su but before inanimate suffixes as -te·-. This noninitial follows such stems as pi·l- "clean" (§6:7), and ka·xk- "dry." Compare the animate nká·xksi "I am dry," ká·xksu "he is dry" and the inanimate ká·xkte·w "it is dry," ka·xkté·yo "the things are dry."

§6:12. Theoretically, each transitive theme calls for a transitivizing suffix. Where such a formative does not actually appear, a zero formative is postulated. Thus, mi·l- plus zero transitivizer before direct marker -a[·w]- (§3:14) in nəmí·la "I gave him something."

§6:13. Stems characteristically precede one or the other of a pair of transitivizers to form correlative transitive animate and transitive inanimate themes (§6:14 ff.). In many cases a given stem may be followed by intransitive as well as by transitive formatives. Rarely, the contrast in goal gender is marked by correlative stems rather than by correlative formatives: nəmóho "I ate him" but nəmi·cí·na "I ate the things"; compare nəmí·tsi "I am eating."

§6:14. Certain stems precede the transitivizers -l, -tu·n. Here, as in the following types, the stem syllable preceding may be slightly altered in accommodation: nníhila "I killed him," nní·tu·n "I killed it" (with long vowel before -tu·n, but two morae interrupted syllable [§1:17] before -l).

§6:15. Certain stems precede transitivizers -h, -tu·n. Before these, the form of the stem is often extended by the addition of -i·-: mpi·lí·ha "I cleaned him," mpi·lí·tu·n "I cleaned it." The stem extensor -i·- is not used before other elements, as intransitive -si, -su, -te· (§6:7; 11). Compare mpé·ha "I wait for him," mpé·tu·n "I wait for it," and mpéhewe "I am waiting" (§2:17 and 6:2). Also without stem extensor: nu·wá·ha "I know him," nu·wá·tu·n "I know it."

§6:16. Certain stems precede the transitivizers -šuw, -tu·n. Compare mpé·šuwa "I brought him," mpé·tu·n "I brought it," and pé·yok "they came" (§6:5).

§6:17. Note the transitivizers -l, -tamən in mpaó·la "I have power from him," mpaó·tamən "I have power from it."

§6:18. Compare with the preceding the transitivizers -aw, -amən in máxkaw "find him!" (with zero imperative suffix), nəmáxkamən "I found it."

The -ən of transitivizers after -am, -ram (§6:17), and other preceding elements in -m is dropped in one type of intransitive derivation (§3:10). The remaining element in -m is followed by -aw in the formation of a theme having two goals (direct and indirect object, one of which is necessarily animate): nəmaxkamáo "I found it for him."

A mediopassive derivation involves in part the animate formative -aw (as -a·- before consonant); -ke is added and the resulting theme is inflected in part as an intransitive: kəmaxka·ʁéhena "we have found our way," entamaxka·ʁé·enk "when we have found our way." But the subordinate third person -t and first person -ak (appearing as -k) follows -am (-an before -k): entamáxkank "when I have found my way" (§2:18).

§6:19. Themes marked for two goals (direct and indirect object, inflected as a transitive animate; compare §6:18) may be formed by the suffix -lx- after animate intransitive themes (§6:2): wi·nəwé·w "he is begging," nəwi·nəwé·lxa "I beg it for her."

Intransitive -e· appears to be replaced by transitivizers -am, -antamən: nəwi·nəwáma "I begged him," nəwi·nəwántamən "I begged it." But on the analogy of somewhat clearer examples (§6:27), -a- can be isolated as an instrumental, "by mouth, by talking," followed by the transitivizer -m for animate goal, -ntamən for inanimate goal. Compare nəwí·cəma "I helped him," nəwí·cəntamən "I helped it," where -m, -ntamən follow the stem without preceding instrumental.

§6:20. Intransitive -i is replaced by transitivizers -m, -tu·n: nšenkí·xi "I'm lying down," nšenkí·xəma "I laid him down," nšenkí·xtu·n "I laid it down."

Some transitivizers suggest a causative function; however, maNi·- plus transitivizer -h (§6:15) is used as a verb of causation before a directive predicator verb (§5:9 ff.): nəmaNí·ha təlišenkí·xi·n "I made him lie down."

§6:21. While there are some dozen different formatives for marking each of the gender goals, the different stem classes call for scores of transitive pair types when the permutations are counted of -tu·n and -l as one pair type (§6:14), of -tu·n and -h as another pair type (§6:15), -tu·n and -m as another (§6:20), and so on.

The lexical form which is restricted to one pair of transitivizers may be a free stem (§6:14 ff.) or a noninitial, as an instrumental. But free stems may precede a wide variety of noninitials, especially those of the instrumental type (§6:22 ff.). some free stems never appear directly before a transitivizer, but always precede an instrumental.

§6:22. The instrumental -ən "by hand" precedes transitivizers zero for animate goal, -əmən for inanimate goal: mpí·ləna "I cleaned him by hand," mpi·lənə́mən "I cleaned it by hand" (compare §6:15).

§6:23. The instrumental -hik "by feet" precedes transitivizers -aw, -amən: mpi·lhíkao "I cleaned him with my feet," mpi·lhíkamən "I cleaned it with my feet." Compare intransitive mpénkwsi "I am dry" and mpenkhwíkamən "I dried it with my feet" (with h transposed before the -w of penkw).

§6:24. The instrumental -a·khw beside -ha·khw "by tool," precedes transitivizers zero, -amən: mpi·la·khómən "I cleaned it with an instrument," mpenkhó·kho "I wiped him dry" (dried him with towel as a tool).

§6:25. The instrumental -s "by heat" precedes transitivizers zero, -mən: mpénkwsa "I dried him by heat," mpenkwsə́mən "I dried it by heat."

§6:26. The instrumental -əl "by shooting" precedes transitivizers -aw, -amən: mpo·kəláo "I broke him by shooting," mpo·kəlámən "I broke it by shooting."

§6:27. The instrumental ᴀ- (§6:19) "by mouth, by talking" precedes transitivizers -m-, -ntamən: mpó·kama "I chewed him up," mpo·kántamən "I broke it
with my mouth."

§6:28. The instrumental -hitehe "by fist, by hitting" precedes transitivizers
-w, -mən: mpo·khitého "I broke him to pieces by hitting him" (-ew plus -a[·w]-
contracts to -o), mpo·khitéhemən ене·šánte·k "I broke the window by hitting it."
Only one free stem has been noted before -w, -mən: nné·yo "I see him," nné·mən
"I see it."

§6:29. The instrumental -h "by intricate movement of fingers" precedes
transitivizers -w, -amən: nkə́pho "I locked him up," nkəphámən skonte·amé·nak
"I locked the gate shut."

A pleonastic instrumental is formed by combining -ələnč "finger," and the
instrumental -h. Thus, nni·skələnčhámən "I dirtied it with my fingers," nni·-
skələ́nčho "I dirtied him with my fingers." This is contrary to the usual semantic
relationship of lexical elements (§6:40; one would here expect the actor, by means
of his fingers, to dirty the fingers of the goal).

§6:30. The instrumental -əsk "by legs, by walking" precedes transitivizers
-aw, -amən: nkwətkə́skao "I sent him back." Compare the intransitive nkwətkíhina
"we went back."

Some instrumentals, notably -əsk, indicate the central event of a predication
(rather than the usual contributory elaboration stating how that event is imple-
mented) when the directive predicator (§5:9 ff.) is added to a transitive theme,
or when intransitive formatives (§6:6) follow the instrumental: mpámska·n "I
walked past him," kaтa·ləmskáhamo héč "do you fellows want to get going?"
alə́mske·w "he began to go."

§6:31. The instrumental -səт beside -t "by ear, by hearing" precedes transitivizers -aw, -amən: nki·msə́тao "I eavesdropped on him," nki·msə́тamən "I got
the secret of it by hearing," nkəlsə́тao "I listen to him," kələ́staw "listen to
him!" (with -səт transposed to -əst). Compare mpə́ntao "I hear him, understand
him" and mpənáo "I look at him, perceive him" (with transitive theme in -aw,
but lacking the preceding instrumental -t).

§6:32. The instrumental -š "by cutting" precedes transitivizers zero, -mən:
nkí·škša "I took off a piece of him by cutting," nki·skšə́mən "I cut off a piece of it."

Compare the inanimate noun kší·кan "knife" which may be a secondary
derivative in -кan from the stem ki·šk- with the sibilant transposed in the sense of
"knife, a thing which takes off pieces." Derivative suffixes (§6:33 ff.) are oriented
in respect to preceding transitivizers (§6:18), indifferent to preceding instrumentals.

§6:33. Secondary derivatives in -кan may be formed on the basis of a free
stem, as in the preceding instance, or on the basis of a theme including an instrumental. Note the free stem kəp- "to close, shut in" with the instrumental -a·khw
(§6:24) in nkəpa·khómən "I locked it," and the inanimate noun with initial syllable

reduplication and vowel change of the aspectual type (§4:1): ke·kpa·khwí·ʀan "lock, thing which shuts in by tool." Often -ʀan replaces the transitivizer without other change: nta·thilu·há·la "I told him a myth," a·thilu·há·ʀan "myth."

§6:34. But the reciprocal -əʀi beside -ti, forming an intransitive verb (§6:7), calls for a preceding animate goal transitivizer. Compare ntalíhilala "I grabbed him," ntalihilaləʀíhina "we grabbed each other"; nkəcu·ltíhina "we came out together in a group" (with underlying transitive theme); nəwi·pé·ma "I sleep with him," wi·péntuwak "they are sleeping together" (with -e·m replaced by -en before -t).

§6:35. Secondarily derived intransitive verbs are formed by -he· (§6:1) after a noun. Compare mpahahší·ʀana "my dried meats," mpahahši·ʀanahéhena "we dried the meat"; čú·lə·ns "bird," ču·lə́·nshe·w "he is hunting birds," ču·lə́·nshe·s "bird hunter" (§4:9); wiyú·s "meat," wiyú·she·w "he has meat."

§6:36. The derivative with base form -i (§6:7) likewise calls for a preceding noun which in some instances follows wə-. Compare i·lá·ok "brave men," i·lá·yuwak "they are brave men"; nəmí·s "my older sister," nu·mí·si "I have an older sister" (nə- contracts with wə- as nu·-); təpčéhele·w "it rolls," ntəpčehelá·-səm "my wagon," nu·təpčehelá·səmi "I have a wagon."

§6:37. In contrast to derivative suffixes (§6:33 ff.), the diminutive is added to transitive animate verbs without changing the paradigm type; -ʀu follows the direct and inverse markers (§3:14) in the independent mode, -ʀi follows the same markers in the subordinate mode and also follows the speaker-addressee suffixes (§3:15), while other inflective suffixes follow the diminutive forms: nu·lhalá·ʀu "I kept the little one," nu·lhalkwə́ʀu "he kept little me," ku·lhalí·ʀi "you are keeping little me," entawəlahalá·ʀian "when you kept the little one." This is really a supplementary paradigm (§5:1 ff.); however, the intransitive and noun diminutives (§6:38; 39) merely form extended themes which call for simple paradigms (§3:1 and 4:1).

§6:38. The diminutive follows the base forms of animate intransitive themes (§6:1), -ʀi forming a new diminutive base form, -ʀu a new word-initial form (§6:7): kpa·tama·ʀíhimo héč "are you little fellows praying?" (compare §6:2), kawí·ʀu "the little one is sleeping" (§6:3; 5), entakəntká·ʀie·kw "when you little fellows were dancing" (6:6), nohtawe·í·ʀi "little I am talking Ottawa" (§6:7), ki·spwí·ʀuwak "the little ones are full" (§6:8).

§6:39. Diminutive -ʀət (-tət, -ʀət) is added to a preceding noun which remains a noun and true to its gender class.

Except for derived nouns and for the small class of nouns which have two forms (word-final -ay, and -e· before suffixes: tə́ntay "fire," tənté·yo "fires"), noun stems are identical with noun themes. Accordingly, suffixes are simply added to the single noun form which in most instances ends in a consonant; the gender of the noun is morphologically apparent only from the inflection (syntactic concordance with verbs also shows gender).

It is possible to speak of an extended noun theme in the relatively rare in-stances of noun composition and in the frequent cases where the diminutive is added.

Thus, with inanimate nouns: háκi "the ground," haκí·Tət "the little ground"; kənáxk "your hand," kənáxktət "your little hand"; ktú·n "your mouth," ktú·nTət "your little mouth"; alú·ns "the arrow," alúntət "the little arrow" (final -s is al-ways dropped before the diminutive).

So also, with animate nouns: mú·xwe·s "the insect," mu·xwe·Tə́rak "the little insects"; wté·ha "his heart," wte·htə́ra "his little heart"; hópan "the lung," hopánTət "the little lung"; nú·x "my father" (with vocative núxa· "oh my father"), nú·xtət "my little father, my uncle"; nú·xwi·s "my grandchild" (with vocative nu·xwí·ri "oh my grandchild"), nu·xwí·Tət "my little grandchild"; nkáhe·s "my mother" (with vocative ána· "oh mother"), nkahé·Tət "my little mother, my aunt."

§6:40. The instrumentals (§6:21 ff.) are characteristically shorter than other types of noninitials (§6:41). Instrumentals generally indicate movement of a body part or activity which requires control by hands or arms. Free stems for body parts are not at all similar in form to these instrumentals, but noninitial by-forms are similar to their correlative free stems.

The noninitial by-forms are followed either by intransitive formatives or by instrumentals which in turn are followed by transitivizers. In the latter case, the noninitial for a body part localizes the portion of the goal toward which the verbal event is directed (§6:29).

§6:41. Most productively, body parts are designated both by free stems and by noninitial by-forms: xkán "bone," nu·xkaná́ma "my bones"; compare the non-initial for "bone," -i·kane, before the instrumental -h (§6:29): nča·ki·kaného "I tapped him on his bone." But some noninitials do not resemble free stems: nnáxk "my hand"; compare the noninitial for "hand, finger," -ələnč before instrumental -h(§6:29) beside -i·lənče before instrumental -ən (§6:22): nkəši·lənčé·na "I washed his hands with my own hands," or as an intransitive (§6:2): nkəši·lə́nče "I washed my hands."

§6:42. Most noun themes include no more than one free stem; this is in some instances followed by a noninitial: nki·tələ́nčak "my thumbs" (ki·t- "big" before -ələnč which may also enter into a verbal theme: §6:41); ləná·pe "Delaware tribe or individual" (lən- meaning uncertain; -a·pe "human being"), nəmata·pe·-íhina "we are nasty," wəla·pé·yu "he is good natured" (mat- "bad," wəl- "good" before -a·pe· followed by verb deriving suffix: §6:36); tópe·kw "well, spring," maná́pe·kw "lake" (meaning uncertain for to- and manə- before noninitial -pe·kw "body of water").

§6:43. Particles also appear to favor free stems. But compare noninitial -a·š which counts as "five" when added to certain preceding stems; and enta (§5:4):

kwəʈá·š "six" (one and five), ni·šá·š "seven" (two and five); compare kwə́ʈi "one," ní·ša "two."

§6:44. Perhaps most noninitials in verbal themes other than those indicating body parts (§6:41) lack a correlative free stem: nkaʈú·səmwi "I am thirsty," nte·ʀú·səmwi "I have enough to drink" (with noninitial ⁻u·səmwi: §6:8); nkaʈúnko·m "I am sleepy," nəwinkúnko·m "I like to sleep" (with noninitial ⁻unko·m: §6:10). Yet many noninitials (as ⁻a·pa "to come" after wink-i⁻ "to like to") are by-forms of free stems (mpá "I came"; §6:5).

THE HOPI LANGUAGE, TOREVA DIALECT

BENJAMIN LEE WHORF

1. INTRODUCTORY

§1. Hopi is a Utaztecan (Uto-Aztecan) language spoken in several pueblos on the Hopi Reservation in northwest Arizona and by a scattering of Hopis at Winslow and other places off the Reservation. There are perhaps 2000 speakers at present and the number is increasing. There are at least four slightly differentiated dialects named by the writer thus: Polacca at the eastern pueblo of Walpi and that vicinity; Toreva (e as in *we*) at the central pueblo so named, its older name being mosáŋnevi, Anglicized as Mishongnovi; Sipaulovi (usually but incorrectly Shipaulovi) at that central pueblo close to Toreva;[1] and Oraibi at that western pueblo, several nearby villages, and the still further western village of Moencopi. Toreva, with fewer speakers than Polacca or Oraibi, on the basis of available data seems to be the most archaic and phonetically complex dialect, though Oraibi has some archaisms it lacks.

§2. The writer's studies have been made over several years with Mr. Ernest Naquayouma, a Hopi of Toreva long resident in New York City, with the aid of funds supplied by the Committee on Native American Languages of the American Council of Learned Societies, checked by a field trip to Toreva and the other dialect regions made with his own funds. He wishes to express his thanks to the Committee, and to Mr. Naquayouma, to whose excellence as an informant he is much indebted.

§3. Hopi is an "inflectional" language with many specialized parts of speech and a technique partly analytic and partly synthetic, the latter largely of suffixation with suffixes often fusing together but seldom fusing with the stem, and with a moderate degree of stem-alteration by stress shift and change or elimination of the final vowel, and a very little prefixing. There is little use of derivation and much of compounding, usually of not over two lexemes, lexemes not occurring free are infrequent, and there is a rich vocabulary of unit-meaning words. Phonemics is rather complex, process phonology fairly simple, with little sandhi or other mechanical changes. Morphology is complex, that of the verb extremely so, with great wealth of modal, aspectual, and voice nuances. A peculiar and distinctive system of ideas, a high degree of integration in terms of this ideology, and an ever-present delicate precision and subtlety of expression, hard indeed to capture and present in a brief

[1] There are a few other central villages of as yet undetermined dialect affiliation.

survey, should be mentioned to complete this introductory picture of a peculiar and remarkable language.

2. PROSODICS

§1. Syllabic structure. Syllables are of the types CV, CVC, and uncommonly CVCC subject to a very limited number of -CC combinations. Thus there is fairly common occurrence of unlimited intersyllable clusters C-C within and between words, while intersyllable CC-C occurs uncommonly between words and rarely and in very limited forms within words. Between adjacent consonants within words (except in certain combinations, e.g., voiceless continuant plus stop) there is open transition, i.e., a murmur-glide between the consonants, while in clusters made by adjacent words there is closed or silent transition. Words may have any number of syllables up to seven or eight, or rarely more, but two, three, and four syllables are most common.

§2. Stress. There are three general levels of force-and-pitch stress, not fixed registers but rather varying with the length of the word: high (', or unmarked), middle ('), and low (unmarked). It is convenient to class the first two as firm stress.[2] A word of three or more syllables may have all three, or certain combinations of any two. A dissyllable has high and low, or middle and low, or two high; when unmarked, high followed by low is to be understood, this type being vastly preponderant. A monosyllable has either high (unmarked) or middle (marked) but in this case there is no contrast between middle and low, the middle-stressed monosyllable being often no louder than the low syllable within a word. High has maximum force and moderately high even pitch, or high pitch falling before a pause; middle and low have about the same low pitch but middle has the greater force.

§3. Vowel-length. Low syllables have only one length, short. Firm syllables may contain vowels of three lengths: long, and two varieties of short (or rather nonlong); medium, which is half-long with a decline of force before any following consonant, and clipped, which is short and staccato, interrupted at full force by the closure of the following consonant, and not occurring in word-final vowels.[3] Clipped vowels are marked thus (a̧), long vowels (a·), others are unmarked. Length and stress are mainly independent, though partly interconnected by features of prosodic or rhythmic patterns of which each word has its own. While subject to changes incidental to morphology, these patterns are essentially fixed in the morphemes composing words, and are not governed by any simple, "mechanical" principle. This is true of stress as well as of length, though the feature of one high stress on the first, or the second nonfinal, syllable of a word may be considered "normal."

[2] The low level is what is often called unstressed or lacking stress, according to which terminology my "firm stress" is merely "stress."

[3] The "clipping" of these vowels is Trubetzkoy's "Silbenschnitt."

3. PHONEMICS

§1. Consonants.

a. Table of Phonemes

	Labial	Alve-olar	Alve-olar Affri-cate	Pre-palatal and Palatal	Labial-ized Palatal	Velar	Glottal
Stops (fortis unaspirated)	p	t	c	k (ḳ)	kʷ	q	
Preaspirates (fortis pre-aspirated)	'p	't	'c	'k	'kʷ	ˌq	
Continuants –nasals	m	n		ɲ	ŋʷ	ŋ	
–vibrants	w v	l	s r	y			
Desonants (voicelsss con-tinuants)	W M	N L		Y		Nˌ	
Laryngeals							h ?

b. Allophones (positional variants)

Phoneme	Syllable-initial Allophone		Syllable-final Allophone
c	[tsʸ] (palatalized)		[ts]
v	[v] (voiced)		[f] (voiceless)
r	[r] (voiced)		[R] (voiceless)
	before a, ε, i	before e, o[4]	
k	[kʸ]	[k]	[k]

It is thought that the above symbols will be self-explanatory with these added notes: ḳ is ordinary k before a, found only in Spanish loan-words; v is unrounded and varies freely between bilabial and labiodental, r is untrilled, retroflex, and slightly spirantal. The preaspirates occur only syllable-initial after a firm-stressed vowel and the desonants only syllable-final; these sounds are phonemically distinct from the plain stops and the continuants, which also occur in these positions. Consonants other than the preaspirates and desonants occur in all positions.[5]

---

[4] Before ö, k does not occur.

[5] The desonants are not found in Sipaulovi and perhaps other dialects, being replaced by the voiced continuants. The preaspirates do not occur in Sipaulovi or Polacca, being replaced by plain stops, preceded by long vowels. In Oraibi the preaspirates do not exist as single phonemes but are represented by h plus stop, h occurring freely before all consonants in Oraibi, whereas in Toreva h-clusters are very rare, and when they do occur, obviously something different from the preaspiration.

§2. Vowel Phonemes.

Vowel Allophones (governed by vowel-length)

	Long	Medium and Low-syllable		Clipped Norm	
a	[a]	[a]		[a]	
ε	[ä]	[ε]		[ε]	
e	[ë to ï]	[ë to ï]		[ï]	
o	[oụ]	[oụ]		[u]	
ö	[ö]	[ö]		[ü]	
		CV syllable	CVC syllable	CV syllable	CVC syllable
i	[i]	[i]	[i to ɩ]	[i]	[ɩ]

The clipped norms are altered by adjacent consonants as follows: labial C[i] > [ï] k or y[a] > [ä, ε] [a]k > [α] [ü]q > [ö, ɔ].

Also [ë] is shifted by preceding labial toward or to [ï], and nonlong i sounds as [ɩα] before q. It is thought that the timbres indicated by the allophonic symbols will be sufficiently clear, with these notes: ë, mid-back-unrounded, approximately vowel of American English "learn" without the r-glide; ï, high-back-unrounded; i, Welsh u or Polish y, between ë and ɩ; ö, nearly as in French "neuf"; ü, nearly as in German "Mütter"; α, as in "up."[6]

4. MORPHOPHONEMICS

§1. Table of Grammatical Techniques or Processes.

Incremental	Internal	Tactical

1) suffixing (very common)
2) prefixing (occasional)
3) reduplication
  a) of stem-initial CV-.
  b) of stem-final -CV.
  c) of word-final V
	4) iotization (ablaut of stem-final V to i)
	5) length-change (occasional)
	6) stress-shift
	  a) of high from stem-initial to stem-final
	  b) regression of high to preceding word or syllable
	7) contraction (defined below)
		8) order of morphemes
		  a) compounding
		  b) word-order patterns
		
		Each process is frequently accompanied by one or more of the others

§2. A word may be said to be in secondary form if in its structure it exemplifies these processes in contrast with a related form (simplex, or primary form) that

---

[6] The symbol e was chosen for the phoneme which has the sounds ë, ï, etc. as an experiment in the freedom of symbolism such as seems desirable to the author, having the advantage of representing an extremely common vowel by a familiar letter instead of loading texts with unfamiliar signs and diacritic marks.

does not. These processes result in changing the phonetic surroundings of some of the phonemes of the primary form, and as this happens the allophones of such phonemes change to accord with the new conditions. In addition phonemes themselves are sometimes altered to other phonemes or lost. Thus k is assimilated to an adjacent q, and secondary i (from iotization) changes a preceding primary t to c, except in the suffix ˑta which becomes ˑti. Many of these morphophonemic alterations are too limited in scope to justify detailing in this survey. Some are indicated by special symbols explained in the grammatical treatment hereinafter. The alterations of phonemes by adjacent phonemes are too infrequent to justify saying that the language shows external or internal sandhi, except when the qualification "to a very small degree." The following alterations however are of wide and regular occurrence:

§3. Elision. When stressˑshift would cause a clipped vowel not in the first syllable to have low stress, that vowel is elided in the form with shifted stress. Sometimes a medium vowel can be thus elided optionally. In the first syllable of a word the vowel merely loses the clipping. If, however, elision would cause a cluster of more than two consonants the stressˑshift cannot occur in that manner.

§4. Contraction. This process applies only to certain morphemes in the lexicon, called contract morphemes, a very large class. In primary form such a word or element ends in a vowel; in contracted form this vowel disappears, and any highˑstressed long vowel in the preceding syllable shortens to medium. The secondarily final consonant if a continuant becomes the corresponding desonant when adjacent to a voiceless stop. In clusters resulting from any other process than contraction (elision for example) continuants are not desonantized. The nasals ɲ, ŋ, ŋʷ all contract to the form ŋ and desonantize to N̦.

§5. Deaspiration. Preaspirates often occur in primary forms, and when the processes yielding a secondary form would move them out of their bounds (specified in III, §1. c) they become the corresponding plain stops, except for ʻp going into syllableˑfinal, when it becomes v.[7]

§6. Lenition. Primary initial p becomes v when it becomes internal to a word or when the word is preceded by another word used as an adjectival or an incorporated verbal modifier, with certain exceptions that need not here be given.

5. WORD CLASSES AND GENERAL SYNTAX

§1. The Hopi lexicon is divided into many selective classes, for which the terms lexeme classes, or parts of speech, are convenient. They are covert classes, i.e., sentences are common in which there is no distinguishing mark of a word's class, either in the form of the word or in that of the sentence. Thus in pạm leˑna "that one is a flute" and pạm peˑna "that one writes it," there are no characteristics that would enable one to say, from these sentences alone, that leˑna is a noun

---

[7] Preaspiration occurs secondarily and rather irregularly in certain reduplications, prefixations, and suffixations, where it will be indicated in the grammatical formulas by the symbol ʻ.

and peˑna a verb. But other sentences are common in which leˑna bears inflections impossible for peˑna, and vice versa. These parts of speech include paradigmatic ones, pronouns, nouns, verbs, and ambivalents, which have extensive systems of inflection; and an analytic group, words which have either no inflections or few or irregular ones. Distinctive traits of word order or word accompaniment, as well as rather strongly marked types of meaning, break up this analytic group into the classes: adjectives, numeratives, indefinitives, interjections, locators, temporals, tensors, modalizers, particles, and conjunctions. It may be convenient to call all but the first four adverbs. The ambivalents partake of both noun and verb nature and can take either inflectional system, but the verb nature is paramount and the verb system preferred. The noun, including the ambivalent in its noun capacity, can be used like an adjective to modify another noun, but an adjective cannot be used as a noun. The locator class overlaps pronouns, most of these words being special uses of case-inflected pronominal bases with or without various bound morphemes. These uses are mostly as postpositions, and when it is convenient the locators will be so termed.

§2. A sentence may be roughly defined as an utterance that may be followed by a long pause without sense of incompleteness. A major sentence is intelligible in itself, e.g., "the man ran"; a minor sentence is intelligible in a recently occurred context, e.g., "yes," or, "a man" in reply to a question "what is that?" A word, in Hopi, may be defined as either a minimal major or minor sentence, e.g., wari "he ran," taˑqa "a man," or a sentence-element of the same juncture-type[8] and lexeme class as such a word. Hopi has two types of major sentences and clauses.[9] A verbal sentence contains a verb, which is the predicative word and occurs usually last, but often medially. A nonverbal sentence has no verb, and the predicator is the last word, which may be of any class except for a few of the analytics. Locators, adjectives, and nouns, in this order, are the frequent predicators, others are occasional. These frequent types express position or motion, qualities denoted by adjectives, like "is red," and predication of a noun, e.g., "is a man." There are no verbs meaning be, have, go, or come. "Be" is the translation of the nonverbal predication when there is no motional meaning. "Have" is expressed by a verb in the possessive voice, a verb derived from the noun of the thing possessed. There are two ways of expressing motion, each within its proper sphere, and they cannot be interchanged. "Motion referred to field," that having an outline defined *only* by reference to field positions, e.g., "go *away*," "go *up*," "go *to* . . . ," "come *from* . . . ," "come *here*," must be denoted nonverbally, with a directional locator, i.e., a postposition or case-form expressing direction like the italicized words, as the predicator. Such a nonverbal sentence means that the subject traverses the

---

[8] The features mentioned under Prosodics distinguish the beginnings and ends of *words*, and thus the passage from word to word, which may be called the juncture-type of *contact*, in contradistinction to the passage between bound morphemes within a word, which may be called *ligature*.

[9] Clause, i.e., sentence connected with another.

course indicated by the locator. "Motion referred to figure," that which has a distinctive outline without reference to field positions, like running, wriggling, stirring from rest, turning, falling, etc., must be denoted by a verb, with or without a directional locator also, the locator in this case being nonpredicative.

§3. A major sentence must have a predicate (predicator and supplementary words) but need not have a subject. If no subject is expressed but is required by the meaning of the predicate, third person subject is understood; or such a subject may at option be expressed by a pronoun. But Hopi has very many verbs denoting events that are essentially complete wholes and need not be analyzed into an agent and an activity. Thus, if a flash of light is to be reported, Hopi need not manufacture a subject for it, either pronominal, as "it flashed," or nominal, as "a light flashed"; its word for "flashed" is enough. A "transitory event," meaning a momentary event that leaves no lasting trace or effect, can be named only by a major sentence (or clause) with its predicator a verb or locator. This important principle controls both syntax and derivation. There can be neither original nor derived nouns meaning "a flash," "a spark," "a wave," "a nod," "a blow," etc.; this of course excludes ambivalents too. Nor can such phenomena as shooting stars, lightning, puffs of smoke, etc., be referred to by nouns, ambivalents, or nouns merely modified by other words, as in our "shooting star." The reply to "what is that?" is not "a man running" or "a flying eagle," but "a man runs," "an eagle flies."

§4. Durative events and any events that leave lasting motionless effects can be named by nouns, ambivalents, and adjectives, as well as verbs and locators. True nouns refer mostly to whatever gives the visual appearance of closed or nearly closed and lasting outlines, including not only tangible objects but inaccessible appearances like clouds and heavenly bodies, certain clear-cut configurations of landscape (e.g., hill, mountain, ground), masses of material, body parts, persons however designated (as by their kinship, function, etc.). Nouns of material (water, dust, meat, food, etc.) refer not to figureless continuums as in English but to vaguely bounded bodies or masses. A water mass is called pa·he when large, flowing, or little confined, ke·yi when small and not flowing. Such nouns are not individualized by names of containers etc. since they are already individual; ke·yi stands for "a glass of," "cup of," "drink of," water.

§5. Adjectives never denote visual outlines or shapes. They denote figureless percepts (white, bright, smooth, hot, etc.) or intellectual concepts, e.g., of size, quantity, emotional and social characters and evaluations. Names of durative outlines and shapes (e.g., round, pointed, notched, crushed, broken, a cleft, a dot, a fascicle, a forking, a gash) make up the class of ambivalents. They are not usually employed as subjects but as predicates. The great majority belong to the k-class of the verb system. Various outlines of landscape, e.g., river, gully or "wash," are ambivalents. The most abstract or intellectual words are usually verbs, expressing various kinds of thinking, desiring, mystical experiences, etc., and the language is rich in them; they are also sometimes nouns or adjectives.

§6. Names of cyclic events and time periods,[10] like summer, morning, full moon, are in the class of temporals, a kind of adverbs. They mean e.g., "when it is summer" and are used to qualify predicates. They are not used as subjects, objects, or at all like nouns.

§7. Place names, while formally nouns, are hardly ever used in the nominative case. They are inflected in locational cases and used adverbially in the predicate. The subject of a sentence would not be such a name, like "Oraibi," but would be the village, people, or something else, "at Oraibi."

§8. Positional (not directional) locators are differentiated in terms of a distinction that elsewhere throughout the language is widespread and fundamental. It is herein called the category of "locus." It is based on the contrast of two notions: "*punctual*" i.e., located at or concentrated around a point, a single small spot (with ambivalents the inception-event; with verbs an inception-event and/or a transitory event are located at a "point-moment"); versus "*tensive*," located either continuously or interruptedly over an extent (in one to three dimensions of space for nouns or in two to four of "space-time" for verbs). The contrast is that between one unitary figure or outline and an extended figuration or a group-figure, like a line, course, progression, plurality, distribution, etc.[11] Numbers, aspects, cases, locators, and vocabulary all must fall in line with this distinction in sentences. Thus if a singular subject is made plural all morphemes, including lexemes, in the predicate that are definitely punctual must be replaced by tensive ones of the proper type. Dual number is punctual.

§9. Many words have an elongated form called the pausal form when they end free sentences (not nonfinal clauses). The full pausal ends in a glottally reduplicated vowel $CV?V$, while the sentence-medial form abbreviates this to either CV or C. On a nonimperative predicator the full form is elided to $C?V$,[12] on a nonpredicating final, to $CV?$. The full form makes the sentence imperative. Words that have no pausal (e.g., most verb forms) glottally reduplicate final vowel for imperative. The final vowel of a sentence, V, becomes $\hat{V}y$ to give an exclamative form, or when followed by the quotative word yàw to indicate the end of a direct quotation.

6. THE PRONOMINAL AND CASE SYSTEM

§1. Hopi has two great inflectional systems, the verb system and the pronominal and case system. Certain portions of these systems are applied to other parts of speech than those to which they typically pertain, verbs and pronouns. The noun inflection is a reduced version of the pronominal system plus a system of

---

[10] Excepting year (noun), day or light, and night (ambivalents), while day and night for measuring time, "nth day," always with an ordinal, is a tensor, q.v. below.

[11] In verbs that have no reference to outline, like "sleep," the contrast is simply between singular-momentaneous and plural or durative.

[12] Sometimes reduced to CV, especially when the medial is C.

THE PRONOMINAL AND CASE SYSTEM*

Pronoun	CASES OF NOUN TYPE			CASES OF LOCATOR TYPE				
	Nominative	Objective	Possessive	Locative (at, in)	Allative (to)	Illative (into)	Ablative (from, in)	Base
'I' med. paus.	ne? ne·?e	ney ne·ye	?i·	?ine·ⁿpɛ ?ine·ⁿpɛ? ?ine·v?ɛ	?ine·mi ?ine·mi? ?ine·mi?ɨ	?ine·miq ?ine·mɪqa ?ine·miq?a	?ine·ŋaq ?ine·ŋaqŏ	?ine·'·
'we'	?itam ?i·tamɛ̀ ?i·tam?ɛ̀	?ita·mey ?ita·meyɛ̀	?ita·'·	?ita·mɛ̀·pɛ etc. as above	?ita·mɛ̀mi etc. as above	?ita·mɛ̀miq etc. as above	?ita·mɛ̀ŋaq	?ita·mɛ̀·
'thou'	?em ?emi? ?em?ɨ	?eŋ ?e·ŋe	?e·'·	?e·pɛ ?e·pɛ? ?ev?ɛ	?emi ?emi? ?e·mi?ɨ	?emiq ?e·mɪqa ?e·miq?ằ	?ŋaq ?e·ŋaqŏ	?e·'·
'ye'	?ema ?ema? ?e·ma?ằ	?emey ?e·meyɛ̀	?eme·'·	?eme·ⁿpɛ etc.	?eme·mi etc.	?eme·miq etc.	?eme·ŋaq etc.	?eme·'·
'he, it'	— —	— —	| |	?ɛv ?ɛpɛ? ?ɛv?ɛ	?aw ?awi? ?aw?ɨ	?ak ?akwa? ?akw?a	?aŋaq, ?aŋk ?a·ŋaqŏ, ?aŋqŏ	?a·'·
'they'	—	—	|	?ame·ⁿpɛ etc.	?ame·mi etc.	?ame·miq etc.	?ame·mɛ̀ŋaq etc.	?ame·'·

'that, he, there'	pạm pạmiʔ pạmʔi	pẹt pẹta pẹt'ʔa	—	pẹv pẹpẹʔ pẹvʔє	paŋso paŋso'ʔ pa'ŋso'ʔô	paŋsok pa'ŋsôqa pa'ŋsok'ʔà	paŋaq, paŋk etc.	pa'·
'those, they'	pema pemaʔ pe'maʔà	pemey pe'meyè	—	—	—	—	—	—
'this, he here'	ʔiʔ ʔiʔʔi	ʔit ʔita ʔitʔa	—	yẹv yẹpẹʔ yẹvʔє	pew pewiʔ pewʔi	yekiq, yek ye'kiqa ye'kiqʔà	yaŋaq, yaŋk etc.	ya'·
'these'	ʔima ʔimaʔ ʔi'maʔà	ʔimey ʔi'meyè	—	—	—	—	—	—
	—	—	—	—	—	—	—	—
'yonder, place'	—	—	—	ʔayɑ'm ʔayɑ'moʔ ʔayɑ'mʔo	ʔayọ'ʔ ʔayọ'ʔo	ʔayɑ'k ʔayɑ'kʷaʔ ʔayɑ'kʷʔa	ʔaya'q ʔaya'ŋqö	ʔaya'
'reflexive and reciprocal'	—	na'·	—	na·v	na·mi na·miʔ na·'miʔi	na·miq etc.	na·ŋk etc.	na'·

* Medial forms followed by first, or simple pausal, and second, or predicative pausal.

its own, and the class of locators also represents the pronominal system. This pronominal system consists of a set of pronominal bases defining person, number
(singular, plural), and demonstrative relations, and a vocabulary of suffixes defining
cases relations. A word can have only one such base but may have two such suffixes. Among the more frequent forms are some quite irregular in form but regular
in meaning according to their place in the system. The first and second persons
also have prefix forms acting as possessive cases when prefixed to nouns and modifiers of nouns. The table herewith shows some very common bases and cases and
illustrates the whole system.

§2. Some important case suffixes not shown in the main table are as follows:

-ŋ(a?a)   locative tensive   -h(o?o)   partitive
-va(a?a)[13]   adessive (on)   -n(i?i)   simulative (like)
-cvi(?o)   supercessive punctual   -mem(a?a)   sociative (with, and)
-cva(a?a)   superessive tensive   -ŋam(i?i)[14]   ethical (for)
-vní'qaY,[14]-'pení'qaY   comparative (more than)

§3. All the suffixes cited thus far are word-final. There are also suffixes that
must be followed by such a final suffix, e.g.: -son- "within" (three-dimensionally),
-'pa- "within" (boundaries or walls). These yield compound cases like -sonvɛ
"within," -sonmi "toward being within," -sonmiq "into within."

§4. In the limits of this survey it is possible to indicate the meaning of these
case relations only in a very general way. They are actually used in terms of a
sort of unconscious ideology of space and movement that is typically Hopi. Thus
the illative does not always mean "into" in our sense, but is used for "to" instead
of the allative whenever the goal of motion is out of sight.[15] It also denotes the
instrumental relation, as though something of the action or actor went *into* the
the instrument. A personal agent however is denoted by the superessive, as if he
were figuratively underneath the phenomenon. Location within a small well-en-
closed interior ("encapsulation") is referred to not by -son- but by the ablative,
as if even reference to such an object partially extracted it from its hiding. The
predicative allative pɛw?i is the ordinary "come" or "come here," but "from there"
is another way of saying "come," especially to add the sense of "coming" to a
formal verb, the ablative being used for short linear paths, the partitive for movements that are longer, more massive, or of vaguer outline. Nominative is the case
of the subject, *noun*-object of an imperative transitive verb,[16] vocative, and noun-
modifier. Objective is the case of the direct object of transitive verbs (except in
imperative as stated) and postpositions, the subject in certain constructions with
the transrelative mode, and the possessor except for the first and second persons,

[13] And -'pa(?a).

[14] After -a-' >-eŋam(i?i), -evní'qaY.

[15] Students may be interested in comparing the various uses of the allative and illative in Finnish.

[16] Finnish also makes a distinction in the case forms of noun objects in **many** cases, depending
on whether or not the verb is imperative.

and even for these as predicative possessive: ne·y(ʔ)e "it is mine." Predicative objective of nouns with animate subject expresses the subject's goal: "I food (objective, predicative)" means "I'm after food." Indirect object is allative.

§5. The distinction between the ʔa·ʿ and pa·ʿ bases in locational sense is that between English unstressed and stressed "there," or between "the place" and "*that* place": pạm ʔawʔi "he *went* there," pạm páŋsoʔò "he went *there*." Besides the bases that are declinable throughout this whole system, there are certain peculiar defective pronouns, e.g., hạn (nom. only) "I" or "I'll," in which it would seem that one's own *unspoken* intention is given a pronoun like a person and contrasted with neʔ the ego, as only neʔ speaks or reports, while hạn is said to be used in one's thoughts as subject of an intention, or spoken in a direct quotation of another's supposed thoughts. For interrogatives and indefinites, see IX §3.

7. THE NOUN SYSTEM

§1. Selective classes. Nouns are divided among three covert selective classes herein called genders; animate, inanimate, and vegetative (plants); distinguished in the inflections of certain plural forms.[17] The words star, cloud, mist, and wind

TABLE OF INANIMATE NOUN INFLECTION

pa·sa "field" (pausal endings in parenthesis)

	SINGULAR		MULTIPLE	
	Nom.	Obj.	Nom.	Obj.
Absolute	pa·sa	pá·sat(à)	pá·vàsa	pá·vàsat(a)
Construct my field	ʔivása	ʔivásay(eʔe)	ʔivá·vàsa	ʔivá·vàsay(eʔe)
thy "	ʔéʿpàsa	ʔéʿpàsay(eʔe)	ʔéʿpà·vasa	ʔéʿpà·vasay(eʔe)
his "	pá·saʔàt(a)	pá·sayàt(a)		
their "	pá·saʔàm(a)	pá·sayàmey(eʔe)		
his or their " reaffirmative,			pá·samàt(a)	pá·samèyatey(eʔe)
his or their "		pá·sày(eʔe)		pá·vasày(eʔe)
our "	ʔitáʿpàsa			
your "	ʔeméʿpàsa			
modifier stem	pas			
base for suffixes	pás·			

our ʔitáʿpàsa, your ʔeméʿpàsa } Inflected like "thy field." Note that the first and second person constructs contain the possessive prefix forms of the personal pronouns.

pa·sa is a "contract" noun

Note the lenition (IV §6) of primary initial p when it is secondarily noninitial, except when secondarily preaspirated (IV §5, footnote 7) by those possessive prefixes which have preaspirating effect, as symbolized by ʿ in the pronominal table.

[17] This applies strictly only to the Toreva dialect. In Oraibi, for example, these gender distinctions are lacking, and the number inflection is somewhat different.

are animate, but not natural phenomena in general. Kinship terms form another type of covert class that includes at least two nonkinship words. Nouns are also selectivity divided into stress-shift (to last-syllable stress), contract, and nonaltering nouns according to the process that makes them modifiers and bases for random bound morphemes. Finally there are classes of nouns in -he, -w(e?e), -ŋ(ʷe?e), the last two nearly all animates, that lose these endings in various inflected forms. These four types of classification all intercross.

§2. Inflections. Nouns are inflected for case (nominative, objective), state (absolute, construct), and number (singular, dual, and two plurals: paucal and multiple). The construct state is inflected for person and singular-plural number of the construct, i.e., term in the relation expressed by English "of," usually possessor. If this construct is also expressed by a detached word the latter is in objective case, a usage which will be called the genitive objective. The table gives the inflection of an inanimate noun, abbreviated to showing only the singular and multiple numbers. The multiple in all nouns has initial reduplication except in the "his or their" form, which is in fact the paucal, as the distinction of the two plurals is lost at this point. The paucal (meaning "some, a few") suffixes -t(e?e) or for some nouns -te(?e), -ht(e?e), -m(e?e), nom., and -tey(e?e), -htey(e?e), -mey(e?e) obj. in the absolute and first, second, persons construct; third construct is like multiple without reduplication. Animates in multiple are paucals with the addition of reduplication, i.e., they have paucal suffixes in all the forms, and also most of them contract the reduplicated stem; cf. ma·na "girl," mult. mamaNt(e?e) with pa·sa, pá·vasà. Some animates use the paucal for all plurals, e.g., ciroht "birds," ḳawáyom "horses." Duals[18] suffix -vit(e?e) nom. -vitey(e?e) obj. in absolute, first person, second person but have no third person, using the paucal instead. The vegetative gender has one general plural which suffixes -qölö, -qlö to the modifier base without reduplication and inflects like singular, while söhȩvi "cottonwood, tree," and -cǫki, -cki "-tree, -bush" can also pluralize like inanimates. Noun singulars can be used as plurals when the meaning is clear, but the strong Hopi feeling for spatial configurations militates against this. The Hopi category of plural applies to things and events that conceivably could appear assembled simultaneously. The count of repetitions that could not be assembled is not plurality in this view; hence temporals and terms like year, day, are not pluralized, and lengths of time are measured by stating the *ordinal* number of the last unit. The declension of the classes whose stems drop characteristic endings in certain forms will be omitted.

§3. The reaffirmative is a special objective third person referring to the subject, e.g., pa·say tȩwa "he saw his (own) field," cf. pá·sayȧt tȩwa "he saw his (another's) field." The genitive objective is seen in e.g., ta·qat pá·sa?ȧt "the man's field" (man-obj. his field). Nouns in general have only two cases, but a number of nouns, e.g., ki·he "house," in their singular absolute can take pronominal case-suffixes on the modifier stem. Demonstratives agree in case with the final case-

[18] Dual number is lacking in Oraibi and perhaps other dialects.

suffix of nouns; e.g., pám ki·he "that house" is declined: obj. pęt ki·het, all. paŋso ki·mi, ill. paŋsok ki·miq, paŋsok kí·sonmiq "into-within that house," etc. Place names can take all the locational suffixes, and when without them, which is rarely, they usually take the special suffix ‑vi, ‑pi, which is replaceable by the locational suffixes. Aside from these special forms, the typical pronominal cases are applied to nouns not directly but through the intermediary of postpositions following the objective. These postpositions (IX §4) are the cases of the pronominal bases, usu‑ ally the ʔa·ʼ base; e.g., ma·nat ʔaw "to the girl," ʔeʻkiy ʔεv "at your house," kí·kihèt ʔaŋ "at (tensive) the houses."

§4. When a noun is preceded by a modifier or modifiers, whether adjectives or nouns, the possessive prefixes are applied to the first such word, the suffixes and reduplication to the noun modified, i.e., the last word.

§5. The kinship‑class nouns occur only in construct state. They can however imply an indefinite possessor, for which purpose the "their" form is used: yęʔam (stem yę‑) "their mother" ="one's mother, a mother."[19]

8. THE VERB SYSTEM

§1. Conjugations. The verb system is applied in its entirety to verbs and ambivalents, which are primarily verbs; and most of it, with certain gaps, may be applied to any word used as predicator, but in a way that makes the conjugation of nonverbs different from any of the conjugational classes of verbs. There are four such classes. Simplex verbs do not change their form of stem as between the simplex and the word extended by suffixes; stress verbs shift stress from first to second syllable and preaspirate certain suffixes, contract verbs contract the stem, k‑class verbs use a stem extended by ‑k‑ for most forms, though they have certain forms that use simplex and contract stems. The conjugation of nonverb predicators is a fifth class, annex verbations, the suffixes being added to a postposed "annex," similar to a suffix, but even more like an auxiliary verb in close‑phrase contact with the predicator.[20]

§2. Resolutions. Verbs fall into two classes of resolution: intransitive and transitive. Roots fall into these classes selectively; and the resolution will also depend on the voice suffix, if any, all voices being intransitive and intransitivizing except the causative, which is transitive and transitivizing, and the possessive, which is the same as its base. There are also two intransitive forms made from transitives by preposed elements: the reflexive by prefix ná·‑, and the incorporative by preposing the modifier stem of a noun, e.g., tav nìna "kills a rabbitt," ciró ninà

---

[19] Cf. English "they say." The stem yę‑ "mother" is irregular in first and second persons: ʔíŋe(ʔè) "my mother," ʔéŋe(ʔè) "your mother."

[20] That the juncture is contact, not ligature (footnote 8), although the group is stressed like one word, is shown by the fact that there is close transition between adjacent consonants, and that the intersyllabic cluster CC‑C occurs in forms found only between words, e.g., in ʔáŋk‑nini "he will come from there," the first ‑ni‑ being the annex, the second the suffix translated "will." This peculiar form of contact will be indicated by a hyphen.

"kills a bird," formed on the identical pattern of adjectival modifying (IX §1) from the modifier stems tav, ciró of the nouns ta·vo, cịro. These "incorporated objects," which formally are modifiers, not objects, are much less common than true noun objects. Transitives imply a definite third person object if none is expressed; indefinite object must be explicitly indicated by words like "something."

§3. Inflection and categories. Inflection is primarily by suffixes, but reduplication along with suffixes is common, initial for all verbs, root-final for k-class verbs; there is also the prefix ná·, and the intensive prefix sẹ́ indicating force, speed,

TABLE OF VERB SUFFIXES AND ANNEXES

WORD SUFFIXES	THEME SUFFIXES	STEM SUFFIXES				
		Position 1 (nearest root)			Position 2	Position 3
·ta₁	·ʳi)n·	·ʳi	·ʳi)na	·la	·ʳi)va	·ʳi)nệmaᶜ
·làweᶜ	·keᶜ	·ʳị)L·ti	·vìwa	·yke	·ta₁ ·ʳi)ma	
·ʔìw·ta₂ʳ	·meᶜ	·ʳị)w·ta₂ʳ	·vẹ̀·L·ti	·tòyna	·ti ·to	
·ʔy·ta₂ʳ	·vte	·ʳìwa	·ʳi)ʔy·ta₂ʳ			

STEM SUFFIXES, continued

Position 4	Position 5	Position 6	Position 7			
·làweᶜ	·ya	·ni	·ʳεʔ(ε)	·qaY(·qà·ʔε)	·kaŋ(o)	·kàkaŋ(o)
		·ŋʷe	·t(a)	·qa	·q(öʔö)	
			·pe	·ve	·pi	

ANNEXES

Singular Subject	Plural Subject	Long-durative
·nị̀· (·ní·ʻ, ·ní··)	·ya, ·ya·	·màn·ta₁ʳ

Some suffixes have special plural forms, viz.: ·ta₁:·tòta, ·ta₂:·yẹŋʷaᶜ, ·ti:·totì, ·làweᶜ:ilàlwa, ·ʳi)ma:·ʳi)wị̀saᶜ, ·to:wị̀saᶜ.

Special symbols: ·ta₁ and ·ta₂ are suffixes that pluralize differently; ·ʳi, ·ʳìwa, the first vowel of the written suffixal form replaces the last vowel of the base (written form is a symbolic device for indicating morphophonemic change, usually iotization, of the last vowel plus addition of a suffix); ·ʳi)na, there is a replacing-vowel i in some paradigms and in others there is merely the suffix ·na; ·làweᶜ, the suffix is contracted before others; ·ʔìw·taʳ, the final suffix is replaceable by stem suffixes of positions two, three, four; ·kaŋ(o), pausal ending in parenthesis. The first two word suffixes are also listed among stem suffixes to show their positions in combinations of suffixes; the other two word suffixes are position one.

and promptness. The suffixes of the verb system are of three kinds. Word suffixes are added to verbs and also to the modifier stems of nouns and adjectives, which they convert to derived verbs, and are not added to annexes (with certain peculiar exceptions). Stem suffixes are added only to verbs and annexes. Theme suffixes are added to verbs, but only in certain forms of certain conjugations, e.g., the -k- element found in the k-class. The table shows all but a few irregular suffixes, and the annexes, and the purely formal arrangement in which they add, alter, and combine with each other. But the meanings and uses cannot be classified neatly in terms of this arrangement, nor in terms of the individual suffixes. They are best treated in terms of a system of overt nonselective grammatical categories along with the covert categories of resolution and locus (punctual and tensive). In this system verbs are inflected for voice, aspect, number, assertion, and mode, and affected by detached words (analytics) for status, injunction, and modality. Annex verbations lack the inflection for voice and are limited as to aspects;[21] otherwise they are the same.

§4. Voices. The *simple* voice (zero form) corresponds to the English active. The *eventive* is the distinctive, almost untranslatable voice of the zero form of the k-class and all ambivalents, sporadically formed in the other classes by -ʳi, yielding a k-class verb in -i. The k-class is a rich vocabulary of CVCV roots, which denote manifestation of characteristic visual outlines and figural arrangements,[22] occurring as moving outlines, or as movements that leave more or less lasting representative outlines, or as simple appearances of figure-and-ground. Eventive roots[23] are punctual, e.g. one break occurs, one slit into an edge occurs, one drop englobes and drips off, one bursting scatters particles; unless they are plural roots, e.g. löhö many units fall at once, nöŋa many units go outside or through to the other side, which are tensive. The temptation to think of these roots as nouns, "a break," "a slit" etc. is misleading from the Hopi standpoint. Not only are they formally distinct parts of speech from Hopi nouns; but a Hopi noun denotes a figure only, these denote a figure surrounded by a more or less hazy local ground or field. A noun

---

[21] Because the distinctions conveyed in the morphemes of locators and other nonverb predicators largely take the place of aspects.

[22] In a few cases, characteristic sounds also, and *very rarely* ideas that seem outside the figural outline category. Verbs of noise and sound, so common in some American Indian languages, are remarkably rare in Hopi. The language constantly emphasizes visual facts, and characteristically never uses them metaphorically for invisible entities. The realm of the psyche has its own vocabulary; in Hopi one does not "grasp" an idea! Onomatopoeia is rare. But there is considerable of what appears to be symbolism by sound of types of shape, outline, and outline of movement, e.g., many verbs and ambivalents beginning pe- and having reference to outlines like the letter V and/or the idea of spreading apart, others beginning me- referring to cylindric form and rolling, etc. This is not merely typical of Hopi but of Utaztecan, though indeed it is found in many languages, being common in Maya; it is along the lines of English slip, slide, slink, slur, slither, slime, slush, sleet, slick, slop, slump.

[23] A "root" is an unanalyzable stem of form CVCV, or less often CV.

predicator is copulative; its subject "is" that noun. An eventive predicator is occurrent; it declares an event. Its subject is that part of the ground or field to which something happens or has happened whereby a new or altered configuration manifests, either fugitively or with lasting effect. Or it may have *no* subject (cf. V §3), while a predicative noun has a subject expressed or implied. If the root denotes a "transitory event," leaving no effect or an effect that rapidly evanesces; if, so to speak, the ground or field returns to its original state after the momentary appearance (a flash, a wave, a nod, a leap, a splash, a flutter, etc.), then the root is a pure verb. If it denotes an event with a stable effect on the field, the root is automatically an ambivalent and may take noun inflections and uses. Thus one can say "his cut," "into a break" etc. but not "his nod" or "into a wave." The *dynamic eventive*, ˊi̧)L̹ti, basically means an event occurring with *added force*, often from outside the subject, e.g., po̧ˀo "leans," pó̧ˀo̧Lti "leans his weight, is thrown into a lean, etc." It seems to us a passive because it passivizes transitives, e.g., ˀeˑta "shuts it," ˀéˑci̧Lti "is shut, caused to shut," but is basically (and paradoxically) an active, the most active of the intransitive voices, often denoting a subject moving energetically of his own accord. The *extended dynamic* voice, ˊi̧wa, is similar but with the "added force" always an external-field tensive influence—"is being ...ed" or "is be...ed" (like e.g., "is bedevilled," "is beclouded") including cases where several agents combine to produce the influence. The *cessative*, ˅i̧wa or ˅ve̹ˑL̹ti according to paradigm, shows the cessation of such an influence—"stops being ...ed," treating the change in condition as a punctual event. The *essive*, ˊi̧w-ta₂ˊ, ˅ˀi̧w-ta₂ˊ, shows a durative state resulting from or preserving the outline of an event, including the state of uniform motion; the nearest English is our form in a-, e.g., is atilt, astride, aswim, afloat, "a-run" (running): ˀéˑci̧wta "is shut (not open)." The *possessive*, ˊi̧)ˀy-ta₂ˊ, applied to nouns means the subject "has" the noun, and may be applied to any number-form—siwáˀyta "has a younger sister," siwáme̹ˀyta "has younger sisters." With noun preceded by modifier it answers to the English e.g., "is long-legged"; one may say e.g., "is pretty-sistered." Applied to transitive stems it means "has it...ed" e.g., sómi̧ˀyta "has it tied" (soma "ties it").[24] The *causative*, -ta₁ for deriving verbs, ˊi̧)na (or sometimes -la, -to̹yna, or -ta₁ replacing -ti) on verbs, makes transitives from intransitive and nonverb bases: peˑhe adj. "new" péˑhetà "renews it"; peˑwi (contract verb) "sleeps," pewna "puts him to sleep"; qöhi (k-class) "breaks," qóhi̧kna "breaks it." Most of our transitives of altering shape or outline are causatives of the k-class eventives.

§5. Aspects. These are formed by the stem suffixes positions two, three, four. Certain aspect suffixes may be superposed giving compound aspects, unlike the the other inflected categories, whose subclasses are mutually exclusive. The *prime* aspect (zero form) is punctual or tensive according to its base, the ingressive is punctual and punctualizing, all others are tensive and tensivizing. The *durative* aspect, -ta₁ "is ...ing" has several varieties marked by stem-alterations, reduplica-

---

[24] The possessive has the resolution of its base, i.e., sómi̧ˀyta is transitive like soma.

tion or contraction or both, or the theme-suffix -n-. The most distinct is the *segmentative*, found in the k-class only, with root-final reduplication, converting the single figural image of the k-class root into a repeating pattern in space-time. The other aspects are frequently formed like secondary derivatives of the various duratives, replacing the -ta by other suffixes (sometimes adding them to -ta) and retaining the stem-alterations. Add to this that these aspects may compound together, and that all but the durative and continuative handle ideas that are utterly strange to English or indeed Indo-European, and one can perhaps imagine the prodigal richness and amazing subtlety of this aspectual system. The *ingressive*, -ri)va, denotes the moment of realization or actualization, of passage from latency (or from "causal power," an important Hopi notion) into manifestation. It is most used on a durative base to denote beginning of a durative state; "begins to be . . . ing." But on "verbs denoting latency" it denotes beginning not of the latency but of its fruition. Thus tenátya "hopes," "is hoped for," or better "uses hoping" whose subject is either hoping person or latent thing, gives ingressive tenátyàva "comes true as hoped for," i.e., "realizes hoping." Contrast the effect with an ordinary verb, as in pewva "goes to sleep," i.e., "realizes sleeping." The *progressional*, -ri)ma, immerses the event in a line of motion. A punctual event (indicated by punctual base) without human agent is shown moving in the natural directional tendency of the phenomenon if it has one: ʔéwìkma "flames up, a flame shoots up" < ʔewi (k-class) "a flame occurs," motion natural to flame being upward. A punctual event with human agent is shown as having occurred during a linear course: somma "has been to tie it." A durative event occurs all along the linear course: sósoMtìma "goes along tying it, them" < sósòMta, dur. of soma; ʔewíwitìma "flames run along" < ʔewíwità "flickering flames occur," segmentative of ʔewi. The *projective*, -to, shows a linear motion or impulse passing into the event: cóʔoktò "launches off into a leap" < coʔo "leaps"; soMto "goes to tie it." The *spatial*, -ri)nèmaᵒ, immerses the event in motion that tours about in space: sósoMtinèma "goes around tying it, them." The *continuative* is a long or indefinitely continued durative, "keeps . . .ing." Its suffix -làweᵒ always replaces -ta₁ and as a word suffix includes the causative force that -ta₁ has with nonverb bases.

§6. Numbers. Plural subject requires -ya except for fixed-number stems and the suffixes that have plural forms (see table). With annex verbations -ya is the annex for plural subject. Dual subject takes a singular verb, and a plural pronoun (pronouns lack dual) with a singular verb indicates dual. Fixed-number stems are numerous, e.g., pọsi "one falls," löhö "several fall." They include transitives that fix the number of the object, either in the root or as causatives, e.g., pọsna "drops one," löhökna "drops several." *Inner plural* is a form confined to the k-class, with -m- (< -meᵒ) in place of the usual -k-, stress-shift, and in the eventive -ti. It pluralizes the single figure of the root within a small local region: poróMti "group of perforated holes occurs" < poro "a perforated hole occurs"; contrast the segmentative porórotà "extended succession of holes occurs."

§7. Assertions. These resemble tenses but refer to realms of validity rather than of time. The *reportive* (zero form) reports an actual occurred or occurring fact; it corresponds to past and present tense. The *expective*, ⸰ni, declares an expectancy, and corresponds to future or incipiency, e.g., somni "he will, wants to, or is about to tie it," except when by context it refers to a past expectancy, "wanted to, etc." The *nomic*, ⸰ŋʷe, declares a general or customary truth, e.g., cįroht péꞏyáwnemyàŋʷe[25] "birds fly."

§8. Modes. The *independent* (zero form) is the mode of an independent sentence or of one of two or more linked clauses. The dependent modes link a clause to another clause, either independent or dependent, each mode in a certain "sense." The *transrelative*, ⸰q(öʔö), links clauses having different subjects; this is not merely an incidental trait but is the "sense" of the mode, patterning with the senses of the other modes. The mode means that a new subject enters, or will enter if the transrelative clause is first. The other modes link clauses with the same subject. The *conditional*, ⸰ʳɛʔ(ɛ), "when, if," states the condition that justifies a nonreportive (expective or nomic) assertion: męʔɛʔ níꞏnáni "when he shoots it he will kill it"; męʔɛʔ níꞏnáŋʷe "when he shoots it he kills it." The dependent clause is in the same assertion as the other clause, as this suffix fuses mode and assertion in one indicator. The *correlative*, ⸰qaY (⸰qàʔɛ), "since, as, etc." denotes causal connection and "accessory to the fact": męʔàꞏqaY niꞏna "having shot it (or, by shooting it) he killed it." On the expective it denotes purpose: méʔanįqaY "in order to shoot it." With special adverbs (tensors or locators) it denotes "until," "as if," "where," and other accessory relations. The *concursive*, ⸰kaŋ(o), ⸰kàkaŋ(o), "as, while," denotes contemporaneous occurrence: méʔakàŋ pǫsi "as he shot it he fell off." Concursive expectancy means priority: méʔanìkaŋ "before shooting it," i.e., "while about to shoot it." The *sequential*, ⸰t(a), "after, and," denotes sequence without implying causal connection: méʔat coʔo "after he shot it he leaped." The *agentive* ⸰qa, forms relative clauses and is inflected as a noun: méʔàꞏqa "he who shot it"; neʔ níꞏnáqat ʔawʔi "I went to him who killed it." It denotes functionary or office on the durative (⸰tàqa), habitual actor on the nomic (⸰ŋʷęqa). The transrelative is used, when there are different subjects, in all these senses, which are secondary to its own sense and distinguished when necessary by adverbs and word order. It is used for indirect discourse and for relative clauses of our type "whom . . . ," also "to whom, from which, etc." with case forms of demonstrative pronouns (Hopi has no relative pronouns). Allied to the modes as position seven suffixes are the verb-derived nouns; of thing effected ("*nomen patientis*") in ⸰pe, ⸰ve, and of place and instrument in ⸰pi.

§9. Status. *Affirmative*, zero form, *negative* in reportive and nomic by qà

---

[25] This verb is in spatial aspect because the prime aspect is punctual, péꞏyála "floats once outspread winglike in air," and of the tensive aspects the spatial best expresses general flying. The verb belongs to a subtype of the simplex class, not treated in this paper, ending in an element ⸰la which changes before certain suffixes.

"not," in expective by soʔon "not." *Interrogative*, by sentence-introducing pè[26] or merely a special restressing of the beginning of the sentence like the pè sentence, interrogative adverbs (indefinitives, IX §3), and interjections or phrases equivalent to "*n'est-ce pas?*" The interjections for replying are ʔowí·y[27] "yes," qąʔɛ or qaʔɛ́·y "no," pí·hí·y "I don't know."

§10. Injunctions. *Imperative* is a pausal inflection of the entire sentence, as explained in V §9. The k-class verb adds its theme suffix to the simplex: wárikeʔè "run!"; contrast wari "he ran." Transitives can make an imperative by simply expressing the nominative object immediately after the verb: mẹʔa cịro "shoot the bird." *Vetative* is the expective with qà instead of sọʔon and the usual objective-case object: cịrot qà mẹ́ʔạni "don't shoot the bird." *Optative* is expective with the adverb nạm, or tẹm which implies "we" subject: tẹm wárịkni "let's run" (dual).

§11. Modalities. These are a system of nuances that express the type of in-tellectual validity of a statement. Thus the reportive assertion denotes the occur-rence of a fact, and in the *indicative* (zero form) this is so without reservation. But in the *quotative* modality, sign yàw, the statement is one of hearsay. The modalities are denoted by a group of detached words belonging to the class of modalizers. There are many modalizers expressing meanings of this sort, but in only seven are these meanings regarded as grammatical categories (modalities). They are so re-garded because of their systematic character—being mutually exclusive for the most part, and coordinated with the modes as part of the apparatus of dependent clauses, though also used in independent sentences. The *concessive*, kẹr, makes the statement a valid assumption, either by evidence or inference, or without evidence but as a postulate for the sake of discussion, hence with conditional or transrela-tive mode it stands for "if," though having many other uses. The *indeterminate*, sɛn "may," i.e., "may or may not" denotes balanced positive and negative possibili-t es. The *suggestive*, kɛ "may after all," "may still," "may really," stresses slightly a positive possibility; with negative it gives "may not." The *inhibitive*, kerhín, is "cannot"; its negative kerhín qà is the *potential*, "can." The *necessitative*, "must," is the double negative sọʔon qà.[28] The *impotential*, ʔạs, is connected with the Hopi notion that I have referred to as "causal power," either in an event already oc-curred, or in any tendency or effort toward later events. It indicates insufficient "power" for further actualization of the end or principle of the action or state. Hence in the reportive or nomic it means that the action or state is in vain, and to be met with frustration or reversal: ʔạs wa·ya "he vainly ran away (but was later caught)," and, if the clause in parenthesis is added, no word for "but" is used, ʔạs in the other clause being its equivalent. It may denote instability of state, as in

[26] Or yà in Oraibi. This pè is not to be confused with the tensor pè̜ʔ, pè̜ʔ.

[27] In rapid tempo often wɛ. A curious likeness to French!

[28] The above translations correspond to the modalities with the expective assertion. They are equally usable with the reportive and nomic, answering then to "perhaps," "could," "had to."

"it *was* here but got taken away."[29] In expective it denotes trying without immediate success: ʔas wá·yáni "he tries (or tried) to run away." With conditional
or transrelative mode it makes a "contrary to fact" conditional clause.[30]

§12. Pronominal Verbs. The pronominal simulative case forms pạ̈n "like
that," yạn "like this," hịn "like what?" yield derived verbs e.g., pạnta "be or
seem like that," pạNti "act like that" and verbs with certain other aspect suffixes
like pạnma "go along like that"; also are prefixed to certain stems not occurring
free, viz. ˊqàwe "say" (páNqàwe "say so"), ˊcàki "do," ˊcàna "do to it." These
pronominal verbs are much and idiomatically used. "What are you doing?" is
ʔem hịncàki.

9. THE ANALYTIC CLASSES

§1. Adjectives. Adjectives are selectively divided into simplex, stress, and
contract adjectives, according to the form of stem used as modifier before nouns as
contrasted with the primary form used as predicator, e.g.: pe·he (simplex type)
"is new," pe·he vọyo "a new knife" (pọyo "knife"); qöca (stress) "is white,"
qöcá voyò "a white knife"; ca·va (contract) "is short," cav vòyo "a short knife."
These changes are the only inflections of adjectives, and together with the stress
patterning of the entire phrase and the lenition of following p- to v- form an *adjectival system*, applicable also to nouns and ambivalents as modifiers, or as first
elements of compounds. A noun, according as it is simplex type, stress, or contract,
will behave exactly as an adjective of similar type,[31] while k-class ambivalents are
of the stress type as modifiers.

§2. Numeratives. These include the numerals and terms like all, many. Some
e.g., the first four numerals, have irregular inflections of plural and objective case,
others are indeclinable. The Toreva dialect has simple numerals up through ten,
and one for twenty, the others being phrase-like composites following the decimal
system. Oraibi has the odd feature of simple numerals up through twenty. All
numerals inflect to give a pausal form, a combining form, and two forms of ordinals,
which are also multiplicatives, or rather the Hopi pattern of ordinal numeration
takes the place of multiplicatives. As explained under nouns, units that cannot be
congregated in space, like days, repetitions, "times," or other successive units of
the same cycle, are counted by ordinals. "Ten days" is not, as with us, treated as
an imaginary aggregate, but as the relation between two events, one on the tenth

[29] In Hopi, ʔas yẹv-nit kẹr hoyo—sequential mode (-t) of annex (-ni-) verbation of yẹv "here,"
kẹr concessive modality because the taking away is an inference, hoyo, k-class, eventive voice, "gets
moved out of previous position."

[30] For a more detailed explanation of the modalities, modes, and assertions, see Whorf, *Some
Verbal Categories of Hopi* (Language, 14, vol., pp. 275–286, 1938).

[31] The noun classes with special suffixes introduce a few minor variations. Sometimes these
suffixes are lost and sometimes not. It may be well to repeat here what was said in V, that while
nouns and adjectives as *modifiers* are entirely similar, adjectives form a distinct class because they
cannot be used completely like nouns, i.e., as independent substantives.

day after the other.[32] Syntactically, cardinals are treated like defective nouns, and ordinals like adverbs.

§3. Indefinitives. It is convenient to treat the interrogative-indefinite "pronouns" as a distinct part of speech, as their inflections, though akin to those of the pronominal system, are irregular and defective. They are formed on the bases: hi- inanimate or impersonal, haki human beings, and fairly regularly with locational suffixes on haqa- for place. They are indefinite (e.g., "something") as well as interrogative ("what?"), the distinction being one of context.

§4. Locators. These are the case-forms (other than objective) of third-person pronominal bases, and of some other bases, already described in VI and VII §3. Many are postpositions, but some are simply adverbs, e.g., ʔáʼpiy(oʼo) "away" or "go away." Many have for bases nonpronominal lexemes not occurring free. Of this type are the important seven orientation terms, i.e., the four compass-points, up, down, and "all directions." Their case-forms are irregular; the allative is the usual name-form of the direction, and in several cases lacks the suffix -mi.

§5. Tensors. As locators correspond to our adverbs of place, so tensors do to adverbs of time and degree. They are sharply distinguished from locators by lacking case suffixes or case distinctions; they never e.g., express time by a locative "in, at," or any other spatial reference. To our notions they seem to be either degree terms, with degree mixed up with manner, or time terms, but it seems probable that in principle they all denote *intensities* of various types.[33] Not only the degree but the kind of intensity is expressed, as to whether it is gentle or rough, punctual or tensive, constant, increasing, decreasing, etc. Incipient intensities are the same as tendencies, and are rendered e.g., "very quickly, right away, now," or "quickly, soon after, soon" etc.; they may be said to be estimators of present or future time. Punctual intensities contain a demonstrative sense and so place an event at a point in the reportive realm, i.e., the past, at more or less remoteness from the speaker, e.g., at *this* event or moment, at *that* event or moment, at that

---

[32] There is a minor exception to this in stating a person's age in years, where Hopi, like French, says he "has" so many years, and cardinals may be used to modify the possessive voice verb derived from "year." Here ordinals are also correct, and for ages in days, using a similar construction, they seem to be required.

[33] This is borne out by lexical study. Hopi does not express intensity, tendency, or duration metaphorically with space and size terms (like much, more, grow, long, etc.)— but has abundant lexical as well as inflectional means for expressing them directly. Tensors show little sign of derivation from space or size terms. Besides tensors, there are certain verbs that express intensity, tendency, and duration directly (e.g., pevéLti "abate in intensity"), again without hint of derivation from spatial terms. Ideas of constant or varying intensities are being continually encountered in this body of lexical material. We have here a large array of lexemes in which denoting of intensities seems to be the leading principle; and tendency, duration, and relative time position seem to be fused with intensity, as with us they are fused with spatial magnitudes—extension, size, and motion. Hence the term "tensor" seems appropriate for these elements that express the intensity-factors of the sentence's ideas.

remote (long past) event, etc. The tensors pę?, pay(e?e), pąsat all may be translated "now" or "then," but pę? corresponds to "this," pay to "it," pąsat to "that"; pay also implies "this becoming that," and as predicator means "become past" or "go" in the sense of "depart, quit the scene": ne? páy·nįni "I'll go" or "now I'll go." Hisat is interrogative "when?" or indefinite "at some time (ago)." Others have repetitive and long durative meaning like "again," "often," "constantly," "all day," "more and more." In general the tensors handle notions allied to those of the verb aspects.

§6. Temporals. These denote points and periods in natural cycles, like summer and the other seasons, morning and other times of day, the moon's phases, the Hopi months, etc. They are wholly adverbial, as more fully explained in V §6. Nevertheless the season terms have an inflection that resembles a nominal objective case, which is in rare use with certain postpositions. Some temporals are transrelative modes of verbs, e.g., "sunset" is the phrase "when the sun enters" (transrelative).

§7. Modalizers. These are the words that denote the modalities, and a good many others of the same type (see VIII §11). ?era, meaning according to memory, and nawes "must" in the sense of "can't very well refuse" are further examples of modalizers.

§8. Particles. The words that denote status and injunction, and miscellaneous nuancing words and sentence-introducers.

§9. Conjunctions. There are but three: the correlative conjunction ni˙qaY, the concursive ni·kaŋ and the transrelative nįq. They consist of the annex ni· with mode suffixes, used as an independent word. They introduce sentences or clauses as though one of these modes had preceded, whether the preceding sentence or clause be in the independent mode or in the same mode that is reaffirmed by the conjunction. They are all rendered "and."

§10. Interjections. These do not differ from interjections in any language. Included here are the reply words, greetings, and clichés of politeness.

§11. Men's and women's speech. The speech of the two sexes differs in a few minor points of vocabulary, largely or entirely confined to the analytics. Thus the sexes use different words for "pretty" (adj.), "greatly" (tensor), and "thank you" (interjection).

§12. Sentence introduction. Sentences and clauses are frequently begun with one, two, three, or even more short analytics—conjunctions, tensors, modalizers, particles, and sometimes an interjection.

10. EXAMPLES OF SENTENCE FORMATION

In order to show the language as functioning, with the maximum of condensation, a small number of analyzed and explained sentences has been preferred to a connected text or to numerous examples scattered through the grammatical description.

§1. ma·na ʔayám ki·vɛ qaté‘qa ʔaŋk wárikìwta. "The girl who lived in yonder house came running": ma·na "girl," unmarried woman" nom. sing.; qaté‘qa nom. sing. agentive of qate (stress-verb) "sing. subj. sits, dwells"; ki·vɛ punctual locative suffix -vɛ added to modifier-stem ki· of ki·he "house"; ʔayám punctual locative of demonstrative pronoun "yonder," ʔaŋk ablative pronoun "from it, from there," changing translation of verb from "was running" to "came running"; wárikìwta essive of wari (k-class verb) "sing. subj. runs," the essive indicating continued states, not only states at rest, but some kinds of motion of a constant, uniform type. Reportive assertion is used here to denote that the living and running are simply reported as individual events. To render "the girl who *lives* . . .came. . .etc." the agentive verb would be nomic, qaté̜ŋʷèqa. Each verb is at the end of its clause, the the normal but not obligatory order. Let us consider now the change produced by pluralizing "girl" and "house."

§2. mamaNt ʔayé̜ʔ kí·kihèt ʔa̜ŋ yɛsqam ʔah yé‘tekiwyè̜ŋʷa. "The girls who lived in yonder houses came running." Every word in the sentence has been changed. From the Hopi standpoint what has happened is that a number of punctual situations have become tensive. MamaNt "girls," multiple plural of ma·na, being animate has suffix -t and contraction in addition to reduplication; yɛsqam, paucal suffix -m is used on agentives for general plural, here on agentive of yɛ·sɛ (contract verb) "plur. subjs. sit, dwell." "House" now being plural it cannot have case suffixes added directly and a postposition must be used for "in"; this is ʔa̜ŋ tensive locative, for location in more than one place is tensive, and is used with objective case in -t of kí·kihè multiple (inanimate) "houses"; ʔayé̜ʔ tensive locative of "yonder"; ʔah "from there" now partitive instead of ablative corresponding to a diffused or distributed removal; -yè̜ŋʷa the plural form of -ta₂, the verb being essive of yeʻte (k-class) "plur. subjs. run." The sentence does not mean that they came running from their houses, as the partitive is not on the "yonder" base.

§3. ta·qa wekónavnày repámnat pay tavíni pa·s ʔeté̜heʔmòqqà̜ʔɛ. "The man unbuttoned his coat and then began to take it off, because he felt so very hot": ta·qa "man" nom. sing.; wekónavnà "coat" a compound of weko adj. (stress-class) "big" and navna "shirt," with reaffirmative objective case suffix -y; repámnat sequential mode (-t) of causative voice (-na) of inner plural theme (-m-) of re‘pa (k-class) "separation, slipping apart occurs," hence "separates or parts at a number of points" i.e., "unbuttons," the reportive assertion indicating a particular event, the sequential that it was followed by action of the same subject indicated by the verb of the next clause, tavíni, expective of ta̜vi (stress verb), transitive, "moves location of singular object," used of one's garment for "takes off." Expective being in context of continued narration refers to moment prior to the event—"was about to" or "began to"; pay, tensor, punctual, but indicating a degree of intensity which manifests not quite immediately but with a slight lag or interval between action and the point of reference, in this case "and then." In the final clause the tensor pa·s, tensive, indicates a continuous, efficient, mild intensity that produces results gently and gradually, as it were by persistent gentle pressure. Often it is translated "soft," "gentle," "slowly" etc., here merely "very"; but it refers to the cumulative effect of the sun's warmth (the sentence is from a Hopi rendering of the story of the North Wind and the Sun). It must not be confused with pas, a tensor meaning "very" in a quite different sense. Finally we have correlative mode (pausal form) ˑqàˀɛ "because" of compound verb formed from ˀetéheˀè adj. (contract) "warm, hot" referring by itself to air temperature but when compounded with moˑki (contract verb) "die," "be wrapped up," "feel dominant sensation," meaning "feel hot."

§4. wíkpàŋʷat sosoMk panis repápatà "He was tying the rope but it was slipping": wíkpàŋʷa "rope," ˑt objective; soma (contract) trans. "ties it" > durative sósòMta (reduplication, contraction, and ˑta₁) in which form the ˑta may be omitted if there is a mode suffix as in the present case; transrelative mode ˑq (morphophonemic change to ˑk after consonant) meaning that the action (tying) is linked with the action of another subject (rope), viz. repápatà, segmentative of reˈpa (k-class) "separate, slip," meaning that a succession of little slips occurs (note deaspiration of primary ˈp as it is moved out of bounds by the stress-shift, as also in repámnat of the previous example); panis, tensor, tensive, meaning an intensity that is exerted persistently for a certain time though the outward effects (action) may be either continuous or interrupted. When its clause is linked to another clause without a distinct reference to later sequence, both clauses being tensive, panis refers to the same period of duration as the other clause, i.e., "while." Note that the "while" of the concursive mode is ruled out by the requirement of transrelative mode for different subjects, and panis takes its place, though panis could also be used in a concursive linkage. This "while" idea also sufficiently expresses the English "but" in this case, there being enough adversative contrast between the ideas of tying and slipping to make an adversative expression unnecessary. The sentence, not being impotential, implies that the tying will triumph over the slipping. If the impotential sign ˀas were before "tying" we could then read "but it persisted in slipping," for this sign would mean that the tying energy or skill was inadequate to cope with the situation, in this case with the slipping tendency. For "he tied it but it (immediately, pèˀ) slipped" we would have ˀas soMk pèˀ reˈpa.

§5. yowyaŋ löqóckit m␛ˀaq neˀ navótk ˀeme "Upon lightning striking the pine-tree I heard it thunder." Here the different Hopi and English adjustments to objective phenomena require wide differences in pattern and in phraseology. The difference is not merely stylistic, being grounded in the grammatical set-up of parts of speech. "Lightning" as an event, being a transitory event (V §3, VIII §4) cannot be a noun or ambivalent. The verb tálwiˈpi composed of taˑla (contract ambivalent) "light" and wiˈpi (k-class verb) "lashes once (like a whiplash)" denotes the occurrence of a lightning flash; the derived ambivalent tálwipìki denotes the outline of lightning as capable of being fixed, and hence a lightning-like design; neither are applicable here, if we are to refer to the blasting of the tree by making "tree" object of a transitive verb. Although eventives need not have a subject, transitives must, as in English. English patterns with "lightning" as an actor, acting upon the tree, but as we have seen, the Hopi "lightning" is a verb, and cannot be an actor. But yowyaŋ "rainstorm" denotes a long-enduring event, could be and is a noun, and can be a subject; it is here treated as the "real" or objective agent. From the Hopi viewpoint "rainstorm" is the common source or cause of all the varied phenomena experienced at such a time; lightning flashes, thunder, falling drops, blasting of trees, etc. If it is desired to speak only of the effect on the tree, the attendant flash need not be alluded to. The verb is a special use of mę̓a "deals it a swift penetrating action, stings, pins, nails, or shoots it." Löqǒcki "pine-tree," compound of löqö (stress-class) "pine" and -cǫki "-tree, -bush" (elision as per IV §3) occurring free as cǫki (k-class ambiv.) "(thing) perched up"; -t objective case. The name of a tree genus used without -coki tends somewhat to imply a piece of the wood. Verb in transrelative mode (-q) denoting dependent linkage with another subject, ne? "I." Verb of next clause is transrelative (-q, morphophonemic change to -k after consonant) of navǫ́ta (contract vb.) "sing. subj. hears it." Final verb is ?eme (k-class), eventive, "loud detonation, or 'boom' occurs," applied to thunder, explosions, guns, etc. whence the Toreva word for gun, ?emékpi (-pi noun of place or instrument, VIII §8). In this type of statement, "he hears that . . . ," and in indirect quotations, it is the verb of hearing, saying, etc., that is put in the dependent mode. This pattern might be rendered in the present instance as "by my hearing it thundered."

AN OUTLINE OF TAOS GRAMMAR

GEORGE L. TRAGER

1. INTRODUCTION

§1:1. *Location*. The Taos language is spoken by about eight hundred Indians constituting the population of Taos Pueblo, two miles north of the Spanish and American town of Taos (hereafter referred to as Taos Village) in northern New Mexico. There are at present no immediate Indian neighbors of the Taos, but there is evidence of various kinds that there were Indian settlements originally at Arroyo Hondo (twelve miles north), at a spot just east of the present Taos Village, and at Ranchos de Taos (six miles south), if not elsewhere.

§1:2. *Dialects and bilingualism*. It can be assumed that the extinct neighbors of Taos spoke dialects similar to that of the present pueblo. But the Taos language now presents no dialectic divisions, being spoken alike, so far as can be ascertained, by all the inhabitants. The oldest people, especially very old women, speak only Taos, but there are few such unilingual individuals; men and women of fifty or over speak Taos and Spanish; those between twenty and fifty years of age speak Taos, English and Spanish, the English improving as age decreases, and the Spanish correspondingly deteriorating; the children from school age (about five) to twenty speak Taos and English. Very young children speak only Taos, though in a few families English is used in the home.

§1:3. *Linguistic relationships*. Taos belongs to the Tiwa subfamily of the Tanoan family of the Azteco-Tanoan stock of languages. Its exact relations, and a brief sketch of historical phonology and morphology will be found in chapter six.

§1:4. *Bibliography*. Partial recordings of the Taos language have been made from time to time by various investigators, and there is some published material.

J. P. Harrington collected linguistic data at Taos in 1907 and 1908, and has a considerable body of text and other material in hand. He has published these papers: *Notes on the Piro Language;* about 180 Taos words are cited in comparison with other Tanoan languages, and the classification of the Tanoan languages into three subfamilies was first made; *An Introductory Paper on the Tiwa Language, Dialect of Taos, New Mexico;* a brief sketch of Taos phonetics and morphology is given, with a text and vocabulary; *Ambiguity in the Taos Personal Pronoun,* a survey of the pronominal prefixes. Several other publications of Harrington's dealing with Tewa or other linguistic and anthropological subjects contain references to or citations of Taos words.

Jaime de Angulo collected Taos material some years after Harrington. I have seen a copy of his manuscript, but have not used the material in my own studies.

I have published the following: *The Language of the Pueblo of Taos, New Mexico* (in phonetic transcription), with a discussion of Taos phonetics, phonetic and phonemic transcriptions of a text ("The Northwind and the Sun," translated from English for me), and a free interlinear translation; the material is now subject to correction in several respects, notably in the phonemic analysis of diphthongs, and in that tones are not noted; *The Days of the Week in the Language of Taos Pueblo, New Mexico*, a discussion of the Spanish loanwords for the weekday names; two Taos tales in text, with interlinear and free translation, as an Appendix to Elsie Clews Parsons' *Taos Tales;* also many Taos words (especially personal and proper names) in footnotes throughout the same volume; *The Comparative Phonology of the Tiwa Languages*, a study of the phonemic correspondences between Taos, Picurís, Sandía, and Isleta, based on a considerable number of common items of vocabulary; *The Kinship and Status Terms of the Tiwa Languages*, a presentation of all the terms of the four Tiwa languages as recorded by me, with phonological reconstruction to Proto-Tiwa, and discussion of meanings and other important points; *Spanish and English Loanwords in Taos*.

BIBLIOGRAPHY ON TAOS

HARRINGTON, J. P., *Ambiguity in the Taos Personal Pronoun* (In Holmes Anniversary Volume, pp. 142–156, Washington, 1916).

An Introductory Paper on the Tiwa Language, Dialect of Taos, New Mexico (American Anthropologist, n.s., vol. 12, pp. 11–48, Lancaster, Pa., 1910).

Notes on the Piro Language (American Anthropologist, n.s., vol. 11, pp. 563–594, Lancaster, Pa., 1909).

PARSONS, E. C., *Taos Tales* (Memoirs of the American Folklore Society, vol. 34, New York, 1940). (Appendix by G. L. Trager, pp. 173–181.)

TRAGER, G. L., *The Comparative Phonology of the Tiwa Languages* (Studies in Linguistics, vol. 1, no. 5, 10 pp., 1942).

The Days of the Week in the Language of Taos Pueblo, New Mexico (Language, vol. 15, pp. 51–55, Baltimore, 1939).

The Kinship and Status Terms of the Tiwa Languages (American Anthropologist, n.s., vol. 45, pp. 557–571, Menasha, Wis., 1943).

The Language of the Pueblo of Taos, New Mexico (in phonetic transcription) (Maître Phonétique, vol. 56, pp. 59–62, 1936).

Spanish and English Loanwords in Taos (International Journal of American Linguistics, vol. 10, pp. 144–158, Baltimore, 1944).

§1:5. *Sources and acknowledgments.* The material for the present Outline was collected partly during the year 1935–1936, while I was teaching in southern Colorado, by means of short trips to Taos periodically, and again during a six-weeks stay at Taos Village in the summer of 1937. The latter stay was made possible by a grant from the Department of Anthropology of Yale University, for whose generous assistance grateful acknowledgment is hereby made.

From November, 1935 to May, 1936, one informant, "A," was used. He was a good worker and knew what was wanted, but refused to continue, through fear of exposure, and another had to be found. This one, "B," proved highly intelligent and very much interested in the work as such; he was used again in 1937 for the whole period. The wives of these two men, especially of "A," also contributed occasional information. In 1937 a third informant, "C," was also used, on part time. A few other individuals supplied occasional words and phrases. Because of the prevailing social situation at the pueblo, the identity of the informants must be carefully guarded, and they will be referred to, when necessary, only by the letters; they were all young men of about thirty years of age. "A" supplied the initial vocabulary of about 600 words, several short texts (including the "The Northwind and Sun" version and text 1 of "Two Taos Tales"), and basic paradigmatic material. "B" checked and corrected, where necessary, all this material, furnished the bulk of the remaining vocabulary (the total being about 2500 items), and a considerable amount of text, with very extensive morphological material, and he recognized the tones and helped in recording them properly. "C" furnished over half of the 1937 texts, including text 2 of "Two Taos Texts," and some other material. To "A," "B," and "C," but especially to "B," and to their wives and families and friends, I extend my thanks for their kindness, interest, and hospitality, and renew my promise to keep their identities hidden so long as they wish it so.

To the memory of Professor Edward Sapir I pay homage, and recall gratefully his interest in my American and other linguistic work, his willingness to publish this Outline, and his sympathy and encouragement.

This sketch was written in 1937, and was revised (principally in the phonology) in 1939. Publication having been delayed, nothing more was done to it until the summer of 1944, when I gave it a final rereading, added some items of bibliography, changed some points of transcription, and made some other changes (chiefly stylistic). I have not been able to return to Taos since 1937, so there has been no new material for me to work on.

I must express my thanks to Cornelius Osgood for including this sketch in the present volume, which he rescued from oblivion by means of the Viking Fund.

§1:6. *Conventions of form.* In this work all Taos linguistic material—phonemes, stems, affixes, words—is in roman type. Translations are in quotation marks, as are words of languages other than Taos used as occasional examples. Phonetic transcriptions are in roman type, within square brackets, the symbols being those suggested or described by B. Bloch and myself in *Outline of Linguistic Analysis,*[1] these being in general the same as the symbols of the International Phonetic Association.

Chapters are numbered and subdivided decimally.

---

[1] B. Bloch and G. L. Trager, *Outline of Linguistic Analysis* (Linguistic Society of America, Baltimore, 1942), pp. 18–37.

2. PHONOLOGY

§2:1. *Definitions, orthography.* The phonology of a language is defined as in-cluding all the phenomena relevant to the production and use of its sounds. It can be subdivided into phonetics and phonemics, and morphophonemics can be treated with it. The phonetics of Taos will be considered within the framework of the phonemic description. Phonemics deals with the phonemes of a language as units of pattern in forming morphemes, without regard to the values of the mor-phemes. Morphophonemics is concerned with the relationship of the phonemes within the pattern of function possessed by the morphemes composed of them.

A phoneme is a class of sounds in a given language, such that it is different from all other similar classes, and serves as a unit of the structure of morphemes; the number of such classes is limited, all sounds used in the language are assignable to one of these classes, and each class may include one or several sounds (which may be called allophones). A morphophoneme is a class of phonemes formed by one or more phonemes functioning in a defined way to give value to a morpheme.

Phonemes constituting parts of syllables in succession are called segmental; in Taos and usually, they are the vowels and consonants. Phonemes applying to syllables as a whole are prosodic; in Taos and usually, they are the various accen-tual phenomena.

The following symbols will be used to write Taos (in alphabetical order): ?, a, ą, b, c, c', d, e, ę, ə, (f), g, h, i, į, k, k', k$_w$, k$_w$', l, ł, m, n, o, ǫ, p, p', pʿ, r, s, t, t', tʿ, u, ų, w, x, x$_w$, y; and with vowels these accents (illustrated with a): ˈa, ˌa, á, à. Punctuation: comma (,) and period (.). See §2:21–2:233 for the values of these symbols. In all my work on Taos previous to the article *Spanish and English Loan-words* (except in the footnotes to Parsons's *Taos Tales*) I used the symbol j for the palatal semivowel instead of y. But I have now decided to use y in all my Tiwa studies, and am making the change definitive here.

§2:2. *Phonemics.*

§2:21. *The sentence, the phrase, the word.*

§2:211. *Sentence and phrase types.* There are no phonemes of intonation ac-companying the sentence in Taos, but only a sentence-marker of intonation. That is, there are no contrasting types, and all sentences have the same intonation. The rise and fall of the voice is governed by the stress-tone combinations of the words, which remain essentially unchanged, and at the end there is a general falling-off—rather abrupt in character—with definite pause. The Taos sentence is not far dif-ferent in intonation from an ordinary English statement. Questions, exclamations, emphatic statements, all have the same intonations, and are distinguished from the declarative sentences, if at all, by special words or particles. The phonemic limita-tions of the beginning and end of a sentence are the same as those of a word (§2:22), and a single syllable may be a full sentence. The end of a sentence is marked by a period (as in the "Appendix" to *Taos Tales*).

Within a sentence of more than one syllable there may be distinguished pauses which correspond to definite syntactic divisions; these pauses are usually shorter than the sentence-final pause, and in every case the preceding syllables have no final falling intonation, but a level or suspended intonation, showing that more is coming. The parts of a sentence between its beginning and such a pause, between two such pauses, and between such a pause and a sentence-final pause, may be called phrases (initial phrase, medial phrase, final phrase); each phrase pause is marked by a comma (as in the "Appendix").

It should be emphasized that the use of any punctuation marks other than the period and comma in Taos would be unwarranted by the phonemic facts of the language as I now know them. It may be that instrumental recordings would indi-cate some variation of the two types of intonation described. But the real varia-tions from intonational monotony in Taos speech are due to the fixed stress and tone patterns, and are less numerous and extensive than the sentence-intonations of most European languages.

§2:212. *The word.* A Taos word must begin in a consonant; it may end in a vowel, or in one of the consonants which may check a syllable (§2:233), or in one of the rare syllable-final two-consonant clusters. It may consist of only one syl-lable, or of as many as eight or even more, though most words are of two, three, or four syllables, and the longer ones always consist of compounds of two or more stems, with various affixes. Each word, whether of one syllable or more, has one loud stress (§2:221); however, some monosyllables that are pronounced with loud stress in isolation may have this replaced by weak stress within the phrase or sentence; the exact conditions of this change have not been determined; these weak-stressed "words" will probably have to be written as enclitics (proclitics), with some symbol connecting them to the next word having a loud stress. Words of two or more syllables have one or more syllables with medial stress or weak stress, in any combination, to any number, and in any position relative to the loud stress, except that a loud stress is not followed by more than three other syllables (§2:223).

From these data it is clear that within a phrase or sentence there are as many words as there are loud stresses. If there is found a cluster of three consonants, there must be word-division between the second and third. But between two con-sonants or between a vowel and a following consonant (itself followed by a vowel), there need necessarily be only syllable division; this syllable division may also be word-division, but does not have to be such. That is, the exact point between two loud stresses at which word-division exists is not always determinable phonemi-cally by my present data. It seems certain however that a consideration of all the kinds of accent-combinations possible, and instrumental recordings of the values of all nonloud-stressed syllables (such as the finals with raised pitch, see §2:223) and of pauses between syllables, would make it possible to state in purely phonemic terms the limits of a word.

On a morphological basis, the minimum free form consisting of a stem, which may itself be a free form, and all its affixes and compounded stems, can be clearly defined. Each such morphological word is found to have one loud stress, and it seems highly probable that the limits determined morphologically would be found to coincide in large part with such phonemic limits as might be found by the procedure just suggested. Accordingly, in all cases other than those of isolated words, word-division has here been determined by morphological criteria when the available phonemic description does not suffice.

The material in the preceding three paragraphs would come under the heading of what I have come to call *juncture phonemes* since this was written. My notes and phonetic data show that Taos has some kind of internal open juncture within many of its longer words, but until the data can be restudied, and new material gathered in the field, the analysis as here given will have to stand.

§2:22. *Prosodic phonemes.*

§2:221. *Stress.* Stress is a phonemic feature of Taos, existing in the form of loud stress, medial stress, and weak stress. The first two may be combined with any one of the three tones. That stress as such is phonemic is indicated by the fact that no rules on a phonemic level can be devised determining the place of the stressed syllables in a word, and such rules as can be laid down for certain morphological combinations are either very complicated or show many exceptions. There are not many instances of words distinguished by the position of loud stress alone (that is, without accompanying tone differences), but there are some: ʔohˈu "*you sg. killed him*": ʔˈohu "*he is washing it,*" ʔạnʔˈo "*they two washed themselves*": ʔˈạnʔˌo "*they two washed him.*" Moreover, many nouns vary the stress patterns as between singular and plural absolute forms, and these changes are as important to correct apprehension of the forms as those in the suffixes. It will be shown in §2:232 how vowel length varies with stress.

Loud and medial stress are phonemically distinct, though there is some mechanical distribution of medial stress (as the "secondary" stress, the loud stress being primary) with normal tone, and a complete complementation of the two (from present evidence) in both the low and high tones (§2:223). Medial stress is found only where a loud stress is present, and only one loud stress is found in a phonemic word. The two are both distinct, of course, from weak-stressed ("unstressed") syllables.

Loud stress is a loudness of the syllable affected as compared with other syllables. Medial stress is a similar loudness, but less in degree. Weak stressed syllables are markedly less loud, and in ordinary speech are considerably slurred, with some obscuring of the clearness of the vowel: nasal vowels especially become rather indistinct under these conditions.

§2:222. *Tone.* There is a threefold distinction of tone in Taos loud- and medial-stressed syllables, the combinations of stress and tone being phonemically distinct. The tones are high, normal, low. The normal is by far the most common, low tone is fairly common in stems, and high tone is limited to a few stems and suffixes (all of these, however, being of frequent recurrence). There are many pairs of words distinguished by tone alone: cˡu̜ "*to pass by*": cù̜ "*to suck*," wˡ ę̨mą "*one*": wę̨mą "*it is real*." In weak-stressed syllables there is only one kind of tone, which is taken to be the normal, as such syllables are usually like normal loud-stressed syllables in pitch.

Normal tone is for the most part at the usual pitch level for an individual's speech, and is of course relative, differing from speaker to speaker. High tone is distinctly higher and sharper. Low tone is distinctly lower and drawling.

§2:223. *Accentual patterns.* The stress and tone types described constitute two separate accentual systems, which, combining in definite patterns, give rise to seven types of syllables (a syllable being further defined segmentally, §2:231). These are: loud normal—written ˡa, medial normal—ˌa, loud low—à, medial low— also à, loud high—á, medial high—also á, weak—unmarked (a). For high and low tones the loud and medial stresses are complementarily distributed, and it is therefore possible to use one symbol in each case and avoid unnecessary graphic complexity.

The stress system takes priority over the tone system, as is shown by the lack of tone distinctions with one of its types (weak stress), and by the fact that the word is definable in terms of the stress of syllables and not of their tone (§2:212).

In a word having a loud normal stress, all other syllables have medial or weak stress. If there is no loud normal, of two low-toned syllables the second is loud-stressed if it is not the last syllable, in which case the first is loud; the same rule holds for two high tones, or for a low and a high, in the absence of a loud normal.

Two-syllable words may have these patterns: tˡana, tˡanˌa, tˡaná, tàna, tànà, tàná, tána, táná—all with loud stress on the first syllable; and tanˡa, tˌanˡa, tànˡa, tánˡa, tˌanà, tˌaná, with loud stress on the second syllable. Three-syllable words may have loud stress on any one of the three syllables, with weak stress or medial stress on one or both of the others. The same holds for four-syllable words. Words of more than four syllables do not seem to have loud stress further back than the fourth syllable from the end. The syllable preceding loud stress may have a medial stress or a weak stress; if it is weak-stressed, then the syllable before it most often has medial stress, usually with normal tone. A third syllable before the loud stress may have medial stress, in which case the two syllables following it are usually both weak-stressed.

Normal loud stress has a rising pitch immediately before a high medial stress. Final weak-stressed syllables two syllables or more after the loud stress are slightly higher in pitch and more prominent than elsewhere, thus constituting a marker of the word final syllable. Final weak-stressed syllables after a low tone are rather higher than the low syllable and somewhat prominent.

§2:23. *Segmental phonemes.*

§2:231. *Structure of the syllable*. Each Taos syllable is delimited first by having one of the seven stress-tone combinations indicated in §2:223. It is further defined by the fact that it begins with a single consonant-phoneme, contains a single vowel or one of the permissible two-vowel clusters, and ends with the vowel or vowel-cluster or in a single consonant or one of the permissible two-consonant clusters. We have the following formulas (C—consonant, V—vowel, Vv—vowel cluster): CV, CVv, CVC, CVvC, CVCC, CVvCC. The first C may be any of the consonant phonemes; the final C may be any of the phonemes designated as sonorants; final CC may consist of a sonant plus a voiced stop (§2:233). V may be any of the eleven vowel phonemes, and Vv any of the five biphonemic clusters (§2:232). All these types of syllables may presumably exist with any stress-tone, and in any position in a word, except that syllables of the type CVCC or CVvCC are always word-final (§2:212); they are also very rare, and examples have not been found for all the stress-tones. It is also true that high tone is almost nonexistent in syllables not ending in a vowel, and that syllables with Vv are rare with weak stress.

In recent loans from Spanish and English, there may occur initial consonant clusters. These are very rare, however, and it seems best to treat them as foreign elements not completely assimilated to the native pattern; structurally they behave as units, but will be written with the symbols of the two Taos phonemes of which they seem to be composed. Those recorded are: pl, pr, tr, kl, kr, and fr (f not occurring otherwise).

§2:232. *Vowels*. There are eleven vowel phonemes in Taos: a, ą, e, ę, ə, i, į, o, ǫ, u, ų. They are all distinct, and may occur in direct contrast; the nasal vowels are units, as syllables of the types tan and tąn both occur.

The permissible vowel clusters are ie, ia, uo, əo, ię. They might be considered unit phonemes, as they are unisyllabic, and little if any longer than a single vowel under the same conditions; they differ from disyllabic vowel sequences, which have ʔ between them phonemically, and from combinations of y, w, plus vowel. But phonetically they clearly consist of two elements, which are identical with single vowels, and by considering the clusters as biphonemic we are able to describe more fully the functioning of the single vowel phonemes and classify them phonemically.

The cluster ie is rare, but sufficiently substantiated. In one Spanish loan word, pꞌueloną "*frying pan*" (informant "A") we find what is apparently a cluster ue, with close second element, [e]; this could be considered as an incompletely assimilated foreign element in the speech of a bilingual, especially as other Spanish loans have uo <ue, as in mꞐuoyaʔꞐana "*steer, ox*" <"*buey.*"

The phonemic functioning of the vowels is as follows: i, u may not occur in the same syllable with following homorganic semivowel (respectively y, w); e is very rare in stems, but frequent in suffixes, and is not found before w or y in the same morpheme; i combines in clusters with following e and a; o combines in clusters with preceding ə and u; į, ų are limited before y, w in the same way as i, u; only į and ę, in that order, may form a nasal-vowel cluster. The following groups can now be defined phonemically, using phonetic labels for convenience: oral—vowels that cluster with each other in symmetrical patterns; nasal—vowels that do not cluster in such patterns; front oral—vowels that cluster as high preceding either of the other two; back oral—vowels that cluster as low following either of the other two; high oral—vowels limited in position before homorganic semi-vowels; mid front oral—rare vowel, limited chiefly to suffixes; mid back oral—the back vowel which is like neither high nor low (by any preceding definition); low front oral—the front vowel that is like neither high nor mid; mid oral—vowels distinguished from the other two in their group (front, back) by partaking of the characteristics of one but not of the other; low oral—those vowels which are neither like high or mid in all their functions; high nasal—like high oral; front nasal—the only nasal vowels that may cluster; mid nasal—vowels that are not found before w in the same syllable, but are found before y; low nasal—the vowel that occurs before both y and w in the same syllable. By taking account of a regular morphophonemic reduplication where an oral vowel is reduplicated as itself, but a nasal is replaced by the corresponding oral (§2:33), we are able further to classify the nasals as: back—corresponding to two of the back oral; neutral—corresponding to a front oral, but not functioning like a front nasal. These relations give the following table:

	ORAL		NASAL		
	Front	Back	Front	Neutral	Back
High	i	u	į		ų
Mid	e	ə	ę		ǫ
Low	a	o		ą	

In each row and each column the phonemes have similar functions. This table, phonemically correct, is also exactly correct phonetically, as we shall now see.

All Taos vowels are long in free syllables when loud-stressed, and are rather short in weak-stressed syllables. Medial-stressed vowels are slightly shorter than loud-stressed ones. Vowels with normal tone and loud or medial stress are usually monophthongal longs, those with low tone are pulsated ('reduplicated') whether the stress is loud or quiet (thus tʼə̀tʼo "by the day" is [tʼˡə̀ə̀tʼa], and tʼə̀ˀləna "day" is [tʼˡə̀ə̀ˀlə·na]); vowels with medial stress and high tone are rather short, those with loud high accent are longer. There are differences in the length of loud-stressed vowels depending on the vowel of the following syllable, but it would lead into too much detail to go into them in a limited description such as the present one.

The exception to the length of loud-stressed vowels is when they are followed by a plain stop, especially p, t, k, when the stop is long and ambisyllabic and the vowel quite short.

In checked syllables the vowels are always short, but less so with the low tone than otherwise, and never as short as weak-stressed vowels.

The clusters are unisyllabic gliding vowels with phonetically clear initial and final elements and a very brief glide from one to the other. They are longer when loud- or medial-stressed than when weak-stressed, but since the length is distributed over two elements, it is not so noticeable as for single vowels; on the other, hand, in checked syllables they are very distinctly short.

The combinations of vowels with syllable-final w and y form phonetic diphthongs, in which the second element is not necessarily entirely nonsyllabic (see the individual vowels, below, for the details). These have been found: iw, aw, ow, əw, ay, oy, əy, uy, i̜w, a̜w, ey, a̧y, o̧y, u̧y. These sequences function just like those of vowel plus syllable-final l, m, n, b, d, g, and moreover are in morphophonemic (and sometimes free) variation with two-syllable sequences of vowel plus w or y plus vowel; this guarantees that our phonemic analysis is correct, and that the sequences are not vowel-clusters (diphthongs) phonemically.

All oral vowels are slightly nasalized before m and n, and all nasal vowels are less nasal than usual before m and n; this is especially true in weak-stressed syllables, and correct recording is often difficult.

i is high front close when loud- or medial-stressed, somewhat more open when weak-stressed; it is still more open in all checked syllables. With syllable-final w, we have [iu] in which the second element is never quite as prominent as the first, though there is not a very marked difference between them. Before intervocalic w, especially on the low tone, there is partial assimilation, so that the effect is as of [iᵘw]; this, however, is distinct from a possible -iww-.

e is mid front open (about as in English "*let*"), but slightly centered, giving a 'dull' quality. It has not been found after initial ʔ, but weak-stressed internally it is common in certain recurring morphemes.

a is low front, almost like English [æ], especially when loud-stressed (not common). Weak-stressed, it recurs in a number of morphemes. The fronted and raised quality is especially noticeable with high tone (as in -yá, future suffix). ay and aw are falling diphthongs, the first element being the same as it is elsewhere.

o is a low back vowel, typically unrounded and like the vowel of Eastern American English in such words as "*hot*." After w, and generally before and after labials, it may be slightly rounded. Before syllable-final m and n the vowel is centered, being much like American English *u* in "*hunt*," and very little different from Taos a̧ and o̧ in similar position. The vowel is extremely common; the writing with o is chosen because of the phonemic patterning of the vowel. In weak-stressed position it is hard for non-natives always to distinguish it from a. oy and ow are falling diphthongs, the latter having often a slightly rounded first element.

ə is a mid back close vowel, i.e., with tongue position of, say, French o in "*pot*," but entirely unrounded; it varies somewhat toward the central position, so that it is often like the vowel of New England r-less speech in "*bird*." Weak-stressed it is more like the second vowel of English "*sofa*." The vowel is quite common. The groups əy and əw are falling diphthongs, with mid-central first element.

u is a high back close rounded vowel when not weak-stressed; but the rounding is often more what might be called an inner rounding than one caused by the
kind of puckering of the lips found in European u-vowels, and occasionally in
rapid recording it was confused with ə and vice-versa. When weak-stressed the
vowel is rather open, as it is often also in checked syllables even when loud-stressed;
before l, m, n in free and checked syllables there is an effect of a very close over-
rounded [o]. uy is a falling diphthong, but the second element is rather prominent.

The nasal vowels are on the whole like the corresponding oral ones; į and ų
are high and close (more open when checked and when weak-stressed), ų being
well rounded; ę is lower and clearer than e, being like the a of English "cant,"
but more nasalized; ą is not at all fronted, but is not a definitely back vowel; ǫ is
very slightly rounded, and further back and higher than ą. Before syllable-final m
or n ą is about like English u in "hunt," and is very much like Taos o in similar
position and only slightly different from ą. The groups consisting of syllable-final w
and y after nasal vowels are phonetically diphthongs with both elements nasalized,
įw and ųy being almost even diphthongs as compared to the others, which are
definitely falling; ęy has a rather closer than ordinary first element.

The clusters ia and uo have the two elements relatively equal in weight in
checked loud- or medial-stressed syllables; in weak-stressed syllables, they are not
common, and the first element is more prominent; with low tone the first element
is more prominent, with high tone the second; in loud normal free syllables the
second element is somewhat more prominent than the first. The cluster ie follows
the same rules. In əo the first element is always more prominent, the second being
much like the vowel of American English "but." In uo the second element is not
more often rounded than is o elsewhere. The nasal cluster įę has the two elements
equally prominent when loud-stressed; weak-stressed, and generally in checked
syllables, especially with low tone, the second element is very short, and is raised
to about the position of English i in "hit."

As is seen, the phonetic element of rounding is consistently present only for u,
and cannot be used as a means of phonemic classification.

§2:233. *Consonants.* The Taos consonant phonemes are: ʔ, b, c, c', d, g, h,
k, k', kᵥ, kᵥ', l, ł, m, n, p, p', p', r, s, t, t', t', w, x, xᵥ, y. For all of them contrasting pairs of words can be cited so that there is no question of their phonemic dis-
tinctness. As for the possibility that some of them may not be units (as p', p'), it
would seem to be ruled out by the phonemic functioning of these entities.

By their phonetic characteristics (see below for details) these phonemes can
be grouped and labeled as follows:

By manner of articulation: plain stops and affricate (voiceless, fortis, unaspirated)—p, t, c, k, kᵥ; aspirated stops (voiceless, fortis)—p', t'; glottalized stops
and affricate (voiceless, lenis, with glottal occlusion)—p', t', c', k', kᵥ', ʔ; voiced
stops (voiced or voiceless according to position, lenis, nonglottalized)—b, d, g;

spirants (voiceless, fortis)—ł, s, x, x$_w$, h; nasals—m, n; liquids—l, r; semivowels—y, w.

By place of articulation: labials—p, p‘, p’, b, m; dentals—t, t‘, t’, d, n, ł, l; alveolars—c, c’, s, r; velars—k, k’, g, x, y; labialized velars—k$_w$, k$_w$’, x$_w$, w; glottals—ʔ, h.

For vowels it was seen that the phonetic and phonemic classifications coincided. This is not so for consonants, which is the reason for giving the expected, phonetically-based classifications first.

Phonemically we have these functions: a) appearing before a vowel only, that is, not at the end of a syllable—p, t, c, k, k$_w$, p‘, t‘, p’, t’, c’, k’, k$_w$’, ʔ, ł, s, x, x$_w$, h; b) before a vowel and also in syllable-final position—b, d, g, m, n, l, r, y, w. Group b), consisting of the consonants which phonetically are voiced at least in some positions, is subdivided first into y, w on the one hand, which do not appear as syllable-finals after a homorganic vowel, and m, n, l, r, b, d, g on the other; and second, into b, d, g, which may appear as syllable-finals not only after vowels but also after one of the other consonants in group b), and m, n, l, r, which may not so appear. From group a) may be separated k$_w$, k$_w$’, x$_w$, which do not appear before u or ų.

These are the only relations to be gotten from purely phonemic functioning. When we consider the morphophonemic interchanges (§2:34) we see, however, that we may set up these further groupings: p, t, c, k alternate respectively with p’, t’, c’, k’ (no evidence for an alternation k$_w$ ∼ k$_w$’); k, x alternate with ʔ, h; m alternates with p, w with k$_w$ and x$_w$, y with c. These are all stem-initial relationships. In the interior of stems, b, d alternate with p, t; y with c and k; m, n with p, t.

From all these possible relations and groupings, we set up the following table, the numbers being explained immediately below:

1	p‘		t‘		ł		s				
	11		12		13		14	15	16	17	
2											
3								x	x$_w$	h	3
4	p		t		c			k	k$_w$		4
5										ʔ	5
6	p‘		t’		c’			k’	k$_w$’		6
7											7
8	b		d					g			8
9	m		n								9
10							y	w			10
	11		12		13		14	15	16		
18			l		r						

Phonemic functional groups: 1, consonants not in any relation to any others, except that they are grouped above the line 7; 2, every consonant within this line is in some relation to one or more of the others; 3, in the relations x $\sim$ x$_w$ and h $\sim$ x, corresponding to k $\sim$ k$_w$ and ʔ $\sim$ k (4, 5); 4, in regular alternation with 6 (no evidence for k$_w$ $\sim$ k$_w$', but as the latter is very rare, this may be merely a statistical lack, and it seems safe to assimilate the pair to the phonetically parallel pairs); 5, in alternation with k, thus like a member of 6, but otherwise joined with h in 17; 6, the reciprocal group to 4; 7, all consonants above this line occur syllable-initially only, while those below (the sonorants) may be both initial and final; 8, voiced stops, may be second in two-consonant final clusters; 9, in alternation with those members of 4 in the same columns; 10, not syllable-final after homorganic vowels; 9 and 10 are the 'sonants'; 11, in the alternations p $\sim$ p', p $\sim$ b, p $\sim$ m; 12, in the alternations t $\sim$ t', t $\sim$ d, t $\sim$ n; 13, in the alternation c $\sim$ c'; 14, in the alternations c $\sim$ y, k $\sim$ y; 15, in the alternations k $\sim$ k', and x $\sim$ x$_w$, k $\sim$ k$_w$ (and k' $\sim$ k$_w$'?); 16, not before u (except w?), where replaced by the members of 15 in the same row, and in the alternations x$_w$ $\sim$ w and k$_w$ $\sim$ w (and k$_w$ $\sim$ k$_w$'?); 17, in the parallel alternations h $\sim$ x and ʔ $\sim$ k; 18, not in any relation to any others, except that they are grouped below the line 7.

All the entities with double articulation—p', t', p', t', c', k', k$_w$', c, k$_w$, x$_w$ function as units in all these relationships and seem clearly definable as unit phonemes.

The foreign clusters pl, pr, tr, kl, kr, fr (f appears only in clusters, for elsewhere Spanish or English f are replaced by p'), when fully assimilated, will create a group l, r characterized not only negatively (18), but positively as phonemes that appear as second elements of initial clusters, will separate p, t, k from the other consonants in group 4 as a subgroup that appears first in two-consonant initial clusters, and will alter the definition of the syllable. But the clusters are so rare and out of the general pattern, that they are best considered as not parts of the system.

Some phonetic details may now be given. The phonemes of group 1 are fortis and voiceless; p', t' are strongly aspirated (almost [p^x], [t^x]), and ł, s have the normal amount of friction. In group 3, x and x$_w$ are almost frictionless, while h has strong friction; acoustically x and h are much alike because of this reversal of the more usual relations in respect to amount of friction. Group 4 consists of relatively fortis stops, initially sometimes slightly aspirated (except k$_w$, which has partially voiced labial release). The phoneme marked 5 is a very weak glottal stop or hiatus, and goes phonetically with group 6. In group 6 we have sounds made with lenis closures in both the glottal and other positions, and nonforceful releases, the glottal release following the other one at an appreciable interval. There is none of the snapping or crackling effect found in the glottalized phonemes of some other languages ("explosive glottalized"), and often, especially between vowels, the effect is that of a nonglottalized voiceless lenis ("intermediate"). The phonemes of group 8 are fully voiced lenis stops between vowels, are less voiced initially, where they appear only in recent loan words, and are voiceless lenis, with long closure, and nonreleased, in syllable-final position. The phonemes of groups 9, 10, 18 are always fully voiced.

Group 11, and p', are made with firm lip-closure, but p' with a few speakers has the free variants [pɸ] or [ɸ]. Group 12, and t', ł, l, are dentialveolar—not as far forward as Spanish t, d, l, n, but further forward than the usual English ones; t' is never [tθ] or [θ]; l is nonfricative, 'neutral' (with [ə]-timbre) between vowels, and 'dark' (u-timbre) in syllable-final. Group 13 are alveolar affricates: c is usually [č], but there is much free variation to [ts$_y$] or [ts], and some speakers consistently use less palatal varieties before e, o than before other vowels; c' is lenis [č'] before the high vowels, and lenis [ts'] elsewhere. The isolated phoneme s goes with these two phonetically, often having a slight effect of [š], especially before i; in rapid speech between vowels it may be slightly lenis; r goes here phonetically, too, being an alveolar single tap, like Spanish short r, whether in English or Spanish loans. The single member of 14 is a nonfricative semivowel before vowels, like English [y]; syllable-final after a vowel it is a nonsyllabic high front vowel (§2:232). The phonemes of 15 are in mid-velar position, with little variation due to following vowels, except slight fronting before i; x is nonfricative and nonrasping (like New Mexican Spanish [x], spelled j). In group 16 we have mid-velar sounds with accompanying labialization: w is a fully rounded nonspirantal semivowel before vowels, and a nonsyllabic high back vowel in syllable final (§2:232); x$_w$ is Taos x plus gradually voiced labialization; k$_w$ has gradually voiced labialization following the midpalatal release; k$_w$' has entirely voiceless labialization, with delabializing simultaneous with the glottal release, and is very lenis with even weaker than usual glottalization. The phonemes of 17 are glottal, h being rather fricative, as stated; ʔ is usually zero initially, but in emphatic speech before a loud-stressed vowel a real glottal stop is heard; between vowels it is a weak glottal stop or hiatus, and after a syllable-final consonant it is like the glottal part of a glottalized stop; but while -at' a is syllabified [a-t'a], -ad ʔa is [ad-ʔa].

The phonetics of syllables not beginning with any phoneme other than ʔ is such that ʔ must be postulated every time; in this way we can clearly account for the phonetic distinctions between [a-na] and [an-a], [a-wa] and [aṷ-a], [ia] and [i-a], and for the fact that phonetic [a-] becomes [(ʔ)a] on addition to a prefix, as [na̧-ʔa].

§2:3. *Morphophonemics.* Under this heading will be listed and described all the alternations between phonemes of a regular nature found to exist in related morphemes. These may be automatic, taking place in all morphemes under similar phonemic conditions, and determined by the phonemic set-up of the language, or conditioned (ablaut), appearing only in certain morphemes or morpheme classes. There are few morphophonemic changes of either kind in Taos, but the latter kind especially are found in some common stems, and are of historical interest.

§2:31. *Sandhi.* There are two types of sandhi in Taos, internal and external.

Internal sandhi takes place between the parts of a word (minimum free form), external sandhi between words.

There are these cases of special internal sandhi: a) The loud stress of a stem
becomes a medial stress when subordinated to another stem in compounding
(§2:32). b) The final vowels of certain kinds of syllables are elided on the addition of suffixes or compounded elements (§2:33); two such vowel elisions may take
place, to form the permitted two-consonant final clusters. c) The suffixes -yá and
-ya (§3:33) combine with such vowel-losing syllables, after loss of the vowel, by
assimilation of y to preceding l, m, n, and by loss of y after b, d; after -a, -yá and
-ya give -ʔá and -ʔa (§2:34). Otherwise, there are no changes in morphemes in
combination.

External sandhi involves no change in words except that a final vowel (usually -a̧, occasionally -u, the cases being the same as those with vowel-loss in internal sandhi) may be lost, so that statistically there are many words with final
consonants in connected speech, these words having one syllable less than normally.
Occasionally the elision seems to be accompanied by accentual change. But there
is considerable free variation in this phenomenon, and a more exact statement is not
now possible. It may be that the elided forms are found in more rapid utterances.

§2:32. *Accentual morphophonemics.* Functioning accentual changes are found
whenever in composition or suffixation a loud stress comes before another loud
stress which takes precedence, so that the first becomes medial; or when a low
tone is final in a word, following another low, in which case the last becomes weak-
stressed (verb forms only). There are also the regular changes in position of the
loud stress as between the singular and plural absolute forms of nouns, especially
in the nouns with stem-vowel reduplication; these changes are taken up in detail
in §3:21.

In inflected forms the stem usually has the loud stress; in compounds the last
stem has the loud stress, the others being medial or weak; but if the last stem is a
verb, it is often weak-stressed. In inflection, changes in stress from stem to suffix
take place before some suffixes; to list them all would be beyond the scope of this
work.

Nonfunctioning changes are found in a few of the ablauting verbs: normal
to low (symbol â) in pʼⁱuy "*he blew*" (intrans.) ∼ pʼùci "*he blew*" (trans.); high loud
to normal medial (symbol ₁á) in tʼó "*he did, danced*" ∼ t₁oʔⁱone "*dance*" (noun), and
tʼę́ "*he cut*" ∼ t₁ęʔⁱene "*act of cutting*"; low loud plus weak to low medial plus normal loud (symbol à⁺) in mà̧pʼǝw "*he squeezed*" ∼ mà̧pⁱǝwma̧ "*it was squeezed*,"
mà̧tʼema̧ "*he hit*" ∼ mà̧tⁱemma "*it was hit*," ʔùpʼuo "*he dropped*" ∼ kùpʼⁱuone "*act
of dropping.*" There is also low to normal (symbol à) in tʼ ò "*he found*" ∼ tʼⁱone "*act
of finding.*" And there are probably others.

§2:33. *Vowel morphophonemics.* Functioning vowel ablaut is found in the
absolute forms of nouns with reduplicating stem vowel, if the vowel is nasal, in
which case the reduplicated vowel is the corresponding nonnasal; or if the stem

has a vowel cluster, in which case the reduplicated vowel is the second of the cluster (i̧ȩ becomes e). See §3:21 for further details.

In internal sandhi stems of two syllables whose second syllable consists of one of the sonorants plus a vowel, usually a̧, lose this vowel on the addition of certain suffixes beginning with a consonant, or in composition with following stems (kᵈlolą "he ate" ∼ kᵈlolhu "he is eating"); this brings about the syllables ending in a consonant. When an apocopated form of this kind enters into combination with the syllable ₋gą (and possibly others beginning with b and d), a second apocopation may take place, giving two-consonant finals, as hᵈiʔąngą "why, because," alternating with hᵈiʔąng. The apocopation of a final vowel can only take place after sonorants, and in the case of double apocopation, the second takes place only after voiced stops. In external sandhi these vowel losses are optional, but in internal sandhi they are regular and automatic.

Nonfunctioning vowel ablaut is found principally in the second vowel of disyllabic verb stems. The most common is ₋ą ∼ i (symbol ąⁱ), for which twenty-nine examples have been found, all in very common words, and to which may be added twelve cases of final consonant (presumably from consonant plus final elidable vowel) alternating with consonant plus i, as indicated in §2:34. The change is from the preterit to the negative preterit, and is found in all the verbs described below that show a consonant change in these forms, and in others: cᵈȩlą "he caught" ∼ wòcᵈȩli "he didn't catch"; kᵈlolą "he ate" ∼ wòk'loli; kʷᵈilą "he shut" ∼ wòkʷᵈili. Other changes are: ₋ą ∼ a (symbol ąᵃ) in p'ₔodą "he lost" ∼ stative p'ₔoda; ₋ą ∼ u̧ (ąᵘ̧) in ʔᵈȩlą "it shook" ∼ ʔᵈȩlu̧ "he shook it"; ₋ȩ ∼ ą (ȩᵃ) in p'ᵈalunȩ "it was burning" ∼ p'ᵈaluną "it was being burned"; ₋i ∼ a (iᵃ) in łᵈəpi ∼ łᵈəba; ₋ǫ ∼ i (ǫⁱ) in xᵈəwǫ "he picked" ∼ wòxᵈəwi, and in two other verbs.

Alternations in the first or only stem vowel are: ə ∼ uo ∼ u (symbol əᵘ⁽ᵒ⁾) in xʷᵈəy ∼ wòxᵈuoki ∼ xᵈuyma; ə ∼ əo (əᵒ) in kə̀wǫ "he swallowed" ∼ wòkə̀owi, and in two other cases; ia ∼ iw (iaⁱʷ) in mo-wᵈia "he gave" ∼ mo-wòwiw; i̧ ∼ i (i̧ⁱ) in wᵈi̧nȩ "he stopped" ∼ stative kʷᵈinemą; uo ∼ u-yą (uoᵘ) in kᵈluo "he put" ∼ wòk'uy, and two other verbs.

§2:34. *Consonant morphophonemics.* Automatic consonant changes are those resulting from the limitation on the appearance of k_w, x_w (and probably k_w') before u, so that k, x (and k') replace them when a vowel ablaut changes the stem vowel to u.' Certain internal losses of ₋y after vowel ablaut resulting in a cluster (as uy >uo) are also probably automatic, as the clusters seem not to be followed by y in stems.

Functioning, but not automatic, are the changes of ₋yá (future suffix) and ₋ya (pronominal suffix in certain third person subject-object combinations): these replace y by l, m, n, after ₋l, ₋m, ₋n, by ʔ after ₋a, and drop it after ₋b and ₋d.

There are two types of consonant ablaut in verbs, neither now functioning. The first affects initial consonants of the stem, the second the internal consonant (in originally disyllabic stems). The words undergoing these alternations are common, so that ablaut recurs frequently.

Initial consonant ablaut takes place in a number of verbs having p·, t·, c·, k·, ?·, h·, m·, w·, y· in the third singular (subject of gender I or III) preterit active form, which is the basic stem of the verb (appearing without prefixes or suffixes). These initials change in the third singular resultative stative, the basic stative stem (usually without prefixes, but often with a suffix), as follows: p·>p·, t·>t·, c·>c·, k·>k·, ?·>k·, h·>x·, m·>p·, w·>k_w·, w·>x_w·, y·>c·. In a few cases there is no stative, but the verbal noun, which is regularly based on the stative stem, shows the ablaut. Examples are (each of the changes is substantiated by from two to seven examples): p'ᵊodą "he lost it" ∼ pᴵᵊoda "it is lost"; t'ᴵ ạmą "he helped him" ∼ tᴵ ammą "he was helped"; t'ó "he danced" ∼ t₁o?ᴵone "dance"; c'ᴵi "he tied it" ∼ cᴵi "it is tied"; k'ᴵolą "he ate it" ∼ kᴵolla "it was eaten"; ?ᴵ ạmą "he did, caused to . . ." ∼ kᴵ ạmmą "it is done" (and in the numerous "causatives" formed with ?ᴵ ạmą as second element); hᴵoy "he took it" ∼ xᴵoymą "it has been taken"; mọ̀ "he brought it" ∼ ną-pọ̀mą "it has been brought"; wᴵoną "he arrived" ∼ kʷₗonᴵene "arrival"; wᴵᵊyą "he took it off" ∼ xʷᴵᵊymą "it has been taken off"; yᴵia "he walked" ∼ c₁ia?ᴵane "a walk." In a few cases, the verb is a compound, or has a prefix, so that the changes appear internally: mą̀p'ᵊw "he squeezed" ∼ mą̀pᴵᵊwmą "it has been squeezed"; t'ᴵahọne "he won" ∼ t'₁axᴵọnemą "it is won." The formula used to indicate these initial changes is ° after the symbol (with the mark of glottalization omitted): p°, t°, c°, k°, ?°, h°, m°, w° for w ∼ x_w, wᵏ for w ∼ k_w.

Internal ablaut affects the second consonant of the basic stem, which changes in the third singular negative preterit (the basic negative and subordinate form). The pairs are: ·b· ∼ ·p·, ·d· ∼ ·t·, ·y· ∼ ·c·, ·y· ∼ ·k·, ·m· ∼ ·p·, ·n· ∼ ·t·, ·zero ∼ ·w·, ·zero ∼ ·y·. In addition there are the cases of preterit in final vowel, and negative preterit with added ·ki, ·li, ·mi, ·pi, ·ti; these look like the ·zero ∼ ·w·, ·zero ∼ ·y· cases, i.e., they may represent an original consonant plus facultatively lost ·ą alternating with ablauted consonant +·i, and are best considered as cases of ablaut rather than of suffixing. Some of the changes are represented so far by only one example, but ·zero ∼ ·mi has sixteen, and others two or more; examples are (wǒ· negative prefix): ? įȩsiabą "he kicked" ∼ wǒ?įȩsiapi "he didn't kick"; p'ᴵᵊodą "he lost" ∼ wǒp'ᴵᵊoti "he didn't lose"; hᴵọy "he said yes, accepted" ∼ wǒhᴵọci; łᴵoy "he sat down" ∼ wǒłᴵoki; mą̀'emą "he hit" ∼ wǒmą̀t'ᴵepi; xʷᴵọną "he beat" ∼ wǒxʷᴵọti; t'ᴵᵊ "he broke" ∼ wǒt'ᴵᵊw; ?u·kᴵo "he planted it" ∼ ?uwǒkᴵowi; pᴵa "he made" ∼ wǒpᴵayi; t'ᴵᵊo "he gathered" ∼ wǒt'ᴵᵊoki; ?ᴵo "he washed" ∼ wǒ?ᴵoli; mụ̀ "he saw" ∼ wǒmụ̀mi; ?ᴵucu "he met" ∼ wǒ?ᴵucumi; p'ᴵᵊo "he caught" ∼ wǒp'ᴵᵊomi; mo·łᴵo "he urinated" ∼ mowǒłᴵopi; mo·cᴵia "he talked" ∼ mowǒcᴵiati. The same type of ablaut, but functioning differently, is found in: łᴵiabą "it broke" ∼ łᴵiapi "he broke it"; c'ᴵᵊodą "he entered" ∼ c'ᴵᵊoti "he brought it in"; p'ᴵuy "he blew" p'ᴵùci "he blew upon . . . " Then we have also: łᴵiaba ∼ łᴵiapi ∼ łᴵiabmą "it is cracked, broken"; and łᴵᵊpi "he stuck it on" ∼ łᴵᵊba" it has been stuck on." These changes are indicated in listing stems by b°, d°, y° (y ∼ c), yᵏ (y ∼ k), m°, n°, ·ʷ, ·ʸ, and +ki, +mi, +pi, +ti.

3. MORPHOLOGY

§3:1. *General*. The morphology of Taos proceeds by combinations of morphemes, and is of two kinds, inflection and word-formation. Inflection consists of paradigmatic changes without change of morpheme class, while word-formation involves change of morpheme class or of basic meaning within the same class.

§3:11. *Morphological processes*. Taos employs the processes of affixation (prefixation, suffixation), stem-compounding, internal (morphophonemic) change, reduplication, and suppletion.

Prefixation is used to express categories (see §3:2 for definitions) of pronominal reference, status, and resolution. Suffixation is used for number, gender, dependence, tense-aspect, mode, voice. Stem-compounding is used for the expression of referential dependence. Internal change appears once to have functioned in expressing voice and status. Reduplication expresses, with suffixes, number and absolute dependence. Suppletion is found in a few cases of verbal number.

§3:12. *Morpheme classes*. The basic division of morphemes in Taos is into dependent and nondependent. Dependent morphemes are the affixes, which, in combination with the nondependent ones, and in sets of greater or less extent, form the paradigms of the language; they never occur by themselves as words, and have no lexical content, being grammatical modulators only. Nondependent morphemes are all others: they may exist as such, or with various affixes, and are divided into classes on the basis of the paradigmatic sets that they are inflected by, or of the lack of inflection. Inflected classes are substantives and verbs; particles are noninflected.

Substantives are divided into nouns, which have full inflection, numerals and demonstratives, with less inflection and different syntax, and nominals, with still less inflection.

Verbs are inflected for different categories and with, on the whole, different paradigmatic sets from nouns. There are some stems which function as both nouns and verbs, but generally a stem is either one or the other, and the affixes always indicate clearly which it is.

Particles are divided into free particles—personal and some other pronouns, and adverbial expressions; and attached particles—the nonparadigmatic suffixes and prefixes.

§3:13. *Morphological categories*. The categories expressed in a language are determined by the paradigmatic sets which are found. The following classification is based entirely on such formal criteria, and function has been considered only in the selection of terms. In the discussion in §3:2 and 3:3 certain functional classifications are used for convenience, but it is clearly shown how they pattern formally.

Categories may be overt or covert. Overt categories are clearly indicated by morphemes in all forms of the paradigm, while covert categories can be recognized only by congruential patterns that appear under certain conditions. Most Taos categories are overt; the covert ones will be indicated.

§3:131. *Number and gender.* Number in Taos is of two kinds: dichotomous and trichotomous. Dichotomous number distinguishes singular from nonsingular (more than one, two+ plural) and is expressed, in combination with gender, by suffixes of nouns and demonstratives. It is also part of the complex category of pronominal reference. In a few verbs dichotomous number is expressed by suppletion, depending on the number of the object of the verb. Trichotomous number distinguishes singular, dual, and three+ plural, and is part of pronominal reference.

There are three genders, designated as I, II, III. Gender I is almost entirely composed of animate nouns, while II and III are both inanimate; there is no way to define these two semantically, as both include the same kinds of words. Gender is expressed, in combination with dichotomous number, by suffixes of nouns and demonstratives, and also as part of pronominal reference.

Place-gender, designated as IIIn, is a subdivision of III; it is a covert category, recognizable only by the special prefixes of pronominal reference applying to these nouns.

§3:132. *Pronominal reference.* This complex category involves the expression of number, gender, and person by means of unit prefixes, and applies to nouns and verbs. There are sets of prefixes expressing person (first, second, third), trichotomous number, and, for the third person, gender, and varying with the dichotomous number and gender of the referent. In nouns the prefixes refer to the possessor and vary with the noun, so that this is a category of possession. In verbs the prefixes refer to the subject and vary with the object.

A special subdivision is reflexive pronominal reference, where the subject is identified with the object, or the possessor is emphatically identified.

§3:133. *Dependence.* This is a category of substantives; absolute dependence is characterized by gender-number suffixes (except for nominals), and expresses the subject and indirect object of a verb; vocative dependence is characterized by the absence of suffixes, and exists only for nouns of gender I used in direct address; referential dependence is characterized by compounding of the noun-stem with verbs and particles, expressing the object of the verb or the referent of the particle.

§3:134. *Status.* This is a category of verbs, and is expressed by prefixes, including zero. Normal status, characterized by zero prefix, expresses an ordinary statement of fact. Negative status expresses negation by a prefix before the stem (or compounded object) and following (occasionally contracting with) the prefixes of pronominal reference; some verbs ablaut the second stem-consonant in the negative status. Narrative status is used in tales and the like for the actor or hero, and is expressed by a prefix following those of pronominal reference and preceding the negative one. Definite status emphasizes the reality of a future or of a temporal subordinate action; its suffix follows the negative one and precedes the stem or compounded object.

The prefixes of the comparative and interrogative statuses precede those of pronominal reference, the interrogative coming first. The comparative expresses greater degree of an "adjectival" notion or greater quantity of a nominal notion: the prefix may also be compounded with the verb, in which case it comes immediately before it, and can no longer be regarded as a paradigmatic prefix. Interrogative status is expressed by the special prefixes only when no interrogative pronoun is present.

§3:135. *Tense and aspect.* These categories of temporal location (tense) and extension (aspect) occur only in certain combinations with each other, and are expressed by suffixes. Present is present-durative, with the aspectual notion more prominent than that of time. Past is durative and nonpresent and nonfuture. Preterit, expressed in the active by zero suffix, is momentary or resultative, with usually definite past connotation. Impending is a durative-inceptive future. Future is a momentary future. The term resultative is used for the stative tense-aspect corresponding to the active preterit.

§3:136. *Mode.* This category indicates objectivity or subjectivity as regards the action on the part of the speaker. It is indicative (zero-suffix), or subordinate; the latter is divided into relative, conditional, temporal, expressed by suffixes; the subordinate employs the negative stem when this is ablauted from the basic stem.

§3:137. *Voice.* This category defines the manner in which the object is affected by the verb. Active voice, expressed by zero suffix, indicates that the object is acted upon by an actor. Stative voice indicates the resulting state or condition of the object as affected by the action of the verb expressed without designating an actor. Stative voice is divided into essive ("passives" of active verbs, "intransitives"), descriptive ("adjectives"), and intensive (special form of "adjectives").

§3:138. *Transitivity.* All Taos verbs are "transitives" in the English sense, but have a partially covert category of transitivity delimiting whether the action may be expressed both with and without an actor, or only without one. Unipersonal transitivity indicates action without an expressed actor, and such verbs can have only an "impersonal" third person singular subject; they correspond to English "intransitives," and have stative voice only: thus, ʔowámą "*I am*" is really "*there performs a being upon me,*" cf. ʔomų̀ya "*he sees me,*" ʔo- in both cases meaning third singular subject plus first singular object. Multipersonal transitivity expresses the actor and such verbs can have "personal" subjects of all three persons; they correspond to "transitives," and have active voice and also (person-limited) stative voice (equal to "passive"). The transitivity of a verb can sometimes be recognized only by the kind of pronominal reference it takes, though most unipersonal verbs have a stative voice suffix identifying them.

§3:139. *Resolution.* This category is entirely covert, and can be deduced only from the pronominal reference of a verb. It is direct or possessive. Direct resolution permits a verb to resolve to a direct object unpossessed. Possessive resolution limits the verb to possessed objects; only unipersonal verbs are found in possessive resolution. Thus: ʔomų̀ya "*he sees me,*" ʔowámą "*I am,*" but ʔąnwámą "*I have it,*" literally "*there performs a being on something of mine*" (ʔąn- "*my*"). Multipersonal verbs may express a possessed object, except when the subject is third person singular, only in absolute or subordinate form: timụ̀hu ʔąnkˡana "*I see my mother*," literally "*I-her-see my-mother*," as compared with tikˌamụ̀hi "*I see the mother*." See chapter 4.

§3:2. *Substantives.* Of the substantives only nouns are inflected for gender, number, pronominal reference, and dependence; demonstratives are not inflected for dependence and not regularly for pronominal reference; some numerals show gender distinctions, but are not otherwise inflected; nominals are restricted to one type of use. Noun inflection will be described, and then the special restrictions of other substantives will be indicated.

§3:21. *Declension.* Nouns are identifiable as to gender and number by the singular and nonsingular absolute forms, which pair into "declensions" on the basis of the manner in which the suffixes are attached to the stem, and of the accentual patterns.

The suffixes for gender I are singular -na, nonsingular -ną and -nemą. Those for gender II are -ną and -nemą in the singular, and -ne in the nonsingular. For gender III (and IIIn) we have singular -na, nonsingular -ne, and indeclinable abstracts and verbal nouns in -ne. The declensions are 1) -na ~ -ną, 2) -na ~ -nemą, 3) -ną ~ -ne, 4) -nemą ~ -ne, 5) -na ~ -ne, 6) -ne. The suffixes may be attached directly to the stem, or by means of a reduplication of the stem vowel: a single oral vowel is reduplicated as such immediately after itself, with intervening ʔ, and nasal vowels and clusters change as stated in §2:33, the ablaut form being separated from the preceding unablauted form by ʔ; thus, kₒʔˡone "*washing*" <ko-, pₒʔˡone "*earth*" <pǫ-, ʔìaʔˡane "*corn*" <ʔìa-; reduplication takes place only in stems ending in a vowel.

The declensions can be subdivided by accentual pattern; in the following table, the hyphen (-) indicates a syllable, ˡ- ˌ- ᷄ ᷅ being the kinds of loud- or weak-stressed syllables (possibility of two kinds of stress thus, ˡ᷅); ʔR is the reduplicated stem vowel. One or more syllables, loud- or medial-stressed, or weak-stressed, may precede the accentual pattern shown. The subdivisions of each declension are designated by letters, the same letter indicating a similar accentual pattern; the first letter refers to the singular, the second to the plural (declension six has no distinction): a) one loud-stressed syllable before the suffix; b) one medial-stressed, one loud-stressed; c) one medial, one weak, one loud; d) two syllables before the suffix, the first loud-stressed; e) one medial, one loud, one weak; f) the third syllable before the suffix loud-stressed; g) one medial-stressed, with the loud stress on the reduplication, before the suffix; h) medial two syllables before the reduplication; i) medial three syllables before the reduplication.

Singular	Nonsingular	Examples
Declension 1, gender I.		
1aa. ˡ-na	ˡ-ną	cˌupˡana "*judge*," cˌupˡaną

1bd. ꞁˊ˴na   ꞁˏ˴ną   kₗayꞁuna "*mother's sister*," kꞁayuną
1ce. ꞁˊˏ˴na   ꞁˊꞁˏ˴ną   cₗibikꞁina "*robin*," cₗibꞁikiną
1cf. ꞁ˄˴na   ꞁ˄ˏ˴ną   tùculꞁona "*humming bird*," tùculoną
1db. ꞁˊ˴na   ꞁˊꞁ˴ną   pꞁloyona "*beaver*," pꞁₗoyꞁoną
1dd. ꞁ˴na   ꞁˏ˴ną   mꞁakuna "*grandchild*," mꞁakuną
1ff. ꞁˏ˴na   ꞁˏ˴ną   nꞁabahuna "*Navaho*," nꞁabahuną
1gd. ꞁˊˀꞁRna   ꞁˏ˴ną   kₗowˀù?ꞁuna "*colt*," kꞁowˀuną
1hd. ꞁˏˀꞁRna   ꞁˏ˴ną   cₗiwyuˀꞁuna "*bird*," cꞁiwyuną
1if. ꞁˏˏˀꞁRna   ꞁˏˏ˴ną   cₗiliyoˀꞁona "*bat*," cꞁiliyoną

Declension 2, gender I.

2aa. ꞁ˖na   ꞁ˖nemą   kꞁana "*mother*," kꞁanemą
2bb. ꞁ˄ꞁ˴na   ꞁˊꞁ˴nemą   lìwꞁena "*woman*," lìwꞁenemą
2bd. ꞁ˄ꞁ˴na   ꞁ˄˴nemą   kₗolꞁena "*wolf*," kꞁolenemą
2db. ꞁˏ˴na   ꞁˊꞁ˴nemą   cꞁiwena "*eagle*," cₗiwꞁenemą
2dd. ꞁˏ˴na   ꞁˏ˴nemą   kᵥꞁlianena "*bitch*," kᵥꞁlianenemą
2gg. ꞁ˄ˀꞁRna   ꞁ˄ˀꞁRnemą   ?ù?ꞁuna "*son*," ?ù?ꞁunemą
2hh. ꞁˏˀꞁRna   ꞁˏˀꞁRnemą   łₗułiˀꞁina "*old man*," łₗułiˀꞁinemą

Declension 3, gender II.

3aa. ꞁ˴ną   ꞁ˴ne   łₗowatꞁuną "*chief's cane*," ꞏtꞁune
3bb. ꞁ˄ꞁ˴ną   ꞁ˄ꞁ˴ne   cₗiatꞁuną "*legging*," cₗiatꞁune
3db. ꞁ˄˴ną   ꞁ˄ꞁ˴ne   ?ₗiałoną "*willow*," ?ₗiałꞁone
3dd. ꞁˏ˴ną   ꞁ˴ne   tꞁlawaną "*wheel*," tꞁlawane
3dh. ꞁˏ˴ną   ꞁˏˀꞁRne   hꞁₗoluną "*lung*," hₗₒluˀꞁune
3fc. ꞁˏˏ˴ną   ꞁˊꞁ˴ne   hꞁₗułoliną "*weapon*," hₗₗułolꞁine
3fi. ꞁˏˏ˴ną   ꞁˏˏˀꞁRne   yꞁₗuwolaną "*skirt*," yₗuwolaˀꞁane

Declension 4, gender II.

4aa. ꞁˏ˴nemą   ꞁˏ˴ne   cꞁinemą "*eye*," cꞁine
4bd. ꞁˊꞁ˴nemą   ꞁˏ˴ne   piakₗənꞁenemą "*chest, heart*," piakꞁənene
4dd. ꞁˏ˴nemą   ꞁˏ˴ne   pꞁlianenemą "*mountain*," pꞁlianene
4gg. ꞁˏˀꞁRnemą   ꞁˏˀꞁRne   yₗo?ꞁonemą "*song*," yₗo?ꞁone

Declension 5, gender III.

5aa. ꞁˏ˴na   ꞁˏ˴ne   kᵥꞁlona "*ax*," kᵥꞁlone
5bb. ꞁˊꞁ˴na   ꞁˊꞁ˴ne   pꞁₗo?ꞁlina "*peach*," pꞁₗo?ꞁline
5bd. ꞁˊꞁ˴na   ꞁˏ˴ne   kᵥꞁₗemꞁlyna "*carpenter's apron*," kᵥꞁₗemyną
5cc. ꞁˊꞁˏ˴na   ꞁˏꞁˏ˴ne   pₗululꞁluna "*plum*," pₗululꞁlune
5ce. ꞁˊꞁˏ˴na   ꞁˊꞁˏ˴ne   cₗapienꞁlena "*yeast*," cₗapꞁlienene
5db. ꞁ˄˴na   ꞁ˄ꞁ˴ne   ?ɔbena "*cherry*," ?ɔbꞁlene
5dd. ꞁˏ˴na   ꞁˏ˴ne   cꞁlunena "*deerhide strip*," cꞁlunene
5gg. ꞁ˄ˀꞁRna   ꞁ˄ˀꞁRne   pₗįe?ꞁlena "*bed*," pₗįe?ꞁlene
5hb. ꞁˏˀꞁRna   ꞁˊꞁ˴ne   cₗiakǫ?ꞁlona "*question*," cₗiakꞁlǫne
5hh. ꞁˏˀꞁRna   ꞁˏˀꞁRne   kᵥꞁₗɛxₗoci?ꞁlina "*bracelet*," ꞏxₗoci?ꞁline
5if. ꞁˏˏˀꞁRna   ꞁˏˏ˴ne   mₗɛsotu?ꞁluna "*church*," mꞁɛsotune (variant; usually mₗɛsotu?ꞁlune, 5ii)
5ii. ꞁˏˏˀꞁRna   ꞁˏˏˀꞁRne   cꞁₗowowo?ꞁlona "*ankle*," cꞁₗowowo?ꞁlone

Declension 6, gender III (pl. form = sg. or collective)

6a.   ꞁˏ˴ne   cꞁlone "*liver*"

6d. lᵕne   h⌐ɔolene "*sickness*"
6g. ⌐ˀlRne   c⌐iˀline "*knot*"
6h. ⌐ᵕˀlRne   m⌐uoliˀline "*return*"

Some of these combinations are rare (sometimes only one example), but most
are frequent. There are also nouns occurring only in the singular (or in the nonsingular) which fit half of these patterns. Finally, there may be other combinations
than those listed, fitting into the same framework of patterns.

§3:211. *Stem forms.* The forms given in the preceding section are absolute
forms. The vocative and referential dependences are expressed by the stem form,
which is usually that part of the word before the suffix. The reduplicated vowel,
if there is one, is not part of the stem; and in many cases an -e- preceding the
suffix, if part of the syllables -be-, -de-, -le-, -me-, -ne-, -we-, is a connecting suffix
and not part of the stem, thus: pòblenemą "*flower*," stem pòb-; ˀòdlenemą "*chin,
jaw*," stem ˀòd-; n⌐ąllenemą "*aspen*," n⌐ąl-; kʷlianena "*bitch*," kʷ⌐ian- (but c'ùnlena
"*coyote*," c'ùnle as vocative and proper name); łìwlena "*woman*," łìw-.

Henceforth nouns will be given with a hyphen after the stem, and a formula
designating the gender and declension, thus: tǫm-lena I.2bb "*father*," which means
that the word for "*father*" has the stem tǫm-, is of gender I, and has a plural
tǫmlenemą.

§3:22. *Possession.* The possessed noun is expressed by prefixes of pronominal
reference, falling into three sets according to the gender of the noun. Expression
of possession by the prefix and the absolute form of the noun is, however, found
only in some cases, especially of direct address. More usual is an expression consisting of prefix, stem, and what at first appears to be a suffix: this turns out to be
the relative subordinate mode of the verb wá "*to be*," so that one really says "*the
one who is my friend*" (or, most literally, "*there takes place a being upon one who is
my friend*"). There is also another "suffix of possession" which has not so far been
identified with any verb stem. For convenience of reference, the following full inflections of possessed nouns will be given in the verb-phrase form with wá.

Gender I. pluy-ena I.2db "*friend*":

Person, No. of Possessor.		Singular Possessed Noun.	Nonsingular Noun.
Singular	1	ˀąnp⌐uywáˀi "*my friend*"	ˀąnąmp⌐uywáˀiną "*my friends*"
	2	kąp⌐uywáˀi "*your friend*"	kąmp⌐uywáˀiną "*your friends*"
	3	ˀąp⌐uywáˀi "*his friend*"	ˀąmp⌐uywáˀiną "*his friends*"
Dual	1	kąnp⌐uywáˀi "*friend of us two*"	kąnąmp⌐uywáˀiną "*friends of us two*"
	2	mąnp⌐uywáˀi "*friend of you two*"	mąnąmp⌐uywáˀiną "*friends of you two*"
	3	ˀąnp⌐uywáˀi "*friend of them two*"	ˀąnąmp⌐uywáˀiną "*friends of them two*"

Plural 1 kip₁uywá ʔi "*friend of us three*⁺"   kimp₁uywá ʔiną "*friends of us three*⁺"
        2 mąp₁uywá ʔi "*friend of you three*⁺"   mąmp₁uywá ʔiną "*friends of you three*⁺"
        3 ʔip₁uywá ʔi "*friend of them three*⁺"   ʔimp₁uywá ʔiną "*friends of them three*⁺"

Gender II. kə̀d⌐ˡenemą II.4aa "*door*":
Singular noun: ʔąnąmkə̀dwá ʔiną "*my door*," kąm⌐, ʔąm⌐; kąnąm⌐; mąnąm⌐, ʔąnąm⌐; kim⌐, mąm⌐, ʔim⌐. Plural noun: ʔąnąwkə̀dwá ʔi "*my doors*," kąw⌐, ʔąw⌐; kąnąw⌐, mąnąw⌐, ʔąnąw; kiw⌐, mąw⌐, ʔiw⌐.
Gender III. kʷˡo⌐na III.5aa "*ax*":
Singular noun: ʔąnkʷ₁owá ʔi "*my ax*," ką⌐, ʔą⌐; kąn⌐, mąn⌐, ʔąn⌐; ki⌐, mą⌐, ʔi⌐.
Plural noun: ʔąnąwkʷ₁owá ʔi "*my axes*," kąw⌐, ʔąw⌐; kąnąw⌐, mąnąw⌐, ʔąnąw⌐; kiw⌐, mąw⌐, ʔiw⌐.

In addition to the above inflections, we have the special forms for place-gender nouns. There is no way to identify these nouns except by this special manner of pronominal reference; for the most part they involve a meaning or connotation of place (see §5:125). Their pronominal reference makes no distinction between singular and nonsingular noun; an example is t'ˡəna IIIn.5aa "*house*":

ʔąnnąt'₁əwá ʔi "*my house, my houses*," kąną⌐, ʔąną⌐; kąnną⌐, mąnną⌐, ʔąnną⌐; kiną⌐, mąną⌐, ʔiną⌐.

Reflexive pronominal reference is expressed by the same sets of prefixes as above, with ⌐mo⌐ after them (but before ⌐ną⌐): ʔąnmop₁uywá ʔi "*my own friend*," ʔąnmoną t'₁əwá ʔi "*my own house*."

To sum up, there are these sets of 'possessive prefixes':

A1—ʔąn⌐, ką⌐, ʔą⌐, kąn⌐, mąn⌐, ʔąn⌐, ki⌐, mą⌐, ʔi⌐, used with singular nouns of genders I and III, the accompanying 'suffix' being ⌐wá ʔi.
A2—ʔąnąm⌐, kąm⌐, ʔąm⌐, kąnąm⌐, mąnąm⌐, ʔąnąm⌐, kim⌐, mąm⌐, ʔim⌐, used with singulars of gender II and nonsingulars of I, with 'suffix' ⌐wá ʔiną.
A3—ʔąnąw⌐, kąw⌐, ʔąw⌐, kąnąw⌐, mąnąw⌐, ʔąnąw⌐, kiw⌐, mąw⌐, ʔiw⌐, used with non-singulars of genders II and III, with 'suffix' ⌐wá ʔi.
A1n—ʔąnną⌐, etc., used with singulars and nonsingulars of IIIn (place-gender) nouns, with 'suffix' ⌐wá ʔi.
A11, A12, A13, A11n—ʔąnmo⌐, etc., ʔąnąmmo⌐, etc., ʔąnąwmo⌐, etc., ʔąnmoną⌐, etc., used as A1, A2, A3, A1n respectively, for reflexive possession.

It may be noted that the various sets are similar and built up of more or less recognizably identical material; this historical insight cannot be further pursued here.

The other 'suffixes' of possession referred to are ⌐k'ˡoyi and ⌐k'oyiną (corresponding to ⌐wá ʔi and ⌐wá ʔiną), as in ʔąn ʔùk'ˡoyi "*my son*"; the example is from a tale, and the rarity of the form otherwise suggests that it is archaic.

§3:23. *Numerals, demonstratives, nominals.* Substantives other than nouns show deviations from the general pattern in some ways. A few of the numerals distinguish gender: wˡęmą "*one*" I, wˡibą II and III; pˡoyuo "*three*" and pʼˡąnyuo "*five*" add -ną for gender I. Apparently numerals are not used in pronominal reference or in dependence, but only in apposition with nouns, so that one says wˡiʔiną ʔąnnątʼ ˌɘwámą "*I have two houses*," literally, "*two I have houses*"; wˡęmą tisˡęonmų "*I saw one man*," literally, "*one I saw a man*"; etc.

Demonstratives show gender and number as do nouns, but, like numerals, are used in appositional constructions, and are not inflected for pronominal reference or dependence (except with attached particles): yˡųna I and III sg., yˡųnemą I pl. and II sg., yˡųne II and III pl., "*this*"; yˡęna, yˡęnemą, yˡęne "*that*" (less remote); wˡoti, wˡonemą, wˡone "*that*" (more remote). The ending of wˡoti is paralleled by that of yˡiati, which means "*that, that yonder*," but for which no other forms were obtained.

Nominals are forms that come close to being adjectives in the Indo-European sense. They exist only as complements of the verb *to be* (or possibly some other "intransitive" verbs), and show the pronominal reference of the noun object to which they refer, but never occur in the absolute form. Thus, "*he is naked*" is kˌipidąwámą, and kˡipidą is given as the translation for "*naked*"; the verbal phrase is then literally "*there takes place a being upon a naked one*." The number of such nominals is not great.

§3:3. *Verbs.* Verbs are conjugated by sets of prefixes (corresponding to the possessive sets for nouns), indicating their pronominal reference. All the categories of a verb take the same set of prefixes under the same conditions, so that the basic stems and the prefix set (or sets), depending on the complement of the verb, are all that is needed to supply any necessary form. The prefix sets will be presented first, then the basic stems, then the paradigmatic suffixes.

§3:31. *Subject-object conjugation.* The prefixes indicating subject and object fall into three main sets of nine forms each, not all different, which will be designated as B1, B2, B3, corresponding to A1, A2, A3. They are shown here with a verb in its basic form, the preterit, the same verb being used for all three: cˡową "*to taste, try, measure*":

B1. Object of verb a singular noun of genders I or III (including nouns of declension 6 in -ne), subjects as indicated:

Person	Singular Subject	Dual Subject	Plural Subject
1	ticˡową "*I tasted it*"	ʔąncˡową	ʔicˡową
2	ʔocˡową	mąncˡową	mącˡową
3	cˡową (zero prefix)	ʔąncˡową	ʔicˡową

B2. Object a singular noun of gender II or a nonsingular noun of gender I:

1	picˡową	ʔąpęncˡową	ʔipicˡową

| 2 | ?ic'ˡową | mąpęnc'ˡowa | mąpic'ˡową |
| 3 | ?ic'ˡową | ?ąpęnc'ˡową | ?ipic'ˡową |

B3. Object a nonsingular noun of genders II or III:

1	?oc'ˡową	kąnc'ˡową	kiwc'ˡową
2	kuc'ˡową	mąnc'ˡową	mąwc'ˡową
3	?uc'ˡową	?ąnc'ˡową	?iwc'ˡową

These forms are much like the possessive prefixes, especially set B3, where the dual and plural are the same as in A3.

The set used when the object is of place-gender is B1n: tiną⸍, ?oną⸍, ną⸍; ?ąnną⸍, mąnną⸍, ?ąnną⸍; ?iną⸍, mąną⸍, ?iną⸍.

When the object is other than third person, we have the following forms, constituting set C1:

			Oʙᴊᴇᴄᴛ			
Subject	Sing. 1st	Sing. 2d	Dual 1st	Dual 2d	Plural 1st	Plural 2d
Sg., Du., Pl. 1	——	?ą⸍	——	mąpęn⸍	——	mąpi⸍
2	may⸍	——	may⸍	——	may⸍	——
3	?o⸍	?ą⸍	?ąn⸍	mąn⸍	?i⸍	mą⸍

When the verb is active, and the subject is ('personal') third person, there is also a suffix ⸍ya, immediately following the stem: omų̀ya "*he saw me*"; this suffix be-comes ⸍la, ⸍ma, ⸍na after stem-final ⸍l, ⸍m, ⸍n; after the future suffix ⸍yá it becomes ⸍?a: ?omų̀yá "*he saw me*," ?omų̀yá "*you 1 will see him*," ?omų̀yá?a "*he will see me*."

From set C1 and the third person subject forms of sets B1, B2, B3 is con-structed the following set ('B4') of 'subject' prefixes for 'intransitive' verbs (i.e., the unipersonal stative verbs, and the stative ['passive'] forms of multipersonal verbs), illustrated with c'ę́mamą "*to be new, young*":

Person	Singular	Dual	Plural
1	?oc'ę́mamą	?ąnc'ę́mamą	?ic'ę́mamą
	"*I am young*"	"*we 2 are young*"	"*we 3+ are young*"
2	?ąc'ę́mamą	mąnc'ę́mamą	mąc'ę́mamą
	"*you 1 are young*"	"*you 2 are young*"	"*you 3+ are young*"
3 I	c'ę́mamą	?ąnc'ę́mamą	?icę́mamą
	"*he is young*"	"*they 2 are young*"	"*they 3+ are young*"
3 II	?ic'ę́mamą	?ąpęnc'ę́mamą	?ipic'ę́mamą
	"*it is young*"	"*they 2 are young*"	"*they 3+ are young*"
3 III	?uc'ę́mamą	?ąnc'ę́mamą	?iwc'ę́mamą
	"*it is young*"	"*they 2 are young*"	"*they 3+ are young*"

As has been indicated, the apparent subject is really the complement of a verb with 'impersonal' third person subject.

When the subject and object are the same, we have a set of reflexive prefixes;

certain verbs are always reflexive, and take these prefixes even when they have a noun object. The set, C11, is illustrated with ?ˈlíęlų "*to run*":

	Singular	Dual	Plural
1	tą?ˈlíęlų "*I ran*"	kąn?ˈlíęlų "*we 2 ran*"	kimą?ˈlíęlų "*we 3+ ran*"
2	?ą?ˈlíęlų "*you 1 ran*"	mąn?ˈlíęlų "*you 2 ran*"	mąmą?ˈlíęlų "*you 3+ ran*"
3	mo?ˈlíęlų "*he ran*"	?ąn?ˈlíęlų "*they 2 ran*"	?imą?ˈlíęlų "*they 3+ ran*"

The dual is like B3; in the plural there is free variation between the forms given and kimoˑ, mąmoˑ, ?imoˑ (by analogy with the third singular?).

§3:311. *Two objects.* When two objects are involved, one "direct," the other "indirect," we get on the whole forms that are identical with those for one object. With the "direct" object third person singular of any gender, the following forms have been found (set D1):

INDIRECT OBJECT (GENDER I)

Subject	Singular			Dual			Plural		
	1	2	3	1	2	3	1	2	3
Sing. 1	tąˑ	kąˑ	tąˑ	?	mąpęnˑ	piˑ	?	mąpimˑ	?ipimˑ
2	mąmˑ	?ąˑ	?ąˑ	mayˑ	mąpęnˑ	?iˑ	mayˑ	?	mąpimˑ
3	?oˑya	?ąˑya	ˑya	?ąnˑya	mąnˑya	?ąnˑya	?iˑya	mąˑya	?iˑya
Dual 1	?	?ąˑ	?ąnˑ	kąnˑ	mąpęnˑ	?ąpęnˑ	?	mąpiˑ	?ipiˑ
2	mayˑ	?	mąnˑ	mayˑ	mąnˑ	mąpęnˑ	mayˑ	?	mapiˑ
3	?oˑya	?ąˑya	ˑya	?	?	?ąnˑ, ?	?ąnˑya	mąnˑya	?
Plural 1	?	?ąˑ	?iˑ	?	?ipiˑ	?ipiˑ	?imąˑ	mąpiˑ	?ipi
2	mayˑ	?	mąˑ	mayˑ	?	mąpiˑ	mayˑ	?	mąpiˑ
3	?oˑya	?ąˑya	ˑya	?ąnˑya	mąnˑya	?ąnˑya	?iˑya	mąˑya	?imąˑ, ?iˑya

It is seen that when subject and indirect object are of the same person the reflexive forms are used (C11). With a third person subject, and an indirect object which is not reflexive, there is consistently the suffix ˑya (here referring to the direct object), and the prefixes are of set 'B4,' i.e., third person subject and first, second, third person object forms. With second person subject, the forms are on the whole those of set C1. With first person subject, the forms are those of sets B1 and B2. There are two forms, mąpimˑ, ipimˑ, not found elsewhere, and there are in the texts other forms which do not quite agree with the above table. Without a more thorough examination of all the collected text material, and consideration of all the possibilities (variation of gender of one or both objects, etc.), it is not possible to give a clearer picture of the two-object situation. This must be left to a future fuller discussion.

§3:32. *Verb-stems.* In order to be able to conjugate most Taos verbs it is only necessary to have the third singular preterit, which is the basic stem, and to know the pronominal-reference prefixes. But for the ablauting verbs it is necessary also to know the negative stem and the stative stem. The negative stem is used for the negative preterit, and also for some relative and temporal subordinate mode forms. The stative stem is used for all "passive" forms and to form the verbal noun. The negative stem might perhaps better be called the "unreal."

The ablaut changes found have been detailed in §2:34. A verb like p'ɩədą̇ "to lose" may be indicated according to the symbols provided there by the following morphophonemic orthography: p°ɩəd°ą̇ ⁱ, where ° after the initial means "glottalization disappears in the stative stem," ° after the medial consonant means "voiced becomes voiceless in the negative stem," and the raised vowel after ą means "final ą becomes i in the negative stem"; that is, we have active p'ɩədą̇, stative pɩəda, negative wòp'ɩəoti. Verbs like mų̇ "to see" are listed as m°ų̇⁺mi (mų̇, pų̇, wòmų̇mi); stem vowel changes are shown in the listing by raised vowels; stative suffixes other than -mą are shown after the stem, separated from it by /, thus hɩu/tá "to kill."

§3:33. *Suffixes.* The preterit tense-aspect has zero suffix regularly. But in the negative status some verbs have a suffix -puo in the preterit, and some of the ablauting verbs have -mi, -ti, etc.: ʔiwɩǫ "the wind blew," ʔiwòwɩǫpuo "the wind did not blow" (wɩǫ "to blow" [of wind], cf. wɩǫnemą II "wind"). I have not as yet analyzed any special meaning attached to -puo or the other suffixes; there is a verb-stem pɩuo "to disappear," so that -puo may not be a suffix.

The present is expressed by the suffix -hu in the affirmative, by -mę in the negative.

The past is expressed by -męʔaną in both affirmative and negative.

The future suffix in the affirmative is -yá; this becomes -lá, -má, -ná after -l, -m, -n of a stem; it becomes -ʔá after -a; it combines with -bą, -dą to give -bá, -dá: k'ɩollá future of k'ɩolą "to eat," p'ɩədá future of p'ɩədą "to lose." The negative future suffix is -pu.

The impending suffix is -hę. The impending is rare in the negative.

The subordinate modes have these suffixes: conditional past -ną, to the negative preterit stem; conditional future, -ʔaną, added to the future; temporal future -xu, to the negative stem; temporal resultative -gą, to the negative stem; temporal past -męgą (and -męxu), to the basic stem; relative present -ʔi added to the appropriate stem (-ʔiną if the subject is II singular or I plural); relative past -męʔi, to the appropriate stem; relative future, -męyáʔi or -mępɩuʔi to the basic stem.

Negative status is expressed by wò- (which combines with preceding -ną- into -nò-); narrative status by wi- (which may combine with preceding -ą- to give -ǫy-); definite status (future only, indicative or subordinate) by -su-; comparative status by ɫıǫy-; interrogative status by po- for an ordinary question and xu- when doubt is implied.

The preterit active has as its equivalent in the stative a resultative, characterized by -mą in the affirmative, but by zero suffix in the negative. Some verbs however have other "passive" suffixes, such as -tá (hʰutá "*he was killed*"). The present stative is not common in the essive, but has the suffix -hu when found. The past (durative) in the stative has -ʔ̜a̜n̜a̜ added directly to the stem. The impending has -he̜, and the future -yá and -pu as in the active.

Descriptive statives have the special present -pʼ ʰihu, but otherwise are like essives. Intensives have -pʰiwhu in the present. The descriptives of color have -wi instead of -pʼ ʰihu.

Verbal nouns, which are used with postpositions to supply 'participial' and 'infinitive' functions, are formed in -ne (III, no distinction of number) from the stative stem.

The verb tʼ ʰa̜o "*to gather, harvest*" may serve to illustrate the suffixes; it is given in the third singular, subject I or III:

	Affirmative	Negative
Active indicative:		
Present	tʼ ʰa̜ohu "*he is gathering it*"	wòtʼ ʰa̜ome̜
Preterit	tʼ ʰa̜o "*he gathered it*"	wòtʼ ʰa̜oki
Past	tʼ ʰa̜omʰe̜ʔa̜n̜a̜ "*he was gathering it*"	wòtʼ ʰa̜omʰe̜ʔa̜n̜a̜
Future	tʼ ʰa̜oyá "*he will gather it*"	wòtʼ ʰa̜opu
Impending	tʼ ʰa̜ohe̜ "*he is about to gather it*"	wòtʼ ʰa̜ohe̜
Active relative:		
Present	tʼ ʰa̜oʔi "*he who gathers it*"	
Past	tʼ ʰa̜ome̜ʔi "*he who was gathering it*"	
Future	tʼ ʰa̜omʰe̜yáʔi "*he who will gather it*"	
Active conditional:		
Past	tʼ ʰa̜okina̜ "*if he gathered it*"	
Future	tʼ ʰa̜oyáʔa̜n̜a̜ "*if he will gather it*"	
Active temporal:		
Future	tʼ ʰa̜okixu "*when he gathers it*"	
Past	tʼ ʰa̜ome̜ga̜ "*when he gathered it*"	
Resultative	tʼ ʰa̜okiga̜ "*when he has gathered it*"	
Stative indicative:		
Present	tʼ ʰa̜ohu "*it is being gathered*"	wòtʼ ʰa̜ohu
Resultative	tʼ ʰa̜oma̜ "*it has been, is gathered*"	wòtʼ ʰa̜o
Past	tʼ ʰa̜oʔa̜n̜a̜ "*it was being gathered*"	wòtʼ ʰa̜oʔa̜n̜a̜
Future	tʼ ʰa̜otáʔá "*it will be gathered*"	wòtʼ ʰa̜otápu
Impending	tʼ ʰa̜otáhe̜ "*it is about to be gathered*"	

(The -tá of the stative future and impending is an irregularity compared with the other forms, but some verbs have it throughout the stative.)

Examples of other statuses are: definite (future) tisutʼ ʰa̜oyá "*I will certainly gather it,*" negative definite tiwòsutʼ ʰa̜opu; narrative (tù̜ "*to say*") cʼùnʰe witù̜hu "*Coyote said (it is said)*"; comparative (kʷʰiawʰalma̜ "*to be strong*") ɫ̜o̜ykʷʰiawᵢalmą "*he was stronger*"; interrogative (mų̀ "*to see*") posᶫɔonmų "*did he see the man?,*" xuˀąmų̀yá "*may I see you?*" (future).

§3:4. *Particles.* The free particles are: personal pronouns: ną "*I, we,*" ˀę́ "*you,*" ˀᶫąwąn(ą) "*he, she, it, they*"; interrogative pronouns: pᶫļ̨ "*who,*" hᶫili "*what*"; and "adverbs," such as hᶫuki "*whether,*" hą "*yes,*" hᶫuoną "*then,*" yᶫuhi "*perhaps,*" and the like. The "adverbs" are numerous.

Attached particles are equivalent in meaning to Indo-European prepositions and adverbs of location, such as ₋tˀo "*in,*" ₋pidą "*back to,*" ₋kiną "*in*" (of time); they are usually added to the stems of nouns: tˀə̀tˀo "*by the day*" (tˀə̀ˀɘna), tˀᶫətˀo "*in the house*" (tˀᶫɘna), pìlkiną "*during the summer*" (pìlᶫena); but ₋mki, ₋tˀoti are added to absolute forms of gender I nouns: sᶫɘonenamki "*for the man,*" sᵢɘonenatˀᶫoti "*from the man*" (but tˀᶫətˀoti "*from the house*").

§3:5. *Word-formation.* Formation of new words in Taos takes place by means of derivation and compounding.

By derivation are obtained verbal nouns and agent nouns: tᶫo stative stem of tˀó "*to dance*" gives tᵢoˀᶫone "*dancing, dance*" and tᵢoˀᶫona "*dancer*" (pl. tᵢoˀᶫonemą); yᵢo₋tˀó "*to sing*" gives yᵢoˀᶫonemą "*song,*" yᵢoˀᶫona "*singer.*" Every verb apparently may give rise to a verbal noun which is an abstract or collective in ₋ne, or a concrete in ₋nemą, and active verbs have agent nouns in ₋na.

Derivatives are also made from particles by adding the noun suffixes: pᵢuoboˀᶫona "*person next in rank*" <pᶫuobo "*near.*"

The stem formatives ₋be₋, ₋de₋, ₋le₋, ₋we₋, ₋e₋ come under the present heading, but an examination of them would take too long and involves too much historical speculation for the present sketch. For the same reason some apparent verb-forming suffixes like ₋tá, ₋puo must be passed over.

Most commonly, new words are formed by compounding. Two or more noun stems may be joined together to give the desired result, the modifying element coming first: kʷᵢiawᵢi₋pᶫļ̨ęna III.5aa "*racetrack*" <kʷᵢiawᶫi₋ne "*race*" and pᶫļ̨ęna "*road*"; kᶫᵢuoˀù₋ˀᶫuna I.1hd "*lamb*" <kˀᶫuo₋na "*sheep*" and ˀùˀᶫuna "*son, off-spring.*" In such compounds the gender is that of the second element; but some-times we have derivation added to compounding, so that a different gender results (where, for instance, the compound is not animate, though the second element is a noun of gender I, or vice versa). Compounds of noun and particle, with noun suffix, are illustrated by pᵢanątˀᶫona III.5aa "*underwear*" <pᶫane "*clothing*" and nątˀᶫo "*underneath.*" In compounds of noun plus verb the verb is always the second element, even though it is the modifier: tˀᵢoy₋ɬo₋na I.1bd "*giant*" <tˀᶫoyna "*person*" and ɬo "*to be big*" (in compounds only). Many free particles are stereotyped com-pounds of noun plus attached particle or of two particles: pᶫiano "*in the middle, among*" <pᶫia₋na "*heart,*" ₋no "*in,*" Compounds of two verbs are frequent: cᶫɘmę́ "*to go hunting*" <cᶫɘ "*to hunt*" + mę́ "*to go.*"

Proper names are for the most part compounds. Many are compounds of one or two stems followed by -ʔù (from ʔùʔ|una) giving a diminutive or affectionate connotation: pòbʔù "*flower-little*," t|opˈ|ayʔù "*dance-red-little*" ="*Red dancer*"; others are two noun stems: ʔə̇ɫ|i "*leaf-grass*"; combinations of noun and verb stems are also found.

4. SYNTAX

In this chapter will be very briefly given the principal statements of the constructions into which the various morphological categories enter. No detail can be attempted within the scope of the present work.

§4:1. *Substantives.* The absolute form of a noun is used as the subject of a verb and as the second of two objects (usually the "indirect" object). It is also found as the direct object of the verb in the plural, when the emphasis is upon the plurality of the noun. When the object is a possessed noun and the subject is not third singular, it must be expressed by the possessed absolute form or by the possessive verb-phrase.

The stem form of a noun is used alone as the vocative. All proper names are therefore in the stem form, even when used in other than vocative function.

The stem form is compounded in referential dependence with the verb when the noun is the object (this includes the "subject" of an "intransitive" verb, i.e., the object of a unipersonal verb). The referential form is also used with attached particles.

The pronominal reference of a noun is always strictly dependent on its gender, and also on its number, with the exception that some nouns of genders II and III are always either singular or nonsingular in pronominal reference as objects of verbs regardless of the fact that as absolutes they possess both forms; thus, "*he shot an arrow*" is ʔuɫ|uotˈ|omą, and with plural object we have the same form, the u- indicating nonsingular object of gender II or III; but the word "*arrow*" has singular and nonsingular forms, ɫ|uonemą, ɫ|uone. The exact conditions when this happens have not been determined.

Numerals and demonstratives are used in apposition with the nouns to which they refer, and agree with them in gender and number, like Indo-European adjectives. Nominals are used only as the object of the verb *to be*, agreeing in pronominal reference with the noun they "modify."

§4:2. *Verbs.* The verb is the center of the Taos sentence, and the nouns and particles depend upon it. The expression of present and past durative and of all kinds of future action is exact; but the preterit form has often a general value in which the time element is subsidiary (cf. English forms like "*he goes*" as opposed to "*he is going*" for a similar phenomenon). In tales the present is used like our narrative present, with or without the narrative status prefix.

There is no imperative, the second person future being used in commands: ʔą̇ʔ|eyá "*go*," literally "*you will go*."

The subordinate temporal modes are of frequent use and the relative construction is common. They are used as equivalents of our subordinate clauses and participial constructions. The subordinate forms may function as nouns and be combined with particles. Equivalents of our adverbial clauses are also formed by the use of verbal nouns with "postpositions": ʔa̧-kʷ₁in⎮en-piw "*to where he was standing,*" literally "*his-standing-towards.*"

Locative and other "adverbial" modifications of verbs are brought about by free particles.

§4:3. *Particles.* The attached particles are "postpositions" for the most part, equivalent to our prepositions and adverbs; they follow nouns and subordinate modal phrases. Free particles are used with nouns and verbs as needed.

§4:4. *Word-order.* The normal order is "adverbial" particles, subject, verb-complex. Examples (from a text) are: huxⵑu ʔa̧na̧mp₁uy⎮enʔow ʔa̧nwⵑonhu "*then they two come up to their friends,*" literally "*then of-them-two — friends — up-to they-two — come — present suffix*"; hobⵑo wⵑiwa wⵑib ʔiwⵑikʼuo "*then again he put one down,*" literally "*then again one he-it — narrative — put-down*"; huxⵑu y₁iatʼⵑoti sⵑɔonena wiʔapⵑiwmę̧ "*and the man went away from there sadly,*" literally, "*and-then there-from man narrative-sad-went.*"

5. VOCABULARY

The purpose of this chapter is to give, in the absence of the complete diction-ary which it is eventually hoped to publish, a brief selection from the Taos vocabu-lary, to indicate the kinds of words and their distribution by meanings and categories, and to serve as material for the comparatist. Nouns are given in the absolute singular, with hyphen after the stem, and indication of gender and declen-sion. Verbs are in the basic stem form, with ablaut indicated where it is present; they are translated by the English infinitive, following the usual custom.

§5:1. *Nouns.* A list of nouns by meaning groups will be given.

§5:11. *Nouns of gender I.* These are all nouns designating persons or animals, with the exception of cʼ₁ipⵑa-na I.1bd "*doll*" and pʼòxʷⵑia-na I.1aa "*egg.*"

§5:111. *Terms for persons:* ʔ₁əwyu-ʔⵑuna I.1hd "*boy*"; kʷⵑę-na I.2aa "*Mexi-can*"; kʷⵑəl-ena I.2dd "*maiden*"; łiw-ⵑena I.2bb "*woman, wife*"; pⵑuy-ena I.2db "*friend*"; pʼonsⵑay-na I.1aa "*white man*"; sⵑɔon-ena I.2db "*man, husband*"; t₁obⵑu-na I.1bd "*governor of pueblo*"; tʼⵑoy-na I.2aa "*person, Indian*"; ʔùɫę̧ɫę̧-ʔⵑena I.1if "*youth*"; ʔup₁ęyu-ʔⵑuna I.1hd "*girl*"; ʔùpʼil-ⵑena I.2bd "*baby.*"

§5:112. *Kinship terms.* I have discussed the kinship and status terms in the paper referred to above (§1:4); the principal terms are listed here for the purpose of giving their declensions:

tǫm-ⵑena I.2bb "*father*"; kⵑa-na I.2aa "*mother*"; ʔù-ʔⵑuna I.2gg "*son, child*"; pʼìw-ⵑena I.2bb "*daughter*"; p₁opⵑo-na I.1bd "*older brother*"; pʼⵑǫy-na I.2aa "*younger brother*"; t₁utⵑu-na I.1bd "*older sister*"; pʼ₁ayu-ʔⵑuna I.1hd "*younger sister*"; mⵑa̧ku-na I.1dd "*grandchild*"; t₁ałułi-ʔⵑina I.1if "*grandfather*"; ʔ₁ału-ʔⵑuna I.1hd "*father's mother*"; ł₁itⵑu-na I.1bd "*mother's mother*"; t₁u̧łu-ʔⵑuna I.1hd "*father's brother, older* cousin"; ʔ˛ị̧ẹmę̧-ʔˡena I.1hd "*father's sister*"; mˌịmˡi-na I.1aa "*mother's brother*"; kˌayˡu-na I.1bd "*mother's sister*"; kˌiłu-ʔˡuna I.1hd "*nephew, niece, younger cousin*"; -mą̧sˡie-na (in composition only, nonsingular -mą̧sieną̧ with stress on first element) "*step-relation*"; k'ˌowa-ʔˡana I.1hd "*relative*"; tˌaʔˡa-na I.1bd "*son-in-law*"; sˌəoyi-ʔˡina I.1hd "*daughter-in-law*"; mˌą̧ku- as first element of compound, "*relation by marriage*" (other than son-in-law and daughter-in-law).

§5:113. *Words for animals, birds, insects:* cˌibikˡi-na I.1ce "*robin*"; cˌiyˡu-na I.1bd "*mouse*"; cˡiw-ena I.2db "*eagle*"; cˌiwyu-ʔˡuna I.1hd "*bird*"; cˌulo-ʔˡona I.1hd "*dog*"; c'àw-ˡena I.2bb "*bluejay*"; c'ˌiliyo-ʔˡona I.1if "*bat*"; c'ùnˡe-na I.1aa "*coyote*"; c'ˌuwala-ʔˡana I.1if "*squirrel*"; hùolˡo-na I.1bd "*quail*"; kˡəo-na I.2aa "*bear*"; kˌol-ˡena I.2bd "*wolf*"; k'ow-ena I.2db "*horse*"; kˌolno-ʔˡona I.1hd "*badger*"; kˌonˡe-na I.2bb "*buffalo*"; kˌosi-ʔˡina I.1hd "*cow*"; kò̧w-ˡena I.2bb "*owl*"; kˌuylulˡu-na I.1ce "*skunk*"; kwˌayˡa-na I.1bd "*magpie*"; lˌilˡu-na I.1bd "*chicken*"; mˌị̧si-ʔˡina I.1hd "*cat*"; pˌẹcu-ʔˡuna I.1hd "*rattlesnake*"; pˡę̧-na I.2aa "*deer*"; pə̀-ʔˡəna I.2gg "*fish*"; pìw-ˡena I.2bb "*rabbit*"; p'òwˌaya-ʔˡana I.1hd "*worm*"; p'ò̧ʔˌọyo-na I.1dd "*spider*"; tˌuxwˡa-na I.1bd "*fox*"; p'ˌị̧w-na I.2aa "*sparrow*"; p'ˌiayˡa-na I.1bd "*louse, flea*"; p'ˌị̧yu-ʔˡuna I.1hd "*fly*"; sùl-ˡena I.2bb "*bluebird*."

§5:12. *Nouns of genders II and III.* As has been indicated, the same kinds of words occur in both of these genders. A selection by meanings is given, no attempt being made to separate the two groups.

§5:121. *Body parts:* cèd-ˡena III.5aa "*anus*"; cˡi-nemą̧ II.4aa "*eye*"; ʔˡę̧-nemą̧ II.4aa "*shoulder*"; ʔˌị̧ẹn-ˡenemą̧ II.4aa "*foot*"; kˡə-na III.5aa "*vulva*"; k'ˡəo-nemą̧ II.4aa "*neck*"; łˌomˡị̧-ną̧ II.3bb "*mouth*"; łˌoxˡoy-na III.5aa "*lip*"; mą̧c'ˡele-na III.5dd "*fingernail*"; mą̧n-ˡenemą̧ II.4aa "*hand*"; ʔòd-ˡenemą̧ II.4aa "*chin, jaw*"; pˡia-na III.5aa "*heart, breast*"; p'ˡi-nemą̧ II.4aa "*head*"; p'ˡəy-na III.5aa "*nose*"; p'ˡo-na III.5aa "*hair*"; t'ˌamˡị̧-na III.5aa "*cheek*"; t'ˡołəo-na III.5dd "*ear*"; t'ˌị̧ẹ-ʔˡena III.5gg "*stomach*"; wˡa-na III.5aa "*penis*"; xˡo-nemą̧ II.4aa "*arm*"; xˡị̧-nemą̧ II.4aa "*leg*"; xˌị̧pˡi-ną̧ II.3bb "*knee*" (<"*leg*" +"*head*").

§5:122. *Plants, trees:* ʔə̀na IIIn.5aa "*leaf*"; hù̧-nemą̧ II.4aa "*cedar*"; hùp'òha-ną̧ II.3dd "*juniper*"; ʔˡiało-ną̧ II.3db "*willow*"; ʔia-ʔˡane III.6g "*corn*"; kwˌẹło-ną̧ II.3db "*oak*"; łˡa-ne III.6a "*tobacco*"; łˡi-ne III.6a "*grass*"; łitˡọ-ne III.6a "*wheat*"; łˌo-ʔˡone III.6g "*wood*"; nął-ˡenemą̧ II.4aa "*aspen*"; pòb-ˡenemą̧ II.4aa "*flower*"; pˡo-na III.5aa "*pumpkin*"; p'òkˡuowoną̧ II.3db "*fir, spruce*"; p'òtukwˌilˡo-na III.5aa "*mint*"; p'ˌuol-ˡenemą̧ II.4aa "*yucca*"; t'ˌą̧-na III.5aa "*bean*"; tˡuło-ną̧ II.3db "*tree, cottonwood*"; t'ˡụłę̧-ną̧ II.3db "*birch*"; wˌiẹ-ʔˡenemą̧ II.4gg "*pine*."

§5:123. *Natural phenomena:* ʔˌị̧ẹkˡọne III.6a "*hail*"; łˌul-ˡene III.6a "*rain*"; nˌạm-ˡene III.6a "*soil*"; pò̧-ʔˡona III.5gg "*land, country, the earth*"; p'ˡian-enemą̧ II.4dd "*mountain*"; p'òcˡia-ne III.6a "*ice*"; p'ˡo-na III.5a(a) "*moon*"; p'òpˡə-na III.5a(a) "*sky*"; p'òxəłˡo-na III.5aa "*star*"; p'òxˡuo-ne III.6a "*steam*"; p'ò̧-ʔˡone III.6g "*water*"; p'ˌia-ʔˡane III.6g "*fire*"; p'ˡị̧ẹ-na III.5aa "*cloud*"; t'ùl-ˡena III.5a(a) "*sun*." The words for "*hail*," "*rain*," "*water*" have corresponding singular and nonsingular forms (III.5aa, III.5aa, III.5gg) meaning "*hailstone*," "*raindrop*," "*drop of* water"; the latter is also used to mean "*river, stream, body of water.*"

§5:124. *Man-made products:* cùd-ena III.5db "*shirt, garment*"; ʔįẹt'u-ną II.3dh "*ladder*"; kə̀d-ˡenemą II.4aa "*door*"; kₗən-ˡenemą II.4aa "*cradle*"; kₗəob-ˡenemą II.4aa "*mocassin, shoe*"; kˡi-nemą II.4aa "*blanket*"; kᵥˡo-na III.5aa "*ax*"; lˡil-ena III-5db "*belt*"; ɫₗot'ˡə-na IIIn.5aa "*boat*"; ɫₗoxᵥˡolo-ną II.3db "*window*"; ɫˡu-na III.5aa ("*piece of) buckskin*"; mǎnmų-ną II.3db "*glove*"; nₗₐxₗu·ʔˡuna III.5gg "*adobe brick*"; pˡa-ne IIIn.6a "*clothing*"; pìę-ʔˡena IIIn.5gg "*bed*"; pₗomˡų-na III.5aa "*trouser leg, trousers*"; pₗuohˡo-na III.5aa "*ball*"; p'ˡįę-na III.5aa "*road*"; p'ȯkˡu-na III.5aa "*(loaf of) bread*"; t'ˡə-na IIIn.5aa "*house*"; xᵥˡil-ena III.5db "*bow*"; yˡuwola-ną II.3fi "*skirt.*"

§5:125. *Place-gender nouns.* Something over fifty nouns have been recorded as being of the place-gender, that is, inserting -ną- after the prefixes of pronominal reference. They cannot be listed here, but some of the meanings are: "*leaf*" (§5:122), "*collar*," "*boat*" (§5:124), "*field*," "*book*," "*house*" (§5:124), "*lock*," "*canyon*," "*fruit*," "*bed*" (§5:124, but the same word as ordinary gender III means "*mattress, sleeping-mat*"), "*work*," "*meal*," "*bitterness*" (literal, not figurative), "*clothes*," "*war*," "*digging*," etc. Nearly all have a definite connotation of place, whether they are concrete objects or verbal nouns of action. The formation is semantically alive, as evidenced by the borrowed words meaning "*canyon*," "*valley*," "*street*," "*bedstead*," "*machine*," "*garter*," "*pocket or purse*," "*store*," "*garden*," and by native words designating recent cultural objects.

§5:13. *Use of compounds.* Compounding being a living process of the language. many notions are expressed by compounds. This is especially true of descriptive terms for natural phenomena, and of terms for man-made objects of all kinds. For recently introduced cultural objects the language is more likely to resort to a descriptive compound than to borrowing. Sometimes the compounds are loan-translations, however, as in the case of cₗip'ȯxᵂₗiliʔˡine (III, nonsingular) "*eye-glasses*" <cˡi-nemą "*eye*" and p'ȯxᵂₗiliʔˡina "*glass.*" Many of the words of the vocabulary, both old and new (like the word for "*glass*"), are evidently compounds in form, but informants are not able to give meanings to some or all of the component parts. A historical study of the Taos vocabulary would prove interesting from this point of view.

§5:2. *Verbs.* As has already been indicated, Taos uses verbs not only to express the usual verbal notions of English and other Indo-European languages, but also for most "adjective" ideas. The number of verbs is thus large, and they play an important part in the expressiveness of the language.

§5:21. "*Transitive*" verbs. Some multipersonal verbs of active meaning are the following: cˡęl(ąⁱ/la ₗ"*to catch*"; cˡə "*to hunt*"; cˡiali "*to sweep, comb*"; cₗiaʔºˡǫ⁺li/la "*to ask a question*"; cₗoyt°ó "*to work*"; cˡǫną "*to grow*"; cºˡəod(ą "*to enter*"; ʔˡę "*to come*"; ʔºˡəl(aⁱ "*to drive*"; hˡəob(ą "*to like*"; hˡǫl(ą "*to breathe*"; hˡu/tá "*to kill*"; kˡo⁺wi "*to plant*"; kˡoyo "*to know*"; kºˡol(ąⁱ/la "*to eat*"; kᵥˡili "*to spill*"; ɫˡəya "*to boil*"; ɫˡoyᵏ(ąⁱ "*to sit down*" (reflexive); ɫˡul(ą "*to rain*"; mǎw "*to *want*"; mạ̀cˈⁱuli "*to press*"; mę̀ "*to walk*"; mⁱuoli "*to return*"; mᵒụ̀⁺mi "*to see*"; nụ̀⁺mi/ma "*to look for*"; ʔᵒloᵗlo "*to wash*"; pⁱęl(ą "*to sew*"; pⁱiawi "*to dye*"; sụ̀ "*to drink*"; tⁱuwiᵃ "*to buy*"; tụ̀⁺puo "*to speak*"; tˈloloᵗpuo "*to hear*"; ʔⁱ*ym*(ę/ma "*to tell*"; wᵒⁱęl(ąⁱ "*to dig*"; wⁱiaⁱʷ "*to give*"; wᵏlon(ą "*to arrive*"; wⁱǫ⁺puo "*to blow*" (of wind); xⁱiᵗmi "*to wait for*"; yᵒloy(i "*to command*" (stative also yloyba); yₗotᵒó "*to sing*."

§5:212. "*Causatives*," "*desideratives*." The verb ʔⁱąmą (neg. ʔⁱąmi, stative kⁱąmmą) "*to do, cause to . . .* " is found compounded as second element with a number of stems, some of which do not exist independently; compounds of this type seem to be freely formed at need, and can be considered causatives, though the formation is lexical and not paradigmatic: hⁱəolʔąmą "*to hurt*" (hⁱəol- "*sick*"), pⁱiʔąmą "*to use*" (pi- not identified), hⁱęyʔąmą "*to mend*" (cf. hₗęywopˈⁱihu "*he is rich*").

In the same way màw "*to want*" is compounded with many verbs to give desideratives, with the meaning "*to want to . . .* "

The verbs mę̀ "*to go, walk*," wá "*to be*," and some others, also enter into numerous fixed compounds.

§5:22. "*Intransitive*" *verbs*. Under this heading will be listed a number of unipersonal verbs of various kinds.

§5:221. *Essives*. These are unipersonal verbs translated for the most part by intransitives: ʔⁱęmą "*to sit*"; kⁱuymą "*to lie down*"; kᵥⁱinmą "*to stand*"; łowmą "*to smell*"; pⁱⁱętá "*to be wrapped*"; tˈləmą "*to dwell*"; wámą "*to be*" (direct resolution) and "*to have*" (possessive resolution). xⁱ*ymm*ą (negative xⁱ*ym*ą) "*to love*" (reflexive possessive); yⁱiawomą "*to be awake*."

§5:222. *Descriptives*. These are unipersonal verbs translated by adjectives; they differ from essives only in having -pˈⁱihu (with medial stress on the stem) in the affirmative present. They are given here in the shorter resultative form in -mą: cˈápumą "*to be bad*"; cˈ*ém*amą "*to be new, young*"; hⁱęywomą "*to be rich*"; kⁱlatimą "*to be silent*"; kⁱⁱimą "*to be thick*"; kⁱlumą "*to be good*" (singular complement only, kⁱⁱuyumą with nonsingular); kᵥⁱiawⁱalmą "*to be strong*"; łⁱəywomą "*to be poor*"; pⁱlayamą "*to be bald*"; xⁱəlimą "*to be round*"; xⁱəlmą "*to be heavy*"; yⁱayimą "*to be crooked*."

Many descriptives have intensive forms in -pⁱiwhu in the present, with -pⁱiwmę negative present, -pⁱiwmęʔ*ąn*ą negative past: kˈₗupⁱiwhu "*he is very good*"; hₗęywopⁱiwhu "*he is very rich*," etc.

§5:223. *Color terms*. Words for colors are either special descriptives with -wi as the suffix in the resultative, or they are free particles ("adverbs") in -hi, used with wámą "*to be*"; -hi usually conveys the idea of -*ish* in English. The most common terms are: cⁱǫlwi "*blue, green*"; cˈⁱulwi "*yellow*"; pˈòhⁱawi "*grey*"; pˈⁱòtˈⁱəwi "*white*"; pˈòxⁱęwi "*brown*"; pˈlaywi "*red*" pˈⁱ*yn*wi "*black*"; the forms pˈòhⁱahi "*greyish*," pˈòxⁱęhi "*brownish*," are used in compound color terms.

§5:3. *Particles*. The most frequent "postpositions" are: -bo "*up against*," ᴧkiną "*in, on*" (time when), ᴧkinʔow "*over*" (but not touching), ᴧkʼəyto "*on top of,*" ᴧmki "*for,*" ᴧmono "*along,*" ᴧmuwo "*throughout*" (space) ,"*during*" (time), ᴧnątʼo "*under,*" ᴧʔogą "*on, upon, into,*" ᴧʔoyą "*on*" (as a wall), ᴧpi "*alongside,*" ᴧpianʔow "*among,*" ᴧpibą "*up,*" ᴧpigą "*down,*" ᴧpiwą "*into,*" ᴧpiwto "*back to,*" ᴧpuobo "*next to,*" ᴧpuotʼo "*near,*" ᴧpʼlialgą "*together with,*" ᴧto "*in, within,*" ᴧtʼo "*at,*" ᴧtʼoti "*from,*" ᴧwagą "*on account of.*"

Many of the free particles are compounded with the above or with nouns, giving fine distinctions of position: cʼlɔotʼo "*in front of (face·at),*" kʼlɔotʼo "*up on top*" (as a hill).

Other free particles are: hliʔ ąngą "*why, because,*" hą "*yes,*" hliyuohu "*hello,*" hoblo "*also,*" hlodą "*and,*" hluki "*whether,*" huxlu "*and so, so then,*" hluoyo "*so much,*" hluoną "*then,*" hluoxeną "*yesterday,*" hluweną "*no,*" klɔwbo "*a long time,*" ʔlolodą "*almost,*" ʔoyxlenhi "*if,*" tą "*then,*" tʼo . . . ᴧneną "*or,*" tʼo . . . tʼo . . . ᴧneną "*either or,*" wlanno "*in, upon,*" wliwa "*again*"; ylodą "*here,*" yluhi "*perhaps,*" ylųy "*suddenly.*"

§5:31. *Place names.* Taos place names are usually composed of a stem with an attached locative particle, or of several stems with a particle: tlɔotʼo "*Taos pueblo,*" literally, "*in the village*"; kᵥęʔogą "*Taos village,*" literally, "*among the Mexicans*"; hlǫlpʼòno "*Santa Fe,*" literally "*shell·water·in.*" Practically all the place names recorded are descriptive and analyzable.

§5:4. *Loanwords.* There are several layers of loanwords in Taos. There are undoubtedly some of Indian origin, though these are of course hard to identify without more knowledge of neighboring languages. The principal loans are Spanish, and there are many English loans too. For a detailed discussion, see the paper referred to in §1:4.

Among the younger and better educated speakers English words are used unaltered; heard in this way were "*stove*" (informant "C"), "*forty·nine cents*" as a unit (informant "B"), and others; "B," who doesn't know much Spanish, is very conscious of the recognizable Spanish loanwords, but mixes in English freely.

6. HISTORY

§6:1. *General.* The history of a language can only be fully written when there are available records of its development over a long span of time. Such records are never available for American languages, and their history can thus never be completely set down. But the soundness of the technique of comparative linguistics is such that reconstructions of the external history can be made with considerable certainty, and much of the internal development can be gleaned from examination and analysis of the vocabulary in relation to the culture of the people speaking the language.

Within the scope of the present work, only a very brief summary of the available evidence for the external history of the Taos language can be presented.

§6:2. *Linguistic relations.* The Taos language is most closely related to the languages of Picurís pueblo, twenty-three miles south of Taos, and of Sandía and Isleta pueblos, respectively fourteen miles north and twelve miles south of Albu-querque. Together these constitute Tiwa, which can be divided into Northern Tiwa—Taos and Picurís, and Southern Tiwa—Isleta and Sandía. According to Harrington, the extinct Piro language in southern New Mexico was close enough to be considered a subgroup of Tiwa, but the evidence is scanty. The Isleta del Sur dialect south of El Paso is now probably extinct, but was practically the same as Isleta, according to Harrington's evidence; this was confirmed by one of my Isleta informants who had been there some years ago and had spoken with the survivors.

The two Tiwa groups are fairly homogeneous: Sandía and Isleta differ very little and are mutually completely intelligible; Taos and Picurís diverge more from each other. Further, the group as a whole is very similar: Taos and Picurís are each intelligible to the other three, and Sandía and Isleta are understood in the north, though with difficulty.

Tiwa is classified as a subfamily; with the Tewa and Towa subfamilies it forms the Tanoan family. Tewa—spoken in Santa Clara, San Juan, Nambé, Tesuke, and by the one surviving Indian family at Pohwake, is very homogeneous, accord-ing to available evidence. Towa now consists only of Jemes, but Pecos is supposed to have belonged to the group. Tewa and Towa are rather different from each other, and widely different from Tiwa.

On the basis of Tanoan and Uto-Aztecan evidence it has been possible to reconstruct an Azteco-Tanoan linguistic stock; see B. L. Whorf and G. L. Trager, *The Relationship of Uto-Aztecan and Tanoan*,[2] where the basic outlines of Azteco-Tanoan phonology and morphology are laid down and about one hundred cognates are cited. Azteco-Tanoan may include Zuni, and probably does include Kiowa; for the latter relationship I have considerable evidence in addition to that pre-sented by Harrington in the past. There is also in hand evidence of a distant rela-tion of Azteco-Tanoan to Penutian, Mayan, and possibly Tunican.

§6:3. *Proto-Tiwa*. On the basis of extensive vocabularies of the three other Tiwa languages collected in the summer of 1937, it has been possible to reconstruct Proto-Tiwa in considerable detail.

The details of the phonology may be found in the papers mentioned above (§1:4)—*Comparative Phonology* and *The Kinship and Status Terms*.

Most of the Proto-Tiwa phonemes remained unchanged in Taos, but these changes did take place: k' >x, initial b >m, initial d >l, ǰ >y; g apparently became y internally under most conditions and x initially, but there are a few cases of internal g left; r >n; ie >i, but a few cases of ie apparently remain; a became fronted; o became low back unrounded; ə changed from high central to mid back; ia changed from low mid central to low mid front; əo changed from high mid central to low mid back; ǫ and ǫǫ both became ǫ (but a few cases of ǫ under conditions not yet determined became ą). The tones remained unchanged. These changes are much less in extent than those that took place in the three other languages, though there too the general lines of the system remain.

Morphologically, the Proto-Tiwa system seems to have been the same as in Taos and Picurís, though there has been some rearrangement of declensional suffixes in Taos. The systems of pronominal reference are the same in Taos and Picurís, but Sandía and Isleta may have only two genders (animate and a single inanimate); the three-gender system must be original, and place-gender looks as if it were the relic of a still older system; the verb is on the whole the same in all four languages, but the southern ones have a preterit suffix which cannot be identified in the northern ones, and which may or may not be original. Proto-Tiwa had the same ablaut system as Taos, but it must already have been nonfunctioning.

§6:31. *Origin of Taos phonemes.* To summarize and reverse the evidence referred to above, we list the origin of the Taos phonemes: p, t, c, k, k_w, ʔ, pʼ, tʼ, pʼ, tʼ, cʼ, kʼ, k_wʼ < the same Proto-Tiwa phonemes; b, d, g < internal Proto-Tiwa b, d, g, accounting for the absence of these sounds initially in native words; ł, s, x_w, h (unchanged from Proto-Tiwa; x <kʼ, and in some cases also probably from Proto-Tiwa or Proto-Tanoan g; m initially from b and m, elsewhere from m; n <n, and in the suffix -na from r; l initially from d, elsewhere from l; y <y, j̈, and internal g; i <i and some cases of ie; ie, ia, e, a, o, ə, əo, uo, u from the same originals, though patterning somewhat differently through phonetic changes; į, įę, ę, ų unchanged; ą from ą and some cases of ǫ; ǫ from ǫ, ǫǫ, and most cases of ǫ.

§6:4. *More remote reconstructions.* From the Tiwa evidence itself, it is possible to reconstruct *qʼ ∼ *q as the original of the ablaut pair ʔ ∼ k, *g_w ∼ k_w for w ∼ k_w, *γ_w ∼ x_w for w ∼ x_w, and possibly others. From the Tanoan evidence as a whole it can be surmised that the vowel clusters originally may have had w, y, or h separating the two elements. Further, the tone system patterns so as to suggest that originally there may have been only stress with differences in length of vowels, and out of these developed the tones, with loss of significant quantity.

The morphology of Taos is obviously archaic and probably differs little from that of Proto-Tanoan.

THE YAWELMANI DIALECT OF YOKUTS

STANLEY S. NEWMAN

BEFORE the coming of the whites, the Yokuts people inhabited the extensive plains and foothills of the southern San Joaquin basin of California.
Even two or three decades ago, traces of about forty Yokuts dialects could
still be found. But, at present, hardly more than a half-dozen dialects continue to
be spoken by the small native communities that have retreated to the foothills.
Among these dialects, Yawelmani exhibits the greatest vitality; it has become the
lingua franca of the Tule River Reservation, the largest of the Yokuts communities,
situated about fifty miles north of Bakersfield.

The relationship of Yokuts to other languages of the Penutian stock, even to
its California neighbor, Miwok, appears particularly remote when viewed from the
narrow perspective of the Yokuts dialects themselves. Except for occasional lexical
differences, manifested in distinct roots and suffixes, the dialects of Yokuts are
practically identical. A description of the Yawelmani dialect is in all essentials a
description of common Yokuts.

Yawelmani is characterized by a singular economy and consistency of form.
Its formal machinery is largely confined to a small number of suffixes employed in
conjunction with a fairly elaborate but strictly regular system of ablaut changes
occurring in stem vowels. The operation of these stem-plus-suffix processes has the
automatic regularity of a paradigm, for the processes appropriate to a given class
of words can be applied to every member of that class. In the formal hierarchy of
the language, every element seems to be rigidly clamped into place: each suffix is
allocated to a specific type of stem; each ablaut change conditioning the stem
vowels is part of a symmetrical system of vowel changes; with its vowels altered
according to an ablaut formula, each stem has its place among the set of stems
formed from a given type of root; each root, in turn, has membership in the configuration of roots comprising a word class.

Two major types of root are to be distinguished. The base (symbolized by an
asterisk, as *de·yi, "lead") is a fundamental, unanalyzable root, which gives rise
to a number of vocalically diversified stems. The theme (symbolized by a diagonal
line, as diya·la·/, "cause to lead") is typically a secondary root composed of a stem
plus a thematizing suffix, the example quoted being made up of the causative ·a·la·/
added to diy-, a stem of *de·yi. As compared with the base, the theme is relatively
limited in its stem formation.

A difference in syllabic structure also distinguishes the base from the theme.

222

There are only two types of syllable in Yawelmani: the open syllable, CV (C =consonant, V =vowel), and the closed syllable, CVC. Bases are disyllabic; they are either biliteral, consisting of two open syllables (CV +CV, as *de·yi, "lead," *xata, "eat"), or triliteral, consisting of an open plus a closed syllable (CV +CVC, as *hulɔ·ṣ, "sit down," *lɔgɔw, "pulverize"). But themes, like words, are made up of any number of open and closed syllables in any combination. Being limited by the two types of syllable, however, words and themes display a striking uniformity in phonetic structure. All words and themes begin in a single consonant followed by a vowel (CV + . . . , CVC + . . .). They may end in a vowel or in a consonant . . . +CV, . . . +CVC). Consonant clusters can occur only in medial position, and the number of consonants in a medial cluster is limited to two (CVC +CV, CVC +CVC). Vowels always occur singly; there are no vowel clusters in Yawelmani.

PHONETICS AND PHONOLOGY

Consonants are sharply distinguished from vowels. There are no phonemes that can function as both consonants and vowels; y or w, for example can never be confused with i or u. The possibilities of syllabic structure, on the one hand, are sufficiently limited to define a given phoneme unambiguously as either a consonant or a vowel by its position in the syllable. In addition, these phonemes are clearly earmarked in the phonological system; whereas root vowels undergo an ablaut change in assuming their appropriate stem forms, the root consonants remain as a fixed unchanging framework throughout the various stems.

Some conception of the consonantal rigidity and the vowel plasticity of Yawelmani can be gained from the following words, composed of suffixes added to various stems of the base *de·yi, "lead"; de·y-en ,"he will lead";[1] dey-hin, "he led"; diy-hatin-hin, "he wanted to lead"; diye·-'iy, "the place where one got the lead" (subjective case); diya·-'an, "he is leading"; deydiy-en, "he will lead repeatedly"; diyidy-i·sa·-hin 'aman, "they led each other repeatedly"; diye·diy-iċ, "one who is leading repeatedly" (subjective case); deyday, "the act of leading repeatedly" (subjective case).

The consonant phonemes of Yawelmani fall into three major sets.

   I. Voiceless
      Stops and Affricatives
         Intermediate: b, d, ḍ, g, ẓ, z
         Aspirated: p, t, ṭ, k, c, ç
         Glottalized: p, t́, ṭ́, k̇, ċ, ç̇
      Fricatives and Sibilants: x, s, ṣ

[1] These examples illustrate predications containing no expressed pronominal reference; a third person singular subject is understood in such instances. Where they are expressed, pronominal references are made by independent words (see page 244).

II. Voiced
    Simple: m, n, w, y, l
    Glottalized: m̓, n̓, w̓, y̓, l̓
III. Faucal: h, ᾿

The voiceless consonants are positionally free; they may occur initially, me-dially (intervocalically, preconsonantally, postconsonantally), or finally in the word. They undergo no changes whatever, and they have no influence on adjacent phonemes. For typographical convenience, voiced symbols are used to indicate the intermediates, which have the nonaspirated quality of French voiceless stops (as in French par, temps, car). The aspirated consonants are pronounced in all positions with a considerable degree of aspiration, much like the English aspirated stops in initial position. A light degree of glottal plosion characterizes the glottal-ized stops and affricatives of Yawelmani; in acoustic effect these consonants are markedly different from the violently glottalized consonants which occur in the languages of the Northwest Coast, such as Nootka or Bella Coola. The subscript dot in ḍ, ṭ, ṭ̓, ẓ, ç, ç̓, and ṣ symbolizes a retroflex aveolar articulation, with the tongue slightly arched and the tip touching the alveolar ridge.

The voiced phonemes exhibit some special features. The glottalized conso-sonants of this set are positionally limited, for they do not occur initially or post-consonantally in the word. In addition, a special phonological process applies to the voiced phoneme; when it occurs as the second consonant of a stem, the voiced phoneme absorbs the floating glottal stop of suffixes, which will be indicated by -᾿. . . in suffixes. The glottal-absorbing process is illustrated in the addition of the agentive suffix, -᾿. . . a·/, to such stems as diy- or huls̱-, resulting in diy̓a·/, "one who is in the lead," and huḷṣa·/, "one who is seated." Here the glottalized pho-nemes y̓ and l̓ are secondary, composed of a fundamental y and l of the stem plus an extrinsic glottal inflection from the suffix. The glottalized voiced phonemes, which also appear as fundamental consonants, likewise absorb the floating glottal stop of suffixes. Such stems as giy̓- (<*giy̓i, "touch") and mun̓- (<*mun̓u, "turn around, turn the back") append the agentive -᾿. . . a·/ to form giy̓a·/, "one who has touched," and mun̓a·/, "one who has his back turned." No other consonants can absorb the floating glottal stop: e.g., xat'a·/, "one who has eaten," 'uṭ'a·/, "one who has stolen," composed of -᾿. . . . a·/ suffixed to the stems xat- (<*xata, "eat") and 'uṭ- (<*'ɔ·ṭu, "steal").

The two faucal consonants also constitute a separate phonemic set. The glot-tal stop, however, presents some phonological peculiarities that do not apply to h. As distinguished from the floating glottal stop of suffixes, the organic glottal stop is a fixed consonant found in roots as well as in suffixes: e.g., *'ɔ·ṭu, "steal,"* ẓu'ub, "divide," -'an, durative present suffix. In contrast to the treatment of the floating glottal stop of -᾿. . . a·/, the initial consonant of -'an is immovable: e.g., huḷɔṣ-'an, "he is sitting down." A third type of glottal stop, an inorganic consonant sym-bolized by ('), is added only to vowel-ending stems when these are followed either by a suffix beginning in a vowel or by a final zero suffix: among the case forms of huɨ̣ṣa·/, "one who is seated," are huɨ̣ṣa·(')-in (-in, possessive case) and huɨ̣ṣa(')-] (-], subjective case).[2] This inorganic element does not appear before suffixes beginning in a consonant: e.g., huɨ̣ṣa··nit (-nit, ablative case).

The glottal stop and h have a similar influence upon vowels. When either of these phonemes occurs intervocalically, the preceding vowel of a stem is assimilated to a strong quality if the following vowel is strong (ɔ·, a·, e·). Thus, to add the agentive -uċ/, a stem is normally demanded whose first and second vowels are respectively weak and strong—u and ɔ·, for example. But the first vowel of a stem assimilates the strong quality of the second vowel when ' or h intervenes: contrast the weak first vowel of the stems in 'uṭɔ·(')-uċ/, "one who is stealing" (<*'ɔ·ṭu, "steal"), and in hulɔ·ṣ-uċ/, "one who is sitting down" (<*hulɔ·ṣ, "sit down"), with the strong-assimilated first vowel in mɔhɔ·(')-uċ/, "one who is diving" (<*muhu, "dive"), and in wɔ'ɔ·y-uċ/, "one who is falling asleep" (<*wɔ·'uy, "fall asleep").

These two consonants also share a positional restriction: neither ' nor h occurs as a root final. These phonemes may, however, appear finally in stems and even in words. Under certain conditions a root with medial ' or h, such as the bases *ma'a, "look down," or *muhu, "dive," will drop the final vowel to form a stem in which the second consonant becomes final, as in ma'-, muh-. With the addition of a final zero suffix to such stems, the ' or h becomes a word final: e.g., ma'-], "the act of looking down" (subjective case), muh-], "the act of diving" (subjective case). The use of an inorganic glottal stop before a zero suffix adds to the possible occurrences of this phoneme as a word final: e.g., muh'a(')-], "one who has dived" (subjective case).

The characteristics of Yawelmani consonants can be summed up briefly. The voiceless consonants are immutable and positionally unrestricted. When occurring as second consonants in stems, the voiced phonemes absorb the floating glottal stop of suffixes, the simple voiced consonants becoming secondarily glottalized by this process; whether secondary or primary, the glottalized voiced consonants are restricted to intervocalic, preconsonantal, and final position in the word. The two faucals are the only consonants which may, under certain conditions, influence the assimilation of stem vowels; in roots these two consonants are restricted to initial and medial position. Of all consonants, the glottal stop is phonologically the most complex, for three phonological types are to be distinguished: 1) the organic glottal

---

[2] Yawelmani possesses three zero suffixes, that is, suffixes with no overt phonetic content. One of these is a final suffix, -], denoting the subjective case. The other two are thematizing suffixes: e.g., the verbal noun suffix -/, as in hulɔ·ṣ- /, "the act of sitting down." No theoretical significance is to be attached to the fact that these suffixes are phonetically zero. Like other suffixes, they have a definite semantic content; they are allocated to specific stems; and the distinction between final and thematizing suffixes applies to them as well as to all other suffixes (see pages 231–232 for a discussion of suffixes).

stop, a fixed phoneme in roots and suffixes; 2) the floating glottal stop of suffixes, which is absorbed by a second voiced consonant of stems; and 3) the inorganic glottal stop, which is employed after vowel-ending stems, a) as the final consonant before a zero final suffix, b) as a hiatus-filling consonant before a suffix beginning in another vowel.

Yawelmani possesses ten vowel phonemes: i, i·, e, e·, a, a·, ɔ, ɔ·, u, u·. These ten phonemes, however, do not have the same phonological status: i·, u·, and e are ablauted forms of root vowels and appear only in stems; the remaining seven vowel phonemes occur in roots as well as in stems. These seven phonologically funda-mental vowels of Yawelmani are patterned as follows:

	Vowel Series			
	ɔ	a	i	u
Light	ɔ	a	i	u
Heavy	ɔ·	a·	e·	ɔ·

The ɔ· phoneme, it will be noted, plays two distinct rôles in this configuration. It is a striking feature of Yawelmani that the only two phonological entities actual-ized in a single vowel phoneme (ɔ· of the ɔ series and ɔ· of the u series) are maximally differentiated in their treatment. For this reason, the phonological principles of vowel harmony and vowel change can best be illustrated by an examination of these two types of ɔ· vowel, as they appear in *dɔ·sɔ, "report," and in *'ɔ·ṭu, "steal."

In one of its aspects, vowel harmony is exhibited in bases, all of which con-tain two vowels belonging to the same vowel series.[3] Because of this harmony in base vowels, the vowel series membership of an ɔ· vowel is defined by the base in which it occurs. Thus, the second vowel of *dɔ·sɔ marks this base as being com-posed of ɔ series vowels; in the same way, *'ɔ·ṭu is identified as a base containing vowels of the u series. There is no base which is ambiguous in its vowel series membership.

Another type of vowel harmony, operating on somewhat wider principles, is imposed upon suffixes by stems. Suffixes occur in twin vocalic forms. For ex-ample, -it, passive aorist, is appended to stems whose last vowel belongs to the ɔ, a, or i series; but if the last stem vowel is of the u series, the suffix takes the form -ut: e.g., dɔ·s-it, "it was reported," but 'ɔ·ṭ-ut, "it was stolen." The dubitative -ɔl is added only to stems having the last vowel in the ɔ series, the twin form -al being employed with stems whose last vowel is in the a, i, or u series: e.g., dɔ·s-ɔl, "he might report," but 'ɔ·ṭ-al, "he might steal." The same harmonic principles apply to suffixes containing more than one vowel in the same series: e.g., dɔ·s-e·ni, "in order to report," 'ɔ·ṭ-ɔ·nu, "in order to steal" (-e·ni and -ɔ·nu, resultative gerundial); dɔs-ɔ·lɔ·/, "cause to report," 'uṭ-a·la·/, "cause to steal" (-ɔ·lɔ·/ and -a·la·/, causa-tive). But if the suffix vowels differ in vowel series, only the first is harmonically varied: e.g., dɔs-'iñay, "while reporting," 'uṭ-'uñay, "while stealing" (-'. . . iñay

---

[3] A more detailed discussion of bases, with examples, will be found on pages 233–234.

and -'. . . uṅay, contemporaneous gerundial); dɔs-hɔtin/, "desire to report," 'uṭ-hatin/, "desire to steal" (-hɔtin/ and -hatin/, desiderative).

The system of suffix vowel harmony is schematized in the following table:

	Series of Last Stem Vowel			
	ɔ	a	i	u
Series of Suffix Vowel	i	i	i	u
	ɔ	a	a	a

As the table shows, each suffix possesses one vocalic form for stems of three vowel series, and another for stems of the fourth vowel series. In citing suffixes hereafter, the practice will be adopted of quoting that vocalic form employed with stems in three of the four vowel series; thus, a reference to the aorist -hin will imply its twin vocalic form -hun, and a reference to -xa, precative, will similarly imply the paired form -xɔ, each member of the suffix pair being distributed among stems in accordance with the principles of suffix vowel harmony.

Stems are formed from roots by processes of vowel change. These processes are to be regarded as operating on two planes: on the one hand, dynamic vowel processes effect ablaut changes that are to be defined in terms of morphological conditions; on the other hand, a few phonetic processes introduce additional vowel changes of a mechanical nature. In the formation of stems these two planes interact; a stem which has undergone dynamic vowel changes may, in turn, be subjected to secondary phonetic changes. For example, dɔsɔ·- and 'uṭɔ·- (stems ablauted from *dɔ·sɔ, "report," and *'ɔ·ṭu, "steal") appear without any secondary vowel changes in dɔsɔ·(')-ič/, "one who is reporting," and in 'uṭɔ·(')-uč/, "one who is stealing." In accordance with the rule that long vowels are shortened in closed syllables, these stems have their last vowel secondarily shortened in dɔsɔ[·]-hnil,/ "place where it was reported," and in 'uṭɔ[·]-hnul/, "place where it was stolen."[4] To the same ablaut type of stem are allocated several suffixes beginning in -'a or -'a· which have an assimilative effect upon the last vowel of vowel-ending stems; but the last vowel of stems ending in a consonant is not subject to this secondary assimilation: contrast the assimilated stem vowel in 'uṭa·-'an, "he is stealing," with the merely shortened stem vowel in hulɔ[·]ṣ-'an, "he is sitting down." Finally, a secondary vowel change, termed glottal-weakening, affects vowels occurring before a final glottal stop: e.g., hulu'ṣu-', "he will cause . . . to sit down," in which the final vowel of the stem hulu'ṣɔ·- is weakened before -' , future; p̓a'a·ṣi(')-], "lake" (subjective case), in which the final glottal stop, even though inorganic, weakens the final vowel of the stem p̓a'a·ṣe-·.

The dynamic vowel processes are configurational in character, for under given morphological conditions the root vowels change in uniform cycles, or sets. The

[4] Brackets will enclose the length sign of an organically long vowel which has been secondarily shortened.

suffix ·'e·y/, for example, demands a stem whose first vowel is ɔ, a, i, or u and whose second vowel is, respectively in each of the four vowel series, ɔ·, a·, e·, or ɔ·:

> dɔsɔ·'e·y/, "that which was reported" (<*dɔ·sɔ, "report")
> xata·'e·y/, "that which was eaten" (<*xata "eat")
> 'ile·'e·y/, "that which was fanned" (<*'ile·, "fan")
> 'uṭɔ·'ɔ·y/, "that which was stolen" (<*'ɔ·ṭu, "steal")

The causative·repetitive ·lsa·/ is suffixed to stems whose first vowel is again ɔ, a, i, or u but whose second vowel is respectively e·, e·, e·, or ɔ·:

> dɔse··lsa·/, "cause to report often"
> xate··lsa·/, "cause to eat often"
> 'ile··lsa·/, "cause to fan often"
> 'uṭɔ··lsa·/, "cause to steal often"[5]

By following different dynamic vowel processes stems may sometimes overlap in objective form. The stems of 'uṭɔ··'ɔ·y/ and 'uṭɔ··lsa·/, in spite of their objective similarity, are differently configurated in the ablaut system; the first stem is aligned with other stems whose vowels are consistently ɔ plus ɔ·, a plus a·, i plus e·, or u plus ɔ·, and the second stem belongs with other stems containing the vowels ɔ plus e·, a plus e·, i plus e·, or u plus ɔ·.

The vocalic form of stems can be most conveniently expressed in terms of an ablaut formula operating upon roots: thus, the suffix ·'e·y/ is added to stems whose formula is W+S (weak first vowel plus strong second vowel); ·lsa·/ is suffixed to W+E· stems (weak first vowel plus E·-induced second vowel). Each of the dynamic vowel sets, with the terms and symbols referring to them, are indicated in the following table. The first line contains the fundamental vowels of roots. Below this, each line represents one of the dynamic vowel sets which, in stems, replaces the root vowels.[6]

Fundamental Vowels	ɔ	ɔ·	a	a·	i	e·	u	ɔ·
F (full)	ɔ	ɔ·	a	a·	i	e·	u	ɔ·
S (strong)	ɔ·	ɔ·	a·	a·	e·	e·	ɔ·	ɔ·
W (weak)	ɔ	ɔ	a	a	i	i	u	u
W' (weak·glottal)	ɔ'	ɔ'	a'	a'	i'	i'	u'	u'
W· (weak·long)	ɔ·	ɔ·	a·	a·	i·	i·	u·	u·
Z (zero)	0	0	0	0	0	0	0	0
I (I·induced)	i	i	i	i	i	i	u	u
E· (E·-induced)	e·	e·	e·	e·	e·	e·	ɔ·	ɔ·

[5] The presence of a long vowel in the closed syllable before ·lsa·/ is one of the two exceptions to the general rule of vowel shortening. The other exception occurs in a rhetorically lengthened vowel (see page 237).

[6] In the table the symbol 0 is used to refer to a zero·grade vowel. The dash indicates that the process does not apply to the root vowel in question: e.g., dulled vowels in the stem are formed only from the light fundamental root vowels (ɔ, a, i, u), not from the heavy vowels (ɔ·, a·, e·, ɔ·).

A (A-induced)	ɔ	ɔ	a	a	a	a	a	a
R (reduced):								
z (zeroed)	0	—	0	—	0	—	0	—
d (dulled)	i	—	i	—	i	—	u	—
z‖ (heavy-zeroed)	—	0	—	0	—	0	—	0
r (retained)	—	ɔ·	—	a·	—	e·	—	ɔ·

The dynamic vowel processes may operate upon each vowel of the root; thus, the W +S—I +Z stem, employed with the agentive -ič/, is an example of the four-fold ablaut change exhibited in stems of reduplicated bases:

doso·dis-ič/, "one who reports often" (<*do·sodo·so, "report often")
xata·xit-ič/, "one who eats often" (<*xataxata, "eat often")
'ile·'il-ič/, "one who fans often" (<*'ile·'ile·, "fan often")
'uṭo·'uṭ-uč/, "one who steals often" (<*'oṭu'oṭ'u, "steal often")

Reduction (R) is the only dynamic vowel process which does not have a uniform effect upon a given type of root vowel; this process is conditioned by variables of phonetic structure, arising from the union of stems and suffixes. In the process of reduction, which operates only upon the last vowel of roots, a light root vowel (L) is zeroed (z) in the stem, unless the stem would end in two consonants and be followed by a suffix beginning in a consonant, in which case the root vowel is dulled (d); a heavy root vowel (H) is retained (r) in the stem, unless the stem would end in a vowel and be followed by a suffix beginning in a vowel, in which case the root vowel is heavy-zeroed (z'). A schematic presentation of the F +R stem of bases, with examples, will clarify the conditions determining the various types of reduction.

Base	F+R Stem	
	preconsonantal	prevocalic
*CVCL (*xata, "eat")	CVCz- (xat-)	CVCz- (xat-)
*CVCLC (*logow, "pulverize")	CVCdC- (logiw-)	CVCzC- (logw-)
CVCH ('ile·, "fan")	CVCr- ('ile·-)	CVCz‖- ('il-)
*CVCHC (*hulo·ṣ, "sit down")	CVCrC- (hulo[·]ṣ-)	CVCrC- (hulo·ṣ-)

The dynamic processes of vowel change have no assignable semantic function. Stems whose vowels have been modified by these processes are employed merely as formal counters for the addition of appropriate suffixes. Examples illustrating the various dynamic vowel processes will be found in the stem table (page 235).

Somewhat parallel to the inorganic consonant ('), which is used to separate verb or substantive stem vowels from suffix vowels, is the inorganic vowel, employed only with substantive stems. This vowel varies in quality according to the theme classification of the substantive and according to the character of the following suffix, a weak inorganic vowel occurring before the monoconsonantal suffix -w, locative, a strong vowel being used before all other suffixes beginning in a consonant. The inorganic vowel is inserted 1) between substantive stems ending in one or more consonants and a monoconsonantal suffix, as in wite·b(a)·w, "toward the child" (<wite·b/, "child"), or in 'axč(i)·w, "toward the bed" (<'axič)/, "bed"); 2) between substantive stems ending in two consonants and a suffix beginning in a consonant, as in 'axč(e·)·nit, "from the bed"; 3) before the last two consonants of substantive stems which, having dropped the last vowel of the theme, would end in three consonants, as in yaw̓(i)lč· (theoretically **yaw̓lč·, a stem of yaw̓lič/, "wolf"). The inorganic consonant and vowel may be regarded as protective devices, for they are employed to separate phonemes which, if combined in accordance with morphological stipulations, would violate the syllabic dictates of the language.

Still another phonological technique for preserving the syllabic regulations is that of suffix truncation. In the process of truncation the first or the last phoneme of a suffix is dropped. Initial truncation, either of consonants or of vowels, fulfills a protective function; thus, the desiderative ·hatin/, which appears in its complete form when suffixed to W+Z stems ending in one consonant (e.g., 'ut̓·hatin/, "desire to steal"), occurs in a truncated form when added to W+Z stems ending in two consonants (e.g., hulṣ·atin/, "desire to sit down"); similarly, the dubitative ·al is employed in its complete form with F+R stems ending in a consonant (e.g., 'ɔ·t̓·al, "he might steal"), but an initially truncated form of this suffix is added to F+R stems ending in a vowel (e.g., 'ile[·]·l, "he might fan"). Final truncation, which has no protective function, applies only to suffix vowels. Certain stems ending in a vowel demand a finally truncated suffix: for example, the imperative ·ka, allocated to F+R stems, appears in its complete form in 'ɔ[·]t̓·ka, "steal!" but in its truncated form in 'ile[·]·k, "fan!" Morphological as well as phonetic conditions determine the occurrence of truncation: impending vowel clusters are avoided by the truncation of initial suffix vowels in certain morphological processes, by the insertion of the inorganic glottal stop in others; in substantives a cluster of consonants is prevented from violating syllabic rules by initial consonant truncation or by the use of an inorganic vowel, depending upon morphological conditions, but verbs consistently employ the truncating technique under the same phonetic circumstances.

In its vowel phonology, then, Yawelmani operates with ten phonemes, of which only seven are the fundamental vowels of roots. Among these seven, however, the vowel ɔ· plays a double rôle, being the heavy member of both the ɔ series and the u series. The fundamental pattern of vowels is based on four series (ɔ, a, i, u), each containing a light and a heavy member. The base root exhibits vowel harmony in that its two vowels belong to the same vowel series; vowel harmony of a somewhat different order operates upon suffix vowels, for a suffix is vocalically harmonized with its stem. The stem itself is formed from the root by means of vowel changes. These changes are of two types. On the one hand, root vowels assume their stem forms by undergoing ablaut changes, each of which is configurated in a set of dynamic vowel processes; these stems, which can be defined in terms of an ablaut formula, may then be subjected to secondary vowel changes, such as shortening, a-assimilation, strong assimilation, glottal weakening. In addition to these changes impressed upon stem vowels, Yawelmani possesses an inorganic vowel inserted after substantive stems to prevent consonant clusters. Under certain morphophonetic conditions, suffix vowels are truncated initially or finally, suffix consonants only initially.

SUFFIXATION

Among the grammatical techniques of Yawelmani, suffixation and ablaut change are the most important. Reduplication is employed to a limited extent in the formation of roots and stems, and a considerable number of roots, particularly substantive themes, are petrified in a reduplicated form. Another grammatical technique, which may be roughly described as proclisis, has an even more limited scope, being restricted to the formation of roots in the small and anomalous word class of -wiyi verbs (pages 236–238). But suffixation and ablaut account for most of the functional expression in Yawelmani; these two processes occur jointly in the formation of every word, even when reduplication or proclisis, or both, also play a part in the same morphological operation.

Each suffix is to be defined, on the one hand, in terms of its stem affiliation: thus, -lsa·/, causative repetitive, demands the W +E· stem; -en, future, demands the F +R stem. In addition, each suffix may be defined with respect to the type of grammatical unit which it forms. On this basis, two major types of suffixes are to be distinguished: 1) thematizing (i.e., theme-forming) suffixes that may be combined with each other or with 2) final (i.e., word-forming) suffixes, of which only one can appear in a word. The unit composed of stem plus thematizing suffix is a theme, which serves as a new point of departure for the formation of stems to which additional suffixes are attached: thus, from the theme 'ile·kič/, "one who is singing" (composed of the thematizing -ič/, agentive, with the W +S stem of *'ilik, "sing") are formed the absolutive case stem 'ile·kič-, the oblique case stem 'ile[·]kč-, the absolutive plural stem 'e[·]lke·č-, the oblique plural stem 'e[·]lkač-. A complete word is formed only by the addition of a final suffix to a stem, whether it be the stem of a base, as in 'ilk-en, "he will sing" (-en, future, with the prevocalic F +R stem of *'ilik), or the stem of a theme, as in 'ile[·]kč-i lanhin, "he hears the one who is singing" (-i, objective case, with the oblique case stem of 'ile·kič/).

To these two major types of suffixes must be added a third special type, the auxiliary suffixes -xɔ·.., durative, and -·...exɔ·.., consequent (referring to the state consequent to an activity). The auxiliary type of suffix, which will be symbolized by two final dots, displays several peculiarities. Like the thematizing suffix, the auxiliary cannot end a word; but the thematizing suffix may be followed by any one of a large number of suffixes, either thematizing, final, or auxiliary in type, whereas the auxiliary is limited in its combinations to one of only five final suffixes. The auxiliary exhibits the phonological peculiarity of not harmonizing vocalically with its stem; instead of possessing the twin vocalic forms that characterize all other suffixes, the auxiliary has only one fixed vocalic form. Furthermore, the dura-tive auxiliary ‑xɔ‧. . causes an irrational shortening of a final stem vowel; and, when added to vowel‑ending stems, a monosyllabic combination of ‑xɔ‧. . plus final suffix has the effect of displacing the word stress to the antepenultimate syllable: note the irrationally shortened stem vowel in 'ili'ke[‧]‑xɔ‧‑nit, "he is being made to sing," and, in addition, the aberrant stress in 'ilí'ke[‧]‑xɔ[‧]‑t, "he was being made to sing."[7] Although they are minor details characterizing the auxiliary, these de-partures from normal phonological practice stand out sharply in a language such as Yawelmani, where phonological rules tend to be uniform and inflexible.[8]

Each suffix type expresses certain of the functional categories. The auxiliaries are purely aspectual in function. The final suffixes include 1) all tense suffixes, whether their tense reference is pure, as in ‑en, future, or mixed, as in ‑'at, which expresses durative aspect and passive voice as well as aorist (past or present) tense; 2) all modal suffixes, as ‑ka, imperative; 3) all gerundial suffixes, which form sub-ordinate verbs, as ‑'. . . iñay, contemporaneous gerundial; 4) all case suffixes, as ‑in, possessive. The thematizing suffixes include 1) all suffixes of modal derivation, i.e., suffixes having a modal reference that is more concrete and external than that of mode proper, as ‑xas/, exclusive ("do nothing but . . . "); 2) all suffixes referring purely to voice, as ‑in/, medio‑passive; 3) all suffixes, other than the auxiliaries, referring purely to aspect, as ‑le‧/, continuative; 4) all nominalizing suffixes, added to the stems of verb roots, as ‑iċ/, agentive; 5) all verbalizing suffixes, added to the stems of noun roots, as ‑'. . . in/, attributive.

WORD CLASSES AND THEIR PARADIGMS

Yawelmani words fall into three major classes: verbs, substantives, particles, and interjections. The verb expresses a predication; if it is the main predication, the verb is marked by a final suffix of tense or of mode; if the verb expresses a sub-ordinate predication, it ends in one of the gerundial suffixes. The substantive, which expresses an entity reference, is formally earmarked by a final case suffix. The particle is an uninflected word, expressing notions that are primarily of an adverbial character.

The three word classes are subdivided as follows:

[7] Stress appears normally on the penult of words. Since it is a mechanical, nonphonemic fea-ture of the language, it will not be marked except in those words having the abnormal, antepenulti-mate stress.

[8] From a configurational point of view, it is interesting to note that the auxiliary has dis-appeared as a distinct type of suffix from the other five dialects of Yokuts that have been studied. All that is left of this exceptional suffix type in most dialects is one final suffix, a petrified combination of the old durative auxiliary plus a final suffix, which still retains the peculiarity of nonharmonic be-havior but does not shorten a final stem vowel or displace the word stress.

    I. Verbs
        A. Basic verbs (verbs having the base as their root)
            1. Primary verbs
            2. ʼwiyi verbs
            3. Reduplicated verbs
        B. Thematic verbs (verbs having the theme as their root)
    II. Substantives (all substantive roots are themes)
        A. Nouns
        B. Personal pronouns and demonstratives
        C. Interrogative pronouns and interrogative demonstratives
    III. Particles and interjections

Each word subclass is formally defined by its configuration of root types, by the paradigm of stems formed from these roots, and by the suffixes affiliated with each stem of the stem paradigm. The main distinction among root types is that between base and theme, a distinction cutting across the word classification of verb and substantive.

Several phonological features of the base and of base types have already been touched upon. Syllabically, bases conform either to a biliteral CVCV structure or to a triliteral CVCVC structure. Vocalically, bases contain two vowels, both of which belong to the same vowel series. Since each of the four vowel series is made up of a light (L) and a heavy (H) member, as i and e· of the i series, the bases are confined to permutations between the two members of the same vowel series. The two vowels in a base may be either L and L, H and L, or L and H (there is no base type containing the fourth theoretical permutation, H and H). These three vocalic possibilities vary independently with the two syllabic possibilities, resulting in six types of base, which may be schematized as follows:

    I. Biliteral bases
        A. With a light last vowel
            1. With a light first vowel   CLCL
            2. With a heavy first vowel   CHCL
        B. With a heavy last vowel   CLCH
    II. Triliteral bases
        A. With a light last vowel
            1. With a light first vowel   CLCLC
            2. With a heavy first vowel   CHCLC
        B. With a heavy last vowel   CLCHC

The following examples will illustrate this configuration of six base types in each of the four vowel series:

IA1)   CLCL: *kɔʼɔ, "strike," *xata, "eat," *wiyi, "say, do," *muhu, "dive"

IA2) CHCL: *dɔ·sɔ, "report," *ṣa·pa, "burn," *de·yi, "lead," *'ɔ·ṭ'u, "steal"

IB)   CLCH: *hɔyɔ·, "name," *xaya·, "place," *'ile·, "fan," *čuyɔ·, "urinate"

IIA1) CLCLC: *lɔgɔw, "pulverize," *pa'aṭ, "fight," *'ilik, "sing," *hubuṣ, "choose"

IIA2) CHCLC: *mɔ·xɔl, "grow old," *'a·mal, "help," *be·win, "sew," *wɔ·'uy, "fall
              asleep"

IIB)   CLCHC: *lɔʒɔ·x, "frighten," *p̓axa·t̓, "mourn," *hiwe·t, "walk," *hulɔ·ṣ, "sit
              down"

The basic verbs draw upon this configuration of bases for their roots. But there are three subclasses of basic verb (see page 233), and each subclass is charac-terized by a somewhat different set-up of bases. The triliteral bases, for example, do not appear in the reduplicated verb subclass, which has as its roots only the biliteral bases in a completely reduplicated form.

The root configuration of primary verbs, however, is made up of the entire set of six base types, in a simple unmodified form. Ablaut changes operating upon these primary verb bases create primary verb stems, which are then ready for the application of secondary phonetic processes and for the addition of suffixes. The primary verb suffixes, which number about fifty, are very unevenly distributed among the stems. Most of the stems of the primary verb paradigm are limited in their productiveness to one suffix. The F+R stem, on the other hand, is the most prolific in the formation of words and themes, for to this stem are allocated the majority of primary verb suffixes.

As the table of stem paradigms indicates (see page 235), some of the stems occur for only certain types of primary verb bases. The biliteral bases do not form W+A, W+W·, W+W', or W+I stems, these being part of a stem-plus-suffix process applied only to triliteral bases. Thus, the repetitive -da·/ is the sole suffix allocated to the W+A stem, and only triliteral bases undergo this process for the repetitive. The same function is expressed for biliteral bases by complete reduplica-tion, which converts the primary verb base into a reduplicated verb base. Similarly, the causative is expressed by -e·/ with the W+W· stem of triliteral bases, but by -a·la·/ with the W+Z stem of biliteral bases. But these instances of a split in the formal expression of a given function are not at all typical of Yawelmani morphol-ogy. For the most part, a function is expressed by a uniform stem-plus-suffix process operating upon all base types.

A few examples will help to actualize the stem-plus-suffix processes of the primary verb subclass:

wiy-hin, "he said": -hin, aorist, with the preconsonantal F+R stem of all primary verb bases.

lɔgw-e·ni, "in order to pulverize": -e·ni, resultative gerundial, with the pre-vocalic F+R stem of all primary verb bases.

xaya·-n/, "act of placing": -n/, verbal noun, with the W+R stem of primary verb bases of type IB. All other base types of the primary verb form the verbal noun by adding the suffix -/ to the W+R stem: e.g., biwin-/, "act of sewing,"

STEM PARADIGMS

Primary Verbs

Base	F+R Stem precons.	F+R Stem prevoc.	W+R Stem	W+Z Stem	W+S Stem precons.	W+S Stem a-assim.	W+S Stem prevoc.
IA1) *wiyi, "say, do"	wiy·	wiy·	wiy·	wiy·	wiye·	wiya·	wiye·(ʼ)·
IA2) *ɔ·ṭʼu, "steal"	ʼɔ[·]ṭʼ·	ʼɔ·ṭʼ·	ʼuṭʼ·	ʼuṭʼ·	ʼuṭʼɔ·	uṭʼa·	ʼuṭʼɔ(ʼ)·
IB) *xaya·, "place"	xaya·	xay·	xaya·	xay·	xaya·	xaya·	xaya·(ʼ)·
IIA1) *lɔgɔw, "pulverize"	lɔgiw·	lɔgw·	lɔgiw·	lɔgw·	lɔgɔ[·]jw·		lɔgɔ·w·
IIA2) *be·win, "sew"	be·win·	be[·]win·	biwin·	biwn·	biwe[·]n·		biwe·n·
IIB) *hulɔ·ṣ, "sit down"	hulɔ[·]ṣ·	hulɔ·ṣ·	hulɔ·ṣ·	hulṣ·	hulɔ[·]ṣ·		hulɔ·ṣ·

Base	W+W Stem	W+I Stem
IIA1) *lɔgɔw, "pulverize"	lɔgɔ·w·	lɔgiw·
IIA2) *be·win, "sew"	biwin·	
IIB) *hulɔ·ṣ, "sit down"	hulu·ṣ·	huluṣ·

Base	S+Z Stem	W+E Stem	W+A Stem	W+W· Stem	W+I Stem
IA1)	we·y·	wiye·w·			
IA2)	ʼɔ·ṭʼ·	ʼuṭʼɔ··			
IB)	xa·y·	xaye··			
IIA1)	lɔ[·]lgw·	lɔge·w·	lɔgɔw·	lɔgɔ·w·	lɔgiw·
IIA2)	be[·]wn·	biwe·n·	biwan·	biwin·	
IIB)	hɔ[·]lṣ·	hulɔ·ṣ·	hulaṣ·	hulu·ṣ·	hulu·ṣ·

Reduplicated Verbs

Base	F+Z—W+Z Stem	F+Z—A+Z Stem	W+Z—A+Z Stem	W+Z—A+Z Stem	W+S—I+Z Stem	W+S—Z+Z Stem	W+I—Z+Z Stem
IA1) *wiyiwiyi, "say often, do often"	wiywiy·	wiyway·	wiyway·	wiyway·	wiye·wiy·	wiye[·]wy·	wiyiwy·
IA2) *ɔ·ṭʼuɔ·ṭʼu, "steal often"	ʼɔ[·]ṭʼuṭʼ·	ʼɔ[·]ṭʼaṭʼ·	ʼuṭʼaṭʼ·	ʼuṭʼaṭʼ·	ʼuṭʼɔ·ʼuṭʼ·	ʼuṭʼɔ[·]ṭʼ·	ʼuṭʼuʼṭʼ·
IB) *xaya·xaya·, "place often"	xayxay·	xayxay·	xayxay·	xayxay·	xaya·xiy·	xaya[·]xy·	xayixy·

'uṭ·/, "act of stealing." These two verbal noun suffixes are the only ones affiliated with the W +R stem.

'uṭ·hatin/, "desire to steal": ·hatin/, desiderative, with the W +Z stem of biliteral primary verb bases. For triliteral bases this suffix appears in an initially truncated form: e.g., lɔgw·ɔtin/, "desire to pulverize."

hulɔ[·]ṣ·'a·hin, "he was sitting down": ·'a·hin, durative preterit, with the preconsonantal W +S stem of triliteral primary verb bases, with the a-assimilated W +S stem of biliteral primary verb bases (see page 227).

wiye·(')-ič/, "one who is saying": ·ič/, agentive, with the prevocalic W +S stem of all primary verb bases.

be[·]wn·a·/, "keep sewing": ·'. . . a·/, continuative, with the S +Z stem of all primary verb bases.

xaye··lsa·/, "cause to place often": ·lsa·/, causative-repetitive, with the W +E· stem of biliteral primary verb bases. This suffix is initially truncated for triliteral bases: e.g., lɔge·w·sa·/, "cause to pulverize often." The W +E· stem is employed only with the causative-repetitive suffix.

biwan·da·/, "sew often": ·da·/, repetitive, with the W +A stem of triliteral primary verb bases. This is the only suffix affiliated with the W +A stem.

hulu·ṣ·ɔ·/, hulu'ṣ·ɔ·/, "cause to sit down": ·ɔ·/, causative, with either the W +W· stem or the W +W' stem of triliteral primary verb bases. These two stems, which are optional in the formation of the causative, are limited to the one suffix.

lɔgiw·le·/, "keep pulverizing": ·le·/, continuative, with the W +I stem of a few primary verb bases of types IIA1 and IIB. There is no other suffix affiliated with the W +I stem. This stem-plus-suffix process is one of the rare instances of a morphological operation applied to only a few representatives of a given base type. Yawelmani morphology, on the whole, is characterized by the free, regular, and machine-like operation of its processes; every base belonging to a given type is, with rare exceptions, subject to the processes appropriate to that type.

The root of the ·wiyi verb, another subclass of basic verbs, is composed of a semiproclitic element plus ·wiyi. The ·wiyi portion of the verb may assume any of the stem-plus-suffix processes that apply to the primary verb base *wiyi, "say, do." With the primary verb examples presented above, compare the following stem-plus-suffix forms of *'uhwiyi, "cough": "uhwiy·hin, "he coughed," 'uhwiy·hatin/, "desire to cough," 'uhwiya·-'a·hin, "he was coughing," 'uhwiye·(')-ič/, "one who is coughing," 'uhwiye·lsa·/, "cause to cough often." As these examples indicate, the proclitic element may remain unchanged while the ·wiyi portion of the verb is subjected to the processes of the primary verb. But there are, in addition, several processes which the proclitic itself undergoes.

According to their proclitic behavior, three types of ·wiyi verb base are to be distinguished, the types being marked by the syllabic structure of the proclitic: the ·wiyi verb base with 1) a biliteral proclitic, 2) a triliteral proclitic, and 3) a quadriliteral proclitic. Of these three types, the -wiyi verb base with a quadriliteral proclitic is the least creative, for the proclitic element is fixed and immutable; this type of -wiyi verb is, in short, limited in its formal behavior to the stem-plus-suffix processes of the primary verb. Most of the quadriliteral proclitics are cast in a double finally reduplicated form: e.g., *simimimwiyi, "keep drizzling," *t'ababab-wiyi, "make fluttering sounds," *'unununwiyi, "shiver." But only a few are actually created by double final reduplication of a biliteral proclitic; *simimimwiyi is reduplicated from *simwiyi, "drizzle," but *t'abababwiyi and *'unununwiyi are petrified in their reduplicated forms. A few of the quadriliteral proclitics do not exhibit a reduplicated form, and these are also petrified: e.g., *ciwak'aywiyi, "turn green."

The biliteral proclitics are somewhat more productive in undergoing formal change. Complete reduplication of the biliteral proclitic serves to express a repetitive function: e.g., *t'apwiyi, "slap," *t'apt'apwiyi, "clap the hands"; *xip'wiyi, "rub once," *xip'xip'wiyi, "rub several times." Double final reduplication of the biliteral proclitic denotes a semelfactive or continuative activity (see the quadriliteral proclitics, discussed above). A rhetorical lengthening of the biliteral proclitic vowel expresses a retardative function: e.g., *t'olwiyi, "get peeled off quickly," *t'o·lwiyi, "get peeled off slowly"; *hik'wiyi, "make a hiccuping sound," *hi·k'wiyi, "make a panting sound." These changes of reduplication and vowel lengthening, which affect the biliteral proclitic of the -wiyi verb base, are the only formal processes applied to this type of -wiyi verb in addition to the stem-plus-suffix processes of the primary verb.

The most productive type of -wiyi verb is that with a triliteral proclitic. This proclitic, like the biliteral type, may be completely reduplicated, and it may have the last vowel rhetorically lengthened: e.g., *gababwiyi, "wave the hand once," *gababgababwiyi, "wave the hand several times";[9] *bidinwiyi, "tumble from a high place," *bidi·nwiyi, "walk over a high place." No creative process, however, is responsible for the finally reduplicated form displayed by a large number of triliteral proclitics, such as *gababwiyi; all of these are petrified in their present form.

In contrast to the other proclitic types, the triliteral proclitic assumes stem forms detached from the -wiyi portion of the verb. The following are examples of the triliteral proclitic stems with their affiliated suffixes:

'ime[·]k-la·/, "cause to drop out of sight": -la·/, causative, with the W +S proclitic stem of *'imik'wiyi, "drop out of sight."

dugg-al/, "that which is straight": -al/, consequent agentive, with the W +Z proclitic stem of *dugugwiyi, "straighten out" (medio-passive).

---

[9] In general, the complete reduplication of triliteral elements is uncongenial to Yawelmani. Biliteral primary verb bases and biliteral proclitics of the -wiyi- verb base undergo complete reduplication quite freely; but the triliteral primary verb bases are totally impervious to this process, and only a very small proportion of the triliteral proclitics may be completely reduplicated.

kɔ·ẏiẏ·it/, "several objects bent sideways": ·it/, distributive, with the S+I proclitic stem of *kɔẏɔẏwiyi, "bend sideways" (medio-passive).

wakwak·iṣ/, "one who always has his mouth open": ·iṣ/, habitual agentive, with the initially reduplicated proclitic stem of *wakakwiyi, "open the mouth."

The ·wiyi verb base with a triliteral proclitic may be regarded as something in the nature of a compound base, for this type of proclitic element has the charac-teristic of a detachable root. Other types of proclitic, however, remain constantly joined to the ·wiyi portion of the verb and, in this respect, are genuinely proclitic in nature. The fact that no grammatical technique resembling either proclisis or compounding occurs elsewhere in the language marks the ·wiyi verbs as a peculiar and anomalous class of words.

Another peculiarity of ·wiyi verbs is their direct expressive force, which stands out sharply in such a highly formalized language as Yawelmani. Many of the proclitics, particularly those of the biliteral type, are patently onomatopoetic, and these combined with the ·wiyi element (obviously related to *wiyi, "say, do") result in a "do so-and-so" type of mimetic reference: e.g., *tuhwiyi, "spit" ("do tuh"), *ga·gwiyi, "cackle" ("do ga·g"), *ṭɔkwiyi, "make a popping sound" ("do ṭɔk"). To the Yawelmani native, at any rate, the ·wiyi verbs have a special and distinct status. They represent a type of linguistic playfulness which is apparently considered to be not quite in keeping with the essential sobriety of adult behavior. These verbs are used by adults only for humorous or grotesque effect; they also appear in the comic portions of mythical narratives, particularly in those describing the antics of Coyote. But in everyday speech the ·wiyi verbs are primarily the linguistic property of children.

A reduplicated form of base with its distinctive stem paradigm characterizes the reduplicated verb, a third subclass of basic verbs. Reduplicated verb bases, which express repetitive notions, are created by complete reduplication of primary verb bases, but it is only the biliteral bases of the primary verb that may be con-verted into reduplicated verb bases. The stem paradigm of the reduplicated verb is presented in the table on page 235.

With minor additions and omissions, the suffixes affiliated with the F+R stem of primary verbs are also allocated to the F+Z—W+Z stem of reduplicated verbs: e.g., 'ɔ[·]ṭ'·hun, "he stole," 'ɔ[·]ṭ'uṭ'·hun, "he stole often"; 'ɔ·ṭ'·al, "he might steal," 'ɔ[·]ṭ'uṭ'·al, "he might steal often." Since these two stems share the ma-jority of verb suffixes, they are the nuclear stems in the creation of words and themes for their respective verb subclasses. Only one or two suffixes are affiliated with each of the reduplicated verb stems other than the F+Z—W+Z stem: e.g., 'ɔ[·]ṭ'·aṭ'·/, "the act of stealing often," contains the suffix ·/, verbal noun, the only one employed with the F+Z—A+Z stem of reduplicated verb bases; wiẏway·a·/ "one who has often said," contains ·'. . . a·/, consequent agentive, the sole suffix allocated to the W+Z—A+Z stem of reduplicated verb bases; xaya·xiy·ič/, "one who often places," contains the agentive -ič/, the only suffix added to the W +S—I +Z stem of reduplicated verb bases.

The root of thematic verbs and of substantives is the theme, which differs in several fundamental respects from the base. The theme is not defined in its phonetic structure by limitations of a syllabic or vocalic nature, such as those applying to the base; like the word, the theme may be composed of any number of open or closed syllables in any combination, and the vowels of these syllables are not restricted to any particular series. For the most part, the theme is a secondary root, made up of a thematizing suffix added to a stem: e.g., 'uṭ'ɔ·lsa·/, "cause to steal often" (-lsa·/, causative-repetitive, with the W +E· stem of *'ɔ·ṭu); xathatin/, "desire to eat" (-hatin/, desiderative, with the W +Z stem of *xata); hɔẏle·xas/, "do nothing but hunt" (-xas/, exclusive, with a stem of the theme hɔẏle·/, "hunt"). As the last example indicates, a thematizing suffix may be added to the stem of a theme as well as to the stem of a base. Theoretically, there is no limit to the number of thematic layers that can lead up to an eventual theme: e.g., xathatinxas/, "do nothing but desire to eat." Not all themes, however, can be demonstrated by analysis to be secondary roots; hɔẏle·/ is an example of a primitive, unanalyzable theme. Such primitive themes are particularly numerous among substantives.

The theme paradigm contains only one characteristic stem—the case stem of substantives, the normal stem of thematic verbs. In this stem it is solely the last vowel which undergoes ablaut change. The theme types and the normal stem of thematic verbs are illustrated in the following table:

Theme Types	Normal Stem	
	preconsonantal	prevocalic
IB) hɔẏle·/, "hunt"	hɔyle·-	hɔyl-
IIA a) pana·mix/, "arrive with"	pana·mix-	pana[·]mx-
b) xatmix/, "eat with"	xatmix-	xatmix-
IIB 'a·ḍay/, "boast"	'a·ḍay-	'a·ḍay-

The treatment of theme vowels in the normal stem corresponds, on the whole, to the treatment of base vowels under the processes of reduction, and it is this correspondence between themes and reduced bases which the numbering of theme types is intended to indicate.[10]

Simple phonetic criteria determine the classification and the stem treatment of theme types among thematic verbs. All themes ending in a vowel are members

[10] The reduction processes are best exemplified in the F +R stem of primary verb bases. This stem is presented in a schematic form and illustrated on page 229; compare the stem treatment of root vowels in *'ile· (base type IB) and hɔẏle·/ (theme type IB), in *lɔgɔw (base type IIA) and pana·mix/ (theme type IIA), in *hulɔ·ṣ (base type IIB) and 'a·ḍay/ (theme type IIB). The correspondence between reduced bases and themes, however, can be more readily demonstrated in the theme configuration of substantives, where the correspondence emerges in more obvious and overt resemblances because of the presence of additional theme types (see page 241 ff.).

of theme type IB, and only a heavy vowel occurs finally in themes; in its normal
stem treatment, this final vowel is retained preconsonantally but assumes the zero
grade prevocalically. Themes ending in a consonant preceded by i or u belong to
theme type IIA; if the penultimate syllable is open, the theme (type IIAa) loses
its last vowel prevocalically; if the penult is closed, the theme (type IIAb) keeps
its last vowel in both the preconsonantal and prevocalic forms of the normal stem.
In the prevocalic normal stem of theme type IIAb, the resistance of the last vowel
to zeroing is due to a syllabic interference rather than to the character of the
vowel itself, for identical processes create verb themes of type IIAa and IIAb,
the examples in the normal stem table (page 239) being composed of ᐧmix/, comita-
tive, with stems of *panaᐧ, "arrive," and *xata, "eat." Finally, themes of type IIB
end in a consonant preceded by a or ɔ; this vowel is retained in both forms of the
normal stem.

The same set of suffixes affiliated with the F+R stem of primary verb bases
and with the F+Z—W+Z stem of reduplicated verb bases are employed with the
normal stem of thematic verbs: e.g., hɔy̆leᐧhin, "he hunted"; pana[ᐧ]mxᐧal nan,
"he might come with me." In addition to these suffixes, the normal stem employs
several others which are identical in function to suffixes affiliated with basic verb
stems other than the F+R stem and the F+Z—W+Z stem: e.g., the agentive
ᐧihneᐧ/, added to the normal stem of thematic verbs, parallels the function of ᐧič/,
agentive, allocated to the W+S stem of primary verbs and to the W+S—I+Z
stem of reduplicated verbs.

The morphological system of thematic verbs, the system of stem-plus-suffix
processes common to all members of this word class, is the normal stem with its
suffixes. But, by analogy, some of the stem-plus-suffix processes appropriate to
basic verbs are sporadically applied to a few thematic verbs. These analogical processes, however, are not to be considered part of the thematic verb paradigm;
for, with the exception of the fake base (see below), no thematic verb can partici-
pate systematically in the processes of the basic verb paradigm. As a matter of fact,
the analogical processes number no more than half a dozen.

Verb themes assume the processes of those verb bases to which they have an
adventitious structural similarity: some processes applied to triliteral primary verb
bases are analogically carried over to triliteral verb themes, and processes operating upon reduplicated verb bases, which are quadriliteral in structure, are similarly
extended to quadriliteral verb themes. Thus, the repetitive ᐧdaᐧ/, regularly allocated to the W+A stem of triliteral primary verb bases (see page 236), is added
to an analogical W+A stem of a few triliteral verb themes: compare 'ilak-daᐧ/,
"sing often" (<*'ilik, "sing") with wilal-daᐧ/, "prepare to depart often"
(<wellaᐧ/, "prepare to depart"); in the same way the agentive ᐧič/, affiliated with
the W+S—I+Z stem of reduplicated verb bases, is suffixed to an analogical
W+S—I+Z stem of a few quadriliteral verb themes: compare dɔsɔ·dis-ič/, "one
who reports often" (<*dɔ·sɔdɔ·sɔ, "report often") with hɔyɔ·nil-ič/, "one who

incites" (<hɔynil/, "incite, rally"), the last example having the same function as hɔynil·ihne·/, in which the agentive ·ihne·/ is added to the normal stem of the verb theme.

The only variety of thematic verb that may undergo the entire gamut of basic verb processes is the fake base, a theme of type IIAa formed by the medio-passive ·in/ appended to the F+R stem of biliteral primary verb bases: e.g., xay·in/, "get placed" (<*xaya·, "place"), he·x·in/, "get fat" (<*he·xi, "fatten").[11] No other thematizing process creates a verb theme which is so base-like in its structure: compare he·xin/ with the base *be·win, "sew." When it is recalled that the normal stem treatment of themes corresponds in certain configurational features to the F+R stem treatment of primary verb bases and that these two stems share most of their suffixes, it will be realized that the fake base is merely a variety of theme which, in its stem-plus-suffix processes as well as in its structure, exhibits a maximal resemblance to the base: compare the normal stem-plus-suffix forms, he·xin·hin, "he got fat," and he[·]xn·al, "he might get fat," with the F+R stem-plus-suffix forms, be·win·hin, "he sewed," and be[·]wn·al, "he might sew." With this fortuitous but farreaching parallelism to the base offering an optimum condition for analogical intrusion, the fake base takes over the entire formal apparatus of the true base: e.g., hixn·atin/, "desire to get fat" (compare biwn·atin/, "desire to sew"), hixe[·]n·'an, "he is getting fat" (compare biwe[·]n·'an, "he is sewing"), hixi'n·e·/, "cause to get fat" (compare biwi'n·e·/, "cause to sew"). But the processes forming he[·]xn·ihne·/, "one who is getting fat," or he·xin·xɔ·hin, "he was getting fat," cannot be applied to *be·win, for the agentive ·ihne·/ and the durative ·xɔ·.. are distinctively normal stem suffixes which are not affiliated with any of the primary basic verb stems. The fake base, in short, is a base-like theme which undergoes the processes of both the basic verb and the thematic verb.

Like the normal stem of thematic verbs, the case stem of substantives appears in two forms, the absolutive case stem corresponding to the preconsonantal normal stem, the oblique case stem corresponding to the prevocalic normal stem. Whereas the divisions of the normal stem are phonetically conditioned, those of the case stem are based upon an alignment of suffixes. To the absolutive case stem is added only the subjective suffix; suffixes expressing the possessive, objective, indirect objective, ablative, and locative cases are added to the oblique case stem. The substantive theme types and their case stems are as follows:

Substantive Theme Types	Case Stem	
	absolutive	oblique
IA kač/, "obsidian"	kač·	kač·
IIB a) pitelse·/, "act of advising"	pitelse··	pitels·
b) ke·xa·/, "money"	ke·xa··	ke·xa··

[11] The suffix ·in/ is also added to the F+R stem of the triliteral type of primary verb base: e.g., lɔgw·in/, "get pulverized" (<*lɔgɔw, "pulverize"). But such thematic verbs are not subject to the basic verb processes; i.e., they are not fake bases.

IIA ćɔnɔ·xis/, "sugar pine"	ćɔnɔ·xis⸴	ćɔnɔ[·]xs⸴
IIB a) ḱile·y/, "cloud"	ḱile·y⸴	ḱile·y⸴
b) silelhal/, "stones"	silelhal⸴	silelhal⸴
c) bɔnɔy/, "two"	bɔnɔy⸴	bɔny⸴

The correspondence of themes to reduced bases is more apparent among substantives than among thematic verbs (see page 239, especially footnote 10). Theme type IA, which does not occur among thematic verbs, is a biliteral substantive theme whose case stem corresponds to the F+R stem of biliteral bases of type IA: compare the F+R stem of *xata, "eat," appearing as preconsonantal and prevocalic xat⸴ (see page 229), with the case stem of ḱać/, indicated in the above table.

Themes of type IB end in a heavy vowel. The IBa substantive theme follows the stem pattern of the IB verb theme (compare hɔý·le·/, page 239) and the IB verb base (compare *ʼile·, page 229) in retaining its final vowel in the absolutive case stem and losing it in the oblique. Peculiar to substantives is the stem pattern for IB roots occurring in substantive theme IBb, which retains its final vowel in both the absolutive and the oblique forms of the case stem. Membership in subtype IBa is morphologically determined: vowel-ending substantive themes composed of a verbal noun suffix added to the normal stem of thematic verbs belong to subtype IBa; all other vowel-ending substantive themes belong to subtype IBb.

Theme type IIA is made up of themes with a final consonant preceded by i or u. Among certain verb themes of this type, a syllabic interference prevents the zeroing of the last vowel in the prevocalic normal stem (see page 240). But substantive themes of type IIA consistently zero their last vowel in the oblique case stem, regardless of syllabic conditions: e.g., in spite of the closed penult in ʼɔnmil/, "daughter-in-law," the last vowel is zeroed and an inorganic vowel is inserted in the oblique case stem ʼɔn(i)ml⸴. The F+R stem pattern of IIA bases is more consistently maintained, therefore, by IIA substantive themes than by verb themes of this type.

Substantive themes of type IIB fall into three subtypes. Like the IIB base with its F+R stem pattern, the IIBa substantive theme ends in a consonant with a preceding heavy vowel, this vowel being retained in the absolutive and oblique case stem. Like the IIB verb theme with its normal stem pattern, the IIBb substantive theme ends in a consonant preceded by a or ɔ, this vowel also being retained in both forms of the case stem. But the IIBc substantive theme, whose last a or ɔ vowel is zeroed in the oblique case stem, is a type of root peculiar to the substantive configuration. This unique theme is a moribund and probably archaic type, for only a handful of IIBc themes occur in Yawelmani. All other theme types are unlimited categories, containing themes formed by thoroughly productive processes.

The entire set of substantive theme types is represented among nouns, one of the three substantive classes (see page 233). The case stem with its six case suffixes is the paradigm common to all nouns. The following examples will illustrate the case paradigm of nouns.

	kac̓/ "obsidian"	ke·xa·/ "money"	c̓ɔnɔ·xis/ "sugar pine"	kile·y/ "cloud"
Subjective	kac̓·]	ke·xa(')·]	c̓ɔnɔ·xis·]	kile[·]y·]
Possessive	kac̓·in	ke·xa·(')·in	c̓ɔnɔ[·]xs·in	kile·y·in
Objective	kac̓·a	ke·xa·(')·in	c̓ɔnɔ[·]xs·ɔ	kile[·]y·]
Ind. objective	kac̓·ni	ke·xa·ni	c̓ɔnɔ[·]xs(ɔ·)·ni	kile[·]y·ni
Ablative	kac̓·nit	ke·xa·nit	c̓ɔnɔ[·]xs(ɔ·)·nit	kile[·]y·nit
Locative	kac̓(a)·w	ke·xa[·]·w	c̓ɔnɔ[·]xs(ɔ)·w	kile·y(a)·w

Among the case suffixes only the objective suffix differs in form according to the theme type of the noun to which it is attached.

Beyond the case paradigm, the stem-plus-suffix processes applied to the noun are extremely sporadic and unproductive. Some of these special processes operate upon only two or three nouns, while others can be applied to as many as a score of nouns; but all of them, in contrast to the processes of the case paradigm, are narrowly limited in scope. In this respect, they have much the same status as the analogical processes of the thematic verb, neither the special processes of the noun nor the analogical processes of the thematic verb being part of the paradigm of thoroughly creative processes that can be systematically applied to every word-class member.

On a functional basis the special processes of the noun may be conveniently divided into verbalizing, nominalizing, and pluralizing processes. Among the verbalizing processes, for example, is the suffix -na·/, "procure, make," added to a W +A stem of a few nouns, to a W +I stem of a few others: e.g., 'inaṭ-na·/, "get magic power" (<'e·niṭ/, "magic power"), ṭalip-na·/, "make arrows" (<ṭala·p/, "arrow"). An example of a nominalizing process is the bahuvrihi intensive -iyin/, whose first consonant varies considerably, sometimes assimilating to the last consonant of the stem and sometimes varying irrationally, added to a W +Z stem of a few nouns: e.g., xisx-iyin/, "one with long fingernails" (<xe·six/, "fingernail"), kuṭṣ-uyun/ or kuṭṣ-uṣun/, "one with a long tail" (<kuṭuṣ/, "tail"), balk-idin/, "one with a large belly" (<balik/, "belly").

Two techniques for pluralizing nouns occur in Yawelmani. One is the addition of a plural suffix to a noun stem, the stem-plus-suffix unit being a theme which is inflected for case like any theme of its type: e.g., sile[·]l-hal/, "stones," is a theme of type IIBb, composed of -hal/, plural suffix, with the W +E· stem of sile·l/, "stone." In contrast to this plural thematizing technique is the formation of a plural stem to which the case suffixes are added, the subjective case suffix being attached directly to the plural stem, the other case suffixes being added to the plural stem with an intervening oblique suffix -h·: e.g., nɔ·sas·, plural stem, and nɔ·sas·h·, plural stem with oblique suffix (<nusɔ·s/, "paternal aunt"). Only a very small proportion of nouns can be formally pluralized, and even in these nouns the plural form is not obligatory for expressing a plural function: e.g., mani' silel, literally "many stone," is as acceptable as mani' silelhal, "many stones."

The personal pronouns and demonstratives constitute another class of substantives, based upon themes of type IBb: na·/, first person, ma·/, second person,
'ama·/, third person; ke·/, "this," ṭa·/, "that." The paradigm of these themes is
made up of a singular, dual, and plural in each of the six cases. The forms of the first
person na·/ will serve to illustrate the paradigm of this substantive class.[12]

	Singular	Dual	Plural
Subjective	na'	na'aǩ	na'an
Possessive	nim	nimgin	nimɔ·gun
Objective	nan	na·nikwa	na·ninwa
Indirect objective	nanni	na·nikwa·ni	na·ninwa·ni
Ablative	nannit	na·nikwa·nit	na·ninwa·nit
Locative	na·naw	na·nikwaw	na·ninwaw

For the first person dual and plural Yawelmani distinguishes between an exclusive
and an inclusive, denoting that the person being addressed is either excluded or
included in the first person reference. The dual and plural forms of the first person
pronoun, as given in the above table, denote the exclusive; the inclusive is expressed by a special paradigmatic inflection of the pronominal theme ma·/, second
person, in the dual and plural cases: compare in their dual subjective forms the
first person exclusive na'aǩ, "we two (he and I), "the inclusive maǩ, "we two (you
and I)," and the second person ma'aǩ, "you two."

The third class of substantives is composed of interrogatives, whose paradigm
is extremely defective. The interrogatives ordinarily appear in three case forms,
to which is attached a constant, enclitic-like element -uk. Although a distinct form
denoting the subjective case occurs for all interrogatives, the oblique case functions are variously combined in their formal expression; usually the indirect objective, locative, and ablative functions are fused in an adverbial case form. Some of the
interrogatives are:

subjective watuk, "who?" possessive wa·tinuk, objective and adverbial
wa·tɔ'uk

subjective ha'uk, "what thing?" objective ha·nuk, adverbial ha·nɔ'uk

subjective hiyuk, "what place?" ablative hiye·tuk, objective, indirect objective, and locative hiyɔ'uk

subjective hawiyuk, "what kind of . . . ?" objective hawyɔ'uk, adverbial
hawye·nɔ'uk

subjective hawṣinuk, "how many?" oblique hawṣe·nɔ'uk

As opposed to verbs and substantives, which constitute the inflected word
classes of Yawelmani, the particles and interjections are uninflected. For the most
part, the particles are primitive elements not derived from verb or substantive

[12] No attempt is made at an analytical presentation of these paradigmatic forms. Although
the pronouns and demonstratives belong to the substantive category, their paradigm, as might
be expected, exhibits a number of special phonetic and morphological details, which cannot be
taken up in this brief sketch.

roots, but a few semantically specialized derivatives appear among the particles: e.g., 'uťťal, "solely, nothing but" (literally, "that which is perched on a summit"), composed of ⁄al/, consequent agentive, with the W +Z proclitic stem of *'uťuťwiyi, "perch on a summit" (see page 237).

According to their function, particles may be classified as 1) predicational modifiers, 2) conjunctives, and 3) sentence words. The predicational modifiers form the largest group among the particles. A number of these express modal ideas: e.g., hina', "perhaps"; 'axam, "probably, it is to be believed that . . . "; 'anaxdi', "it is to be doubted that . . . "; 'ahmun, "it is to be expected that . . . "; 'e·man, "to no avail, without success"; 'ax, "unintentionally, unwittingly"; 'aṣ, "actually, really"; wiľ, "of course, certainly"; miẓna', "indeed, surely"; na'aṣ, a dubitative tag, always employed in a sentence containing a verb with the dubitative suffix ⁄al. Some examples in context are:

'axam xata nimɔ·gun 'ɔ·ťɔn, "probably he will steal our food"
cawhin 'e·man, "he shouted, to no avail"
'angi ma' ṭan 'aṣ dɔshin, "did you actually report it?"

Particles with a temporal force are also numerous among the predicational modifiers: e.g., hiya·mi', "a long time ago"; 'alid, "some time ago"; walan, "yesterday"; he·ẓi'," today"; ṭiymi, "right now"; canum, "immediately"; 'aca·wis, "in a short while"; mi'in, "soon"; wisa, "not yet, after a while"; hiya', "later on."

hiya·mi' kew na'an hɔy̓le·hin, "a long time ago we hunted here"
xaten na' ṭiymi, "I shall eat right now"
mi'in hulɔshun, "soon he sat down"

Several particles convey notions of an aspective nature: e.g., xɔ·nɔw, "always"; ṭa'aṣ, "continuously"; hiyam, "already." The interrogative is expressed by 'angi, which is placed at the head of a sentence to interrogate the entire predication, and by gi, which follows the word that it interrogates: e.g., ma' gi ṭan dɔshin, "was it you who reported it?" Negation is expressed by 'a·ni with verbs containing the suffix ⁄ka, imperative, and by 'ɔhom in all other instances: e.g., 'a·ni ṭan wiy̓ka, "don't do that!" 'ɔhom na' na'aṣ taxnal, "I might not come."

The conjunctive particles have the function of coordinating or subordinating predications or the parts of a predication. The particle 'ama', "and, then," which occurs at the beginning of a sentence, is employed only as a coordinator of predications; yɔw, "and, also, again," may be used in the same way, but it also acts as a word coordinator: 'ama' binethin kay̓wa, "and he asked Coyote"; yɔw 'aman ilek'an, "and they are singing"; 'ama' kay̓iw yɔw be·mamguc pana·hin, "and Coyote and Humming Bird arrived." Other conjunctive particles are: dab, "next, on the other hand"; 'i', 'ɔ', "or"; wa'aṣgi, "therefore"; me'ẓi', "because"; wilṣin, "but, in spite of that"; 'aṅum, "at any rate, at least"; ṭaw, "if"; ki, "when."

kay̓iw 'ɔ' be·mamguc taxnen, "Coyote or Humming Bird will come"
'ama' hɔy̓le·hin me'ẓi' 'e·dilhin, "and he hunted because he got hungry"
ṭaw ma' xaten 'ɔhom 'edlen ma', "if you will eat, you will not get hungry"

The sentence words include the negative 'ɔhɔm, "no, not," which is employed also as a predicational modifier; the affirmative hɔ·hɔ', "yes," pronounced with nasalized vowels;[13] the exclamatory híydege', expressing surprise; and the greeting hiyuk, "hello," a special usage of the interrogative demonstrative meaning "what place?" (see page 244).

Interjections, regarded as appropriate only in women's speech, are earmarked by protracted vowels: e.g., wi . . . expresses annoyance; 'ina . . . is an exclamation of fear; 'e . . . expresses amazement and surprise.

SYNTAX

Yawelmani is singularly bare and simple in its syntax. Because the verb expresses no pronominal references, it is free of any ties of concord to its subject or object. Nor is the syntactic relationship between the words in a sentence indicated by word order; with the exception of certain particles, some occurring at the head of a sentence and others following the term they modify, words may take any position within the sentence. In its syntactic style, as a matter of fact, Yawelmani is even more loose-jointed than the formal description of its unambitious syntax might suggest, for the few devices offering a means of syntactic elaboration tend to be used sparingly. Typical Yawelmani prose consists of a sequence of independent simple sentences.

The sole obligatory feature of Yawelmani syntax is the expression of case in the substantive. The obligation, however, is morphological as well as syntactic: the inflected words (verbs and substantives) must end in a final suffix, and suffixes referring to case are the only final suffixes in the substantive paradigm; consequently, substantives must appear with a final case suffix. There are six cases— subjective, possessive, objective, indirect objective, ablative, and locative. The subjective case suffix, -] with the absolutive case stem, -i with certain plural stems and -a with others, is appended to substantives acting as the subject of a predication.

mam lanhin kay̓iw-], "Coyote heard you"
la·nit kay̓iw-], "Coyote was heard"
nɔ·sas-i 'amin pana' ṭew 'amin, "his paternal aunts will arrive at his house"
Substantives in a copulative predication and substantives used absolutively are also marked by the subjective case suffix.

'ama' nɔ·ċɔ(')-] be·mamguċ-], "and a clever fellow (is) Humming Bird"
'anṭuw-] wiyhin kay̓iw, " 'the shaman,' said Coyote"
Ownership or possession is expressed by the possessive case suffix, -in.

ṭa kay̓w-in t̓ulɔs, "that (is) Coyote's bow"
Agency in a passive construction is also indicated by the possessive case.

'axam̓ hɔ·yet diya·(')-in, "probably he was sent by the leader"

---

[13] Nasalized vowels are not classified as phonemes, for they appear only in the affirmative particle.

Nonfinite verbal forms, such as gerundials and verbal nouns, cannot take a gram-matical subject; in these instances the possessive case is used to denote agency.

ʼiliktaw ʼan(u)ṭw-un huloṣhun kayʼiw, "at the shaman's singing, Coyote sat down"; ʼanuṭwun, in the possessive case, is the logical subject of the gerundial verb ʼiliktaw.

lanhin ʼilka ʼan(u)ṭw-un, "he heard the shaman's singing"; here ʼanuṭwun is the logical subject of the verbal noun ʼilka, which, being the object of the predica-tion, appears in the objective case.

The direct object of a predication takes the objective case suffix, which varies in form according to the theme type membership of the substantive (see page 243).

miʼin ʼɔ·ṭɔn kaća min, "soon he will steal your obsidian."
Substantives may stand in an objective relation to other substantives having a predicational force.

ṭa ʼuṭ'a kʼe·xa·(ʼ)-in, "that (is) the one who has stolen the money."

hina' bine[·]t-] min kayʼw-a lanhin, "perhaps he heard your asking Coyote"; kayʼwa is the object of the verbal noun binet which, in turn, is the object of the main predication.

The locative -w and the ablative -nit have the function of expressing location or direction, the locative denoting "to, toward, into, in, at, on," the ablative "away from, out of."

ʼama' kayʼw(a)-w tanhin, "and he went toward Coyote"
ʼangi ma' laga' nim ṭe[·]-w, "will you spend the night at my house?"
ʼama' ṭa·-nit pil-nit yɔ'ke·hin ʼaman, "and from that road they returned"
ṭan piçewʼan ʼilk(a·)-nit, "he is pulling it out of the water."

The locative case has some special uses. It frequently expresses temporal location or duration.

wɔy(ɔ)-w ʼamin, "at his birth"
yɔw ʼilken ʼaman bɔny(ɔ)-w tɔynɔ[·]-w, "and they will sing for two nights"
Place names always have a locative form, regardless of their syntactic function in the sentence.

ťulɔnʼan ʼa[·]lt(a)-w, "Altaw is burning"; the place name ʼaltaw is the loca-tive form of ʼa·lit/, "salt grass"

The indirect objective -ni expresses a variety of indirective relational notions not covered by the locative or ablative.

ʼama' ṭaw pana·hin kayʼw(a·)-ni, "and there he arrived with Coyote"
dinhin naʼan nɔ·n̄ɔ·ʼin ťunɔ[·]l-nu, "we shielded the man from the wild-cat"
ʼangi nan kaćni wa·nen, "will he give me obsidian?"
ʼa·n̄i ʼuguʼnɔk nan ʼilk(a·)-ni, "don't make me drink water!"

Substantives in apposition agree in case: see above, the locative bɔnyɔw tɔynɔw, "for two, for night," i.e., "for two nights," and the ablative ṭa·nit pilnit, "from that, from road," i.e., "from that road." Substantival phrases that have an attributive or limiting function may likewise appear in apposition to other sub-stantives.

pana' diẏa·(')-in ṭew yɔlɔ[·]wċ-in yɔkɔ·ċi, "he will arrive at the house of the leader, of the one who is assembling the people"

Although the substantive carries the heaviest syntactic load, there are some purely syntactic functions that may be expressed in the verb. These are subordinating functions, indicated by gerundial suffixes attached to the verb.

'ama' cawhin 'amiċ-mi, "and he shouted, having approached"; -mi, consequent gerundial

taxan'an kew mam bine·t-e·ni, "he is coming here to ask you"; -e·ni, resultative gerundial

'amiċ-tin kaẏwin ga·gwiyhin, "being approached by Coyote, he cackled"; -tin, passive gerundial

Gerundials are true verbs in that they do not appear in any of the case forms. In this respect they differ from verbal nouns, which are also used to express subordinate predications.

xat(a)-w nim 'ilikhin, "during my eating, he sang"; -w, locative (of time), with the verbal noun xat/

Several of the conjunctive particles express ideas of a subordinating nature (see page 245). The use of these, however, entails no syntactic complications in the verb: e.g., pana·hin na', "I arrived," ki pana·hin na', "when I arrived..." Consequently, it is only the gerundial suffixes which formally mark the verb as a syntactically subordinate element.

YUMA

A. M. HALPERN

INTRODUCTION

YUMA is now spoken by approximately 750 members of the Yuma tribe, living on the Fort Yuma Indian Reservation in California. The reservation was established in 1859, but some of the Indians continued to live off the reservation at the town of Algodones, in Mexico, until 1912. The name Yuma is supposedly of Spanish origin. The Yuma call themselves kʷacá·n, or ʔaxám kʷacá·n, which is translatable as "Those who descended by way of the river." The reference is to the migration down the Colorado river from ʔaví· kʷamé·, where the original creation took place.

In former times the tribe consisted of three local divisions, an eastern, a northern, and a southern. Each division is said to have spoken a slightly different dialect. At present Yuma is a single language without dialectic differentiation, except that certain features are said to be characteristic of the southern (Algodones) dialect.

PHONOLOGY

§1. General remarks.

The word may be monosyllabic: mó· "well, now," té·k "he brings it closer"; or it may have as many as eight syllables: alʸnʸi·nʸa·xʷílʸvətəxalʸa "I would associate with you." The word, even when monosyllabic, always has an accented syllable: xú·lʸ "cholla cactus"; and may have two accented syllables: ʔawíyú "let me do it."

§2. System of consonants.

Table I represents the consonantal phonemes of Yuma and indicates their phonetic characteristics.

For purposes of discussion it is convenient to divide the consonants into the four following groups: a) stops, spirants, and affricate, b) liquids, c) palatalized liquids, and d) semivowels.

a) The stops, spirants, and affricate, as a class, show no systematic positional variations. A few individual phonemes, however, undergo changes in some phonetic contexts.

kʷ is delabialized before the vowel u·: kʷu·cécənʸ "the leader," kʷu·xamí· "the procreator." In this context kʷ is phonetically undistinguishable from k in the same context. The orthography kʷ will be retained, however, because a labialized pronunciation of kʷ is accepted as over-careful. kʷa (kʷ +vowel a) is pro-

TABLE I. CONSONANT PHONEMES

	Unaspirated Voiceless Stops	Voiced Fricatives	Voiceless Fricatives	Voiceless Affricate	Voiced Nasals	Voiced Laterals	Voiceless Laterals	Semivowels	Tip-trill
Bilabial	p	v			m			w	
Interdental		δ							
Dental	t		s	c	n	l	ł		
Palatalized dental	tʸ				nʸ	lʸ	łʸ		
Cacuminal	ṭ		š		ŋ				
Prepalatal	kʸ							y	r
Palatal	k		x						
Labialized palatal	kʷ		xʷ						
Velar	q								
Labialized velar	qʷ								
Glottal	ʔ								

nounced as ku when followed by a bilabial consonant or by kʸ, k, or kʷ:kʷapáy "the carrier," kʷakxó· "woodpecker." Again the orthography kʷ is retained because an overcareful pronunciation is acceptable.

xʷ is similarly delabialized before the vowel: u· xʷu·nʸó·vənʸ "his dodging," xʷu·ʔá·vənʸ "her jealousy."

The affricate c varies in pronunciation from a dental to an alveolar affricate. When followed by t in rapid speech, c is pronounced as s: aʔíctaʔa "so they said."

b) The phonemes m, n, ŋ, l, ł, and r constitute the class of liquids. Of these, m, n, l, and r share a certain kind of positional variation, while ŋ and ł are of such rare occurrence that little can be said about them.

The phonemes m, n, l, and r occur in long form 1) when preceded by an accented short vowel: naqámək "he touches," acénək "he descends," salasál "porous," tamaʔórək "it is full"; 2) when following a short vowel and preceding an accented vowel: namák "he leaves," anák "he sits," alú·k "he smears," arúvək "it is dry"; and 3) when following a short vowel and preceding another consonant: kamló "flirtatious woman," ʔankʸí· "grass sp.," xatalwé "coyote," ʔarkúyk "he conceals," with the exception that m or n followed by a homorganic stop is not so geminated: a·ʔámpək "he bends over," ʔantamák "we leave." In all other contexts m, n, l, and r occur as short consonants.

The phoneme r usually occurs as a tip trill similar to the Spanish r, but when preceded by š and an unaccented short vowel it has a retroflex pronunciation: šaréq "he grasps," mašaráyk "he is angry."

c) The palatalized liquids are nʸ, lʸ, and łʸ. When two palatalized liquids come in contact with each other, the first loses its palatalization but is articulated at a point slightly higher than that of the corresponding unpalatalized liquid: nuˑmínʸnʸa "their passing by," alʸnʸiˑδúˑck "he thinks," kʷatxasíłʸnʸa "that corˑ rugated one." A palatalized liquid may also (but not uniformly) lose its palatalizaˑ tion when followed by c: uˑδúcənʸc "his actions," xaˑlʸcaδúˑm "Halchidhoma."

d) The semivowels, w and y, occur in consonantal form when in the initial position in the word, when intervocalic, and as final members of consonant clusters: waˑrávək "he forbids," awíˑm "he does," aˑcwísk "he sneezes," yaˑlák "goose," ayúˑk "he sees." They occur in vocalic form when in the final position in the word and as initial members of consonant clusters: ʔaʔáw "fire," aδáwk "he takes," vatáy "big," kaméˑyk "he brings for him." Vocalic w and y are never treated as vowels: they are never accented and are treated as consonants for purposes of syllabification.

§3. Positions of consonants.

Consonants may occur in six positions in the word: 1) initially, 2) finally, 3) intervocalically preceding an unaccented vowel, 4) intervocalically preceding an accented vowel, 5) as first member of a consonant cluster, and 6) as final member of a medial consonant cluster. Most consonants occur in all six positions. Some, however, are defective in that there are some positions in which they do not occur.

There are two classes of defective consonantal phonemes. Class I includes the phonemes δ, kʸ, kʷ, xʷ, qʷ, and ʔ. These do not occur in the final position, and with the exception of kʷ they do not occur as initial members of consonant clusters. Class II includes the phonemes ł, łʸ, and tʸ. These do not occur in the initial posi tion, intervocalically preceding an accented vowel, or as final members of medial consonant clusters.

The distribution of the phoneme ṭ is similar to that of defective phonemes of class II. Like them, it occurs in the final position, intervocalically preceding an unaccented vowel, and as initial member of a consonant cluster. It occurs in the initial position only once (ṭáw ṭáw "bird sp.") and intervocalically preceding an accented vowel only once (uˑṭáw "to defeat"), and does not occur as the final member of a medial consonant cluster.

§4. Consonant clusters.

Consonant clusters may occur medially or finally in the word but never ini tially. Medial clusters may be biconsonantal or triconsonantal. Final clusters are never of more than two consonants.

Altogether 242 medial biconsonantal clusters are actually found.

The absences are accounted for by the following considerations: δ, kʸ, xʷ, qʷ, and ʔ do not occur as initial members of consonant clusters; tʸ, ṭ, ł, and łʸ do not occur as final members; ŋ, a very rare phoneme, does not occur as initial or final member; v is absorbed by a following m, v, or p; p is absorbed by following p. All other absences must be regarded as fortuitous.

Medial triconsonantal clusters of two types are found: 1) with ʔ as final member, e.g. aδíctʔaš "it has gone to seed," ʔawétkʔaš "therefore I did it"; and 2) containing (usually as medial member) kʷ, nʸ, or lʸ, e.g. ʔanʸkʷcuˑmpáp "we four," ʔašlʸmák "my back," ʔanʸcxáˑṭ "my horses." Both types are of rare occurⲵrence.

The following final consonantal clusters are found:

tp, mp, np;
ct, št, xt, nt;
pk, tk, tʸk, ṭk, ck, sk, šk, xk, nʸk, lʸk, wk, yk;[1]
sq, šq, nʸq, lʸq;
tc, ṭc, nʸc, lʸc, wc, yc;
wš.

§5. Vowels: general remarks.

Vowel phonemes occur in two quantities, short and long. The distinctiveness of length as a phonemic feature of the vowel is shown by such contrasts as ʔaˑvé "snake" and ʔaˑvéˑ "mouse," iˑδó "eye" and iˑδóˑ "tooth." Initial vowels are proⲵnounced with an aspirated attack: iˑmáˑṭ "body," aváˑk "he arrives." Final acⲵcented short vowels are released with a sharp, clearly audible aspiration: ʔamó "mountain sheep," ʔakʷé "cloud."

The vowel may occur in three positions in the word: accented, preaccentual, and postaccentual.[2] The positional variants of a given vowel phoneme may deⲵpend on its position in the word. Some vowels are limited in respect to the positions in which they may occur.

§6. Accented vowels.

Ten vowel phonemes, five long and five short, occur in the accented position:

á (as a of German Mann): ʔamáṭ "land," atápk "he throws"
é (as e of English pet): namé "wildcat," axʷélʸk "he digs"
í (as i of English pit): awík "he helps," ʔapílʸ "hot"
ó (as o of German Gott): ʔampóṭ "dust," aδóxa "he will do"
ú (as u of English put): ašúc "younger brother," amúlʸ "name"
áˑ (as a of English father): ayáˑk "he goes," ʔaxʔáˑ "cottonwood"
éˑ (same quality as é): ʔaméˑ "high," téˑk "he brings closer"
íˑ (as ea of English bead): ʔacíˑ "fish," maníˑš "scorpion"
óˑ (same quality as ó): atóˑk "he is sated," xóˑr "gravel"
úˑ (as oo of English food): aštúˑm "he gathers," ayúˑk "he sees"

§7. Preaccentual vowels.

The vowels aˑ, iˑ, uˑ, oˑ, a, e, i, o, and u are found in the preaccentual position.

---

[1] q and k preceded by a vowel absorb a following final k: ʔanóq <*ʔanóqk "it is small," anák <*anákk "he sits."

[2] That is, in relation to the primary accent of the word. In words containing two accents, the first accent is primary. The vowel bearing the primary accent is in the accented position. All vowels in the preaccentual position are unaccented. Vowels in the postaccentual position may be unacⲵcented or may bear a secondary accent.

a· has the quality of accented á· and is found preceding all accented vowels: a·δápk "he splits it," a·mélək "he wears it as a belt," a·nʸórək "he writes," ta·pí·ṭ "blanket."

When preceding an accented á, á·, í, í·, ú, or ú·, i· has the quality of accented í·: ʔaci·mák "he dances," i·xú· "nose," mi·sí·lʸ "thigh." When preceding an accented é, é·, ó, or ó·, i· has the quality of accented é·: vi·yémək "he goes away," i·δó "eye." If, however, an unaccented a· intervenes between i· and an accented é, é·, ó, or ó·, or if i· is followed immediately by another unaccented vowel, i· has the quality of accented i· regardless of the quality of the accented vowel: nʸi·ka·taqʷérək "follow him," wi·u·vsó·yk "he curses him."

When preceding accented á, á·, í, í·, ú, or ú·, u· has the quality of accented ú·: u·šák "he stings him," u·lʸík "he crushes it," u·tú·rvək "he plays shinny." When preceding accented é, é·, ó, or ó·, u· has the quality of accented ó·: u·kʷépšək "he stretches it," u·cu·yó·yk "he shows." If an unaccented a· intervenes between u· and the accented vowel, u· has the quality of accented ú· regardless of the quality of the accented vowel: u·pa·xkʸé·k "he arranges them by sevens."

Unaccented o·, with the quality of accented ó·, is found in the preaccentual position in a very few words. In all cases it can be shown to be derived from o + a: δo·tárək (< *δoatárk) "he is blind," δo·láwk (< *δoaláwk) "he turns his head."

Unaccented a usually has the quality of accented á, but when preceded or followed by a dental, cacuminal or prepalatal consonant it ranges in pronunciation towards the quality of accented é and í. This variation in quality is optional, and a pronunciation with the quality of á is always acceptable.

Unaccented e, i, o, and u have the qualities of the corresponding accented vowels. They occur most frequently in themes formed by reduplication.

§8. Postaccentual vowels.

The vowels a, e, i, u, a·, i·, and u· are found in the postaccentual position. All have the qualities of the corresponding accented vowels regardless of phonetic context.

§9. Inorganic ə.

A semiwhispered vowel of variable quality (ə) occurs in the postaccentual position in certain specific contexts. It occurs most frequently with the phonetic character of a murmur or shwa, but after bilabial consonants it may have an u tinge and after dental and cacuminal consonants it may have an e tinge. The vowel ə in all its occurrences is inorganic, i.e. morphologically unnecessary. It never occurs in the final position and never bears an accent.

The vowel ə occurs in the following types of context: a) preceding a final consonant and preceded by a consonant which cannot combine with the final consonant to form a final consonant cluster: a·ʔávək (< *a·ʔávk) "he hears," cá·məlʸ (< *cá·mlʸ) "all of them"; b) following a medial consonant cluster and followed by a single consonant: a·ʔámpək (< *a·ʔámpk) "he bends over," mašéctəxa (< *mašéctxa) "they will call you"; c) following a single consonant and followed

by a consonant cluster nʸc, nt, nk, or ct: u·δúcənʸc (<*u·δúcnʸc) "his actions,"
awétəntik (<*awétntik) "he did it again," aʔétənka (<*aʔétnka) "did he say so?",
alʸnʸá·pəctaʔa (<*alʸnʸá·pctaʔa) "they threw me in"; d) following a single consonant preceded by ə and followed by a single consonant: caxí·rməcəxa
(<*caxí·rmcxa) "they will burrow through," xʷa·δú·cvəcək (<*xʷa·δú·cvck)
"they dodge"; e) following a consonant cluster and followed by a consonant
cluster nʸc, nt, or a consonant cluster ending in ʔ: u·táqšənʸc (<*u·táqšnʸc) "his
jumping," asó·ctəntik (<*asó·ctntik) "they ate again," aδúctəkʔaš (<*aδúctkʔaš)
"they did so"; and f) between two single consonants which may combine to form
a medial or final consonant cluster: u·tá·pək (<*u·tá·ppk) "they throw," u·šíʹ·tək
(<*u·šíʹ·tvk) "they name," aʔépək (<*aʔépak) "he indeed says," walʸaδómətəxa
(<*walʸaδómatxa) "he will be unable."

The occurrence of ə in the first five of these contexts may be accounted for
in terms of the rules governing consonant clusters. It occurs a) between two consonants which cannot form a final consonant cluster, b) between the second and
third, or c) between the first and second of a series of three consonants which
cannot form a consonant cluster, d) following the second and the third, or e) between the second and the third of a series of four consonants which cannot form
a consonant cluster. In all these contexts ə is in contrast with other postaccentual
vowels (aδótəm "he doing so" and aδótum "he always does so," acéntək "he
descended" and acéntik "he lays down again") and in complementary distribution
with zero (šaxá·ck "it melts" and šaxá·ccək "they melt," aʔétk "he said" and
aʔíctək "they said").

The occurrence of ə in context (f) cannot be accounted for by the rules governing consonant clusters. In this context, furthermore, ə is in contrast with zero
(atá·pk "he throws them" and u·tá·pək "they throw"; ašíʹ·tk "he names them" and
u·šíʹ·tək "they name"), not in complementary distribution with zero. Analysis of
the forms in which ə occurs in this context shows that the single consonant preceding ə is derived from a morphophonemic consonant cluster (u·šíʹ·tək <*u·šíʹ·tvk)
or from a morpheme consisting of consonant +vowel whose vocalic element has
been syncopated (see §11). Single consonants of these types are "strengthened,"
i.e., treated phonologically as consonant clusters. For example, themes ending in a
vowel or a (morphophonemic) single consonant take the hortatory tense-modal
suffix -ú; themes ending in a consonant cluster or a "strengthened" single consonant take the hortatory tense-modal suffix -iyú, e.g. kacu·náv14yú (<*kacu·návvviyú)
"let them tell" (cf. kaná·vú <kaná·vú "let him tell"), walʸaʔémiyú (<walʸaʔ-
émaiyú) "let him not be" (cf. ʔanayémú <ʔnayémú "let us go away"). The occurrence of ə in context (f) is thus congruent with its occurrence in contexts (b)
and (d).[3]

[3] An inorganic vowel a occurs in the preaccentual position, especially between the first two
consonants of a word: taʔaxʷéṭk <*tʔaxʷéṭk "he reddens it," calʸaví·k <*clʸaví·k "he fits it,"
ʔaʔanʸéwxa <*ʔʔanʸéwxa "I will disappear." It has the same phonetic character and occurs in the
same contexts as organic a.

§10. Contacts between vowels.

Contacts of vowel with vowel within the word are of four types: a) between unaccented a and a preceding or following vowel, b) between postaccentual u or u· and a preceding vowel, c) between two unaccented long vowels in the pre-accentual position, and d) between an unaccented long vowel and a following accented vowel.

a) a is always absorbed by a preceding or following long vowel: nʸa·ʔí·m (<*nʸa·a·ʔí·m) "when he says," vi·vák (<*vi·avák) "he is here," wu·kavárǝk (<*wau·kavárk) "he causes him to like it." a is also absorbed by a preceding short vowel but lengthens the short vowel in which it is absorbed without changing the latter's quality: ka·ʔétám (<*kaa·ʔétám) "how is it?" ðo·tárǝk (<*ðoatárk) "he is blind," aðú·s (<*aðúas) "he might do," aʔí·s (<*aʔías) "he might say."

b) when á, á·, ó, ó·, ú, or ú· is followed by u or u·, a w-glide appears between the two vowels: amáwum (<*amáum) "he might eat," u·nó·wú·m (<*u·nó·ú·m) "would they be present," aštúwú (<*aštúú) "let him gather." When é, é·, í, í·, or postaccentual i is followed by u or u·, a y-glide appears between the two vowels: takʷéyú (<*takʷéú) "let him awake," aðí·yú (<*aðí·ú) "let him come," masó·-tǝntiyum (<*masó·tntium) "you might eat (meat) again."

c) the following contacts of type (c) occur: i· +a·, i· +u·, a· +u·, and u· +u·. i· is shortened or absorbed by a following a·: nʸia·taqʷérǝk (<*nʸi·a·taqʷérk) "he follows," nʸa·ðí·k (<*nʸi·a·ðí·k) "bed." i· and a· in some cases are shortened or absorbed by a following u·: nʸiu·cmá·nǝk (<*nʸi·u·cmá·nk) "he cures them," nʸu·šmá·m (<*nʸa·u·šmá·m) "when they are asleep"; in other cases, i· and a· change following u· to wa: ʔa·wakó·yǝnʸ (<*ʔa·u·kó·ynʸ) "her agedness," ʔi·wamácǝnʸ (<*ʔi·u·mácnʸ) "my dancing." u· alternatively is absorbed by a following u· or changes a following u· to wa: šu·ðáwǝnʸ or šu·waðáwǝnʸ (<*šu·u·ðáwnʸ) "his waiting," cu·cécǝnʸ or cu·wacécǝnʸ (<*cu·u·cécnʸ) "his spreading."

The vocalic element of wa <*u· is not absorbed by a following vowel: a·waé·mnʸa (<*a·u·é·mnʸa) "his pushing away of it," a·waí·mnʸa (<*a·u·í·mnʸa) "his recklessness."

d) the following contacts of type (d) occur: a· followed by á·, é·, í·, ú·, and ó·: i· followed by á·; u· followed by á·, é·, and í·. a· is shortened to a when followed by á· but is not changed when followed by other accented vowels: nʸaá·mǝk (<*nʸa·á·mk) "when he passes," a·é·mǝk (<*a·é·mk) "he pushes it away," a·í·mǝk (<*a·í·mk) "he heedlessly does," a·ú·x (<span. aguja) "needle," ʔa·ór (<span. oro) "gold." i· changes a following á· to yá: nʸi·yápk (<*nʸi·á·pk) "he throws them," vi·yámǝk (<*vi·á·mk) "he passes by." u· changes a following á· to wá and tends, but not consistently, to shorten following é· and í·: u·wámpǝk (<*u·á·mpk) "he leaves a remainder," tu·é·mǝnʸ or tu·émǝnʸ (<*tu·é·mnʸ) "his pushing away of it," nʸu·íl ʸǝnʸ (<*nʸu·í·lʸnʸ) "its blackness," nu·í·mǝnʸ (<*nu·í·mnʸ) "his insistence."

§11. Syncope of vowels.

Syncope of vowels occurs under the following conditions

a) Initial a rarely occurs preceding an accented vowel by more than one syllable. An initial a of a verb theme is syncopated when it occurs in this position: šu·mácənʸ (<*ašu·mácnʸ <theme *ašmá) "his sleeping," vu·ˀácək (<*avu·ˀácvk <theme *avˀá·) "they walk."

b) A number of suffixes composed of consonant+vowel occur as such when in the final position in the word but have the vocalic element syncopated when followed by another suffix: ˀa·véva "this snake (absolutive)," >ˀa·vévəc (<*ˀa·vévac) "this snake (nominative)," aδóxa "he will do" >u·δóxənʸ (<*au·δóxanʸ) "his future action," ˀamáyva "sky, atmosphere" >ˀamáyvi (<*ˀamáyvai) "up above, in the sky."

c) An accented final vowel of a noun theme may be syncopated before the locative suffix ·i: vaδí (<*vaδái, cf. vaδác "this one") "here," makʸí (<*makʸéi, cf. makʸéc "who?") "where?"

d) Series of more than two short vowels or two short and one long vowel separated by single consonants are generally avoided, preceding the accented syllable, by syncopation of the second vowel of the series: šamaδí·k (<*šmaδí·k) "he does not know" >mašmaδí·k (<*mšmaδí·k) "you do not know," natu·má·k (<*natu·má·kk) "they abandon" > ˀantu·má·k (<*ˀnatu·má·kk) "we abandon." Series of one long and two short vowels, or a long, a short and a long vowel, separated by single consonants may occur preceding the syllable bearing the accent: nʸa·matapúyk "when you kill," nʸi·natu·má·k "they abandon them."

e) Unaccented a may be syncopated between two consonants the first of which is a palatalized liquid: ˀanʸkó (<*ˀnʸakó)" my father," walʸmúlʸmiyú·m (<*walʸamúlʸmaiyú·m) "would it be nameless?"

§12. Vowel-semivowel combinations.

The following combinations of an accented vowel with the vocalic form of a semivowel are found:

áy	éy		óy	úy
á·y	é·y		ó·y	ú·y
áw	éw	íw	ów	
á·w	é·w	í·w	ó·w	

Though íy and í·y do not occur, the phoneme í· in some of its occurrences is derived from morphophonemic *íy or *í·y. No other explanation accounts for the ablaut of í· to á·y (e.g., alʸaskʸí·k <*alʸaskʸíyk "he continues the same" >alʸaskʸá·yk "they continue the same") or to é·y (e.g., xamí·k <*xamí·yk "he is born" >xacmé·yk "they are born").

§13. Vocalic ablaut.

Ablaut (change in quality, length, or both) of the accented vowel is a frequently employed grammatical process, and should really be discussed as a grammatical rather than a phonological process. It seems useful, however, to append here tables showing the types of vocalic ablaut which occur. Table II shows the

TABLE II. ABLAUT OF THE ACCENTED STEM VOWEL

Singular	Collective Plural		Distributive Plural		Distributive Object		Adaptive Verbal Abstract	
		with ʼc/ʼt		with ʼc/ʼt		with ʼc/ʼt		with ʼc/ʼt
á >	á·	á·	á·	á·	á·	á·	á·	á·
é >	á·		á·	á·	á·	á·	á·	
é >	í·	í·	í·	í·	í·	í·	í·	í·
é >						í		
í >	á·		á·		á·			
í >	í·		í·		í·		í·	
í/é >			é·					
í/é >				í·		í·		í·
ó >	ó·		ó·					
ó >	ú·		ú·	ú·	ú·	ú·	ú·	
ó >						ú[1]		
ú >	ó·[2]		ó·[2]		ó·[2]		ó·[2]	
ú >	ú·		ú·		ú·		ú·	
ú/ó >			ó·					
ú/ó >				ú·				
á· >		á	á	á	á	á	á	
á· >		é		é				
é· >			é	é		é		
é· >			á·		á·			
í· >			é		é			
í· >					í	í		
í· >			á·		á·			
í· >			é·		é·			
ó· >			ó		ó			
ó· >		ú[1]		ú[1]				
ó· >			á·[1]		á·[1]			
ú· >			ó		ó			
ú· >			ú	ú		ú		
áy >	á·		á·		á·	á·		
áy >		á		á		á		
áw >			á·		á·			
áw >				ó		ó		
éw >			á·		á·			
éw >		ó[1]						
á·y >			á·					
é·y >						é[1]		
ó·y >						ó[1]		

[1] Occurs in only one stem.   [2] Occurs only in stems ending in ʼúy in the singular.

kinds of vocalic ablaut found in conjugation of the verb theme for the various
plurals and in the formation of the adaptive verbal abstract. "with ‑c/‑t" at the
head of a column indicates that the verb stem is concurrently modified by the
addition of a consonantal increment ‑c or ‑t immediately following the accented
vowel. Semivowels immediately following the accented vowel of the stem are
often, sometimes optionally, syncopated when the vowel is ablauted. Table III

TABLE III. ABLAUT OF THE ACCENTED STEM VOWEL
PLUS SUFFIXATION OF ‑y

		With Benefactive ‑y	With Attributive ‑y
á	>	á·y	á·y
é	>	á·y	á·y
é	>		í·(í·y?)
í/é	>	é·y	
ó	>		ú·y
ó	>		úy
ú/ó	>	ó·y	
á·	>		áy
á·	>		éy
é·	>		í· (í·y?)
ó·	>		úy
ó·	>		ú·y
ú·	>	ó·y	

shows the kinds of vocalic ablaut found in the formation of verb themes from noun
themes by suffixation of attributive ‑y and in the formation of the benefactive verb
theme by suffixation of benefactive ‑y to an existing verb theme.

§14. Accent.

Accent is an inherent feature of certain morphemes. It falls on the last vowel
of the verb or noun stem, whether this vowel is final in the word or is followed by
one or several syllables, and on certain inherently accented suffixes (e.g. hortatory
‑ú, future possible interrogative ‑ú·m) which must occur in the final syllable of the
word. The word, then, may contain one accent, that of the stem; or two accents,

the first being the accent of the stem and the second that of an inherently accented suffix.

In a word containing only one accent, the accented syllable is pronounced on a high falling tone: kaná·vək "he tells." In a word containing two accents, the first (stem) accented vowel is pronounced on a high tone, the second (suffix) ac-cented vowel on a high falling tone: kaná·vú "let him tell."

§15. Syllabification.

The syllable may begin with a vowel or a single consonant and may end in a vowel, a single consonant, or a consonant cluster. The following types of syllable are found:

	v	vc	vcc
c	cv	cvc	cvcc

§16. Sandhi.

Sandhi forms occur in rapid speech when a) a word ending in a consonant is followed by a word beginning in a vowel, b) a word ending in -k is followed by a word beginning with v-, and c) a word ending in a vowel is followed by a word beginning in a vowel.

a) A final consonant of one word is often pronounced as the initial consonant of a following word which begins with a vowel: matxá cá·mək <matxác á·mək "the wind passes," ʔaxtóṭ maδí·k < ʔaxtóṭəm aδí·k "he came through the red-berry bush."

b) Final k of one word plus initial v- of a following word becomes initial kʷ- of the second word: aʔét kʷi·yá·k <aʔétk vi·yá·k "so saying he went," atápəm kʷi·v ʔáwk <atápmək vi·v ʔáwk "standing here he threw it."

c) A final vowel of one word combines with initial a- of the following word into a long vowel having the quality of the first vowel: nʸá·nʸi·mánək <nʸá·nʸi amánək "there he starts," ayú·lʸa ʔémək <ayú· alʸa ʔémək "he does not see." Initial u·- and i·- of a word become wa- and ya- respectively when the preceding word ends in an accented vowel: ʔaxá wasícənʸ < ʔaxá u·sícənʸ "his drinking of water," kʷa·pá yayá· <kʷa·pá i·yá· "Cocopa language."

MORPHOLOGY

17-20. GRAMMATICAL PROCESSES

§17. Word classes.

The word consists of two types of immediate constituents: a theme and non-thematic elements. The word usually contains one or more nonthematic affixes, but may contain none or only such as are phonetically zero.

The syntactic function of the word depends on its nonthematic affixes. These are of two types, nominal and verbal. Three syntactic classes of words may thus be distinguished: a) nouns, i.e., words constructed of a theme plus nominal affixes or the absolute forms of themes to which nominal affixes may be added; b) verbs, i.e., words constructed of a theme plus verbal affixes or the absolute forms of themes to which verbal affixes may be added; and c) interjections, i.e., words constructed of a theme (generally of exclamatory meaning) to which no affixes can be added.

A similar threefold classification of themes may be made. Noun themes are those themes which may take only nominal affixes and from which verb themes may be derived by specific grammatical processes. Verb themes are those themes which take verbal affixes and from which noun themes (verbal abstracts) may be derived. Interjectional themes cannot be manipulated grammatically.

Any verb theme may be used as a noun theme, but the reverse is not true. Thus the theme *vatáy "to be big" may serve as the theme of a verb (vatáyk < zero third person pronominal prefix +vatáy "to be big" +·k present-past suffix, "he is big") or of a noun (vatáyəc <vatáy "big" +·c nominative case suffix, "the big one"). The rather numerous examples of themes which may be used without phonetic modification as either verb or noun themes are best explained as cases of the formation of verbal abstracts. Sometimes the noun theme thus formed serves as the base from which another verb theme is derived: *ʔi·pá· "to be a man" > ʔi·pá· "man, male" >*ʔi·páy "to be alive, to be human."

A verb theme plus verbal nonthematic elements may also be used as a noun theme. Thus some noun themes contain elements which are in origin nonthematic. The word kaʔaδómək in the expression kaʔaδómək ʔaδúwú·m? "How shall I do it?" (lit. "how-am-I-able? would-I-do?") is a verb whose theme is *aδóm "to be able" and whose nonthematic elements are ka- interrogative prefix, ʔ- first person pronominal prefix, and ·k present-past suffix. The word kaʔaδóməc in the expression kaʔaδóməc ʔaδúwú·m "What kind of person would I be?" (lit. "I-able-to-do-what would-I-do?") is a noun whose theme is kaʔaδóm "I able to do what" and whose nonthematic element is the nominative case suffix ·c.

§18. Word formation.

The mechanics of word formation are simple. The only processes employed are prefixation and suffixation. The noun theme may occur in the absolute form or with various combinations of affixes. The verb theme usually occurs with a pronominal prefix and a predicative suffix (ʔayú·k <ʔ- first person pronominal prefix +ayú· "to see" +·k present-past suffix, "I see"), but in some types of verbal phrase the predicative suffix may be omitted (ʔayú· ʔaʔí·m "I am going to see," lit. "I-seeing I-say"), while in others the pronominal prefix and predicative suffix may both be omitted (páq aʔí·m "it makes a popping noise," (lit. "pop it-says," cf. apáq <zero- third person pronominal suffix +apáq "to burst (into bloom)" +·k present-past suffix, "flower blooms").

The use of nonthematic verbal prefixes other than the pronominal prefixes is for the most part optional. There are, however, some verb themes which occur only with specific nonthematic prefixes or are altered in meaning when in association with specific nonthematic prefixes. These may be designated as verb themes with adhering prefixes. An example of the first type is the theme *atí·š, which occurs only with the adhering prefix nʸi·-, as in nʸi·tí·šk (nʸi·- adhering prefix +zero- third person pronominal prefix +atí·š +-k present-past suffix) "he deceives." An example of the second type is the theme *ʔi·páy, by itself meaning "to be alive, to be human," but with the adhering prefix wa- (wa-*ʔi·páy) meaning "to be en- livened, to come to life." The adhering prefixes occupy the positions of and in some cases are phonetically identical with substantive and locative verbal prefixes. In the majority of cases, no definite meaning can be ascribed to the adhering prefix itself; it is only the combination of adhering prefix and theme which has meaning.

§19. Formation of nonthematic elements.

Nonthematic elements are for the most part unanalyzable unit morphemes. Some substantive and locative prefixes of the verb, however, are complex and must be regarded as composed of a pseudo-thematic or theme-derived element together with some exclusively nonthematic elements. The substantive prefix ʔac- "things" occurs in simple form in the word ʔacaδú·m "he does things" (aδú·m "he does") the prefix ʔack-, as in ʔacku·vá·k "he stays about, in various places" (u·vá·k "he is present) consists of ʔac- plus the locative case suffix -k. Similarly the adhering prefix wanʸm-, as in wanʸmayá·k "he enjoys," contains a pseudo-thematic element wa- (possibly <i·wá· "heart") plus a demonstrative suffix -nʸ plus the ablative case suffix -m.

§20. Theme formation.

In regard to the processes employed and the relationship between the com- ponent parts, complex nonthematic elements follow the same patterns of formation as words, more especially nouns. The mechanics of theme-formation differs from the mechanics of word formation in both these respects.

The processes employed in the formation of the theme and in the modifica- tion of the theme for grammatical purposes are affixation (prefixation, infixation, and suffixation), reduplication, vocalic ablaut, and composition. The association between the component parts of the theme is much firmer than that between a theme and nonthematic elements in that both the structure and the meaning of the theme are determined or altered by the grammatical processes mentioned. Affixes which thus affect the theme will be called thematic affixes to distinguish them from nonthematic elements.

Affixation is more characteristically employed with the verb theme (both in formation and grammatical modification) than with the noun theme. The scope of the process is indicated by the following series of forms: *aδáp "to be split" is a verb theme consisting of a stem alone; from it is derived, by prefixation of the thematic prefix t-, the theme *taδáp (*t-aδáp) "to split"; the gerund of *taδáp is tu·δáp (*t-a<u·>δáp) "his splitting"; the distributive plural form of taδáp is tatu·δá·p (*t-a<t><u·>δá·p-p) "many split."

The chief use of affixation with the noun theme is in the formation of derived verb themes: e.g. *n^{y}u·tí·šv "to be equipped with a bow" is derived from the noun theme ʔu·tí·š "bow" plus the thematic affix-complex n^{y}-. . .-v.

The process of infixation calls for some comment. It is not used with noun themes proper (i.e. noun themes other than those derived from verb themes) but only with verb themes. The term infix is here used to refer to morphemes which occupy such positions with respect to the stem of a verb theme that under certain conditions they are included within it. Some infixes occupy a position immediately preceding the first consonant of the stem, others a position immediately preceding the consonant which precedes the accented vowel of the stem. With stems of the types vcv́ and vccv́ both types of infix are included within the stem: e.g. tatu·sú·l^{y} (*t-a<t><u·>sú·l^{y}, stem *asúl^{y}) "many gouge," cacxu·táṭv (*c-a<c>x<u·>-táṭ-v, stem *axtá·ṭ) "many crawl." With stems of the type v́ both types of infix precede the stem: ya-šatu·wál^{y}v (ya-*š-<t><u·>á·l^{y}-v, stem *á·l^{y}) "many crave." With stems of the type cvcv́ infixes of the first type precede the stem while infixes of the second type are included within it: šatku·ví·rv (š-a<t>ka<u·>ví·r-v, stem *kavér) "many overcome."

Reduplication is employed as a theme-forming process with both verb and noun themes. There are two types, both involving complete reduplication of the stem element. In the first type, the stem is reduplicated in de-accented form and, under the appropriate conditions (see §11a), with loss of the initial vowel: toxatóx (<stem *atóx) "to be spotted," x^{w}ecax^{w}éc (<stem *ax^{w}éc ?) "oriole," axlakaxlák (<stem *axlák) "to be intertwined," axnaraxnár (<stem *axnár ?) "turtle." In the second type, found only in noun themes, the stem is repeated with retained accent, so that the result resembles a nominal phrase: xál xál "wagtail (bird sp.)." The treatment of such forms is analogous to that of single nouns rather than that of nominal phrases.

Vocalic ablaut, alone or together with other grammatical processes, is employed chiefly for grammatical modification of the theme, less often as a theme forming process. It is characteristically used with the verb rather than the noun theme.[4]

Composition is employed only in the formation of the noun theme. The verb theme never contains more than one stem; the noun theme may be composed of two stem elements. Some of these are modified forms of stems which are noun themes in themselves: δo-šu·n^{y}á "eye-lash" (cf. i·δó "eye"), ʔavu·tó "center of the house" (cf. ʔavá "house" and ató "center"). Others are not etymologizable.

21–26. THE NOUN

§21. General remarks.

The noun form may consist of a theme alone or of a theme plus affixed nonthematic elements. The nonthematic elements are of four types: a) pronominal

[4] For table of vocalic ablaut series, see §13.

prefixes, b) demonstrative suffixes, c) the locative suffix -i, and d) case suffixes. No two affixes of the same type may occur in the same word. Pronominal prefixes may not occur in the same word with the locative suffix -i.

The tabulated analysis in Table IV of a few typical forms indicates the relative positions occupied by the several elements of the noun form.

TABLE IV. POSITIONAL ANALYSIS OF NOUN FORM ELEMENTS

Pronominal Prefix	Theme	Demonstrative Suffix	Locative -i	Case Suffix	Form and Meaning
ʔanʸ- "I, we"	camʔaδúlʸ "ant"			-c nominative	ʔanʸcamʔaδúləc "we ants"
	ʔa·vé "snake"	-va "this"		-c nominative	ʔa·vévəc "this snake"
m- "your"	i·δó "eye"	-nʸ "that"		-c nominative	mi·δónʸc "your eye"
	ʔamáy "above, sky"	-sa "that"	-i	-lʸ allative	ʔamáysilʸ "up into the sky"
	vaδá "this one"		-i		vaδí "here"

§22. The noun theme.

Three types of noun theme[5] are found:

a) Simple noun themes consist of a single unanalyzable stem element: ʔaxá "water," takšé "gopher."

b) Reduplicated noun themes consist of a repeated single stem element, with or without loss of accent (see §20).

c) Compound noun themes consist of two stem elements. Some of the stem elements found in compound noun themes are etymologizable, others are not. They may be classified as first- and second-position elements according to the positions which they must occupy in the word. The following are typical:

First-position elements:

i·- (used in body part terms)

  i·δó· "tooth," i·má·ṭ "body," i·mé "foot," i·šá·lʸ "hand," i·ʔé "hair," i·pálʸ "tongue."
kam-

  kamcú·ləq "green berry sp.," kamnálʸ "boulder," kamʔu·tá "dipper."
malʸ-

---

[5] I.e., noun theme proper, excluding those derived from verb themes.

malᵞka·téš "gnat," malᵞʔú·v "wild tobacco," malᵞxó "pipe," malᵞpú· "umbilical cord."
xam·
    xamkᵞé "swallow," xamsúlᵞ "chameleon," xamʔu·kᵞé "pestle" (poss. cf. kʷasʔu·kᵞé
       "pottery paddle").
ya·· (cf. i·yá· "mouth")
    ya·vu·mé "beard," ya·xaʔáw "jawbone," ya·xu·pó "side of thorax," ya·saδúlᵞ "gums."
ʔi·· (cf. ʔaʔí· "wood")
    ʔi·δó· "willow," ʔiδú·ṭ "wild turnip," ʔi·sáv "arrowweed."
ʔavu·· (cf. ʔavá "house")
    ʔavu·lᵞpó "house post," ʔavu·mák "back of house," ʔavu·yá· "door," ʔavu·cúlᵞ
       "smoke-hole."

Second-position elements (listed here are a few which occur in more than one theme. A large number of others can of course be extracted from themes containing isolable first-position elements):

·mák (cf. amák "behind")
    šalᵞmák "back," ʔavu·mák "back of house."
·táṭ (connotes "spiny")
    ʔatáṭ "thorn," malᵞtáṭ "viznaga cactus," axtáṭ "backbone, back," ʔu·táṭ "spear."
·tóṭ
    ʔaxtóṭ "red-berry bush," xalᵞtóṭ "spider."
·póṭ (cf. verb stem *apóṭ "to be scattered")
    ʔampóṭ "dust," xalᵞpóṭ "Dispersal (clan name)."

The noun theme generally may have either a singular or a plural significance: ʔi·δó· "my tooth" or "my teeth," maxʷá· "badger" or "badgers." A suffix ·c is added to the theme when respective possession is indicated or when the members of a group are referred to severally: ʔi·δó·ca "our (respective) teeth," ma·maxʷá·ca "you (who are) badgers" (both forms with vocative case ending ·a).

§23. Pronominal prefixes.

Possessive pronominal prefixes indicate first, second, third, and indefinite third (someone's) person possessor, but do not indicate number. The first person possessive pronominal prefix may be translated as "my" or "our," etc. There are two sets of possessive prefixes:

	I	II
1 pr.	ʔ·	ʔanᵞ·
2 pr.	m·	manᵞ·
3 pr.	zero·	nᵞ·
indef. 3 pr.	kʷ·	kʷanᵞ·

The first set is used chiefly with body part and kinship terms, the second chiefly with natural objects and artifacts, but also with certain body part terms. The distinction, however, is not quite identical with that between inalienable and alienable possession: i·kʷé "his horn" may refer to a deer's own horn or to a person's deer horn.

A few themes, most of them having ˀ- as initial consonant, have a possessed form which differs from the absolute form: ˀakmé "bag" > ˀanʸkamé "my bag," ˀaxná·lʸ "gourd" > ˀanʸxaná·lʸ "my gourd," ˀavu·spó "abandoned home" > ˀanʸvu·sapó "my abandoned home," taškʸén "cookpot" > ˀanʸtašakʸén "my cookpot." In some cases the change is optional: ˀamáṭ "land" > ˀanʸmáṭ or ˀanʸˀamáṭ "my land," ˀaˀú·v "tobacco" > ˀanʸˀú·v or ˀanʸˀaˀú·v "my tobacco."

A few themes occur only with possessive prefixes: *-u·ˀá·lʸ in nʸu·ˀá·lʸ "his clothes," *-i·xʷéṭ in nʸi·xʷéṭ "his blood."

Referential pronominal prefixes are ˀanʸ- for the first person singular or plural and ma·- (>ma- when preceding ˀ-) for the second person singular or plural: pa ˀi·pá· "person, people," ˀanʸpa ˀi·pá· "I (who am a) person, we people," ma·pa ˀi·pá· "you (who are a) person, you people."

§24. Nonthematic nominal suffixes.

The demonstrative suffixes are -va "this (nearby)," -sa "that (far off)," and -nʸ "that (location unspecified)."

The locative suffix -i has approximately the meaning of English "at, the vicinity of." It is usually affixed to the noun theme plus demonstrative suffix: i·mé šamá·vi (i·mé "foot," šamá· "root" +-va "this" +-i "at") "at his feet, under-foot," lit. "at the root of his foot." Noun themes of demonstrative meaning may take the locative suffix -i directly: va δí (<va δá "this" +-i "at") "here."

The noun theme in the absolute form is used as the object of a verb, as the possessor of a following noun, or as a member of a nominal phrase: xatalwé kaná·vək "he tells about coyote," lit. "coyote he-tells-of"; xatalwé nʸa ˀú·v "coyote's to-bacco," lit. "coyote his-tobacco"; xatalwé šalʸ ˀáy "sand coyote," lit. "coyote sand." The theme with case suffixes functions as the subject of a verb, as an adverb, or (with vocative -a) as a predicative expression: šalʸ ˀáyc ˀamé·k "the sand is high," lit. "sand it-is-high"; šalʸ ˀáyəm aδí·k "he came through the sand," lit. "sand-through he-came"; šalʸ ˀáya "the sand!"

The case suffixes are:

-c nominative
-k locative ("at, from")
-lʸ allative ("to, into")
-m ablative ("through, by means of")
-a vocative

The following suffix combinations are found (-nʸ being taken as representative of the demonstrative suffixes):

Absolute	-zero	-nʸ	-i	-nʸi
Nominative	-c	-nʸc		
Locative	-k	-nʸk	-ik	-nʸik
Allative	-lʸ	-nʸəlʸ	-ilʸ	-nʸilʸ
Ablative	-m	-nʸəm	-im	-nʸim
Vocative	-a	-nʸa		

Themes with the plural suffix -c occur in the absolute form, with nominative suffix, and with vocative suffix, but take no other suffixes except these.

§25. Demonstratives, pronouns, and adverbs.

Noun themes of demonstrative and pronominal meaning take no pronominal prefixes and are limited to certain suffix combinations. The following forms of vaδá- "this one (nearby)" illustrate the suffix combinations taken by it and by the themes avá- "this one (a short distance away)," savá- "that one (far off)," and makʸé "who?, anyone?"

Absolute	—	vaδánʸ	vaδí	—
Nominative	vaδác	—	—	—
Locative	—	—	vaδík	—
Allative	—	—	vaδílʸ	—
Ablative	vaδám	—	vaδím	—
Vocative	—	—	—	—

The theme makʸíp "which one?, someone?" occurs only in the following forms:

Absolute	makʸíp	—	—	—
Nominative	makʸípəc	—	—	—
Locative	—	—	—	—
Allative	—	—	—	—
Ablative	makʸípəm	—	—	—
Vocative	makʸípa	—	—	—

The theme nʸá·- "that" occurs only with demonstrative suffixes: nʸá·va "that one here," nʸá·sa "that one there," nʸá·nʸ "that one (location unspecified)." The following forms of nʸá·nʸ indicate the suffix combinations with which the theme nʸá·- may occur:

Absolute	—	nʸá·nʸ	—	nʸá·nʸi
Nominative	—	nʸá·nʸc	—	—
Locative	—	—	—	nʸá·nʸik
Allative	—	—	—	nʸá·nʸilʸ
Ablative	—	nʸá·nʸəm	—	nʸá·nʸim
Vocative	—	nʸá·nʸa	—	—

Free pronominal themes indicating first and second person singular and plural are somewhat irregular in treatment. The following forms occur:

	1 pr. sing.	1 pr. plural	2 pr. sing.	2 pr. plural
Absolute	ʔanʸép, ʔanʸá·p	ʔanʸéc	má·nʸ[6]	—
Nominative	ʔanʸá·c	ʔanʸécəc	má·nʸc	mácəc
Locative	—	—	—	—

[6] I.e., má· +demonstrative -nʸ.

Allative	—	—	—	—
Ablative	ʔanʸépəm	—	máˑnʸəm	—
Vocative	ʔanʸépa	ʔanʸéca	máˑnʸa	máca

Adverbial themes (themes of place and time reference), e.g., amák "(the) behind" maxák "(the) underneath," ʔaxkʸé "(the) across," take no pronominal prefixes, but otherwise are treated as normal noun themes.

§26. Derivation of verb themes from noun themes.

Verb themes are derived from noun themes in several ways.

a) From noun themes ending in an accented vowel, by suffixation of attributive -y with or without concurrent ablaut of the accented vowel:

ʔaxá "water" > *ʔaxáy "to be damp"
ʔanʸáˑ "sun" > *ʔanʸáˑy "to be bright"
ʔaxʷé "enemy" > *axʷáˑy "to be hostile"
ʔiˑδóˑ "willow" > *ʔiˑδúy "to be willow-covered"

If the accented vowel of the noun theme is preceded by a consonant cluster, a vowel a may be intercalated between the two consonants of the cluster:

ʔaxʔáˑ "cottonwood" > *ʔaxaʔáy "to be cottonwood-covered"
masʔéˑ "mud" > *masaʔíˑ (*masaʔíˑy ?) "to be muddy"
kʷaxʔóˑ "ashes" > *kʷaxaʔúˑy "to be ashy"

But cf. xalʸʔá "moon" > xalʸʔáy "to be moonlit."

b) From noun themes ending in a consonant and having the accented vowel preceded by a consonant cluster, by intercalation of a vowel a between the two consonants of the cluster:

kamnálʸ "boulder" > *kamanálʸ "to be heavy as stone"
salʸʔáy "sand" > *salʸaʔáy "to be sandy"
ʔampóṭ "dust" > *ʔamapóṭ "to be dusty"

c) From noun themes ending in an accented vowel, by suffixation of possessive -v to the attributive form:

ʔaxʷé "enemy" > *ʔaxʷáˑyv "to be at war with" (cf. *ʔaxʷáˑy "to be hostile")
yaˑvuˑmé "beard" > *yaˑvuˑmíˑv (*yaˑvuˑmíˑyv ?) "to be bearded"
iˑtó "belly" or ató "center" > *atúyv "to be pregnant"

d) By prefixation of nʸ- (third person possessive pronominal prefix) and suffixation of possessive -v to the noun theme:

kuˑpéṭ "quiver" > *nʸakuˑpéṭv "to be equipped with a quiver"
-iˑxʷéṭ "blood" > *nʸiˑxʷéṭv "to bleed"
xuˑmár "child" (cf. verb theme xuˑmár "to be young") > *nʸaxuˑmráv "to have a child, to be a father."

TABLE V. POSITIONAL ANALYSIS OF VERB FORM ELEMENTS

4 Substantive Prefix	3 Locative Prefix	2 Conditional Prefix	1 Pronominal Prefix	Theme	1 Aspective Suffix	2 Aspective Suffix	3 Tense and Tense-Modal Suffix	4 Modal Suffix	5 Syntactic	Word and Meaning
av- "thus"			ʔ- 1 pr.	aδ "to do (static)"	-t assertive	-apat oneself	-k present-past			avʔaδótapatk "thus I also do"
ka- "what"			m- 2 pr.	aʔɛ "to say"			-xa future	-ᵞa optative		kamaʔɛxalᵞa "what would you say?"
ka- "what"		nᵞaˑ- conditional	m- 2 pr.	awém "to be able to do"			-m subordinate			kanᵞaˑrmawémam "if you can do anything"
	alᵞ- "into"		nᵞ- "he-me"	áˑpc "to throw (collective plural)"	-t assertive			-ʔaš evidential		alᵞnᵞáˑpctʔaš "they threw me in"
	alᵞ- adhering prefix		nᵞinᵞ- "I-ye"	axʷilᵞv "to associate with"	-t assertive		-xa future	-ᵞa optative		alᵞnᵞinᵞaxʷilᵞvtxalᵞa "I would associate with you"
av- "thus"			ʔ- 1 pr.	alᵞʔɛ "to think, believe"	-t assertive		-k present-past		-aʔa (end of phrase)	avʔalᵞʔɛtkaʔa "that's what I think"
	nᵞiˑ- "there"	nᵞaˑ- conditional	zero- 3 pr.	namák "to leave behind"			-k present-past			nᵞinᵞaˑrnamák "when he left it there"
ʔac- "things"			ʔ- 1 pr.	kanáˑv "to tell, relate"	-t assertive		-xa future			ʔacʔakanáˑvtxa "I will tell about things"
maṭ- reflexive	nᵞiˑ- adhering prefix	nᵞaˑ- conditional	zero 3 pr.	acéw "to make something out of"	-t assertive		-k present-past			maṭnᵞiˑnᵞaˑcéwtak "when he had transformed himself"
av- "thus"			ʔ- 1 pr.	aʔɛ "to say"			-xa future	-as dubitative		avʔaʔɛxas "whatever I may say"
walᵞ- adhering prefix			zero 3 pr.	áˑrmc "to not desire (collective plural)"			-k present-past			walᵞáˑrmacǝk "they do not care for it"

e) With the adhering prefix alʸ⁻, verb themes of these types have the meaning "to turn into . . . ," "to become . . . ."

ʔamó "mountain sheep" >alʸ⁻*ʔamúy "to turn into a mountain sheep"
kamnálʸ "boulder" >alʸ⁻*kamanálʸ "to become heavy as stone"
šamá· "root" >alʸ⁻*šamáyv "to take root" (i.e., "to become possessed of a root" ?).

27–45. THE VERB

§27. General remarks.

The complete verb form ordinarily consists of a theme and two nonthematic elements, a pronominal prefix and a predicative suffix,[7] but may contain more than two nonthematic elements. The theme is the relatively invariant portion of the verb form, i.e. that portion which remains unchanged in structure and meaning irrespective of the presence or absence of specific nonthematic affixes. The positions of the various nonthematic elements with respect to the theme and to one another are fixed. The order in which they may occur is substantive prefix-locative prefix-conditional prefix-pronominal or imperative prefix-theme-position 1 aspective suffix-position 2 aspective suffix-tense or tense-modal suffix-modal suffix-enclitic. Nonthematic elements may thus be classified according to relative nearness to the verb stem. A third-position (tense or tense-modal) suffix may follow the theme immediately if no first- or second-position suffixes occur in the same word, but must follow a first- or second-position suffix that does occur in the same word. In some cases two substantive or two locative prefixes occur in the same word, but no two nonthematic affixes of any other positional class may co-occur in a single word.

The tabulated analysis in Table V indicates the relative positions of the several elements of the verb form.

§28. Types of verb theme.

The verb theme[8] itself may be either a simple or a complex element. Themes may be classified according to three levels of development. On the simplest level the theme consists of a stem (an unanalyzable thematic element) alone or a reduplicated stem. On the next higher level of complexity the theme consists of a simple or reduplicated stem to which are added thematic prefixes. On the third level are themes of either the simple-stem or prefix-stem types to which are added thematic infix-suffix complexes.

The classification of theme types may be expressed in tabular form.

·I. Themes based on stem alone
   A. simple-stem theme
   B. reduplicated-stem theme

---

[7] But see §18; 36.

[8] In this discussion of theme types, only the singular form of the theme will be considered. The various plural forms of the theme are derived from the singular form in definable ways which depend largely on the type to which the latter belongs.

II. Prefix-stem themes
    A. single prefix plus simple or reduplicated stem
    B. two prefixes plus stem
III. Developed themes
    Theme of type I or II plus thematic infix-suffix complex

The theme may be further modified on any of these levels by the addition of thematic suffixes. Since these exercise no influence on the type of grammatical modification to which the theme is subject, no subclassification is necessary.

§29. The verb stem.

Verb stems are classified primarily according to the number and character of the phonemes preceding the accented vowel, secondarily according to the number and character of the phonemes following the accented vowel.

The following types are found.

Accented vowel preceded by—	-zero	-c	-cc
zero-	v́	v́c	v́cc
c-		cv́c	
vc-	cv́	vćc	vcv́cc
vcc-	vccv́	vccv́c	vccv́cc
cvc-	cvcv́	cvcv́c	cvcv́cc
cvcc-	cvccv́	cvccv́c	cvccv́cc
vcvc-	vcvcv́		
cvcvc-	cvcvcv́	cvcvcv́c	cvcvcv́cc
cvccvc-	cvccvcv́	cvccvcv́c	

About ninety percent of all verb stems are disyllabic.

The verb stem normally has the same form with all nonthematic suffixes. Some stems ending in an accented vowel which take the present-past suffix -ᵛm[9] have two singular forms. One form (the present-past stem) is used with second-position aspective suffixes, the present-past suffix -ᵛm, and underlies the collective plural form. The other form (the future stem) is used with first-position aspective suffixes, the future tense suffix -xa, and most thematic suffixes. When the accented vowels of the present-past stem are -ú and -í, the accented vowels of the future stem are -ó and -é respectively.[10]

§30. Reduplication of the verb stem.

Reduplication adds to the meaning of the stem the element of repetitive or intermittent activity. Only vcvc and vccvc type stem are reduplicated. The initial

---

[9] Rather than the more common present-past suffix -k; see §44.
[10] A table of these changes is to be found in §44c.

vowel of vcv́c type stems is syncopated in the reduplicated form. The initial vowel
of vccv́c type stems is retained.

atóx "to have a spot" (cf. šatóx "to make a spot on"), toxatóx "to be spotted"
aspúk "to be curled" (cf. kaspúk "to curl (self) up"), aspukaspúk "to be kinky (hair)"

§31. Thematic prefixes.

Thematic prefixes, when a definite meaning can be ascribed to them, are for
the most part causative. There are, however, some to which no definite meaning
can be ascribed. The following are typical and common:

k- "to cause with foot, with a large or heavy instrument, or with great force"
kasúlʸ (*k-asúlʸ, cf. asúlʸ "to be ripped") "to rip with great force"
ka?ák (*k-a?ák) "to kick"
c- "to cause with the teeth"
cakʸéw (*c-akʸéw) "to bite"
canʸé (*c-anʸé) "to chew on" (cf. kanʸé "to press down lightly with the foot")
c- "to cause a bunch of objects"
ca?úlʸ (*c-a?úlʸ) "to carry a bunch of objects in the hand" (cf. ta?úlʸ "to carry in the
hand")
caδú·n (*c-aδú·n) "to dip a bunch of small objects" (cf. taδú·n "to dip small object")
c- generalized causative
cayá· (*c-ayá·, cf. ayá· "to go") "to send"
canálʸ (*c-análʸ, cf. análʸ "to drop off") "to lose"
t- "to cause (general), to cause by means of an instrument"
tayú·š (*t-ayú·š, cf. ayú·š "to be cool") "to cool (it)"
taqʷeraqʷér (*t-qʷeraqʷér, cf. qʷeraqʷér "to be sharp-pointed") "to sharpen to a
point"
š- "to cause a small object, to cause with the hand or with a small instrument"
šalwax (*š-alwáx) "to punch a hole with the finger" (cf. kalwáx "to kick a hole
through")
šaréq (*š-aréq) "to hold, grasp"
a·- "to cause a long object"
a·vkʸéw (*a·-avkʸéw) "to carry long heavy object"
a·?úlʸ (*a·-a?úlʸ) "to carry long object in the hand" (cf. ta?úlʸ "to carry in the hand")
With numerals a·- has a special significance.
a·xavík (*a·-xavík, cf. xavík "to be two") "to do twice"
u·- "to cause or induce a condition without altering the nature of the object"
u·δí· (*u·-aδí·, cf. aδí· "to come") "to bring"
u·vatáy (*u·-vatáy, cf. vatáy "to be big") "to exaggerate" (cf. also tava·tá·y "to en-
large")
a·c- causative (?)
a·cmanʸé· (*a·c-manʸé·, cf. manʸé· "to be sweet") "to relish"
nʸam-a·clʸu·vév (nyam-*a·c-lʸu·vév, cf. lʸu·vév "to be equal") "to match against something"
u·c- causative, especially with numerals

nʸi·ᵁ·cxamók (nʸi·*ᵁ·c·xamók, cf. xamók "to be three") "to divide into three parts"
u·clʸu·vév (*u·c·lʸu·vév, cf. lʸu·vév "to be equal") "to divide in halves"

    a·c' and u·c' are sometimes used alternatively:

a·cu·pís or u·cu·pís (*a·c/u·c·a<u>pís, cf. apís "to suck") "to give suck"

v· "to do in standing position"
    vakʸá·v (*v·akʸá·v) "to walk around" (cf. cakʸá·v "to place objects around")
    vé·m (*v·é·m, stem *é· "to be in motion") "to move back (in standing position)"

m· "to do on account of"
    manʸúv (*m·anʸúv, cf. anʸúv "to fight with someone") "to fight over something"
    maxán (*m·axán) "to admire"

n· "used chiefly in kinship terms
    napí· (*n·apí·) "to call someone father's sister"
    nakʷí· (*n·akʷí·) "to call some one mother's brother"

nʸ· ?
    nʸu·wíc (*nʸ·u·wíc) "to own"
    nʸaváy (*nʸ·aváy, poss. cf. ʔaváy "house") "to inhabit"

xʷ· "to do in a hostile manner" (?)
    xʷanʸó·v (*xʷ·anʸó·v) "to dodge, to flinch"
    xʷa?á·v (*xʷ·a?á·v) "to be jealous"

x· ?
    xamí· (*x·amí·) "to be born"
    xalʸqíc (*x·alʸqíc) "to grab small object"

s· ?
    samá·v (*s·amá·v) "to borrow"
    sakʷalʸxé (*s·kʷalʸxé) "to tie a knot"

kʷ· ?
    kʷí· (*kʷ·í·) "to give"
    kʷakʸé (*kʷ·akʸé) "to ask for, to request"

§32. Compounding of prefixes.

The prefix-stem theme may contain two prefixes. The most frequent combination of prefixes is causative u· plus some other prefix.

u·caqáw (*u·c·aqáw, cf. caqáw "to eat fruit") "to feed fruit to"
u·takanáy (*u·t·kanáy, cf. takanáy "to stop overnight") "to provide a stopping place"
u·maxán (*u·m·axán, cf. maxán "to admire") "to cause to admire"
u·kʷí· (*u·kʷ·í·, cf. kʷí· "to give") "to buy"

    Other combinations are rare.

a·sakʸév (*a·s·akʸév, cf. sakʸév "to be half full") "to fill half full"
taqʷalayéw (*t·qʷ·layéw, cf. qʷalayéw "to become morning") "to do all night"
u·cavašáw (*u·c·v·ašáw, cf. vašáw "to guard") "to post a guard"

§33. Stem modification in prefix-stem themes.

The stem, as in most of the examples already cited, usually undergoes no changes when incorporated in a prefix-stem theme. Under some circumstances, however, modification of the stem occurs.

a) In prefix-stem themes with prefix t-, š-, or c- an element <a·> may be in-fixed before the consonant immediately preceding the accented vowel of the stem.

ta·šáy (*t-a<a·>šáy, cf. ašáy "to be fat") "to fatten"
tama·δó·lʸq (*t-ma<a·>δó·lʸq, cf. maδó·lʸq "to be sweet") "to sweeten"
ca·táqš (*c-a<a·>táqš, cf. atáqš "to jump") "to flip"
taxva·šú· (*t-xava<a·>šú·, cf. xavašú· "to be blue") "to make blue"
　　The accented vowel may be concurrently ablauted.
ta·ní·x (*t-a<a·>ní·x, cf. anéx "to be quiet") "to do quietly"
ta?a·qó·l (*t-?a<a·>qó·l, cf. ?aqól "to be long") "to lengthen"

b) In themes with prefix a·c- or u·c- an element <u·> may be infixed before the consonant immediately preceding the accented vowel of the stem.

u·cu·yó·y (*u·c-a<u·>yó··y, cf. ayú· "to see") "to show"
a·cvu·kʸéw or u·cvu·kʸéw (*a·c-/u·c-av<u·>kʸéw) "to give someone a long heavy object to carry" (cf. a·vkʸéw <*a··avkʸéw "to carry a long heavy object")
a·ckolu·kól (*a·c-kola<u·>kól, <stem *akól) "to lay one long object on top of an-other"

c) When u·- is prefixed to stems containing an unaccented i·, the i· may change to u·.

u·xu·pán (*u·-xu·pán, cf. xi·pán "to be near") "to bring near"
u·kʷas?u·δí· (*u·-kʷas?u·δí·, cf. kʷas?i·δí· "to be a doctor") "to make into a doctor"
　　But cf.:
u·si·pxú·k (*u·-si·pxú·k, cf. si·pxú·k "to be in groups of seven") "to arrange by sevens"

d) Some stems add a consonantal increment -c when incorporated in prefix-stem themes.

kacpác (*k-acpác, cf. acpá "to emerge") "to drive out"
taman^yé·c (*t-man^yé·c, cf. man^yé· "to be sweet") "to sweeten"
šapa?i·páyc (*š-pa?i·páyc, cf. pa?i·páy "to become alive") "to make into a human being"

§34. The developed theme.

A simple-stem theme or prefix-stem theme may be further developed in two ways.

a) By infixation of <u·> before the consonant preceding the accented vowel of the stem plus suffixation of a thematic suffix -v/-p.[11] The meaning of the de-veloped theme is then "to be one who does . . ." or "to have been doing . . . ."

u·šúcv (*a<u·>šúc-v, cf. ašúc "to call someone younger brother") "to have a younger brother"
ku·nácv (*k-a<u·>nác-v, cf. kanác "to order, summon") "to be one who orders"

---

[11] -v after vowels and most consonants, -p after m and p. The closest analogue of this suffix appears to be the possessive thematic suffix -v (see §26c, d, e).

wiˑaˑvukʸáwv (wiˑ-*aˑav<uˑ>kʸáwˑv, cf. wiˑaˑvkʸáw "to call someone paternal half-sibling") "to have a paternal half-sibling"

nʸiˑaˑtuˑqʷerv (nʸiˑ-*aˑ-tˑa<uˑ>qʷérˑv, cf. nʸiˑaˑtaqʷér "to follow") "to be a follower, to have been following"

b) By infixation of <iˑ> before the consonant preceding the accented vowel of the stem plus suffixation of a thematic suffix ˑv/ˑp.[11] The meaning of the developed theme is "to be worthy or capable of doing . . . or of having . . . done to one."

aˑcqiˑ δáˑyv (*aˑcˑaq<iˑ>δáˑyˑv, cf. aˑcaqδáˑy "to slip") "to be slippery"
waˑniˑmiˑlv (waˑ-*nˑa<iˑ>míˑlˑv, cf. namíˑl "to coax") "to be a nuisance"

The accented vowel of the stem may be concurrently ablauted:

mašiˑ δéˑv (*mˑaš<iˑ>δéˑˑv, cf. mašδé "to fear") "to be fierce, dangerous, terrible"

The stem may be further modified by addition of a consonantal increment ˑc:

aˑcxiˑnúcv (*aˑcˑax<iˑ>núcˑv) "to be contagious" (cf. aˑxnó<*aˑˑaxnó "to become infected")

§35. Thematic suffixes.

The following are the most important thematic suffixes:

a) Directional ˑk "towards self or speaker" and ˑm "away from self or speaker" are found with simple-stem and prefix-stem themes.

acpák (*acpáˑk) "to come out"; acpám (*acpáˑm) "to go out" (cf. acpá "to emerge")
téˑk (*tˑéˑˑk) "to bring closer"; téˑm (*tˑéˑˑm) "to move away" (<stem *é "to be in motion")

b) medio-passive ˑv/ˑp[12] is found rarely with simple-stem themes, fairly frequently with prefix-stem themes.

δamˑayúˑv (δamˑ*ayúˑˑv, cf. ayúˑ "to see") "to be plain, manifest"
uˑspérv (*uˑˑaspérˑv, cf. uˑspér "to tie tight," aspér "to be strong") "to exert oneself"

Themes with prefix t- and medio-passive suffix often have the meaning "to do while sitting," and themes with prefix aˑ- and medio-passive suffix the meaning "to do while walking or lying." With themes with prefix v- "to do while standing" they form a triad of themes in which position is indicated.

tapéṭv (*t-apéṭˑv) "to sit in front of"
aˑpéṭv (*aˑˑapéṭˑv) "to lie in front of"
vapéṭ (*vˑapéṭ) "to stand in front of"

The medio-passive suffix always follows a directional suffix occurring in the same theme.

téˑkv (*tˑéˑˑkˑv) "to come closer (sitting)"
téˑmp (*tˑéˑˑmˑp) "to move back (sitting)"

----

[12] ˑv after vowels and most consonants, ˑp after m and p.

c) Benefactive ⸢y occurs with simple⸍stem and prefix⸍stem themes. The ac⸍
cented vowel of the stem may or may not be ablauted.

aδá·y (cf. aδá· "to gather greens") "to gather greens for someone"
acá·y (cf. acé "to lay a bunch down") "to lay down for someone"
tará·y (cf. tará· <*t⸍ará· "to kindle") "to kindle for someone"
kamé·y (cf. kamí/é <*k⸍amí/é "to bring") "to bring for someone"

Benefactive ⸢y is compulsory in some themes with u·⸢ prefix.

u·só·y (cf. asó· "to eat meat") "to feed meat to"
u·šamá·y (cf. šamá· <*š⸍amá· "to dream") "to empower"
u·má·y (cf. amá "to eat") "to feed"
u·tak\u02B7á·y (cf. tak\u02B7é <*t⸍ak\u02B7é "to awake") "to wake, revive"

d) The suffix ⸢m "to be able" occurs only with five themes, all of the simple⸍
stem types. It occurs with the future stem of bimorphous stems.

aⸯém (cf. aⸯí/é "to say") "to be able to say"
awém (cf. awí/é "to do") "to be able to do"
aδóm (cf. aδú/ó "to do, be") "to be able to do, be"
ayúm (cf. ayú· "to see") "to be able to see"
aⸯám (cf. aⸯáv "to hear") "to be able to hear"

e) Intensive ⸢pa occurs with simple⸍stem and prefix⸍stem themes.

ašmápa (cf. ašmá "to sleep") "to be sound asleep"
kaná·pa (cf. kaná·v <*k⸍aná·v "to tell") "to tell all"
a·ví·rpa (cf. a·ví·r <*a·⸍aví·r "to finish") "to finish completely"

f) Privative ⸢ma occurs with all types of themes. An adhering prefix wal\u02B8⸢ is
usually affixed concurrently.

wal\u02B8⸢á·rma (cf. á·r "to desire") "to have no desire for"
wal\u02B8aδóma (cf. aδú/ó "to do, be") "to be unable"
wal\u02B8tayú·šma (cf. tayú·š <*t⸍ayú·š "to cool") "to have not cooled"
wal\u02B8⸢ci·vá·ma (wal\u02B8⸢*c⸍a<i·>vá·m·p⸍ma, cf. cavá·m <*c⸍avá·m "to probably not be")
     "to be impossible"

§36. Reduction of the theme.
The verb themes cited heretofore are used with nonthematic affixes. Many
themes occur in a reduced form which takes no nonthematic affixes but is predi⸍
cated by an auxiliary verb (generally a form of aⸯí/é "to say") in which nonthematic
affixes occur. The reduced theme plus auxiliary verb has a momentaneous meaning.
If the theme begins in a short vowel followed by a single consonant, the
initial vowel is dropped in the reduced form.

šá\u0163 aⸯí·m "straight down he comes!" (cf. tašá\u0163 <*t⸍ašá\u0163 "to set upright")
x\u02B7í·r aⸯí·m "long object comes out slowly" (cf. u·x\u02B7í·r <*u·⸍ax\u02B7í·r "to draw long ob⸍
     ject out of matrix")

If the theme begins in a short vowel followed by a consonant cluster, a long vowel, or a consonant, the reduced form is the same phonetically as the full form.

aklét aʔíˑm (<stem aklét) "it rises on its hind legs!"
aˑδéˑv aʔíˑm (cf. aˑδéˑv "to step aside") "aside he moves!"
manamán aʔíˑm (cf. amán "to arise") "it goes up and down"

§37. Plural forms of the verb theme.

Verb themes of intransitive meaning are normally conjugated for the collective (subject) and distributive (subject) plurals. Verb themes of transitive meaning are normally conjugated for both these plurals and for distributive object (with singular subject). Themes consisting of a reduplicated stem only and developed themes are conjugated only for the collective plural. See §39; 40.

The collective plural form indicates action taken by a group of people together, on a single object, or at the same place and time. The distributive plural form indicates action taken by a number of people severally, or each on an object of his own, or at different places and times. The distinction emerges clearly in such forms as nʸuˑwíck "he owns it," coll. plu. nʸuˑwíccək "they own jointly," nʸacuˑwíˑcək "they own severally." For the sake of convenience, the collective plural will be glossed as "two (subj.) . . . ." and the distributive plural as "many (subj.) . . . ."

The distributive object form indicates primarily action performed on a number of different objects: nʸiˑkáˑmək "he conquers him," dist. obj. nʸiˑkacámək "he conquers them." It may also indicate action performed on a number of successive occasions: aˑδápk "he makes an incision," dist. obj. aˑcδáˑpk "he makes several incisions"; in several places successively: axʷélʸk "he digs," axʷáˑlʸk "he digs here and there"; or by habit, inclination or profession: ʔaciˑmák "he dances," dist. obj. ʔaciˑcmáˑck "he is a dancer," aˑnʸórək "he writes," dist. obj. aˑcnʸúˑrək "he is a clerk."

The method by which the theme is conjugated for the plurals depends on the structure and meaning of the theme. Only regular types of conjugation will be discussed here. Partly or wholly aberrant types of conjugation are numerous, but outside the scope of this paper.

§38. Distributive object conjugation.

The theme may be conjugated for distributive object by one of three methods: a) by ablaut of the accented vowel of the stem; b) by infixation of <t> or <c> before the first consonant of the stem; and c) by ablaut and infixation both. In all three types of conjugation the stem may be concurrently modified by the addition of a consonantal increment ˑc or ˑt.[13]

---

[13] The infix <c> is used with simple-stem themes and with prefix-stem themes with prefix kˑ, cˑ, aˑˑ, uˑˑ, aˑcˑ, uˑcˑ, vˑ, xˑ, xʷˑ, kʷˑ, nʸˑ, or mˑ. The infix <t> is used with prefix-stem themes with prefix tˑ, šˑ, sˑ, or nˑ. In themes containing two prefixes, the choice of infix is governed by the prefix which stands closest to the stem. If the infix directly precedes a consonant cluster of the stem, an inorganic vowel a occurs between the infix and the following consonant.

All three types of conjugation are used with both simple-stem and prefix-stem themes. Type (b) is the least frequent. Types (a) and (c) are of about equal frequency with simple-stem themes. Type (c) is much the most frequent with prefix-stem themes.

a) The following forms illustrate type (a):

ašílʸ "to fry" >ašíˑlʸ "to fry many"
taspér (*t-aspér) "to tighten" >taspíˑr "to tighten many"
ta?ora?ór (*t-?ora?ór) "to make spherical">ta?ura?úˑr "to make many spherical"

With consonantal increment:

b) The following forms illustrate type (b):

anʸúv "to fight" >acnʸúv (*a<c>nʸúv) "to be a fighter"
cakʸéw (c-akʸéw) "to bite" >cackʸéw (*c-a<c>kʸéw) "to bite several times"

With consonantal increment:

šéˑk (*š-é-k) "to bring closer" >šatéˑck (*š-<t>é-cˑk) "to bring many closer"
uˑšá (*u-ašá) "to sting" >uˑcšát (*u-a<c>šát) "to sting several times"

c) The following forms illustrate type (c):

axér "to tie up" >acxíˑr (*a<c>xíˑr) "to tie up many"
xʷa?áˑv (*xʷ-a?áˑv) "to be jealous" >xʷac?áv (*xʷ-a<c>?áv) "to have a jealous nature"
uˑtalaxóx (u-t-laxóx) "to empty" >uˑtatlaxúˑx (*u-t-<t>laxúˑx) "to empty many"

With consonantal increment:

así/é "to drink" >acsíˑc (*a<c>síˑc) "to drink habitually"
casvé (*c-asvé) "to wipe" >cacasvíˑc (*c-a<c>svíˑc) "to wipe many"
cašé (*c-ašé) "to challenge" >cacšíˑt (*c-a<c>šíˑt) "to challenge many"

§39. Plurals of simple-stem themes.

Simple-stem themes[14] of intransitive meaning are conjugated for the collective plural in one of three ways:

a) By ablaut of the accented vowel:

ayér "to fly" >ayáˑr "to fly (two)"
mavís "to be soft" >mavíˑs "to be soft (two)"
?ora?ór "to be spherical" > ?ura?úˑr "to be spherical (two)"

b) By ablaut of the accented vowel plus addition of a consonantal increment -c:

atóˑ "to be sated" >atúc "to be sated (two)"
vatáy "to be big" >vatác "to be big (two)"
apám (*apá-m) "to fall down" >apáˑcm (*apáˑc-m) "to fall down (two)"

[14] And reduplicated-stem themes.

278 VIKING FUND PUBLICATIONS IN ANTHROPOLOGY: 6

c) Five themes only are conjugated for the collective plural by prefixation of u·:

ašmá "to sleep" >u·šmá (*u·ašmá) "to sleep (two)"
acpá "to emerge" >u·cpá "to emerge (two)"
acpák (*acpá·k) "to come out" >u·cpák (*u·cpá·k) "to come out (two)"
acpám (*acpá·m) "to go out" >u·cpám (*u·acpá·m) "to go out (two)"
av?á· "to walk" >u·v?á· (*u·av?á·) "to walk (two)"

Simple-stem themes of transitive meaning are conjugated for the collective plural by suffixation of a thematic suffix ·c.

á·y "to give" >á·yc (*á·y·c) "to give (two)"
á·pm (*á·p·m) "to throw away" >á·pmǝc (*á·p·m·c) "to throw away (two)"
alʸúl "to cook" >alʸúlʸc (*alʸulʸ·c) "to cook (two)"
ašá·m (*ašá··m) "to see in the distance" >ašá·mc (*ašá··m·c) "to see in the distance (two)"

Simple-stem themes are conjugated for the distributive plural in one of two ways:

a) By infixation of <u·> before the consonant preceding the accented vowel plus (optional) suffixation of a thematic suffix ·v/·p,[15] usually with concurrent ablaut of the accented vowel of the stem, and sometimes with concurrent modification of the stem by addition of a consonantal increment ·c or ·t. The following subtypes are thus found:

1) with neither vocalic ablaut nor consonantal increment:

á·r "to desire" >u·wárv (*<u·>á·r·v) "to desire (many)"
alʸáy "to call some one female cross cousin" >u·lʸáyv (*a<u·>lʸáy·v) "to call etc., (many)"
avsúc "to urinate" >vu·súcv (*av<u·>súc·v) "to urinate (many)"

2) with consonantal increment only:

apám (*apá·m) "to fall down" >u·pácm (*a<u·>pác·m) "to fall down (many)"
xʷa·acpá "to advance hostilely" >xʷa·cu·pácv (xʷa·*ac<u·>pác·v) "to advance hostilely (many)"

3) with vocalic ablaut only:

así/é "to drink" >u·sé·v (*a<u·>sé··v) "to drink (many)"
ašá·m (*ašá··m) "to see something far off" >u·šámp (*a<u·>šá·m·p) "to see something far off (many)"
?aqʷá·s "to be tired" > ?u·qʷásv (*?a<u·>qʷás·v) "to be tired (many)"

4) with both vocalic ablaut and consonantal increment:

a?í/é "to say" >u·?í·cv (*a<u·>?í·c·v) "to say (many)"

[15] ·v after vowels and most consonants, ·p after m and p.

ató· "to be sated" >u·túcv (*a<u·>túc·v) "to be sated (many)"
ašé "to name" >u·ší·tv (*a<u·>ší·t·v) "to name (many)"

b) Of the five themes which take the collective plural in u·, two are conjugated for the distributive plural by prefixation of a· plus addition of a consonantal increment ·c.

ašmá "to sleep" >a·šmác (*a·ašmác) "to sleep (many)"
acpá "to emerge" >a·cpác (*a·acpác) "to emerge (many)"

Two others are conjugated by this method plus ablaut of the accented vowel.

acpák (*acpá·k) "to come out" >a·cpá·ck (*a·acpá·c·k) "to come out (many)"
acpám (*acpá·m) "to go out" >a·cpá·cm (*a·acpá·c·m) "to go out (many)"

The fifth is conjugated by method (a).

av?á· "to walk" >vu·?á·cv (*av<u·>?á·c·v) "to walk (many)"

§40. Plurals of prefix-stem themes.

Prefix-stem themes[16] are conjugated for the collective plural in one of two ways.

a) By suffixation of a thematic suffix ·c:

kanʸó (*k·anʸó) "to trail" >kanʸóc (*k·anʸó·c) "to trail (two)"
té·k (*t·é·k) "to bring closer" >té·kc (*t·é·k·c) "to bring closer (two)"
maši·δé·v (*m·aš<i·>δé··v) "to be fierce" >maši·δé·vc (*m·aš<i·>δé··v·c) "to be fierce (two)"

b) A limited number of themes are conjugated by infixation of <t> or <c>[17] before the first consonant of the stem plus infixation of <a> before the consonant preceding the accented vowel of the stem plus (evidently optionally) suffixation of a thematic suffix ·v/·p.[18] Two subtypes are found, depending on whether the accented vowel of the stem is or is not ablauted.

1) without vocalic ablaut

namák (*n·amák) "to leave behind" >natamák (*n·a<t><a>mák) "to leave behind (two)"
šamé· (*š·amé·) "to miss" >šatamé·v (*š·a<t><a>mé··v) "to miss (two)"

2) with vocalic ablaut

a·ví·r (*a·aví·r) "to finish" >a·cavér (*a·a<c><a>vér) "to finish (two)"
šamaδí· (*s·maδí·) "to not know" >šatmaδá·v (*š·<t>ma<a>δá··v ?) "to not know (two)"
mu·δúcv (*m·a<u·>δúc·v) "to be a practical joker" >mu·caδú·cv (*m·a<u·><c><a>δú·c·v) "to be (two) practical jokers"

---

[16] And developed themes.
[17] For the rules governing the choice of infix <t> or <c>, see §38, footnote 16.
[18] ·v after vowels and most consonants, ·p after m and p.

Prefix-stem themes are conjugated for the distributive plural by infixation of <t> or <c>[17] before the first consonant of the stem plus infixation of <u·> before the consonant preceding the accented vowel of the stem, plus (optional) suffixation of a thematic suffix -v/-p;[18] the accented vowel of the stem is usually ablauted and a consonant increment -t or -c may be added to the stem. Four sub-types are thus found.

1) with neither vocalic ablaut nor consonantal increment

nʸi·ká·m (nʸi·-*k-á·m) "to conquer" >nʸi·kacu·wámp (nʸi·-*k-<c><u·>á·m-p) "to conquer (many)"

xalʸqíc (*x-alʸqíc) "to grab" >xaclʸu·qícv (*x-a<c>lʸ<u·>qíc-v) "to grab (many)"

2) with consonantal increment only

tawé (*t-awé) "to grind" >tatu·wécv (*t-a<t><u·>wéc-v) "to grind (many)"

3) with vocalic ablaut only

tayú·š (*t-ayú·š) "to cool" >tatu·yúšv (*t-a<t><u·>yúš-v) "to cool (many)"

a·lʸʔí/é (*a·-alʸʔí/é) "to consider" >a·clʸu·ʔé·v (*a·-a<c>lʸ<u·>ʔé·-v) "to consider (many)"

u·taraʔúy (*u-t-ra?úy) "to prepare" >u·tataru·ʔó·yv (*u·-t-<t>ra<u·>ʔó·y-v) "to prepare (many)"

4) with both vocalic ablaut and consonantal increment

šamá· (*š-amá·) "to dream" >šatu·mácv (*š-a<t><u·>mac-v) "to dream (many)"

casvé (*c-asvé) "to wipe" >cacsu·ví·c (*c-a<c>s<u·>ví·c) "to wipe (many)"

cakaná (*c-kaná) "to decide" >cacku·ná·cv (*c-<c>ka<u·>ná·c-v) "to decide (many)"

u·šá (*u·-ašá) "to sting" >u·cu·šá·tv (*u·-a<c><u·>šá·t-v) "to sting (many)"

§41. Plurals of themes indicating position.

Themes indicating position are of three types, simple-stem themes, themes with prefix v-, and themes with prefix t- or a-- and medio-passive suffix. All three types are conjugated for the collective plural by prefixation of n- and for the distributive plural by prefixation of a-- or a·k-, the latter two prefixes being used alternatively in some cases.

With simple-stem themes, the prefixes n- and a--/a·k- are simply added to the theme.

acén "to descend," coll. plu. nacén, distr. plu. a·cén

xi·pán "to be near," coll. plu. naxi·pán, distr. plu. a·xi·pán

With themes with prefix v-, v- is replaced by the prefixes n- and a--/a·k-.

vakʸá·v "to walk around" coll. plu. nakʸá·v, distr. plu. a·kʸá·v or a·kakʸá v

vakamé· (*v-kamé·) "to stand on the edge," coll. pl. nakamé·, distr. plu. a·kamé·

With themes of the third type, the prefix t- or a·- is replaced by the prefixes n- and a·-/a·k- and the medio-passive suffix is dropped in the plural forms.

takamé·v (*t-kamé·-v) "to sit on the edge," coll. plu. nakamé·, distr. plu. a·kamé·
alʸ-a·xʷílʸ-v (alʸ-*a·-ₐax̌ʷílʸ-v) "to associate with someone," coll. plu. alʸ-nax̌ʷílʸ, distr. plu. alʸ-a·kax̌ʷílʸ

§42. Plurals of reduced themes.

Reduced themes are usually conjugated for the plurals by conjugation of the auxiliary verb rather than of the theme.

lá·x aʔí·m, "it flashes," lá·x aʔíck "they two flash," lá·x u·ʔé·vək "they many flash"
manamán aʔí·m "it goes up and down," manamán aʔíck "they two go up and down," manamán u·ʔí·cək "they many etc."

Reduced forms of themes indicating position are, however, conjugated for the plurals, the auxiliary verb remaining singular.

vaδé· aʔí·m "he steps aside," naδé· aʔí·m "they two step aside"
vaná·lʸ aʔí·m "he stands off," naná·lʸ aʔí·m "they two stand off," a·ná·lʸ aʔí·m "they many stand off"

§43. Nonthematic prefixes of the verb.

The positional classes into which nonthematic prefixes of the verb fall have already been indicated in §27.

a) Prefixes of the first position are the pronominal prefixes and the imperative prefix. The subjective pronominal prefixes (zero—third person, m—second person, and ʔ—first person) and the imperative prefix k- indicate person but not number, number being indicated in the theme. The following forms of *ayér "to fly" indicate the use of these prefixes.

	Singular	Coll. Plural	Distr. Plural
3 pr.	ayérək	ayá·rək	u·yá·rək
2 pr.	mayérək	mayá·rək	mu·yá·rək
1 pr.	ʔayérək	ʔayá·rək	ʔu·yá·rək
imper.	kayérək	kayá·rək	ku·yá·rək

Objective pronominal prefixes cannot be isolated as such. Instead there are pronominal prefixes in which both singular pronominal object and pronominal subject are indicated simultaneously. The following table shows the use of these prefixes with the theme *ayú· "to see" and the present-past suffix -k.

Subject	Object (Singular)		
	1 pr.	2 pr.	3 pr.
1 pr.		nʸ‑ayúˑ‑k	ʔ‑ayúˑ‑k
2 pr.	ʔan‑ʸm‑ayúˑ‑k		m‑ayúˑ‑k
3 pr.	nʸ‑ayúˑ‑k	m‑ayúˑ‑k	(zero‑)ayúˑ‑k
imper.	ʔan‑ʸk‑ayúˑ‑k		k‑ayúˑ‑k

An element nʸiˑ‑ (>nʸi‑ before ʔ) is prefixed to the pronominal object‑subject prefixes to indicate plural pronominal object.

Subject	Object (Plural)		
	1 pr.	2 pr.	3 pr.
1 pr.		nʸiˑnʸ‑ayuˑ‑k	nʸiˑʔ‑ayúˑ‑k
2 pr.	nʸiˑʔan‑ʸm‑ayúˑ‑k		nʸiˑm‑ayúˑ‑k
3 pr.	nʸiˑnʸ‑ayúˑ‑k	nʸiˑm‑ayúˑ‑k	nʸiˑ‑yúˑ‑k
imper.	nʸiˑʔan‑ʸk‑ayúˑ‑k		nʸiˑk‑ayúˑ‑k

b) The second prefix position is occupied by the conditional prefix nʸaˑ‑ (>nʸa‑ before ʔ), indicating true to fact condition.

nʸaˑrúvəm ("when‑it‑was‑dry") aˑkʸéṭk ("he‑cuts‑it") aδáwk ("he‑takes‑it"), "When it was dry, he cut a piece off and took it."

ʔanʸʔiˑpá ("my‑arrow") nʸaʔakʸémək ("when‑I‑shoot") uˑráˑvtəxa ("there‑will‑be‑lightning"), "When I shoot my arrow, lightning will flash."

c) The third prefix position is occupied by prefixes of locative meaning.

alʸ‑ "in, into, onto, away"

ʔakʷiˑšá ("shade") xalʸkʷáˑk ("he‑seeks") alʸapáˑm ("he‑lies‑down‑in") alʸaδík ("he‑is‑(lying)‑in"), "He sought out a shady place and lay down in it."

alʸkaˑpáxmək, "Throw it away!"

viˑ‑ (>vi‑ before ʔ) "here, nearby, in this direction"

viˑδíˑm ("it‑coming‑here") ayúˑk ("he‑sees"), "He sees it coming."

ʔaˑíˑmək ("I‑do‑regardless") viʔayáˑtxa ("I‑here‑will‑go"), "Nevertheless I will go on."

siˑ‑ (>si‑ before ʔ) "there, in that direction"

ʔamáṭ ("land") ʔaméˑc ("high") siˑváwum ("it‑might‑be‑situated‑there"), "There might be high land there."

siˑkavák, "Stay there!"

nʸik‑ (<nʸiˑ‑ plus locative case suffix ‑k ?) "on that side, from there"

nʸikcacénək "he brings it down on that side"
nʸikaδí·k "he comes from there"

The prefixes alʸ- and nʸi·- occur also as adhering prefixes.

alʸapá·m (<theme alʸ-*apá) "he makes a mistake"
nʸi·tí·šk (<theme nʸi·-*atí· š) "he deceives him"
alʸnʸi·δú·ck (<theme alʸnʸi·-*aδú·c) "he thinks"

d) The fourth prefix position is occupied by 1) substantive prefixes and 2) a group of prefixes found only as adhering prefixes.

Typical substantive prefixes are:

ʔac- "things, objects"
    ʔacʔakaná·vək "I tell about things"
    ʔacnʸa·matapúyk "if you kill things"
ʔack- (<ʔac- plus locative -k) "at places"
    ʔackamu·vá·xa "You will stay at (different) places"
nʸam- (<nʸ- "that?" plus ablative -m) "thereby"
    nʸama·ckʸé·k "He guides him with it."
maṭ- or ma·ṭ- (cf. i·má·ṭ "body") reflexive and reciprocal
    maṭu·pó·yk "He pretends to be dead" (lit. "he causes himself to die")
    ma·ṭá·yk "They give to each other."
av- "whatever"
    avawí·m "What (ever) he does."
    avʔá·mək "Wherever I pass by."
ka- "what?, anything"
    kaʔaδóxa ("I-shall-do-what") ʔašmaδí·k ("I-do-not-know") "I don't know what I shall
      do."

Typical adhering prefixes are:

δo- (cf. i·δó "eye")
    δó·tárək (<theme δo-*atár) "he is blind"
    δonʸamé·k (<theme δo·*nʸamé·) "he is dizzy"
wa- (cf. i·wá· "heart")
    wakaʔi·páyk (<theme wa-*ʔi·páy) "be lively!"
    wanʸašqʷí·ck (<theme wa-*ašqʷé) "they two dislike me"
walʸ- (coupled with privative thematic suffix -ma)
    See §35f.
wi·-
    wi·ʔanʸmu·vsó·yk (<theme wi·-*u·avsó·-y) "you curse me"
    wi·a·vkʸáwk (<theme wi·-*a·avkʸáw) "he calls him his paternal half-sibling"

§44. Nonthematic suffixes of the verb.

The five positions in which nonthematic affixes of the verb occur are outlined in §27.

a) Suffixes of the first position are aspective in meaning. Of those cited below, assertive ᵕt is not normally predicative and is usually followed by a predicative suffix; the others are predicative and are never followed by another suffix.

ᵕt assertive. The verb form with assertive ᵕt is used in answer to a question, in emphasizing the truth of an assertion, and in conveying information previously unknown.

> acénta?a "He did descend"
> maséctəxa "They will (surely) name you̬."

ᵕtum (following an accented vowel) /ᵕtiyum (following a consonant or ə) usitative; the interrogative forms of this suffix are ᵕtú·m and ᵕtiyú·m.

> amátum "He always (usually) eats."
> ?alʸaqʷáqtiyú·m "Is it always bitter?"

ᵕtʸa (following an accented vowel) /ᵕtiya (following a consonant or ə). The verb form with ᵕtʸa/ᵕtiya indicates completed action or that which is obviously, naturally, or universally so.

> ?avá·mtək ("I·arrive") ?aδútʸa ("I·did·so"), "I have arrived."
> xalʸ?áytiya "There is (normally) moonlight."

b) Suffixes of the second position are aspective in meaning. They are never predicative but must be followed by another suffix or an auxiliary verb.

ᵕnti "again"
> ?akaná·vənti ?a?í·m "I am going to tell of it again."
> ?awétəntixa "I will do it again."

ᵕapat / ᵕnʸpat "oneself, in turn, also"
> mawétapatxa "you in turn will do so"
> ?ama·wí·tənʸpatk "we also call him kin"

ᵕnʸ "until now"
> vi?u·nó·nʸk ("we·are·engaged·in·doing·until·now") ?anʸu·páyk ("we·are·depleted"), "We have gone on in this way until now we are depleted."

ᵕxay "still, no sooner than"
> vi?u·nó·xayk "I am still engaged in doing so"
> saví ("there") apákxayk ("he·no·sooner·arrives") amí·m ("he weeps"), "No sooner did he arrive there than he wept."

c) Suffixes of the third position are of tense or tense·modal meaning. All are predicative. Present·past ᵕk and future ᵕxa may be followed by other suffixes.

ᵕk present·past
> atápk "He throws, threw it."
> kawíntik "Do it again!"

ᵕᵛm present·past. This suffix is used to the exclusion of ᵕk with all themes having stems ending in final ᵕú/ó or ᵕí/é and with some themes having stems ending in final ᵕá or ᵕé, provided that no other suffix, thematic or nonthematic, occurs be-

tween the stem and the present-past suffix. The following table indicates the treatment of such themes in the singular and collective plural forms with present-past,
hortatory, and future suffixes and zero- third person pronominal prefix.

	Theme	Present-past	Hortatory	Future
sing.	amá "to eat"	amá·m	amáwú	amáxa
c. plu.	amá-c	amáck	amácú	amácxa
sing.	ašmá "to sleep"	ašmá·m	ašmáwú	ašmáxa
c. plu.	u·ašmá	u·šmá·m	u·šmáwú	u·šmáxa
sing.	akʸé "to shoot"	akʸá·m	akʸá·wú	akʸéxa
c. plu.	akʸé-c	akʸéck	akʸécú	akʸécxa
sing.	c-amí/é "to place"	camí·m	camíyú	caméxa
c. plu.	c-amí-c	camíck	camícú	camícxa
sing.	aštú/ó "to gather"	aštú·m	aštúwú	aštóxa
c. plu.	aštú-c	aštúck	aštúcú	aštúcxa

-xa future

  ma?ávəctəxa "You two will hear."
  apúyxalʸa "He would die."

-ú (following single consonants and, with an intervening w- or y-glide (see §10b),
vowels) /-iyú (following consonant clusters and strengthened consonants) hortatory

  ?a?ávú "Let me hear!"
  atáqšiyú "Let him jump!"

-um (following single consonants and, with an intervening w- or y-glide (see §10b),
vowels) /-iyum (following consonant clusters and strengthened consonants) future
possible. The interrogative forms of this suffix are -ú·m/-iyú·m.

  ?alá·yum "He might be bad."
  walʸ?ašémiyú·m "Would I not name it?"

-ám interrogative. This suffix is used only with verbs in the first and third persons.
The present-past form of the verb is used with interrogative meaning in the second
person.

  nʸi·mu·má·yám "Did he feed ye?"
  ka?a?étám "What did I say?"

-m subordinating. The following sentence illustrates the uses of the subordinate
verb form.

viˑyáˑk ("he-goes-along") ayúˑm ("he-seeing-it") xaˑsaʔílʸ ("sea") atók ("from-the-middle") acpákəm ("it-coming-out") ayúˑk ("he-sees"), ayúˑm ("he-seeing-it") axávək ("it-goes-in") ácpáktəntik ("it comes-out-again") láˑx aʔétk ("it-flashes") axávəm ("it-going-in") ayúˑk ("he-sees"), "As he went on he saw (something) come out from the midst of the sea: looking at it, he saw that it went in (to the water), came out again, flashed, and went in."

d) Suffixes of the fourth position are modal in meaning. All are predicative and may be preceded by other (predicative or nonpredicative) suffixes.

ˈʔaš evidential
    ʔawétʔaš "I did it."
    kamétəntiʔaš "He brought it again."
ˈlʸa optative
    ʔayóˑvlʸa "We would like to see."
    kamaʔéxalʸa "What would you say?"
ˈva "perhaps"
    nʸaˑðúˑva "perhaps it is so"
    ʔayémxava "perhaps I will go away"

ˈas dubitative. Translatable as "although . . ." or "if (contrary to fact) . . ."

    avʔáˑkas "if it were to walk"
    nʸašéxas "although I will name you"
ˈnka / ˈmka interrogative
    tiˑnʸáˑmənka "Is it dark?"
    maʔéxamka "Will you say?"

e) Suffixes of the fifth position have a syntactic rather than a semantic function. For example:

ˈa/ˈaʔa end of phrase.
    nʸavánʸ ("his-house") ayúˑk ("he-sees") aʔétk ("he-says") kanáˑvtaʔa ("he-told-of-it"), "He saw his house, and so he told of it."

§45. Derivation of noun themes from verb themes.

As noted previously (§17) any verb theme may be used in unaltered form as a noun theme. There are also certain specific grammatical methods by which verbal abstracts may be formed. Of these, the three most important are the adaptive, the definite, and the gerund.

a) The adaptive is formed from the singular verb theme by infixation of <aˑ> before the consonant immediately preceding the accented vowel of the stem plus ablaut of the accented vowel. In some cases the stem is concurrently modified by addition of a consonantal increment ˈc. The resulting noun theme has the meaning "that which is capable of, worthy of, fit for doing . . . or having . . . done to it."

    axér "to tie" >aˑxíˑr (*a<aˑ>xíˑr) "rope"

takanáy "to stop overnight" >taka·ná·y (*t·ka<a·>ná·y) "a stopping place"
amá "to eat" >a·má·c (*a<a·>má·c) "food, that which is edible"

b) The definite is formed by prefixation of the definite prefix kʷ to the theme
either in the singular or any of the plural forms.

apúy "to die (sing.)" >kʷapúy "the dead one"
u·xacmé·y (distr. obj. form of *u·x·amí· "to procreate") >kʷu·xacmé·y "the pro·
creator"
kacu·náv (distr. plu. form of *k·aná·v "to tell") >kʷakcu·návənʸc "those who tell"

The nominal series of referential pronominal prefixes is used with the definite
verbal abstract. Verbal nonthematic prefixes and suffixes may also occur as part
of the noun theme, the non·thematic prefixes preceding the referential pronoun.

vi·kʷaδíkva "this one that lies here" <noun theme *vi·kʷaδík< verb theme *aδík "to
be lying" plus verbal nonthematic affix vi·· "here" and definite kʷ·.
avʔanʸkʷá·mənʸc "I who pass by any places" <noun theme *avkʷá·m< verb theme
*á·m "to pass by" plus verbal nonthematic prefix av· "whatever" and definite
kʷ·.
ma·kʷu·vá·xəc "you who will remain here" <noun theme *kʷu·vá·xa< verb theme
*u·vá· "to remain" plus verbal nonthematic suffix ·xa future and definite kʷ·.

c) The gerund is formed from the verb theme in any person or number by
infixation of <u·> before the consonant immediately preceding the accented
vowel of the stem (see §10c). In some cases the stem is concurrently modified by
addition of a consonantal increment ·c. As with the definite, verbal nonthematic
affixes may become part of the noun theme. The gerund usually occurs with the
demonstrative nominal nonthematic suffix ·nʸ.

The meaning of the gerund is approximately that of English verbal abstracts
in ·tion; e.g., u·céwənʸ "his creation" (<*acéw "to create") means either "his act
of creation" or "that which he has created."

The following examples illustrate the formation of the gerund.

á·r "to desire" <u·wárənʸ (<u·>á·r+·nʸ) "his desire"
á·rc (coll. plu.) >u·wárcənʸ (<u·>á·r·c+·nʸ)
u·wárv (distr. plu.) >u·wárvənʸ (<u·><u·>á·r·v+·nʸ)
*amán "to arise" >u·mánənʸ (*a<u·>mán+·nʸ) "his arising"
*amá·n (coll. plu.) >u·má·nənʸ (*a<u·>má·n+·nʸ)
*u·má·nv (distr. plu.) >u·má·nvənʸ (*a<u·><u·>má·n·v+·nʸ)
*ašmá "to sleep" >šu·mácənʸ (*aš<u·>mác+·nʸ) (see §11a) "his sleeping"
*u·šmá (coll. plu.) >u·šu·mácənʸ (*u·aš<u·>mác+·nʸ)
*a·šmác (distr. plu.) >a·šu·mácənʸ (*a·aš<u·>mác+·nʸ)
*aʔí/é "to say" >u·ʔícənʸ (*a<u·>ʔíc+·nʸ) "his saying"
*aʔíc (coll. plu.) >u·ʔíccənʸ (*a<u·>ʔíc·c+·nʸ)
*u·ʔí·cv (distr. plu.) >u·ʔí·cvənʸ (*a<u·><u·>ʔí·c·v+·nʸ)
Cf. however:

*a·ʔéˑxa "to say (future)" >uˑʔéxən^y (*a<uˑ>ʔéˑxa+n^y) "his future saying, what he will say"

*a·ʔícˑxa (coll. plu.) <uˑʔícxən^y (*a<uˑ>ʔícˑxa+n^y)

*uˑʔíˑcvəˑxa (distr. plu.) >uˑʔíˑcvəxən^y (*a<uˑ><uˑ>ʔíˑcˑvˑxa+n^y)

The formation of the gerund from themes in the distributive object form is irregular in some cases. When the distributive object infix <c/t> occurs following a short vowel and preceding the consonant which precedes the accented vowel of the stem, the gerund infix <uˑ> precedes the infix <c/t>.

*taδáp "to split" >tuˑδápən^y (*ta<uˑ>δáp+n^y) "his splitting," "that which he has split"

*tatδáˑp (distr. obj.) >tuˑtδáˑpən^y (*ta<uˑ><t>δáˑp+n^y)

*tatuˑδáˑp (distr. plu.) >tatuˑδáˑpən^y (*ta<t><uˑ>δáˑpˑp+n^y)

When the vowel preceding the infix <c/t> is long, or when the infix <c/t> falls in some other position than that regularly occupied by the gerund infix <uˑ>, the gerund of the distributive object theme is formed regularly.

*aˑδáp "to make an incision" >aˑwaδápən^y (*aˑa<uˑ>δáp+n^y) "his incising of it"

*aˑcδáˑp (distr. obj.) >aˑcuˑδáˑpən^y (*aˑa<c><uˑ>δáˑp+n^y)

*aˑcuˑδáˑp (distr. plu.) >aˑcuˑδáˑpən^y (*aˑa<c><uˑ>δáˑpˑp+n^y)

*aˑlʸʔák "to befriend" >aˑlʸuˑʔákən^y (*aˑalʸ<uˑ>ʔák+n^y) "the one has he befriended"

*aˑcalʸʔáˑk (distr. obj.) >aˑclʸuˑʔáˑkən^y (*aˑa<c>lʸ<uˑ>ʔáˑk+n^y)

*aˑclʸuˑʔáˑk (distr. plu.) >aˑclʸuˑʔáˑkən^y (*aˑa<c>lʸ<uˑ><uˑ>ʔáˑk+n^y)

*šakavér "to overpower" >šakuˑvérən^y (*šˑka<uˑ>vér+n^y) "his overpowering of him"

*šatkavíˑr (distr. obj.) >šatkuˑvíˑrən^y (*š<t>ka<uˑ>víˑr+n^y)

*šatkuˑvíˑr (distr. plu.) >šatkuˑvíˑrən^y (*š<t>ka<uˑ><uˑ>víˑr+n^y)

SUMMARY

Since the primary interest of this paper has been in sketching the salient morphological features of Yuma, practically no material has been presented to show the ways in which words are combined into larger predicative constructions. A discussion of syntax would have had to deal with situations too complicated for adequate presentation within the limits of space.

If any one morphological feature may be said to be basic, I should say that in Yuma it is the sharp distinction of nouns and noun themes from verbs and verb themes. This distinction is based not only on the difference in syntactical use of the two word classes, but also on the relative simplicity and immutability of the noun theme in contrast to the verb theme and the existence of definite techniques for the deriving of noun themes from verb themes and vice versa. The distinction between verb and noun states a configuration; other morphological features fill in the details. The verb conveys most of the nuances of meaning and most of the indication of relations, both grammatical and notional. The primary function of the noun is to supply relatively simple referential content.

TONKAWA

HARRY HOIJER

THE Tonkawa appear to have been an important and war-like tribe who lived in central Texas during most of the 18th and 19th centuries. The remnants of this group, less than forty in all, today live in the vicinity of Tonkawa, Oklahoma.

The first linguistic material on the Tonkawa was collected by two German travelers to Texas. This data was turned over to Dr. A. S. Gatschet, who reported on it in three short papers.[1] Later (ca. 1884) Dr. Gatschet collected additional material which has, as far as I know, never been published.

Powell classified Tonkawa as an independent linguistic stock, presumably on the basis of the data gathered by Gatschet.[2] In 1915, Swanton compared Tonkawa with the scanty materials available on the Coahuiltecan languages. As a result of this comparison, he set up a new Coahuiltecan stock with two subdivisions, one including Coahuilteco proper, Comecrudo, and possibly Karankawa; and the other, Cotoname and Tonkawa.[3] In 1920, Sapir made a comparison between the Coahuiltecan of Swanton and the California Hokan languages. This brought out the important fact that Tonkawa and the Coahuiltecan languages may be remotely related to the Hokan languages of California.[4]

My material on Tonkawa was collected in 1928 and 1929 from one of the six remaining speakers of the language. A descriptive grammar based upon this data has been published[5] but I have not yet had the opportunity of testing either of the above-mentioned hypotheses in the light of my more complete data.

The sketch that follows is essentially a brief summary of the longer descriptive account. I have, however, made several important changes in both the orthography and the phonological discussion. My earlier account of the phonology was in

[1] A. S. Gatschet, *Die Sprache der Tonkawas* (Zeitschrift für Ethnologie, vol. 9, pp. 64–73, 1877), *Remarks upon the Tonkawa Language* (Proceedings of the American Philosophical Society, vol. 16, 1876, pp. 318–327); *Zwölf Sprachen aus dem Südwesten Nordamerikas* (Weimar, 1876).

[2] J. W. Powell, *Indian Linguistic Families of America North of Mexico* (7th Annual Report of the Bureau of American Ethnology, 1891), p. 125.

[3] John R. Swanton, *Linguistic Position of the Tribes of Southern Texas and Northeastern Mexico* (American Anthropologist, n.s., vol. 17, 1915, pp. 17–40).

[4] E. Sapir, *The Hokan and Coahuiltecan Languages* (International Journal of American Linguistics, vol. 1, 1920, pp. 280–290); *The Hokan Affinity of Subtiaba in Nicaragua* (American Anthropologist, n.s., vol. 27, 1925, pp. 491–527).

[5] Harry Hoijer, *Tonkawa, An Indian Language of Texas* (In Handbook of American Indian Languages, pt. 3, 1933, pp. 1–148).

many respects poorly done; the revision, I believe, takes care of most of its defects. The orthographic changes may briefly be summarized as follows:

Old	New	Old	New
b	p	ʔ	ʔ
d, t	t	c, s	s
g, k	k	xw	xʷ
gw, kw	kʷ	dj, dz, tc	c

m, n, w, y, and l are the same in both orthographies. The sounds t' and k' have been eliminated; it is clear that glottalized stops occur only in abnormally slow speech. kw', c', x', xw', m', n', w', y', l', and t'c have throughout been interpreted as the clusters kʷʔ, sʔ, xʔ, xʷʔ, mʔ, nʔ, wʔ, yʔ, lʔ, and cʔ, respectively.

1. THE PHONOLOGY

§1. The consonants.

POSITION OF ARTICULATION	VOICELESS			VOICED	
	Stops	Affricates	Spirants	Nasals	Frictionless Continuants
Bilabial	p			m	w
Dental	t	c	s	n	l
Palatal	k		x		y
Labiopalatal	kʷ		xʷ		
Faucal	ʔ		h		

p, t, k, and kʷ are voiceless, unaspirated, and lenis. In the final position of the word or syllable they may be unexploded as well. There is no noticeable variation otherwise. Examples: pax "just," hacip "hole," kopul "round"; tan "tail," hexʷit "belt," na·ton "mountain"; kapay "nothing," ʔok "hide," makik "yellow"; kʷa·n "woman," na·kʷ "go ahead," kʷa·kʷan "woman."

The glottal stop is clearly pronounced and does not vary noticeably in pronunciation: ʔa·x "water," ʔoʔoʔ "owl," ʔo·ʔon "blood veins."

c may be heard in either the dental or blade-alveolar position, though the latter is probably most common. The variation appears to be wholly random. In final position c, like the stops, is often unexploded. Examples: cakow "river," ha·c "land, earth," yacak "small, little."

s, too, is pronounced either as a blade-alveolar spirant (roughly similar to the initial of ship) or as a dental. The former pronunciation is especially characteristic of final s; the latter, varying with the former, of s in the initial position. Examples: samox "red," losos "all," ?awas "buffalo."

x is a palatal spirant not unlike the ch of German lachen and x^w is the same sound plus strong labialization. Both vary in position of articulation, being front-palatal before e and i and mid- or back-palatal before a, o, and u. Examples: xa· "fat, grease," xe·cwal "alligator," hoxolo·ko "shell," henox "pretty"; x^we·nkoxo? "he puts on his pants," hex^wit "belt," c?ax^w "cloth."

h is a light faucal aspiration which occurs only initially and medially. Examples: henox "pretty," ?ahen "daughter."

m and n are roughly similar to the initials of mad and neck, respectively, except that n is dental rather than alveolar. In final position both m and n become syllabic. Examples: maslak "white," hemaxan "chickens," me·m "cheeks"; nekak "vine," hanil "rat," hayon "itchy."

w, l, and y are similar to the initials of war, light, and young, respectively, except that l is pronounced in the dental position. In final position l becomes syllabic and w and y are vocalic rather than consonantal. Examples: waxes "surely," haway "long," ?aw "deer"; yamas "lips," hayon "itchy," ?asoy "stomach"; losos "all," keles "spotted," hewil "thickly clustered."

§2. The vowels.

Tonkawa vowels are distinguished according to quality and length, as follows.

i·, high, front, unrounded, and long. Similar in quality to cardinal i. ?i·s?a "minnow."

i, lower-high, front, unrounded. Similar to the vowel of English bit (Midwestern American dialect). pix "sweet."

e·, higher-mid, front, unrounded, and long. Similar to cardinal e in quality. ta·?e·k "spouse."

e, lower-mid, front, unrounded. Similar to the vowel of Midwestern American English bed. hetec "how?, in what manner?"

a, a·. Both of these vary in position of articulation from low central unrounded to low back unrounded. The variation appears to be random. wa?an "right, exactly," sa·xal "doorway, entrance."

o, lower-mid, back, rounded. Similar to the o of standard German voll. losos "all, many."

o·, higher-mid, back, rounded. Similar to the o of standard German Sohn. yo·m?o? "it rains."

u, u·, high, back, rounded. Similar to cardinal u in quality though the short u is sometimes a bit lower. hecu· "what?"; noxlul "screech owl."

Vowels followed by y and w are raised slightly in position of articulation. haway "tall," ?aw "deer," hewil "thickly clustered," xa·sey "leaf," ?oyuk "sack," k^wa·low "big." u and u· do not occur in this position.

§3. Word and sentence prosody.

Tonkawa utterances consist of a succession of more or less evenly stressed syllables. In no case does it appear that either stress or pitch accent plays any significant role in the word. Disyllabic forms, however, are generally pronounced with a somewhat heavier stress on the final syllable, whereas in polysyllabic words the main stress moves to the penult.

It is my impression that pitch-stress patterns, in kind not unlike those of English, function in Tonkawa phrases and sentences. I do not, however, possess data with which to describe and illustrate this point.

§4. Consonantal combinations.

Both the word and the syllable in Tonkawa invariably begin with a consonant, though they may terminate in either a consonant or a vowel. The syllabic is always a vowel or a vowel plus semivowel. Vowels never occur in sequence without an intervening consonant.

Consonants, however, do occur before or after other consonants. There are two types of consonantal combinations. The first and most frequent results when a syllable terminating in a consonant immediately precedes one begininng with a consonant. Any consonant may begin a syllable and all but h may end one. It would appear, then, that consonantal combinations of the first type may consist of any consonant but h plus a slight hiatus marking the point of syllabic division plus any consonant. However, as a result of certain morphophonemic processes, certain combinations never or rarely appear. Thus: combinations of identical consonants always unite to form a single consonant; ʔ plus consonant is very rare; stop plus ʔ occurs only in slow speech (in normal speech the glottal stop is absorbed to the preceding stop); an h following another consonant always disappears; and consonant plus y is rare. Other combinations are also infrequent because the consonants involved occur but seldom.

Examples: hop·cow "soft," ʔa·x·pix "cider"; net·xal "tongue," yak·toʔ "they sit about"; sok·noʔ "he owns it," tic·kan "people"; yakʷ·tos·wan "water fall," ʔaw·kʷa··low "elk"; ya·kaʔ·na··woʔ "he swings," xac·ʔan "stingy"; he·coc·xo·k "frightful," nax·can "fire"; nam·ʔek "fire-wood," kat·ma·ʔac "meadow-lark"; tan·kol "back of the head," yox·noʔ "he flies away"; mas·lak "white," ʔa·pan·su·s "house-fly"; nox·lul "screech owl," nok·xol "heel"; toxʷ·na·woʔ "it smells," ket·xʷa·noʔ "he smells me"; naw·loʔ "he spreads it out," ka·l·wan "wagon"; he·xal·ʔoy "ants," hak·la·nan "sharp"; may·ʔan "land terrapin," nes·ye·xem·yo·n "money."

A second type of consonantal combination is found within the syllable. Such clusters are pronounced without an intervening hiatus and, with a few exceptions (viz. ʔs, lʔ, yʔ, and sʔ), may only begin the syllable. The initial consonants of such clusters are kʷ, c, m, n, s, x, xʷ, l, and y; the final consonant is always the glottal stop. In slow speech the combinations pʔ, tʔ, and kʔ may also be heard but these always become p, t, and k, respectively, in normal speech.

It may also be noted that clusters of type two, when placed between vowels, become ambisyllabic just like the consonant combinations of type one. Thus, the cluster xʷ?, is pronounced without hiatus in xʷ?e·lo? "he misses him" but becomes ambisyllabic in kexʷ-?e-lo? "he misses me." Clusters of type two, then, may be found as initials of syllables beginning an utterance, as initials of syllables immediately preceded by a syllable terminating in a consonant, and, in the case of the exceptional combinations ?s, l?, y?, and s?, as syllable finals in syllables terminating an utterance.

Examples: kas-kʷ?as "five times"; c?axʷ "blanket," ?a-wa-k-c?e·k "gum"; m?e·-tan "lightning," nen-m?e-no? "he roasts it"; n?a·n-wo? "it is ground," ?a-was-n?a·n "sausage"; s?a·c "finger-nail," hen-s?o·y-to? "he stretches himself"; x?a·y "mother," hec-x?o-mo? "he pulls his foot back"; xʷ?e·-lo? "he misses him," nes-xʷ?e·-lo? "he causes him to miss him"; yak-l?a-xo? "he breaks it"; y?a-co? "he vomits," wen-y?e-co? "he milks them"; yak-pan-wa·s? "I strike him (right now)," yak-po?s "I strike him," ?al? "all right!" hey? and he-hey? "yes!"

§5. The syllable.

It is now evident that there are five types of syllable in Tonkawa. These may be exemplified as follows:

1) Consonant plus vowel: ?e-xʷa "buzzard," ka·-la "mouth."

2) Consonant, vowel, consonant: ?ok "skin, hide," ne·l "penis," tan-kol "back of the head," ka·l-wan "wagon," na-so·n-ti "Caddo Indians," hen-ca·n "pond, lake."

3) Consonant cluster (type two) plus vowel: s?a-ko? "he scrapes it," yak-l?a-xo? "he breaks it," s?e·-do? "he cuts it," nes-x?e·-po? "he makes him take it off."

4) Consonant cluster (type two), vowel, consonant: s?et-xʷa-no? "he chokes," hec-x?ol-?o? "he pulls his hands back," m?e-t-no? "lightning strikes him," hen-s?o·y-to? "he stretches himself."

5) Consonant, vowel, and ?s, l?, y?, or s?. Syllables of this type are found only in the final position. yam-xo?s "I paint his face," yak-pan-wa·s? "I strike him (right now)," ?al? "all right!" hey? and he-hey? "yes!" These examples are exhaustive.

2. MORPHOPHONEMICS

§6. Initial stem syllables beginning with h drop the h when a prefix syllable is added. If the prefix syllable has the form cv, its vowel is lengthened and given the quality of the vowel of the stem syllable. Examples: hap-lo? "they attack him" but ka··pi-lo? (<ke-hap-lo?) "they attack me," hew-lo? "he catches it" but ke··wi-lo? (<ke-hew-lo?) "he catches me," hep-co? "several fall" but xe··pa-co? (<xa-hep-co?) "several fall hard," ho·-?o-xa-wo? "he steals it" but ko·-?o-xa-wo? (<ke-ho·-?o-xa-wo?) "he steals me."

When the prefix syllable ends in a consonant, the vowel of the initial stem syllable forms a new syllable with the final consonant of the prefix. Examples:

ne·sew·lo? (<nes·hew·lo?) "he causes him to catch it," ne·so·-?o·xa·wo? (<nes·ho·-
?o·xa·wo?) "he causes him to steal it."

Some initial theme syllables beginning with y behave in a similar fashion
when preceded by certain prefixes of the type cv. Thus, ya·ko·na· "to hit with the
fist" but ha·ko·na· (<he·ya·ko·na·) "to box."

§7. Final stem syllables having the form cvw or cvy become co· when followed by a suffix beginning with a consonant. Examples: ?e·-?e·yaw· "to work" in
?e·-?e·ya·wo? (< ?e·-?e·yaw·o?) "he works" and ?e·-?e·yo·no? (< ?e·-?e·yaw·no?) "he
is working." xal·?oy· "to cut" in xal·?o·yo? (<xal·?oy·o?) and xal·?o·no? (<xal·
?oy·no?) "he is cutting it."

Similarly, the suffixes -we, declarative mode; -wes?, plural subject; and -a·dew,
future tense; are heard -o· or -o, -o·s?, and -a·do·, respectively, except when preceded by a long vowel or, in the case of -a·dew, followed by a vowel. Examples:
ya·ce·-we·? "he sees you" but ya·c·o·? (<ya·c·we·?) "he sees him" and ya·c·o·ka
(<ya·c·we·-?e·ka)"you see him"; ya·ce·-wes?·o·? "they two see you" but ya·c·o·s?·o·?
(<ya·c·wes?·we·?) "they two see him"; ya·c·a·dew·o? "he will see him" and
ya·c·a·dew·a·we? "he will see you" but ya·c·a·do·no? (<ya·c·a·dew·no?) "he
will be seeing him."

§8. Vowels in Tonkawa are morphophonemically of two types. One group,
which we shall distinguish by italic a, a·, e, e·, i, i·, o, o·, u, and u·, are found only
in stems. The second group are written a, a·, e, e·, i, i·, o, o·, u, and u· and may occur
in any portion of the word.

Vowels of the first type, when they occupy an even numbered position in
the word, are reduced one mora in length. Short a, e, i, o, and u then become zero
and long a·, e·, i·, o·, and u· are shortened. Examples: yamaxa· "to paint someone's
face" in yamx·o? "he paints his face," ke·ymax·o? "he paints my face," nes·yamx·o?
"he causes him to paint his face." ka·na· "to throw away" in ka·n·o? "he throws
it away," xa·kan·o? "he throws it far away," nes·ka·n·o? "he causes him to throw
it away."

Final vowels of stems, it will be noted, are elided if followed by a vocalic
suffix (e.g., yamaxa· in yamx·o? "he paints his face") but are retained, regardless of
their position, if the suffix begins with a consonant (e.g., yamaxa· in yamxa·no? "he
is painting his face," ke·ymaxa·no? "he is painting my face").

When final in a word, the last vowel of the stem is dropped and the penultimate vowel retained. Examples: notoso· "to hoe" in nots·o? "he hoes it," we·ntos·o?
"he hoes them," notso·no? "he is hoeing it" and notos "hoe."

A syllable containing a vowel of type one, when reduplicated, sometimes
repeats both consonant and vowel and sometimes only the consonant. Examples:
topo· "to cut" in top·o? "he cuts it," ke·tp·o? "he cuts me," totop·o? "he cuts it
repeatedly"; yakapa· "to hit" in yakp·o? "he hits him" ke·ykap·o? "he hits me,"
yakakp·o? "he hits him repeatedly." In neither case does the addition of a prefix

to the reduplicated form alter the vowel of the reduplicated syllable: ke·totop·o? "he cuts me repeatedly," ke·ykakp·o? "he hits me repeatedly."

§9. The following examples illustrate the preceding morphophonemic rules.

necepaw- in necpaw·o? "he touches him," ke·ncepaw·o? "he touches me," necpo··no? "he is touching him," ke·ncepo··no? "he is touching me."

tanxoy- in tanxoy·o? "he takes it from him," ke·tanxoy·o? "he takes it from me," tanxo··no? "he is taking it from him," ke·tanxo··no? "he is taking it from me."

naxʷece- in naxʷc·o? "he rattles it," we·nxʷec·o? "he rattles them," naxʷexʷc·o? "he rattles it repeatedly," we·nxʷexʷc·o? "he rattles them repeatedly," naxʷec "rattle."

na·ta- in na·t·o? "he steps on it," we·nat·o? "he steps on them," nanat·o? "he steps on it repeatedly," we·nanat·o? "he steps on them repeatedly."

ya·lo·na- in ya·lo·n·o? "he kills him," ke·yalo·n·o? "he kills me."

s?e·ta- in s?e·t·o? "he cuts it," we·s?et·o? "he cuts them," s?es?et·o? "he cuts it repeatedly," we·s?es?et·o? "he cuts them repeatedly."

m?aye- in m?ay·o? "he sets fire to it," we·m?ay·o? "he sets fire to them."

y?oco- in y?oc·o? "he pinches him," ke·y?oc·o? "he pinches me," y?oy?oc·o? "he pinches him repeatedly."

salke- in salk·o? "he pulls it out," we·salk·o? "he pulls them out," sasalk·o? "he pulls it out repeatedly," we·sasalk·o? "he pulls them out repeatedly."

xaclew- in xaclew·o? "he becomes angry," xaclo··no? "he is getting angry," ke·xaclew·o? "I become angry," ke·xaclo··no? "I am getting angry," ke·xaxaclew·o? "I become very angry."

hayoxo- in hayx·o? "he mounts (a horse)," ka·yox·o? (<ke·hyox·o?) "he mounts me," hayoyox·o? "he mounts (a horse) repeatedly," ka·yoyox·o? (<ke·hayoyox·o?) "he mounts me repeatedly."

hatxese- in hatxes·o? "he knows him," ka·txes·o? (<ke·hatxes·o?) "he knows me."

hapaxa- in hapax·o? "he looks up," ka·pax·o? (<ke·hapax·o?) "I look up."

3. MORPHOLOGY

§10. Tonkawa morphemes may be divided into the following classes.

I. Themes
  A. Free themes.
  B. Bound themes.
II. Affixes
  A. Transformative affixes; i.e., affixes by means of which a theme may be altered in function.
  B. Verbal affixes; i.e., affixes which can be added only to verbs.
  C. Noun and pronoun affixes.

III. Enclitics; i.e., bound forms which may be added to gerundial verb forms, nouns, or pronouns.

It is clear from this list that affixation is an important grammatical process in Tonkawa. Suffixation is, however, far more important than prefixation.

Word order is grammatically negligible in differentiating between subject and object since these relations are indicated by means of noun endings. There is, however, a regular order: subject, object, verb, which is normally maintained. And word order functions grammatically in distinguishing between certain other form classes. For example, the free theme cʔel "up, above" functions differently in each of the following examples: cʔel-ʔa·yʔik ha·noʔ "he goes to the top" (ha·noʔ "he goes"), na·ton-cʔel-ʔa·yʔik ha·noʔ "he goes to the top of the mountain" (na·ton "mountain"), cʔel ha·noʔ "he goes upward." In the first example, cʔel occurs with two noun suffixes, -ʔa·, definite article, and -yʔik, dative of arrival, and functions therefore as a noun. In the second example, cʔel appears between a noun (na·ton) and its suffixes (-ʔa·yʔik) and functions therefore as an adjective. And, in the last example, cʔel occurs independently and directly preceding a verb, functioning therefore as an adverb.

Compounding is very common in Tonkawa. Verb compounds generally involve only bound verb themes. No more than two themes are combined and, in all cases, the second theme is the modifying element. Examples: hawawne-taxka- "to carry [several] to this place" (hawawne- "to carry a burden," taxka- "several arrive"), yakaw-ka·na- "to kick away" (tr.; yakaw- "to kick," ka·na- "to throw away"), henkʷay-silwe- "to run about here and there" (henkʷay- "to run," silwe- "to wander about"), taʔan-aycona- "to pull up" (taʔan- "to grasp, to seize," haycona- "one moves up"). Some themes occur only as second elements of verb compounds: yak-ay- "to pierce by shooting" (yake- "to shoot," -ay- "[to] pierce"), yats-ay- "to pierce by stabbing" (yats- "to stab"), so·l-to·xa- "to drip onto" (so·l- "to drip," -to·xa- "[to fall] on"), ta·kona-tol- "to search in vain" (ta·kona- "to search," -tol- "in vain"), yako·n-yapalʔ- "to knock down" (yako·n- "to strike," -yapalʔ- "down"). Most of these secondary themes serve an adverbial function in the compound.

Other than verb themes appear rarely in verb compounds. ho·s-taxsew "to be morning" is a combination of ho·s "early" and taxsew- "day breaks"; na·x-sokna- "to guide, to reconnoitre" is a compound of na·x "road" and sokna- "to put away, to have"; tap-ecne- "to lie on one's side" is tap- "on one's side" which is found compounded only with hecne- "to lie down."

Noun compounds may involve two or three free themes. Examples: ʔa·x-pix "cider" (ʔa·x "water," pix "sweet"), ʔaw-kʷa·low "elk" (ʔaw "deer," kʷa·low "big"), ʔawas-esʔaw "camel" (ʔawas "meat," hesʔaw "little"), tan-maslak "rabbit" (tan "tail," maslak "white"), yakwan-ʔoyuk "leggings" (yakwan "leg," ʔoyuk "sack"), tan-ʔok-apay "opossum" (tan "tail," ʔok "hair," kapay "none"), tolʔaxan·o·ʔoxo·n·a·x "the Milky Way" (tolʔaxan "corn," ho·ʔoxo·n "that which is stolen," na·x "road").

Sometimes, however, a bound theme occurs in a noun compound: ʔawas·nʔa·n "sausage" (ʔawas "meat," ·nʔa·n· <nʔa·nwe· "to be ground"), ʔekʷans·xaw "horse" (ʔekʷan "dog," ·s, instrumental suffix, ·xaw "to move far [?]"), maslak·taxso· "frost" (maslak "white," taxso·· "day breaks"), cʔaxʷ·yapec "thread" (cʔaxʷ "cloth," yapce· "to sew"). And, as in the verb, several noun themes occur only in compounds: ʔa·x·yaycan "kingfisher" (ʔa·x "water"), tas·ʔok "pubic hair" (ʔok "hair"), tan·soytat "squirrel" (tan "tail"), yoxanan·kamlew "bat" (yoxanan "wings").

Reduplication affects verb themes for the most part. Generally only one of the syllables of the theme is repeated. Reduplication symbolizes repeated action, plural subject, or rarely, vigorous or intense action. Examples: totop· "to cut repeatedly" (top· "to cut"), wawana· "several fall forward" (wa·na· "to fall forward"), sosoyana· "several swim away" (so·yana· "to swim away"), xaxaclewa· "to be very angry" (xaclewa· "to be angry"), sasalke· "to pull out repeatedly" (salke· "to pull out"), napopoxa· "to blow at repeatedly" (napoxa· "to blow at"), walalapa· "to boil vigorously" (walapa· "to boil"), yaypax· "to slap repeatedly" (yapxa· "to slap").

In noun themes, reduplicated forms occur rarely: nantoʔon "a range of mountains" (na·ton "mountain"), kʷa·kʷan "women" (kʷa·n "woman") hosaʔas "young [referring to plural noun]" (hosas "young [referring to one]"), henoʔox "pretty [referring to several]" (henox "pretty [referring to one]"), ʔo·ʔon "blood veins" (ʔo·n "blood").

THE THEME

§11. Themes, as has been indicated, are of two major types, free and bound. In general, free themes function as nouns and modifiers, bound themes as verbs and pronouns. There are, however, a number of free themes which may function as either nouns or verbs depending upon the suffix type added. Thus, the theme notox "hoe" functions as a noun when found with noun suffixes (e.g., notox·ʔa··la "the hoe"; ·ʔa·, definite article, ·la, nominative singular) and as a verb when verb suffixes are added (e.g., notx·o·ʔ "he hoes it"; ·o, declarative mode suffix, ·ʔ, third person, present tense). Other themes in this category are: mʔe·tan "lightning," mʔe·tn· "lightning strikes"; tolʔaw "dough," tolʔaw· "to knead"; naxʷec "rattle," naxʷce· "to rattle, to shake a rattle"; yakaw "spurs," yakwa· "to kick, to spur"; yawey "field," yawya· "to plant."

Similarly, there are some free themes functioning as demonstrative pronouns: helʔa·t "that one," heka·t "those," we·lʔa·t "that one," wa·taʔas "this time," and two that function as interrogative pronouns: hecu· "what?" (presumably to be analyzed into he·, interrogative prefix, and ·cu·, but the latter does not occur independently) and hetwan "how many?"

Certain themes (both free and bound) may change in function only when transformative affixes are added. Thus, a number of free themes may function as verbs if either the suffix -ʔe or -wa is added (in addition, of course, to the regular verbal suffixes). Examples: yatin "scraper," yatin-ʔe· "to scrape"; palʔil "brains," palʔil-ʔe· "to smear [e.g., brains on skin]"; ʔasoy "stomach," ʔasya-wa· "to be pregnant"; taxas "day," taxse-wa· "day breaks"; xa· "fat," xa·-wa· "to be fat"; yo·c "foam," yo·c-wa· "to foam."

Similarly, many bound themes can be made noun themes by the addition of a suffix -an. Examples: heylapa-"to stand erect," heylap-an "tree"; yakwa-"to kick," yakw-an "leg"; katwe-"to give birth to," katw-an "female animal"; xʔene-"to sweep," xʔen-an "broom"; sʔe·ta-"to cut," sʔe·t-an "rope." The gerundial verb suffix -k also serves this function in a few cases: hecocxo·-k "an evil one" (hecocxo·-"to be feared"), taxso·-k "tomorrow" (taxso·-"day breaks"), ta·ʔe·-k "spouse" (ta·ʔe·-"to marry"), hekto·-k "singing" (hekto·-"to sing"), The -k suffix has other functions as well.

This process is particularly well illustrated in the pronouns where, by the use of transformatives, demonstrative themes can be made to function as demonstrative adverbs, interrogatives, and indefinite pronouns. Examples: te·- "this," te·-ca "this place," te·-l "this direction" te·-c "this way, in this manner," he-te-ca "in what place?" he-te-l "where?" he-te-c "in what manner?" he-te-ca-ʔax "somewhere," he-te-c-ʔax "in some way, somehow."

§12. Most themes cannot be analyzed. In a few of them, however, certain elements appear which can be isolated. The most free of these isolable elements are the suffixes -na "away" and -ta "hither." They are found either as an essential part of the theme or in themes that may also be used without them. Examples: ha·-na-"one person goes," ha·-ta-"one person comes" (ha·-"one person moves," not used alone); ka·-na-"to throw away," ka·-ta-"to throw this way"; wa·-na-"to fall forward," wa·-ta-"to fall backward"; yox-na-"to fly away," yox-ta-"to come flying"; so·ya-na-"to swim away," so·ya-ta-"to come swimming"; cetxa-na-"to jump away," cetxa-ta-"to jump this way." The following themes may be used with or without the directives: topo-"to stalk, to creep up on," top-na-"to go along stalking," top-ta-"to come stalking"; he·sa-"to point at," he·sa-na-"to point over there," he·sa-ta-"to point here"; ya·ce-"to see," ya·ce-na-"to look away," ya·ce-ta-"to look here."

A third suffix -xa "arrival at" is found with only two themes: xa·-xa-"one person arrives at a distant point" (xa-, theme prefix "with force, to a distant point," -a·- from ha·-"one person goes") and xat-xa-"several arrive at a distant point" (-t- from -ta-"several move"; cf. ta-na-"several go").

Certain other suffixes alternate with the -na and -ta suffixes and may, for this reason, be isolated. yak-e· (<*yak-ʔe·) "to shoot," yak-na-"to shoot away," yak-ta-"to shoot this way"; yasyak-e· (<*yasyak-ʔe·) "to tear," yasyak-na-"to go along tearing." From these two examples the suffix -ʔe may be isolated. Its meaning, however, is not too clear unless we can associate it with the transformative suffix -ʔe (see §11).

Another suffix, -ʔa, may be isolated in the same way. Thus, yakew-ʔa- "to make," yakew-na- "to go along making"; co·l-ʔa- "to defecate," co·l-na- "to go along defecating." Here again the meaning of -ʔa does not appear clearly.

It is a possible hypothesis that -ʔe and -ʔa are verb forming suffixes of the type of the transformatives described in §11. The suffixes -na, -ta, and -xa may also have served a similar function in addition to their adverbial use. But there is no way of proving this hypothesis on the basis of Tonkawa materials alone.

§13. An interesting set of what may be called secondary stems can be isolated from the following themes: ha-yco-na- "one person goes up," ha-yco-ta- "one peson comes up," ta-yco-na- "several go up," ta-yco-ta- "several come up," ha-kla-na- "one person goes down," ha-kla-ta- "one person comes down," ta-kla-na- "several go down," ta-kla-ta- "several come down," ha-kxo-na- "one person goes in," ha-kxo-ta- "one person comes in," ta-kxo-na- "several go in," ta-kxo-ta- "several come in," ha-txil-na- "one person goes out," ha-txil-ta- "one person comes out," ta-txil-na- "several go out," ta-txil-ta- "several come out," ha-yxe-na- "one person goes across," ha-yxe-ta- "one person comes across," ta-yxe-na- "several go across," ta-yxe-ta- "several come across."

Here the initial elements ha- and ta- are most certainly related to the initial morphemes of the themes ha·-na- "one person goes" and ta-na- "several go," respectively. The final elements, -na and -ta, are the directives "away" and "hither," respectively. That leaves a set of adverbial secondary stems, only one of which occurs in another connection. kox-na- "several go in" seems to be a combination of the full form of -kxo- with the directive suffix -na. It is possible, therefore, that the themes described above may be old compounds, the second constituents of which have lost independent existence.

§14. Certain initial theme elements occur with sufficient frequency to be regarded as prefixes. The most frequently occurring of these are he-, ya-, and ne-. Of the three, he- is easiest to define. Examples: ha·kona- "to box" (=he- plus yakona- "to hit with the fist"), ha·xaxkosa- "several go in single file" (=he- plus the reduplicated form of yaxkosa-"to follow"), ha·tasa-"a fight with knives takes place" (=he- plus yatsa- "to stab"), he-tay ʔew- "to join a group" (tay ʔew- "to mix"), he-ns ʔo·yto- "to stretch oneself" (cf. ʔey-nos ʔo·yto- "to stretch"), he ntitxew ʔa- "to move about nervously, to tremble," (cf. ʔey-netitxew ʔa- "to move"). From these examples, it is clear that he- gives a mediopassive significance to the verb theme. It may also be noted that the reflexive pronoun has exactly similar form (see §21). The he- themes, therefore, may be themes in which the reflexive pronoun has become fixed.

ya- themes occur with less frequency than he- themes and the function of ya-

is not easily defined. Alternate forms are rare; the following are practically exhaustive. ya-kpa- "to strike" (tr.), nes-kapa-, "to close, to shut," (nes-, causative
prefix). Here a form -kapa- seems isolable with the meaning "[two objects] come
together, to bump" (act. intr.). If that is true, then ya- in yakpa- could be interpreted as a causative. Compare also ya-tke- "to be frozen" (intr.) and nes-tike- "to
freeze." It is possible that -tike- means "to be cold" and that the two verbs above
are causatives at different stages in the history of the language.

Another ya- prefix is found which is similar to the preceding in all but one
respect. Where the former possesses an a-vowel (i.e., morphophonemic type one)
(e.g., yakp-o? "he strikes him," ke-ykap-o? "he strikes me"), the latter has the
a-vowel (e.g., yasxaw-o? "he frightens him," ke-yasxaw-o? "he frightens me").
The latter is, however, definitely a causative as the following examples show:
xamce- "to be broken," ya-xmac- "to break" (tr.); saxwa- "to be frightened,"
ya-sxaw- "to frighten" (tr.); ?atsaw- "to revive, to come to life," ya-?atsaw- "to
revive, to bring to life" (tr.). It also occurs in a number of themes for which there
are no alternates: yatmaxe- (-yatmaxe-) "to break" (tr.), yatxalka- (-yatxalka-) "to
hang up" (tr.), yalmete- (-yalmete-) "to deceive" (tr.), yalxilna- (-yalxilna-) "to run
away," yatsan- (-yatsan-) "to think of" (tr.). In these forms it has become a part
of the theme much in the same way as has the previously discussed ya- except that
it does not elide its vowel. Perhaps it is possible to associate the two ya- prefixes;
the first ya- having become indissolubly a part of the theme to the extent of obeying
the rules of elision characteristic of theme elements and the second having fused
with some themes to a lesser extent and still being freely movable in others.

ne- themes occur with still less frequency and alternate forms are practically
nonexistent. However, among the forms discussed by Gatschet[6] is a word paxka
which he defines "tobacco" and asserts is a borrowing from English. The form I
recorded for tobacco is nepaxkan, a noun derived from the verb nepaxka- "to
smoke" (tr.). My informant assured me, however, that this was a recent word for
tobacco and that the archaic form was na?acwawk. If this is true, Gatschet's analysis is probably correct and we have a test form for ne-; i.e., ne-paxka- "to smoke"
from an original paxka "tobacco."

One other alternation involving ne- may be mentioned. nam?ene- "to broil
[meat] over coals" (tr.; possibly derived from nam?e-k "firewood," -k being a noun
suffix) and ne-nm?ene- "to barbecue [meat]" (tr.). This alternation does not agree
in meaning with the one above, however.

Finally, there is a difference between the two causative prefixes in Tonkawa
which may have a bearing upon the meaning of ne-. nes- symbolizes the regular
causative (see §22) and hes- a mediopassive causative. Thus, nes-?ek-o?s "I make
him give it to him" (?eke- "to give to") and hes-?ek-o?s "I ask for it" (literally "I

[6] A. S. Gatchet, *Remarks upon the Tonkawa Language* (Proceedings of the American Philosophical Society, vol. 16, 1876), p. 318.

make him give it to me"). It is possible that the ne- of nes- is cognate with the ne- of the ne- themes and the he- of hes- with the mediopassive he-.

§15. In addition to the more or less regular phonetic-semantic similarities described in the preceding, there are a number of less frequently occurring similarities in form and meaning between themes. Lack of space does not permit an exhaustive discussion of these; the following samples will serve to illustrate the type.

na-m ʔe-k "firewood," na-m ʔe-ne- "to broil [meat] over coals" (tr.), ne-n-m ʔe-ne- "to barbecue" (tr.), ha-m ʔa-m ʔa- "to burn," m ʔa-ye- "to set fire to" (tr.), m ʔe-·lne- "to shine, to glow," m ʔe-·lcicen "sheet lightning." From these examples, we can isolate the elements -m ʔe-·, -m ʔe-, and -m ʔa-, all of which seem to have some reference to fire, heat, or light. Further analysis is impossible.

tol-ʔaxe- "to cut corn kernels from cob" (tr.), kay-ʔaxe- "to disjoint, to dismember" (tr.), som-ʔaxe- "to skin, to flay" (tr.), yakl-ʔaxe- "to break [e.g., neck]" (tr.), ʔey-tam-ʔaxe- "to smash" (tr.), ʔey-pas-ʔaxe- "to burst by pressure" (tr.), ʔey-kel-ʔaxe- "to smash" (tr.). In this series there seems to be a common element -ʔaxe- referring to cutting, breaking, or chopping. The first elements may be incorporated nouns defining the object. Some evidence for this point may be found in the series: tol-ʔaxe- "to cut kernels of corn from the cob" (tr.), tol-ʔawe- "to knead [bread dough]" (tr.), ya-tal-pa- "to make [corn] bread."

so-ya-na- "to swim away," so-ya-ta- "to come swimming," nen-so-ya-wa- "to swim with a burden, to ferry" (tr.), so-na "duck" so-·la- "[liquid] drips onto [something]." From the first three examples it seems possible to isolate a stem so-ya- referring to movement through the water. The functions of the other elements are not clear. A comparison of so-ya- with so-na and so-·la- indicates a possible further analysis.

§16. The only conclusion that can be drawn from the preceding survey of theme morphology is that there is some slight evidence that the Tonkawa theme is composed of smaller morphologic units. It is probable that the basic unit is a stem composed of two phonetic elements (cvcv) and that this stem is often modified by the addition of various affixes. In most cases, however, the theme is now the functional unit and has been so for a long time. This has no doubt led to a phonetic fusion of stem and affix which, together with changes in the meanings of themes, makes it difficult to isolate, from Tonkawa evidences alone, the theme constituents.

Comparison with other Coahuiltecan languages and with the Hokan languages will no doubt aid greatly in understanding the structural history of the Tonkawa theme. Such a comparison is, however, beyond the scope of this paper.

NOUN SUFFIXES

§17. The noun suffixes may be summarized as follows:

	Indefinite		Definite	
	Singular	Plural	Singular	Plural
Nominative	-la	-ka	-ʔa·la	-ʔa·ka
Accusative	-lak	-kak	-ʔa·lak	-ʔa·kak
Genitive	-ʔan		-ʔa·lʔan[7]	
Dative (arrival)			-ʔa·y·ik[8]	
Dative (approach)			-ʔa·wʔan[8]	
Instrumental	-es		-ʔa·las[9]	-ʔa·kay
Conjunctive	-ʔen		-ʔa·lʔen[9]	

Examples: ha·ʔako·n-la ha·noʔ "a man goes away"; ha·ʔako·n-ka tanoʔ "several men go away"; ha·ʔako·n-lak yakpoʔ "he strikes a man"; ha·ʔako·n-kak yakpoʔ "he strikes men"; ha·ʔako·n-ʔa·la ʔekʷan-ʔa·lak ya·lo·noʔ "the man kills the dog"; ha·ʔako·n-ʔa·ka ʔekʷan-ʔa·kak ya·lo·noʔ "the men kill the dogs"; hepayxʷetan-ʔa·lʔan xa·y-ʔa·la "the young woman's mother"; ha·ʔako·n-ʔa·lʔan macxanan-ʔa·la "the man's sweetheart"; xalo·nde·-la kʷa·n-ʔan ʔo·nbaxcoʔ "this knife is all [covered with] a woman's blood" (kʷa·n "woman"); na·ton-ʔa·yʔik xa·xoʔ "he arrived at the distant mountain"; na·ton-ʔa·wʔan ha·noʔ "he went toward the mountain"; yanʔa·nwan-elʔa·t-as neskʷitoʔ "he bound him with that chain" (yanʔa·nwan "chain"; helʔa·t "that"); saxʔay-ʔa·las yakoʔ "he shot him with the arrow"; ʔekʷan-es hexsasoʔ "he yelped like a dog" (ʔekʷan "dog"); he·tyan-ʔa·kay taʔancenesʔoʔ "they held him by his arms" (he·tyan "arms"); heykʷecan-ʔen heyxaxalʔan-ʔen taʔanoʔ "he picked up rings and ear rings"; he·tyan-ʔa·lʔen yakwan-ʔa·lʔen yawoʔ "he tied up the [his] arms and the [his] legs."

PRONOUNS

§18. The independent personal pronoun is used only for emphasis since person and number are regularly indicated by the verb form (see §25 to §27). Following

[7] If the noun is followed by a demonstrative, the definite article suffix -ʔa· may be dropped and -lʔan suffixed directly to the demonstrative theme.

[8] -ʔa·yik denotes an ending-point relationship, -ʔa·wʔan a relationship of approach (see the examples following). Here, also, the -ʔa· is dropped if the noun is followed by a demonstrative.

[9] -ʔa· is dropped if the noun is followed by a demonstrative.

are the personal pronoun themes plus the case suffixes employed with them:

		Nominative	Accusative	Genitive
Singular	1	sa·ʻya	sa·ʻsik	sa·ken
	2	na·ʻya	na·ʻyak	na·ʻxen
	3	ʔa·yeʻla	ʔa·yeʻlak	ʔa·ʻxen
Dual	1	kewʻsa·ʻya	kewʻsa·ʻsik	—
	2	weʻna·ʻya	weʻna·ʻyak	—
	3	ʔaʻweʻla	ʔaʻweʻlak	—
Plural	1	kewʻsa·ʻka	kewʻsa·ʻkak	kewʻsa·ken
	2	weʻna·ʻka	weʻna·ʻkak	naʻwenexen
	3	ʔaʻweʻka	ʔaʻweʻkak	ʔaʻwxen

In addition to these forms are found the following: sa·ʻxʷa "I also," na·ʻxʷa "you also," ʔa·ʻxʷa "he also," kewʻsa·ʻxʷa "we also," weʻna·ʻxʷa "you (plural) also," ʔaʻwaʻxʷa "they also"; sa·ʻcos "by myself," na·ʻcos "by yourself," ʔa·ʻcos "by himself," kewʻsa·ʻcos "by ourselves," weʻna·ʻcos "by yourselves," and ʔaʻwaʻcos "by themselves."

§19. The demonstrative pronouns are as follows:

	Nominative	Accusative	Dative	
Singular	wa·ʻʔa·la	wa·ʻʔa·lak	wa·ʻyʔik	wa·ʻwʔan
Plural	wa·ʻka	wa·ʻkak	—	—
Singular	te·ʻla	te·ʻlak	—	te·ʻwʔan
Plural	te·ʻka	te·ʻkak	—	—
Singular	heʔeʻla	heʔeʻlak	heʔe·ʻk	heʔe·ʻwʔan
Plural	he·ʻka	he·ʻkak	—	he·ʻwʔan
Singular	—	—	we·ʻyʔik	we·ʻwʔan

From this it can be seen that there are four demonstrative themes, wa·ʻ "that one aforementioned," te·ʻ "this," heʔe (or heʔe·ʻ or he·ʻ) "that," and we·ʻ "that one yonder." The suffixes are similar in form and meaning to those employed with the noun (see §17).

Four other demonstratives occur in my material: helʔa·t "that one," heka·tʻkak "those" (ʻkak, plural accusative noun suffix[?]), weʻlʔat "that one near, it, that," and waʻtaʔas "this particular time." All of these may function either as demonstratives (in which case they require the proper noun suffixes) or as demonstrative adverbs.

Other demonstrative adverbs may be formed from the four bound demonstrative themes by the addition of the suffixes ʻca, "place," ʻl, "direction," and ʻc, "manner." Thus: wa·ʻca "that place aforementioned," te·ʻca "this place," heʔeʻca "that place," te·ʻl "this direction," heʔeʻl "that direction," we·ʻʔil (an irregular formation) "that direction yonder," te·ʻc "this manner," he·ʻc "that manner" and we·ʻc or we·ʻtic "that manner." There is apparently no difference in meaning between the last two forms and he·ʻc.

§20. The interrogative pronouns are characterized by a prefix he·ʻ. Most of them are formed from the demonstrative theme te·. Thus he·te·l "where?" (·te· reduced form of te· "this"; ·l, direction suffix), he·te·w·ʔan "which way?" (·w·ʔan, dative suffix), he·te·c "how?" (·c, manner suffix) and he·te·ca "where?" (·ca, place suffix). Three other interrogative pronouns occur which cannot be so analyzed: hecu· "what?" hecu·ʔet "why, for what reason?" and hetwan "how many?"

The indefinite pronouns are formed from the interrogatives by the addition of a suffix ·ʔax. Thus: hecu··ax "anything, anyone, something"; hetwan·ʔax "several"; hetec·ʔax "somehow"; heteca·ʔax "somewhere"; and hetew·ʔan·ʔax "in some direction, in any direction."

VERB PREFIXES

§21. Four of the verb prefixes express pronominal concepts. These are: ke·, first person pronoun object, we·, plural pronoun object, kew·, first person plural pronoun object (obviously a combination of ke· and we·), and he·, a reflexive pronoun. Examples: yakpoʔ "he hits him," ke·ykapoʔ "he hits me," we·ykapoʔ "he hits us," and he·ykapoʔ "he hits himself."

Ordinarily the form he· is sufficient for the reflexive in all persons. When, however, it is necessary to emphasize person in the reflexive, the prefixes sa· "me," na· "you," ʔa· "him," kewsa· "us," and wena· "you (plural)" may be added before the reflexive pronoun. Examples: sa·he·ykapoʔs "I hit myself," na·he·ykapo·ka "you hit yourself," ʔa·he·ykapoʔ "he hits himself," etc.

The prefix he·, the affixes he·. . .·wa and he·. . .·wa, and the suffix ·wa are found in some verbs to express the notion of plural subject or repeated action. Examples: he·y·ay·ʔace· "to vomit repeatedly" (y·ʔace· "to vomit"), he·ykakawa·wa· "several dance" (yakwa· "to dance"), he··nanace·wa· "several bite" (nace· "to bite"), nececepa·wa· "to touch repeatedly" (necpa· "to touch"). It will be noted that in all these examples the theme is reduplicated. In many themes, the affixes need not be used, reduplication being sufficient.

The reciprocal pronoun is expressed by the affix he·. . . yew· (he·. . . ·yo·) or he··. . .·yew (he··. . .·yo·). The variation between ·yew and ·yo· is phonetic (see §7); the variation between he·· and he·, however, cannot be explained. Neither can it be proven that this prefix is the same as that discussed in the preceding paragraph. Examples: he··ʔensa··yew·oʔ "they are jealous of one another" (ʔensaw· "to be jealous"), he··ʔensa··yo··noʔ "they are being jealous of one another," he·cocna·· yew·oʔ "they are sleeping with each other" (coxna· "to sleep").

§22. There are two freely movable causative prefixes, nes·, the regular causative, and hes·, the mediopassive causative. Examples: nes·ʔeke· "to cause to give to" (ʔeke· "to give to"), nes·ʔace· "to cause to become sick" (ʔace· "to become sick"), hes·ʔeke· "to ask for" (literally, "to cause to give to oneself").

In some themes, nes· and hes· have become a part of the total form; i.e., the theme cannot be used without them. Examples: nes·pece· "to fill," nes·tewe· "to

call by name," nes·tike· "to be freezing," hes·kekte· "to be tied in score" (cf. nes·
kete· "to count"), hes·kʷace· "to like."

§23. The postposition ta·· "with, to" occurs in two other forms tas· and tasa·.
Examples: tasa·yela· "to sit with" (yela· "to sit"), tas·ecne· "to lie with" (hecne·
"to lie"), ta··notso· "to stand with" (notso· "to stand"). Only one theme is found
in which this prefix is apparently "frozen": ta··kona· "to search for, to hunt."

The prefix xa· "with force, to a distance": xa·kana· "to throw with force, to
throw to a distance" (ka·na· "to throw"), xa·ykapa· "to hit hard" (yakpa· "to hit"),
xa·soyana· "to swim to a distance" (so·yana· "to swim away"), xe·cne· "to fall
down" (<xa· plus hecne· "to lie down"), xe·nkʷa·na· "to run far away" (<xa·
plus henkʷa·na· "to run away").

If a theme with the directional suffix ·ta "hither" employs this prefix, the
meaning of the two becomes "in a circle." Examples: ka·ta· "to throw here,"
xa·kata· "to swing" (i.e., "to throw in a circle"); so·yata· "to swim here," xa·
soyata· "to swim in a circle."

The prefix ya· is probably an older causative prefix than that discussed in §21
since it occurs as a freely movable prefix with but few themes and is apparently an
immovable part of several others. The relationship between this prefix and the
theme element ya· has already been discussed (see §14). Examples: xamce· "to be
broken," ya·xmace· "to break" (tr.); saxwa· "to be frightened," ya·sxawa· "to
frighten." See §14 for other examples.

VERB SUFFIXES

§24. ·ape, ·ap, negative suffix. Ordinarily this suffix immediately follows the
theme. When the verb employs the second person pronoun object, however, this
is inserted between the theme and the negative suffix (see below). Examples:
yakp·ap·oʔ "he does not strike him" (yakp· "to strike," ·oʔ, declarative mode, pres·
ent tense, third person) yakp·a·p·oʔ "he does not strike you" (the length of ·a··
is due to the second person pronoun); yakp·ape·noʔ "he is not striking him" (·n,
continuative suffix).

The second person pronoun is expressed by adding one mora of length to the
vowel of the preceding morpheme. Normally it follows the future tense suffix but
when the negative suffix is used, the second person suffix comes between it and
the theme (see above). Examples: yamxa·weʔ "he paints you" (cf. yamxoʔ "he
paints him"; yamxa· "to paint"; ·weʔ, declarative mode, present tense, third per·
son), yamxa·poʔ "he does not paint you"; yamxa·tewa·weʔ "he will paint you"
(cf. yamxa·tewoʔ "he will paint him"); yamxa·pa·tewoʔ "he will not paint you"
(cf. yamxapa·tewoʔ "he will not paint him").

·nesʔe, ·nesʔ, dual subject. Examples: hecne·nesʔ·oʔs "we two lie down";
hecne·nesʔ·o·ka "you two lie down"; hecne·nesʔ·oʔ "they two lie down"; hecne·
nesʔe·s "we two shall lie down!" This suffix follows the negative suffix, the future
tense suffix, and the second person object pronoun.

ˑwesˀe, ˑweˀ, ˑoˑsˀe, ˑoˑsˀ, plural subject. This suffix has the same position as the dual subject suffix. It occurs in the first and second persons of all modes. Third person plurals have a different form. Examples: kaˑnˑoˑsˀoˀs "we throw it away," kaˑnˑosˀoˑka "you plural throw it away," ˀekeˑˑwesˀoˀs "we give it to you," ˀekˑoˑsˀeˑs "we give it to him!"

ˑaˑtew, ˑaˑtoˑ, future tense suffix. Examples: yakpˑaˑtewˑoˀ "he will hit him"; yakpˑaˑtoˑnoˀ "he is going to hit him"; ˀaˑtoˑnes "I'll do it!"

ˑno, ˑn, continuative suffix. Examples: waˑnaˑnˑoˀ "he is falling" (cf. waˑnˑoˀ "he falls"); waˑnaˑtoˑnˑoˀ "he is going to fall" (cf. waˑnaˑtewoˀ "he will fall"); waˑnaˑnoˑk "he, falling."

§25. ˑwe, ˑoˑ, ˑo, declarative mode suffix. This suffix always appears with either the present tense suffix ˑˀe (ˑˀ) or the past tense suffix ˑˀey (ˑˀeˑ, ˑˀe). The declarative present tense conjugation is as follows: yakpˑoˑˀs "I strike him," yakpˑoˑka "you strike him" (the tense suffix is completely elided), yakpˑoˑˀ "he strikes him," yakpaˑnesˀoˑˀs "we two strike him," yakpaˑnesˀoˑka "you two strike him," yakpaˑnesˀoˑˀ "they two strike him," yakpˑoˑsˀoˑˀs "we strike him," yakpˑoˑsˀoˑka "you (plural) strike him," and yakpˑoˑˀoˑyuk "they strike him." The continuative aspect of this tense mode is formed by inserting the continuative suffix ˑno, ˑn: yakpaˑnˑoˑˀs "I am striking him," etc. Similarly, the future tense suffix may be inserted, forming a near future tense: yakpˑaˑtewˑoˑˀs "I shall strike him," etc.

The declarative past tense conjugation is as follows: yakpˑoˑˀoˑˀ "I struck him," yakpˑoˑˀoyˑno "you struck him," yakpˑoˑˀo "he struck him," yakpaˑnesˀoˑˀoˑˀ "we two struck him," etc., yakpˑoˑsˀoˑˀoˑˀ "we struck him," and yakpˑoˀoˑlok "they struck him." The continuative suffix may also be inserted as before. The future tense suffix, used with this paradigm, denotes a remote future.

Both the preceding paradigms may be put into the interrogative by omitting the declarative suffix and adding, at the end, a suffix ˑˀ. Thus: yakpaˑkaˑˀ (<yakpaˑˀkaˑˀ) "are you striking him?" and yakpˑeyˑno "did you strike him?" The dual and plural forms are built up as before. Both the continuative and the future tense suffixes may also be used. The final ˑˀ (interrogative suffix) is dropped if the form is preceded by an interrogative pronoun.

§26. The assertive mode is conjugated as follows: yakpˑaˑnˀes "I strike him!" yakpˑaˑnˀey "you strike him!" yakpˑaˀa "he strikes him!" yakpaˑnesˀaˑnˀes "we two strike him!" etc., yakpˑoˑsˀaˑnˀes "we strike him!" etc. There is no third person plural form. The continuative and future tense suffixes may be used with this mode: yakpaˑnaˑnˀes "I am striking him!" etc., and yakpˑaˑtewˑaˑnˀes "I am going to strike him!" etc.

The following interrogative paradigm seems somewhat related to the above. yakpaˑyaˑˀaˑˀ "did you strike him?" yakpaˑlˑˀaˑˀ "did he strike him?" yakpaˑnesˀeˑyaˑˀaˑˀ "did you two strike him?" and yakpˑoˑsˀeˑyaˑˀaˑˀ "did you (plural) strike him?" As before, the final glottal stop (suffix for the interrogative) is dropped when the form is preceded by an interrogative pronoun.

§27. The declarative-assertive mode is conjugated as follows: yakpa·nwa·ˑsʔ "I strike him," yakpa·nwa·ˑnʔey "you strike him," yakpa·nwaʔ "he strikes him," yakpa·nesʔe·nwa·ˑsʔ "we two strike him," etc., and yakpo·sʔe·nwa·ˑsʔ "we (plural) strike him," yakpo·sʔe·nwa·ˑnʔey "you (plural) strike him," yakpa·nwaʔa·nik "they strike him." The continuative and future tense suffixes may be added: yakpa·no·nwa·ˑsʔ "I am striking him," etc., and yakpa·to·ˑnwa·ˑsʔ "I shall strike him."

§28. The difference in function between the declarative, assertive, and declarative-assertive seems to be mainly one of emphasis. The declarative is used to denote a simple statement of fact or occurrence. ʔekʷanwixwanlak nenxalo·sʔoʔs "we found a little dog" (nenxal- "to find"), nacekla ʔeykanxayconoʔs "when the fish bit, I pulled him up" (ʔeykanxaycon- "to pull up"), we·yik ta·taxkoʔ "he brought her here." It will be noted that the declarative suffix is always combined with a tense suffix. The tenses distinguished are the present, the past, the near future, and the remote future: cakawʔa·yʔik yaxasto·ka "you are near the river" (yaxast- "to be near"), hetopoʔa·lak ʔeywencakanesʔoʔo·ʔ "we two have killed the Osage," taxas wa·taʔas na·ʔeya·tewo·snoʔs "we are going [home] this very day" (na·ʔey- "several go"), ha·na·tewoʔo·ʔ "[someday] I'll go away."

The assertive is used when the statement of fact or occurrence is made with emphasis: sa·ya ʔe·na·nʔes "it is me!" to·nanaʔa "he lies!" te·l ʔe·naʔa "here he is!" Only the future tense is distinguished in this mode: we·paka·tewa·nʔes "I shall tell them!"

The declarative-assertive is apparently used of statements of fact or occurrence without reference to time. Thus: kokonwa·lʔan ʔahenʔa·la ʔe·nwa·sʔ "I am the chief's daughter." Examples of this usage are rare, however. More often the future form of the declarative-assertive is found denoting an occurrence to take place at some definite future time: taxso·kʷa ya·lo·na·to·nwaʔ "tomorrow she will kill him," yaxasʔok neswalʔan keykewʔa·to·nwaʔ "if I eat it, I shall become a fish," ʔo·sʔeyoʔok sosko·na·to·nwaʔanik "if you (plural) do that, they will hear of it."

§29. The suffix -kʷa, used only in the third person singular, denotes an exclamation. The continuative suffix and the future tense suffix may be used with it. Examples: ha·ˑas heykewta·kʷa "many [people] are coming!" kʷa·low yo·mʔa·to·ˑno·kʷa "it is going to rain hard!" ʔawasʔa·la hetoxa·kʷa "the meat is all gone!" hexalʔoyka kence·no·kʷa "ants are biting me!"

There are two suffixes denoting the intentive mode: -a·haʔa and -a·ʔ. The former apparently defines the simple intentive, the latter an emphatic intentive. Both may be used only in the first person, singular, dual, or plural. Examples: hewl·a·haʔa "I will catch him," ʔo·ʔo·kʷa ya·lo·n·a·haʔa "tonight, I will kill him," cʔa·mow ya·lo·n·a·ʔ "leave him alone, I'll kill him," teyeyʔa·lak yaxapew sa·ya yax·a·ʔ "don't eat the liver, I intend to eat it."

The imperative mode is formed by the suffix -w. It is found only in the singular, dual, or plural second person. Examples: ʔanco·w "wake up!" kecn·o·sʔo·w "[you plural] let me go!" te·lak soko·w "put this away!"

The suffix -e·l appears only in the third person singular, dual, and plural and appears to characterize an exhortation or command. Examples: ham ?amto·x·a·tew-e·l "let him be burned up!" xa·n·e·l "there he goes!" we·?ispax xastew-e·l "[do it] once more!"

§30. The following three subordinating suffixes are added to themes conjugated for person and number.

-ka?ak "but, when, while, as": yaxa·s·ka?ak "I ate it but," yaxa·ne·ka?ak "you ate it but," yaxa·l·ka?ak "he ate it but," yaxa·nes?e·s·ka?ak "we two ate it but," etc., and yax·o·s?e·s·ka?ak "we ate it but," etc. Examples: yaxaneykak ta·yaxa·l·ka?ak hetlo·no? "he offered him food but he refused it" (ta·yaxa· "to offer food, to feed"); hakoxa·nes?e·l·ka?ak ta?ancenes?o? "when those two became tired, two [others] held him."

-?ok "when, as, if": nesexwe·s·?ok "when I scream," nesexwe·yo·?ok "when you scream," nesexwe·l·?ok "when he screams," nesexwe·nes?e·s·?ok "when we two scream," etc., and nesexw·o·s?e·s·?ok "when we scream," etc. Examples: ke·sya·ce·yo·?ok ya·lo·na·tewa·no?s "when you see me, I shall kill you."

-kʷa "as soon as, when": ya·ce·kʷa·nes "when I see him," ya·ce·ken "when you see him," ya·ce·kʷa "when he sees him," ya·ce·nes?e·kʷa·nes "when we two see him," etc., and ya·c·o·s?e·kʷa·nes "when we see him," etc. Examples: wa·na·kʷa·nes kenesyaxaw "as soon as I fall, feed me," hakxona·ken yalxilno? "as soon as you went in, he ran away," na·?e·kʷa ta?ano? "as they went away, he picked it up."

§31. Four other subordinating suffixes occur which are added to the unconjugated theme. Person and number are expressed for the combination in the principal verb.

These suffixes, -ta, -?an, -l?ila, and -t, all express a consecutive occurrence of two or more actions. -ta expresses simple conjunction between otherwise unrelated acts: no·ta ha·no? "he said [thus] and went away"; neskapa·ta haxeyno? "he closed [the door] and went away"; ta?ane·ta hanpilno? "he picked it up and went over there."

The other three indicate conjunction also but with varying degrees of dependence of the final action upon the initial action. When -?an is used, this dependence seems to be least marked: nex?ew?a·lak nok·an (<nok·?an) ?eywencakano? "he took the gun and killed them" (nok· "to take"), ha·n·?an m?e·tno? "as he went off, he was struck by lightning" (ha·n· "one person goes"), ?awaskak ya·lo·n·?an ?oyuka·lak nespeco? "killing [several] buffalo, he filled the sack [with meat]" (ya·lo·n· "to kill").

-l?ila denotes a closer dependence of principal concept on subordinated concept: hemaya·l?ila no·no? "it is his ghost talking" (hemaya· "to be a ghost"), ?aweykak ya·lo·na·l?ila ta·yaxano? "whenever they killed many deer, they ate together" (ya·lo·na· "to kill"), hetec ?eye·nokye coxna·takʷe·l?ila "how do you act when you are fast asleep" (coxna·takʷe· "to be fast asleep").

Finally, when -t is used, the relation of the two concepts is closest, in some cases approaching the unity of a compound. na·ton?a·y?ik haycona-t, heylapo? "climbing the mountain, he stood there" (haycona- "one climbs, moves upward"); hakxona-t "hecu· ?e·kʷa." noklakno?o "entering [the tipi], he said, it is said, 'What's the matter!'" (hakxona- "one enters, goes into"); haklana-t tekalak yaxʷkayce-t, kaxaw nesam?am?ata sokota coxno? "descending, chopping off a piece of wood, he burned it black and put it away and went to sleep" (haklana- "one descends"; yaxʷkayce- "to chop off").

§32. -n absolutive verb suffix (cf. -an noun forming suffix, §11). Examples: hetlo·no? yaxa-n "he doesn't want to eat" (yaxa- "to eat"), hetlo·no·ka yakpa-n "you don't want to hit him" (yakpa- "to strike"), hecna-n ha·csokonayla "coyote lying down" (hecna- "to lie down"), hepakew ?e·ta-n "tell him to come" (?e·ta- "to come"), hatxilna-n yoxno? "going out, he flew away" (hatxilna- "to go out"). This suffix, added to the theme plus the continuative suffix, also expresses a horta-tory: ta·taklana-no-n "let's take him down," hecocxa·yo·-no-n "let's go to sleep," wa·teca ?e·-no-n "let's stay right here."

§33. A suffix -k is attached to themes conjugated for person and number: yakpa-se-k "I having struck him," yakpa-ne-k "you having struck him," yakpa-k "he having struck him," yakpa-nes?e·se-k "we two having struck him," yakpa-nes?e-ne-k "you two having struck him," yakpa-nes?e-k "they two having struck him," yakp·o·s?e·se-k "we having struck him," yakp·o·s?e-ne-k "you (plural) hav-ing struck him," yakpa-n "they having struck him." Note that the third person plural employs an -n suffix (see §32). The continuative and future tense suffixes may also be employed in this paradigm.

-k forms are used with or without noun suffixes. In the latter case, they func-tion as modifiers; hexal?oy ha·?as ?e·-no-k kenana·co·nokʷa "there are many ants biting me." In this example, hexal?oy ha·?as ?e·nok "there are many ants" functions as a substantive phrase modifying kenana·co·kʷa "they are biting me." This is a rare usage; more often -k forms are found with noun suffixes and function either as verbal nouns or as subordinated forms: xa·xa-k-la haklanat panxow newo? "he hav-ing arrived, they said: 'Go down and bathe'!" (xa·xa- "one person arrives"), ?o·?o·-k-la hecno? "night having come, they lay down" (?o·?o·- "night falls"), yaxto·xa-k-la yalxilno? "having eaten it all, he ran away" (yaxto·xa- "to eat all"), ta·tanano? he·sokyo·k-wa·y?ik "he was bringing him to that place aforementioned where he had fought" (he·sokyo·- "to fight"), sosko·no? hekto·-k-wa·?a·lak "he listened to that singing aforementioned" (hekto·- "to sing"), xa·xo? he·pano·-k-wa·y?ik "he arrived at the council" (he·pano·- "to discuss, to hold council").

ENCLITICS

§34. Enclitics are bound morphemes that may be suffixed to -k forms of verbs, to nouns, or to demonstratives. They express certain modal concepts.

The declarative enclitic -aw (-a·we). Examples: tickankalaka kew?eyweycak·aw "the enemy have captured us" (ʔeyac· "to capture"), hecu·ʔax ʔeye··no·k·aw "something has been happening to you" (ʔeye· "to do to"), na·ya ta·haple·ne·k·aw "you have helped her" (ta·haple· "to help"), cakaw·eʔe··k·aw "there is the creek" (cakaw "creek," he·ʔe·k "to that place"), na·yak helʔa·t·aw "yours is over there" (he·ʔa·t "over there").

The interrogative eclitics ·ye and ·yelkʷa. Both of these take the interrogative suffix ·ʔ unless preceded by an interrogative pronoun (see §25 to §26). The first may be translated "have [you done] . . ." and the second "are [you] certain of . . . ." Examples: hetec ʔa·to·ne·k·ye "how will you behave?" heteca ye·la·k·ye "where are they?" heteca yamka··k·ye "to what place were you called?" (yamka· "to call"), waxes ʔekʷan·yelkʷa·ʔ "are you sure it's a dog?" (ʔekʷan "dog"), xam·aleʔela cʔaw·ʔal·ye·ʔ "is that prairie wide?" (cʔaw·ʔal "wide"), hetec ʔa·to·ne·k·yelkʷa "are you sure you will do it?"

The resultative ·coʔ. Examples: te·c ʔa·to··se·k·coʔ "[if someone chased me] I should behave in this manner," we·yʔik kesʔetalʔok ke·waw·a·to·k·coʔ "if I am cut there, then I will die," keyacantitsʔanʔok ya·tet keyacenesʔe·k·coʔ "if they want to see me, they must come here to see me."

The hortatory ·e·. Examples: tana·se·k·e· "let's go," tayxena·se·k·e· "let's go across," yakexaycona·se·k·e· "let's push it up," ya·lo·na·se·k·e· "let's kill him."

The quotative ·noʔo and the narrative ·laknoʔo may be added only to verb forms in ·k. Examples: cane·ne·k·noʔo "it is being said that you left her," ya·lo·na·k·noʔo "it is said that he killed him," xa·xa·k·laknoʔo "he arrived, it is said," yaxa·k·laknoʔo "he ate it, it is said." The narrative enclitic must be added to every verb form employed in a myth not in direct discourse or having a subordinating suffix. It distinguishes events known to the raconteur on the authority of cultural tradition from those which he has personally experienced.

There are three subordinating enclitics, ·a·lakit "because," ·ay "as, while," and ·latoy "but." They may be added only to verb forms in ·k and are not commonly used. Examples: ya·ce·se·k·a·lakit yalxilnoʔ "because I saw him, he ran away" (ya·ce· "to see"), yalxilnoʔ yakpa·ne·k·a·lakit "he ran away because you struck him," hecne·k·ay ʔatsawoʔ "as he lay there, he recovered consciousness," cʔaw·ʔal tana·nesʔe·k·latoy yancicxa·xoʔ "they had gone far but he ran and caught them" (tana· "several go"), ʔe··k·latoy ha·ʔako·nwa·ʔa·la "all were there except that man aforementioned" (ʔe·· "to be there").

PARTICLES

§35. The great majority of Tonkawa particles are composed of the verb theme ʔe··, probably identical with the theme ʔey·, ʔe·· "to be, to do" plus one or more verb suffixes. Thus, ʔe··t "then, and" (·t, subordinating suffix, §31), ʔe··ta "and then" (·ta, §31), ʔe··k·la "then, it being so" (·k, §33; ·la, noun suffix used with ·k verbs, §33), ʔe··no·k·lak "it happened then" (·no, continuative; ·k·lak, §33), ʔe··la "just as, when" (·la, noun suffix, here irregularly attached directly to a verb theme), ʔeˑnoˑla "after, before" (ˑno, continuative, and ˑla [see the preceding]), ʔeˑlka "thus, in consequence of" (ˑlka, a unique suffix), ʔeˑlkaʔak "whereupon, at that, when" (ˑlkaʔak, §30), ʔeˑyoʔok "then, at that point, upon so doing" (ˑyoʔok, §30), and ʔeˑlʔok "but, and" (ˑlʔok, §30).

Other particles, not analyzable, are as follows: ʔenik "then," and the inter-jections ʔana "look there!" ʔaˑkay "no!" ʔalʔ "all right!" ʔeyew "agreed!" ʔoˑko "no!" naˑkʷ "go ahead!" newey "hurry!" heʔeˑwa "don't know!" hey? "yes!" hehey? "yes!" hecocoˑk "be still!" waʔan "wait!" waʔanaˑlesuk "just a moment!" weˑʔil "let's go!"

CHITIMACHA

MORRIS SWADESH

1. INTRODUCTION, PHONETICS

§1:1. There is only one person who can speak the Chitimacha language among sixty or so who constitute the present population of the tribe on Bayou Teche in southern Louisiana. In 1698, when first encountered by the French, the tribe numbered about 2600.[1] Soon after their first appearance in history, the Chitimacha engaged in a war of several years with the French and their Indian allies, and suffered heavily in killed and captured, the latter being sold into slavery. After the war, the tribe lived peacefully under the successive rule of France, Spain, and the United States. The smallness of the tribe at present is perhaps as much due to dispersion as to war and disease. The Chitimacha have been very conservative as to their language, which they continued to use in spite of close contacts with the French around them. In time, however, French came to be used more and more until, a few generations ago, only the more conservative families continued to use the Indian tongue as their principal language. The passing of the old language has taken place in a time when the French language was in turn being crowded out by English.

§1:2. Remarkable in the terminal history of Chitimacha is the purity with which it was preserved. Benjamin Paul, who died in 1934, used only one borrowed word when speaking Chitimacha, kahpi "coffee," not to speak of four names of non-native peoples, kačen "Accadian," hespani "Spaniard," ʔinkiniši "Englishman, American," yah "German." The last word was said to be based on the ja which characterizes the speech of Germans. It is seen that foreign sounds have been eliminated from these words, but on the other hand l and r are used in bird calls, as čilink čilink čilink čiri · ·, call of an unidentified bird called the chinsh, and či · · ri · ·, call of the robin. This is not to say that European contacts did not affect the Indian language. We find native names made to apply to new concepts, as in the case of ka·nuš "master white man," ka·nuš niki "Frenchman" <"genuine white man," kiš ʔatin "horse" <"large dog," pu·p ʔatin "sheep" <"large rabbit," nanu ʔatin "apple" <"large persimmon," pe·špe·šn "fluttering; ribbon." Especially interesting are words like ʒo·t ʔatin "turkey" <"large chicken," yukš ʔatin "wild cat" <"large cat," waš·tik šandun "buffalo" <"wild bovine," suseygs ʔo· ǯi·pu "oppossum" <"woods hog." In these cases we may guess that the names of native animals were first transferred to newly introduced animals, and that the latter came

[1] Swanton's estimate, *Indian Tribes of the Lower Mississippi Valley and Adjacent Coast of the Gulf of Mexico* (Bureau of American Ethnology, Bulletin 43, Washington, 1911), p. 45.

to be so common that it was necessary to modify the term when referring to the native animals.

With regard to grammar Chitimacha shows no signs of influence by French or English, nor is there anything suggestive of internal disintegration, unless the presence of alternate equivalent forms is such a symptom. Since we have no record of the language before it came into extensive contact with French, we must judge on the basis of the present nature of the language. The grammatical structure, though not wholly different from that of modern Indo-European languages, is nevertheless quite distinctive, and the fullness of the grammar suggests that little has been lost.

In characterizing the purity of Chitimacha as spoken by Benjamin Paul, it must also be noted that the other recent speaker, Delphine Decloux, does interlard English words and frequently substitutes translation forms for proper native names, as žah pinun (("red bird")) for dipno "cardinal." The speakers of a generation ago probably included careless speakers such as Mrs. Decloux, but there must also have been something of a tradition of unadulterated Chitimacha.

§1:3. Only one dialect of Chitimacha has ever been recorded. Duralde's vocabulary of 1803, Gatschet's material recorded in 1886, that of Swanton and the author's, both recorded in the 20th century, show hardly any differences, certainly nothing greater than certain minor differences found in the speech of Mr. Paul and Mrs. Decloux.

There are no closely related languages. If Tunica and Atakapa are related to Chitimacha, as Swanton is perhaps correct in suggesting,[2] the relationship is not a close one.

§1:4. A Chitimacha word consists of one or more syllables recognizable as a unit by prosodic and other phonetic features. The first syllable of a word, unless it is a monosyllable ending in a short vowel, has greater stress than medial and final syllables. Within the sentence, the words are grouped into phrases which have one of two intonational patterns, one characterized by high tone on the final syllable, the other by high tone on the penult (sometimes the antepenult) and a low-pitched ultima. The final syllable of a phrase is heavier than medial syllables not in word-initial position. All syllables have a single initial consonant and a single vowel or m or n as syllable nucleus; they may be open, ending in the vowel, or closed by a consonant or a series of consonants. Open syllables are lighter than closed ones, short-voweled syllables are lighter than those with long vowels. If an otherwise open syllable with short vowel is followed by an open light syllable, the consonant of the following syllable leans on the preceding, which is thereby closed, e.g., pini-kank "red (pl.)."

§1:5. The phonemes of Chitimacha consist of the following vowels, consonants, and phrase melodies.

[2] John R. Swanton, A Structural and Lexical Comparison of the Tunica, Chitimacha, and Atakapa (Bureau of American Ethnology, Bulletin 68, 1919).

Vowels, short: i, e, a, o, u; long: i·, e·, a·, o·, u·

Obstruent consonants, aspirates: p, t, c, č, k; ejectives: b, d, ẓ, ž, g; oral
spirants: s, š; glottals: ʔ, h

Sonorant consonants: y, w, m, n

Phrase-melodies: high-final ´; high-prefinal `

i and i· are high narrow front unrounded, except for minor variations due to
position, particularly in that i is somewhat more open in closed syllables and in
very light syllables. Similarly, u and u· are high narrow back rounded except for a
parallel positional variation. a, a· and o, o· vary little in quality; the former is low
back unrounded, the latter mid narrow back rounded. e· is a little lower than mid
wide front unrounded. e has a range of quality between that of e· and mid narrow
front unrounded. The open quality is found in phrase-final position and in the
word initial syllable when followed by m, n, or h. In open syllables other than
those mentioned the close quality occurs, and in closed syllables there is an intermediate quality.

The series of stops and affricates which may be called aspirates are mildly
aspirated before vowels, heavily aspirated before consonants within the word, but
not aspirated in word final position. Those called ejectives are lenis in articulation
and marked by glottalization only in syllabic initial position; in syllabic final position, in which they occur only after vowels and sonorant consonants, the glottal
closure comes before the oral closure. ʔ and h occur only immediately before or
after a vowel, except that ʔ may also occur in word final position after a sonorant,
e.g., neyʔ "earth." y and w occur only in contact with a vowel, except that they
may be separated from a preceding vowel by h, e.g., ka·hw "tongs"; in the latter
position they are voiceless, When m and n occur not flanked by a vowel, they
make a syllabic nucleus, e.g., way-tm "winner, more so," but this is not true in a
case like haym-ʔa-si·g "lion" involving a preceding semivowel. n before a k or g
in the same word has a palatal instead of a dental position, e.g., ʔinkinišingiš "just
an American."

2. FORMATIONAL MECHANICS

§2:1. The principal morphological techniques are juxtaposition and suffixation. Juxtaposition is used in syntax, lexeme-building, and to a limited extent in
inflection (i.e., for periphrastic inflection). Suffixation is used in inflection and to a
limited extent in lexeme-building; also in syntax, in that certain postpositions are
suffixed to the preceding word. In certain cases juxtaposed words may optionally
be combined into a single unit, e.g., ʔišiš or ʔiš hiš "by me"; this process, used to a
limited extent in syntax and to a greater extent in lexeme-building, may be called
amalgamation. Suppletion serves in the function of inflection in some cases instead
of the more usual suffixation. Irregularities, or nonuniform methods of formation,
are quite common in some inflectional formations, such as noun and adjective
plurals.

§2:2. Phonology.

§2:21. A peculiarity of Chitimacha is the presence of a number of cases of alternate equivalent forms, not different as to meaning. In most of the finite verb forms there are equivalent "brief" and "full" forms, as getik or getiki "I struck him," geti or geti?i "he struck him," getnuk or getnaka "we struck him," getna or getna?a "they struck him," gečuk or gečuki "I shall strike him," and so on. Other types of alternations in verb forms are getnakun or gedišnaka or gedišnakun "we are beating him," getuyi or getuymiš "he used to beat him." In the adjective there are often three or more forms for the singular, as žiwi, žiwgi, ži·niš, žiwa, žiwg(š) "bad"; the plural of this adjective is either ži·kank or ži·ki·g. Equivalent alternation is not restricted to inflectional forms but is also found in the case of a few nouns and particles: ka·nuš or ka·nš "master, White," yo·tiš, yo·tš "roach," segis, seygs "interior, inside," hin?iš, hinš "only," ki·saktiš, ki·saktš "on the left side."

§2:22. Suffixation and amalgamation are accompanied by phonological changes. The phonological changes connected with suffixation are not always consistent for all suffixes, but the changes for any given suffix are regular. The rules must then be stated partly in terms of the particular suffix, which is easily possible since the number of suffixes is limited. The most extensive regular inflec- tional formations are those of verb and adjective conjugation. The verb stem and the verbiform stem of the adjective do not occur alone, but always with suffixes. Furthermore, the phonology of suffixation obscures the ending of the stem itself. However, it is possible to abstract stem forms in such a way that it is then possible to state the combinations of stem final with suffix initial in terms of regular rules, leaving only a limited number of exceptions, irregular verbs. The verb stem ends either in a consonant, other than an ejective, or in a vowel. Monosyllabic stems end only in consonants. Vowel-finals of stems are either i, a, or e (never o or u) and the frequency of the three endings is in the order given. A number of the suf- fixes, called iotizing suffixes, have the effect of changing the stem-final vowel to i. Other suffixes cause the loss of stem-final i. If the suffix begins with a vowel, the stem-final vowel is lost. ·?iš· of the continuative contracts with a preceding vowel to ·a·š·. Stem-final t is lost before ·č· of the future singular. Postconsonantic final t is lost before initial n or m of suffixes.

The foregoing is not a complete statement of the phonology of suffixation but gives some of the more important changes and some idea of the nature of the proc- ess.

§2:23. The phonology of amalgamation is relatively uniform: a final short vowel of the preceding word is lost and certain consonant clusters are simplified; for example, gituygi "parched" <giti "dry" +huygi "good," waštežin "Sunday, week" <wašta "day" +hežin "holy," kipinun "mulatto" <kipi "body" +pinun "red," gušdatin "glutton" <gušti "food" + ?atin "large," ?o·ksžiniš "thief" < ?o·ksni "to steal" + žiniš "bad," ke·bup "to bed" <ke?e·b hup. We may note that h never occurs after a consonant in the same word, so that the rule that h

is always dropped after a consonant is to be expected. Similarly, the rule that ʔ is contracted with a preceding aspirate to the corresponding ejective is in agreement with the rule that ʔ never occurs after a stop or affricate in the same word. On the other hand, the simplification of *kippinun to kipinun and *ʔoʼksnžiʼniš to ʔoʼksžiʼniš is not phonologically necessary (cf. kappa "light," ni kaʼmsn "malicious one").

§2:24. In syntax we observe a phenomenon of phonology which we may call contextual variation. Certain words vary in their phonetic form according to whether they occur in sentence-final or nonfinal position, and according to whether they are found in phrase-final or nonfinal position. All words ending in ʔ lose this consonant except in sentence-final position. Words of the form cvʔ, furthermore, lengthen the vowel in phrase nonfinal position; thus, hus šaʔ "his mouth" but hus šaʼ ki "in his mouth." Words having the vowels of their last two syllables separated only by ʔ, when in phrase nonfinal position, usually contract the vowel group into a single long vowel of the quality of the first vowel, e.g., henškaʔe "it is true," henškaʼ gan "it is not true"; keʔeʼb "bed," keʼb ki "in bed." A final a in a polysyllable may be replaced by i except in phrase-final position, e.g., kiča "woman," kiči hup "to the woman." Word-final iyi or uwi may be replaced in phrase nonfinal position by iʼ or uʼ, e.g., piya "cane-reed," piyi gan or piʼ gan "no cane-reed."

§2:3. Syntactic combination. In syntax words are put in sequence with no change other than contextual variation affecting certain kinds of words (see above), a limited amount of amalgamation, and some sibilant assimilation. Amalgamation in syntax is limited to combinations of pronouns with the postpositions hiš "by" and hup "to" and a few other combinations with hup: ʔišiš "by me," ʔišup "to me," ʔušiš "by us," etc. huʼhup "to the lake," keʼbup "to bed," čaʼdup "to the bayou," siʼtup "to the seashore," nusup "to the west," pegup "upward" (<pegis "up"), segup "inward" (<segis "inside"). With pronouns and occasionally with other substantives, there is sibilant assimilation of postpositions giš "just, only" and hiš to an s of the preceding word, e.g., hus gis "only he," hunksis "by them."

§2:31. The addition of postpositions is partly by juxtaposition, partly by suffixation. Some postpositions are always phonetically independent, e.g., kin "with"; some are always suffixed, e.g., (-n)k emphatic. In addition there are postpositions like (-n)giš which are suffixed after vowels, separate after consonants, e.g., kičangiš "only a woman," kič giš "only women." (-n)kš teʼt "like" consists of a suffixed element and a following independent element, e.g., šušʼkš teʼt "like a tree." Several postpositions have slightly different forms according to whether a consonant or a vowel precedes; they have an n after vowels that is absent after consonants; t is inserted after n, e.g., kamčin-tkš teʼt "like a deer."

§2:32. Demonstratives vary in form according to whether they occur in the independent or proclitic position: proclitic sa "that," ha "this," ho "these," we "that, the"; independent saʼs or saʼks, haʼš or haʼkš, hoʼš or hoʼkš, wey or weyš or weykš. Examples: sa yukšʼ hi ʔamʔaʼ "look at that cat," saʼsʼ hi ʔamʔaʼ "look at that one." We may note in this connection that only proclitics (demonstratives and preverbs) and postpositions may have the phonetic form cv; the minimum form for other words is cvc.

§2:33. Phrasing has a bearing on syntax, in that it may help to indicate the syntactic relations of elements in the sentence. The phrases do not coordinate with the syntactic groupings completely, for elements spoken in separate phrases may be construed together and separate syntactic elements may be spoken in a single phrase. But there is a general correlation, such that phrasing may indicate relationships in otherwise doubtful cases. We may best show this with an example of sentences having the same wording but different phrasing:

we panš′ kiš′ hi geti?i "That man′ dog′ thither he-killed-him′": "That man killed a dog"

we panš kiš′ hi geti?i′ "That man dog′ thither he-killed-him′": "That man's dog killed him" or "He killed that man's dog"

we panš′ kiš hi geti?i′ "That man′ dog thither he-killed-him": "That man killed a dog"

The use of a phrase melody marks the phrase. The choice between the two phrase melodies depends on the make-up of the phrase. Thus the interrogative postposition te requires the high prefinal intonation. The interrogative forms of verbs and the simple imperative also take the high prefinal, and two exclamative particles take it. In all other cases the high-final intonation is used. Chitimacha contrasts with English and other European languages in using a rising intonation for statement and a falling one for interrogation.

§2:4. Verb inflection. There are differences in inflection as between the auxiliaries and the normal verbs. The inflection of the auxiliaries, while it involves recurrent features, is most easily indicated by a list of the forms. In the case of the normal verbs one can easily abstract a series of suffixes which make the different tense-mode and person forms. For present purposes, we select the two auxiliaries hi(h)- "to be (in neutral or unindicated position)—sg." and na(h)- "to be—pl." and the normal verb get- "to beat." For brevity's sake we give one form for each entry of the paradigm, even in cases where there are two or more alternate equivalent forms. Abbreviations in the following are sg. =singular, pl. =plural, F =first person, NF =nonfirst person.

	Aorist		Continuative		Usitative	
sg. F	hik	getik	?išik	gedišik	—	getuyki
NF	hi	geti	?iši	gediši	—	getuymiš
pl. F	naka	getnuk	?išnuk	gedišnuk	—	getuynuk
NF	na	getna	?išna	gedišna	—	getuymank
	Future		Necessitative		Conditional	
sg. F	hihčuk	gečuk	hihčukingš	gečukingš	hihčukiš	gečukiš
NF	hihčuy	gečuy	hihčuyingš	gečuyingš	hihču·š	geču·š

pl. F	nahdinuk	gedinuk	nahdinakangš	gedinakangš	nahdinakaš	gedinakaš
NF	nahdina	gedina	nahdinangš	gedinangš	nahdina·š	gedina·š

Imperative		*Hortative*		*Permissive* ('*let me . . .* ')	
ni hi	geda	?	getu	?	getku

Participle		*Prior Participle*		*Gerundive*	
hi·g	getk	—	getu·t	sg. —	getmiš
				pl. —	getmank

	Gerund		*Personal Participle*		*Desiderative*	
sg. F	—	getka	—	getkite	higa	getga
pl. F	—	geta	—	?	?	geda
NF	hi?i	geti	—	getite	—	—

So far as can be determined, the continuative-like forms of the auxiliary represent only an alternate mode of expressing the aorist; they are listed with the continuative in the table for the purpose of comparison.

§2:41. The interrogative is indicated for some of the paradigmatic forms by the addition of the particle te with high prefinal tone, for some of the forms by this tone without the postposition, e.g., hi· te` "Is he?" getuymiš te` "did he use to beat?" but geti` "did he beat?" gečuki` "will be beat?" nana` "are they?" Sometimes modification in form is involved, as in the last example.

§2:42. The conjugation of the normal verb includes a set of stem extensions, expressing voice, occurrence number, and first person object. The extensions are added to the verb stem and the extended stem is then conjugated in the same way as the basic stem, except for some irregularities. The following list gives the extensions in the order in which they are added. In each of the four groups the elements are mutually exclusive, but elements from each of the groups may be combined, e.g., getpama·ki "he caused him to beat for me."

1) Causative -pa-
2) plural -ma-, plurimal -mama-
3) indirective -a?-
4) F sg. object -ki-, F pl. -kuy-

In several verbs, the causative is made by suppletion, as:

wiš- "to burn"		?ici- "to burn . . ."	
tus- "to hide"		?iki- "to hide . . ."	
gušt- "to eat . . ."		nokšte- "to feed . . . to . . ."	
ka·čt- "to drink . . ."		hakte- "to give . . . to . . . to drink"	
nu·p-, pl. tuw- "to die"		get-, pl. dema- "to beat, kill . . ."	

The last pair of words has suppletive plurals. Other cases of suppletive plural are: čuw-, čuy-, pl. dut- "to go": ?eh-, pl. ?uy- "to arrive."

§2:5. Inflection of nonverbs. The adjective has a substantival singular and plural and singular and plural verbiform stems, the latter being inflected like verbs. The principal parts of the adjectives are formed in a variety of ways and there are often alternate forms. The element -ka- or something similar is frequently found in the plural both of the substantival and verbiform. A few examples:

ʔatin, ʔati(gi), pl. ʔatkapa, ʔatkin, ʔatkank; ʔati·, pl. ʔatka· "large"

ǯiwin, ǯiwi, ǯiwgi, ǯi·niš, ǯiwg(š), ǯiwa, pl. ǯi·kank, ǯi·ki·g; ǯiw·, pl. ǯi·ka·
"bad"

ʔuǯin, ʔuǯi(gi), pl. ʔuǯikank; ʔuǯi·, pl. ʔuǯika· "rotten"

pinun, pl. pinikank; pi·hne·, piniwa·, pl. pinika· "red"

bakbakn(iš), pl. bakbakmank; bakte·, pl. baktema· "flat"

§2:51. Nouns are uninflected except for about thirty of them, including rela-tionship terms and some others referring to persons, which distinguish a singular and plural form. The only inflected noun not referring to a person is ʔuca, pl. ʔuc "oar." The plural formative is most often ·kank or ·kampa or ·mank, but several other formations occur. Like ʔuca, pl. ʔuc are kiča, pl. kič "woman," kici nahẓibu, pl. kič na·kš "girl," and ʔasi, ʔayš "man," with abbreviation used to indicate the plural. kiča, pl. kičkampa "wife" differs from "woman" in the plural. Some other cases are: hewʔu, pl. hewmank "nephew, niece"; ta·din, pl. ta·dinkank "younger sibling or maternal first cousin"; napšžank, napšžikank "Negro"; nada, pl. natga "chief, sheriff, judge"; ʔa·yʔ, pl. ʔa·yʔampa "mother"; ʔapš kiče, pl. ʔapš kičemank "married couple"; ʔamʔ, pl. ʔamkampa "female cousin of self or parent, sister of parent or grandparent"; gimniš pl. ginkgank "young woman."

§2:52. The numerals from "two" to "ten" make secondary forms by the addi-tion of suffixes as kištkami·g "the seventh," kištkamink "the seventh time," kištkaminki "on the seventh (e.g., day)" <kišta "seven."

§2:53. The demonstratives, as stated in §2:32, distinguish a proclitic and an independent form. The two forms combined, one preceding and one following the modified word, make the emphatic, e.g., ha hana ha·š "this house here." In addition there are locative and directional forms made by the addition of the postpositions ·nki and ·nk to the enclitic form, e.g., hanki "here," hank "hither." (These differ from postposition combinations with the independent form, e.g., ha·š ki "in this one.") There is also inflection for number and position in the demonstrative of near deixis: ha "this" (neutral as to position), han "this (sitting position)," hač "this (standing)," ho plural. han and hač have no independent forms.

Some of the interrogative-indefinites also distinguish proclitic and independ-ent forms. The differentiation is suppletive, e.g., ʔam panš "which person?" ʔuči "who?"

§2:54. Two particles are inflected for number: weytem, pl. weytemank "of that kind," kaye, pl. kayemank "alive." All remaining classes of words are unin-flected.

§2:6. Lexeme building.

§2:61. Lexeme building is accomplished mainly by readaptation of lexemes, paradigmatic forms, or syntactic constructions to new uses without change of form. Examples: kiča "woman" >"wife"; pešmank "fliers" >"duck"; kiš ʔatin "big dog" >"horse." However, properly considered there is often a change involved, and we may recognize inflectional change, form fixation, order fixation. Our first two examples illustrate inflectional change. While "wife" and "woman" are homonymous in the singular, there is a difference in the plural. We must therefore say kiča, pl. kič "woman" >kiča, pl. kičkampa "wife." In the meaning "fliers," pešmank is part of the conjugation of peš- "to fly," it is the plural gerundive. pešmank "duck" is uninflected, and like most nouns has the same form for singular and plural. The use of a plural adjective or gerundive as a noun not distinguishing number is fairly characteristic in the formation of names for plant and animal species.

Form fixation is a variety of inflectional change, and is illustrated by kiš ʔatin "horse." Where the adjective "large" has several alternate forms (ʔatin, ʔati, ʔatigi), only one of these is ever used in the word for horse. From a multiform element we change to a uniform element. Such a case as the present one also involves inflectional change in another sense: while ʔatin as an adjective is singular, as part of the derived noun lexeme it is not capable of inflectional change.

Order fixation is involved in the case of composites (lexemes derived from syntactic constructions) if a construction of indifferent order comes to be used as a derived lexeme with fixed order. For example "they bury people" is either ney nučmpuyna' panš' or panš' ney nučmpuyna'; "cemetery" is panš ney nučmpuyna with the words always in this order.

§2:62. There are a number of cases of amalgamated composites. This of course serves to formally distinguish the composite from the construction from which it is derived. Another distinguishing mark is formal irregularities. An excellent example is hanšaʔa "door" if it is derived from hana šaʔ "house's mouth."

§2:63. Suffixation is used in lexeme building in one type of formation, called root extension. To certain roots are added certain suffixed root determinants. Special rules of phonetic combination apply to root extension, the most important of which is that m elides a preceding n, e.g., šamt- "pl. go out" <šan- +-mt-.

3. LEXEME CLASSES AND INFLECTION

§3:1. Under lexemes are included simplexes and composites. According to inflection and syntactic usage, they fall into a number of classes and our task now is to indicate the more important groups into which they fall, as a basis for further discussion of the grammar.

§3:11. We may first distinguish a fairly large class of words inflected for tense, number, voice, mode, and other features, some of whose forms are predicative, indicating a subject and in some cases also expressing or implying an object. This class may be called verbs. It has to be subclassified into auxiliary verbs and normal verbs, and normal verbs may be further subclassified according to basic aspect and voice.

§3:12. Very much like certain kinds of verbs is the adjective, part of whose inflection coincides with that of the verb, but which has two additional forms called the substantival singular and plural. Moreover, it is precisely the substantival forms which are the most commonly used. A number of other lexeme types have in common the fact that they may serve the syntactic function of terms, a function which they share with certain forms of the verb. If we use the term substantives for all words having this function as their outstanding characteristic, we find that this class includes the following subclasses distinguished in details of inflection and syntax: adjectives, quantitatives, nouns, particle-nouns (lexemes which function like nouns and like particles), pronouns, demonstratives, interrogative-indefinites. Pronouns, particle-nouns, and most nouns are uninflected.

§3:13. The remaining word classes are most difficult to classify. They are almost without exception uninflected, and serve a variety of syntactic functions. They can be divided fairly readily, according to position of occurrence, into proclitic, postclitic, and independent particles. The proclitics are fairly homogeneous, being used with verbs to indicate direction and other modifications of the action or state; we may call them preverbs. The postpositions include those that express qualifying relations (relating one syntactic element to another in such a way as to qualify the first, e.g., A in B), inclusional relations (indicating that the second entity is included with the first, whether expressed or implied), predication of the governed element, modification of the governed element. Independent particles include interpolative elements, like exclamatives, imitatives, and sentence words; predicative elements, which predicate something; and modifying particles, including elements that stand in the predicate and modify the subject and modifiers of the verb and sentence. Some independent particles have more than one function which gives them characteristics of more than one subclass; usually it is still possible to assign such an element to one group to which it seems more characteristically to belong. There is a class of elements used both as postpositions and as independent modifiers, and these are called postpositive-independents.

§3:2. Entity number and position. These inflectional categories are found in different word classes, and so it is convenient to give them separate treatment.

§3:21. Inflection for entity number is found in the subject and in the first person object of verbs, in adjectives, some nouns, one demonstrative, and two particles. The numbers distinguished are singular and plural. The singular applies to a single entity, e.g., we panš' ʔap čuyiʔi' "The man, he came," or to a continuum including a mass of small things conceived as a continuum, e.g., we ku·kš' kas čuˑšiʔi' "the water, it is receding," gasma' noˑgš hin' "the corn, it is ripe," we po· či·š' pehnem' načpa·ši' "The leaves of that herb, it cures fits." The plural applies to two or more entities, whether referred to by a single noun (plural, if an inflected noun) or by a combination, e.g., we panš' ʔap dutnaʔa' "The people,[3] they came," we panš ne' we kiči ne' ʔapš wa·čminaʔa' "The man and the woman, they married."

---

[3] Not explicitly plural.

§3:22. A generic reference, applying to a whole class of entities may be either singular or plural. If an independent pronoun is used it is hus "he, she, it" or hunks "they," except that a singular reference to people may be expressed by him? "thou." Examples: to·tuš' že·m' hapšžepi gayši', husk' ša· gayši' "The cuckoo doesn't build a nest, he doesn't sleep," panš pinikankš' siksiš' dempi gayšna?a' "The Indians do not kill eagles," hunks' hin?iš' hi hokma·šna?a' "They leave them alone," nenču?u' gušču·š' "if you eat too much."

§3:23. Position, horizontal, vertical, and neutral, is indicated in the auxiliary verbs and in one demonstrative (han, hač, ha). In addition several verbs made up of root plus determinant and expressing movement distinguish position in the determinant, but they show only horizontal and vertical position, e.g., huhdi· "to enter horizontally," huhčwa· "to enter vertically."

The literal meanings of the positions come rather infrequently into play. Instead there are affective meanings which tend to be more prominent.[4] When applied to persons, the horizontal or lying position is derogatory or abusive and the vertical, in a milder way, is respectful. The unspecified position, being affectively neutral, is the most commonly used. nu·pk pen "he lies dead" should properly be said only of an animal. Applied to a person it would be very disrespectful. Instead one should say nu·pk hi?i "he is dead" or even nu·pk či?i "he stands dead." The range of nuances of the horizontal position includes insult, sarcasm, disparagement, joking, abuse, defiance. To the example given we may suggest the following additional illustrations: a person says disparagingly ni·ki·g peken "I am horizontally sick," someone says defiantly hankipeken "Here I am (whether you like it or not)," han haksigam' žah ni ša?o·niš' ka·či kas hukuntinkš te·t' ?učka·ši' "This horizontal young fellow is treating me as the mocking bird (did in) fooling the owl" (this was stated by Mr. Paul in telling a story to make fun of "this horizontal young fellow"). That the actual literal meaning of the positions has little effect on usage in connection with persons is shown by the fact that one can say such things as nuhčwi·g peken "I am horizontally standing." The root plus determinant verbs use the vertical forms for both polite and neutral reference in contexts where the affective element might enter in other contexts; they are used literally more often than the auxiliaries of corresponding position.

§3:3. The verb.

§3:31. The tense-modes of the verb include five finite tense-modes of time and aspect, the future, the aorist, the periphrastic aorist, the continuative, the usitative; two derivative finite modes, the necessitative (I, you, etc., must . . .) and the desiderative, limited to the first person and expressing "I, we want to . . ."; four evocative modes, calling for action, the imperative, the polite imperative, the hortatory (let's . . .), and the permissive (let me . . .); four relational modes, the

[4] Morris Swadesh, *Chitimacha Verbs of Derogatory or Abusive Connotation with Parallels from European Languages* (Language, vol. 9, Baltimore, 1933, pp. 192 ff.).

participle, the personal participle, the prior participle, and the conditional; two term-reference modes, the gerund and the gerundive. The future states that action will take place in the future, the other simple finites refer to the present-past time period. The periphrastic aorist of all verbs and the simple aorist of static verbs refers to the existence of a state. The aorist of active verbs makes a simple reference to an action. The continuative and the usitative are virtually limited to active verbs; when one finds them used with static verbs, they seem to be synomymous with the aorist. The continuative refers primarily to an action in progress either in the present or at some time in the past. The usitative expresses a customary or usual action.

The point of departure in the use of the future and the aorist tenses may be either the present or some contextually indicated time, e.g., ču·čuk′ "I'll go," hi te·ti?i′ hi ču·čuyi′ "He said he'd go," hi te·ti?i′ hi čuyi?i′ "He said, he had gone." The future is also used to state the consequence of an unreal condition, e.g., ni wopmakiču·š′ we wa·bit′ hi ?a?ik′ "If he had asked me, I would have given him the money." Another important function of the future is the indication of purpose or desired action in subordinate clauses, e.g., wey ?učik′ we panš′ ne·mpičuki′ "I did it, I would scare that man" ="I did it to scare that man," gihčuk′ him hi ču·čuy′ "I want you to go," ?un kun′ tuptiki′ guščuk′ "I found something to eat" ("I found something I'd eat").

The derivative finite modes and the evocative modes are self-explanatory. Of the relational modes, the participle expresses an action as related temporally, causally, or otherwise to the superordinate verb, e.g., panš ?ami·g′ hi čuyi?i′ "Seeing the man, he left" may mean "he left when, while, because, although, by means of the fact that he saw the man." If the subject of the participle is different from that of the superordinate verb, this may be indicated by the use of the personal participle, e.g., huhčwite′ kap nuhčwiki′ "He entering, I arose." The prior participle expresses a temporal relation, referring to an action or state that precedes that of the superordinate verb, e.g., gasma′ gastu·t′ his kečti?i′ "After having planted corn, he waited." The meaning of the prior participle is within the range of meaning of the simple participle, but is explicit where the latter is general. The conditional expresses a condition whether unreal and purely hypothetical or actually possible, e.g., hanki′ hihču·š′ natmičuk′ "If he were here I'd tell him" or "If he's here I'll tell him." The time of the condition is indifferent and can be past, present, or future. Our illustrative sentence, in the appropriate context, might have to be translated, "if he had been here," or "if he will be here."

The gerund has three syntactic functions: 1) term-reference, 2) complement to certain verbs, 3) finite. In the last meaning the gerund is somewhat equivalent to the aorist but its range of use tends to be more restricted, for it is preferred only in clauses governed by a postposition and in relative clauses, e.g., nučmpakanki "when I worked" or wašta nučmpaka "the day I worked." Furthermore, the temporal meaning is more general than that of the aorist, so that we should per-

haps define nučmpakanki as "during my work." For the other two syntactic functions of the gerund, only the nonfirst person is used and it has nonpersonal meaning.
In term-reference the action of the verb or something produced by it is referred to
as a term and the syntax of terms applies, e.g., ʔiš nučmpa' gaypiʔi' "I lost my
work." The gerund also serves to complement certain verbs including giht- "to
want," kap nacpikma- "to begin," kaniwi- "to try," e.g., gušti gihtiʔi "he wants
to eat."

The gerundive makes a term referring either to a subject or object of the verb,
necessarily the former in the case of an intransitive verb but to either in the case
of a transitive. It may refer to a one-time subject or to a habitual doer of the act,
thus našmam "hunter" in the senses "one who hunted, is hunting, is or was in the
habit of hunting." The same word may mean "a hunted thing"; in reference to the
object the gerundive implies that the action has been (successfully) completed.

§3:32. A fundamental subclassification of normal verbs is that into active and
static, according to whether the meaning has to do with action (change) or state.
Active verbs express resultant state in the periphrastic aorist, e.g., nu·piʔi "he
died," nu·pk hiʔi "he is dead," getiʔi "he killed him," getk hiʔi "he has killed
him." The static verb expresses state in the aorist; its periphrastic aorist has the
same meaning, and may be more frequent than the simple aorist. The continuative
and usitative tenses of static verbs is not ordinarily used. On the other hand a
complete active inflection (usually marked by the preverb kap) is possible in the
inceptive meaning, e.g., hamči·g hiʔi or hamčiʔi " he has it," kap hamčiʔi "he gets
it," kap hamča·ši "he is acquiring it," hamčpuymiš "he used to get it." A few
further examples of static verbs will serve to indicate the nature of the class:
ka·kwa- "to be able; to know, to understand . . ." ti·kst- "to hate, dislike . . ."
ka·kte- "to extend across," ga·še- "to be bent, inclined, dishonest," siʔ- "to have
an odor."

§3:33. All verbs are inflected for person and number of the subject. Singular
and plural number are distinguished and first and nonfirst persons. The latter includes reference to either second or third person and the actual reference in particular situations depends on the context. Ambiguity may be avoided by the use of the
personal pronouns himʔ "thou," was "you," hus "he," hunks "they," but apparently the possibility of confusion is not as great as one might suppose, for sentences
without independent pronouns are very common.

Some of the tense-modes have less than the full number of person-number
distinctions. There is a nonpersonal participle, much more commonly used than
the personal which distinguishes neither person nor number. The prior participle,
too, is nonpersonal. The personal participle and the gerund do not distinguish
singular from plural in the nonfirst person. The same is true of the imperative,
which does not have a first person. The desiderative has only first person forms,
the permissive has only a first person singular, the hortatory only a first person
plural. The gerundive distinguishes number but not person.

§3:34. All the finite modes with the exception of the desiderative have inter-rogative forms. The relational modes and the term reference modes are subject to interrogation by means of the postposition te', as are nonverbal lexeme classes, e.g., nučmi·g te' kač huygi kap ʔehi' "Was it by working that he became rich?" našmam te' "Is he a hunter? was it hunted?"

§3:35. Normal verbs are inflected for a set of notions which may be called occurrence number and which include a singular, a plural, and a plurimal. In con-trast with entity number, applying to the subject, occurrence number is more in-timately connected with the nuclear meaning of the verb, indicating the number of times the action or state takes place or exists. Occurrence plurality applies either to a series of recurrences, e.g., we ʔukš' we kiča gahmi' "the snake bit the woman (several times)," or to a number of simultaneous occurrences, e.g., deminaʔa "they killed them." In the latter meaning it is closely related to entity number, for a plural subject or object may imply occurrence plurality. As a matter of fact we find that intransitive verbs tend to have plural occurrence number with plural sub-ject and transitive verbs usually have plural occurrence number with plural object.

Occurrence singular refers to one instance, plural to more than one instance. The plurimal implies a great many or more than one might expect. Its meaning cannot be stated in terms of a definite number but is a matter of subjective empha-sis. The use of the plural is far from consistent; one finds cases of plural occurrence referred to by a singular.

§3:36. Two voice modifications may be applied to normal verbs, the causa-tive and the indirective. The former introduces a new subject, the causing subject, which is indicated as exerting inducing or permissive influence on the subject of the action or state, e.g., geti "he beat him," getpi "he caused (allowed) him to beat him," huhčwi "he entered," huhčupi "he had him enter." The indirective, limited to active verbs, indicates that the action is performed for the sake of some one, e.g., našmaʔi "he hunted for his sake," tučaʔi "he cooked for him," tučpaʔi "he caused him to cook for him." Note that the causative may be indirectivized.

§3:37. Transitive verbs are those that imply an object, e.g., tuči- "to cook . . ." Some verbs imply two objects, e.g., nošte- "to feed . . . to . . ." ʔaʔi- "to give . . . to . . ." In some cases there is reason to assume an implied object in verbs which require a postposition when the object is expressed, as natmaʔ- (čun, hup) "to tell (about . . . , to . . .)": natmi "he told him about it," panš hup' neka čun' natmi' "he told the people about the devil."

If the object of a transitive verb or of a causative or indirective is first person, this is expressed as part of the inflection, e.g., geti "he beat him," getki "he beat me," ni·kpaki "he made me sick," natmaki "he told me," natmakuyi "he told us." When more than one object is implied by the basic verb, context indicates which of the objects is represented by the first person object, e.g., waštik' ʔap ʔa·kiʔi' "he gave me a cow." In the case of a causative or indirective, the first person object is preferentially the object of the causation or indirection, e.g., tučpaki "he made me cook it," tuča·ki "he cooked it for me."

§3:38. Certain verbs express a first person subject as an object, e.g., dadiwaki' "I feel cold," nu·pkiču·š "if I die." These verbs, which may be called deponent, refer to bodily states or bodily changes; further examples: kap ʔašiše- "to become wearied," kap ʔagihte- "to be greedy," wokt- "to taste, feel . . ." teki- "to suffer pain," ša ʔ- "to sleep, fall asleep," ga·ste- "to shiver." The normal inflection may be used as well as the deponent.

§3:39. Auxiliary verbs are much more limited in inflection than normal verbs. Like static verbs they lack the continuative and usitative tense-modes but also lack the gerundive. They lack voice inflection and do not make an inchoative. They may be said to show occurrence number, in that there are separate stems for singular and plural. The three singular auxiliaries are distinguished by notions of position: hi(h)- "to be (neutral or unindicated position)," či(h)- "to be (standing)," pe(h)- "to be (lying)." The plural na(h)- does not show this differentiation.

§3:4. Substantives.

§3:41. The adjective inflection includes verb-like forms as well as substantival forms. The verbiform inflection is like that of static intransitive verbs except that plurimal occurrence number is not found. The existence of primary substantival forms and the preponderance of their use, even in cases where the verbal forms could be used, distinguishes the adjective from the static intransitive. "He is good" is almost always huygi hiʔi, rather than the finite verbal form huyiʔi. As a matter of fact the use of adjective verbiforms is essentially confined to a few of the inflectional categories as the hypothetic tense-mode (huyču·š "if it is good," one also says huygi hihču·š) and the causative voice (huypi "he made it good," also huygi ʔuči).

Like that of Latin, the Chitimacha adjective is a substantive and not a mere modifying particle as the English adjective. huygi really means "a good one" rather than "good." ʔasi huygi means "a man, a good one" rather than "a good man" and huygi hiʔi means "he is a good one" rather than simply "he is good." This interpretation is based on the fact that the adjective has the same syntactic functions as the noun, thus with the foregoing examples compare panš ʔasi "a male person" and ʔasi hiʔi "he is a man"; further compare huygi' ʔap čuyi' "a good one came," with ʔasi' ʔap čuyi' "a man came" and huygi ʔinži "a good one's father" with ʔasi ʔinži "a man s father."

§3:42. The noun is uninflected except that a number of nouns make a plural (see §2:52). Its syntactic functions have been indicated in connection with the discussion of the adjective. We may recognize a special subclass of nouns referring to age and sex, e.g., ʔasi, pl. ʔayš "man," which, as illustrated above in panš ʔasi "male person," are very frequent in the syntactic function of postposed appositional modifier, but this function is not restricted to these nouns.

Another subclass is constituted by nouns referring to relationship and located parts, which are not used except with a preceding possessive modifier, e.g., ʔiš ʔinǯi "my father," ʔiš keta "my friend," we hana ʔapš kudihn "the region around that house, that house's environs." Such nouns may be called dependent nouns. A unique instance of the class is ʔeypi, which is used only with pronouns to refer to anything contrasting with a similar entity already in the context, e.g., ʔiš waši' him ʔeypi hi waytm' ʔatkapa' "My hands are larger than yours."

§3:43. Quantitatives include the numerals from one to ten, pu·p "hundred," pu·p ʔašinǯada, pl. pu·p ʔašinǯatka ("old hundred") "thousand," ʔapš nehe "half" (also "middle"), ʔaniš ke "a few, a small part," ʔaniš te' "how many? how much?" ʔupinak "both," ʔo·nak "all," huynak "the entire." They are much like the adjective and noun in syntactic usage. Only the numerals from two to ten are inflected; they make an ordinal (e.g., ʔupkami·g "the second one"), a temporal ordinal (ʔupkamink "the second time"), and a temporal locative (e.g., wašta ʔupkaminki "on the second day"). The ordinal corresponding to "one" is the adjective šama "new, fresh." pu·p and pu·p ʔašinǯada are used only with numerals, e.g., pu·p ʔungu "one hundred."

The word for "one" is also used in the sense of "some," whether singular or plural is referred to. A paired reference is by repeated ʔungu or by waʔa "other," e.g., panš ʔungu ... panš ʔungu or panš waʔa "some person (people) ... (an) other person (people)."

§3:44. Particle-nouns are lexemes of locative reference, which differ from ordinary nouns in syntactic function by the fact that they may also function as postposed or independent relaters, e.g., hana segis "the inside of the house, inside the house," segis hiʔi "he is inside." The class includes haktiš "side, direction; in the direction of," hisgis "under part; under ..." kamis "hind part; behind ..." samis "front part; in front of ..." pegis "top, over ..." and a few others. There are location nouns which do not behave in the same way syntactically, the locative relation being expressed by a postposition, e.g., hana keta·nki "beside the house."

§3:45. The personal pronouns are ʔiš "I," ʔuš "we," him? "thou," was "you," hus "he, she, it," hunks "they." Their syntax is more restricted than that of the noun, for they cannot be preceded by a possessive modifier (cf. we panš ney "that person's land") and have only one modifying function, that of preposed possessive, e.g., ʔiš hana "my house."

§3:46. There are three demonstratives, two for near and far deixis (ha "this," sa "that") and one for contextual reference (we "that aforementioned"). All the demonstratives distinguish a proclitic, an independent, and an emphatic form (see §2:54). The inflection includes a locative and a directional, e.g., hanki "here," hank "hither." ha alone is further inflected for position in the singular of the enclitic and has a distinct plural.

§3:47. Interrogative-indefinites have a very irregular differentiation of forms. The meanings to be distinguished are a) interrogative (ʔuči "who?"), b) selective interrogative (ʔaštem "which one?"), c) indefinite (neš kun "someone"), d) indefinite unknown (ʔuči ke "someone or other"), e) indefinite hypothetical or indifferent (ʔaštemin "anyone at all"), f) negative (ʔuči +negative). There are special forms for inanimate reference: a) ʔam ("what?"), b) ʔaštem (same as an.), c) ʔun kun, ʔam, d) ʔam ke, e) ʔamin, f) ʔun kun or ʔamin +neg. The proclitic form is ʔam for (a) to (c), (d) ʔam .. ke, (e) (?), (f) ʔamin .. +neg. The proclitics do not distinguish animate and inanimate.

§3:5. Postpositions.

§3:51. Qualificative postpositions express spatial location, direction, temporal location, means, purpose, and other relations, used in connection with terms, or with predications, e.g., hana·nki "in the house," we hana huhčwi·nki "when he entered the house." Many of them have more than one function. The most important postpositions are: (·n)ki 1) spatial location "at, in, on, among . . ." 2) temporal location, used with terms, "at, in, during . . ." or predications "while when . . ." 3) partitive "of, from, among . . ."; kin 1) reciprocal location or mutual participation "with . . . ," 2) "in connection with, in the matter of . . ." 3) "and . . ." (this is an inclusional relation); hup 1) movement "toward, to . . ." 2) communication, bestowal "to . . ." 3) location "near, in the region of, facing the direction of . . ." 4) temporal location "at about . . ."; hiš 1) indicating subject of an active verb, 2) "by means of . . . instrument, material"; čun 1) "for the sake, benefit of . . . , substituting for . . . ," 2) "in order to get . . ." 3) with expressions of mental and communicative process "about concerning . . . " 4) with expressions of quality indicating basis of comparison or person whose judgment or needs are considered "by reference to . . . , in the estimation of, for . . ." 5) "because of, on account of . . ." with gerund "because . . ." 6) temporal duration "for . . . time"; (·n)kite·t "since, after . . ."; gan ki "before . . ."; (·n)kš te·t "like . . . , as . . . is, does," with numerals "approximately," with adjectives "rather, fairly . . ." with expressions of temporal location "approximately . . ."

§3:52. Inclusional postpositions indicate that the governed element is to be taken with some other element, expressed or understood, thus ne in ʔasi′ kiči ne′ "a man and a woman," kiči ne′ "a woman also." kin, otherwise a relational postposition meaning "with . . ." may also be used in this way. When the elements combined are expressed ne or kin may be expressed with one or all of them, e.g., ʔasi′ kiči ne, ʔasi, ne′ kiči ne′ (note that ʔasi ne′ kiči kin′ or ʔasi kin′ kiči ne′, as well as ʔasi′ kiči kin or ʔasi kin′ kiči kin′, are possible). The postposition (·n)gis "only" is one of negative inclusion, and may be translated ". . . and nothing else": hi šaniš "in excess" is used in numeral constructions, as hey ẓi husa′ husa hi šaniš′ "ten five′, five in·excess′": "five tens and five" = "fifty·five." nak is used at the end of enumerations in the meaning "and so forth."

ne and giš are frequently used as emphatic elements, in which case their force may be suggested by "even" and "just." nehe is used in an emphatic or reflexive sense with pronouns. (·n)k(š) is a mildly contrastive emphatic, its meaning being something on the order of ". . . on the other hand." Perhaps to be included here is a postposition -š which is quite common at the end of phrases, but which seems to have no meaning at all.

§3:53. There are four predicational postpositions: hugu "it is . . ." te` "is it . . . ?" gan "it is not . . ." -ga "how about, what of . . . ?" The last-mentioned is rarely used, being found mainly in an exchange of greetings; to huygi hi· te` "Are you well?" one responds huygi' ʔišk' him ga' "I am well (or some other response), how about you?" gan is not solely predicational having also the modifying and relational meanings of "not" and "without . . ." The most characteristic and important function of the first three predicational postpositions may be called that of selective predication. They are added to one of the syntactic segments of an otherwise complete predication and draw the logical emphasis of the predication to that element, e.g., ʔiš hiš' wey ʔakik' "I saw that," ʔiš hiš hugu' wey ʔakik "It was I who saw that."

§3:54. There are a few postpositions which modify the term they govern. These are: weytem, pl. weytemank "of that kind, nature," wa·ne "strange, foreign, different," niki "genuine." These elements differ from adjectives and other substantives in that they are never used independently. weytem is the only inflected postposition.

The postposition keystigi "very" is used with modifiers, especially adjectives, to express high degree, e.g., huy keystigi "very good."

§3:55. There are a few particles, called postpositive-independents, which are used either as postpositive relaters or as independent modifiers, e.g., hana nugus' hi čuyiʔi' "he went behind the house," nugus' hi ču·ši' "he was going along behind." Other such particles are: niwis "to one side," pan ki "before . . . , first" hi waytmiš "more than . . . is, does, more than one does to . . . , more, most."

§3:6. Preverbs. Except for a few special usages, the particles called preverbs are used only with verbs, which they always precede. There are seven freely used preverbs, as follows: ʔap "hither," hi "thither"; ʔapš 1) "returning hither" 2) "moving together" 3) reflexive, reciprocal, 4) "moving about, round and round, at random"; kas 1) "moving back thither" 2) "reversing a process" 3) "apart"; kap 1) "up" 2) inchoative of adjectives and static verbs; ni 1) "down" 2) used with the imperative 3) with substantives, in a meaning not understood; his 1) "redoing" 2) "doing in response." In addition to their free use, the preverbs occur as a fixed element of many verb composites, e.g., his he·čt- "to meet, join . . ." kap ʔo·ni- "to deprive . . . of . . ."

§3:61. There is a considerable stylistic emphasis on the indication of direction of action by means of preverbs, particularly as to the directions "hither" and "thither." "He struck him" is usually expressed as ʔap geti or hi geti according to the direction in which the action is conceived as moving.

§3:62. A sequence of preverbs does not occur. If a preverbal meaning is to be expressed with a verb already having a preverb as a bound composite element, the phenomenon of preverb displacement may take place: the free preverb is used and the bound one omitted, e.g., "he came and met me," might be expressed as ʔap he·čtki although the preverb his is otherwise a necessary part of the verb "to meet."

§3:7. Independent particles.

§3:71. Interpolative particles, which are syntactically independent interpolations not directly construed with other elements in the context, include: a) sentence words, like ʔe·he "yes," gayi "no," huyukt "very well," huya` "thanks," nito "let's go"; b) exclamatives, like ʔi·ha` excitement, admiration, fear, kap ʔišt impatience, mahy "presto!" indicating a very sudden effect; c) imitative vocables, as ye·pye·p sound of fluttering, ku·psku·ps song of the cuckoo, wa·s sound of the cricket.

§3:72. There are a few particles, called predicative particles, which express predication, like verbs, but lack inflection. They are not restricted as to person and number of subject. The predicative particles are: ka·kun "is able, has permission, reason to . . ." (may be complemented by a verb gerund); ka·han "is unable, is not permitted to . . ."; ʔiška 1) "says . . ." 2) occasionally used for kunugu quotative particle; ʔamta` "What is it?"; weydšin, sa·dšin "that is all" (indicating the end of a story or account).

§3:73. Modifying particles show quite a range of meanings and syntactic functions. First of all there are a few particles which serve as predicate modifiers: kaye, pl. kayma "alive," toktok "scattered about, pell-mell," suksuk "atremble," žeyt "straight," kap ʔungunk 1) "without difference, alike, equal," 2) heterogeneous ones "together," 3) "just as well, equally satisfactory." Like English "afire," "aglow," "alone," and the like, these elements modify terms, but only in the predicate.

Connectives particles include wetk "then, and so," very frequent in narrative, tutk "then, thereupon," tewe "however, but, nevertheless, in spite of that, at any rate." These elements are similar in function to numerous other particles which modify the predication, including temporal particles, e.g., hači?i "now"; particles of cause and purpose, e.g., wey ži·g "therefore," hacp ʔungu "expressly for that," hinš čun "in vain," ʔam ʔuč "why?"; modal particles, as ʔaštka "perhaps," huš optional imperative element, nidik "it seems," kunugu "it is said" (sometimes used for ʔiška "he says . . ."). Particles of spatial location and direction e.g., ʔan žit "where?" pekup "up," nuk "outside," either modify the verb or the predication. Particles of manner and means include: ʔašt ʔuči·g "how?" weyt "thus," žuwa "quickly." ʔašt expresses either manner, in the meaning 1) "how?" or degree 2) "to what extent" as a modifier of modifiers. nenču?u "too much" and ʔapš kanime "enough" modify either verbs or modifiers. hin?iš "just, only" is an inclusional modifier applying to predications and compares with giš used with terms.

4. SYNTAX

§4:1. The sentence. The sentence is made up of one or more predications, but the compound sentence is not common. Instead subordination, particularly participial subordination, is used. For example, a closely connected sequence of events is commonly put into a series of participial clauses except for the last one, which is expressed as the main clause, e.g., ʔiš susbi ʔiš gampi neʹ gaptkʹ, huʹhupʹ čuʹgʹ, huʹtankiʹ nahpiʹgʹ, gastank hupʹ našmiʹgʹ čuʹgʹ, ǯuʔunkʹ kamčin getikiʹ "Taking my gun and my ammunition, going to the lake, crossing over in a boat, I hunted toward the north, and soon killed a deer." The same device is used in the connection of ideas into a subordinate group, e.g., we nuš gaptkʹ, him susbiʹ wey hišʹ hi kaʹtemiʹgʹ, wetkʹ našmiʹgʹ čuʹcuʹšʹ, ʔaštkanki ʔoʹnakʹ ʔun kun gecuyʹ "Taking that stone, rubbing your gun with it, if you then go hunting, you'll soon kill something."

Insofar as compound sentences are used, they are not formally marked except by prosody, e.g., hana hupʹ čuyiʔi nenčuʹ waʹkstiʹ, hi ʔehiʔiʹ "He went to the house, he arrived too late." The particles weyǯiʹg "therefore" and tewe "nevertheless" are found in the second member of a compound sentence, but the same elements are used in unipredicational sentences also. The most frequent type of compound sentence is that involving an interjectional element as one of its units, e.g., ʔeʹheʹ ʔučpi kaʹhanʹ "Yes, I can do it," ʔiʹhaˋ kap tohʔišiʹʔiʹ "Oh, it's breaking."

§4:2. The predication. There are normal predications and interjectional predications. Normal predications include predicator predications, characterized by a finite normal verb or a predicational particle, and predicate predications, in which the nuclear predication is indicated in a predicate modifier.

From the point of view of self-containedness, there are full predications and complementive predications. Complementive predications are answers to questions and corrections of or additions to previous statements, such as: ʔaštkankiʹ čuʹčuyʹ— waštmenkʹ "When will you come?"—"Tomorrow"; hokuʹ ʔučiʔiʹ, ʔam ni kihcpuyna neʹ "He made a mortar. Also a pestle." Some interjectional predications are complementive in nature in that they are intelligible only if the context indicates their application; thus, ʔeʹhe "yes," gayi "no," huyukt "very well."

§4:21. Interjectional predications are made up of a single element, a sentence word, an exclamative, or an imitative. We may also class vocatives as interjectional predications. These are made up of terms (§4:3) whether simple or complex in structure. Sometimes the postposition ne is used to mark the vocative, e.g., him haksigam neʹ ʔam ʔučiʹ sankiʹ "You young fellow, what are you doing there?"

§4:22. The normal predicator predication has as its nuclear and sometimes its only component, a finite verb or verbiform adjective or a predicational particle (§3:72). The nucleus contains, expressed or implied, a pronominal subject and object. The subject and object may be expressed by explicit terms, which then stand in apposition to the pronominal references of the verb. The subject of an active verb may be specifically marked by the postposition hiš. For some verbs the object is also marked by a postposition (§3:37). There may also be modifiers of the verb and of the predication as a whole. Certain verbs and particles, as ka·kwa- "to be able," giht- "to want," ʔapš kaniwi- "to try," kap nacpikma- "to begin," ka·kun "is able," ka·han "is unable," take a verbal gerund as a complement. In this case the superordinate verb does not have an object and the gerund may have one; the gerund may also have modifiers or a gerund complement, but does not have a subject aside from that of the superordinate verb.

§4:23. The essential element of a predicate predication is a predicate element, which may in all cases be regarded as a modifier. The fact of predication may be specifically indicated by an auxiliary verb or a postposition, but the sentence is complete without such an element, thus "it is a dog" is either kiš hiʔiʔ or simply kiš. If interrogation is to be indicated, there has to be an explicit predicator, either kiš teʾ or kiš hi· teʾ "Is it a dog?" Likewise if other tense-modes than the aorist are to be specifically indicated, an auxiliary is necessary, as ʔatin hihčuy "it will be large." In addition to the predicate and the predicator, there may also be an explicit subject and predication modifiers, e.g., ʔišʔ nadaʔ da·tʔ "I am now chief," husʔ ču·ču·šʔ, huygiʔ, "If he comes it is good."

§4:24. Predications serve directly as main propositions of sentences or, with or without relaters, as modifiers (see §4:36, 4:1). There are, furthermore, predication-like constructions whose verb is in a relational mode; we may call these relational predications. Such constructions have the same syntax as finite-verb predications, but differ from these in that they can only function as modifiers and this without the addition of relaters. If the verb is a gerund, the construction can serve only as the complement of a suitable governing verb.

§4:25. The order of the segments of the sentence, the verb, verb-complement, the subject, the object, modifiers, is mainly indifferent. A preverb, functioning as a modifier of a verb, precedes it immediately except in the case of a few verbs allowing an object term to intervene, thus kap panš pinikank teyi "He became an Indian." A gerund complement ordinarily precedes its governing verb immediately, but occasionally follows it immediately. One rule is fairly rigid: the parts of a syntactic segment are generally kept together. An exception is a quotation functioning as an object of a verb of communication, e.g., ʔiš ketaʔ, hi te·tiʔi, ʔučičukʔ him čunʔ " 'My friend,' he said, 'I'll do it for you'."

Though the order is not rigid, there are some general tendencies. The nuclear verb or predicate tends to come last. The subject usually precedes the object, the latter tending to come just before the verb. Modifiers come in between or at the beginning. These general tendencies are almost regular in dependent clauses preceding the main verb. If a postposition governs a predication, it is attached to the verb, which stands last.

§4:3. The term. Term is the designation for the type of syntactic element that serves as the subject and object of verbs. With relating postpositions they form modifiers and are in the predicate used without explicit relaters as modifier. There are two kinds of term constructions, quotations and term-nucleus terms.

The former type consists of anything given as a repetition or an imitation of an utterance or other sound. Such terms function in syntax only as the object of verbs or particles or communication, thought, sound production, e.g., huygi hi· te⸴ hi te·ti′ (or ʔiška′) " 'How are you?' he said"; ye·pye·p ʔučiʔi′ "It went flap-flap." Otherwise terms are made up of a nuclear term with or without modifiers.

§4:31. There are uninuclear terms, with one nucleus, and plurinuclear, or compound terms. The units in a compound term are put in sequence without any formal mark of the relationship, or the postpositions kin or ne are used, e.g., kiš ʔatin (ne, kin) waštik (ne, kin)′ hamčmiʔi′ "He had a horse and a cow." A special case of the compound term is that in which one of the units is negated, e.g., panš pinikank gan′ ka·nuš′ ʔučiʔi′ "Not an Indian (but) a White man did it." We may term as anaphoric compound term the case of one of the elements being referred to in the inclusional postposition instead of being explicitly included, e.g., panš pinikank ne′ "the Indians also" (i.e., "the Indians in addition to those already mentioned"), panš pinikank giš "only the Indians" (i.e., "the Indians and no one else").

§4:32. The nucleus of a term may be any kind of substantive or a verbal gerund or gerundive. The possible modifiers include preposed possessive or demonstrative (mutually exclusive), postposed appositional, following relative. If the nucleus is a demonstrative, it may be modified only by a relative construction, e.g., weyš′ ha hananki′ namkina′ "they who live in this house." If the nucleus is a pronoun, it cannot have a preposed possessive or demonstrative but may have postposed appositionals and relatives, e.g., ʔuš panš′ ha hananki′ namkinada′ "We people who live in this house." Any other nucleus may have the full range of possible modifiers, and, indeed, there may be more than one postposed appositional, e.g., we panš ʔayš ʔatkapangiš ke·ta′ šuš hup′ dutnaʔa′ "Those eight large male persons who went to the woods."

§4:33. There can be only one preposed modifier, either a simple demonstrative (proclitic form) or a term standing in a possessive relation to the following nucleus. The possessive relation is indicated only by position, e.g., we ʔasi ʔinǯi "that man father" ="that man's father." The relation called possessive is of quite a wide range, including relationship of ownership, part, kinship, association generally, e.g., ʔiš hana "my house (which I own, or occupy, or which I have charge of)," ʔiš kut "my head," ʔiš keta "my friend," ʔiš nučmpa "my work." The term serving as preposed modifier is generally of limited complexity, never having a relative modifier and tending to have but few postposed appositionals. There is, however, a substitute form of construction in which there is no limitation on the complexity of the possessive construction. The device consists of summarizing the possessive in a third person pronoun which then immediately precedes the nucleus, e.g., we panš kiš ʔatigi′ we pu·p geti′ hus kut′ "That man's large dog who killed the rabbit, his head." The same device may be used to avoid ambiguity as to what is the nucleus, thus we panš ʔatigi would normally be taken to mean "that

large man"; to express "that man's large one" one would say we panš' hus ʔatigi'
"that man, his large one."

§4:34. A postposed appositional may serve a noun, an adjective, a gerundive,
or a quantitative, e.g., panš kiča "person woman" ="female person," panš kač
huyniš "a rich person," panš nu·pn "a dead person," panš ʔo·nak "all people."
As already indicated there may be a series of postposed appositionals, in which
case they follow the general order indicated, e.g., panš kič nu·pn ʔo·nak "all the
dead women." There may be more than one adjective or gerundive, but such complicated constructions are infrequent. In the expression of number, the quantifier
may be either a simple numeral for the numbers up to ten, or a numeral construction for numbers above ten.

§4:35. The tens from twenty to ninety are expressed by a numeration of
hey ǯi "ten," e.g., hey ǯi ʔupa "twenty." The hundreds from 100 to 900 are expressed by a numeration of pu·p "hundred," e.g., pu·p ʔungu "a hundred," the
thousands by a numeration of pu·p ʔašin ǯada. The numbers between the even tens
and hundreds are expressed by adding to the nearest lower ten or hundred, the
particle patniš "in excess" being used to indicate the addition, e.g., hey ǯi hatka'
meša patniš' "six tens, four over" ="sixty-four." An additional feature of numeral
usage is that the numerated term frequently takes the postposition giš ("just")
before the numeral or numeral construction, e.g., panš giš hey ǯi ʔupa' ʔupa patniš'
"twenty-two people."

§4:36. A relative modifier consists of a predication referring to the modified
term. One may use in this function any predication which might be made involving
the modified term, usually as subject or object, but occasionally also in other relations, as, for example, the object of a postposition. The relation of the term to the
modifying predication is not explicitly indicated. Examples:

we panš' we nučmpa ʔučiʔi' "the man (who) did that work"
we hana' ʔiš ʔakik' "the house (which) I saw"
we panš' hunks ni ti·kmiš' "the man (who was) their leader"
we hana' hu·h si·h ki' "the house (which is) on the edge of the lake"
we hana' namkinaka' "the house (in which) we lived"

When the term has the subject relation to the relative modifier, the whole construction has the form of a predication, thus the first, third, and fourth examples.
In other cases word order or the nonuse of relaters identifies the construction. In
any event, the larger context indicates the function. The term with relative modifier is like other term constructions. It may even be governed by a postposition,
as we panš' we nučmpa ʔuči· hiš' ʔo·nak' wey čun' natmiʔi' "The man who did that
work, told all about it."

§4:4. Modifiers of predications and verbs; predicate modifiers.

§4:41. Elements and constructions which may serve as predication modifiers
include: independent particles, term plus postposition, predication plus postposi-

tion, relational predication (one involving a verb in a relational mode), a future-tense predication expressing purpose. Examples: hanki nučmik' da·t "I work here now"; wey čun' nučmik' "I work on account of that"; hunks' šušeyanki' wa·ǯikinanki' nučmik' "While they played in the enclosure, I worked"; hana ʔakstk' ʔiš yaʔa' hi ʔaʔik' "Buying a house, I gave it to my child"; wey ʔučik' him waččuk' "I did it, I'll tease him" ="I did it to tease him."

§4:42. Verb modifiers are not always distinguishable from predication modifiers. Expressions of time, cause, and attendant circumstance probably always modify the predication as a whole. Expressions of direction and manner modify the verb, and expressions of location usually do. Verb modifiers then include: independent particles, preverbs, the direction and location states of demonstratives, term or predication plus postposition; examples: weyt ʔuči "he did it thus"; hi čuyi "he went away"; hank ʔap čuyi' "he came here"; him-up hi čuyi "he went to you"; šuš ǯita·šinks te·t' ʔučiʔi' "He acted as though he were cutting trees."

§4:43. Predicate-modifiers include some syntactic elements like those used as verb and predication modifiers, e.g., hanki hiʔi "He is here," ka·cpankš te·t' "(He is) like a stick." There are a few particles used only as predicate-modifiers (§3:73), as kaye "alive." In addition, terms of all kinds are used. In this case there is an implicit relation between the subject and the predicate term, a relation of identity, class, inclusion, or the like, e.g., ʔiš hiki "It is I," yukš hiʔi "it is a cat." And finally a modified term construction, made up of a simple nuclear term, referring to a body part, with a simple appositional modifier, may be used in an implicitly changed sense to characterize an individual. For example, kut ʔatin hiʔi may mean either "it is a large head" or "he has a large head."

5. LEXEME BUILDING

§5:1. New lexemes are made mainly from paradigmatic forms of other lexemes and from syntactic constructions. The composite tends not to be complicated, most often consisting of two words. The lexeme-building process of root-extension, is limited in scope.

Secondary lexemes are found in all or most of the lexeme classes, but only nouns and verbs have any great number of instances. The present treatment, for the sake of brevity, is limited to these word classes.

§5:2. Noun formations. The types of formation are mentioned and examples given. Nouns derived from simple nouns: waštik name of a dog <"cow," kiča "wife" <"woman," nuš "earthenware" <"rock." Nouns from adjectives: gasda "north," gasti "catarrh" <gasti "cold," ša·čniš name of a town from ša·čn(iš) "empty," ʔižiti "bile" <ʔižitem "yellow." Nouns from gerundives and gerundive constructions: pešmank "duck" <"fliers" (pl.), kučmank "knuckles, fist" <"butters, punchers," may gušmam "mosquito hawk" <"mosquito eater," šuš hacmam man's name <"wood measurer." Nouns from gerunds and gerund constructions: ʔu·šti "clothing" <ʔu·št- "to dress," kucpa "hat" <kuci- "to cover up . . . , to get

covered," kut paktmpa "scissors" <kut "head" +paktma· "to shave (pl.) hair."
Nouns from possessive noun +nuclear noun construction: hihmu nema "beeswax,"
suseygs ʔo·ẓi·pu "opossum" <"woods hog," kiš panʔ name of a month <"dog
month," wams ʔukš "watersnake" <"catfish snake," nehti poʔ "sarsparilla" <
"bruise medicine." Nouns from noun +appositional modifier construction: nanu
ʔatin "apple" <"large persimmon," ku· pinun "wine" <"red liquid," ča·d pinun
"Red River" <"red bayou," neyt hapinniš "cigar" <"rolled tobacco," nu·p niki
"yam" <"genuine potato." Nouns from noun +relative modifier: siksi čaka ʔatin
"eagle of a certain variety" <"eagle (who has) a large breast," po· ko· gamkin
"golden rod" <"herb (which has) long stems," nakti kas šagiti "apron" <"dress
(which) hangs," denu wa·hyti "bullfrog" <"frog (which) asks."

Most of the formations are from syntactic terms. We also find nouns derived
from predications, e.g., ša·hken ʔapš ẓakšẓepuynaʔa "weave-tightener" <"they
tighten baskets," panš ney ʔnučmpuynaʔa "cemetery" <"they bury people,"
makta kap šahi "trousers" <"the rump goes in," keta šakšmank <"(it has) scored
sides."

§5:3. Verb formation.

§5:31. Root-extension affects a limited number of root elements, denoting
mainly direction of movement, as: *huh- "indoors," *šah- "into an enclosure or
container," *šan- "out," *ni- "into water," *ku(y)- "into a vehicle," *nen- "out
of water, out of a vehicle," *neh- "down," peh- "on," and several others. The determinants, which are also limited in number, express manner of movement or
transportation, as: -čwa- "moving erect, walking," -di- "moving horizontally,
crawling," -duwi- "rushing, moving violently" -čt- "to carry . . ." -tgešt- "to
dump . . ." Examples of derived verb stem from the root *huh- are: huhčwa- "to
walk indoors," huhdi- "to crawl indoors," huhduwi- "to rush indoors," huhčt-"to
carry . . . indoors," huhtgešt- "to dump . . . indoors."

§5:32. Composite verbs are derived from verb constructions. Elements commonly found coupled with verbs in this way include preverbs, nouns, adjectives,
ša· gušt- "to kiss . . ." <"to eat mouth," na·kšt ẓa·t- "to play cards" <"to spear
(with) paper," ney nučma- "to bury . . ." <"to fix earth," ni huyi wa·hyte- "to
ask to be excused" (<ni +"to ask good"), huyi ʔuči- "to benefit . . ." <"to do a
good thing."

A GRAMMATICAL SKETCH OF TUNICA

MARY R. HAAS

1. INTRODUCTORY REMARKS

THE Tunica Indians[1] were always a comparatively small tribe and at the present time their numbers have been reduced to a mere handful living near Marksville, Louisiana. Of these, there is only one individual, Mr. Sesostrie Youchigant (born c. 1870), who has the ability to speak the language with any degree of fluency and it was from him that the grammatical and textual material on Tunica was obtained.[2] The present sketch, though completed first, is more or less a condensation of a larger grammar published in 1941, entitled *Tunica* (in Handbook of American Indian Languages, vol. 4, pp. 1–143). Two other manuscripts ready for publication are: *Tunica Texts* and *A Dictionary of the Tunica Language* (Tunica-English and English-Tunica).

To the reader who would prefer to get a general idea of the morphology of the language before taking up the phonetics, it is suggested that section four can be read before section two without hindrance to the understanding of the sketch as a whole.

2. PHONETICS

The unit phonemes, the syllabic phonemes, and the phrasal phonemes of Tunica are listed and described below.

§2:1. The unit phonemes.
§2:11. The vowels.
§2:111. Vocalic Table:

---

[1] In his book entitled *Indian Tribes of the Lower Mississippi Valley and Adjacent Coast of the Gulf of Mexico* (Bureau of American Ethnology, Bull. 43, 1911), Dr. John R. Swanton presents what is known of the history and ethnology of the Tunica (pp. 306–337). Swanton has also published a sketch of the Tunica language: *The Tunica Language* (International Journal of American Linguistics, vol. 2, pp. 1–29, 1923), based primarily on the notes of Albert S. Gatschet. Since Gatschet's notes were recorded in 1886, they contain many of the phonetic inaccuracies that were commonly made at that time. His material is particularly weak in that he did not record glottal stops. For this reason a better understanding of the phonetics of the language coupled with the great amount of new grammatical and text material obtained from Youchigant has contributed much toward making possible a fuller and more adequate analysis of the language.

[2] Most of my field work was done during the summer of 1933 under the auspices of the Committee on Research in American Native Languages. The same committee has also provided me with appropriations for the preparation of my three books on the Tunica language.

	UNROUNDED		ROUNDED BACK	
	Front	Mixed		
High close	i			u
Mid close	e			o
		ε	ɔ	
Low		a		

§2:112. Vowels occur after and between consonants but not after other vowels. Moreover, they may not initiate the syllable. While i, a, and u occur fre-quently in all positions, the remaining vowels are rare except in stressed syllables. All vowels are normally short, but vowels occurring in stressed syllables are some-what lengthened, particularly if such syllables are open. Vowels occurring before n in the same syllable are nasalized, e.g., yu′nka "rope." All of the vowels are fully voiced in all positions except that u in phrase-final position after k or hk is voiceless in the event that the phrase-final melody is placed on the vowel of the penultimate syllable, e.g., ʔi′manàhku "like me" (see: §2:31).

§2:113. i is a somewhat close high front vowel; e is a somewhat close mid front vowel; ε is a low vowel, slightly closer than the a of English cat; a is a low mixed vowel; ɔ is a rounded low back vowel, but not quite so low as a in English all; o is a rounded somewhat close mid back vowel; u is a rounded somewhat close high back vowel. Examples: mi′li "red"; me′li "black"; nε′ra "ghost"; ʔa′la "cane"; čɔ′ha "chief"; mo′lu "full"; pu′na "ball."

§2:12. Consonants.

§2:121. Consonantic Table:

	Bilabial	Labio-dental	Alveolar	Palatal	Mid-palatal	Glottal
STOPS						
Voiceless	p		t	č	k	ʔ
Voiced	b*		d*		g*	
CONTINUANTS						
Voiceless Spirants		f*	s	š		h
Semivowels	w			y		
Nasals	m		n			
Lateral			l			
Trill			r			

Note. In the above table phonemes occurring only in a few isolated words (of foreign or probable foreign origin) are followed by an asterisk.

§2:122. Consonants occur most frequently before and between vowels (e.g., lɔ'taku "he runs"), but they also occur after vowels (e.g., ti'riš "to her home") and before, between, and after consonants (e.g., ru'šta "a rabbit"; wi'škʔohku "a robin").

Although every syllable, every word, and every phrase must begin in a consonant, only one consonant is permitted in these positions. In word- or phrase-medial position, clusters of two consonants are fairly common, clusters of three consonants are somewhat rare, while clusters of more than three consonants are not permitted at all. In phrase-final position not more than two consecutive consonants are permitted.

Most instances of word- or phrase-medial double consonant clusters come under one of the following rules: 1) ʔ may be preceded by any consonant except itself (e.g., ču'hʔuhki "he spat"); 2) any voiceless stop may be preceded by any continuant except y, w, or m (e.g., wi'sta "sweet"; ši'lka "a blackbird"); 3) any consonant may be preceded by n, including n itself (e.g., yu'nka "rope"; ʔunna'šiku "he leads them").

Most instances of word- or phrase-medial triple consonant clusters fall under the following rule: A double consonant cluster consisting of a continuant (except y, w, and m) plus a voiceless stop may be followed by ʔ (e.g., wi'škʔohku "a robin").

Occurrences of phrase-final consonants are fairly common but ʔ, s, y, and w are not permitted in this position. Occurrences of phrase-final clusters of two consonants (never more) are rare and always consist of h plus a voiceless stop.

§2:123. The voiceless stops p, t, č, and k are fortis in all positions and aspirated in all positions except before ʔ (e.g., in te'titʔɛ "a highway," the first and second t's are aspirated, the third, unaspirated). The voiced stops b, d, and g are lenis in all positions and occur only in words of foreign or probable foreign origin (e.g., ʔi'ngrasa "an Englishman, American").

The voiceless spirants s, š, and h are fortis in all positions (e.g., so'su "muscadine"). The spirant f is found only in one stem ka'fi "coffee" (<Fr. café).

The semivowels y and w and the bilabial nasal m are voiced in all positions (e.g., ya'mawi "he dressed"). The alveolar nasal n, the lateral l, and the trill r, on the other hand, are voiced in certain positions but voiceless in others. Their voiced variants occur before and between vowels and before ʔ (e.g., nɛ'laku "he rolls"; ha'rʔuhki "he sang"). Their voiceless variants occur before any consonant except ʔ and in phrase-final position (e.g., ma'nku "four"; ʔa'mʔilta "both"; ta'rkuš "to the tree"; ši'kur, apocopated form of ši'kuri "knife").

§2:2. The syllabic phonemes.

The syllabic phonemes pertain to stress. There are stressed syllables and unstressed syllables, the former being distinguished from the latter by having an acute sign (') placed after their vowel, e.g., ha'raku "he sings." Although every word has one or more stressed syllables (e.g., ʔu'runʔa'hkini "I have whooped"), two stressed syllables may not occur consecutively. A further limitation is found in the fact that a stressed syllable may not occur in phrase-final position.

§2:3. The phrasal phonemes.

§2:31. The vowel of the ultimate syllable, or, in certain instances, the vowel of the penultimate syllable of the last word in every phrase is subjected to a phrase-final melody. The following melodies occur:

1) High, indicated by an acute sign (´) placed over the vowel,[3] e.g., ha′rakú "he sings."

2) Low, indicated by a grave sign (`) placed over the vowel, e.g., ha′rakɔ′nì "he was singing, they say."

3) Rising, indicated by an inverted circumflex (ˇ) placed over the vowel, e.g., ʔi′mapăn "I, too."

4) Falling, indicated by a circumflex (ˆ) placed over the vowel, e.g., šu′čʔikî "Shoot!"

5) Falling-rising, indicated by a tilde (˜) placed over the vowel, e.g., hõn "Yes."

In case the final vowel is u preceded by k or hk, the low and the rising melodies may be placed on the penultimate vowel, if desired, e.g., to′nìku "the man," la′hontŏhku "early"; in this event the u is unvoiced (cf. §2:112). The remaining melodies, however, must be placed on the final vowel without exception, e.g., pi′takú "he walks."

§2:32. The high phrase-final melody is used only on the last syllable of the predicative word of a main clause in the indicative mode. This word must have this melody whether it stands in sentence-final position or not. Note to′nisɛ′măn, hi′pʔɔntá as against hi′pʔɔntá, to′nisɛ′màn "the people danced."

The low phrase-final melody is used as follows:

1) It occurs on the last syllable of the predicative word of a main clause in the quotative mode, e.g., hi′pʔɔnta′nì "they danced, they say."

2) It also occurs on the last syllable of the last word of every sentence unless that word is a predicative which requires some other type of melody, e.g., hi′pʔɔntá, to′nisɛ′màn. Note that two low phrase-final melodies will occur in a sentence in the quotative mode unless the predicative word of the main clause is also the last word in the sentence. Note hi′pʔɔnta′nì, to′nisɛ′màn as against to′nisɛ′măn, hi′pʔɔnta′nì "the people danced, they say."

The rising phrase-final melody is used as follows:

1) It occurs on the last syllable of the predicative word of a main clause in the interrogative mode, e.g., ka′tăn, wi′yăn "Where are you going?"

2) It also occurs on the final syllable of a phrase- or clause-final word (including predicatives in dependent clauses) unless such phrase- or clause-final word is also the last word in the sentence, e.g., to′nisɛ′măn, hi′pʔɔnta′nì.

---

[3] Note that the diacritics indicating the phrase-final melodies are placed over the vowel while the diacritic indicating stress is placed after the vowel.

The falling phrase-final melody is used as follows:

1) It occurs on the final syllable of the predicative word of a main clause in the imperative mode, e.g., hopi'ʔikî "Come out!"

2) It also occurs on the final syllable of any exclamative word except hōn, e.g., ʔahâ "No!" dâ "Now! Ready!"

The falling-rising phrase-final melody, however, occurs only with the one monosyllabic word, hōn "Yes."

§2:4. Pause forms.

All stems having a stessed final syllable (i.e., monosyllabic stems and composite stems ending in a monosyllabic stem) have special pause forms (i.e., forms occurring only in phrase-final position). These pause forms add on an extra syllable consisting of ʔ plus a vowel having the same quality as the stem vowel plus an incremental consonant -n plus the low or rising phrase-final melody, e.g., sa'ʔàn, sa'ʔăn "a dog" (<sa', context form); la'spiri'ʔìn, la'spiri'ʔĭn, "a bank") (<la'spiri', context form).

All phrase- or clause-final words ending in a vowel (except predicative words in main clauses) also have special pause forms. These are made by the addition of the nasal increment together with the low or rising phrase-final melody, e.g., to'nisɛ'màn, to'nisɛ'mân "the people" (<to'nisɛ'ma, context form). When such words end in a consonant, however, they cannot take the nasal increment; hence their pause forms are indicated solely by the fact that they have the low or rising phrase-final melody, e.g., to'nisɛ'màt, to'nisɛ'măt "the people, on their part" (<to'nisɛ'mat, context form).

Predicative words of main clauses are marked as pause forms by the use of the high, low, or rising phrase-final melodies but cannot take the nasal increment even though they may end in a vowel, e.g., ha'rakú "he sings."

All examples of Tunica words quoted in this sketch are pause forms when their phrase-final melody is marked (e.g., ha'rakatí "she sings"); examples quoted without a phrase-final melody are context forms (e.g., ha'raka'ti "she sings"; see §3:26).

3. SANDHI

§3:1. Because of widespread external sandhi phenomena, the smallest phonetic group of Tunica is the phrase, which may consist of a single word or of several words. In most cases a distinction is made between internal sandhi (morphophonemic changes operating when grammatical elements are combined into words) and external sandhi (morphophonemic changes operating when words are combined into phrases).

§3:2. Internal sandhi.

§3:21. The most important morphophonemic processes employed in internal sandhi are vocalic contraction, vocalic assimilation, vocalic syncope, consonantic syncope, and stress losses and shifts.

§3:22. There are two types of circumstances under which vocalic contraction may occur. The first of these is when an element ending in a vowel is combined with an element beginning in a vowel. In this case the following contractions occur:

1) a+a >a (e.g., nara′ni "it is a snake"[4] <na′ra "a snake" +a′ni, quotative enclitic particle).[5]

2) i, e, or ε+a >ε (e.g., milε′ni "it is red" <mi′li "red" +a′ni).

3) i+e >e (e.g., ʔe′htini "it is mine" <ʔi· "my, mine" +e′htini "it is . . .'s")

4) u or ɔ+a >ɔ (e.g., molɔ′ni "it is full" <mo′lu "full" +a′ni).

5) u+e >o (e.g., ʔo′htini "it is his" <ʔu· "his" +e′htini).

The second type of circumstances under which vocalic contraction occurs is as follows: When a suffix beginning in h plus a vowel is attached to a polysyllabic (i.e., nonmonosyllabic) stem or word ending in a vowel, the h is lost and the vowels thus coming together contract. In this case the following contractions occur:

1) a+a >a (e.g., ʔi′nimat "we, on our part" <ʔi′nima "we" +·hat "on . . .'s part").

2) i+a >ε (e.g., ʔu′wεt "he, on his part" <ʔu′wi "he" +·hat).

3) u+a >ɔ (e.g., ma′šɔpawi "he had already made" <ma′šu "to make" +·hapa· "to have already . . .·ed" +·wi "he").

4) i, a, or u+i >i (e.g., lɔ′tilawi "he was about to run" <lɔ′ta "to run" +·hila· "to be about to . . ." +·wi).

After a monosyllabic stem, however, the h is not lost and contraction cannot occur (e.g., ma′hat "you, on your part" <ma′ "you" +·hat).

§3:23. There are two types of circumstances under which vocalic assimilation occurs. Under the first type it is found that when a suffix or an auxiliary verb beginning in ʔ is attached to a stem ending in a vowel, the vowel following the ʔ assimilates to the preceding vowel. If the vowel preceding the ʔ is in an unstressed syllable, it is syncopated (§3:25). The following assimilations occur:

1) a after i, e, or ε >ε (e.g., mi′lʔεhε "not red" <mi′li "red" +·ʔaha "not").

2) a after o or u >ɔ (e.g., mo′lʔɔhɔ "not full" <mo′lu "full" +·ʔaha).

Under the second type of circumstances requiring vocalic assimilation it is found that whenever the first vowel of an ·aha· group has changed its quality by contraction with or assimilation to a preceding vowel, the second vowel of the ·aha· group assimilates to the first, as follows:

1) a after ε >ε (e.g., tε′hεyaku "her brother" <ti· "her" +a′haya "brother" +·ku, masc. sg. suff.).

2) a after ɔ >ɔ (e.g., la′pʔɔhɔ "not good" <la′pu "good" +·ʔaha).

---

[4] Lit., "it is a snake, they say." To conserve space the quotative enclitic particle, which always means "they say," is usually not translated in the examples of its use which occur in this sketch.

[5] Note that the term "enclitic particle" as used in this sketch is equivalent to the term "postfix" used in the larger grammar, *Tunica*.

§3:24. Summary chart of vocalic contraction and assimilation.

	Contraction or Assimilation			Contraction		
First Vowel	i, e, ε	a	u, o, ɔ	i, e	u	i, a, u
Second Vowel	a	a	a	e	e	i
Resulting Vowel	ε	a	ɔ	e	o	i

§3:25. In the combination of grammatical elements into words a vowel in an unstressed syllable which would come to stand before ʔ is regularly syncopated, e.g., ʔaʹkʔuhki "he entered" (< ʔaʹka "to enter" + ʔuʹhki "he did").

In addition, stems ending in hki, ši, ni, li, or ri may syncopate the i (except when their penult is stressed) when they come to stand before a grammatical element beginning in a consonant, e.g., ʔɔʹškačeʹhkintʔε "a large pot" (< ʔɔʹškačeʹhkini "a pot" + -tʔε, augmentative suff.). This latter type of syncopation, though very common, is not obligatory and ʔɔʹškačeʹhkinitʔε is therefore just as acceptable as ʔɔʹškačeʹhkintʔε.

In the analyses of the examples quoted below a syncopated vowel is placed in parentheses.

§3:26. The following types of consonantic syncope occur:

1) An h which would come to stand between a continuant and a voiceless stop is dropped, e.g., taʹhalta "on the ground" (< taʹhal(i) "the ground" + -hta "on").

2) A k which would come to stand between an h and a voiceless stop is dropped, e.g., tiʹtihtʔε "a river" (< tiʹtihk(i) "a bayou" + -tʔε).

3) An hk group which would come to stand before a continuant, other than h, is dropped, e.g., ʔaʹšumeʹli "Easter day" (< ʔaʹšuhk(i) "day" + meʹli "black"). When the continuant following the hk is h, the next rule applies.

4) An h which would come to stand after an hk group is dropped, e.g., yuʹkihkεʹra "you are cooking" (< yuʹki "to cook" + -hk-, habitual thematic suff., + hεʹra "you (fem.) lie").

§3:27. Every stem, whether monosyllabic or polysyllabic, has an intrinsic stress on its initial syllable. In addition, a few monosyllabic prefixes and a few disyllabic (but not monosyllabic) suffixes and enclitic particles have an intrinsic stress on their initial syllables. When grammatical elements are put together to form words, their intrinsic stresses are retained if possible, but since two stressed syllables may not occur consecutively, certain accommodations (consisting of stress losses and shifts) are necessary under certain circumstances. Other instances of stress losses and shifts are induced by the fact that two of the phrase-final melodies of Tunica do not permit a stress on the penultimate syllable of the word with which they are used. The following rules cover the conditions under which stress losses and shifts occur.

1) When a monosyllabic stem or a syncopated disyllabic stem is juxtaposed with another stem or combined with a disyllabic suffix or enclitic particle having an intrinsic stress, the second element loses its stress, e.g., po'ʔɔki "she looked" (<po' "to look" + ʔa'ki "she did"); ha'rʔaki "she sang" (<ha'ra "to sing" + ʔa'ki); po'kati "she looks" (<po' + ka'ti "she").

2) When a stem is combined with a monosyllabic prefix having an intrinsic stress, the stem loses the stress of its initial syllable, e.g., ta'naraku "the snake" (<ta'-, the articular pref., + na'ra "a snake" + ku, masc. sg. suff.). In contrast, note ʔuna'raku "his snake" (< ʔu- "his" + na'ra + ku).

3) When a monosyllabic stem is preceded by a monosyllabic prefix which does not have an intrinsic stress, the stress of the stem shifts to the prefix under the following circumstances: a) when the monosyllabic stem would stand in word-final position, e.g., ti'riš "to her house" (<ti- "her" + ri' "house" + -š "to"); b) when the monosyllabic stem is juxtaposed with another stem or combined with a suffix having an intrinsic stress, e.g., ʔu'yata'hkiš "his deerskin" (< ʔu- "his" + ya' "deer" + ta'hkiš "skin"); ti'sasi'nima "her dogs" (<ti- "her" + sa' "dog" + -si'nima, fem. du.-pl. suff.).

4) When a stem or word having a stressed penult is combined with a suffix or enclitic particle which begins in a vowel and has an intrinsic stress, the stem or word loses the stress on its penult, e.g., mile'ni "it is red" (<mi'li "red" + -a'ni, quotative encl. part.). In contrast, note ši'hkale'ni "it is a rock" (<ši'hkali "a rock" + -a'ni) wherein no loss of stress is required.

5) When a stem or word with a stressed penult has a prefix in front of it, the stress of its penult will shift to the prefix as soon as the stem or word is combined with an enclitic particle which begins in a vowel and has an intrinsic stress, e.g., te'mile'ni "it is red all about" (<te- "all about" + mi'li + -a'ni); ho'powe'ni "he looked out" (<hopo'wi "he looked out" + -a'ni). In contrast, note howe'sawe'ni "he jumped out" (<howe'sawi "he jumped out" + -a'ni) wherein no shift in stress is required.

6) The high and the falling phrase-final melodies do not permit a stress on the penult of the words with which they are used. Hence when they are added to words having a stressed penult they cause the loss of the stress on this syllable, e.g., ha'rawihkí "you have sung." In contrast, note ha'rawi'hkïhč "when you have sung" wherein the rising phrase-final melody is used without causing loss of stress. As an example of the effect of the falling phrase-final melody, note poʔin "look!" (<po'ʔi "you look" + -n, imperative encl. part.).

§3:3. External sandhi.

§3:31. The most important morphophonemic processes employed in external sandhi are vocalic apocope, consonantic apocope, and stress losses. These processes function only within the phrase.[6]

---

[6] In this sketch and in *Tunica Texts* words within a phrase are not separated by spaces, but

§3:32. When a word ending in a vowel is followed by a word beginning in ?, the final vowel of the first word is apocopated, e.g., toʼnik?iyuʼw?ik?ihč "if you give me the man" (<toʼniku "the man" + ?iyuʼw?ik?ihč "if you give me"). Unlike the similar rule applied in internal sandhi (§§3:23 and 3:25), vocalic assimilation does not accompany the application of the rule in external sandhi.

Words ending in hki, hku, ši, ni, li, or ri (unless they have a stressed penult) usually lose the i or u when followed by another word in the same phrase, e.g., šiʼkurčuʼwihč "when he took a knife" (<šiʼkuri "a knife" + čuʼwihč "when he took").

§3:33. When words which have lost a final i or u though apocope end in a consonant group hk, they may undergo consonantic apocope according to rules that are similar to the rules of consonantic syncope in internal sandhi (§3:26). The rules are:

1) A k which would come to stand between a continuant and a voiceless stop is dropped, e.g., tiʼtihpiʼr?utak?ahčá "it will turn into a bayou" (<tiʼtihk(i) "a bayou" +piʼr?utak?ahča "it will turn into").

2) An hk group which would come to stand before a continuant is dropped, e.g., kaʼnaraʼp?ănč "if I kill something" (<kaʼnahk(u) "something" +raʼp?anč "if I kill").

§3:34. As in the case of the word, two stressed syllables may not occur con-secutively within the phrase. Hence when an apocopated word having a stressed penult is placed before a word having a stressed initial syllable, the first word losses the stress on its penult, e.g., kat?uʼna "where he sits" (<kaʼta "where" + ?uʼna "he sits"). But if the second word does not have a stress on its initial syl-lable, the first word retains its stress, e.g., ?uʼw?onɛʼnì "He is a person" (< ?uʼwi "he" + ?onɛʼni "it is a person").

It will be noted that this rule for the loss of stress in the juxtaposition of words within the phrase is the reverse of the rule for the loss of stress that applies in the case of the juxtaposition of grammatical elements within the word (see §3:27, rule 1).

4. GENERAL REMARKS ON THE STRUCTURE OF THE LANGUAGE

§4:1. The Tunica language is mildly synthetic in structure. In its technique of synthesis it is for the most part agglutinative, but it also employs a limited amount of fusion. The morphological processes used are juxtaposition, affixation (prefixation, infixation, and suffixation), reduplication, and suppletion. Of these,

---

in the larger grammar, Tunica, they are so separated. Since all words within a phrase are actually run together without any break or pause, the writing without spaces is beyond question the more exact method of representation. However, in the larger grammar so much illustrative material was given that it was felt the use of spaces might make it easier for the reader to follow the details of analysis.

prefixation and suffixation, particularly the latter, are exploited to a greater extent than are the other processes.

§4:2. The structural elements of the word are a stem and one or more affixes. Stems may be primary or secondary. Secondary stems are built up by means of the formational techniques of affixation (i.e., the addition of an affix to a primary stem) and juxtaposition (i.e., the placing together of two primary stems). In either case the result is a new stem whose meaning is particularized from the sum of the meanings of the component elements. Once such a new stem has been formed, it may in turn serve as the basis for other new formations in the same way that a primary stem does.

Affixes are of two main types, derivational and syntactic. Derivational affixes, as indicated above, are added to primary stems to make secondary stems. Syntactic affixes are best subdivided into the inflective type and the noninflective type. Inflective affixes are always appended to stems while noninflective affixes may be appended only to formally complete words. Once the necessary inflective affixes are appended to a stem, the result is a word which is, by means of these affixes, fully defined as to its relation to other words within a phrase or sentence. Such affixes are employed extensively for purposes of inflection and define person, number, gender, possession, aspect, and, in one instance, modality. Noninflective affixes consist of the preverbs and the enclitic particles (postfixes). The former indicate direction of movement while the latter indicate a wider range of notions, including subordination, tense, and additional types of modality.

§4:3. The word classes of Tunica, which have been worked out on the basis of syntactic and inflectional considerations, are as follows: the independent personal pronouns, nouns, the interrogative-indefinite pronouns, adjectives, the auxiliary verbs, active verbs, static verbs, adverbs, postpositions, quantitatives, comparatives, sentence connectives, and exclamatives. The inflected classes are the independent personal pronouns, nouns, and the three classes of verbs. The remaining classes, which some might prefer to group together as noninflected particles, are distinguished here because of definitive differences in syntactic usage (see §7:3).

5. INFLECTION

§5:1. General remarks on inflection.

Inflection is accomplished almost exclusively by means of syntactic affixes of the inflective type. However, suppletion and reduplication are employed in the inflection of the auxiliary verbs and the periphrastic inflection of active verbs is accomplished by juxtaposition with the auxiliary verbs.

The paradigmatic categories of the verb consist of the semelfactive, habitual, and repetitive aspects, and the conditional mode. Each of these categories comprises a separate paradigm and the inflectional categories of each paradigm consist of person, number, and gender.

Two paradigms of personal pronouns are distinguished, the dependent and the independent. Here, too, the inflectional categories employed are person, number, and gender.

The paradigmatic categories of the noun are the indeterminative and the determinative. The former consists of a simple uninflected noun stem. The latter is marked by the use of the articular prefix or a pronominal prefix and, in addition, makes use of two embryonic case-categories, the subjective-objective and the locative. The subjective-objective category makes use of the two inflectional categories of gender and number. The locative category, however, is not inflected beyond what is required for all determinatives unless one should count the locative suffixes and the postpositions as individual inflectional elements.

With respect to the categories of person, number, and gender, the following remarks are pertinent. There are three persons (first, second, and third), three numbers (singular, dual, and plural), and two genders (masculine and feminine). Number distinctions are made in all three persons. Gender distinctions, however, are made in the second and third persons but not in the first. The independent personal pronouns and all of the types of personal pronominal affixes used with nouns and verbs are thus inflected for the following fifteen forms:

Singular	Dual	Plural
1	1	1
2M	2M	2M
2F	2F	2F
3M	3M	3M
3F	3F	3F

§5:2. Pronominal inflection.
§5:21. Paradigm of the personal pronominal prefixes.

	Singular	Dual	Dual=Plural	Plural
1	ʔi-		ʔin-	
2M	wi-		win-	
2F	hi-; he-		hin-; hen-	
3M	ʔu-	ʔun-		si-
3F	ti-		sin-	

Note. With the exception of the 3M forms, the dual and plural forms of this paradigm fall together. The 1D-P, 2MD-P, 2FD-P, and 3MD forms are made up of the corresponding singular forms plus the dual infix -n-. The 3FD-P form appears to be related to the 3MP form in the same way.

An h is regularly inserted between a pronominal prefix (with the exception of those ending in n) and a stem beginning in a voiceless stop provided the stem has a stress on its first syllable. For example, one says ʔihti'rahči "my cloth" (< ʔi-h-+ti'ra "cloth" +-hči, FS gender suffix) but ʔi'kiku "my uncle" (< ʔi- +-'ki "uncle"

+ku, MS gender suffix). Between a pronominal prefix and a stem beginning in ʔ a consonant group ʽhkʼ is regularly inserted except after prefixes ending in n where only ʽkʼ is permitted. For example, one says ʔihk ʔa'lahči "my cane" (< ʔi·hkʼ + ʔa'la "cane" + ʽhči) but ʔink ʔa'lahči "our cane" (< ʔin·kʼ + ʔa'la + ʽhči). Moreover, when the pronominal prefixes are appended to a stem beginning in a vowel the vowel of the prefix contracts with this initial stem vowel (§3:22), e.g., ʔo'siku "his father" (< ʔuʼ + ʽe'si "father" + ʽku).

The pronominal prefixes are used as possessives with nouns (§5:73) and as direct objects with active verbs (§5:543). In addition, they are used as grammatical objects (with the logical function of subjects) in the inflection of static verbs (§5:61).

§5:22. Paradigm of the independent personal pronouns.

	Singular	Dual	Dual=Plural	Plural
1	ʔi'ma		ʔi'nima	
2M	ma'		wi'nima	
2F	hɛ'ma		hi'nima	
3M	ʔu'wi	ʔu'nima		sɛ'ma
3F	ti'hči		si'nima	

Note. As in the case of the pronominal prefixes, all of the dual and plural forms of this paradigm fall together with the exception of the 3M forms.

Space does not permit a full analysis of this paradigm, but the reader will note at once that many of the forms are based on a stem *ʽma or *ʽama to which the pronominal prefixes are attached; he will also note that the sign of the dual is ʽniʼ in place of the ʽnʼ characteristic of the pronominal prefixes.

The discussion of the uses to which these pronouns are put belongs properly to the section on syntax (§7:31).

§5:3. Verb inflection.

On the basis of certain fundamental differences in method of inflection Tunica distinguishes three classes of verbs: the auxiliary verbs, active verbs, and static verbs. Of these the active verbs are by far the most numerous class. The special inflectional peculiarities of each class are given in §§5:42, 5:51, and 5:61.

§5:4. The inflection of the auxiliary verbs.

§5:41. The primary paradigmatic categories of the auxiliary verbs are the semelfactive and repetitive aspects and the conditional mode. Each verb has a separate paradigm for each of these notions except that the causative auxiliary lacks a repetitive paradigm; each paradigm is inflected for the person, number, and gender of the pronominal subject. The basic paradigm of each verb is its semelfactive one and the repetitive and conditional paradigms are formed from this basic paradigm according to regular rules (§§5:45 and 5:46).

§5:42. The special inflectional peculiarities of the auxiliary verbs may be summarized as follows: 1) Their semelfactive paradigms are all irregular and this fact precludes the possibility of setting up any general rules for their construction. While the pronominal element referring to the subject can often be isolated, this is not invariably the case. In some cases this element is a pronominal prefix (§5:21), in other cases it is an inflectional ending of the semelfactive paradigm of the active verb (§5:521), and in still other cases it is not to be isolated. 2) Certain of these irregularities in inflection are caused by the use of suppletion, a process not used by any other word-class of the language. While most cases of suppletion involve number only, a few cases involve person or gender or both. 3) Reduplication is regularly employed in the formation of the repetitive paradigms of these verbs, and like suppletion, is not employed elsewhere in the language. 4) All of these verbs are used in the periphrastic inflection of active verbs (§5:522) although all but the causative auxiliary may also be used independently.

§5:43. Due to the irregularities exhibited by the semelfactive paradigms of these verbs, each auxiliary except la'ka (an anomalous plural verb) is referred to by its 3MS semelfactive form. The complete list of the auxiliary verbs is as follows:

ʔu'hki "he is, was; he exists, existed"
ʔu'ra "he lies, lay; he is, was in a lying position"
ʔu'na "he sits, sat; he dwells, dwelt; he is, was in a sitting position"
ʔu'sa "he comes, came; he is, was coming"
ʔu'wa "he goes, went; he is, was going"
-ʔu'ta "he causes, caused"
la'ka "they live, lived; they dwell, dwelt; they are, were living, dwelling" (an anomalous third person plural verb).

The definitions given above cover the semantic range of the independent usage of these verbs; the semantic range of their dependent usage is a separate problem (§5:523).

§5:44. Semelfactive paradigms of the auxiliary verbs.
§5:441. ʔu'hki "he is, was; he exists, existed."

	Singular	Dual	Plural
1	ʔa'hkini	ʔi'nihki	ʔɔ'nʔiti
2M	wi'hki	wi'nihki	ʔɔ'nawi'ti
2F	hi'hki; he'hki	hi'nihki; he'nihki	ʔɔ'nahi'ti; ʔɔ'nahe'ti
3M	ʔu'hki	ʔu'nihki	ʔɔ'nta
3F	ʔa'ki	si'nihki	ʔɔ'nasi'ti

§5:442. ?u'ra "he lies, lay; he is, was in a lying position."

	Singular	Dual	Plural
1	?a'rani	?i'rana	
2M	wi'ra	wi'rana	
2F	hɛ'ra	hɛ'rana	
3M	?u'ra	?u'rana	na'?ara
3F	?a'ra	si'rana	na'?ara

Note. This paradigm lacks plural forms for 1, 2M, and 2F; possibly the 1, 2M, and 2F dual forms could be used to supply the lack. It should also be noted that the 3M and 3F plural forms are identical. The paradigm of the immediately following auxiliary has the same peculiarities.

§5:443. ?u'na "he sits, sat; he dwells, dwelt; he is, was in a sitting position."

	Singular	Dual	Plural
1	?a'nani	?i'nana	
2M	wi'na	wi'nana	
2F	hɛ'na	hɛ'nana	
3M	?u'na	?u'nana	?u'k?ɛra
3F	?a'či	si'nana	?u'k?ɛra

§5:444. ?u'sa "he comes, came; he is, was coming."

	Singular	Dual	Plural
1	?a'sani	?i'nasa; ?i'nsa	?i'tani
2M	wi'sa	wi'nasa; wi'nsa	wi'tani
2F	hɛ'sa	hɛ'nasa; hɛ'nsa	hɛ'tani
3M	?u'sa	?u'nasa; ?u'nsa	?a'tani
3F	?a'sa	si'nasa; si'nsa	si'tani

§5:445. ?u'wa "he goes, went; he is, was going."

	Singular	Dual	Plural
1	?a'ni	?i'yana	?i'taši
2M	wi'ya	wi'yana	wi'taši
2F	hɛ'ya	hɛ'yana	hɛ'taši
3M	?u'wa	?u'wana	?a'taši
3F	?a'ta	si'yana	si'taši

§5:446. ⸗ʔu'ta "he causes, caused."

	Singular	Dual	Dual=Plural	Plural
1	⸗ʔa'tani; ⸗hta'ni		⸗ʔi'nta	
2M	⸗wi'ta		⸗wi'nta	
2F	⸗he'ta		⸗he'nta	
3M	⸗ʔu'ta	⸗ʔu'nta		⸗ʔa'nta
3F	⸗ʔa'ta		⸗si'nta	

Note. With the exception of the 3M forms, the dual and plural forms of this paradigm fall together. It should also be noted that the 3FS form is homonymous with the 3FS form of the auxiliary verb given immediately above. The forms of this paradigm never stand alone but are used only in the inflection of causative active verbs (§5:532). Of the two 1S forms ⸗hta'ni is used only in causative semelfactive paradigms while ⸗ʔa'tani is used only in causative habitual paradigms.

§5:447. The anomalous auxiliary verb la'ka.

The verb la'ka is anomalous in that it is exclusively a third person masculine and feminine plural verb meaning "they live, lived; they dwell, dwelt; they are, were living, dwelling." It is classed with the auxiliary verbs because, like them, it has a repetitive form made by reduplication (§5:45).

§5:45. The repetitive paradigms of the auxiliary verbs.

The repetitive paradigms of these verbs are used both as repetitives and as usitatives. As has already been pointed out, the causative auxiliary lacks a repetitive paradigm. The formation of the repetitive paradigms of the remaining auxiliary verbs is accomplished by reduplication which is applied to the inflected semelfactive forms of these verbs according to the following rules:

1) With the exception of the plural forms of ʔu'ra and ʔu'na, the reduplication consists in repeating the first consonant and vowel of the inflected semelfactive form and in shifting the stress to the reduplicated element, e.g., ʔa'ʔaki "she used to exist" (rdpl. form of ʔa'ki, 3FS of ʔu'hki, §5:441); wi'wisa "you keep, kept coming" (rdpl. form of wi'sa, 2MS of ʔu'sa, §5:444); la'laka "they always dwell, used to dwell" (rdpl. form of la'ka, §5:447).

2) The repetitive forms of na'ʔara and ʔu'kʔera (the plural forms of ʔu'ra and ʔu'na, respectively) are made by reduplicating the first consonant and vowel of the element *⸗ʔara, giving the forms na'ʔaʔara "they always lie, used to lie" and ʔu'kʔeʔera "they always sit, dwell, used to sit, dwell," respectively.

§5:46. The conditional paradigms of the auxiliary verbs.

The conditional paradigms of these verbs are formed according to the following rules:

1) With the exception of the 1S forms, the fusional conditional forms of the auxiliary verbs (in all persons, numbers, and genders) are made by the insertion of a ʔ between the last consonant and vowel of their corresponding semelfactive

forms, e.g., wi'hkʔi "if you exist" (smlf. form: wi'hki, 2MS of ʔu'hki, §5:441); ʔi'yanʔa "if we go" (smlf. form: ʔi'yana, 1D of ʔu'wa, §5:445).

2) The 1S fusional conditional form of ʔu'wa follows the rule given above and is accordingly, ʔa'nʔi "if I go" (smlf. form: ʔa'ni, §5:445). The 1S form of -ʔu'ta is made by replacing the 1S semelfactive ending -ni with a special conditional form -ʔan, thus: -hta'ʔan "if I cause" (smlf. form: -hta'ni, §5:446). The 1S fusional forms for the remaining auxiliaries do not occur in the available material. Nonfusional conditional forms for them, however, may be formed according to the rule given below.

3) Alternative nonfusional conditional forms for all of the auxiliary verbs may be made by the addition of the conditional enclitic particle -kʔi to the semelfactive forms of these verbs. Such alternative forms are used just as often as are the fusional forms. For example, a form like wi'yakʔi "if you go" (<wi'ya, 2MS smlf. of ʔu'wa, +-kʔi) occurs just as often as the equivalent fusional form wi'yʔa.

§5:47. A few examples of the independent use of the auxiliary verbs are given below.

ta'riki'čŭn, ʔuna'nì. "He was sitting in the house." (ʔuna'ni < ʔu'na, 3MS smlf. of ʔu'na, +-a'ni, quotative encl. part.)

ta'wakăku, ʔu'ʔuhkɛ'nì. "(There) used to be a commander." (ʔu'ʔuhkɛ'ni < ʔu'ʔuhki, 3MS repet. of ʔu'hki, +-a'ni).

ta'rkuki'čŭn, le'yutăn, wi'yanʔăhč . . . . "if you go straight into the woods . . . ." (wi'yanʔahč <wi'yanʔa, 2MD cond. of ʔu·wa, +-hč, subordinating encl. part.)

§5:5. The inflection of active verbs.

§5:51. Active verb stems fall into two main categories, the noncausative and the causative. Moreover, both categories fall into five subclasses: the intransitive, the transitive, the impersonal, the transimpersonal, and the personificative. All active verb stems are inflected for pronominal subject while transitive and transimpersonal stems undergo additional inflection for pronominal object. The distinction between noncausative and causative stems is maintained only in the type of subjective inflection each uses (§5:52 and 5:53); in objective inflection the two types fall together.

Unlike the stems of auxiliary and static verbs, the stems of active verbs may be used independently; in this usage they are infinitives.

The primary inflectional categories of both noncausative and causative verbs are the semelfactive, the habitual (also used as a progressive), and the conditional. The repetitive aspect may be expressed only periphrastically (§§5:522 and 5:523). In noncausative verbs inflection for pronominal subject is accomplished by suffixation (§5:521) or by juxtaposition (§5:522). In causative verbs, on the other hand, inflection for pronominal subject is accomplished exclusively by juxtaposition (§5:531).

§5:52. The subjective inflection of noncausative active verbs.

§5:521. The nonperiphrastic inflection of noncausative verbs is accomplished by the use of the three sets of inflectional endings characteristic of these verbs, namely, the semelfactive set, the habitual set, and the conditional set. These are given below.

The Semelfactive Set of Noncausative Inflectional Endings:

	Singular	Dual	Plural
1	-ni	-ʔi'na	-ʔi'ti
2M	-ʔi	-wi'na	-wi'ti
2F	-ʔa	-hi'na; -he'na	-hi'ti; -he'ti
3M	-wi	-ʔu'na	-ta
3F	-ti	-si'na	-si'ti

The Habitual Set of Noncausative Inflectional Endings:

	Singular	Dual	Plural
1	-ka'ni	-hkʔi'na	-hkʔi'ti
2M	-ki	-wi'na	-wi'ti
2F	-ka	-hi'na; -he'na	-hi'ti; -he'ti
3M	-ku	-hkʔu'na	-ka'ta
3F	-ka'ti	-si'na	-si'ti

Note. A number of the inflectional endings of the habitual paradigm are identical with those of the semelfactive paradigm, viz., the 2MD, 2FD, 3FD, 2MP, 2FP, and 3FP. While it is possible to trace an interesting historical connection between the semelfactive and the habitual endings, space does not permit such a digression in the present sketch.

The Conditional Set of Noncausative Inflectional Endings:

The conditional set of endings are based on the semelfactive set in much the same way that the conditional paradigms of the auxiliary verbs are based on their semelfactive paradigms (§5:46). The rules for the formation of the conditional endings are as follows:

1) With the exception of the 1S, 2MS, and 2FS forms, the conditional endings are made by the insertion of a ʔ between the last consonant and vowel of the corresponding semelfactive endings, e.g., -wʔi, 3MS cond. ending (cf. -wi, corresponding smlf. ending); -ʔi'nʔa, 1D cond. ending (cf. -ʔi'na, corresponding smlf. ending).

2) The 1S conditional ending is -ʔan, consisting of an element -ʔa-, plus the semelfactive ending -ni which is always apocopated to -n in this case.

3) The 2MS and 2FS forms are -ʔikʔi and -ʔakʔi, respectively, and are made up of their corresponding semelfactive endings plus the conditional enclitic particle -kʔi.

4) With the exception of the 2MS and 2FS forms (whose only conditionals are nonfusional) there are alternative nonfusional conditional forms for all persons, numbers, and genders which consist of the semelfactive endings plus the enclitic particle ‑kʔi.

§5:522. The periphrastic inflection of noncausative verbs is accomplished by placing the stem of an active verb in front of the semelfactive, repetitive, or conditional paradigms of any of the auxiliary verbs except the causative. In addition the notion of the habitual aspect may be expressed by placing a semelfactive form of an auxiliary verb after an active verb stem which has been extended by the habitual thematic suffix ‑hk‑. However, this suffix cannot be used before an inflected form of the auxiliary verb ʔuʹhki.

§5:523. When the auxiliary verbs are used in periphrastic inflection their primary meanings are subdued or lost entirely. The special meanings assumed by each auxiliary under these circumstances are as follows:

1) The auxiliary ʔuʹhki (§5:441) is regularly employed to express the notion of priority in time. It covers the simple past tense, the present perfect tense and the past perfect tense. Smlf. ex.: haʹtikăn, yaʹkʔahkiní. "I have come back again." (yaʹkʔahkini "I have come back" <yaʹka "to come back" +ʔaʹhkini, 1S smlf.). Repet. ex.: piʹhkayunsaʹhkun, čuʹʔuʔuhkɛʹnì. "He always took one copper." (čuʹʔuʔuhkɛʹni "he always took" <čuʹ "to take" +ʔuʹʔuhki, 3MS repet., +‑aʹni, quot.).

2) The auxiliary verbs ʔuʹra (§5:442) and ʔuʹna (§5:443) are used to express the notion of durativity. Two types of durativity may be expressed, the immutable and the mutable. To express the immutable durative either of these auxiliaries is used with a nonhabitual form of an active verb stem (i.e., any stem which is not extended by ‑hk‑). To express the mutable durative either of these auxiliaries is used with the habitual theme (formed by the suffix ‑hk‑) of an active verb. Examples of the immutable durative are: teʹtĭn, hoʹnʔɔraʹnì, taʹnahtahaʹlùht. "(There) was a path going down under the bank." (hoʹnʔɔraʹni "it (lit., she) was going down" <hoʹnu "to descend" +ʔaʹra, 3FS smlf. of ʔuʹra, +‑aʹni); piʹhʔunaʹnì. "He stayed hidden" (<piʹhu "to hide" +ʔuʹna, 3MS smlf., +‑aʹni). In the first example note particularly that the path does not undergo any change by virtue of its "going down"; instead, it stays perpetually in a "going down" position.

Examples of the mutable durative are: hiʹpuhkʔuraʹnì, hɔʹwàš. "He was dancing outside." (<hiʹpu "to dance" +‑hk‑, habitual suff., +ʔuʹra+‑aʹni); piʹtahkʔunaʹnì, seʹhiyuʹrùhč. "He was walking all day long." (<piʹta "to walk" +‑hk‑ +ʔuʹna, 3MS, +‑aʹni).

A repetitive example occurs in ʔɛʹmahkʔaʹʔaraʹnì. "It (the fire) would burn and burn." (<ʔɛʹma "to burn" +‑hk‑ +ʔaʹʔara, 3FS repet. of ʔuʹra, +‑aʹni).

3) The auxiliary verbs ʔuʹsa (§5:444) and ʔuʹwa (§5:445) retain their literal meanings (§5:43) in periphrastic inflection. They are widely used with active verb

stems expressing the idea of a change of position, such as, ho·. . pi′ "to emerge," ʔa′ka "to enter," ho′nu "to descend," sa′ka "to cross." When ʔu′sa and ʔu′wa are used with such active verb stems they express the notion of hitherward and thitherward direction, respectively, so that ʔa′kʔusa means "he comes, came in" and ʔa′kʔuwa means "he goes, went in."

§5:53. The subjective inflection of causative active verbs.

§5:531. The inflection of causative verbs is always periphrastic. The semel‑factive, habitual, and conditional paradigms require the use of the causative aux‑iliary. Other types of periphrastic inflection (involving the use of the other aux‑iliaries) are also possible with causative stems provided certain special formational rules are applied (§5:533).

§5:532. The component elements of the semelfactive, habitual, and condi‑tional paradigms of causative verbs are as follows:

1) A causative stem plus the semelfactive paradigm of the causative auxiliary (§5:446) makes up the semelfactive paradigm of a causative verb, e.g., ʔu′rʔuta "he whooped" (< ʔu′ru . . c . "to whoop" +‑ʔu′ta, 3MS). (Note that ʔu′ru . . c . is to be read ʔu′ru, causative active verb stem.)

2) A causative habitual theme (<a caus. stem +suff. ‑hk‑) plus the semelfac‑tive paradigm of the causative auxiliary makes up the habitual paradigm of a causa‑tive verb, e.g., ʔu′ruhkʔu′ta "he whoops, would whoop" (< ʔu′ru . . c. + ‑hk‑ + ‑ʔu′ta).

3) A causative stem plus the conditional paradigm of the causative auxiliary (§5:46) makes up the conditional paradigm of a causative verb, e.g., ʔu′rʔutʔa "if he whoops" (< ʔu′ru . . c . + ‑ʔu′rʔa, 3MS cond.).

§5:533. In case it is desired to use one of the other auxiliary verbs with a causative stem the following rule applies: A causative theme (<a caus. stem + the caus. thematic suff. ‑n‑) is placed in front of the semelfactive, repetitive, or condi‑tional paradigms of any noncausative auxiliary verb, e.g., ʔu′runʔu′hki "he has whooped" (< ʔu′ru . . c . + ‑n‑ + ʔu′hki, 3MS). The special meanings of the non‑causative auxiliaries when used with causative stems are the same as when they are used with noncausative stems (§5:523).

§5:534. A synopsis showing the chief differences in inflection as between a noncausative and a causative stem is given below.

Stem	Noncausative	Causative
	pa′ta "to fall"	pa′ka . . . c. "to reply"
3MS smlf.	pa′tawi "he fell"	pa′kʔuta "he replied"
3MS hab.	pa′taku "he falls"	pa′kahkʔu′ta "he replies"
3MS past	pa′tʔuhki "he has fallen"	pa′kanʔu′hki "he has replied"

§5:54. The inflection of the subclasses of the active verb.

§5:541. As has already been pointed out, both noncausative and causative verbs fall into five subclasses: the intransitive, the transitive, the impersonal, the transimpersonal, and the personificative. While none of these subclasses makes use of any special inflectional elements, each of them (except the transitive) is restricted in a different way as to which of the total number of inflectional elements it may use. The essential characteristics of each of these subclasses are presented in the following paragraphs.

§5:542. Intransitive verbs may be inflected only for pronominal subject and the rules for the subjective inflection of active verbs already given cover all that can be said of the inflection of this subclass.

§5:543. Transitive verbs are inflected not only for pronominal subject but also for pronominal object. Inflection for pronominal subject is the same as for intransitive verbs. Inflection for pronominal object is accomplished by the use of the pronominal prefixes (§5:21) or by the use of the reciprocal prefix (ʔa- before all stems except those beginning in ʔ; before the latter, ʔak-). Examples of the objective inflection of transitive verbs are: ʔihpɛ'kʔuhkí "he has hit me" (< ʔi-h-, 1S pron. pref. used as obj., + pɛ'kʔuhki "he has hit"); ʔapɛ'kʔunihkí "they have hit each other" (< ʔa-, reciprocal pref., +pɛ'kʔunihki "they (MD) have hit").

§5:544. Impersonal verbs may be inflected only for third person feminine singular subject. Any of the 3FS inflectional endings and any of the 3FS forms of auxiliary verbs may be used. This 3FS subject implies an impersonal agent, as in, ti'hikati'sihkŭn, pi'ratĭhč "when it got to be seven years" or "seven years later" (pi'ratĭhč "when it got to be" <pi'ra "to get to be" +-ti, 3FS smlf. ending, + -hč, subordinating encl. part.).

§5:545. Transimpersonal verbs may likewise be inflected only for 3FS subject. In addition, however, they must be inflected for pronominal object by means of the pronominal prefixes, e.g., sɛ'mapăn, siho't ʔɔkɛ'nì. "They, too, have become extinct," i.e., "an impersonal agent has finished them" (siho't ʔɔkɛ'ni "they have become extinct" <si-, 3MP pron. pref., +ho'tu "to become extinct" +ʔa'ki, 3FS of ʔu'hki).

It will be noted that impersonal verbs are to intransitive verbs as transimpersonal verbs are to transitive verbs.

§5:546. Personificative verbs may be inflected only for 3MS subject. These are without exception verbs meaning "to rain," "to snow," "to hail," and the like. They are called personificative verbs because in Tunica mythology the Thunder Being (who is personified as a man) is thought to control this type of weather manifestation, hence, sa'čʔuhkí "it has rained" (<sa'či "to rain" + ʔu'hki) carries the implication that "he (i.e., the Thunder Being) has rained."

§5:6. The inflection of static verbs.

§5:61. Static verb stems are inflected by means of the pronominal prefixes (§5:21) and may not be used without them. Grammatically speaking, these prefixes must be construed as objects, but logically speaking they may be interpreted as subjects, e.g., ʔi'yaší "I am angry" (< ʔi-, 1S pron. pref., + -ya'ši "to be angry").

A number of static verb stems begin in vowels and in this case the vowel of the prefix contracts with the initial vowel of the stem, e.g., ʔoʹhtini "he owns; it is his" (< ʔu-, 3MF pref. + -eʹhtini "to own, to belong to . . . ").

§5:62. Certain static verbs may have special inchoative forms which contain not only a pronominal prefix but also a 3FS subjective element, i.e., either a 3FS inflectional ending (normally attached to active verb stems, §5:521) or the 3FS form of the auxiliary ʔuʹhki. Ex.: ʔiyaʹšʔɛkí "I became angry" (< ʔi- + -yaʹši + ʔaʹki, 3FS of ʔuʹhki). Due to the fact that inchoative forms contain an element which must be construed as the grammatical subject, the pronominal prefixes are construed as grammatical objects not only in the inchoative forms but in the non-inchoative forms as well, even though in the latter case there is no element which can be construed as a grammatical subject.

It will be noted at once that the inchoative forms of static verbs are constructed like transimpersonal active verbs (§5:545). The difference between the two types lies in the fact that while transimpersonal verbs cannot be used without an expressed 3FS subject, all static verbs have noninchoative forms in which no expressed grammatical subject may be used (§5:61).

§5:7. Noun inflection.

§5:71. The paradigmatic categories of the noun are the indeterminative and the determinative. The indeterminative category consists of the simple uninflected noun stem, e.g., ruʹšta "a rabbit, rabbits."[7] The determinative category, however, is marked by the use of the determining prefixes and the relational suffixes. These are as follows: the articular prefix (§5:72), the pronominal prefixes (§5:73), the gender-number suffixes (§5:74), and the locative suffixes (§5:75). An unmodified noun in the determinative category is preceded by the articular prefix or a pronominal prefix and is followed by a gender-number suffix, a locative suffix, or a postposition. Thus the articular prefix and the pronominal prefixes are mutually exclusive, and the gender-number suffixes, the locative suffixes and postpositions are likewise mutually exclusive.

§5:72. The articular prefix has the force of a definite article. It regularly appears in the form taʹ- before all noun stems except those beginning in ʔ or t. Before stems beginning in ʔ it takes the form t- with consequent loss of the stem-initial ʔ. Before stems beginning in t the articular prefix is usually omitted haplologically, though instances of the use of taʹ- also occur. Examples: taʹruštaku "the rabbit" (<taʹ-+ruʹšta "a rabbit" + -ku, MS suff.); toʹniku "the man" (<t- + ʔoʹni "a person" + -ku); tɔʹrahkiku "the ice" (<tɔʹrahki "ice" + -ku) or taʹtɔrah-kiku "the ice."

All proper nouns must always be used with the articular prefix, e.g., taʹwišimiʹliku "Red River" (<taʹ- + wiʹši "water" + miʹli "red" + -ku).

----

[7] Nouns in the indeterminate category are not defined as to number; therefore they may be translated either as singulars or as plurals, whichever the context demands. To conserve space, however, they are hereafter translated as singulars only, rather than as both singulars and plurals.

Possessed noun stems (§5:73) cannot occur without the pronominal prefixes. Since the pronominal prefixes and the articular prefix are mutually exclusive, it follows that these noun stems cannot take the articular prefix.

§5:73. The pronominal prefixes (§5:21) may be used with any noun stem, when desired, to denote its possessor, e.g., ʔuhčɔ'haku "his chief" (< ʔu·h·, 3MS pref., +čɔ'ha "a chief" +·ku). In addition, there are a special class of nouns, known as possessed nouns, which refer to entities conceived to be inalienably possessed and this class of nouns cannot be used without pronominal prefixes, e.g., ʔo'siku "his father" (< ʔu·, 3MS pref., +·e'si "father" +·ku). Most possessed noun stems are body-part terms or terms of relationship. It should also be noted that many possessed noun stems begin in a vowel and in this case the vowel of the prefix contracts with the initial vowel of the stem (§5:21).

§5:74. The gender-number suffixes indicate not only the gender and number of the noun but also the subjective-objective case. These suffixes are as follows:

	Singular	Dual	Dual=Plural	Plural
M	·ku	·ʔu'nima		·sɛ'ma
F	·hči		·si'nima	

Note. The same feminine form is used both as a dual and as a plural.

Examples: ta'čɔhaku "the chief" (<ta'·+čɔ'ha "a chief" +·ku); ta'čɔhʔu'nima "the (two) chiefs"; ta'čɔhasɛ'ma "the (several) chiefs"; ta'nisarahči "the girl" (<ta'·+ni'sara "a young person" +·hči); ta'nisarasi'nima "the (two or more) girls."

§5:75. The locative suffixes are ·hta "on" and ·š(i) "to, at," e.g., ta'halta "on the ground" (<ta'·+ha'li "ground" +·hta); ta'riš "to the house" (<ta'·+ri' "house" +·š(i)). As has already been noted, the locative suffixes, the postpositions, and the gender-number suffixes are mutually exclusive.

§5:76. The salient features of Tunica noun classification are as follows: All nouns are either masculine or feminine. This classification into masculine and feminine may be termed the outer or "grammatical" classification. The criteria needed in determining the gender-class of any given noun, however, reflect an inner or "teleological" classification which is based on a certain few selected natural characteristics of the entity to which the noun refers. These are conveniently grouped into a set of interweaving dichotomies as follows:

	Animate		*vs.*	Inanimate
Human	*vs.*	Nonhuman		
Male *vs.* Female		Male *vs.* Female		Integral *vs.* Continual

Before one can determine the gender-class of a given noun, then, one must answer the questions raised by the above sets of dichotomies; in addition, one must know whether the noun is to be used in the singular, dual, or plural number class. The

singular number class, moreover, is subdivided into 1) true singulars and 2) collec-
tives. The rules of classification based upon the above criteria are as follows:

1) Nouns referring to human or nonhuman male animates in the sg., du., or
pl. number are masculine in gender, and nouns referring to human or nonhuman
female animates in the sg., du. or pl. number are feminine in gender, e.g., ta'čɔhaku
"the chief"; ta'čɔhʔu'nima "the (two) chiefs"; ta'čɔhasɛ'ma "the (several) chiefs";
ta'nisarahči "the girl"; ta'nisarasi'nima "the (two or more) girls."

2) Nouns referring to human male and female animates in the collective, du.,
or pl. numbers are masculine in gender, e.g., ta'čahtaku "the Choctaw (as a tribe)";
ta'nisarʔu'nima "the young people (a pair)"; ta'čahtasɛ'ma "the Choctaws (several individuals, male and female)."

3) Nouns referring to nonhuman male and female animates in the du. number
are masculine, but nouns referring to nonhuman male and female animates in the
collective or pl. number are feminine in gender, e.g., ta'yorumʔahʔu'nima "the
beasts (a pair)"; ti'sahči "her dogs (as a collective)"; ti'sasi'nima "her dogs (as individuals, male and female)."

It will be noted that it is only in connection with the last two rules that the
dichotomy of human vs. nonhuman has significance.

In a number of cases the gender classification of nouns referring to inanimates
is arbitrary, but the following rules take care of the majority of inanimate nouns:

4) Most nouns referring to integrals in the sg. number, and only such nouns,
are masculine in gender, e.g., ta'šihkaliku "the stone." However, some nouns referring to integrals are feminine in gender, e.g., ta'rihči "the house," and since no
rules can be made to cover these instances, the classification of such nouns is to be
considered arbitrary.

5) All nouns referring to continuals in the sg. number are feminine in gender,
e.g., ta'wišihči "the water."

6) Integrals which are classed as masculine in the sg. are likewise classed as
masculine in the du., e.g., ta'šihkalʔu'nima "the (two) stones." In the pl. number
integrals are classed as feminine, regardless of whether they are masculine or
feminine in the sg., e.g., ta'šihkalsi'nima "the stones"; ta'risi'nima "the houses."

7) Nouns referring to continuals are not dualized nor pluralized.

6. STEM FORMATION

§6:1. Verb stem formation.

§6:11. Verb stem formation as a productive process occurs most widely with
active verb stems. The most important elements used are the purposive suffix and
the thematic suffixes.

§6:12. The purposive suffix is -wan "in order to . . ." It is added to active
verb stems (infinitives) and the resultant form may not be inflected, e.g.,
te'hinʔuhkɛ'nì, ʔuhkɔ'sawàn "he went around (the deer) in order to skin it"
(ʔuhkɔ'sawan "in order to skin it" < ʔu-h-, 3MS pref., +kɔ'sa "to skin . . ."
+-wan).

§6:13. The thematic suffixes fall into two classes, the restricted and the non-restricted. An active verb stem plus a restricted suffix results in a theme which may be inflected only periphrastically. An active verb stem plus a nonrestricted suffix, however, results in a theme which may be inflected in all of the ways in which an active verb stem may be.

The two most widely used thematic suffixes are -hk-, the habitual-progressive suffix, and -n-, the causative suffix. Both are restricted. The rules for their use have already been discussed in connection with the inflection of active verbs (for -hk-, see §§5:522 and 5:523; for -n-, see §§5:533 and 5:534). There is also another restricted suffix, namely -tahk- "to repeatedly . . . ; to be constantly . . .-ing," e.g., ʔamɛ'katahkʔu'ʔunaná "they were constantly quarreling" (theme: mɛ'katahk- <mɛ'ka "to quarrel" +-tahk-). The two most important nonrestricted suffixes are -hapa- "to have already . . .-ed" and -hila- "to be about to . . . ," e.g., ʔura'pap-ʔonta'nì "they had already killed him" (theme: ra'papa- <ra'pa "to kill . . ." +-hapa-); ʔuhta'pilatĭhč "when she was about to seize him" (theme: ta'pila- <ta'pi "to seize . . . " +-hila-).

§6:2. Noun stem formation.

§6:21. Secondary noun stems are of three main types: 1) augmentativized or diminutivized stems, 2) composite stems, and 3) agentives.

§6:22. Augmentativized and diminutivized noun stems are derived from primary noun stems by means of the augmentative suffix -tʔɛ and the diminutive suffix -to'hku (or -to'hok), respectively, e.g., ru'štatʔɛ "a sheep" (<ru'šta "a rabbit" +-tʔɛ); ya'ruhto'hku or ya'ruhto'hok "a hatchet" (<ya'ruhki "an ax" +-to'hku, -to'hok).

§6:23. Composite noun stems are formed by juxtaposition and are of two main types:

1) noun stem plus adjective stem composites (e.g., ʔo'nrɔwa "a white person" (< ʔo'ni "a person" +rɔ'wa "white").

2) noun stem plus noun stem composites (e.g., ya'nɛrana'ra "an ocean snake (mythical)" (<ya'nɛra "an ocean" +na'ra "a snake").

§6:24. Agentive noun stems are derived from active verb stems by means of the agentive prefix ta'- (not to be confused with the articular pref., §5:72, with which it is homonymous), e.g., ta'hara "a singer" (<ta'- +ha'ra "to sing").

7. SYNTAX

§7:1. The sentence.

§7:11. Sentences may be simple, compound, or complex. Compound sentences are rare. Complex sentences, however, are quite common and consist of a main clause and one or more dependent clauses which are always indicated by having one of the subordinating enclitic particles attached to their predicative word.

§7:12. The syntactic elements of the sentence are a predicative word, an independent subject, an independent object, a predicate modifier, a predicate complement, and a sentence connective. Every sentence (except those consisting of an exclamative, §7:39) must have a predicative word and may consist of only this word (see next paragraph).

The predicative word may be a substantive (§7:31), an adjective (§7:32), or any one of the three classes of verbs (§7:33), e.g., ši'hkalí "it is a stone"; yu'pahtá "it is cold"; ha'rʔuhkí "he sang."

The independent subject (i.e., a word used as subject as opposed to the sub- jective pronominal element of the verb) and the independent object (i.e., a word used as object as opposed to the objective pronominal element of the verb) may be any substantive (§7:31), e.g., ʔu'wĭn, hi'pʔuhkí "he danced" (with ʔu'wi "he," an independent personal pronoun, used as independent subject); to'nĭku, hi'pʔuhkí "the man danced" (with to'niku "the man," a noun, used as independent subject); ʔu'wĭn, ʔuhpɛ'kʔahkiní "I hit him" (with ʔu'wi used as independent object); to'nĭku, ʔuhpɛ'kʔahkiní "I hit the man" (with to'niku used as independent object).

Predicate modifiers are of three types:

1) Adjectives, which are used as modifiers of nominal predicatives, e.g., ta'yoronĭku, ʔo'nilapú "the Tunica are good people" (la'pu "good," used as modi- fier of the nominal predicative ʔo'ni "people").

2) Comparatives, which are used as modifiers of adjectival and static verb predicatives, e.g., ta'kafĭhč, la'pupanú "the coffee is very good" (pa'nu "very," used as modifier of the adjectival predicative la'pu).

3) Adverbs and adverbial phrases, which are used as modifiers of auxiliary or active verb predicatives, e.g., ʔu'nana'nì, hɔ'wàš "they were sitting outside" (hɔ'waš "outside," adverb, used as modifier of the auxiliary verb ʔu'nana'ni "they were sitting"); ta'riki'čŭn, ʔa'kʔuwa'nì "he went into the house" (ta'riki'ču "in the house," adverbial phrase, used as modifier of the active verb ʔa'kʔuwa'ni "he entered").

Predicate complements are substantives (§7:31) and are used as complements of static and transimpersonal verb predicatives, e.g., hi'čutʔɛn, ʔuhpi'rʔakɛ'nì "he became an eagle" (hi'čutʔɛ "an eagle," used as the complement of the trans- impersonal verb ʔuhpi'rʔakɛ'ni "he became").

Sentence connectives are used to establish a loose conjunctive, contrastive, or disjunctive connection between a sentence and the sentence that precedes it, e.g., hi'nahkʔɔhčăt, ta'yoronĭku, ta'hčʔihi'pŭhč, hi'pukɔ'nì "For this reason the Tunica dance the Sun-dance" (hi'nahkʔɔhčat "therefore, for this, that reason").

§7:13. The following rules and tendencies of word order should be noted:

1) If a sentence connective is used it precedes all the other elements of the sentence (see the last example above).

2) The predicative word of either a main or a dependent clause tends to take clause-final position, tɔ'katɛ'kahăku, yu'kawĭhč, ta'hičutʔɛhč, ʔa'čɛhɛ'nì "When the orphan boy arrived, the eagle was not there." (yu'kawĭhč, predicative word of the dependent clause tɔ'katɛ'kahăku, yu'kawĭhč; ʔa'čɛhɛ'ni, predicative word of the

main clause ta'hičut?ĕhč, ?a'čɛhɛ'nì). This order is not too rigidly adhered to since predicate modifiers often come last, as in ?a'k?uwa'nì, ta'riki'čùn "he went into the house" (?a'k?uwa'ni, predicative word). See also 6) below.

3) The independent subject tends to precede all other syntactic elements in the clause except the sentence connective, e.g., ta'ruštăku, tɔ'mahkăku, ?uhpɛ'k?uhkɛ'nì "Rabbit hit the alligator" (ta'ruštaku, independent subject). Hence if both an independent subject and an independent object occur in the same clause, the latter will normally follow the former, as in the sentence just quoted wherein tɔ'mahkaku is the independent object.

4) Adjectives must always immediately follow the noun they modify, e.g., ta'yoronĭku, ?o'nilapú "The Tunica are good people."

5) Comparatives must always immediately follow the adjective or static verb they modify, e.g., ta'kaſĭhč, la'pupanú "The coffee is very good."

6) Predicate modifiers (i.e., adverbs or adverbial phrases) usually immediately precede or immediately follow the verb they modify. If there is only one predicate modifier either order is equally good, e.g., ta'rkuki'čùn, ?a'k?uwa'nì "he went into the woods" (ta'rkuki'ču "in the woods") or ?a'k?uwa'nì, ta'rkuki'čùn. On the other hand, if there are two predicate modifiers, one will ordinarily precede the verb while the other will follow it, e.g., ta'rkuki'čùn, ?a'k?uwa'nì, la'hontòhku "he went into the woods early" (la'honto'hku "early").

7) A predicate complement usually precedes the verb it complements, e.g., hi'čut?ĕn, ?uhpi'r?akɛ'nì "he became an eagle."

§7:14. Summary chart of word order.

	SC	PM	IS	IO	PM	PC	PW	PM
1							pi'tahk?una'nì. He was walking.	
2						lɔ'ta To run	wiwa'năn. do you want?	
3					hɔ'wăš, Outside		howɛ's?uhkɛ'nì. he jumped out.	[hɔ'wàš.]
4			ya'?ăn A deer				?uwe'n?uhkɛ'nì. he found him.	
5			ta'ruštăku, Rabbit				?u'š?ɛpa'nì. he was glad.	
6			to'nĭku, The man	ta'yak the deer			?ura'p?uhkɛ'nì. he killed him.	
7	h-hč Then		?u'wĭn, he		ma'hon just		?una'nì, he was sitting	?u'rìš. at home.
8	h-hč Then	ha'tikăn, again	ta'ruštăku, Rabbit	tɔ'mahkak Alligator		?uhpɛ'kawan to hit him	yakɔ'nì. he was doing.	

§7:15. In sentences of two or more clauses the dependent clauses usually precede the main clause, e.g., ta'yăku, pa'tawĭhč, ta'yarɔ'hpanyu'kawĭhč, ʔuhkɔ'-sawante'hinʔuhkɛ'nì. "When the deer fell, when he got near the deer, he went around (it) in order to skin it." (ta'yăku, pa'tawĭhč, first dependent clause; ta'yarɔ'hpanyu'kawĭhč, second dependent clause; ʔuhkɔ'sawante'hinʔuhkɛ'nì, main clause.)

§7:16. The following are the circumstances under which agreement in person, number, and gender is essential:

1) Between an independent subject and the pronominal subjective element of the verb of which it is the subject, e.g., ta'nisarăhč, ha'rakatí "the girl sings" (3FS subjective element -ka'ti agreeing with the feminine singular noun ta'nisarahč "the girl").

2) Between an independent object and the pronominal objective element of the verb of which it is the object, e.g., ʔi'măn, ʔihpɛ'kʔuhkí "he hit me" (1S objective element ʔi-h- agreeing with the 1S independent personal pronoun ʔi'ma).

3) Between the nominal possessor of a noun and the pronominal possessive element attached to the noun that is possessed, e.g., to'nikʔu'rĭhč "the man's house" (3MS possessive element ʔu- agreeing with the masculine singular noun to'niku "the man").

§7:2. The preverbs and the enclitic particles (postfixes).

The preverbs and the enclitic particles are discussed in connection with the section of syntax, first, because they are appended only to formally complete words, and secondly, because for the most part the rules for their use are based on the syntactic classification of the words to which they are attached.

§7:21. The preverbs may be attached to any predicative word (§7:12), e.g., teha'hpaya'nì "there was noise all about" (<te-, preverb meaning "about, all about" +ha'hpaya'nì "there was noise"); tewɛ'sasitɛ'nì "they were jumping about" (<te-+wɛ'sasitɛ'nì "they were jumping"); te'milɛ'nì "it was red all about" (<te-+milɛ'nì "it was red"). The remaining preverbs are ki- "in, into," ho- "out, out of," and ha- "up."

§7:22. There are some thirty enclitic particles expressing the future tense, various modes, negation, and a variety of other notions. Some of these may be used with any predicative word while the use of others is restricted to a single word class. Some of the modal and tense enclitic particles used with verbs require that the verbs be in the semelfactive aspect. One of these is -kʔahča, denoting the future

Note 1. The explanation of the abbreviations used in the chart opposite is as follows: SC, sentence connective; PM, predicate modifier; IS, independent subject; IO, independent object; PC, predicate complement; PW, predicative word. In addition h-hč is an abbreviation for hinya'tihč "then, now" and the word hɔ'waš "outside" is once placed in brackets to show an alternative position for the predicate modifier.

Note 2. The translations of the analyzed sentences are as follows: 1) pi'tahkʔuna'nì. "He was walking." 2) lɔ'tawiwa'năn. "Do you want to run?" 3) hɔ'wăš, howɛ's?uhkɛ'nì (or) howɛ's?uhkɛ'nì, hɔ'wăš. "He jumped outside." 4) ya'ʔăn, ʔuwe'nʔuhkɛ'nì. "He found a deer." 5) ta'ruštăku, ʔu'š?epa'nì. "Rabbit was glad." 6) to'nĭku, ta'yakʔura'pʔuhkɛ'nì. "The man killed the deer." 7) hinya'tĭhč, ʔu'wĭn, ma'honʔuna'nì, ʔu'rĭš. "Then he was just sitting at home." 8) hinya'tĭhč, ha'tikăn, ta'ruštăku, tɔ'mahkakʔuhpɛ'kawanyakɔ'nì. "Then Rabbit tried to hit Alligator again."

tense, e.g., lɔ'tʔinakʔahčá "we shall run" (<lɔ'tʔina "we run," smlf. aspect, +-kʔahča). In general it can be said that all of the enclitic particles have their own peculiarities and restrictions as to usage, and, for this reason there will not be space to do more than list the most widely used ones. They are: -kʔahča, future tense; -kʔi, conditional mode (see §§5:46 and 5:521); -pa, concessive mode; -ki, imperative mode; -n, interrogative mode; -a'ni, quotative mode; -ʔaha and -aha, negation (-ʔaha being used with certain word-classes, -aha with certain others); -štukʔɔhɔ "to be unable to . . . "; -hč "when, as, after," i.e., general subordination; -škan "although," contrastive subordination; -ʔama "and," coordination; -hat "on . . . 's part"; -nahku "resembling, like . . . "; -tahki "nothing but . . . "; -pa "too, also."

In certain cases more than one enclitic particle can be attached to the same word and in this event the order of the elements is fixed. For example, -a'ni, quotative mode, must always come last in a sequence of enclitic particles, e.g., pa'nuwištukʔɔhɔ'nì "he could not get past, they say" (<pa'nuwi "he got past" +-štukʔɔhɔ "to be unable to . . . " +-a'ni).

§7:3. The syntactic uses of the word classes.

The word classes of Tunica (cf. §4:3) are the independent personal pronouns, nouns, the interrogative-indefinite pronouns, adjectives, the auxiliary verbs, active verbs, static verbs, adverbs, postpositions, quantitatives, comparatives, sentence connectives, and exclamatives. These are discussed below in this order.

§7:31. The independent personal pronouns (§5:22), nouns (§5:7), and the interrogative-indefinite pronouns (ka'nahku "something, anything, what"; ka'ku "someone, anyone, who"), which must be distinguished as separate word classes on the inflectional level, may be classed together as substantives on the syntactic level. Substantives are used in the following ways:

1) As predicative words, e.g., ʔu'wʔɛhɛ́ "it is not he" (<ʔu'wi "he" +-ʔaha "not"); ti'šlinahčɛ'nì "it was the Stone Witch" (<ti'šlinahči "the Stone Witch" +-a'ni, quot.); ka'nahkupʔahá "there is nothing" (<ka'nahku "something" +-pʔaha "no . . . ").

2) As subjects of predications, e.g., ʔu'wʔonɛ'nì "he is a person" (ʔu'wi "he"; ʔonɛ'nì "it is a person"), to'nĭku, hɔ'wašʔuna'nì "the man was sitting outside" (to'niku "the man"); ka'kŭn, ʔuwi'ʔutʔăhč "if anyone hears him" (ka'ku "anyone").

3) As objects of transitive and transimpersonal verbs, e.g., ʔi'măn, ʔihpɛ'k-ʔuhkí "he has hit me" (ʔi'ma "me").

4) As objects of postpositions, e.g., ta'riki'čùn "in the house" (<ta'ri "the house" +ki'ču "in").

5) As complements of transimpersonal and static verbs, e.g., ʔu'wĭn, ʔušpi't-ʔokɛ'nì, ti'hčìn "he forgot her" (ti'hči "her," used as the complement of the static verb ʔušpi'tʔokɛ'nì "he forgot"); ʔu'wăn, ʔuhpi'rʔakɛ'nì "he became a hoot owl" (ʔu'wa "hoot owl," used as the complement of ʔuhpi'rʔakɛ'nì "he became").

§7:32. Adjectives are used in the following ways:

1) As predicative words, e.g., te'sĭnč, milɛ'nì "her head was red."

2) As modifiers of nouns and interrogative-indefinite pronouns, e.g., ta'-yoronĭku, ʔo'nilapú "the Tunica are good people" (ʔo'ni "people," modified by la'pu "good"); ka'nala'puyu'kʔɛ̆nč "if I cook something good" (ka'nahku "something," modified by la'pu).

§7:33. The auxiliary verbs and the static verbs are always inflected and must always be used as predicative words, e.g., ʔu'naná "they (two) are sitting" (aux. vb.); ʔe'rusá "I know" (st. vb.). Active verbs, when inflected, are also used as predicative words, e.g., ʔihpɛ'kʔuhkí "he has hit me." Uninflected active verbs (i.e., infinitives), on the other hand, are used as static verb complements and then only when the implied subject of the infinitive is the same as the logical subject (grammatical object, §5:6) of the static verb, e.g., lɔ'tasi'waná "they want to run" (lɔ'ta "to run"; si'waná "they want").

§7:34. Adverbs are always used as verbal modifiers, e.g., hi'hčĭn, ʔuná "he is sitting here" (hi'hči "here"); hɛ'ʔɛ̆š, ya'kawikʔahčá "he will come today" (hɛ'ʔɛš "today"); hi'štahahkʔu'ʔuwa'nì "he still keeps on going" (hi'štahakhi "still, yet").

§7:35. Postpositions always govern substantives, e.g., ʔi'marɔ'hpànt "beside me" (rɔ'hpant "beside . . . "); ta'hkɔraha'yihtàn "on the table" (ha'yihta "on, on top of . . . "). Postpositional phrases (i.e., postpositions plus the substantives they govern) are used as predicate modifiers, e.g., ʔi'marɔ'hpănt, ʔu'kʔihčân "sit beside me!"

There are some postpositions which may be used both as adverbs and as postpositions. Note ha'yĭš, na'rʔata'nì "she flew above" (ha'yiš "above") as against ta'riha'yĭš, na'rʔata'nì "she flew above the house" (ha'yiš "above . . . ").

§7:36. Quantitatives include the numerals and ho'tu "all." They are used as follows:

1) In all the ways that substantives are used, e.g., sa'hkŭn, ʔuhta'pʔɛkɛ'nì "she caught one" (sa'hku "one," used as an independent object), ho'tŭn, lu'pʔɔnta'nì "all of them died" (ho'tu "all," used as an independent subject).

2) As modifiers of nouns, e.g., kohkʔe'nihkŭn, ma'riwĭhč "when he picked up three turtles" (ʔe'nihku "three," modifying ko'hku "turtle").

3) As modifiers of active verbs, indicating the number of times an event takes place, e.g., ʔi'lĭn, ʔihpɛ'kʔuhkí "he hit me twice" (ʔi'li "two, twice").

§7:37. Comparatives are used in the following ways:

1) As modifiers of adjectives, e.g., la'pupanú "it is very good" (pa'nu "very," used as a modifier of la'pu "good"); yu'pahtari'kiní "it is too cold" (ri'kini "too . . . ," used as a modifier of yu'pahta "cold").

2) As modifiers of those static verbs whose meaning permits it, e.g., ʔišʔɛ'pa-panú "I am very glad" (pa'nu "very," modifying ʔišʔɛ'pa "I am glad").

§7:38. Sentence connectives are used as sentence or word conjunctives, contrastives, and disjunctives, e.g., hi'nahkŭhč, ʔuwa'nì "Then he went on."

(hiʼnahkuhč "then, after that"); hiʼnahkuškăn, hakaʼlʔɛkɛʼnì "Nevertheless she stood up." (hiʼnahkuškan "nevertheless, in spite of that"); ʔaʼhakʔĭhč, wihpɛʼkanik-ʔahčá "Otherwise I shall hit you." (ʔaʼhakʔihč "otherwise, if not, or"); ʔonʔiʼlĭn, ʔaʼhakʔĭhč, ʔeʼnihkŭn, simiʼrukɔʼnì "He would swallow two or three people."

§7:39. Exclamatives are always used as little sentences within themselves. They include true exclamatives, such as ʔahâ "No!" dâ "Now! Ready!" hōn "Yes" and also imitatives, such as yuwénš imitating the sound of cicadas, čuwí, imitating the call of the killdeer.

THE MILPA ALTA DIALECT OF AZTEC
WITH NOTES ON THE CLASSICAL AND THE TEPOZTLÁN DIALECTS

BENJAMIN LEE WHORF

1. INTRODUCTORY

§1. Aztec is by far the largest language of the Utaztecan (Uto-Aztecan, UA) stock in number of speakers. For that matter, it is the largest native language of North America, approached only by Maya in size. In the classification of the stock by the author and J. Alden Mason, Aztec is the name given to a number of closely similar, mutually intelligible dialects of Central Mexico, all distinguished by λ ('tl') as representing original UA *t before UA *a. This linguistic area merges into a fringe of dialects closely related to Aztec, but having t in place of λ. There is less mutual intelligibility among these dialects than within Aztec itself, and some of the dialects well distant from the central territory rank as separate, mutually un-intelligible languages, Pochutla being probably the most distinct. Aside from these the group forms in a broad sense one language, Nahuatl, and including these a subfamily, Nahuatlan, of the Aztecoidan family (containing also Cora and Huichol) of Utaztecan. The following is a simplified version of Mason's and Whorf's classi-fication of Nahuatlan:

Nahuatlan
- Nahuatl
  - Aztec
    - Central: Classical, Milpa, Alta, Xochimilco, Tezcoco, etc.
    - Eastern: Puebla, Tlaxcala, etc.
    - Southern: Tepoztlán, Cuauhtla, etc.
    - Western: various
  - Nahuat—not a linguistic unity; collective term for the t-dialects. The southernmost is Pipil (Nicaragua).
- Pochutla (of Pochutla, Oaxaca, few speakers, perhaps now extinct) perhaps a few others—unclassified

§2. The speakers of Nahuatlan are believed to number something over a mil-lion, of whom the greater part, probably nearly a million, are speakers of Aztec. "Aztec" is a familiar word, deriving from the Aztec astekaλ "person of asλan" (the legendary home of the Aztecs) and adopted into all European languages (Azteco, Aztèque, Aztekisch, etc.). This familiarity and traditional use in a sense substantially like that above make "Aztec" the logical term for the language, far preferable to "Nahuatl," which has often been used for all dialects besides Classical

367

Aztec. In Mexico however the term Aztec is little used, the language being called in Spanish usually Mexicano, and in Aztec itself ma·sewalkopa "in Indian fashion."

§3. "Classical Aztec" (Cl) at the time of the Conquest was the dialect of populous Mexico City (meši ʔko or teno·čtiλan) and the surrounding Valley of Mexico. Soon reduced to writing, it became a notable literary vehicle; and the mass of chronicles, town annals, traditional histories, songs, poems, grammars, the great dictionary of Molina, and the native ethnographic texts gathered by Sahagún form a literature of great interest to the Americanist. The language is no longer spoken in Mexico City, though various scholars there keep alive its literary traditions, but it is still the native speech of Indian towns in and around the Valley. The dialect of the village of Milpa Alta, D.F., spoken by a few hundred people, is one of these survivals, in my opinion one of those which are most like Cl.

§4. My studies of Cl were pursued from documentary evidence away from Mexico, until by means of a Grant-in-Aid from the Social Science Research Council, New York, I was able to visit Mexico and study the dialects of Milpa Alta and Tepoztlán, Morelos, in the winter and early spring of 1930. My main informant at Milpa Alta was Milesio Gonsales, with some material also from Luz Jiménez and Pedrita Jiménez. I obtained further valuable insights from Professor D. Mariano Rojas of the National Museum, himself a native of Tepoztlán, but well acquainted with Milpa Alta and a most learned and scholarly exponent of the classical speech. I must record my thanks to all these, and to Miss Anita Brenner for her assistance in finding such excellent informants.

§5. On account of the interest, especially in Mexico, in Cl and the many local dialects, I have tried to make this sketch serve as a guide to them also, taking advantage of the close similarity between Milpa Alta and Cl. Footnotes and remarks in the text have been used to point out the more important differences between MA (Milpa Alta) and Cl. Many differences must of course be ignored in a work of these dimensions. Finally, a note is appended on the markedly different dialect of Tepoztlán, since that town is a favorite field for ethnologists, folklorists, and students of the impact of the old Aztec and the modern cultures.

§6. Aztec is a highly inflecting language using both prefixing and suffixing, the latter to the greater extent, with little internal change and that incidental to affixing processes. Its lexicon is divided into well-marked parts of speech, reminiscent of Indo-European on the whole, yet with differences that the traditional treatment has tended to obscure. Cl especially developed derivation to an astonishing pitch; it is one of the world's most "deriving" languages; compounding also is most abundant and free, and in power of coining new words the language in classical times must have had few equals on the globe. Its vocabulary then was enormous, and pre-Conquest culture had already developed an extensive system of religious, philosophical, and similar 'abstract' terminology. Phonetically simple, morphologically it is complex by the standard of Western European tongues, yet it is one of the simpler of the Utaztecan languages on this score. Mexican Spanish has borrowed heavily from it; and it has given to all modern languages many words, e.g., chocolate, cacao, copal, tomato, istle, chicle, sapote, aguacate, teosinte, peyote, guayule, atlatl, tonalamatl. Finally, the euphony and liquid flowing character of its words, it melodious tonal patterns, its poetic styles and wealth of allusion to the picturesque antique culture of Middle America, add to the enthusiasm with which most students of Aztec, in or out of Mexico, regard it.

2. PROSODICS

Note. These prosodic principles apply only to the native Aztec words. Words borrowed from Spanish may show all the syllabic and accentual possibilities of Spanish.

§1. Syllables. Syllables are of the forms V, VC, CV, CVC. Consonant clusters are hence limited to intersyllabic C-C. They are pronounced with close transition. Geminate clusters are rare except for the extremely common ll, a long l of two pulses. Vocalic clusters occur in syllabic sequences of types V·V and V·VC. They are limited to the common (i+any other V) and the uncommon ao, eo— which however occur in some common words, e.g., λaon 'what?' and teo·λ 'God' and its many derivatives. At first it might seem that (o+any other V) occurs, but it can be shown that such utterances are owV. On the other hand the iV utterances are not iyV, which also occurs, but sounds slightly different in rapid talk, the y then becoming prominent, so that λapiyani approaches λapyani, while in the rapid pronunciation of ia, the common instance of iV, the i tends toward (ı), and in the case of ·tia· with stressed a the result in rapid speech is (tᵊa) with a very short glide ə, or even (t·a), ki·ctiaya becoming ki·ctᵊaya, ki·ct·aya. Moreover the behavior of iyV and iV in certain morphophonemic alternations in which V disappears is different, and the behavior of owV in similar alternations is analogous to that of iyV.[1]

§2. Accent.

§2:1. MA has a stress accent with associated pitch differences. Words over one syllable have primary accent on the penult. This accent consists of loud stress together with one of two varieties of tone-pattern. In 'normal tone-pattern' these varieties are: 1) words ending in ·C, including ʔ, have high tone on penult and low tone on ultima, e.g., í·nòn síwà·λ; 2) words ending in ·V have on penult a tone falling from medium high (less high than the high of pattern one) to medium (higher than 'low') and remaining medium on ultima, e.g., kisâya, kwepô·ni; except that the ultima may show a further slight fall before a pause. Words ending in ·lli e.g., kalli tend to show a compromise with pattern one by often having a nonfalling high tone on the penult, the fall seeming to occur on the long l. One-syllable words usually have stress and a moderately high tone, but a few, marked thus, kà, have low tone and optional stress. This tone-feature alone distinguishes kà "with, by"

---

[1] Viz. ·ia >·i =·owa >·ow (with voiceless w) =·iya >·iš (š a voiceless continuant analogous to voiceless w and probably stemming from pre-Aztec voiceless y).

from ka (high tone) "is": kà no-tómìn "with my money," ká no-tómìn "it is my money."

§2:2. Secondary accents and unaccented syllables have a medium tone and the former a louder stress than the latter, nearly approaching the stress of the primary accent. Secondary accent occurs on: 1) an ultima ending in -C; 2) the first syllable of a long word; 3) alternate syllables before the primary accent except that a short-V open syllable is usually hurried and does not count, and two in succession count as one, e.g., o·'nonokʷep?ia″ya, where no, no, kʷe, and pi are thus hurried.

§2:3. Emphatic tone-pattern. On a word to be emphasized, or the last word of a clause to be emphasized, the stress-feature of the primary accent is unchanged or made louder, but the tone-pattern alters. The last two syllables become low and the antepenult, if any, high and less hurried; e.g., normal ayê″mo "not yet," emphatic áyè″mò! Emphasis appears to be connected with *low-toned* loud stress. There may perhaps be other slight alterations of tone-pattern for questioning and other nuances of the speaker's attitude. Questions do not differ in form from state-ments. They often have the emphatic tone-pattern, and may possibly be signalized by some subtle modification of this pattern, such as I have not yet discovered.

§3. Vowel length. Vowels are "inherently" (morphophonemically) either short or long, and these lengths are maintained in actualization regardless of posi-tion in the word, subject to the following minor alterations: 1) a primary-accented long vowel tends to lose some of its length, especially in rapid speech (though on the contrary long vowels *without* primary accent tend to compensate for their lack of accentual prominence by holding their length well); 2) a primary-accented short vowel is slightly lengthened; 3) there is, increasing with speed of talk, the hurrying of short-V open syllables mentioned in §2:2(3). In some common expres-sions such a vowel may disappear, though initially only when a sibilant-stop clus-ter results, e.g., škawa "wait!" ški?ta "see it!" for šikawa, šiki?ta. Long vowels are marked thus: a·. Because of the confusing effect of (1) and (2) to a nonnative, it cannot be guaranteed that vowel length is always correctly shown in this sketch, though I have tried to achieve reasonable exactitude.

§4. Word limits.

§4:1. A word is a prosodic entity in MA, word division always being clear from the penultimate accent. Coordinated with this are other features: secondary stress on beginning of a long word, hurrying occurring only within the word, lack of external sandhi, weakening of word-final n, and restrictions in word-final pho-nemes. No native word ends in -m, and probably none in -e (apparent -e being -e?, -ey), and only a very few in -t. The common C-finals are w, n, s, λ, l, k, ?; others are relatively infrequent. There are different limitations on syllable-final C within words, e.g., no syllable ends in λ within a word. No native word begins in l, nor in ?, though possibly V-initial corresponds to ?-initial—yet there is not, word-initially, the contrast between V and ?V that is possible within words.

§4:2. There is an "enclitic" (possibly a few others), which is prosodized as part of the preceding word and alters the accent like a suffix, but is grammatically grouped in a class of words, i.e., ʻon "that" (syn. of iˑnon), which may refer to preceding or following word but is always prosodized with preceding word, e.g.ʻ siwaˑλon "that woman" but oˑkʻiˀtakon siwaˑλ "he saw that woman." The mor, phological unit λasoˀkamati "thank you" is usually prosodized as λasoˀkamat ì, with primary accent on ka.

§4:3. It follows from the rarity of such distortions that prefixes and suffixes are easily distinguished from independent words, and hence that the bound lexeme of an affix-bearing word is itself easily distinguished from its affixes. To help the reader follow this native ease of analysis I shall henceforth place a hyphen before the lexeme of each prefix-bearing word, thus exposing the initial letter of the lexeme, which will facilitate alphabetic reference, and understanding of cited forms. Thus, certain above-cited forms become- kˑiˑctiaya, oˑnono-kʷeˀkʷepiaya, ši-kawa, šik-iˀta. When it is desired to cite in isolation a lexeme always preceded by some prefix it will be done thus: e.g., ʻiˀta "sees it."

3. PHONEMICS

§1. Consonant phonemes (native).

§1:1. Table of correlated groups.

		Labial	Alve- olar	Alve- olar Lateral	š Position	Mid- Palatal	kʷ Position	Glottal
Voiceless,	Stops	p	t			k	kʷ	?
fortis,	Affricates		c	λ	č			
lightly	Continuants		s	l	š			
aspirated	Semivowels	w				y		
	Nasals	m	n					

§1:2. Allophones. All sequences referred to are sequences in the same word.

1) l, w, syllable-final, unvoiced (but y is not).
2) w, p, word-final, followed by brief voiceless i as off-glide:
   oˑkʷep:(oˑkʷepI̥), oˑ-pew:(oˑpeWI̥).
3) clusters of l, n +w, y, both consonants unvoiced.
4) in ˀw, w unvoiced.
5) k, kʷ before C:x, xʷ.
6) n before k, kʷ:ŋ.
7) k, l before e, i fronted, before a, o receded.

8) unvoiced l after e, i spirantal (ł), after a, o only slightly so, or nonspirantal.

9) ʔ ("aleph" or "saltillo") is postaspirated, strongly so before voiceless
C (λeʔko:[λeʔhko]), so that ʔ sounds somewhat like h and is sometimes written as h. Nevertheless the glottal check can always be
heard before the aspiration except in word-final, when this check is
quite faint. Aztec ʔ must not be likened too much to ʔ in many other
languages, for in Aztec it is in general type a *voiceless* consonant,
strange as that may seem. The glottal feature is a mere check, not a
sonant twang, and is accompanied always by voiceless breath.

§1:3. Speed effects. In moderately rapid speech word-final n tends to become
a nasal echo-vowel: iˑpan >iˑpaᵃ. Before a quickly-following voiceless C the echo-
vowel is unvoiced and resembles a soft voiceless m, n, or ŋ, accommodated to the
following C. In slower speech n usually remains n, though some speakers tend to
drop word-final n entirely; there seems to be a colloquial alternation between this
n and zero, which might be compared to the alternation in English between -iŋ
and -in.

§2. Vowel phonemes (native).

§2:1. These phonemes are: a, e, i, o.

§2:2. Allophones.

	Short Vowel	Long Vowel
e	[ɛ] (lax)	[e] but somewhat lax, and ap-proaching [ɪ]
o	[o] lax and open, but less open than [ɔ] except that before syllable-final l and before ll very close, practically [u]	[o] close, but somewhat lax
i	is always [i] except in the speed-form of ia described in II, §1.	

The speed effects mentioned in II, §1 and 2:2, are the only ones noted of vowels.

§3. Introduced phonemes. Appearing only in loanwords from Spanish are the
introduced phonemes b, δ, g, f, r, rr, h or x, and vowel u, representing Sp. b or
v, d, g, f, r, rr, j, u. Spanish j varies between h and x, and will be written always h,
which sometimes represents not only j but the Spanish vocalic beginning, e.g.,
haˑseyte "oil," Sp. aceite. r patterns after l in being unvoiced in syllable-final and
in unvoicing a following w, which results from Aztec inflection of Spanish loanwords, e.g., tikm-atrabesarwis "you (respectful) will traverse it." Some words introduced early into Aztec were Aztecized in form, e.g., awaš "broad-beans" <Sp.
habas.

4. MORPHOPHONEMICS

§1. Grammatical operations within bound forms:
§1:1.

Incremental	*Internal*	*Tactical*
Affixing (prefixing, suffixing).	Ablaut of stem-final	Compounding.
Reduplication (of word-initial syl.):	vowel (see below).	
a. Simple.		
b. Infixed (with inserted ?, e.g.,	Contraction (see	
k^{w}epa > k^{w}e?k^{w}epa).	below).	

§1:2. A secondary form (sec.) is a form that shows one or more of the above operations in contrast to a related form (primary, pr., or simplex) that does not.

§1:3. Reduplication. It is regularly infixed, but many lexemes are exceptions and use simple reduplication. The distinction appears to be in the lexeme. In simple reduplication the first vowel is usually long, but there are also exceptions to this.

§1:4. Ablaut. a) pr. stem-final -a > sec. -i (iotization, the most common form of ablaut); b) pr. stem-final -a or -i > sec. -o.

§1:5. Contraction. This is loss of final vowel of the pr. in the sec., leaving the sec. ending in C or i.[2] Morphemes which contract are indicated when neces-sary by . . . °.

§2. Automatic morphophonemic processes. 1) pr. m, becoming in sec. sylla-ble-final, becomes n except before p; e.g., -ʎami +contraction > -ʎan. 2) pr. ʎ > sec. t if the morphophoneme (ʎ/t) is not followed by a in the sec.; e.g., ʎaʎa +iotization +-a > ʎatia, a·weweʎ(i) +-ʎan >a·wewetiʎan. 3) pr. 1+pr. ʎ > sec. ll, e.g., kal- +-ʎi <kalli. Process (2) precedes (3), e.g., kal-ʎi-ʎan >kaltiʎan. 4) pr. iw +k > sec. i?k, e.g., -či·wa +contraction +-ke? > -či· ?ke? (this process not in Cl).

§3. Processes incidental to prefixing.

§3:1. The types of prefixes are: 1) *simplex*, which are invariable in form. 2) *contract*, which contract before a vowel, e.g., ni°-a?si >na?si. 3) the prefix ki-, which contracts *after* a V (e.g., ni-k-mati) and *before* i and the prefix on- (k-on-ana) but otherwise is simplex (ki-ana). 4) *duplex*, e.g., i·n^m-, a^y-, the superscript showing the form before V: i·m-a·kal, i·n-ta?cin; a-k^{w}alli, ay-okmo. The n^m type however can be regarded as simplex, and will be written with m, which then >n automati-cally by §2.(1).

§3:2. Initial i followed by C-cluster is eclipsed by differing V of a prefix, even a contract prefix, e.g., mo°- +-i?ta, -ilpia, -ikši >mo·-?ta, no-lpia, mo-kši (a few irregular exceptions, e.g., m-i?towa instead of expected mo-).

§4. Processes incidental to suffixing.

[2] Sometimes also a long V in primary syllable before the vowel to be lost becomes short in the contracted secondary.

§4:1. The types of suffixes are: 1) *regular*, which do not alter the regular forms of the stem. 2) *eliding*, with verbs only, before which ⸐ia⸐ > ⸐i⸐ and ⸐owa⸐ (with certain exceptions) > ⸐o⸐, denoted by superscript zero, e.g., ⸐miktia + ⸐⁰lia > ⸐miktilia. 3) A few suffixes are modified in special ways, herein treated as irregularities. In Cl, ⸐yo > ⸐lo after l, and > ⸐o after a sibilant. This still holds in MA, but also the form ⸐lyo has been restored by analogy, e.g., λapalyoλ "color," Cl λapalloλ.

§5. Processes incidental to compounding. 1) A V-sequence resulting from compounding is broken by interposed ʔ, except for the sequence i +any other V. 2) If the first element of a compound is a noun stem of the contract class (VII, §3:1) it is usually contracted.

§6. Processes in derived forms. Among derivations (IX) are found sporadically changes not accounted for by any of the above principles. These forms date from an earlier stage of the language, preserving certain processes no longer operative because at a previous period they came to be felt as vocabulary items rather than as results of free synthesis. Most of them are easily explained on historical principles, for which a certain amount of historical treatment of the language would be needed. Thus at one time contraction of a stem ending in ⸐i did not completely remove the i but left the stem ending in ⸐y or something similar, which palatalized preceding t, c, s, to č, č, š. Hence, corresponding to te·si "grind" we have te·šλi "flour." In a short descriptive treatment such changes seem best treated as irregularities. The above-mentioned change may be called "palatalization."

5. LEXEMIC CLASSES AND GENERAL TRAITS OF EXPRESSION

§1. Lexemic classes.

§1:1. The lexicon is divided into the following lexemic classes (parts of speech) and subclasses. Three classes are paradigmatic, having extensive systems of inflection except in two subclasses, adjectives and uninflected entitives. Three classes are analytic, or uninflected.

§1:2.

Lexemic classes		Subclasses
1) pronominals		a. pronouns (personal)
		b. pronominal cases, including prepositions
Paradigmatic 2) entitives		a. nouns
		b. adjectives (including adverbials)
		c. uninflected entitives
3) verbs classes of resolution, or resolutions		a. intransitives
	transitives	b. direct terminatives
		c. first causatives
		d. second causatives
		e. applicatives

	4) conjunctions	a. introducers
		b. connectives
Analytic	5) adverbs	
	6) interjections	

§1:3. Selection and overtness. The lexemic classes and subclasses are *selective*, i.e., each is a group of stems not coterminous with the whole lexicon and except to very small extent not overlapping in membership any other group of coordinate rank. Each belongs in just one of the subclasses of one of the main classes and cannot be inflected or handled syntactically except in the manner of that subclass. All these selective groups are moreover overt, not covert as in Hopi. That is, in nearly all sentences there is another indicator of the class and subclass besides selection of the lexeme, an indicator either in the collocation of word neighbors, or in the paradigmatic classes usually by the paradigmatic affixes, which are seldom either zero or like those of another subclass. These affixes cannot be applied to any lexeme, but only to one of the proper sublcass. Change in subclass may be made by the operation of *derivation* (IX), which requires usually different affixes from the paradigmatic ones.

§1:4. Absolutive suffix. In most cases the primary form of the noun paradigm is marked by a special suffix called the absolutive suffix, denoted by the formula -λ(i), which is actualized when word-final after V as -λ, word-final after C as -λi, and word-internal as morphophonemically altered to -ti-, which before V other than a is usually contracted to -t-. Besides occurring in the primary form of most nouns, its internal variant may occur in sec. forms and in the lexeme (stem) of non-nouns derived from nouns. It also occurs final on some adjectives, some uninflected entitives, and the full forms of the pronouns, which syntactically are like entitives, though differently inflected. Hence it may be said to denote the end of an entitive stem.

§2. Types of reference. On the whole the lexemic classes do not refer to distinctly different types of reference, as in Hopi. Both verbs and entitives may refer to action having movement, with only the difference that a verb refers to a particular action as occurring in a particular situation, while an action-entitive ("direct participial," IX §2:1) refers to a class of particular actions (as also does the verb) without like the verb denoting that a particular representative of the class is being singled out for attention. There is also a distinction in type of reference between the two entitive subclasses of nouns and adjectives, but not quite the same distinction as in Western European. It is treated in §3:2.

§3. Entitives.

§3:1. An entitive, noun, adjective, or other, has two *moduli*,[3] the modulus of a *substantive*, and that of a *modifier*. The mark or *signature* of each modulus is

---

[3] Categories freely producible by either inflectional or collocational techniques are called *moduli* in the system used by the author for describing Utaztecan languages. Thus numbers, tenses, aspects, and categories denoted by definite and indefinite articles are moduli.

simply word order. The meaning of the moduli is difficult to define, but fortunately it is a familiar one; in most cases it is very similar to what we understand by substantive and modifier, or head and attribute, in English and Western European generally. An entitive not adjacent to another is a substantive. When two or more entitives or entitive stems are in immediate sequence, bound or free, the last is a substantive, the others all its modifiers—exactly like English, where in e.g., "brick chimney top," "top chimney brick," and "top brick chimney" the last word is a substantive, the others modifiers. Moreover, as in the case of English "red brick chimney" and "brick chimney red," the matter of whether these terms are selectively and paradigmatically nouns or adjectives has no bearing on the substantive and modifier distinction.

§3:2. There is also a semantic distinction between all nouns and all adjectives that deserves some attempt at description since it could scarcely be inferred from Western European analogies, though the author cannot hope to achieve any very good brief definement of the matter. An adjective seems to denote a portion of the objective field of space having a vague outline in which is localized a quality; while a noun denotes 1) portion of the objective field with definite or semidefinite outline (e.g., "house," "man") or 2) generalized class of objective situations (e.g., "running," "color," "whiteness") or 3) generalized class of subjective experience (e.g., "happiness," "anger"). When an adjective is a modifier its sense of vague outline is lost, but when it is a substantive this reference to some specific though vague patch of the external scene seems to be present, and might need to be translated by "something"—which would include "somebody." Thus the adjective "white" as substantive would not mean "whiteness" or "the color white" but rather "white effect" or "something white." "Happy" as substantive would not mean "happiness" but some objective localizer of this quality, "somebody or something happy."[4] If my *Sprachgefühl* is equal to the task of predicting what such a collocation as "brick chimney red" might mean, assuming that it can be said, I should be inclined to think that it would not mean a shade of red like that of a brick chimney but rather a patch of red which turns out to be a brick chimney. Red in the sense of redness is not the substantive adjective but a derived noun.

§3:3. When a quality which we think of as adjectival itself denotes a semidefinite outline, i.e., implies a certain kind of shape, it is referred to usually by a passive participial (IX, §2:2), an entitive derived from a verb and formally a noun. Passive participials are combined with other nouns in bound groupings, i.e., compound words, and in a manner called herein "reversed construction." The participial is treated as the substantive and placed last, the other noun before it as modifier. Thus "narrow" in the sense of long and narrow, is expressed as "narrowed," and "narrow road" as "road narrowed-effect." As passive participials are

---

[4] This is not to be confused with the more specific use of Romance languages in which the adjective denotes a person. Thus čipawak is neither "la hermosa," "the beauty," nor "lo hermoso," "the beautiful"; "cosa hermosa," or "thing of beauty," or "something beautiful" come nearer to it.

described in IX §2:2, it will be noted that they bear prefixes λa- or te-. These are usually omitted in combinations with another noun. "Something narrowed" is λa-picakλi, "road" is o?λi, its bound stem is o?-, hence "narrow road" is o?-picakλi.

§4. Sentences.

§4:1. Types. A sentence may be roughly defined as an utterance that is intelligible though followed by a long pause. A minor sentence is intelligible only with the aid of a recently-occurred context, e.g., the minor sentence "a man" which is intelligible as answer to a question such as "what is that?" A major sentence does not need the support of such a previous context, e.g., "the man ran." Aztec has two types of major sentence, verbal and nonverbal. A verbal sentence contains a verb, the minimal verbal sentence being simply one verb. A nonverbal sentence contains at least two words, representing subject and predicate. The subject comes first and is usually the full form of a pronoun, but may be a noun, especially a construct (i.e., possessed) noun, like "his name." An unpossessed noun as subject is usually followed by a full-form pronoun referring to it; e.g., "John is a man" is expressed "John he man" (hwa·n ye?waλ λa·kaλ). A third person pronoun subject without noun is usually followed by enclitic -on "that," e.g., ye?waλon λa·kaλ "he is a man." A nonverbal sentence cannot be conjugated, expresses a general truth, a predication always applicable to the subject, and is used to translate Spanish ser. A sentence with the verb ka "be" can be conjugated, reports the condition in a particular situation, and is like Sp. estar.

§4:2. Sentence technique. The verb is usually the first paradigmatic word in a verbal sentence, though it is usually preceded by conjunctions (X §2). The verbs "be," "go," and "come" however usually follow the noun subject and are followed by the complement or the word expressing place with reference to motion. With transitive verbs, noun subject and noun object usually follow verb, and it seems to make little difference which comes first. In complex sentences (X) clause connection may require placing either subject or object after the verb. Hence there is much irregular order, and one might think this would make it hard to tell what is subject and object, since nouns have no cases. But probably such confusion rarely occurs, for various reasons. Obviously many combinations of verb, subject, and object are not reversible, e.g., "man eats bread." In many more, e.g., "king punishes slave," the reversal is so improbable that it would be accompanied by an explanatory context. Aztec has extended such lexical particularization as compared with many languages. If "kills bear man" would be ambiguous, one can say "shoots and kills bear man" or use a particularized verb that implies that a nonpersonal object is killed; or the verb inflections which show number of both subject and object may indicate the relation. The "shoots and kills" type of sentence, called "twin verbs," the verbs bearing identical inflections and juxtaposed without any connective, was very common in Cl, not only to give clarity but as a general pattern. Such verbs often were almost or quite synonymous, e.g., "shapes, molds, the workman the clay," the couplet being used like a unitary vocabulary item, and giving greater richness of meaning than a single verb. In fact this syntactic coupling is what corresponds in Aztec to the compounding of bound stems, when the stems to be combined are all verbal. The pattern is still found to some extent in MA.

§5. Compounding. Compounding requires that all stems in the compound but the last must be entitive stems; the last may be either an entitive or a verb. It is a common and freely used technique, but there is not enough combination of ele-ments for it to be called polysynthesis; compounds are essentially binary, and in most cases only two stems are combined. When more than two are combined, it is as a binary whose parts are compounds. The parts stand in the modifier-modified relation, and the modifier-substantive construction already described may be worked out either as a compound or as a syntactic group. The two are easily dis-tinguished since the compound is one word by its accent and morphophonemic processes, but they have practically the same meaning. When the first term is an adjective the syntactic group is preferred; when a noun, the bound compound, although the syntactic group may still be used. The first term of a compound is usually a bare noun stem, contracted if the noun is of the contract class, or it may be a noun with absolutive suffix in form -ti- (this type is associated today with derived verbal nouns, also found in old petrified compounds), or an adjective, usu-ally in adverbial form with suffix -ka-. If the final is a transitive verb the antece-dent may refer to its object ("incorporated object") in which case the verb is inflected like an intransitive, without pronominal object, e.g., mepam-po?powa "weeds agave-row(s)," <mepami°-λ <me-λ "agave," pami°-λ "row." But the an-tecedent is basically a modifier, and its equivalence to an object is conditioned by grammatical logic; e.g., λe·-kʷepo·ni (intransitive verb, no object) "bursts *from the action of* fire (λe-λ)." Cl λa-šoči?-i?kʷilowa (transitive with transitive inflection) "paints or engraves something (λa-) *with* flowers, floral designs (šočiλ "flower')."

§6. Reverentials and diminutives. Aztec abounds in polite and respectful forms of verbs and nouns, for which the term "reverential" of the old grammarians will be used. In verbs, the reverential is a technique of using two-object verbs, explained in VIII §10:6 and has no diminutive sense. In nouns it is formed by the suffix -cin(-λi), an "affective," having a sort of diminutive sense, for which the term "diminished augmentative" may be used. It implies that a thing is great but the speaker's contact with it is of diminished degree, modest, humble. Used of a person or his possessions it thus implies respect. It also has a very limited use with natural phenomena, apparently in the sense that a small portion of some great and wide-spread phenomenon is being dealt with; e.g., water in domestic use, or the water of a tank or well is a·-cinλi, <a·-λ, water in nature; while "a day" is tonal-cinλi <tonal-li "sun, daytime, light." Another diminutive, -ton(-λi) is not reverential and means that the thing is small, e.g., piltonλi "boy." In MA the reverential is largely confined to verbs and nouns and second person subject or possessor and has become equated to the Spanish use of Usted. It is impolite to use the reverential of oneself; thus "my house" is no-kal; "your house," polite, is mo-kalcin. But where

"my" does not refer to ownership but to kinship or a social relation, it is no bar to polite use of the revential. "My mother" is always no-nancin.

§7. Intrusions from Spanish. Spanish has contributed various prepositions, conjunctions, and adverbs, e.g. para, por, pos or pwes; ko·sa, <cosa, is an adverb "very." The Spanish element que is usually dropped: mientras for mientras que. There are loan translations of many Spanish or Mexican Spanish idioms, e.g., ika ni·kan "this way," ika ompa "that way" (por acá, por allá); kà kema, kà amo (que sí, que no); a·ša·n kema (ahora sí); kenin amo "certainly" (como no); k-iʔtosneki "it means" (quiere decir); use of ye "already" with preterite for a past perfective (Sp. ya with preterite). Spanish verbs are used by adding -owa to the infinitive: ki-atrabesarowa "he traverses it" (Sp. atravesar). These Hispanisms have not made for any substantial alteration in Aztec grammar.

6. THE PRONOMINAL AND CASE SYSTEM

§1. Pronouns (personal pronouns).

§1:1. Table of forms

	Full form (independent word)	Base (bearing suffixes, or used as prefix)	Other forms
Singular			
1	neʔwaλ, or neʔwa?	no°-	The system of verb prefixes,
2	teʔwaλ, teʔwa?	mo°-	subject, object, and reflexive,
3	yeʔwaλ, yeʔwa?	i·-	listed under Verb System,
Plural			VIII (the verbal first &
1	teʔwantin, teʔwan	to°-	second person reflexives are
2	ameʔwantin, ameʔwan	am-	identical with bases in pre-
3	yeʔwantin, yeʔwan	i·m-	ceding column)
	Indefinite te-		

§1:2. Full forms are used chiefly as subjects of nonverbal sentences (V §4:1). Bases are used as prefixes to nouns, in which case they are possessive pronouns (VII §3:2), and as bases for the suffixes of the case system, e.g., no-teč "to me," i·-pan "at it."

§2. Case system.

§2:1. This system is a vocabulary of suffixes, of which some of the commonest are:

-teč (third sing. -ʔteč) to, for, pertaining to
-pan in, at (locative)
-ʔitik (third sing. i·tik) within
-ka (third sing. ika, kà, or i·k) by (with)
-kpak over, & in the direction over
-cinλan under, & in the direction under

-kopa in the manner of
-pampa for (ethical)
-λakʷ with (sociative)
-na·wak near
-xwan and (chiefly used in third sing. i·wan or wan)

§2:2. Sometimes suffixes are added to noun stems, e.g., ma·sewalkopa "in the manner of Indians, in Aztec (language)" < ma·sewalli "commoner, Indian." In general this is not done. Usually such a form as kalpan "in the house," λe·kʷilpan "on the hearth" is archaic or literary, or it might be idiomatic in that particular case, much as in English "homeward" is idiomatic but "dogward" is not, though a possible form. To apply the case relations to nouns in general, the third sing. (third plural rarely, even for plural nouns) base form is used as a *preposition*, e.g., i·pan kalli, i·pan λe·kʷilli. Some case forms seem to be used only on third singular base, e.g., i·ʔki (Cl i·w, i·wki) "like it, likewise, like ...."

§2:3. The ideas of "to" and "from," purely motional or directional, are not handled by cases, but by the verb, which is given (if it does not have lexically) a centrifugal or a centripetal (VIII §1:3 on, wal, VIII §5 ·tiw, ·kiw) sense, and the noun is placed after the verb, before which is often one of the adverbs ompa "there, thither," ni·kan "here, hither," onkan "there, thence," e.g., ompa o·ni·ya no·kal "I went to my house," lit. "thither went my house." The noun is not the verb's object and is not represented by an objective prefix.

§2:4. Suffixes with directional meaning are attached to the base λa- (VIII §1:6) for directional adverbs, e.g., λakpak "upward, up," λacinλan "downward, down," and through Spanish analogy we find e.g., ika λakpak "por arriba."

§2:5. Aztec place names are *ipso facto* in a locational case-relation and end in a case suffix, e.g., kʷaw·na·wak "Cuernavaca" or rather "at Cuernavaca," lit. "near tree(s)." Usually place names do not have a "regular" suffix like ·na·wak (though ·pan is common) but special ones which are found in MA only on place names and derived common nouns of place in ·λan, ·kan, etc. (IX §3). These suffixes are ·k, ·ko, ·λan, ·λa, ·kan, ·yan, ·ya. It is idiomatic to relate speaker's position to place by an adverb, e.g., ompa meši·ʔko "in Mexico City" (speaker in Milpa Alta), ni·kan meši·ʔko id., speaker in Mexico City. These suffixes are found attached either to a noun, e.g., to ama·λ "Ficus tree" or to its stem (ama·-): ama·tiλan or ama·λan "(at) Ficus-grove," Amatitlán, Amatlán.[5]

7. THE ENTITIVE SYSTEM

§1:1. Entitives contrast among themselves in three ways: 1) nouns/adjectives/uninflected entitives, 2) substantives/modifiers, 3) radical entitives/derived entitives. For (1) and (2) see V §1:2, 3:1. Radical entitives are determined selectively (in the lexeme) as nouns, adjectives, or uninflected entitives. Derived entitives are determined as nouns or adjectives by derivative suffixes. Any entitive, radical or derived, can be converted from noun or adjective to the other by derivation or superposed derivation; theoretically derivations can be superposed indefinitely (IX).

[5] The Spanish accent on ultima applies only to the Hispanized version of Aztec place names; in Aztec they are accented on the penult.

§1:2. The *absolute suffix* -λ(i) is attached to the absolute state singular of all nouns with the minor exceptions noted in §3:4 and to some radical adjectives, e.g., kʷalli "good," yekλi "right." When it is word-final after V, (-i) does not occur, e.g., λa·ka·λ "man," though λaka?·λi "day." Derivative suffixes usually add to the absolutive suffix, which then becomes -ti- (IV §2 (2)). Sometimes however these suffixes add directly to the stem (contracted if a contract noun), the absolutive suffix being dropped.

§2. Inflections and categories.

§2:1. Nouns have the moduli of *state*, absolute and construct (the latter inflected for person and number of possessor); of *number*, singular and plural; of the *affectives*, all the foregoing determined inflectionally; and of *determination*, indefinite and definite, for which the signatures are special modifiers (articles).

§2:2. Adjectives have two moduli: *primary* and *adverbial*, to be referred to for simplicity as adjectives and adverbials. The ideas of comparison are expressed unsystematically by various lexemes, thus not being grammatical categories in Aztec.

§3. Nouns.

§3:1. Nouns occur in three isosemantic classes ('declensions'): *simplex class*, in which the "construct base" is the primary stem (the word minus -λ(i)), e.g., kalli "house" >no·kal "my house"; *contract class*, in which it is the stem contracted, e.g., komiλ "pot" >no·kon "my pot"; and w-class, in which it is the stem extended by -w, e.g., siwa·λ "woman, wife" >no·siwa·w "my wife." Stems ending in -C are simplex, those in -V are selectively apportioned among the three classes. Nouns not using -λ(i) are simplex except that those in -ki are w-class, construct base in -kaw.

§3:2. The *construct state* consists of the construct base with a pronominal base as prefix: no·kal "my house," t-a·kal "our boat," i·kone·w "his child," te·si? "somebody's grandmother"—the base te- means "somebody's, one's, people's." Also to- "our" can be used in an indefinite sense, e.g., "our father" as "the father of any one of us." Kinship terms occur in context only as construct, but their *absolute state* (nonconstruct) can perhaps exist in isolation as the "official" name form of the word, as in dictionaries. For a noun possessor, e.g., "the child's house" the form is "the child his house": kone·λ i·kal. In the plur. of w-class nouns, -w becomes -wan: no·kone·wan "my children"; -wan is also added in the plural of a few simplex nouns. The subject prefixes of the verb system (VIII §1:2) are sometimes added to absolute state nouns with the meaning of a pronoun in apposition: ti-knoλaka? or ti-pobres "we poor people." In Cl (at least) they could be added to constructs: tino·kniw "thou my friend."

§3:3. Plural. Nouns are divided into several selective classes according to formation of plural, as follows, these classes being distinct from the three classes of construct base.

Plural class and membership	*Operation from singular > plural*
a. many stems in ⸱V, few in ⸱l, ⸱n	⸱λ(i) > ⸱me⁊ (sometimes + reduplication)
b. many stems in ⸱C	⸱λ(i) > ⸱tin (< ⸱me⁊, loss of ⁊, added upon ⸱λ(i) and contracted)
c. many contract nouns	construct base + ⸱tin
d. derived nouns in suffixes viz.:	⸱k, ⸱ki > ⸱ke⁊ ⸱wa⁊ > ⸱wa⁊ke⁊ ⸱(y)o⁊ > (y)o⁊ke⁊
e. many stems in ⸱V	⸱λ(i) > ⸱⁊ (usually + reduplication)
f. various, see §§3:4(2), 3:6	reduplication alone
g. Spanish loans, except "horse"	Spanish plural in ⸱s
h. few, e.g., kawayo "horse"	irregular, e.g., > kawa⁊tin

These rules apply to the absolute state. In construct the only difference is that ⸱me⁊ and ⸱tin become ⸱wan, ⸱ke⁊ becomes ⸱kawan, rarely ⸱wan is added irregularly. The Aztec plural appears to be an optional modulus, and is often not used when the plural sense is otherwise clear, as with a numeral or a modifier connoting plurality. This is less true of the borrowed plural in ⸱s, which is generally used as it would be in Spanish, but not always, e.g., na·wi pe·so "four pesos."

§3:4. The absolutive suffix is not found in 1) derived nouns in ⸱k, ⸱ki, ⸱wa⁊, ⸱(y)o⁊, ⸱ni (type a. plural ⸱nime⁊), or place⸱suffixes; 2) nouns in ⸱lin (type f.) and a few in ⸱in, ⸱an (λackan); 3) affectives, with some special exceptions; 4) in Cl, some personal names, especially stems in ⸱l, e.g., teskawicil (personal names in Milpa Alta today are all Spanish).

§3:5. Determination. A singular noun is in either definite or indefinite determination. Definite, similar in meaning to a noun with definite article, is the zero form, either absolute or construct. The indefinite cannot be construct and is the absolute state preceded by the indefinite article senteλ or sente or its substitutes, e.g., se "one," oksenteλ "another." In the plural the whole category of determination is absent.[6]

§3:6. Affectives. These forms indicate feeling⸱attitude toward the referent. They are the diminutives ⸱ton, ⸱pil, the diminished augmentative and reverential

[6] This system of two determinations with the *indefinite* article, the one expressed, is rather unusual and historically interesting. It derives from Spanish un, una, but disregards the Spanish el, la, as well as the plural unos, unas, and it reverses the system of Cl. In Cl the indefinite was the zero form, the definite was either the construct or the absolute preceded by in "this" (unemphatic) used like a definite article (it was also used frequently before personal proper names). The later imitation of Spanish may have arisen through trade, where there was much counting and saying "one"; for Cl sente "one unit" (lit. "one⸱stone") was used as a counter. It was evidently Spanish un, and not the contrasting el, that struck the Aztecs as most significant. This fitted the pattern of Aztec verbs, in which the subject "*the* one, he" is unexpressed (zero form) but "*a* one, someone" as subject is expressed by an uninflected entitive. Hence imitation of Spanish seems to have reversed the Aztec pattern and at the same time made it more Aztec, or more internally consistent, and less Spanish, than before!

-cin, and in Cl the augmentative -pol. In MA only -ton and -cin are widely used (see V §6). The suffix adds to the stem, sometimes the contracted stem. The final -λ(i) is omitted except in certain words, e.g., a·cinλi "(some) water," λe·cinλi "(a) fire," siwa·pilli "lady," piltonλi "boy," but however siwanton[7] "girl." Plural re-duplicates both stem and suffix: pipiltoton "boys," sisiwantoton "girls." Redupli-cation of stem alone yields a more diminutive and colloquial form of singular: pipiltonλi, sisiwanton.

§4. Adjectives. Adjectives are determined either by the derivational opera-tions -k, -ti-k contrasting with primaries not showing these operations, or selec-tively, in which case they often show the suffix -k though there is no contrasting primary, or again they may lack -k and have -λ(i), e.g., kʷalli "good." Substantive adjectives have no number and state distinctions like nouns. Occasionally, in imita-tion of Spanish, adjectives take the affective -cin, usually with reduplication: kʷakʷalcin "pretty," imitating Sp. bonito.

§4:1. The *adverbial* is denoted by -ka (adjectival -k > -ka), e.g., yekλi > yektika "rightly," čikawak "strong" > čikawaka "strongly." This adverbial is also the "adjectival base" for derivation, e.g., yekλi + deriv. -yoλ > yektikayoλ "right-ness."

§5. Uninflected entitives. These words behave syntactically like entitives and may be substantitives or modifiers in the same way, but cannot take case suffixes like pronouns and have no systematic inflections, though a few have op-tional plurals, adverbials, etc., which are rather supplementary lexemes than inflec-tions. Here are many words traditionally called pronouns, herein termed *substitu-tions*, and the *quantifiers*, including the numerals and words like miyak "much, many," noči "all,"[8] keškič "how much?" The numerals actually have inflections, though not those of the entitive system, denoting combining-forms, ordinals, and repetitives. The substitutions may be classified as demonstratives, interrogatives, indefinites, relatives, and (indefinite) articles, e.g., "a," "a one," "another," which are also in a sense quantifiers.

8. THE VERB SYSTEM

§1. Prefix-system of the verb.

§1:1. The verbal prefix-system denotes the modulus *of pronominal reference* (consisting of subject, object, and reflexive references), and certain noncategorized notions. It is thus tabulated:

[7] The first n in siwanton, < siwa·λ "woman," is perhaps an importation from the branch of Aztec represented by the Tepoztlán dialect (Southern Aztec), in which it could be accounted for his-torically.

[8] Cl moči or i·skič, the latter also found in MA.

position 1	position 2 pron. subject	position 3 definite pron. object	position 4 direction, optional	position 5 reflexive object	position 6 indefinite pron. object	position 7 verb stem
	singular	singular		singular		
o·	1 ni°	1 ne·č	centrifugal	1 no°	impersonal	
ye o·	2 ti°	2 mi·c	on	2 mo°	λa	
or yo·	3 ẕero	3 ki	centripetal	3 mo°	personal	
	plural	plural	wal	plural	te	
	1 ti°	1 te·č		1 to°		
	2 am	2 ame·č		2 mo°		
	3 ẕero	3 kim		3 mo°		
	imperative			ne (indefinite as to person)		
	2 ši° (sing. or plur.)					

§1:2. Peculiarities of the prefix ki are treated in IV §3:1(3). Before k·on, ni, ti, ši assimilate to nokon, tokon, etc.; on before no, mo loses n. o·, yo· denote past time (§3:2).

§1:3. Use of on and wal is optional and often greatly changes the sense: wal "hither" changes ideas of going, sending, to those of coming, bringing; on intensifies the idea of onward, away. Both can be used a) with verbs of motion, b) with most transitives, giving a directional idea to the transference from subject to object, e.g., kon·ana "onward·gets it, goes and gets it." These elements inserted among preposed pronominals are strikingly comparable to French y and en.

§1:4. Resolutions. Use of the pronominal prefixes depends on the two categories of *resolution*, transitive and intransitive, every verb form being one or the other. These are either selective (in the lexeme) or modulated, i.e., determined by the moduli of voice or terminative; e.g., passive voice is always intransitive. Subject prefixes are not affected by resolution and are obligatory, even with an independent pronoun subject.

§1:5. Subject number is also shown by final plural suffix of verb, an element tied up with the prefix·system. These suffixes are: for preterite, perfective and future ·keʔ (save in a few irregular verbs), for imperative ·kan, otherwise ·ʔ. These pluralizers distinguish "they" from "he" and "we" from "thou."

§1:6. Object prefixes (including reflexive and indefinite) are used only with transitives and are obligatory with them, e.g., ki·či·wa kalli "he makes the house" (one cannot say simply či·wa). For indefinite object, te "someone, people" is used for persons, λa "something, things" for impersonals (things, animals), e.g., λa·či·wa "he makes something," te·λasoʔλa "he loves someone": contrast k·iʔkʷilowa "he writes it" and λa·ʔkʷilowa "he writes"; k·iʔtowa "he says it" and λa·ʔtowa "he speaks." As the total scheme of meanings is often well summed up by the indefinite and reflexive uses alone, a convenient form of lexical citation is e.g., ·polowa: λa· "lose, destroy," mo· "be lost, be lacking, fail" etc. The unspecified reflexive ne "oneself, self" appears in derivatives, e.g., mo·miktia "kills himself" >ne·miktilisλi "killing oneself, suicide."

§2. Isosemantic verb classes (conjugations).

§2:1. Class A. Preterite stem by contraction of primary (e.g., temi >ten, ·či·wa >·či·w), with word·final y >š: ·piya >·piš, ·yokoya >·yokoš, (and ·ˀ added to V, e.g., ·λalia >·λaliˀ. This only in Cl).

Note. Aztec has a few irregular verbs, some with suppletion in certain forms, which cannot be described fully in this sketch. Most have an irregular preterite of the contractive type: yaw "go" > ya, walaw "come" >wala, wi·c "come" >wi·c, ami "hunt" >aˀ, ay "do" >aš.

§2:2. Class B. Pret. stem by eliding·suffix ·⁰k, e.g., ·nami >namik, λalia > ·λalik, čolowa > čolok. All passives are class B: či·walo > či·walok.

Note. In MA nearly all verbs in ·ia, ·owa are B, but in Cl all were A, e.g., ·λali, čolow. A very few irregular verbs have pret. in ·ka, e.g., ka "be" >katka, mani "extend" >manka.

§2:3. Thematic conjugation. Some of these verbs are A, some B, but all form one group on another level of similarity. The stem is a "theme" consisting of the ultimate lexeme ("root") plus a "theme suffix": ·wa, ·na, ·ca, which are A, ·wi, ·ka, which are B, ·ni which is A unless it contrasts with ·na on the same root, when it is B. A long vowel becoming final in sec. shortens. Thus kʷepo·ni >kʷepon, ·koto·na >·koton, koto·ni >koto·nik. The suffixes are a part of the derivational system (see IX) that is too complex to be treated herein; some make transitive verbs, some intransitives, and they have other slight nuances of difference; a given suffix is constant throughout a paradigm except in certain types of *aspect* (§4) but may change in derivatives. Many of the thematic verbs are of a type of meaning (outline or shape manifestation) recalling the k·class verbs of Hopi.

§3. Tense·aspect system.

§3:1. There are seven tense·aspects, unit forms which are systematically related as the product of three implicit tenses and three implicit primary aspects, less two forms missing. The tenses are past, present, future; Cl had a fourth, remote past (called "pluperfect"), with suffix ·ka; it may still exist in moribund condition. Besides the three primary aspects of this system, some one of which is always present, verbs can receive as secondary aspects: two repetitive aspects, two transference aspects, ten auxiliary aspects. The three primary aspects are *simple, imperfective, perfective*. The simple denotes a single act or a motion or state of short duration, unless durativized by one of the secondary aspects. The imperfective is durative, a continuing action or state, either unterminated or terminated in the past. Its present tense form includes the idea of having begun in the past, or in dependent clauses is timeless, time being shown by the main clause. In main clauses its *present* tense usually denotes *past* action, being used much like the Spanish imperfect. Its past tense emphasizes the past idea. Its present can express a usitative nuance, without time distinction. Future imperfective is a future durative. Perfective denotes completion in either recent or remote past ("has done, had done") and is a loan translation of Spanish. "Preterite" will be used for convenience in-stead of "simple past." In the following table, pr. denotes "primary" (="present stem"), pr·st. "preterite stem."

§3:2. Tabulation of tense-aspect system and its formative operations:

Primary aspects	Present	Past	Future
simple	(pr.)	o·-(pr·st.)	(pr.)-ºs
imperfective	(pr.)-ya	o·-(pr.)-ya	o·-(pr.)-ºsskia
perfective	lacking	ye o·-(pr·st.) or yo·-(pr·st.)	lacking

Note. Irregular verbs wi·c "come," -wikac "bring ' have no future, except suppletion by verbs walaw and -walmika of similar meaning. With ka "be," future is yes on suppletive stem ye-.

§4. Repetitive aspects. 1) *frequentative*, denoting continued pulsing of the action, when the stem meaning does not preclude this, is formed by reduplication. In thematic verbs the theme suffix -ni (and sometimes -wi or others) is replaced by -ka: kʷeyo·ni "flashes (once)" >kʷeʔkʷeyo·ka "is flashing." 2) *intensive frequenta-tive*, only in thematic verbs, increases the idea of intensity or force in the frequenta-tive, from which it differs only by substituting -ca for all other theme suffixes: kʷeʔkʷeyo·ca "is flashing violently or intensely."

§5. Transference aspects. 1) centrifugal: (pr.) +-ºtiw present (-ºtiweʔ plural). -ºto past, -ºti imperative (see §7). 2) centripetal: similarly -ºkiw, -ºkiweʔ, º-ko, -ºki. The imperfective row and future column of forms is lacking. 1) Denotes motion away to be ended in the action ("goes to do it"); 2) denotes motion hither to be ended in the action ("comes to do it"); e.g., -či·wa >ki-či·watiw "goes to make it," -λalia >o·mo-λaliko "came to seat himself."

§6. Auxiliary aspects. These are compounds of an entitive base derived from the verb with ten independently existing verbs, the auxiliary verbs. The sense is derived from the meaning of the auxiliary, but in Cl, which richly developed these forms, they practically constituted a set of aspects supplementing the other aspects and extending their powers of expression. The auxiliary is suffixed to (pr.) -ºti·, e.g., with auxil. ka "be" and mo-λalia "sits," o·mo-λalitikatka "he was sitting," mo-λalitiyes "he will be sitting." The auxiliaries are: 1) ka "be" =continuative; 2) nemi "walk, travel" ="goes along doing it"; 3) wi·c "come" ="comes doing it"; 4) mani "extend, lie" ="goes around doing it, does it all around (over an area), extends around in such a state," e.g., kiyawtimani "rains all around"; 5) ikak "stand" ="stands in such a state" of things erect; 6) ewa "lift" =nondurative, moves or starts into the action, or simply an inceptive, kon-anatewa "starts for-ward to get it" (-ana); 7) momana and 8) mote·ka, both "settle down," the former with an idea of spreading also, idiomatic in use; 9) kisa "go forth" and 10) weci "fall," nondurative and vigorous launching-forward inceptives, e.g., -kʷitiweci "dashes upon and takes (-kʷi)." Only the -ka form and perhaps a few others seem to be common now in MA.

§7. Imperative. Formed with imperative subject prefix ši-, present stem with final -ia, -owa > -i, -o, (and for the transference aspects as in 5), to which for plural subject is suffixed -kan. A related form called optative in Cl grammars is of doubtful existence in MA; the same may be said of a Cl form called subjunctive.

§8. Order of suffixes with reference to any stem or base taken as origin, is 1), nearest to the stem, derivatives, 2) terminatives, 3) derived entitive stem in -ti-, 4) auxiliary aspect, 5) voice, 6) transference aspect, 7) tense-aspect, 8) number. Thus, taking from §6 above the form k-on-ana-t-ewa, pref.-pref.-stem (ana)- (3) to (4), and adding the applicative suffix -ili (a terminative, 2), and the simple future 7) and plural 8) suffixes, we get k-on-ani-li-t-ewa-s-ke?.

§9. Voices: *Direct voice*, zero form, corresponds to the English active, but in some cases has a stative meaning, e.g., maya-na "is hungry." *Passive voice* can be formed from any transitive direct voice, and intransitivizes it and reverses subject and object like the English passive. It is formed by -ᵒlo, e.g., ki-λatia "burns it," λatilo "is burned," except that thematic verbs in -na, -ka, and some anomalous verbs in -a passivize by -a > -o. The *essive* occurs in Cl, may or may not be present in MA; by contraction +-tok, from transitives; it intransitivizes and reverses but indicates resulting state, inactive, e.g., ki-λapana "breaks it" > λapantok "lies broken." It is defective as to tense-aspects, and has only this form, probably a preterite but capable of a present sense.[9]

§10. Terminatives.

§10:1. The terminatives; direct (i.e., primary transitive), causatives, and applicative, are moduli of the transitive resolution, indicating a relation of action to object. Similarly the voices, considering the direct voice only when it is intransitive, are moduli of the intransitive resolution. Just as the voices may be applied to transitives, making them intransitives, the nondirect terminatives may be applied to intransitives, except essives and some passives, transitivizing them.

§10:2. The *direct* terminative, zero form, is simply the ordinary selective transitive, considered as a member of the system of terminatives instead of simply as a resolution or transitive. Thus -či-wa "makes," -λasa "throws" are inherently or selectively transitive, i.e., direct terminatives.

§10:3. The *first causative* makes a transitive from an intransitive: "causes it to be ..." (the condition denoted by the intransitive), e.g., kaša-ni "becomes loose" > ki-kaša-nia "loosens it." Usually the first causative must be learned along with its primary as a lexical item, the formation being various (sometimes irregular) as follows: 1) thematics in -ni, -wi often by -i > -a. 2) some others by -i > -a. 3) verbs in -iwi > -owa. These (1, 2, 3) are simply pairs of parallel ablaut verbs in -i and -a, and either or both forms could be considered primary. From the standpoint of general pattern consistency and also the historical standpoint the -i forms ap-

---

[9] It should also be said that the reflexive pronominal reference often has a medio-passive sense and, while formally a transitive, it is much used as the semantic equivalent of intransitivizing a transitive; but it is not formally a voice.

pear more secondary (iotizations), but from the standpoint of applying the causa-tive technique they are the primary. 4) by either ˑi or ˑa >ˑia (this is common, even for thematic verbs in ˑni). 5) by contraction +ˑtia, 6) by ˑ⁰ltia. Passives in ˑlo are transitivized by method 5, the contraction of ˑlo yielding this same form ˑltia, which form has probably spread by analogy and become an independent suffix. 7) a few in ˑo and ˑowa >ˑwia. 8) some quite irregular, but ending in ˑtia, ˑlia, ˑwia; several show ˑlowa >ˑločtia.

§10:4. The *second causative* uses methods 4, 5, 6, 7, or 8 to make a verb al-ready transitive into a two-object transitive, "causes him (or it) to . . . it": ki-či·wa "makes it" >ki-či·waltia "makes him make it, makes him do it." If the prefixes referring to the two objects would be the same, only one is used, if ki-kim, only kim is used, otherwise both are used. In combinations with another objective prefix the indefinites and the reflexive are always the object of the lexeme idea, e.g., kiλa-či·waltia "makes him make something"; apparently one cannot say "make someone make it." Transitives of over two syllables in ˑowa use method 7 >ˑwia, most others 6 (ˑltia), some 4, 5, 8.

§10:5. The *applicative* converts a transitive into a two-object transitive with direct and indirect objects (indirect in sense of "to, for"), with prefixes used as in the second causative, e.g., ki-či·wilia "makes it for him," kiλa-či·wilia "makes some-thing for him." The formative methods are: a) most often, iotization, and to the result ˑ⁰lia (this may be denoted ˑⁱlia). b) verbs in ˑlowa, ˑrowa, >ˑlwia, ˑrwia. c) sometimes ˑ⁰ltia like (6) for causatives. d) sometimes aside from (b) like (7) for causatives. e) a few quite irregular, e.g., k-iˀtowa "say it" >k-iˀtalwia "says it to him." In methods (b), (c), (d) the applicative would be like the second causative, but these are mostly verbs in which second causative would not be used, or ˑ⁰lia may be added, giving applicatives in ˑlwilia, ˑlitlia, ˑwilia. The verbs k·ilwia "says it to," ki-maka "gives it to," ki-nanankilia "answers (it to) him" are applicatives without underlying direct forms.

§10:6. The *reverential* is the use of a two-object transitive in reflexive, making it equivalent to a one-object transitive, or of a first causative in reflexive, equating it to an intransitive. Thus to say "you walk" one would say "you cause yourself to walk." The idea seems to be "you deign to walk" and so indicates respect (see V §6). For a transitive reverential, with two-object transitive, the applicative is generally used rather than the second causative, e.g., tikmo-ma·kištilis "you will set him free (ˑma·kištia)." The idea seems to be that here the *reflexive* object is the indirect one: "you will set him free for yourself," i.e., if you think it to your inter-est, "if you please," you will set him free. Suppletive reverential stems are used in the case of yaw "go" (>mika) and ka "be" (reflexive of ˑe·ctika, an auxiliary aspect in ˑka). For reverential reflexives the regular reflexive is used suffixing ˑ⁰cinowa, e.g., timo-λalicinos "you will sit down (seat yourself)."[10]

---

[10] The source of this form seems to be a verb ˑcinowa meaning "apply the suffix ˑcin to, treat politely or considerately."

9. THE DERIVATIONAL SYSTEM

§1. Derivation.

§1:1. In Aztec the derivation of lexemic classes (parts of speech) from other ones, or of one lexemic subclass from another, is of great importance, in contrast to Hopi, where it is of little importance. In fact the extent of derivation and the huge vocabulary built up out of a small number of roots is perhaps the outstanding char-acteristic of Aztec.

§1:2. Definition. For the purposes of Aztec, derivation may be defined as formation from a relative primary of a secondary such that there is a change in lexemic class or subclass and that from the secondary may be formed a tertiary that restores the original class or subclass but not the equivalent of the original primary. To illustrate from English, though the definition is not framed for Eng-lish, from the primary "care," a noun, may be formed the secondary "careful," which is a derivative because it is an adjective and because it can yield the tertiary "carefulness" which is a noun but not the equivalent of the original "care." An example of class change which is not derivation in this sense is the Hopi annex-verbation, which makes a noun or adjective formally equivalent to a verb, but which verb cannot be reconverted to noun or adjective without removing the an-nex-verbation and restoring the original noun or adjective. The Aztec derivational processes are so coordinated as to form practically one system. The terminative forms are in an ambivalent position by being part of this system as well as inflec-tions of verbs; thus the first causative technique may be applied not only to verbs but to entitives also, forming derived transitive verbs, though the applicative may not be so applied.

§1:3. Types. The basic types of derivation will be denoted by formulas, e.g., the type (verb > entitive) by the formula V-E; these formulas will be used for brevity in referring to the types. The basic types, then, are:

V-V verb > verb—changing from one subclass of verb (V §1:2) to another; this has described under vb. terminatives.

V-E verb > entitive—yielding deverbal entitives, or participials; these are formally nouns, not adjectives.

E-E entitive > entitive—changing subclass, e.g., noun > adjective, or vice versa.

E-V entitive > verb—yielding de-entitive verbs.

§2. V-E Participials.

§2:1. Direct participial, noun of action and active state. a) regularly by -⁰lis, after which, as noun, -λi. b) in certain irregular cases by -⁰s(λi), e.g., mi·ki "dies" > mi·kisλi "dying, death." When formed from a transitive the prefixes λa, te, or ne are generally used to imply the sort of objects to be understood; they become a fixed part of the new derived lexeme and are no longer operational prefixes, hence will not be hyphenated; e.g., -kʷa "eat" > λakʷalisλi "eating," tekʷalisλi "man-eating; cannibalism"; -miktia "kill" > λamiktilisλi "killing (of animals)," temiktilisλi "murder," nemiktilisλi "suicide." One may go on deriving from the new lexeme; thus by E-V, λa-temiktilistia "causes something (e.g., explosives) to commit murder, kill someone," from which could be formed still another noun, e.g., λatemiktilistikan "place where things are caused to kill people"—a likely name for a mine-field, for instance! This participial answers to our abstract noun, e.g., te-λaso?λa "loves someone" > teλaso?λalisλi or λaso?λalisλi "love" (when the root idea connotes chiefly people te is not always required), and it would seem to be also the name-form of the verb, corresponding to the Spanish infinitive used as name-form.

§2:2. Passive participial: a) regularly by contraction of the passive with nominal -λi and inclusion in lexeme of indefinite prefix, e.g., miktilo "is killed" > temiktilli "someone killed," or as modifier, or when combined with a noun in "reversed construction" (V §3:3), simply "killed." From a passive not in -lo; e.g., pepeno "is chosen" > λapepenλi "thing chosen." b) often when the passive is not in -lo but the direct voice is in -Ca, this participial is formed in -alli as if from such a passive. c) sometimes irregular, e.g., -kʷikʷi "carve" > λakʷikʷiλ "thing carved." This participle may also have the meaning "suitable to be . . . ed," e.g., λakʷalli "food" as well as "thing eaten." If verbs are rederived from these participials by E-V they will end in -ltia, -tia, or -lowa and be related to the original verbs as second causatives; this is probably the source of these second causative suffixes.

§2:3. Agentive participial, or agentive, by -ni, one of the types of nouns not taking -λ(i). Formed from a transitive it usually attaches the indefinite prefixes, except that for reflexive it uses mo instead of ne: λakʷani "eater," tekʷani "man-eater; cannibal," temiktiani "murderer," momiktiani "suicide (person)." It means either immediate or customary agent, and as modifier like an English present participle, e.g., weckani siwanton "the laughing girl"; as predicate substantive it is often equivalent to the English adjective, e.g., kone-λ ko·sa mawiltiani "the child is much the player, is very playful." A subtype of agentive is the *instrumentive*, or agentive of a passive, a noun denoting nonpersonal instrument or means, e.g., -teki "cut" > passive teko > tekoni or λatekoni "means by which something is cut, knife." Also -⁰loni, originating from the -lo passive, may be used as instrumentive suffix on reflexives, e.g., -ilpia "bind," mo-lpia "binds, girds himself" > nelpiloni "means of girding oneself, belt" (no longer a strict agentive, it takes ne instead of mo). Agentives are also formed by -ki, pl. -ke?, often on contracted stem, e.g., -piya "have, keep" > λapiški "keeper, guard, soldier," pl. λapiške?.

§2:4. Place participials. The suffixes -⁰kan, -⁰λan, -yan or -ya applied in the now familiar V-E technique form nouns denoting place of action or state, e.g., te-λamačtia "delights one" > teλamačtikan "where it delights one, (at the) delightful spot"—like all Aztec place names these contain an adverbial or locative-case sense. The -yan or -ya is also used on passive bases to denote "instrumentive place," place used for a purpose or instrument which provides a place for the action, e.g., pa·ko "is washed" >λapa·koyan "place for washing things, washbowl, etc."; mo·λalia "sits" >neλaliloya "sitting·place, seat, chair."

§2:5. Compounding with participials. Participials are freely used in com-pounds, and modifying nouns usually represent subjects of intransitives and ob-jects of transitives, e.g., for the former tonalli "sun," kisa "go forth" >tonalkisayan "where the sun rises, east." With modifier representing object the λa or te are usually omitted since a definite incorporated object has been substituted for the indefinite one, e.g., ikšiλ "foot" +(·λa)pa·koyan >ikšipa·koyan "place, bowl, for foot·washing." See also V §3:3.

§3. E·E. The following list is representative and incomplete. Superscript ᶜ means that the suffix usually replaces ·λ(i); otherwise it usually adds to the latter. 1) ·k adjective, meaning usually "having quality of": seλ "ice" >setik "cold." (The noun as modifier has more then meaning of "pertaining to.") Many adjectives are of this form though the base does not occur free, e.g., kostik "yellow," etik "heavy." 2) ·ᶜyo·λ (with morphophonemic changes, ·lo·, ·o·) noun, name of the quality of the primary, e.g., kʷalli "good" >kʷalloλ "goodness"; kostikayoλ "yel-lowness" (see VII §4:2). 3) ·ᶜwaʔ, ·ᶜyoʔ (and ·oʔ) noun, person having the primary or its quality. 4) ·λan, ·kan, ·yan noun "(at) place of": a·weweλ "cypress" (Taxo-dium sp.) >a·wewetiλan "(at) cypress grove." In a sense these are not derivatives (they do not change subclass) but the special case in which case·suffixes are ap-plicable to nouns, however they are conveniently treated here. 5) ·teka·λ, ·ᶜteka·λ noun, person living at or native of the place of the primary, gentilic modifier (the ·tec of Aztec, Zapotec, Mixtec, etc.).

§4. E·V de·entitive verbs: 1) ·a added after ·λ(i) forms a transitive, usually with causative sense, which when reflexive may mean producing the thing denoted by the base: teλ "stone; egg" >ki·tetia "stone·izes it, rigidifies it," mo·tetia "lays egg(s)." 2) ·ᶜowa, replacing ·λ(i) on C·ending and contracted stems, forms similar transitives, also transitives meaning using the thing in question upon something, or if reflexive, simply using it. This suffix converts the borrowed Spanish infinitive, treated as a noun, into an Aztec verb.[11] There are other such formatives, while compounding of entitives with verbs of somewhat general meaning, e.g., ·λalia "put, set," ·keca "put upright," ·te·ka "lay, pour," ·či·wa "make," is much used as a quasi·derivative process, yielding verbs with meanings more precisely related to the base than the regular de·entitives. A feature which should be mentioned is the compounding of ·neki "want" with the future of another verb as if the latter were a noun, which I believe is the only case in which a verb is used as antecedent

---

[11] Note that the causative inflections of verbs are simply de·entitive verbs made from entitive bases derived from the verb. By treating the verb stem or contracted verb stem as a noun to which is then added ·λ(i) (though there may be no such noun in isolation) it can be again verbified to yield the form in ·tia. Similarly, from the passive participial in ·lli come the forms in ·ltia, ·lowa. It is also pos-sible that the applicative in ·lia is derived from an entitive base in ·li which appears plus nominalizing ·ᶜs in the direct participial ·lisλi.

in a compound without conversion to an entitive stem, e.g., ki-či·wasneki "wants to make it."

§5. Modifying prefixes. A small number of true prefixes, found as bound pre-posed elements only, are used in word building and are accessory to the deriva-tional system, though formally the results of such prefixing are a type of compounds rather than true derivatives. The chief is aʸ-, negative, which is much used, some ideas being given only in negative form, e.g., akʷalli for "bad" (or amokʷalli with amo "not," which is more common in MA). Much more numerous are certain entitive stems used in an extended meaning; e.g., i·š-, stem of i·šλi "face" is widely used in the sense of "external" somewhat like Latin ex-; yol-, root of yolloλ "heart, mind," in the sense of "mental" etc. Free prepositions and adverbs are also used as bound prefixes in a manner reminiscent of Indo-European, e.g., neteč "to each other" (case-suffix -teč on base ne-) like Latin inter-: Cl netečewa (lift to each other) "contend, quarrel." The free adverb wel "well, intensely, strongly" is used much like Greek eu-, e.g., λaneštia "shine" >Cl wellaneštia "shine as well-polished, etc."

§6. The above is the barest sketch of this vast derivational system, which employs many other less frequent affixes and complicated ways of superposing derivatives, using of bases formed by contraction, and other operations not treated herein. The system is rather inactive in modern MA, due to the pressure of Spanish, the Indians preferring to use Spanish terms for new things and ideas instead of the power of free coinage given by the system. Nevertheless the impress of the system remains in the structure of the vocabulary and in a transparency of etymology and an effect of interrelatedness binding together the whole of the vocabulary. In Cl times the system was fully alive and in active use. For seemingly many centuries the building of words had gone on till much of the original Utaztecan vocabulary had been superseded by new syntheses. Probably the majority of all lexical items is derived ultimately and to a large extent transparently from 200 or fewer roots, which in turn are largely, even without using Utaztecan comparisons, clearly re-ducible to a much smaller number of subradical elements. I have used the term "oligosynthetic" to denote a lexicon of this type. The vocabulary of modern chem-istry with its vast number of names coined from a comparatively few roots and affixes, would also be an example of oligosynthesis.

10. SYNTAX OF CLAUSES AND PHRASES

§1. Section V dealt with word classes and certain general principles of sen-tence syntax and phraseology, such as conveniently precede the discussion of entitive and verb morphology. This section is a continuation of the syntactic dis-cussion·in V. It was noted in V that there are two types of major sentence, verbal and nonverbal. The nonverbal sentence is of limited use, principally for cases in which Spanish would use ser—except that unlike ser the nonverbal sentence can-not be conjugated, and to express aspect and tense distinctions must be changed to a verbal one, using perhaps ka "is," which is not wholly similar to estar, or perhaps mo-kawa "remains," mani "extends, lies," ikak or mo-keca "stands," etc.

§2. Clauses.

§2:1. Major sentences consist of one or more main clauses with or without one or more dependent clauses, or they may consist only of linked clauses, all equally dependent. Except when a main clause begins a sentence or follows a be-ginning clause that is marked as dependent, and often even in these cases, a main clause begins with the type of conjunction called introducer. A verb not preceded by such an introducer and occurring in the midst of a sentence (except in special cases noted presently) constitutes a dependent clause, e.g., wan o·ne·č-ilwik ki-piya λao·lli "and (wan, introducer) he said to me (-ilwia "say to") that it held (lit. "holds," -piya) corn." When an introducer is followed by an entitive and then two or more verbs, it is the type of sentence consisting simply of linked clauses, in which it may be merely a matter of translation which we consider main, e.g., wan i·non kone·λ o·nik-i·ctiaya o·k-ik ci·cikicin "and that child whom I was watch-ing (-i·ctia) drank (-i "drink") a little bit," or "and that child I was watching her as she drank a little bit." In such linkage without explicit connective words the nature of the connection is of course left rather vague, just as it would be in a gerund type of linkage, which Aztec, at least MA, does not use. For more explicit connec-tion dependent clauses may be begun (and are so begun if they start sentences) with the other type of conjunction, the connective, or with a relative entitive (who, etc.). If such a marked dependent clause begins a sentence the next verb con-stitutes a main clause without needing an introducer.

§2:2. Introducers. Some of the common main-clause introducers are:

i·wan, wan	and	sani·man	and then, next
ni·man	then	pwes, pos	so, well
san	only, but	no·, no· i?ki	also
a·ša·n[12]	now	noso	or

§2:3. Connectives. Some common dependent-clause connectives are:

para, inik	with future; so that, in order to	i·kʷak, kʷak	when, whenever
para	with nonfuture; inasmuch as	i·man, i·ma	when, while
		λa?	if
		ka?λi	who, whom
kampa	where, at which	ke	like Spanish que

§2:4. Tense-aspects in clauses. The tense-aspect of a dependent verb is not controlled by an absolute view of time but by the sort of distinction between the situation which it describes and the situation described by the verb of the main clause or the verb of the preceding linked clause. In this distinction as treated by

[12] Cl aškan.

Aztec, aspect is more important than absolute time and the aspect feature in the tense-aspect of the dependent verb is rather to the fore. A distinction that may be called *modality* is also important. There are two modalities, future and nonfuture. Future modality is expressed by the simple future tense-aspect (rarely by the imperfective future) and includes the meaning not only of future time but of purpose, end, goal, desire, wish, intention, assumption, or hypothesis. Whenever this future modality appears, which usually is in dependent clauses, the tense feature of the verb is future. The greatest variety of dependent clauses occurs in narrative type of discourse when the main verb is in the preterite. In that case we have this general scheme:

to express	tense-aspect of dependent clause
1) nondurative event following main-clause event	—preterite
2) nondurative or static event concurrent with main-clause event	—simple present
3) durative event begun prior to main-clause event	—imperfective (present or past)
4) durative event beginning with or after m-c event	—imperfective future
5) "future modality" dependent on main-clause event	—simple future

Continuative auxiliary aspect in -ka and other durative secondary aspects may replace imperfective. If the main verb is simple present the scheme is generally similar with certain shifts to bring tense-features into line; thus the dependent clause in 1) is either simple present or simple future, in 2) and 3) unchanged, with the added possibility of a nondurative event completed before the main-clause event denoted by preterite or perfective. If the main verb is imperfective there is another readjustment of the general scheme, as likewise if it is future.

§2:5. Use of connectives. In MA para seems to be the most common connective by far. With the future it expresses purpose much as in Spanish with the infinitive, e.g., wan ki-λalia i·pan λe·cinλi para kʷakʷəlakas "and he puts it (-λalia) on the fire to (that it may) boil" (future frequentative of thematic verb kʷala-). With nonfuture para indicates a vague contingent relation like an Indo-European participle or gerund clause, e.g., sani·man o·ni·tekλe?kok para o·nik·i·ckik oksenteλ o?λi "next I circlingly-climbed (tekλe?ko) *having taken* (inasmuch as I took, para +-i·ckia) another road." Another interesting example is ko·sa n·e·wa kʷalkan para ni·yaw nik·kʷis i·non ne·kʷa·λ "extremely (ko·sa) I rise (n·e·wa, colloquial abbreviation of nin·ewa) early (kʷalkan) inasmuch as I go (yaw) to get (-kʷi) (that I may get) that maguey·sap," i.e., "I rise very early because I go out to get that maguey·sap." Here a para is omitted, as it usually may be, from a clause, in this case the future clause of purpose. A relative clause is often indicated only by context plus the fact that the noun subject or object of a marked main clause stands before the dependent verb, as in an example above (§2:1, wan i·non kone·λ etc.). Or again such a clause may be linked by a relative entitive, e.g., wan kone·λ o·ki·tilan ša?šalo?ton ka?λi o·ki·piyaya nekʷλi "and the child pulled (tila·na, thematic verb) the little mug *which* (ka?λi) held (·piya) the pulque."

§3. Entitive phrases. Entitive phrases, i.e., sequences of grammatically inter-coordinated words other than verbs, are of the following main types: 1) two or more entitives, the last a substantive, the others modifiers (V §3:1). 2) two or more entitives and/or pronouns in apposition. 3) an entitive preceded by a preposition. 4) entitives and/or pronouns linked by conjunctions. 5) noun of possessor followed by construct of noun possessed, e.g., "John his·book." An adjective ordinarily precedes as a modifier the noun it refers to, forming a phrase of type (1), but in special cases it may be placed after its noun, in which case it is formally a substantive entitive in apposition, type (2). This order may be used to link the adjective to following words in a phrase or clause, e.g., pwes i·non ičkaλ ki·λapalwia? kà λapalli či·čiltik (adj.) wan λi·ltik (adj.) ki·či·waltia? "then that wool they dye with dye scarlet and black which they develop (or fix on the wool, ·či·waltia "cause it to make")." An adjective with a construct noun is usually bound to it as a compound: i··λi·llapal "his black dye." Adjectives borrowed from Spanish are usually placed after the noun.

§4. Verb phrases.

§4:1. A verb phrase, i.e., a sequence of grammatically inter-coordinated words including a verb or verbs, not including subject, object, or conjunctions, and not forming more than one clause, is chiefly of the types: 1) verb and adverb or adverbial, 2) verb preceded by preposition (uncommon in MA), 3) two or more parallel verbs.

§4:2. In (1) the adverb or adverbial regularly precedes verb but may sometimes occur after it for connecting with the next phrase or clause. The adverbial is easily formed from a noun by adjectival derivation, and in Cl served as a sort of general oblique case, and especially instrumental case, of the noun, e.g., tekolli "charcoal" > tekoltika λa·?kʷilowa "charcoalwise he writes, he writes with charcoal."

§4:3. 2) is the relic of a construction common in Cl, in which a preposition expressing relation of its object to the action of a verb was placed before the verb and its noun·object after the verb; thus "falls into water" was literally "into falls water," i·pan weci a·λ.

§4:4. 3) is the "twin verb" construction discussed in V §4:2. It is distinguished from verbs forming successive clauses by close similarity of meanings in the verbs and identical inflections (except for possible difference as to reflexive prefix, which might be medio·passive with one verb and lacking with the other), also any short adverbs are usually repeated. Two verbs so juxtaposed form a close semantic association and are like a verbal compound: ko·sa ni·λaokoya ko·sa nino·tekipačowa "greatly I sorrow and grieve."

§5. Adverbs. Aztec has a large number of adverbs which express time, place,

etc. rather in the modern European manner, and also some expressing modal nuances that in the European manner are denoted by auxiliary verbs. These in MA
tend to be negative in form, e.g., awelli "cannot," ayewelli "can no longer," but
instead of the implied *welli "can," I have found actual verbs "is able," "knows,"
etc. Many adverbs have a negative form in aᵞ. "Not" and "no!" are both amo.

§6. Interjections and clichés. Aztec interjections are remarkable only for their
rarity compared to many languages. But polite phrases, clichés, and sentence-con-
densations abound. A few of the most serviceable are: ke·ma "yes," amo "no,"
λaso?kamat ì "thank you" (II §4:2), m·i·špancinko lit. "in your (august) presence"
=please excuse me, with your permission, etc., šimo·pano·lti "please proceed,"
"that's all right," etc.—reply to the one preceding.

11. NOTES ON THE TEPOZTLÁN DIALECT

§1. This dialect (T) differs from MA appreciably, especially in phonology.
The differences are such as to indicate that T does not, like MA, stem from the Cl
of the Mexico City vicinity, but from a different branch of Aztec. The outstanding
differences may be summed up as follows:

§2. Prosodics. 1) p, m, w, t, n, k after accented short vowel are geminated.
2) Although accent is normally penultimate it tends to shift forward in certain
phrasal groups. The tone patterns, while generally similar, do not occur in the same
way; the pattern high-low occurs on words ending in V and is not universal on
those ending in C.

§3. Phonemics. 1) š is a cacuminal s with a suggestion of untrilled voiceless r
(though č is not cacuminal, but the ordinary sound, as in MA). 2) ? is nearly or
quite h (perhaps always h before C). 3) k is not spirantized before C as in MA.
4) word-final n is less lightened than in MA but has closure farther back than in
other positions, and after e, i especially in rapid speech may be almost or quite ŋ.
5) syllable-final w is lacking, see §4(1). 6) ao is lacking, replaced by ayo, but eo
exists.

§4. Morphophonemics. 1) w becoming secondarily word-final >n;[13] sec. before C >? (or h), e.g., ki·či·wa > pret. o·ki·či·n, pret. plur. o·ki·či·?ke? (this last
also MA, but T applies it to all cases, e.g., ki·senkawa >o·ki·senka?ke?, MA
o·ki·senkawke?). The other important morphophonemic rules are as in MA.

§5. Morphology, syntax, and vocabulary. On the whole these are much as in
MA but with less intrusion of Spanish features; native conjunctions are used instead of the continual para of MA. There is comparatively little Spanish vocabulary and more archaic words are preserved; in vocabulary, T is more like Cl than

---

[13] Probably the historical reason for this change is that many of the noninitial w's of Aztec,
including probably the final -w of the construct of w-class nouns, come from Utaztecan *ŋʷ, which
in the branch represented by T could have become n when word-final, the pattern then being extended to all w's.

is MA, though structurally it is much further from Cl. The centrifugal aspect suffixes are ˈtin, plur. ˈtiwa, pret. ˈta instead of ˈtiw, ˈtiweʔ, ˈto; probably the cenˈtripetal is analogous. A form of the Cl optative occurs like the imperative, but with the indicative subject prefixes and the adverb ma or man (this may also exist in MA but is not common). "What?" is λen where MA would use λaon. The inˈdefinite article is usually sente; MA prefers senteλ.

CHIPEWYAN

LI FANG-KUEI

§1. The following sketch is prepared from material gathered by the author at Fort Chipewyan, Alberta, Canada in the summer of 1928. Orthography has been slightly altered to conform to a more phonemic presentation, and therefore differs from my previous publications on this language.

PHONOLOGY

§2. Consonantal system:

	STOPS AND AFFRICATIVES			NASAL	FRICATIVES	
	Inter-mediates	Aspir-ated	Glottal-ized		Surds	Sonants
Labials	b			m		
Dentals	d	t	t'	n		
Gutturals	g	k	k̠		x	γ
Labio-gutturals	gw	kw	k̠w		xw	γw
Interdentals	dδ	tθ	t'θ		θ	δ
Dental Sibilants	dz	ts	t's		s	z
Prepalatal Sibilants	dj	tc	t'c		c	y
Laterals	dl	tł	t'ł		ł	l
Glottals	ʔ				h	
Tongue Tip Trill						r

The intermediates are voiceless lenis. Aspirated stops are strongly aspirated with a guttural spirantal glide; aspirated affricatives are also strongly aspirated, but without the guttural spirantal glide. y as a syllabic initial is pronounced like the English y, but finally is pronounced with a good deal of friction. g is often pronounced with a γ-glide. The labio-gutturals exist before or after o, u, and some-times before a. γw is frequently weakened to [w], in the prefix syllables and also finally in the stem syllable. h is labialized to [w] after u.

Distribution of the consonants: All consonants listed above can be used as the initial of a syllable except r which cannot be used as an initial unless preceded by other syllables. r and h are never used as the initial of a stem syllable.

The finals of a syllable are limited to the nasal ‑n, the fricatives ‑γ, ‑θ, ‑δ, ‑s, ‑z, ‑y, ‑ł, ‑l, ‑h, and ‑r.

m occurs only once in my material as the initial of a stem in homą "it stinks."

§3. Vocalic system:

Short vowels:	a	ɛ	e	i	o	u
Long vowels:	a·	ɛ·		i·		u·
Nasalized short vowels:	ą	ɛ̨		į		ų
Nasalized long vowels:	ą·	ɛ̨·		į·		ų·
Diphthongs:	ai		ei		oi	ui
	ąi				ǫi	ųi

e varies between [e] and [ə]:[e] in open syllables or when followed by ł or l, sometimes s or z; [ə] in the diphthong ei or when followed by a voiced final conso‑ nant particularly n, r, γ, y. After the strongly aspirated t, k, and x, γ, [ə] is more often heard.

The diphthongs occur only in syllables followed by a voiceless spirant, except ei which may occur in open syllables. There are also a number of pseudo‑diphthongs which are results of two vowels fallen together, and can be bettter designated as two vowels. Long vowels are often the result of coalescence of two vowels, al‑ though it is difficult sometimes to identify the separate elements.

§4. Tones: There are two registers in this language, the high pitch which is marked by an acute accent and the low pitch which will not be marked in this sketch. Coalescence of elements of different pitches sometimes gives a rising or falling inflection which is marked by ˇ and ˆ respectively. In the prefix syllable the low pitch is slightly more elevated in pitch than the low pitch in the stem syllable.

§5. Syllables: There are two types of syllables, the stem syllable which re‑ ceives more weight in pronounciation, and the prefix or suffix syllables. The stem syllable does not have as its initial h or r, may possess any one of the diphthongs which do not occur in the prefix or suffix syllable, and often alternates between a light and a heavy form.

A light syllable is either an open syllable or ends in a voiceless consonant and a heavy syllable always ends in a voiced consonant. The alternation between a heavy and a light syllable plays a great part in the morphology of the language, particularly in the verbs. We have the following types of alternating forms:

‑θ:‑δ	nirɨłtcuθ "you are picking up a fabric"
	nirɨłtcúδ "you have picked up a fabric"
‑s:‑z	niúhʔás "you (dual) get up"
	niúhʔaz "you (dual) have got up"
ił:‑l	hídił "it is turning red"
	hídíl "it has turned red"
‑ih:‑y	nįnesdzaih "I am bringing it (grain‑like object)"
	nįni·dzáy "I have brought it (grain‑like object)"

ʿːγ   tįba "you start off on war path"
         tįbáγ "you have started off on war path"

ʿˏːⁿ   súnįγų "growl at me!"
         súnįγun "it has growled at me"

In many cases the heavy form appears when a suffixed vowel is added, the light form appears when standing alone or in composition with other stems, for example, tsą́ "excrement": seˑtsą́n-é "my excrement"; seˑna-δᴐ́δ "my eye-lid": seˑnaγ-á "my eye"; tɬuɬ "string": tɬul-e "rope."

§6. Alternation of voiceless and voiced fricative initials: The fricative initial of a stem syllable is always in the voiceless form when standing alone, and is voiced when a prefix is added, thus θų̂θ "spear"; be-δų̂θ "his spear"; seγ "spittle"; se-zeγ-é "my spittle"; cen "song"; seˑyen-é "my song"; ɬą "many"; ho-ɬą "many times"; xaɬ "club" ho-γaɬ "a heavy club for pounding things." The only exception seems to be the initial y- which sometimes may stand alone, such as ya "sky," yá "louse," yaθ "snow." We may distinguish morphophonemically two kinds of y-, one which alternates with c-, and one which does not become a c- in absolute initial positions.

The voiced initial fricative will be unvoiced when immediately preceded by a voiceless fricative, thus θiˑˑγar "I shake it"; θuh-xar "you (pl.) shake it"; ne-δaθ "you singe it"; γwa-s-θaθ "I shall singe it"; niˑˑyą "I have grown up"; yeˑné-ɬ-cą "he has raised him up," etc.

Whenever the voiced initial of the stem syllable is preceded by a voiceless fricative and yet it does not become unvoiced, it always means that the preceding voiceless fricative is of voiced origin, secondarily unvoiced due to contraction, thus, ná-s-zé "I am hunting" <ná-s-l-zé; yeˑkó-deˑné-ɬ-yá "he has learnt it" <yeˑkó-deˑné-θ-l-yá.

§7. Simplification of double consonants: When identical consonants come to-gether, they are simplified to a single consonant. There are no true long or double consonants, thus teˑsáih "I split" <teˑs-sáih <teˑs-záih; hįˑlaɬ "go to sleep!" >hįˑl-laɬ, etc.

§8. Dropping and weakening of consonants in the prefix syllables: ʔ, k, h, and γ sometimes disappear in intervocalic positions in rapid speech, for example, ʔekwâˑdi for ʔekwáʔadi "he says so"; hě·δdel for heheδdel "they have started off"; he-déɬ for heγedéɬ "they are going along."

d is often weakened to r in intervocalic positions, thus desį "I say," but ʔekwáresį "I say that, say so"; déθgai "there is a white spot," but náréθgai "there is a white stripe, it is white-striped"; benayudéɬni "it disappeared in a distance again," but beyuréɬni "it disappeared in a distance."

Such dropping and weakening occur only in the prefix syllables and never occur in the stem syllable.

§9. Assimilation of vowels: The suffix vowel -e is assimilated to a after a or aγ, i.e., θaγ-a "grey eagle" <θaγ-e; se-dzaγ-á "my ear" <se-dzaγ-é; se-zä̀· "my watch" <se-zà-é; se-tsä· "my hat" <se-tsa-é.

A vowel may be nasalized in the neighborhood of a nasalized vowel, i.e., kų́·ę "home, house, fort" <kų́·ɛ; sɛ·lį·ę "my daughter" <sɛ·lį·ɛ; bɛ·tcąɣ·ą́ "his ribs" <bɛ·tcąɣ·ɛ́, ʔįłáɣ·į "one (person)" < ʔįłáɣ·į, etc. Occasional nasalization of a vowel because of a following n is common in the prefixes, i.e., cų́·nílya "we (pl.) have started to eat" <cɛ́·ú·ní·l·lya.

§10. Nasalization of ɛ, e to į: į is the regular nasalized form of ɛ, e, for example, nén "land" but nį́·hołɛ "on the land"; sįlá "my hand" <sɛ·n·lá; nįdáih "sit down!" <nɛ·n·dáih. Chipewyan ɛ, ɛ́ is a secondary form largely due to contraction, i.e., hɛ·słał "I am falling asleep" from hį·hɛ·s·łał; yųtθɛ́ "to the north, out on the lake" <yų·tθį́·ɛ́, cf. yų·tθį́ "at a certain place in the north, outside."

MORPHOLOGY

§11. The word: A word in Chipewyan may consist of a single stem syllable, with or without prefixes or suffixes. Two or more stems may form compounds. Prefixes, suffixes, consonant alternation, vocalic alternation, and pitch alternation may be employed to express various grammatical functions.

Word classes: There are three main classes of word, the noun, the verb, and the particle. The noun may be inflected according to its possessor, and often presents a possessed form different from the free form. The verb may be inflected according to aspect, mode, person, number, voice, etc. The particle rarely changes its form, and includes a large number of words of diverse meanings, such as the pronouns, the numerals, and other syntactic particles.

NOUNS

§12. Nouns may be a) simple monosyllabic stems without any prefix or suffix, i.e., ʔi "coat, dress," bes "knife," bér "meat," des "river," tθe "stone, pipe," sa "sun, watch," xai "root," tłoɣ "grass," tsą́ "excrement," kún "fire," tu "water"; b) with an inherent prefix i.e., dɛ·ne "person, Indian," dɛ·tcin "wood, stick, tree," łɛ·ní "taste," łɛ·zen "a speck," ho·tɛθ "portage," ho·ba "twilight," etc.; or an inherent suffix, i.e., ʔóɣw·ɛ "eddy," bą́n·ɛ "war party," ten·ɛ "trail," tłul·ɛ "rope," łuɣw·ɛ "fish," θaɣ·a <θaɣ·ɛ "grey eagle," tel·i "kettle," θah·i "pole, tepee pole," łur·i "The Scabby One (man's name)," cf. łur "scab," sá·ł "hook," cf. ·sáih (verb stem) "to hook" and ·zɛ́ (verb stem) "to hook at," dló·ł "smile" cf. dlóɣ "laugh, laughter," kú·ł "that which is vomited" cf. ·kui (verb stem) "to vomit," etc.; c) nouns which must be possessed, mostly body parts and kinship terms, i.e., sɛ·ɣú "my tooth," nɛ·tθí "your head," bɛ·dá "his lip," etc. d) verbal nouns, either abstract nouns such as ná·tser "strength" also "he is strong," ho·tsį́ "gesture" also "he signals"; ná·zɛ́ "hunting," cf. ná·l·zɛ́ "he hunts," ya·tei "word, language," cf. ya·ł·tei "he speaks" (abstract without the l or ł classifier which is present in the verb); dɛ·l·gú "a hooping noise" also "it hoops" (abstract with the l classifier); or d) relative nouns formed with the relative suffix ·i such as ya·ł·tey·i "preacher, priest," cf. ya·ł·tei "he speaks," dɛ·l·dδér·i "a rattle," cf. dɛ·l·dδér "it rattles"; and e) compounds; possessive compounds such as tsá-záł "beaver hook," cf. tsá "beaver" and sáł "hook," tsá-dąn-é "beaver food," cf. tsá "beaver" and dąn-é "food," hotél-ʔená "Eskimo," cf. hotél "barren land" and ʔená "enemy," dene-na-tú "tear" cf. dene "person" -na- "eye," and tu "water"; descriptive compounds such as tθe-tsóγ-é "boulder," cf. tθe "stone" and de-tsóγ "it is round," djíye-tθoγ-é "orange," cf. djíye "berry" and de-l-tθoγ "yellow," łį-tcil-e "small or little dog," cf. łį "dog" and se-tcil-e "my younger brother," etc. The second member of these compounds often presents a distinctly possessed form (cf. §14).

§13. Possessive prefixes: Any one of these nouns may theoretically have one of these possessive prefixes and some nouns (§12c) must be always possessed. In Chipewyan there is a distinct tendency to use a paraphrastic expression to denote possession for those nouns except §12c, i.e., łį setsį "my dog < dog me-form." The possessive prefixes are:

se- "my"	nuhe- "our"
ne- "your"	nuhe- "your (pl.)"
be- "his, her, its"	hube- "their"

ye- "his, her, its their, when the subject of the sentence is also in the third but not the same person"

ʔe- "indefinite possessor"

ʔede- "one's own, my own, your own, his own, etc."

The vowel ε of these prefixes is dropped if the following noun stem begins with a vowel, i.e., bą < b(ε)-ą "his mother."

§14. Possessed forms: when the possessive prefix is added to a noun stem, the stem form may remain the same but sometimes may show a different form. For those nouns which are always possessed, the nonpossessed form must be looked for elsewhere when the stem is used, for instance, as a member of a compound, thus, se-γú "my tooth" (possessed): se-γu-tθén "my gum (< tooth-flesh)" (non-possessed), se-dá "my lip" (possessed): se-da-γá "my whiskers (< lip-hair)" (non-possessed). There are the following types of possessed forms:

a) Without change of form, except for the voicing of the initial fricative (§6); θuθ "spear"; be-δuθ "his spear," kį "a mound, heap": ʔe-kį "beaver lodge," bą́n-e "edge"; be-bą́n-e "its edge."

b) With the adding of the possessive suffix -é: t'θen "bone"; se-t'θen-é "my bone," del "blood": se-del-é "my blood," tsą́ "excrement": be-tsą́n-é "his excrement" (cf. §5), sa "watch": se-zǎ- "my watch" (cf. §9).

c) When the noun has an original suffix -e (cf. §12b), the possessed form is formed by changing this -e to -é: łuγw-e "fish": se-łuγw-é "my fish," bą́n-e "war party": dene-bą́n-é "a war party of Indians."

d) Without the suffix -é, but with a shift of tone of the stem from low to high: t'a "feather": be-t'á "its feather," ke "moccasins": be-ké "his moccasins."

e) With the possessive suffix and with a shift of tone: tu "water": kún·tú·έ "liquor (<fire·water)," dzέ "gum": tθε·dzεγ·έ "tar (<stone·gum)."

§15. Vocative suffix: Vocatives are formed either by adding a suffix ·į· with the dropping of the last vowel if the noun ends in a vowel, or by lengthening the last vowel with a falling tone, i.e., sεtcilį· "my younger brother!" from sεtcilε "my younger brother," ?εnį· "my mother!" from ?εné "my mother," sεtâ· "my father!" from sεtá "my father," datsątθį· "Raven·head (man's name)!" from datsątθí.

§16. Postpositions: Postpositions are local nouns and therefore belong to the same class of words as the nouns, cf. bε·bą́n·ε "around it =its edge," bε·yáγ·a "in it =its inside," etc. Like the nouns it may consist of a monosyllabic stem, such as ·a "for," ·έł "with, in company with," ·?ą́ "off on one side, at a distance from," ·ba "for, waiting for," ·ta "among," ·t́á "by means of," ·γá "giving to, for," ·k̇ε "on," ·t́sén "toward," ·t́si̧ "from," ·yέ "in," ·yε "under," ·t́ca "away from." It may have an inherent suffix ·ε (cf. §12b), such as ·bą́n·ε "around," ·tεθ·ε "passing over, above," ·gεz·ε "between," ·yaγ·a "under, below," ·yáγ·a "in, inside of," ·djáγ·a "in the middle of" (for ·a instead of ·ε see §9).

§17. Pronominal objective prefixes: The pronominal objects of these post· positions are identical in form with the possessive prefixes of the nouns, for ex· ample, sε·t́sén "toward me," nε·t́sén "toward you," bε·t́sén, yε·t́sén "toward him, etc.," nuhε·t́sén "toward us, you (pl.)," hubε·t́sén "toward them," ?εdε·t́sén "to· ward one's self." Aside from these there are a few others of common occurrence.

ho· referring to place, time, event, etc., such as ho·γą "at it (a place)," ho·t́sén "toward it (a place)"

?εł·, ?εłε· referring to mutuality, reciprocality, such as ?εł·k̇ésį "like each other, alike," ?εłε·t́cazį "away from each other"

yų· in the direction of, such as yų·yaγa "down below," cf. bε·yaγ·a "under it," yų·naθε "next," cf. sε·naθε "in front of me."

Some of the so·called adverbs are really postpositions with a prefix such as those listed above, i.e., ?εłε·na, ?εł·na "in turn," yų·daγa "above," yų·yaγa "down be· low," etc.

§18. The pronominal prefixes are dropped when the object immediately pre· cedes, and the noun and the postposition form a sort of compound much like the possessive compounds, thus sas·γą "at the bear, to the bear," sas·t́sén "toward the bear";[1] some of such compounds become regular nouns, such as xíł·t́sén "evening (<darkness·toward)," dzi̧·dizε "noon (day·at·the·middle)." Two or more post· positional stems may also be compounded to express various relations, such as bε·naθε·t́sén "better than him (<him·in front of·toward)," ?εłε·k̇έ·t́ca "different

---

[1] For postpositions with a vocalic initial, the pronominal prefix is replaced by x·, thus, bέł ("with it"): sas·xέł ("with the bear"), ba ("for it"): sas·xa ("for the bear").

from each other (<each other·on·away from)," ʔɛłɛ·na·ťca·sį "one on each side, i.e., of the river (<each other·in place of·away·from)."

§19. Postpositional suffixes: The following suffixes may be added to the post-postional stems and sometimes to noun stems, but they never take directly the pronominal objects and do not act as regular stem syllables:

·sį "towards, in the direction of," probably the weakened form of ·ťsén, i.e., ťa·sį "backwards," cf. ťa "back," nį·sį "to the ground," cf. nén "ground," bɛ·ḱɛ·sį "like him."

·sį "from," probably the weakened form of ·ťsį, i.e., yų·ní·sį "from behind," cf. yų·ní "back of, behind," yų·da·sį "from above" cf. yų·da·ɣa "above."

·zį "along," i.e., ho·ba·zį "in the same line as," cf. ·ba "for, waiting for," bɛ·ḱɛ·zį "after him, following him," cf. bɛ·ḱɛ "on him," bɛ·ťca·zį "away from him." cf. bɛ·ťca "away from him (at a distance)."

·zį in dɛnɛ·ni·zį "among the people," bɛ·ḱɛ·zį "on it (formerly)."

·zɛ "in the middle" dzį·di·zɛ "noon," cf. dzį "day," sį·ni·zɛ "my waist," cf. sɛnɛn·ɛ "my back."

·rɛ "place around, along," i.e., bɛ·la·rɛ "along its top," cf. ·layɛ "top," bɛ·zí·rɛ "along its side (of a canoe)," cf. ·zí "body."

·θɛ "ahead," probably the weakened form of ·tθɛ "before, in front of," i.e., bɛ·na·θɛ or bɛ·na·tθɛ "in front of it."

§20. Some stems by means of an alternation of tone or a suffix ·ɛ seem to denote motion, such as ·ḱɛ "on": ·ḱɛ́ "on, along (moving)," ·ťca "away from (at a certain distance)": ·ťcá "away from (moving away)," yų·da·ɣa "above": yų·da·ɣ·á "upwards," yų·ya·ɣa "down below": yų·ya·ɣ·á "downwards," yų·ʔá "off on one side": yų·ʔán·ɛ́ "away to one side."

VERBS

§21. The verb in Chipewyan is a complicated structure, consisting of a stem and a number of prefixes. It may also take suffixes. The modes, the aspects, the person, and the number form the conjugation of the verb, and are expressed by prefixes as well as stem variations. Other prefixes are present in all aspects and persons, and form with the stem a verbal theme. The meaning of the verb is determined by such themes, for example, ya·. . .·tei is a theme meaning to "to speak," from which we may get ya·s·tei "I speak," ya·ł·tei "he speaks," etc. To analyze such a theme into a prefix ya· and a stem ·tei does not lead us to a solution of either the meaning of the stem or of the prefix. Another theme, as ná·. . .·tɛ "to dream" is composed of a prefix ná· "here and there, about" which requires the continuative forms of the stem, and a stem ·tɛ "a living being lies around (continuative)." From this theme we may have ná·s·tɛ "I dream," ná·θi·tį "I have dreamt," etc. Although this theme can be analyzed into two separate elements, the meaning of "to dream" depends on the theme as a whole.

§22. There is a series of verb stems describing the nature of the object handled, i.e., to handle a round, solid object, a long stick-like object, a living being, liquid in a vessel, grain-like object, a fabric, or several objects, each requiring a distinct stem. The manner of handling such as to pick up, to put down, to carry around, to hold, etc., depends upon the prefixes which form with the stems themes.

Some stems have an intrinsic number idea in themselves and can only be used either in the singular, in the dual, or in the plural. In so far as the number idea refers to the subject of the verb, there are three types of stems, a) stems which can only be used in the singular, requiring a different stem each for the dual and the plural; b) stems which can be used both in the singular and the dual, requiring only a special stem for the plural; and c) stems which can be used in the singular only, requiring a special stem for both the dual and the plural. For example,

a) nį-dáih "sit down!" (sing.), ní·kɛ "we are sitting down" (dual), du-ł-t'θi "sit down!" (pl.).

b) ná-s-θer "I am staying" (sing.), ná-uh-θer "you are staying" (dual), ná-í-de "we are staying" (pl.).

c) θi··tį "I am lying" (sing.), θí·tɛz "we are lying" (dual or pl.).

Similarly the stem may refer to the object in regard to number, thus "to kill one person" requires a different stem from "to kill several persons," and so on. For example, łɛγá-ni-ł-θer "I killed him," but łɛγá-ni-ł-dɛ́ "I killed them (several persons)," sa θi-ł-tsį "I made a watch," ǩá γi··γą "I made several arrows." Sometimes by means of a causative formation, the number which refers to the subject of the verb may be shifted to the object, thus łɛγá-ni··δer "I died" and łɛγá-ni-ł-θer "I killed him (I caused him to die)," lɛγá-ní·-dɛ́ "we died," and łɛγá-ni-ł-dɛ́ "I killed them (I caused them to die)."

§23. Aspects and modes: There are three aspects and five modes. The three aspects are the imperfective, referring to an action which is going on; the perfective, referring to an action which has been done; and the future, referring to action which is to take place. The five modes are the neuter, the momentaneous, the continuative, the customary, and the progressive. The neuter verb refers to the state or the position and includes such verbs as "to lie (in a lying position)," "to sit (in a sitting position)," "to stand (in a standing position)," and verbs of adjectival nature such as "to be yellow," "to be black," "to be big," etc. The momentaneous verb refers to a rapid action or transition from one state to another and includes such active and inchoative verbs as "to sit down," "to lie down," "to come to a stand," "to become yellow," "to become black," and so on. The continuative verb refers to an activity which lasts for a certain length of time, such as "to stay," "to own," "to go for a visit." The customary verb refers to an action which is customary or repeated. The progressive verb refers to an activity which is kept on particularly while one is moving along. For example, from the stem "to handle a living being," we have in the neuter "a living being is in position, i.e., to lie";

in the momentaneous "a living being gets into position or acts, i.e., to lie down"; in the continuative "a living being acts continually, i.e., to dream (<to lie around)"; in the customary (transitive) "to handle a living being customarily or repeatedly, i.e., to carry it around"; in the progressive (transitive) "to keep on handling a living being, i.e., to hold it." Each of these modes may have the three aspects, thus:

Neuter: θi·tĮ "I am lying," γi·tĮ "I had lain (no longer lying)," γwa·s·té "I shall lie."

Momentaneous: nɛs·téih "I am lying down," ni·tĮ "I have lain down," nu·s·té "I shall lie down."

Continuative: ná·s·tɛ "I dream," ná·θi·tĮ "I have dreamt," ná·γwa·s·té "I shall dream."

Customary: dzɛ́rɛ́·s·teih "I am carrying it around," dzɛ́rɛ́·γi·ł·teih "I have car-ried it around," dzɛ́rɛ́·γwa·s·teih "I shall carry it around."

Progressive: da·γɛ·s·teł "I am holding it," da·γi·ł·teł "I have been holding it," da·γwa·s·teł "I shall hold it up."

Some stems have all the five modes, others may have only four, three, or two of them.

§24. Stem variations: The stem may vary according to the aspects. The cus-tomary and the progressive stem does not vary usually according to aspects, but in the other modes often varies in numerous ways. We may briefly summarize them into the following types, stems being listed in this order: imperfective, perfective, and future:

a) Invariable: ·ʔar, ·ʔar, ·ʔar "to throw, handle violently cloth-like object," ·bá, ·bá, ·bá "to go to war (continuative forms)."

b) Tonal alternations: ·dɛ, ·dé, ·dɛ "to clean ,wash," ·cĮs, ·cĮs, ·cĮs "to whistle," ·t's is, ·t's ís, ·t's ís "to caress," ·dą, ·dą, ·dą́ "to drink."

c) Vocalic modifications: Alternations of ɛ:a, Į:ą, e:ɛ, ɛ:o, u:o, i:e, ɛ are represented in the following examples. They may be accompanied by a shift of tone. Thus, ·lɛ, ·la, ·lɛł "to handle several objects," ·t'lĮ, ·t'lá, ·t'lá "to lean," ·bɛ́r, ·bér, ·bɛ́r "to bend," ·xɛ́r, ·xwór, ·xɛ́r "to bend," ·γuł, ·γwoł, ·γuł "to become warped," ·δir, ·δer, ·δir "to be, act, do," ·yił, ·yeł, ·yił "to make a thundering noise," ·dĮ, ·dą, ·dą́ "to be drowned (sing, or dual)."

d) Alternation of syllabic types, light:heavy:light (cf. §5). Such alternations may further be accompanied by tonal alternations as well as vocalic modifications.

1) Without tonal changes	2) With tonal changes
·bąθ, ·bąδ, ·bąθ "to roll (a wheel, barrel)"	·ba, ·báγ, ·ba "to go to war (momentaneous)"
·ní, ·níy, ·ní "to buy"	·dił, ·díl, ·dił "to become red"
·γų, ·γun, ·γų "to growl at"	·ʔás, ·ʔaz, ·ʔás "two persons go"

3) With vocalic changes

ʾzέ, ʾzáγ, ʾzέ "to hook at"
ʾne, ʾnaγ, ʾne "to throw a body"
ʾtθiθ, ʾtθaδ, ʾtθiθ "to extinguish a fire"
ʾtsił, ʾtsel, ʾtsił "to soak"
ʾǩέθ, ʾǩέδ, ʾǩέθ "to fire a gun"
ʾθú, ʾθóγ, ʾθú "to fold a hard sheet"
ʾťcuł, ʾťcel, ʾťcuł "to burst, to split"

4) With vocalic and tonal changes

ʾzέ, ʾzaγ, ʾzέ "to bristle up (hair, grass, etc.)"
ʾdέł, ʾdel, ʾdέł "several persons go"
ʾxáł, ʾxel, ʾxáł "to throw a club"
ʾxέł, ʾxel, ʾxέł "darkness comes"

§25. The momentaneous imperfective sometimes takes a diphthongal form i.e., ai from stems with an a and sometimes ε, e vowel; ei from stems with an ε or ei; ui, oi from stems with a u or o vowel, and similarly for the nasalized diphthongs ąi, ųi, and ǫi. Sometimes the future may take the same form as the imperfective. For example,

ʾʔáih, ʾʔą, ʾʔał "to handle a round solid object"
ʾkéih, ʾkε, ʾkέ "to sit (dual)"
ʾʔóih, ʾʔóγ, ʾʔóih "water rushes, whirls as if boiling"
ʾkáih, ʾką, ʾkáih "to burn"
xaił, ʾxał, ʾxaił "to make a dent, to dent once"

The final ʾh is always present in stems which do not end in a consonant, and is the trace of an old suffix which causes such diphthongization. If the stem has a final ʾr, it is changed to ʾy, for example,

ʾgay, ʾgar, ʾgar "to shake"
ʾťθiy, ʾťθer, ʾťθiy "to start to fall"
ʾdjúy, ʾdjúr, ʾdjúy "to make it give a deep hollow noise"

§26. The perfective is sometimes formed by nasalizing the vowel, usually with a low tone, while the imperfective and the future are not nasalized, for example,

ʾbí, ʾbį, ʾbέ "to swim (sing. or dual)"
ʾkáih, ʾką, ʾkał "to handle liquid in a vessel"
ʾθε, ʾθą, ʾθε "to tan hide"
ʾlέ, ʾlį, ʾlέ "to be, become"

§27. In some perfectives we find the dropping of a final ʾr or ʾθ (rarely also in the future), and the dropping of a final ʾn with the nasalization of the vowel (often also in the future), for example,

ʾgεr, ʾgέ, ʾgεr "to crawl on all fours"
ʾyur, ʾyú, ʾyu "to chase"
ʾťéθ, ʾťε, ʾťéθ "to roast"

ʾʔen, ʾʔį, ʾʔį́ "to examine"
ʾten, ʾtą, ʾtą́ "to handle a long stick-like object (cont.)"
ʾδen, ʾδį́, ʾδį́ "to think"

§28. The future is often the same as the imperfective, sometimes the same as the perfective, and sometimes different from both usually by an alternation of tone. It may sometimes take the suffix ˑł as in the progressive mode (cf. below §32). For examples see §24 to §27.

§29. Suppletive stems: Some verbs have for their perfective a different stem, for example, ʔasnɛ "I become so," ʔasdjá "I have become so," ʔaɣwasnɛ "I shall become so."

§30. Stem variations according to modes: Different modes demand different sets of stems. They are highly irregular and too complicated to be stated in this sketch. The following list will give some idea.

	Neuter	Momentaneous	Continuative	Customary	Progressive
"to handle a round solid object"	ˑʔa̜, ˑʔá̜, ˑʔá̜	ˑʔáih, ˑʔa̜, ˑʔał	ˑʔa, ˑʔá, ˑʔá	ˑʔaih	ˑʔał
"to handle a long stick-like object"	ˑta̜, ˑtá̜, ˑtá̜	ˑtį̈, ˑta̜, ˑtá̜	ˑten, ˑta̜, ˑtá̜	{ˑtį̈ ˑtį	{ˑtį̈ł ˑtį̈ł
"to handle a fabric"	ˑtcúδ, ˑtcúδ, ˑtcúδ	ˑtcuθ, ˑtcúδ, ˑtcuθ	ˑtcúδ, —, ˑtcúδ	ˑtciθ	ˑtcɛθ
"to handle grain-like object"	ˑdzáy, ˑdzáy, ˑdzáy	ˑdzaih, ˑdzáy, ˑdzaih	ˑdzáy, —, ˑdzáy	ˑdzaih	ˑdzał
"to handle a living being"	ˑtį, ˑtį̈, ˑté	ˑtéih, ˑtį, {ˑté ˑteł	ˑte, ˑtį, ˑté	ˑteih	ˑteł
"to handle liquid in a vessel"	ˑka̜, ˑká̜, ˑká	ˑkáih, ˑka̜, ˑkał	ˑka, —, ˑká	ˑkaih	ˑkał
"to handle several objects"	ˑla, ˑlá, ˑlá	ˑlɛ, ˑla, ˑleł	ˑla, —, ˑlá	ˑli	ˑleł
"to go to war"	—	ˑba, ˑbáɣ, ˑba	ˑbá, ˑbá, ˑbá	—	—
"to roll"	—	ˑba̜θ, ˑba̜δ, ˑba̜θ	ˑba̜δ, ˑba̜δ, ˑba̜δ	ˑba̜iθ	—
"to be, to act (sing. or dual)"	—	ˑδir, ˑδer, ˑδir	ˑδer, ˑδer, ˑδer	ˑδiy	ˑδeł
"to be, to act" (pl.)	—	ˑde, ˑdɛ́, ˑde	ˑdɛ́, ˑdɛ́, ˑdɛ́	ˑdaih	ˑdał
"to sit" (sing.)	ˑda, ˑdá, ˑdá	ˑdáih, ˑda, ˑdá	—	ˑdaih	—
"to sit" (dual)	ˑkɛ, —, ˑkɛ́	ˑkéih, ˑkɛ, ˑkɛ́	—	ˑkéih	—
"to stand" (sing. or dual)	ˑyį̈, ˑyį̈, ˑyį̈	ˑyį̈, ˑyį̈, ˑyį̈	—	ˑdjį̈	ˑyį̈ł
"to be white"	ˑgai	ˑgai, ˑgái, ˑgai	—	ˑgaih	—
"to be fat"	ˑk̉a	ˑk̉a, ˑk̉á, ˑk̉a	—	ˑk̉aih	—
"to be yellow"	ˑtθoɣ	ˑtθu, ˑtθú, ˑtθu	—	—	—
"to be angry"	ˑt̉coɣ	ˑt̉cɛ, ˑt̉cɛ́, ˑt̉cɛ	—	ˑt̉coih	ˑtcoł

The neuter imperfective is often the same as the momentaneous perfective sometimes even with the perfective prefix θɛˑ (§37a). The neuter and the continuative forms either do not alternate their forms according to the aspects or simply alternate the tone, rarely by other means; the momentaneous form varies according to various different types mentioned above; and the customary and the progressive practically never change their forms.

§31. The formation of the customary stem: The customary stem exists in three forms, a) with a simple vowel, i, u, or į, u̜ from the stems with i, e, ɛ or į, en, u̜; b) with a diphthong like some momentaneous imperfective forms, i.e., ai from stems with a or sometimes ɛ, e; ei from ɛ, ei; ui, oi from u, o, similarly for the nasalized diphthongs a̜i, o̜i, u̜i; c) with a final ˑy from stems with a final ˑr. For example,

a) ˑní from ˑnį, ˑníy, ˑní "to buy"

ᐧδį from ᐧδen, ᐧδį, ᐧδį "to think"

ᐧʔiθ from ᐧʔєθ, ᐧʔέδ, ᐧʔєθ "to make a kick at"

ᐧgú from ᐧgú, ᐧgwóz, ᐧgú "to make a rush at"

ᐧk̇ʋs from ᐧk̇ʋs, ᐧk̇ʋ́z, ᐧk̇ʋs "to blush, to redden"

b) ᐧdaih from ᐧdє, ᐧdέ, ᐧdє "to clean, to wash"

ᐧʔáis, from ᐧʔás, ᐧʔaz, ᐧʔás "several animals walk"

ᐧkéih from ᐧkéih, ᐧkє, ᐧké "two persons sit"

ᐧdjuih from ᐧdju, ᐧdjú, ᐧdju "to dishevel (hair)"

ᐧtɫóih from ᐧtɫóγ, ᐧtɫóγ, ᐧtɫóγ "to make a splashy noise"

ᐧgạih, from ᐧgạ, ᐧgạ, ᐧgą́ "several people fight"

ᐧγwọih from ᐧγun, ᐧγun, ᐧγun "to snarl"

ᐧt'θụiθ from ᐧt'θụ́θ, ᐧt'θụ́θ, ᐧt'θụ́θ "to suck"

c) ᐧʔay from ᐧʔar, ᐧʔar, ᐧʔar "to throw, handle violently cloth-like object"

ᐧbíy from ᐧbєr, ᐧbér, ᐧbєr "to bend"

ᐧtuy from ᐧtur, ᐧtur, ᐧtur "to mix with water"

§32. The formation of the progressive stem: Suffix ᐧɫ is often added to the stem to form the progressive, except stems having a final ᐧθ, ᐧs, or ᐧɫ where this progressive suffix does not appear. The ᐧɫ rarely disappears in other stems. Vocalic modifications may also accompany this suffix.

ᐧtįɫ from ᐧtį, ᐧtạ, ᐧtą́ "to handle a long stick-like object"

ᐧδeɫ from ᐧδir, ᐧδer, ᐧδir "to be, act, do"

ᐧdzạɫ from ᐧdzaih, ᐧdzáy, ᐧdzaih "to handle grain-like object"

ᐧʔiθ from ᐧʔєθ, ᐧʔέδ, ᐧʔєθ "to make a kick at"

ᐧtceθ from ᐧtcuθ, ᐧtcúδ, ᐧtcuθ "to handle a fabric"

ᐧdéɫ from ᐧdéɫ, ᐧdel, ᐧdéɫ "several persons go"

ᐧde from ᐧdє, ᐧdέ, ᐧdє "to clean, to wash"

The importance of recognizing these five modes is that further derivations such as causative, medio-passive, etc., are strictly based upon these sets of stems. The neuter as well as the momentaneous may have its causative, for example, θi-ɫ-ʔạ "I have it lie there," γi-ɫ-ʔą́ "I had it lie there," causatives derived from the neuter ᐧʔạ, ᐧʔą́, ᐧʔą́ "a round solid object lies"; sєᐧneɫᐧcє "he is raising me up" sєᐧnéɫᐧcạ "he has raised me up," causatives derived from the momentaneous ᐧyє, ᐧyạ, ᐧyє "to grow," etc.

VERBAL PREFIXES

§33. There are two classes of of prefixes, the conjunctive and the disjunctive. The conjunctive prefixes occur immediately before the stem and after the pronominal objective prefixes, and a conjunct form of the second person (singular) subjective prefix is used after them. There are also frequent contractions of these prefixes when they come together. The disjunctive prefixes occur before the pronominal objects and are less connected with the stem, they require a disjunct form of the second person subjective and do not as a rule contract with the conjunctive prefixes.

§34. The position which these prefixes occupy in the verb can be briefly demonstrated by the following diagram:

Disjunctive prefixes	Pronominal subject (third person) and objects	Conjunctive prefixes	Stem
1) Incorporated post- positions with their pronominal objects	5) Third person pro- nominal subjects	7) Modal prefixes	11) Stem
		8) Aspectival pre- fixes	
2) Local and adver- bial prefixes	6) Pronominal ob- jects	9) Pronominal sub- jects	
3) Iterative prefix		10) Classifiers	
4) Incorporated noun stems			

We shall proceed from the prefixes nearest to the stem.

§35. Classifiers: There are four classes of verbs according to whether they possess a zero, ·d·, ·ł·, or ·l· immediately before the stem. These classifiers often combine with the initials of the stem, and sometimes drop out. The d classifier drops out before all initials except, 1) ·d+ʔ· > ·ťʼ·, 2) ·d+n· > ·d·, 3) ·d+γ· > ·g·, 4) ·d+ẟ· > ·dẟ· or rarely ·d·, 5) ·d+z· > ·dz·, 6) ·d+y· > ·dj·, 7) ·d+l· > ·dl·. The ł classifier is regularly kept and causes the unvoicing of the following fricative initial (cf. §6). Sometimes under unknown conditions it may combine with the following n to form a ł, for example, xahorełi "he is fearing," but xahorełni "there is fear." The l classifier is also regularly kept, but in some cases it combines with a following n or y to form an l, for example, ʔanεlε "you are making it so," ʔanεlá "you have made it so," ʔaɣwụlε "you will make it so," from ·l·nε, ·l·ya, ·l·nε, cf. ʔaílnε "we are making it so," ʔaílyá "we have made it so," ʔaɣwúlnε "we shall make it so."

The function of these classifiers is to denote whether the verb is transitive, intransitive, causative, medio-passive, etc., but in many cases we have stereotyped uses of these prefixes where these functions are difficult to demonstrate.

a) zero class: Intransitive, transitive and neuter.

nε·yε "he is growing up" (intransitive)
yε·nε·ʔa "he is fooling him" (transitive)
dε·bér "it bends easily, is pliable" (neuter)

b) ł class: Mostly transitive and causative.

sε·nε·ł·cε "he is raising me up" (causative of "to grow")
kún θε·ł·tsị "he has made the fire" (transitive)

c) d class: Mostly passive, medio-passive, and reflexive derived from the zero class verbs. It is also used in the first person plural and dual and the third person indefinite forms of the zero class verb, and used sometimes in the customary forms and the "again-form."

neɣeťá "one is fooled" <neɣed‑ʔá (passive), cf. ne‑ɣi‑‑ʔá "I fooled him"

céɣes‑ti̧ "I have eaten" <céɣes‑d‑ti̧ (medio‑passive, meaning "to handle food to one's self")

nǐ‑‑ťás "we are getting up (dual)" <ni‑ǐ‑‑d‑ʔás, cf. ni‑úh‑‑ʔás "you are getting up (dual)"

na‑he‑s‑dzus "I slide down customarily, one time after another" <na‑he‑s‑d‑zus (customary), cf. ho‑dá‑hi‑‑zúz "I started to slide down"

na̧‑s‑ťa "I own it again (a round solid object)" <ná‑na‑s‑d‑ʔa (again‑form), cf. ná‑s‑ʔa "I own it"

d) 1 class: Mostly passive, medio‑passive, and reflexive derived from ɫ class verbs. It is also used in the first person plural and dual and the third person indefinite forms of the ɫ class verbs, and sometimes used in the "again‑form."

hǐ‑l‑záih "it is being hooked" (passive), cf. hi̧‑ɫ‑sáih "hook it!"

ke‑ná‑‑ʔe‑ne‑l‑de "he is washing his own face" (medio‑passive), cf. ye‑ke‑ná‑ɫ‑de "he is cleaning it"

né‑θǐ‑‑l‑ya̧ "we have raised him," cf. ni‑ɫ‑ca̧ "I have raised him"

zǐ‑l‑záih "one is hooking it" (third person indefinite)

na̧‑ne‑l‑ten "you own it (a sack, kettle, etc.) again" <ná‑na‑ne‑l‑ten (again‑form), cf. ná‑ne‑ɫ‑ten "you own it"

It seems clear that the relation of l to ɫ is similar to that of d to zero.

A few peculiar uses of these classifiers can be illustrated by the following examples: ná‑e‑ké θ "it (a long object) is dropping," but ná‑ɣi‑ɫ‑keδ "I (in a sack) have dropped," θe‑ti̧ "it (a living being) lies there," but θe‑ɫ‑ti̧ "a corpse lies there," θe‑ta̧ "it (a stick) lies there," but θe‑ɫ‑ta̧ "it (a sack, vessel, kettle) lies there"; and θǐ‑l‑ta̧ "you are floating in a canoe."

§36. Pronominal subjects: There are two sets of pronominal subjective prefixes, one for the zero and the ɫ class verbs and the other for the d and the l class verbs. These prefixes appear immediately before the classifiers and sometimes coalesce with them.

	zero class and ɫ class	d class and l class
Imperfective		
1st. sg.	‑s‑	
2nd. sg.	ne‑ (disjunct), ‑(n)‑ (conjunct)	
3rd. sg.	—	
1st. pl. or dual	‑ǐ‑‑(d)‑, ‑ǐ‑(l)‑	
2nd. pl. or dual	‑uh‑	
3rd. pl. or dual	—	
Perfective		
1st. sg.	‑i‑‑, ‑i‑(ɫ)‑	‑s‑
2nd. sg.	‑(n)‑ (conjunct)	
3rd. sg.	—	

1st., 2nd. and 3rd. pl. or dual same as imperfective.

Future

1st. sg.	ʾsʿ
2nd. sg.	ʿ(n)ʿ (conjunct)
3rd. sg.	—
1st. pl. or dual	ʾúʿʿ(d)ʿ, ʾúʿ(l)ʿ
2nd. pl. or dual	ʾuhʿ
3rd. pl. or dual	—

The first person singular ʿsʿ contracts with the ł and l classifier to form ʿsʿ, is assimilated to ʿcʿ when followed by the initial djʿ, tcʿ, or ťcʿ, and coalesces with a following yʿ to form ʿcʿ, except when the s is from s+l, for example, héctcé <héʿsʿlʿtcé "I got angry"; nįnecdja <nįʿnaʿneʿsʿdʿya "I came back"; ʔeléγwacás < ʔeléγwaʿsʿyás "I shall knot it together"; húce <húʿsʿłyε "I call it, name it," bekóresyą <beʿkéʿhoʿdeʿsʿlʿyą "I know it."

The disjunct form of the second singular is used when there is no prefix or only disjunctive prefixes preceding it, the conjunct form is used when there is a conjunctive prefix preceding it. The ʿ(n)ʿ of the conjunct form regularly disappears with a nasalization of the preceding vowel.

The first plural or dual requires the d classifier in the zero and d class verbs, and the l classifier in the ł and l class verbs. The vowel ʿuʿʿ, ʿuʿ, in the future is due to contraction with the future prefix γwaʿ (§37d).

The h of the second plural or dual contracts with the ł and l classifier forming ł. The vowel of this as well as the first person plural or dual prefix often displaces the ε of the preceding prefix, and sometimes contracts with the other vowels.

The third singular subject is not denoted by any prefix, but the plural or dual is expressed by a prefix not in this position, cf. §40g.

§37. The aspectival prefixes are placed immediately before the pronominal subjects, and they are:

a) θεʿ perfective. It has a durative force and is used often in the imperfective with many neuter verbs denoting position. These neuters are perfective in form, and may be called perfective presents. This θεʿ disappears after the conjunctive prefixes but reappears sometimes in the first plural or dual and the third person forms. In the third person forms when preceded by a conjunctive or pronominal objective prefix (§40a) it will lose its vowel and appear as δ in the zero class verbs, as θ in the d class verbs, and will contract with ł and l classifier forming ł. It often raises the pitch of the preceding low-pitched conjunctive or pronominal objective prefix.

b) γεʿ perfective. In the third person forms it remains as γεʿ in the d and l class verbs and becomes γįʿ in the zero and ł class verbs.

c) neʿ momentaneous. It is used in the imperfective as well as in the perfective, but not in the future. In the third person forms it is dropped with the nasalization of the preceding prefix in the imperfective and sometimes also in the perfective when the verb belongs to the d or l class. In zero or ł class verbs it becomes nį̈· in the perfective. It often raises the pitch of a preceding conjunctive prefix.

d) γwa· future. In the second singular γwa +(n)· becomes γwų·, in the second plural or dual γwa +uh· becomes γwuh·, and in the first plural or dual γwa +í· >γwú··. When preceded by a conjunctive or pronominal (objective or subjective) prefix, it is contracted with the preceding vowel forming ·u·.

e) γε· progressive.

f) A peg element hε· is added to the verb in this position when there is no other prefix preceding the pronominal subjective prefixes. This element does not appear in the second singular where we have nε·, and is regularly dropped in the perfective, the future etc., where we require other prefixes preceding the pronominal subjects.

§38. The following paradigms will illustrate the various aspectival and pronominal subjective prefixes together with the classifiers, and their contractions. The stem or the theme will be given first with its meaning, and then the paradigm. If there is a disjunctive prefix, it is placed before the bar / to distinguish it from the conjunctive prefixes.

1) ·(γε·perf.)·(zero class)·tsaγ "to cry"; with a peg element hε· in the imperfective.

	Imperfective	Perfective	Future
1 sg.	hεstsaγ	γi·tsaγ <γ(ε)·í·tsaγ	γwastsaγ
2 sg.	nεtsaγ	γįtsaγ <γ(ε)·n·tsaγ	γwųtsaγ <γwa·n·tsaγ
3 sg.	hεtsaγ	γįtsaγ	γwatsaγ
1 pl. or dual	hí·tsaγ <h(ε)·í·d·tsaγ	γí·tsaγ <γ(ε)·í·d·tsaγ	γwú·tsaγ <γwa·í·d·tsaγ
2 pl. or dual	huhtsaγ <h(ε)·uh·tsaγ	γwuhtsaγ <γ(ε)·uh·tsaγ	γwuhtsaγ <γwa·uh·tsaγ
3 pl. or dual	hεhεtsaγ	hεγįtsaγ	hu·tsaγ <hε·γwa·tsaγ

2) Theme cέ·/·(γε·perf.)·(d class)·tį "to eat."

1 sg.	cέstį	cέγεstį	cέγwastį
2 sg.	cέnεtį	cέγįtį	cέγwútį
3 sg.	cέtį	cέγεtį	cέγwatį
1 dual	cí·tį <c(ε)·í·d·tį	cέγí·tį	cέγwú·tį
2 dual	cúhtį <c(ε)·uh·d·tį	cέγwuhtį	cέγwuhtį
3 dual	cέhεtį	cέhεγεtį	cέhu·tį <cέ·hε·γwa·d·tį

3) Theme nε·(θε·perf.)·(zero class)·téih "to lie down (sg.)"; with a change of stem to ·tés for the dual and plural.

1 sg.	nεstéih	ni·tį <nε·θε·i·tį	nusté <nε·γwa·s·té
2 sg.	nįtéih <nε·n·téih	nįtį <nε·θε·n·tį	nųté <nε·γwa·n·té
3 sg.	nεtéih	nέδtį	nuté <nε·γwa·té
1 pl. or dual	ní·tés <n(ε)·í·d·tés	nέθí·tεz	nú·tés <nε·γwa·í·d·tés
2 pl. or dual	nuhtés	nuhtεz <nε·θε·uh·tį	nuhtés <nε·γwa·uh·tés
3 pl. or dual	hεnεtés	hεnέδtεz	hεnutés

4) ·(θε·perf.)·(ł class)·tsi "to make it (one object)"; with the peg element hε· in the imperfective; the third person forms require the third person pronominal object yε· (§40a).

1 sg.	hɛstsi < hɛ·s·ł·tsi	θiltsị < θ(ɛ)·i·ł·tsị	γwastsi
2 sg.	nɛltsi	θịltsị < θɛ·n·ł·tsị	γwụltsi
3 sg.	yɛltsi	yɛ́ltsị < yɛ·δ·ł·tsị	yu·łtsi < yɛ·γwa·ł·tsi
1 pl. or dual	híltsi	θíltsị	γwúltsi < γwa·í·l·tsi
2 pl. or dual	hułtsi < h(ɛ)·uh·ł·tsi	θułtsị	γwułtsi < γwa·uh·ł·tsi
3 pl. or dual	hɛyɛltsi	hɛyɛ́ltsị	hɛyu·łtsi

5) Theme tu·/·nɛ·(θɛ·perf.)·(d class)·dị́(< d classifier + nị́) "to be drowned."

1 sg.	tunɛsdị́	tunɛsdạ	tunụsdạ́
2 sg.	tunịdị́	tunịdạ	tunụdạ́
3 sg.	tunɛdị́	tunɛθdạ	tunụdạ́
1 dual	tuní·dị́	tunɛ́θí·dạ	tunú·dạ́
2 dual	tunühdị́	tunuhdạ	tunuhdạ́
3 dual	tuhɛnɛdị́	tuhɛnɛθdạ	tuhɛnudạ́

6) Theme hɛ·(θɛ·perf.)·(l class)·zɛ "to start to hunt."

1 sg.	hɛszɛ < hɛ·s·l·zɛ	hɛszɛ́ < hɛ·θɛ·s·l·zɛ́	huszɛ < hɛ·γwa·s·l·zɛ
2 sg.	hịlzɛ	hịlzɛ́ < hɛ·θɛ·n·l·zɛ́	hụlzɛ < hɛ·γwa·n·l·zɛ
3 sg.	hɛlzɛ	hɛ́lzɛ́ < hɛ·θ·l·zɛ́	hulzɛ < hɛ·γwa·l·zɛ
1 dual	hílzɛ	hílzɛ́ < hɛ·θɛ·í·l·zɛ́	hŭ·lzɛ < hɛ·γwa·í·l·zɛ
2 dual	hułzɛ < hɛ·uh·l·zɛ	hułzɛ́ < hɛ·θɛ·uh·l·zɛ́	hułzɛ < hɛ·γwa·uh·l·zɛ
3 dual	hɛhɛlzɛ	hɛhɛ́lzɛ́	hɛhulzɛ

7) Theme t́sɛ·/·(nɛ·momentaneous)·(zero class)·δir "to wake up."

1 sg.	t́sɛnɛsθir	t́sɛni·δer	t́sɛγwasθir
2 sg.	t́sɛnịδir	t́sɛnịδer	t́sɛγwụδir
3 sg.	t́sɛ·δir < t́sɛ·n(ɛ)·δir	t́sɛnịδer	t́sɛγwaδir
1 dual	t́sɛní·dδir	t́sɛní·dδer	t́sɛγwú·dδir
2 dual	t́sɛnuhθir	t́sɛnuhθer	t́sɛγwuhθir
3 dual	t́sɛhɛ·δir < t́sɛ·hɛ·n(ɛ)·δir	t́sɛhɛnịδer	t́sɛhu·δir

8) Perfective present (θɛ·perf. as imperfective) (γɛ·perf.)·(zero class)·tị "one living being lies there."

1 sg.	θi·tị	γi·tị́	γwastɛ́
2 sg.	θịtị	γịtị́	γwụtɛ́
3 sg.	θɛtị	γịtị́	γwatɛ́

9) ·(zero class)·bɛł "to swim along (progressive stem)."

Progressive

1 sg.	γɛsbɛł
2 sg.	γịbɛł
3 sg.	γɛbɛł

§39. Modal prefixes: These prefixes are also conjunctive prefixes placed immediately before the aspectual prefixes.

a) tɛ· or hɛ· inceptive. tɛ· and hɛ· seem to be interchangeable, probably hɛ· is the weakened form of tɛ·. They usually require the momentaneous stem, and take the θɛ· in the perfective. For example, tịγaih or hịγaih "you start off," tɛγaih or heɣaih "he starts off," tįya or hįya "you started off," téδya or héδya "he started off"; see also §38 (6).

b) hí- or -í- inchoative. This prefix does not require the perfective prefix. The vowel is changed to ε before the first person subjective prefix s, and is contracted with the future ɣwa- forming u. For example héctce "I am getting angry," híltce "he is getting angry," héctcé "I got angry," híltcé "he got angry," húctce <hí-ɣwa-s-tce "I shall get angry"; dígai <d(ε)-í-gai "it is becoming white," dígái "it has become white," dúgai <d(ε)-í-ɣwa-gai "it will become white," cf. delgai "it is white."

c) ne- completive. It is used with verbs of a great variety of meaning. It requires often the momentaneous stems, the θe- perfective, and is used in all three aspects, differing from the momentaneous ne-, which is used only in the imperfective and perfective. For examples, see §38 (3) and (5).

d) ne- adjectival. It is sometimes dropped with the nasalization of the preceding vowel, but not dropped after a disjunctive prefix. For example, nedáδ "it is heavy," nenéδ "it is long," nezų "it is good," hųzų "it is good (a place)," nelɣus "it is boiling (neuter)," nesxus <ne-s-ł-nus "I am boiling it (caus. of the neuter)."

e) de- adjectival. When used with the l classifier it often denotes a sound. For example, debạδ "it is round," debér "it bends easily, is pliable," denur "it is soft," delba "it is grey," deldél "it is rattling," delɣus "it barks."

f) łe- adjectival. łeka "it is fat," łekan "it is sweet."

g) de- (-re-) meaning obscure, often used with other prefixes; beba nâurįl?į "you are waiting for him," yeba nâurél?į "he is waiting for him," yeba náhodél?į "they are waiting for him."

h) dí- (-rí-) often used together with ni- "up," with xá- "out," yé "in," etc. (cf. §43f, g). It seems to denote a local relationship. for example, beyérįl?εθ "you put them on (snow shoes)," beyéxárįl?εθ "you step out of them," nirés?áih "I am picking it up (a stone)," niyerį?ạ "he picked it up."

i) δe- "exhaustion." δįlɣį "you are exhausted," δélɣį <δé-θ-l-ɣį "he is exhausted."

j) hu- or -u- "pointing at, toward, against"; often used with ne- (§39c) or de- (§39g), for example, hustás "I am shooting at him," yúnįłtáz <y(ε)-ú-nį-ł-táz "he has shot at him," húníldel "we made a rush at them."

k) hį- in hįhesłał or he̦·słał "I am falling asleep," hįhesłál or he·słál "I have fallen asleep."

§40. Pronominal objective prefixes and third person pronominal subjective prefixes: these prefixes are placed between the disjunctive and the conjunctive prefixes.

a) Pronominal objects are identical in form with the pronominal possessive prefixes of the nouns. The third person object is omitted when the subject is in the first or second person, ye- is used when the subject is in the third person. If the object immediately precedes, the ye- is often omitted. For example,

t́sesénįłθer "he waked me up"	t́senuhúnįłθer "he waked us or you (dual) up"
t́senénįłθer "he . . . you"	t́sehubį́nįłθer "I waked them (dual) up"
t́seyį́nįłθer "he . . . him"	sa hełtsi "he makes a watch"
t́senįłθer "I . . . him"	yełtsi "he makes it"

The raised pitch is due to the ne᷍ momentaneous prefix, which also nasalizes the vowel of some of them, but not all.

b) ʔe᷍ indefinite object. ʔeldéł "he is eating (several objects)," cf. yeldéł "he is eating them"; ʔesdą "I am drinking," cf. hesdą "I am drinking it."

c) de᷍ "for one's self." It requires the d or l classifier; łeɣádénesδer "I killed it for myself," cf. łeɣániłθer "I killed it"; nideyerį́tą "he has picked it (a stick) up for himself," cf. niyerį́tą "he has picked it up."

d) ʔede᷍ reflexive, requiring d or l classifier: łeɣâ·dénesδer < łeɣá·ʔedénes·l·δer "I killed myself."

e) łe᷍ "mutual, each other, requiring d or l classifier: łeɣáłehį́lδer < łeɣá·łe·hé m(e)·l·δer "they (dual) killed each other."

f) ho᷍ third person indefinite subject or object referring to a place, an event, etc., hóδʔą "it is there (place, event)," cf. θeʔą "it (a rock) lies there," huzų "it is good (a place)," cf. nezų "it is good."

g) he᷍ third person plural or dual subjective prefix, for examples see §38 paradigms.

h) t́se᷍ third person indefinite subject, referring to one or a group of persons. It often requires the d or l classifier, and coalesces with the following modal prefixes (de᷍, ne᷍) to form ze᷍ or (with te᷍, he᷍) se᷍. For example, nát́sedé "people are staying," cf. nádé "they are staying," hezelʔá < he·ts(e)·nel·ʔá "one has been mistaken about it," cf. benį́lʔá "you have been mistaken about it," séθdel "people have started" < t́s(e)·hé·θ·d·del, cf. hehéδdel "they have started."

§41. Incorporated noun stems: A large number of nominal stems may be incorporated into the verb in this position, such as tθí᷍ "head," na᷍ "eye," bá᷍ "war party," sa᷍ "sun," xa᷍ "hair," xu᷍ "tooth," cį᷍ "song," etc. Some stems, however are no more used as independent nouns in Chipewyan, such as cé᷍ "food," tθį᷍ "flight," tįba᷍ "running, rapid movement," etc. They are placed before the pronominal objective and subjective (third person) prefixes, and are disjunctive, i.e., they require the disjunct form of the second singular subject if there is no other conjunctive prefix, and do not as a rule coalesce with the conjunctive prefixes. The following are some examples,

yįdátθíni·tθiy "I have poked my head in," cf. ʔetθí "head" and net́sén nįni·tθiy "I pointed a stick at you"

nábą́hǔ·déł "we shall go on war path," cf. bą́ne "war party" and hǔ·déł "we shall go"

nitįbahį́ɣaih "you are getting up rapidly," cf. nihį́ɣaih "you are getting up" beyą nίyatini·ʔą "I passed the words to him," cf. yatei "word" and ʼʔą perfective of "to handle a round solid object"

§42. The iterative prefix na·: It means "again," "back again," and "customarily" when used with the customary stems. It often, though not always requires, the d or l classifier according to whether the original verb is zero or ł class. It is dropped after certain prefixes and pulls the tone to the low pitch with the nasalization of the preceding vowel. For example,

nánadδer "he is staying again," nánadδiy "he is staying customarily" cf. náδer "he is staying"

nąsťa "I own it again (a round object)" <ná·na·/·s·d·ʔa cf. násʔa "I own it"

xąlʔóih "water rushes out (cust.) as if it were boiling" <xá·na·/·l·ʔóih cf. xálʔóih "water rushes out"

nįhįdel "they returned" <nį̇·na·/·hɛ·n(ɛ)·del cf. nįhįdel "they came"

§43. Local and adverbial prefixes: The number of such prefixes is extremely numerous. They often go with certain other prefixes and sometimes require certain stem forms such as the continuative, the customary, and so on. Only a limited number of examples will be given below to illustrate their use in the verbal structure.

a) dá· distributive. It indicates the plurality of the subject, or of the object and is used sometimes adverbially.

dáhułtsi "you (pl.) all make it" <dá· "distributive" /·h(ɛ)· "peg element," ·uh· "second plural subject," ·ł· "classifier," ·tsi "to make one object." dá· here only emphasizes the plurality of the subject.

xádárɛθgai "it is white·spotted" <xá· "out," ·dá· "distributive" / ·dɛ́ "adjectival," ·θ· "perfective, used as neuter imperfective," ·d· "classifier," ·gai "to be white." It is built upon a primary theme dɛ́·θ·gai "there is a white spot."

ʔełťsįdánełsus "you split several objects" <ʔeł· "mutual, postpositional object," ·ťsį· "from, postposition," ·dá· "distributive" / ·nɛ "second singular subject, disjunct form," ·ł· "classifier," ·sus "to split." It is built upon a theme, ʔeł·ťsį· / ·ł·sus, cf. ʔełťsįnełsus "you split it." dá· here refers to the object.

beyé xádána ʔesdzis "I sip out of several vessels (cust.)" <beyé "in it," xá· "out," ·dá· "distributive," ·na "iterative" / ·ʔɛ· "indefinite object," ·s· "first singular subject," ·d· "classifier, used with the iterative," ·zis "to sip (customary form)," cf. beyé xąna ʔesdzis "I sip out of it (cust.)" <be·yé xá·na/ ·ʔɛ·s·d·zis.

b) da· "up." tθɛ dayɛʔał "he is holding a rock up" <tθɛ "rock," da· "up," ·yɛ· "progressive," ·ʔał "to handle a round solid object (progressive form)."

c) ná· continuative. It means "here and there, about" and requires the continuative stem.

násθer "I am staying," nánɛδer "you are staying," built upon the theme ná· / ·δer "to stay," from the stem ·δer "to do, to act (continuative form)."

násʔa "I own it (a round solid object)," nánɛʔa "you own it," built upon the theme ná- / -ʔa "to own," from the stem -ʔa "to handle a round solid object (con-tinuative form)."

d) ná- "across." náni·bį "I have swum across" <ná- "across" / -n(ε)- "mo-mentaneous," -i- "first singular perfective subject," -bį "to swim."

nániʔa "it extends across" <ná- "across" / -nį "momentaneous, third person perfective," -ʔa "to have extension."

e) nį- terminative, "arriving at."

níni·ya "I have come, arrived" <nį- "terminative" / -n(ε)- "momentaneous," -i- "first singular subject perfective," -ya "one person goes, perfective."

ʔεyεr níɣwaʔá "it will extend to that place" <ʔεyεr "there" nį- "termina-tive" / -ɣwa- "future," -ʔá "to have extension, future."

f) ni- "up." It is often used with the inchoative hí-(í-) or dí-(-rí-).

nǐ·ɣaih "he is getting up" <ni- "up" / -hí- "inchoative," -ɣaih "one person goes, imperfective."

niyεríʔáih "he is picking it up" <ni- "up" / -yε- "third person object," -d- see §39h, -ʔáih "to handle a round solid object."

g) xá- "out." xálʔóih "water rushes out as if it were boiling " <xá- "out"/-l- "classifier," -ʔóih "water rushes, whirls."

xánaɣεsduδ "I have crawled out again" <xá- "out," -na- "iterative" / -ɣε- "perfective," -s- "first singular subject," -d- "classifier," -duδ "to creep."

h) dzέrέ- "around." It requires the customary stem.

dzέrέnεʔaih "you are carrying it around (a round solid object)" <dzέrέ- "around" -nε- "second singular subject disjunct form," -ʔaih "to handle a round solid object (customary form)."

dzέrέhεdíl "they are walking around" <dzέrέ- "around" / -hε- "third person plural subject," -díl "several persons go (customary form)."

i) yįdá- "inside of a tent, house, etc."

yįdánįltį "you have brought him in" <yįdá- "in" / -nε- "momentaneous," -(n)- "second singular subject, conjunct form," -ł- "classifier," -tį "to handle a living being."

yįdąyénįltį "she has brought him in again" <yįdá- "in," -na- "iterative" í -yέ- "third person object," -nį- "momentaneous, third person perfective," -ł- "classi-fier," -tį "to handle a living being."

j) łεɣá- "death." łεɣánεsθir "I am dying" <łεɣá- "death" / -nε- "momentane-ous," -s- "first singular subject," -θir "to do, to act," built upon the theme łεɣá-/— (zero class) -θir "to die."

łεɣánilθer "I killed him," causative of the preceding.

k) ʔa- "so, thus." -ʔasʔį "I am doing so" <ʔa- "so" / -s- "first singular subject," -ł- "classifier," ʔį "to do."

ʔaʦεdεlʔį "one is making one's self thus" <ʔa- "so" / -ʦε- "third person in-definite subject," -(ε)dε- "self," -l- "classifier, because of the reflexive," -ʔį "to do."

l) ʔą- "back home." ʔąhįłʔa "you send him home" <ʔą- "back home" / -hε-

"inceptive," ⸰(n)⸰ "second person singular subject," ⸰ɬ⸰ "classifier," ⸰ʔa "to command."

ʔą̆hέθdja "he went home" < ʔą̆⸰ "back home" / ⸰hέ "inceptive," ⸰θ⸰ "perfective," ⸰d⸰ "classifier," ⸰ya "one person goes."

m) ʔεkwá⸰ "thus, like that." ʔεkwáneťε "you are like that" < ʔεkwá⸰ "like that" / ⸰nε⸰ "second singular subject," ⸰ťε "to be."

§44. Incorporated postpositions with their objects: These postpositions may be accompanied by their pronominal objects or may be used alone. The number of such postpositions are also numerous, the following are some examples.

a) ⸰έ "at, against." bέrįdí "you are feeling it, i.e., a pain by pressing hard against it" < b(ε)⸰ "third person postpositional object," ⸰έ "at, postposition" / ⸰dε "local relation," ⸰(n)⸰ "second singular subject," ⸰dí "to feel (d class)."

bέnεlʔį "you are imitating him, mocking him" < b(ε)⸰ "third person postpositional object," ⸰έ "at" / ⸰nε⸰ "second singular subject," ⸰l⸰ "classifier," ⸰ʔį "to imitate."

b) xá⸰ (⸰γá⸰) "to, for." xáyεrlέtį "he has taken her for himself" < xá⸰ "for" / ⸰yε⸰ "third person object" ⸰dέ "self," ⸰n(ε)⸰ "momentaneous," ⸰l⸰ "classifier," ⸰tį "to handle a living being, perfective."

bεγáyέniɬtį "I have given her to him" < b(ε)⸰ "third person object of the postposition," ⸰γá⸰ "to" / ⸰yέ "third person object used when there are two third person objects," ⸰n(ε)⸰ "momentaneous," ⸰i⸰ "first singular subject," ⸰ɬ⸰ "classifier," ⸰tį "to handle a living being."

c) na⸰ "in place of." yεnahεγaih "he replaces him (cust.)" < yε⸰ "third person object of the postposition," ⸰na⸰ "in place of" / ⸰hε⸰ "peg element," ⸰γaih "one person goes (customary form)," cf. bεnanεγaih "you replace him (cust.)," bεnaniγaih "you replace him (momentaneous)."

d) ǩa⸰ "following, after." bεǩaθíldel "we have followed him" < bε⸰ "third person object of the postposition," ⸰ǩa⸰ "following" / ⸰θ(ε)⸰ "perfective," ⸰i⸰ "first plural subject," ⸰l⸰ "classifier," ⸰del "several persons go."

e) ǩε⸰ "on, at." ǩεnεʔar "you are untying it" < ǩε⸰ "on" / ⸰nε "second singular subject," ⸰ʔar "to untie."

bεǩεnεsťáθ "I am cutting it off" < bε⸰ "third person object of the postposition," ⸰ǩε⸰ "on" / ⸰nε⸰ "momentaneous," ⸰s⸰ "first singular subject," ⸰ťáθ "to cut."

VERBAL SUFFIXES (OR POSTPOSED PARTICLES)

§45. These suffixes are more or less detached from the verb itself, and may be called postposed particles although they do not have as a rule an independent existence. The following are some examples.

a) ⸰i relative suffix. The verb with this suffix is often introduced by the particles ťahi "the thing that," ťą̆hį "the one who," and ťahú "the time when" (§47). Many nouns are formed by this suffix (§12d).

ťąhį   sas·xéł   θeťį·i   "the one who was sleeping with the bear"
the one bear·with he is sleeping·who
ťahú   sas·xéł   néδťį·i   hoťsį "since the time when he slept with the
the time bear·with he has lain down·when it·from   bear"

b) ·ixa future purpose or simple future, used with the imperfective forms.

sas   łeγął̇θir·ixa   hı́le   "he will not kill a bear"
bear   he kills·in the future   not

c) ·į future intention used with future forms.

łuγwe   hú·ldéł·į   "we shall eat fish"
fish   we shall eat·future intention

d) ·hú, ·ú gerundive suffix.

ʔeťsı́naθé tθiyé   yerįγįłcel·ú   yeťcazı́   téδya
finally in the fire he having thrown it away from it   he started off

"finally when he had thrown it into the fire, he went away"

yenįδen·ú ʔįγą́ nihı́ya "when he thought of that, quickly he got up"
he thinking quickly he got up

e) ·nį past tense, sometimes with the meaning of contrary to fact when used
with a conditional clause.

xaunelten·nį   "one was taught"
one is taught·in the past
setθue   bedį·dé   γesna·ixa·hı́le·nį   "if without my grandson.
my grandson without him·if I live·in the future·not·in the past I would not have lived"

f) ·dé if.

sas·γą cı́·lyi·dé "if we eat the bear"
bear·at we eat·if

g) ·nį·dé expressing a wish especially when followed by the verb "to think."

γįna·nį·dé   yenesθen "I wish that you live, would that you live!"
you live·wishing   I think

h) ·dé·kúlú even if.

netcá·hı́le·dé·kúlú "even if it is not big"
it is big·not·even·if

i) ·hı́le not.

nezų·hı́le   "it is not good"
it is good·not
łeγánįłθir·hı́le "do not kill him!"
kill him·not

j) -húsą́ interrogative.

nínįya-húsą́   "did he come?"
he came-interrogative suffix

k) -sąná future prohibitive, used with future forms.

łeɣánųłθir-sąną   "you shall not kill him!"
you shall kill him-shall not

Other suffixes such as -sî·, -ląsî· "whoever, whatever," used in the same way as the relative -i, -ɣwalí "it will be, used to form the paraphrastic future," -lesą́, ląsą́ "probably," -sį "to be sure," sų̂·ni "probably, presumably," hįtŭ· "while," -t'θe "it is heard," -sni "it is said," -hiƙé "it is found out," etc., are used much in the same way.

INDEPENDENT PARTICLES

§46. The independent particles consist of the pronouns, the numerals and the adverbial and syntactic particles.

§47. Pronouns. The personal pronouns have only the first and the second person; the third person pronouns are demonstratives.

si "I"   nuhni "we"
nen "you"   nuhni "you (plural)"

The demonstratives are:

diri "this, these"   ʔeyi "that, those, he, they, etc."
dją "here"   ʔeyer "there"
noɣwe "that over there"   ʔedųni "the other one"
noɣwį "that one (person) over there"   ʔełasųni "another"
yuɣwe "over there"

There is a third person reflexive, ʔedįni "he himself, they themselves."

The interrogatives are formed from a stem -dlá-, -dláɣ-, or -dlį́- with the indefinite possessive prefix ʔe- and with other suffixes or stems.

ʔedláɣe "what?"   ʔedlą́ɣį "who?"
ʔedláɣeka "why, what for?"   ʔedláú "when?"
ʔedlį́ni "where?"   ʔedlásį́, ʔedlį́sį́ "where to?"
ʔedlą́·t'ŭ, ʔedlą́·t'e "how?"

The relative pronouns are t'ahi "that which," t'ą̃hį "the one who," t'ahú "the time when," which are used to introduce a relative clause, for examples see §45a.

The indefinite pronouns are: t'asî· "anything, something," nahèi "something, some of the things," ną̃·ne "some one, some of them," etc.

§48. The numerals are divided into two sets, one used in counting things and the other used in counting persons. The set used in counting persons is formed

by a suffix -ne (cf. dɛne "person"), which sometimes takes the weak form -(n) causing the nasalization of the preceding vowel, such as in numeral one and in some
pronouns (§47).

ʔiɬáɣɛ "one"	ʔiɬáɣį "one person"
nákɛ "two"	nádɛne "two persons"
taɣɛ "three"	tane "three persons"
diɣį "four"	dįne "four persons"
sasuɬáɣɛ "five"	sasuɬáne "five persons"

Numerals beyond five are compounds formed from these simple numerals, ʔɑɬkɛ́-
taɣɛ "six <each side three," ʔiɬásį-diɣį "seven <one side four," ʔɑɬkɛ́-diɣį "eight
<each side four," ʔiɬáɣɛ-yaɣaútą "nine <one finger bent down," ʔiɬá-unéną "ten,"
ʔiɬáɣɛ-ʔɛʦadδɛɬ "eleven <one left over," ná-unéną "twenty," ná-unéną naθɛʦén
ʔiɬáɣɛ "twenty-one <one more than twenty," ta-unéną "thirty," dį-unéną "forty,"
sasuɬá-unéną "fifty," etc.

§49. Chipewyan makes use of a great number of adverbial and syntactic particles, which may be simple stems, or stereotyped postpositions or verbs. The following is a list of some of the common ones.

ʔąɬa "together"	kúʦa "enough"
ʔaɬŭ· "still, yet"	kúlú "but"
ʔáɬkɛ́ "separate, each"	kaɬdąnɛ́ "already"
ʔɛʦaxą "suddenly"	káɬdjįne "nearly, almost"
ʔɛyiʦá "therefore"	húɬdúú "then, afterwards"
ʔɛʦsįnaθɛ́ "finally"	θá "long"
ʔiɣą́ "quickly"	θani "alone"
ʔoteyɛ́ "quite, well"	ʦθi "also"
dɛdąnɛ́ "immediately, at once"	θúú "in vain, unable"
dŭ·, duhú "now"	hodɛlyŭu "all"
dúyɛ́ "difficult, impossible"	ʔɛ̌· "yes"
tău ... tău "either ... or"	ʔiíle, or ʔihíle "no"
nárį "repeatedly"	
nąde "the last"	
kú·, ʔɛkú· "so, then"	

WORD ORDER

§50. The verb which is an essential part of the sentence always stays at the
end of the sentence or clause, the other parts of the sentence are placed before it.
The order is usually thus: subordinate clause, particles, subject, postposition with
its object, object, verb. For example,

setθuɛ	sa	kún	θɛltsį	"my grandson made a fire for me"
my grandson	for me	fire	he made	

t'ahú   sas-xél   neðtį-i   hot'sį, ʔɛkú· hųłdų́ú   sas yɛt'sén
the time bear-with he has lain down-when it-from then afterwards bear him-to
xáyaɣįltei "Since the time when he slept with the bear, only then the bear spoke to him"
he spoke

BIBLIOGRAPHY

GODDARD, P. E., *Chipewyan Texts and Analysis* (Anthropological Papers of the American Museum of Natural History, vol. 10, pts. 1 and 2, pp. 1–65 and 69–168, New York, 1912).

LEGOFF, L., *Dictionnaire français-montaignais* (Lyon, Marseille, Rome, 1916).

  Grammaire de la langue montagnaise (Montreal, 1889).

LI, F. K., *Chipewyan Consonants* (In the *Tsai Yuan Pei Anniversary Volume*, Bulletin of the Institute of History and Philology of the Academia Sinica, suppl. vol. 1, pp. 429–467, Peiping 1933).

  A List of Chipewyan Stems (International Journal of American Linguistics, vol. 7, nos. 3 and 4, pp. 122–151, New York, 1932).

PETITOT, E., *Dictionnaire de la langue dènè-dindjié* (Paris, 1876).